THE BICENTENNIAL EDITION
OF THE
WORKS OF JOHN WESLEY

General Editor RICHARD P. HEITZENRATER

Textual Editor FRANK BAKER

THE WORKS OF
JOHN WESLEY

VOLUME 19

JOURNAL AND DIARIES

II

(1738–43)

EDITED BY

W. REGINALD WARD
(JOURNAL)

AND

RICHARD P. HEITZENRATER
(DIARIES)

ABINGDON PRESS

NASHVILLE

1990

The Works of John Wesley, Volume 19
JOURNAL AND DIARIES, II, 1738–43

Library of Congress Cataloging in Publication Data

(Revised for vol. 19)

Wesley, John, 1703-1791.
The works of John Wesley.

Includes bibliographical references and indexes.
Contents: v. 1. Sermons I, 1-33 — v. 2. Sermons II, 34-70 — [etc.] — v. 19. Journal and diaries II (1738-43) / edited by W. Reginald Ward and Richard P. Heitzenrater.
1. Methodist Church—Collected works. 2. Theology—Collected works—18th century. I. Outler, Albert Cook, 1908-1989. II. Ward, W. Reginald. III. Heitzenrater, Richard P. IV. Davies, Rupert. V. Title.
BX8217.W5 1984   252'.07   83-22434

ISBN 0-687-46222-3 (v. 19)
ISBN 0-687-46214-2 (v. 9)
ISBN 0-687-46221-5 (v. 18)
ISBN 0-687-46213-4 (v. 4)
ISBN 0-687-46212-6 (v. 3)
ISBN 0-687-46211-8 (v. 2)
ISBN 0-687-46210-X (v. 1)

THE MONOGRAM USED ON THE CASE AND HALF-TITLE IS
ADAPTED BY RICHARD P. HEITZENRATER FROM ONE OF
JOHN WESLEY'S PERSONAL SEALS

MANUFACTURED IN THE UNITED STATES OF AMERICA

THE BICENTENNIAL EDITION OF
THE WORKS OF JOHN WESLEY

THIS edition of the works of John Wesley reflects the quickened interest in the heritage of Christian thought that has become evident during the last half-century. A fully critical presentation of Wesley's writings had long been a desideratum in order to furnish documentary sources illustrating his contribution to both catholic and evangelical Christianity.

Several scholars, notably Professor Albert C. Outler, Professor Franz Hildebrandt, Dean Merrimon Cuninggim, and Dean Robert E. Cushman, discussed the possibility of such an edition. Under the leadership of Dean Cushman, a Board of Directors was formed in 1960 comprising the deans of four sponsoring theological schools of Methodist-related universities in the United States: Drew, Duke, Emory, and Southern Methodist. They appointed an Editorial Committee to formulate plans, and enlisted an international and interdenominational team of scholars for the Wesley Works Editorial Project.

The works were divided into units of cognate material, with a separate editor (or joint editors) responsible for each unit. Dr. Frank Baker was appointed textual editor for the whole project, with responsibility for supplying each unit editor with a critically developed, accurate Wesley text. The text seeks to represent Wesley's thought in its fullest and most deliberate expression, in so far as this can be determined from the available evidence. Substantive variant readings in any British edition published during Wesley's lifetime are shown in appendices to the units, preceded by a summary of the problems faced and the solutions reached in the complex task of securing and presenting Wesley's text. The aim throughout is to enable Wesley to be read with maximum ease and understanding, and with minimal intrusion by the editors.

This edition includes all Wesley's original or mainly original prose works, together with one volume devoted to his *Collection of Hymns* (1780) and another to his extensive work as editor and publisher of extracts from the writings of others. An essential feature of the project is a Bibliography outlining the historical

settings of the works published by Wesley and his brother
Charles, sometimes jointly, sometimes separately. The Bibliography also offers full analytical data for identifying each of the two
thousand editions of these 450 items that were published during
the lifetime of John Wesley, and notes the location of copies. An
index is supplied for each unit, and a General Index for the whole
edition.

The Delegates of the Oxford University Press agreed to
undertake publication, but announced in June 1982 that because
of severe economic problems they would regretfully be compelled
to withdraw from the enterprise with the completion in 1983 of
Vol. 7, the *Collection of Hymns*. The Abingdon Press offered its
services, beginning with the publication of the first volume of the
Sermons in 1984, the bicentennial year of the formation of
American Methodism as an autonomous church. The new title
now assumed, however, refers in general to the bicentennial of
Wesley's total activities as author, editor, and publisher, from
1733 to 1791, especially as summarized in the first edition of his
collected works in thirty-two volumes, 1771–74.

Dean Robert E. Cushman of Duke University undertook
general administration and promotion of the project until 1971,
when he was succeeded as President by Dean Joseph D. Quillian,
Jr., of Southern Methodist University, these two universities
having furnished the major support and guidance for the
enterprise. During the decade 1961–70, an Editorial Committee
supervised the task of setting editorial principles and procedures,
and general editorship was shared by Dr. Eric W. Baker, Dean
William R. Cannon, and Dean Cushman. In 1969 the Directors
appointed Dr. Frank Baker, early attached to the project as
bibliographer and textual editor for Wesley's text, as Editor-in-
Chief also. Upon Dean Quillian's retirement in 1981, he was
succeeded as President of the project by Dean James E. Kirby,
Jr., also of Southern Methodist University. In 1986 the Directors
appointed Richard P. Heitzenrater as General Editor to begin the
chief editorship of the project with the *Journal and Diaries* unit.

Other sponsoring bodies have been successively added to the
original four: The United Methodist Board of Higher Education
and Ministry, The Commission on Archives and History of The
United Methodist Church, and Boston University School of
Theology. For the continuing support of the sponsoring
institutions the Directors express their profound thanks. They

gratefully acknowledge also the encouragement and financial support that have come from the Historical Societies and Commissions on Archives and History of many Annual Conferences, as well as the donations of The World Methodist Council, The British Methodist Church, private individuals, and foundations. On June 9, 1976, The Wesley Works Editorial Project was incorporated in the State of North Carolina as a nonprofit corporation. In 1977, by-laws were approved governing the appointment and duties of the Directors, their Officers, and their Executive Committee.

The Board of Directors

David L. Watson, Board of Discipleship, Nashville, Tennessee
Charles Yrigoyen, Jr., Executive Secretary of The Commission
   on Archives and History of The United Methodist Church,
   Drew University, Madison, New Jersey

CONTENTS

SIGNS, SPECIAL USAGES, ABBREVIATIONS

[ ]   Indicate editorial insertions or substitutions in the original text, or (with a query) doubtful readings.

< >   Indicate conjectural readings in manuscripts where the original text is defective.

. . .   Indicate a passage omitted by the writer from the original and so noted by Wesley, usually by dash.

[. . .]   Indicate a passage omitted silently by Wesley from a text he was quoting, to which the present editor is drawing attention; the brackets are not used in editorial annotations and introductions.

(( ))   Enclose passages within a manuscript struck through for erasure.

[[ ]]   Enclose passages supplied by the present editors from cipher or shorthand, from an abstract or similar document in the third person, or reconstructed from secondary evidence.

a,b,c   Small superscript letters indicate footnotes supplied by Wesley.

1,2,3   Small superscript figures indicate footnotes supplied by the editor.

Cf.   Before a scriptural or other citation by Wesley, indicates that he was quoting with more than minimal inexactness, yet nevertheless displaying the passage as a quotation.

See   Before a scriptural citation indicates an undoubted allusion or a quotation which was not displayed as such by Wesley, and which is more than minimally inexact.

Wesley's publications. Where a work by Wesley was first published separately, its title is italicized; where it first appeared within a different work such as a collected volume, the title appears within quotation marks. References such as 'Bibliography, No. 3' are to the forthcoming Bibliography in this edition (Vols. 33–34), which has a different numbering system from Richard Green's *Wesley Bibliography*.

Book-titles in Wesley's text are italicized if accurate, and given in roman type with capitals if inaccurate. If a title consists of only one generic word which forms a major part of the original title, it is italicized; but if it is inaccurate (such as 'Sermons' for a volume entitled *Discourses*), it is printed in lower case roman.

Abbreviations. In addition to many common and fairly obvious abbreviations, the following are used in the notes: A[nswer], Conf[erence], Meth[odis]m, Meth[odist], Q[uestion], Wes[leyan].
Works and institutions frequently cited are abbreviated thus:

BCP   The Book of Common Prayer, London, 1662.

Bibliography	Frank Baker, *A Descriptive and Analytical Bibliography of the Publications of John and Charles Wesley* (in preparation), Vols. 33–34 in this edn.
Curnock	Nehemiah Curnock, ed., *The Journal of the Rev. John Wesley, A.M.*, 8 vols., London, Epworth Press, 1938.
CWJ	Thomas Jackson, ed., *The Journal of the Rev. Charles Wesley, M.A.*, 2 vols., London, Wes. Meth. Bookroom, 1849.
Jackson	Thomas Jackson, ed., *The Works of the Rev. John Wesley*, 4th edn., 14 vols., London, Mason, 1840–42.
JW	John Wesley (1703–91).
JWJ	John Wesley's *Journal.*
Loeb	The Loeb Classical Library, London, Heinemann; Cambridge, Mass., Harvard Univ. Press.
OED	Sir James A. H. Murray et al., *A New English Dictionary on Historical Principles*, 11 vols., Oxford, Clarendon Press, 1884–1933.
SPCK	Society for Promoting Christian Knowledge.
SPG	Society for the Propagation of the Gospel.
Telford	John Telford, ed., *The Letters of the Rev. John Wesley*, 8 vols., London, Sharp, 1931.
Works (1771–74)	John Wesley, *The Works of the Rev. John Wesley, M.A.*, 32 vols., Bristol, Pine, 1771–74.
WHS	*The Proceedings of the Wesley Historical Society*, 1898– .

A N

EXTRACT

OF THE

Rev^d. M^r. JOHN WESLEY's

JOURNAL,

From *August* 12, 1738,

To *Nov.* 1, 1739.

---

*If this Counsel or this Work be of Men, it will
come to nought : But if it be of* GOD, *ye cannot overthrow it ; least haply ye be found even
to fight against* GOD.

Acts v. 38, 39.

BRISTOL: Printed by *Felix Farley*,

And sold at his Shop in *Castle-Green*, and by *John
Wilson* in *Wine-street:* In LONDON, by *Thomas Trye*
near *Gray's-Inn-Gate*, and *Thomas Harris* on the
Bridge ; and at the Foundery in *Upper-Moor-Fields*.
M.DCC.XLII.

The Preface[1]

1. When at first men began to lay to my charge things which I knew not, I often thought, 'Had I but two or three intimate friends who knew what my life and conversation were, they 5 might easily speak what they had seen and heard, and all such aspersions would fall to the ground.' But I perceived my mistake as soon as I had two or three who were friends indeed, not in name only. For a way was easily found to prevent their being of any such use as I once imagined they would be. This was done at 10 a stroke, and that once for all, by giving them and me a *new name:* a name which, however insignificant in itself, yet had this peculiar effect, utterly to disable me from removing whatever accusation might for the time to come be cast upon me, by invalidating all which those who knew me best were able to say 15 in my behalf. Nay, which any others could say. For how notorious is it that if any man dare to open his mouth in my favour, it needs only be replied, 'I suppose you are a Methodist, too,' and all he has said is to pass for nothing.

2. Hence, on the one hand, many who knew what my 20 conversation was were afraid to declare the truth, lest[2] the same reproach should fall upon them: and those few who broke through this fear were soon disabled from declaring it with effect by being immediately ranked with him they defended. What impartial man then can refuse to say, 'It is permitted to thee to 25 answer for thyself'?[3] Only do not add, but 'thou *shalt not* persuade me, though thou *dost* persuade me: I am resolved to think as I did

---

[1] The Preface makes clear JW's intention to write a defence of 'What it is the Methodists (so called) have done, and are doing now.' Curnock was probably right (II.66) to suppose that JW meant the preface to stand before the entry for Sept. 17, 1738, but that the printer, finding that he had more pages in the German journal than he had proposed to produce for 8*d.* (three or four times the price of a chap-book), simply transferred the surplus to the next volume. At a later stage he was simply to destroy the additional matter.

[2] The 1742 original, like the version in the *Works* (1774), uses the spelling 'least', but in the errata to the *Works* JW notes: 'r[ead] lest, and in 100 places'. Actually the spelling 'least' remained in use occasionally as an alternative, but JW clearly preferred what has become the modern usage.

[3] Cf. Acts 26:1.

before.'[4] Not so, if you are a candid man. You have heard one side already. Hear the other. Weigh both. Allow for human weakness. And then judge as you desire to be judged.

3. What I design in the following extract is openly to declare to all mankind what it is that the Methodists (so called) have done 5 and are doing now—or rather, what it is that God hath done and is still doing in our land. For it is not the work of man which hath lately appeared. All who calmly observe it must say, 'This is the Lord's doing, and it is marvellous in our eyes.'[5]

4. Such a work this hath been in many respects as neither we 10 nor our fathers had known. Not a few whose sins were of the most flagrant kind, drunkards, swearers, thieves, whoremongers, adulterers, have been brought 'from darkness unto light, and from the power of Satan unto God'.[6] Many of these were rooted in their wickedness, having long gloried in their shame, perhaps 15 for a course of many years, yea, even to hoary hairs. Many had not so much as a notional faith, being Jews, Arians, Deists, or atheists. Nor has God only made bare his arm in these last days in behalf of open publicans and sinners, but many 'of the Pharisees' also 'have believed on him',[7] of the 'righteous that needed no repentance',[8] 20 and having 'received the sentence of death in themselves, have then heard the voice that raiseth the dead',[9] have been made partakers of an inward, vital religion, even 'righteousness and peace and joy in the Holy Ghost'.[10]

5. The manner wherein God hath wrought this work is as 25 strange as the work itself. In any particular soul it has generally, if not always, been wrought in one moment. 'As the lightning shining from heaven', so was 'the coming of the Son of man',[11] either to bring peace or a sword; either to wound or to heal, either to convince of sin or to give remission of sins in his blood. And the 30 other circumstances attending it have been equally remote from what human wisdom would have expected. So true is that word, 'My ways are not as your ways, nor my thoughts as your thoughts.'[12]

6. These extraordinary circumstances seem to have been 35 designed by God for the further manifestation of his work, to

---

[4] Cf. Aristophanes, *Plutus, l.* 600, *Non persuadebis, etiamsi persuaseris,* one of JW's favourite quotations. See Sermon 4, *Scriptural Christianity,* IV.2, 1:159-80 in this edn.
[5] Ps. 118:23; Matt. 21:42.   [6] Acts 26:18.
[7] Cf. John 7:48.   [8] Cf. Luke 15:7.
[9] Cf. 2 Cor. 1:9.   [10] Rom. 14:17.
[11] Cf. Matt. 24:27.   [12] Cf. Isa. 55:8.

cause his power to be known, and to awaken the attention of a drowsy world. And yet even from these some have drawn their grand objection against the whole work. 'We never saw it', say they, 'on this fashion.'[13] *Therefore* the work is not of God. To prove
5 which farther, they have not only greatly misrepresented many circumstances that really were, but have added many that were not, often without any regard either to truth or probability. A bare recital of those facts which were 'not done in a corner'[14] is the best answer to this sort of objections. To those which have been
10 judged to be of more weight I have occasionally given a more particular answer.

7. Yet I know even this will by no means satisfy the far greater part of those who are now offended. And for a plain reason, because they 'will never read it': they are resolved to hear one
15 side, and one only. I know also that many who *do* read it will be just of the same mind they were before, because they have fixed their judgment already and 'do not regard anything' which such a fellow can say. Let them see to that. I have done my part. I have delivered mine own soul.[15] Nay, I know that many will be greatly
20 offended at this very account. It must be so from the very nature of the things which are therein related. And the best appellation I expect from them is that of a fool, a madman, an enthusiast. All that in me lies is to relate simple truth, in as inoffensive a manner as I can. Let God give it the effect which pleaseth him and which
25 is most for his glory!

8. May 'he who hath the keys of the house of David, who openeth and no man shutteth',[16] open 'a great and effectual door'[17] by whom it pleaseth him, for his everlasting gospel! May he 'send by whom he will send',[18] so it may 'run and be glorified'[19]
30 more and more! May he 'ride on, conquering and to conquer',[20] until 'the fullness of the Gentiles be come in',[21] and 'the earth be full of the knowledge of the glory of the Lord, as the waters cover the sea'![22]

[13] Mark 2:12.
[14] Acts 26:26.
[15] One of JW's favourite expressions, based on Ezek. 14:20, which formed the closing statement of his *Nature, Design, and General Rules of the United Societies* (1743). For other examples in the *Journal,* cf. Apr. 1, 1785, and Mar. 6, Apr. 2, 1787, where it is applied to preaching.
[16] Cf. Rev. 3:7.   [17] Cf. 1 Cor. 16:9.   [18] Cf. Exod. 4:13.
[19] 2 Thess. 3:1. This was the translation which JW later used in his *Explanatory Notes upon the New Testament* (1755); see Vol. 6 in this edn.
[20] Cf. Rev. 6:2.   [21] Rom. 11:25.   [22] Cf. Hab. 2:14.

Journal

From August 12, 1738, to November 1, 1739

Saturday, Aug. 12, about seven in the evening, we came to Neukirch, a town about twenty-four miles from Herrnhut. Mr. Schneider (the minister of it, who had desired us to take his house 5 in our way)[1] was not at home, but we found one Mr. Manitius[2] there, the minister of a neighbouring town, who walked with us in the morning ten miles to Hauswalde, where he lived. He told us that the Lutherans as well as the Papists were irreconcilable enemies to the Brethren of Herrnhut; that the generality of the 10 Lutheran clergy were as bitter against them as the Jesuits themselves; that none of his neighbours durst go thither (unless by stealth), being sure of suffering for it if discovered; that to prevent any of Herrnhut from coming to them the Elector had forbid, under a severe penalty, any number of persons exceeding 15 three to meet together on a religious account;[3] and that he himself, for having a little society in his own parish, had been summoned to appear before the consistory at Dresden. Yea, let 'the kings of the earth stand up, and the rulers take counsel

[1] For David Schneider, see Aug. 10, 1738, n., 18:279 in this edn.

[2] Orig., 'Manoetius'. Johannes Bogislav Manitius (1689–1748) who had been a theological student at Halle 1709–14. A former follower of Konrad Dippel, he had been converted by the witness of the Herrnhuters. Hauswalde was a village near Bischofswerda, 20 miles E. of Dresden.

[3] To the general causes of friction between the Electoral government and the community at Herrnhut — the pressure of the emperor to stop the abduction of his subjects, the connexion between Liberda in his next parish of Gross Hennersdorf and the Prussian government, and the resistance of the Saxon Lutheran Orthodox to the intrusion of an ecclesiastical foreign body — must be added the severe local friction here hinted at. Zinzendorf had cultivated the Huldenbergs, the proprietors of Neukirch, a village where there were already numerous adherents of Herrnhut in the early 1730s. Huldenberg (the British envoy in Vienna), however, turned violently against them and their 'secret gatherings', and was believed by Zinzendorf not only to have been prejudiced against him by the interests of Halle after the expulsion of Spangenberg, but to have brought on him the second commission of inquiry by the Saxon government in 1736. This inquiry led to new legislation against conventicles in 1737, and Zinzendorf's own expulsion from Saxony for the second time in 1738. See F. S. Hark, 'Der Konflikt der kursächsischen Regierung mit Herrnhut und dem Grafen von Zinzendorf', *Neues Archiv für Sächsische Geschichte und Alterthumskunde* 3 (Dresden, 1882), pp. 1-65; also Ferdinand Körner, *Die kursächsische Staatsregierung dem Grafen Zinzendorf und Herrnhut bis 1760 gegenüber* (Leipzig, 1878).

5

together against the Lord and against his anointed! He that sitteth in heaven shall laugh them to scorn; the Lord shall have them in derision.'[4]

We left Hauswalde in the afternoon, and in the evening came 5 to Dresden. But the officer at the gate would not suffer us to come in; so that we were obliged to go on to the next village; which leaving early in the morning, on Thursday in the afternoon we came to Leipzig.

We were now kept only an hour at the gate, and then conducted 10 to Mr. Arnold's,[5] who had invited us when we were in the town before, to make his house our home. A few we found here, too, who desire to 'know nothing but Jesus Christ and him crucified'.[6] And from them we had letters to Halle, whither we came on Friday 18. But the King of Prussia's tall men (who kept the gate) 15 would not suffer Mr. Brown to come in. Me they admitted (in honour of my profession) after I had waited about two hours; and one of them went with me to the Prince of Hesse,[7] who after a few questions gave me leave to lodge in the city. Thence he showed me to Mr. Gottschalck's[8] lodgings, to whom I had letters from 20 Leipzig. He read them and said, 'My brother, what you find here you will use as your own. And if you want anything else, tell us, and you shall have it.'

I told them my companion was without the gate. They soon procured admittance for him. And we were indeed as at 25 home, for I have hardly seen such little children as these, even at Herrnhut.

Sat. 19. I waited on Professor Francke, who behaved with the utmost humanity; and afterwards on Professor Knappe,[9] to whom

---

[4] Ps. 2:2, 4 (BCP, with 'sitteth' retained from AV).

[5] The identity of this Mr. Arnold is uncertain, but it may well have been Theodorus Arnold of Fleischer Gasse, one of three teachers of the English language at Leipzig. *Das jetzt lebende und jetzt floriende Leipzig* (Leipzig, 1723), p. 61.

[6] Cf. 1 Cor. 2:2.

[7] The two chief lines of the family of Hesse were those of Hesse-Cassel and Hesse-Darmstadt, in 1738 represented respectively by Frederick (1676–1751) who became King of Sweden in 1720 and Count of Hesse-Cassel in 1730, and Ernest Lewis (1667–1739) who became count of Hesse-Darmstadt in 1678.

[8] It is not clear whether this Gottschalck is the same as the one who was among the German Brethren in London formed into a separate congregation in 1744 (Daniel Benham, *Memoirs of James Hutton* [London, Hamilton, Adams, 1856], p. 130), and evangelized Maryland and Virginia in 1747 (J. Taylor Hamilton, *A History of the Church Known as the Moravian Church or The Unitas Fratrum* [Bethlehem, Pa., Times Publishing Co., 1900], p. 140).

[9] Johann Georg Knappe (1705–71), a pupil of Buddeus at Jena, had a varied career as pedagogue, preacher to the royal corps of cadets at Berlin, and (from 1737) an

also I am indebted for his open, friendly behaviour. Between ten
and eleven, seven of the Brethren set out with us, one of whom
went with us two days' journey. It was the dusk of the evening on
Sunday 20 when, wet and weary, we reached Jena.
Mon. 21. We visited the schools there, the rise of which (as we 5
were informed) was occasioned thus:

About the year 1704 Mr. Stoltius,[10] a student at Jena, began
to speak of faith in Christ, which he continued to do till he took
his master's degree and read public lectures. About twelve or
fifteen students were awakened and joined with him in prayer 10
and building up one another. At this (after various calumnies
spread abroad and persecutions occasioned thereby) the
consistory was offended and issued out a commission to
examine him. In consequence of the report made to the
consistory by these commissioners he was forbid to read any 15
public lectures or to hold any meetings with his friends. Not
long after an order was given by which he was excluded from
the Holy Communion. He was also to have been expelled from
the university; but this he prevented by a voluntary retirement. 20
Yet one of the commissioners who had been sent by the
Duke of Weimar (one of the lords of Jena), informed the Duke
that according to his judgment Stoltius was an innocent and
holy man. On this the Duke sent for him to Weimar and fixed
him in a living there. There likewise he awakened many and 25
met with them to pray and read the Scriptures together. But it

extraordinary professor of divinity at Halle. In the year following JW's visit he became
co-director of the Orphan House. When G. A. Francke died in 1769, he became director
of the Orphan House and the royal Pädagogium. He had a reputation for great personal
simplicity and modesty and for edifying preaching. See Gottlieb Anastasius Freyling-
hausen, *Wohlverdientes Ehrengedächtniss, gestiftet dem weiland und hochgelahrten Herr Johann
Georg Knapp* . . . (Halle, 1772).
  [10] Johann Ernst Stolte (1672–1719), Magister in Jena (1694–1715), pastor at the Jacobi
Kirche, Weimar, 1715. Bengel describes how in 1713 he 'was introduced to a man of
approved piety and of no common learning, who received me under his roof, and treated
me as one of his family; his name is Stolthe. He has great talent for awakening and stirring
up others, by which he has been useful to many of the young, and his usefulness in this way
is daily increasing. Many suspect or envy him, and consequently hate him; but others are
most affectionately attached to him, are glad to have his guidance in their studies, and are
in closest communion with him by mutual prayer. Every Lord's Day he holds a
prayer-meeting in his house, and another for exposition daily after dinner. To students
preparing to communicate at the Lord's table, he gives instruction for several weeks
beforehand, by particular exposition of subjects from the catechism' (J. C. F. Burk,
Memoir of the life and writings of John Albert Bengel [London, 1837], p. 25).

was not long that the city could bear him. For he boldly rebuked all vice, and that in all persons, neither sparing the courtiers nor the Duke himself. Consequently his enemies everywhere increased, and many persecutions followed. In 5 fine, he was forbid to have any private meetings and was to have been deposed from the ministry; when God, calling him to himself, took him away from the evil to come.

Before Stoltius left Jena, Buddaeus[11] also began to preach the real gospel, as did Christius[12] soon after; whereby some 10 awakening continued till the year 1724. A few of the townsmen then agreed to maintain a student to be a schoolmaster for some poor children. They afterwards kept several school-masters. But about 1728, all of them going away, the school was broke up, and the children quite neglected. Professor 15 Buddaeus being informed of this, earnestly recommended the consideration of it to the students in his house; and about ten of them, among whom was Mr. Spangenberg,[13] took upon themselves the care of those children. Their number soon increased, which gave great offence to the other schoolmasters 20 in the town, and not long after to the magistrates of the town and to the senate of the university. The offence soon spread to the pastors, the professors, the consistory, and the princes who are lords of Jena. But it pleased God to move one of them, the Prince of Eisenach,[14] who had the chief power there, to stop the 25 open persecution by forbidding either the senate or consistory

---

[11] Johann Franz Buddeus (1667–1729), professor of civil and moral law at Halle (1693–1705), professor of theology at Jena from 1705. Taking a middle position between pietism and orthodoxy, he pointed also, despite a conflict with Wolff, towards the Enlightenment. He was highly esteemed by friends of Zinzendorf, won Spangenberg for evangelical religion, was in personal touch with Spener and Francke, and was attacked by the Orthodox as a patron of pietists. That this was not so, in no way reduced their chagrin at the way the Jena theological faculty which, as an Orthodox stronghold had reached a low ebb, was raised to a new glory by men like Buddeus and the Franconian Fuertsch (Karl Heussi, *Geschichte der Theologischen Fakultät zu Jena* [Weimar, 1954], pp. 154-62). Buddeus's *Elementa Philosophiae Theoreticae* was translated and abridged by JW to form the nucleus of his own *Natural Philosophy* (see Vol. 17 of this edn.).

[12] The Magister Friedrich Christ (in 1727 a pastor in Drakendorf, and in 1730 of Pösneck) was one of a series of young men who kept the revival awake in Jena, especially among students, after the departure of Stolte, and began free schools for the children of the poor. Gerhard Reichel, *August Gottlieb Spangenberg, Bischof der Brüderkirche* (Tübingen, 1906), pp. 19, 48; reprint in *Nikolaus Ludwig von Zinzendorf: Materialen und Dokumente*, 2 R., 18, pp. 35, 64.

[13] On Spangenberg see Feb. 7, 1736, n. 37, 18:145-46 in this edn.

[14] William Henry (1691–1741) became Duke of Sachsen-Eisenach 4 Jan. 1729. *Jährliches Genealogisches Handbuch*, ed. Gottlieb Schuman (Leipzig, 1747).

to molest them. He likewise wholly exempted them from the jurisdiction of both, ordering that all complaints against them for the time to come should be cognizable only by himself. But during the persecution the number of schools was increased from one to three (one in each suburb of the city), the number 5 of teachers to above thirty, and of children to above three hundred.

There are now thirty-one constant teachers, ten in each school, and three or four supernumerary, to supply accidental defects. Four of the masters are appointed to punish, who are 10 affixed to no one school. Each of the schools being divided into two classes, and taught five hours a day, every one of the thirty masters has one hour in a day to teach. All the masters have a conference about the schools every Monday. They have a second meeting on Thursday, chiefly for prayer. And a third 15 every Saturday.

Once in half a year they meet to fill up the places of those masters who are gone away. And the number has never decreased, fresh ones still offering themselves, as the former leave the university. 20

The present method wherein they teach is this:

There are always two classes in each school. In the lower, children from six to ten or twelve years old are taught to read. They are then removed to the other class, in which are taught the Holy Scriptures, arithmetic, and whatever else it may be 25 useful for children to learn.

In the morning from eight to nine they are all catechized and instructed in the first principles of Christianity, either from Luther's smaller catechism, or from some texts of Holy Scripture. 30

From nine to ten the smaller children are taught their letters and syllables, and the larger read the Bible. From ten to eleven those in the lower class learn and repeat some select verses of Holy Scripture, chiefly relating to the foundation of the faith. Meanwhile those in the upper learn arithmetic. 35

In the afternoon from one to two all the children are employed, as from nine to ten in the morning. From two to three the smaller children learn and repeat Luther's smaller catechism, while the larger are taught to write.

Every Sunday there is a public catechizing on some text of 40 Scripture, at which all persons who desire it may be present.

In the afternoon we left Jena, several of the Brethren accompanying us out of town. At five, having just passed through Weimar, we met Mr. Ingham going for Herrnhut. We all turned aside to a neighbouring village, where, having spent a comfortable 5 evening together, in the morning we commended each other to the grace of God and went on our several ways.

We breakfasted at Erfurt with Mr. Reinhardt, spent the evening with some Brethren at Saxe-Gotha, and by long journeys came to Marienborn on Friday, August 25.

10 Mon. 28. I took my leave of the Countess[15] (the Count being gone to Jena) and setting out early the next morning came about three in the afternoon to Frankfurt.[16] From Mr. Böhler's we went to the society, where one of the Brethren from Marienborn offered free redemption through the blood of Christ to sixty or 15 seventy persons.

Wed. 30. In the afternoon we came to Mainz,[17] and agreed for our passage to Cologne[18] by water, for a florin per head, which was but half what we gave before, though (it seems) twice as much as we ought to have given.

20 Thur. 31. We spent half an hour in the great church,[19] a huge heap of irregular building, full of altars, adorned (or loaded rather) with abundance of gold and silver. In going out we observed a paper on the door, which was of so extraordinary a nature that I thought it would not be labour lost to transcribe it. 25 The words were as follow:

Volkommener Ablass für die arme Seelen im Feg-feuer
Seine Päbliche Heiligkeit, Clemens der 12te, haben in diesem Jahr 1738,
den 7 Augustin, die Pfarr Kirche des Sancti Christophori in Mentz
gnädigsten Privilegirt, dass ein jeder Priester, so wohl secular als

---

[15] Erdmuthe Dorothea (1700–56), first wife of Count Zinzendorf (1722). Like her brother, Count Henry XXIX of Reuss Ebersdorf (through whom she met Zinzendorf), and her elder sister, she was deeply influenced by Spener. Her strength was finally sapped by incessant travelling and labours for the Brethren and by giving birth to twelve children, most of whom died young and none of whom survived to a mature age.

[16] Orig., 'Franckfort'.

[17] Orig., 'Mentz'.

[18] Orig., 'Cölen' (Köln), here and below.

[19] St. Martin's Cathedral, Mainz, originally built 975–1009, had been rebuilt several times and received accretions from several architectural styles. A century later Murray remarked in a style similar to Wesley that the cathedral was 'less interesting for any beauty of architecture (as it is built in the massive round arched Gothic style) than for its great antiquity' ([Murray's] *Handbook for Travellers on the Continent: being a guide through Holland, Belgium, Prussia and Northern Germany* [3rd ed., London, 1839], p. 265).

regularischen stands, der am aller Seelen-tag, wie auch an einem jedem tag
in derselben Octav; so dann am zweien vom Ordinario tagen einer Jeden
woch das Jahr hindurch, für die Seel eines Christglaubigen verstorbenen an
zum Altar Mess lesen wird, jedesmahl eine Seel aus dem Feg-feuer erlösen
könne.   5

A full Release for the poor Souls in Purgatory
His Papal Holiness, Clement the XIIth, hath this year 1738, on the
seventh of August, most graciously privileged the Cathedral Church[20]
of St. Christopher in Mentz, so that every priest, as well secular as
regular, who will read Mass at an altar for the soul of a Christian 10
departed, on any holiday,[21] or on any day within the octave thereof, or
on two extraordinary days, to be appointed by the Ordinary, of any
week in the year, may each time deliver a soul out of the fire of
purgatory.

Now I desire to know whether any Romanist of common sense 15
can either defend or approve of this?
At eight we took boat and on Saturday, September 2, about
eleven, came to Cologne, which we left at one, and between seven
and eight reached a village an hour short of Neuss.[22] Here we
overtook a large number of Switzers, men, women, and children, 20
singing, dancing, and making merry, being all going 'to make
their fortunes in Georgia'.[23] Looking upon them as delivered into
my hands by God, I plainly told them what manner of place it was.
If they now leap into the fire with open eyes, their blood is on their
own head.   25
Mon. 4. Before noon we came to Kleve,[24] and to Nijmegen[25] in
the evening. The next night we lay at a little village near Tiel,
which leaving early in the morning, we walked by the side of many
pleasant orchards, and in the afternoon came to Ijsselstein.[26] We
stayed only one night with the Brethren (in the new house called 30
Heerendyk,[27] an English mile from the town) and hasting forward
came the next afternoon to Dr. Koker's at Rotterdam.

---

[20] Actually, 'the parish church'.
[21] Actually, 'on All Souls' Day'.
[22] Orig., 'Neus'.
[23] In Coulter and Saye's not quite complete *List of the Early Settlers of Georgia* in the first
decade of the colony, almost half of those sent on the Trustees' charge were foreign
Protestants (839) of whom 142 were Swiss. But others went at their own charge, including
Samuel Ausperger, engineer and land surveyor of Bern, who contracted to recruit labour
in Germany and Switzerland. Egmont, Earl of, *Diary of Viscount Percival, afterwards First
Earl of Egmont*, 3 vols. (London, Historical MSS Commission, 1920–23), III.114, 224.
[24] Orig., 'Cleve'.   [25] Orig., 'Nimwegen'.
[26] Orig., 'Ysselstein'.   [27] Orig., 'Herndyke'.

I can't but acknowledge the civility of this friendly man all the time we stayed in his house. In the morning, Friday 8, we went to the English Episcopal Church, which is a large, handsome, convenient building. The minister[28] read prayers seriously and
5 distinctly to a small, well-behaved congregation. Being informed our ship was to sail the next day (Saturday), we took leave of our generous friend and went to an inn close to the quay,[29] that we might be ready when called to go aboard. Having waited till past four in the afternoon, we stepped into the Jews' Synagogue,
10 which lies near the water-side. I do not wonder that so many Jews (especially those who have any reflection) utterly abjure all religion. My spirit was moved within me at that horrid, senseless pageantry, that mockery of God which they called public worship. Lord, do not thou yet 'cast off thy people'![30] But 'in Abraham's
15 seed let them also be blessed'![31]

The ship lingering still, I had time to exhort several English, whom we met with at our inn, to pursue inward religion: the renewal of their souls in righteousness and true holiness.[32] In the morning a daughter of affliction came to see me, who teaches a
20 school at Rotterdam. She had been for some time under deep convictions, but could find none to instruct or comfort her. After much conversation we joined in prayer, and her spirit a little revived. Between nine and ten we went on board. In the afternoon I read prayers and preached in the great cabin. The wind being
25 contrary, we did not get out of the river till Wednesday, nor to London till Saturday night.

Sunday, September 17, I began again to declare in my own country the glad tidings of salvation, preaching three times and afterwards expounding the Holy Scripture to a large company in
30 the Minories.[33] On Monday I rejoiced to meet with our little society, which now consisted of thirty-two persons. The next day I went to the condemned felons in Newgate and offered them free salvation. In the evening I went to a society in Bear Yard,[34] and

---

[28] Richard Lowther, minister in Rotterdam, 1719–40.
[29] Orig., 'key', although in later years JW used 'quay'.
[30] Cf. Ps. 94:14.
[31] Cf. Gen. 22:18.   [32] Eph. 4:24.
[33] This was a property belonging to Peter Sims, butcher (b. 1716), where one of the largest religious societies assembled. A fortnight before Charles Wesley had preached there 'to above two hundred people' (CWJ, I.129). The Minories is a road running north and south, linking Aldgate with the Tower.
[34] This second mention of religious societies in successive days emphasizes one of the links between the early Methodists (it is still too soon to speak of Methodism) and an

preached repentance and remission of sins. The next evening I spoke the truth in love at a society in Aldersgate Street. Some contradicted at first, but not long, so that nothing but love appeared at our parting.

Thur. 21. I went to a society in Gutter Lane, but I could not declare the mighty works of God there, as I did afterwards at the Savoy[35] in all simplicity. And the word did not return empty.

Finding abundance of people greatly exasperated by gross misrepresentations of the words I had spoken, I went to as many of them in private as my time would permit. God gave me much love towards them all. Some were convinced they had been mistaken. And who knoweth but God will soon return to the rest and leave a blessing behind him?

On Saturday 23 I was enabled to speak strong words both at Newgate and at Mr. E[xall]'s[36] society; and the next day at St. Anne's, and twice at St. John's, Clerkenwell,[37] so that I fear they will bear me there no longer.

informal religious past. Growing up in the late 1670s in response to the ministry of Anton Horneck (1641–97), the German preacher at the Savoy, the religious societies provided a spiritual discipline and a scope for the philanthropy not unlike that of the Holy Club. Becoming numerous in London after the 1688 Revolution, they attracted members of very varying brands of churchmanship and some Dissenters also. At that time a good deal of the religious life of London went on in these societies and in the ministry of lecturers whose appointment they secured. Little is known of their condition at this stage of their history, but the *Journal* makes it clear not merely that they still existed but that they continued, like the pietist *Stunden* in many parts of Protestant Germany, to provide a common forum for earnest members of the establishment and others.

[35] The Chapel Royal, Savoy, the scene of Horneck's ministry in London, in the vicinity of which a religious society still met.

[36] The name appears as Exall in the original letter of Sept. 21, 1739, and appears as Exall or Extell constantly in the diaries at this time. William Exall was one of the members of the Fetter Lane Society who threw in his lot with JW. WHS 16:145.

[37] Few churches have had a more eventful history than St. John's, Clerkenwell. Built in the twelfth century by the Order of St. John (the Knights Hospitallers), it was burned down in the Peasants' Revolt of 1381, then rebuilt and enlarged in the early sixteenth century. At the Dissolution, the nave was blown up to provide stone for Protector Somerset's new house in the Strand, but it was rescued by Lady Burleigh, wife of the grandson of Elizabeth's Lord High Treasurer, to whom ownership passed, and it was opened for worship in 1623 as a private chapel. It later passed to the Earl of Aylesbury who used the crypt as a wine-cellar. In 1706 it became a Presbyterian meeting-house, only to be gutted by the mob in the Sacheverell riots. Rescued this time by two local people, it was sold in 1723 to the Commissioners for Fifty New Churches, who made it into the parish church it continued to be for two centuries. Its parish was then absorbed by St. James's, Clerkenwell, when it became once more the Grand Priory Church of the Order of St. John. Burned out by enemy action in 1941, it was restored and rededicated in 1958. (Mervyn Blatch, *A Guide to London's Churches* [London, 1978], pp. 333-34.) The rector, 1738–69, was Stephen Aldrich.

Tue. 26. I declared the gospel of peace to a small company at Windsor.[38] The next evening Mr. H.[39] preached to the societies at Bow, but not 'the truth as it is in Jesus'.[40] I was afraid lest 'the lame' should 'be turned out of the way',[41] but God answered the thoughts of my heart and took away my fear, in a manner I did not expect, even by the words of Thomas Sternhold.[42] They were these (sung immediately after the sermon):

Thy mercy is above all things,
　O God; it doth excel:
In trust whereof, as in thy wings,
　The sons of men shall dwell.

Within thy house they shall be fed
　With plenty at their will;
Of all delights they shall be sped,
　And take thereof their fill.

Because the well of life most pure
　Doth ever flow from thee;
And in thy light we are most sure
　Eternal light to see.

From such as thee desire to know
　Let not thy grace depart;
Thy righteousness declare and show
　To men of upright heart.

[38] This meeting took place in the house of that 'excellent man John Thorold, Esq., . . . a gentleman of fortune, a very worthy and truly Christian man; who, not being ashamed of the Gospel and its followers, had from the year 1738, attended the evening meetings of the society in [James] Hutton's house, expounded the holy Scriptures, with singing and prayer for the work of the Lord, particularly among the Brethren', but who had sharp differences with them in 1742 (Benham, *Hutton*, pp. 82-84). Despite much evangelical speculation, there seems no reason to identify this John Thorold of Windsor with the Sir John Thorold, Bart., of Gainsborough, into whose fellowship at Lincoln College JW was elected, and who remained the friend of JW and the Countess of Huntingdon.

[39] Curnock surmised, apparently without evidence, that this sermon was preached in St. Mary-le-Bow, and was preached not to religious societies but to the SPCK and SPG. It is, however, likely that Mr. H. may be the Jeph. Harris to whose religious society Charles Wesley had been taken by Bray on Aug. 16, 1738 (CWJ, I.126), and whose doctrine he had confuted.

[40] Cf. Eph. 4:21.

[41] Heb. 12:13.

[42] Thomas Sternhold (d. 1549), joint versifier of the Psalms with John Hopkins. The verses quoted are from the metrical version of Ps. 36:7-10, which is in fact ascribed to Hopkins.

Sat. 30. One who had been a zealous opposer of 'this way'[43] sent and desired to speak with me immediately.[44] He had all the signs of settled despair, both in his countenance and behaviour. He said he had been enslaved to sin many years, especially to drunkenness; that he had long used all the means of grace, had 5 constantly gone to church and sacrament, had read the Scripture, and used much private prayer, and yet was nothing profited. I desired we might join in prayer. After a short space he rose, and his countenance was no longer sad. He said, 'Now I know God loveth *me* and has forgiven *my* sins. And sin shall not have 10 dominion over me, for Christ hath set me free.' And according to his faith it was unto him.

Sun. Oct. 1. I preached both morning and afternoon at St. George's-in-the-East.[45] On the following days I endeavoured to explain the way of salvation to many who had misunderstood what 15 had been preached concerning it.

Fri. 6. I preached at St. Antholin's once more. In the afternoon I went to the Rev. Mr. Bedford[46] to tell him between me and him alone of the injury he had done both to God and his brother, by preaching and printing that very weak sermon on *Assurance*,[47] 20 which was an *ignoratio elenchi*[48] from beginning to end, seeing the assurance we preach is of quite another kind from that he writes against. We speak of an assurance of *our present pardon*, not (as he does) *of our final perseverance*.

---

[43] Acts 9:2.

[44] The diary indicates that this was a Mr. Jennings. Cf. CWJ, I.131.

[45] St. George's-in-the-East was a flight of fancy created by Hawksmoor, 1714–26, to serve a riverside district when the huge parish of Stepney was being subdivided. The scene of antiritual riots, 1859–60, it was burned out by enemy action in 1941. Between 1960 and 1964 the walls were repaired, a small modern place of worship created in the eastern part of the old nave, and flats, a parish hall, and other amenities formed in other parts of the building (Blatch, *London's Churches*, pp. 399–403). The rector, 1729–64, was William Simpson, D.D.

[46] Arthur Bedford (1668–1745), educated at Brasenose College, Oxford, and incumbent of Newton St. Loe, Somerset, from 1701. As a young man he was chaplain to the Duke of Bedford, a crusader against the stage; he had a lifelong interest in chronology, mathematics, and other topics of scientific and doctrinal interest. In 1724 he was appointed chaplain to the Haberdashers' Company at Hoxton and late in life became chaplain to Frederick, Prince of Wales. Long afterwards JW spoke highly of him (JWJ, Mar. 18, 1781).

[47] *The Doctrine of Assurance: or, the case of a weak and doubting conscience. A Sermon preached at St. Lawrence Jewry . . . on Sunday, August 13, 1738.* No copy of the first edition appears to be extant. The second edition appeared in June 1739. See JW's letter to Bedford on this work, Sept. 28, 1738, *Letters*, 25:562–66 in this edn.

[48] 'Ignoring the pearl', i.e., leaving out the chief point in an argument.

In the evening I began expounding at a little society in Wapping. On Sunday 8, I preached at the Savoy Chapel (I suppose the last time) on the parable (or history rather) of the Pharisee and publican praying in the temple.[49] On Monday 9, I set
5 out for Oxford. In walking I read the truly surprising narrative of the conversions lately wrought in and about the town of Northampton in New England.[50] Surely 'this is the Lord's doing, and it is marvellous in our eyes'![51]

An extract from this I wrote to a friend, concerning the state of
10 those who are 'weak in faith'.[52] His answer, which I received on Saturday 14, threw me into great perplexity, till after crying to God I took up a Bible, which opened on these words: 'And Jabez called on the God of Israel, saying, O that thou wouldst bless me indeed and enlarge my coast! And that thine hand might be with
15 me, and that thou wouldst keep me from evil, that it may not grieve me! And God granted him that which he requested.'[53]

This, however, with a sentence in the Evening Lesson, put me upon considering my own state more deeply. And what then occurred to me was as follows:
20 'Examine yourselves, whether ye be in the faith.'[54] Now the surest test whereby we can examine ourselves, whether we be indeed in the faith, is that given by St. Paul: 'If any man be in Christ, he is a new creature. Old things are passed away. Behold all things are become new.'[55]

---

[49] See Luke 18:9-14.

[50] Jonathan Edwards, *A Faithful Narrative of the Surprising Work of God, in the Conversion of many hundred Souls in Northampton . . .*, ed. by Isaac Watts and John Guyse (London, 1737; 2nd edn., 1738). This, perhaps the most famous of all the revival tracts, was repeatedly published in both England and New England (also in Magdeburg, 1738) and was abridged by JW in 1744.

[51] Ps. 118:23 (BCP).

[52] The reference is to Rom. 4:19. Edwards's narrative had described how 'many times persons under great awakenings were concerned because they thought they were *not* awakened, but miserable, hard-hearted, senseless, sottish creatures still, and sleeping upon the brink of hell . . . . That calm of spirit that some persons have found after their legal distresses, continues some time before any special and delightful manifestation is made to the soul of the grace of God as revealed in the gospel. But very often some comfortable sweet view of a merciful God, of a sufficient Redeemer, or of some great and joyful things of the gospel immediately follows, or in a very little time . . .' (*The Works of Jonathan Edwards*, ed. H. Rogers, S. E. Dwight, and E. Hickman [London, 1837] I.351, 353).

[53] 1 Chron. 4:10.

[54] 2 Cor. 13:5.

[55] 2 Cor. 5:17. A few years later Wesley preached a sermon from this text against Moravian claims to sinless perfection, very different in tone. The anxiety of the last section of this self-examination is replaced by the confident assertion that 'there are in every

First, his judgments are new: his judgment of himself, of happiness, of holiness.

He judges himself to be altogether fallen short of the glorious image of God; to have no good thing abiding in him, but all that is corrupt and abominable; in a word, to be wholly earthly, sensual, 5 and devilish[56]—a motley mixture of beast and devil.[57]

Thus, by the grace of God in Christ, I judge of myself. Therefore I am in this respect a new creature.

Again, his judgment concerning happiness is new. He would as soon expect to dig it out of the earth as to find it in riches, honour, 10 pleasure (so called), or indeed in the enjoyment of any creature. He knows there can be no happiness on earth but in the enjoyment of God and in the foretaste of those 'rivers of pleasure which flow at his right hand for evermore'.[58]

Thus, by the grace of God in Christ, I judge of happiness. 15 Therefore I am in this respect a new creature.

Yet again, his judgment concerning holiness is new. He no longer judges it to be an outward thing, to consist either in doing no harm, in doing good, or in using the ordinances of God. He sees it is the life of God in the soul; the image of God fresh 20 stamped on the heart; an entire renewal of the mind in every temper and thought, after the likeness of him that created it.

Thus, by the grace of God in Christ, I judge of holiness. Therefore I am in this respect a new creature.

Secondly, his designs are new. It is the design of his life not to 25 heap up treasures upon earth, not to gain the praise of men, not to indulge the desires of the flesh, the desire of the eye, or the pride of life;[59] but to regain the image of God, to have the life of God again planted in his soul, and to be renewed after his likeness, in righteousness and all true holiness.[60] 30

This, by the grace of God in Christ, is the design of my life. Therefore I am in this respect a new creature.

---

person, even after he is justified, two contrary principles, nature and grace, . . . even though babes in Christ are *sanctified*, yet it is only *in part*. In a degree, according to the measure of their faith, they are *spiritual;* yet in a degree they are *carnal*' (Sermon 13, *On Sin in Believers*, V.1, 1:332 in this edn.). This was ground not for lack of assurance, but for 'diligence in "fighting the good fight of faith"' (ibid., V.2, 1:333 in this edn.).

[56] Jas. 3:15.

[57] A current phrase found not merely in the Wesley hymn, 'Jesu, the sinner's friend, to Thee' (1739), but in many other contemporary writers.

[58] Cf. Pss. 16:1; 36:8.

[59] See 1 John 2:16.

[60] Eph. 4:24.

Thirdly, his desires are new, and indeed the whole train of his passions and inclinations. They are no longer fixed on earthly things. They are now set on the things of heaven. His love and joy and hope, his sorrow and fear, have all respect to things above.
5 They all point heavenward. Where his treasure is, there is his heart also.[61]

I dare not say I am a new creature in this respect. For other desires often *arise* in my heart. But they do not *reign*. I put them all under my feet through Christ which strengtheneth me.[62]
10 Therefore I believe he is *creating* me anew in this also, and that he has begun, though not finished, his work.

Fourthly, his conversation is new. It is 'always seasoned with salt',[63] and fit to 'minister grace to the hearers'.[64]

So is mine, by the grace of God in Christ. Therefore in this
15 respect I am a new creature.

Fifthly, his actions are new. The tenor of his life singly points at the glory of God. All his substance and time are devoted thereto. 'Whether he eats or drinks, or whatever he does',[65] it either springs from, or leads to, the love of God and man.
20 Such, by the grace of God in Christ, is the tenor of my life. Therefore in this respect I am a new creature.

But St. Paul tells us elsewhere that 'the fruit of the Spirit is love, peace, joy, long-suffering, gentleness, meekness, temperance.'[66] Now although, by the grace of God in Christ, I find a
25 measure of some of these in myself, viz., of peace, long-suffering, gentleness, meekness, temperance; yet others I find not. I cannot find in myself the love of God or of Christ. Hence my deadness and wanderings in public prayer. Hence it is that even in the Holy Communion I have rarely any more than a cold attention. Hence
30 when I hear of the highest instance of God's love, my heart is still senseless and unaffected. Yea, at this moment, I feel no more love to him than to one I had never heard of.[67]

Again, I have not that 'joy in the Holy Ghost';[68] no settled, lasting joy. Nor have I such a peace as excludes the possibility
35 either of fear or doubt. When holy men have told me I had no

---

[61] See Matt 6:21; Luke 12:34.   [62] Phil. 4:13.
[63] Col. 4:6.   [64] Eph. 4:29.
[65] Cf. 1 Cor. 10:31.
[66] Cf. Gal. 5:22-23.
[67] *Works* (1774) omitted the last two sentences and closed the previous one: 'I have frequently no more than a cold attention.'
[68] Rom. 14:17.

faith, I have often doubted whether I had or no. And those doubts have made me very uneasy, till I was relieved by prayer and the Holy Scriptures.

Yet, upon the whole, although I have not yet that joy in the Holy Ghost, nor that love of God shed abroad in my heart,[69] nor the full 5 assurance of faith,[70] nor the (proper) witness of the Spirit with my spirit that I am a child of God,[71] much less am I, in the full and proper sense of the words,[72] in Christ a new creature;[73] I nevertheless trust that I have a measure of faith and am 'accepted in the Beloved':[74] I trust 'the handwriting that was against me is 10 blotted out',[75] and that I am 'reconciled to God through his Son'.[76]

Sun. 15. I preached twice at the Castle, and afterwards expounded at three societies. Wednesday evening I came to London again, and on Friday met a society (of soldiers chiefly) at Westminster. On Sunday 22 I preached at Bloomsbury in the 15 morning, and at Shadwell[77] in the afternoon. Wednesday 25 I preached at Basingshaw Church;[78] on Friday morning at St. Antholin's; on Sunday at Islington[79] and at London Wall.[80] Strange doctrine to a polite audience!

[69] See Rom. 5:5.

[70] Heb. 10:22.

[71] See Rom. 8:16.

[72] *Works* (1774) abridged to read: 'Yet, upon the whole, although I have not yet that joy in the Holy Ghost, nor the full assurance of faith, much less am I, in the full sense of the words . . .'.

[73] 2 Cor. 5:17; Gal. 6:15.

[74] Eph. 1:6.

[75] Cf. Col. 2:14.

[76] Cf. Rom. 5:10.

[77] St. Paul's, Shadwell, was built in 1656 as a chapel of ease to St. Dunstan's, Stepney, and replaced by another building in 1820. The incumbent, 1736–40, was John Nash, M.A.

[78] St. Michael, Basinghall (or Bassishaw), the rector of which, 1730–42, was George Lavington, who as Bishop of Exeter began a celebrated controversy against Methodism in 1749. The parish was joined to that of St. Lawrence Jewry in 1892 and the church demolished in 1900. Blatch, *London's Churches*, pp. 100, 20.

[79] St. Mary's, Islington, certainly existed in the twelfth century and was rebuilt in the fifteenth. Efforts to secure a more adequate building succeeded only with the passing of a local act in 1750; this church was destroyed by a bomb in 1940 and replaced in a new style in 1956. The church had a strong Protestant tradition and was to be important in the early stages of the revival. The vicar, 1738–40, was George Stonehouse, M.A.

[80] All Hallows, London Wall, began on a long and narrow fringe of land in the twelfth century and was replaced in the thirteenth by the church in which JW preached. It consisted of a nave and aisle raised well above street level and behind a retaining wall. This church was replaced 1765–67 by a building subsequently damaged severely in the Second World War. This was restored under the Guild Churches Act in 1962 and houses the Council for Places of Worship. The rector, 1736–58, was Samuel Smith, LL.B.

In the evening, being troubled in what some said of 'the
kingdom of God within us',[81] and doubtful of my own state, I
called upon God and received this answer from his Word, 'He
himself also waited for the kingdom of God.'[82] 'But should not I
5 wait in silence and retirement?' was the thought that immediately
struck into my mind. I opened my Testament again, on those
words, 'Seest thou not how faith wrought together with his works?
And by works was faith made perfect?'[83]

Finding the same doubts return on Tuesday, I consulted the
10 oracles of God again and found much comfort from those words,
'They which be of faith are blessed with faithful Abraham.'[84]

Fri. Nov. 3. I preached at St. Antholin's. Sunday 5, in the
morning at St. Botolph's, Bishopsgate,[85] in the afternoon at
Islington, and in the evening to such a congregation at I never saw
15 before at St. Clement's in the Strand.[86] As this was the first time
of my preaching here, I suppose it is to be the last.

On Wednesday my brother and I went, at their earnest desire,
to do the last good office to the condemned malefactors.[87] It was
the most glorious instance I ever saw of faith triumphing over sin
20 and death. One observing the tears run fast down the cheeks of

---

[81] Cf. Luke 17:21.

[82] Cf. Luke 23:51.

[83] Cf. Jas. 2:22.

[84] Gal. 3:9.

[85] St. Botolph's without Bishopsgate was apparently built on the site of a Saxon church
and is first mentioned in the documents in 1212. It survived the Great Fire but became
ruinous and was demolished in 1724. A new church, built by James Gold, was consecrated
in 1728. Subsequently restored seven times, St. Botolph's suffered no more than the
destruction of the west windows in the Second World War. A piece of land to the north of
the church was given to found the Priory of St. Mary of Bethlehem in 1247; after the
Dissolution this was converted to the celebrated Bedlam, the Bethlehem Hospital for
Lunatics (Blatch, *London's Churches*, p. 48). The rector, 1730–43, was William Crowe,
D.D.

[86] St. Clement Danes, supposedly so called as a church for Danes with English
wives, permitted by Alfred the Great to settle between Ludgate and Westminster in A.D.
886. An old timber-framed church was replaced by a stone building *c.* 1022, the
remains of which are still visible. The church was partly rebuilt in 1640 and survived
the Great Fire. Wren, however, pulled it down and completely rebuilt it — the only
church outside the city he reconstructed in this way. In 1719 Gibbs added an upper
stage to Wren's tower, which survived when the church was burned out by enemy
action in 1941. In 1955 the RAF rebuilt the church for their own use, and the parish
was joined to St. Mary-le-Strand (Blatch, *London's Churches*, p. 204). The rector,
1721–73, was Thomas Blackwell, A.B.

[87] JW's diary makes it clear that the brothers were at Newgate on Tuesday as well as
Wednesday. Charles Wesley noted: 'At Newgate I was melted down under the word I
spoke' (CWJ, I.134). On Nov. 8, eleven malefactors were executed at Tyburn, mostly for
murder and other crimes of violence. *Gentleman's Magazine* (Nov. 1738), VIII.602.

one of them in particular, while his eyes were steadily fixed upwards, a few moments before he died, asked, 'How do you feel your heart now?' He calmly replied, 'I feel a peace which I could not have believed to be possible. And I know it is the peace of God which passeth all understanding.'[88]

My brother took that occasion of declaring the gospel of peace to a large assembly of publicans and sinners. 'O Lord God of my fathers', accept even *me* among them and 'cast me not out from among thy children!'[89]

In the evening I proclaimed mercy to my fellow-sinners at Basingshaw Church and the next morning at St. Antholin's. Friday 10, I set out, and Saturday 11 spent the evening with a little company at Oxford. I was grieved to find *prudence* had made them leave off singing psalms. I fear it will not stop here. God deliver me, and all that seek him in sincerity, from what the world calls 'Christian prudence'!

Sun. 12. I preached twice at the Castle. In the following week I began more narrowly to inquire what the doctrine of the Church of England is concerning the much controverted point of justification by FAITH. And the sum of what I found in the Homilies I extracted and printed for the use of others.[90]

Sun. 19. I only preached in the afternoon at the Castle. On Monday night I was greatly troubled in dreams, and about eleven o'clock waked in an unaccountable consternation, without being able to sleep again. About that time (as I found in the morning) one who had been designed to be my pupil, but was not, came into the porter's lodge (where several persons were sitting) with a pistol in his hand. He presented this, as in sport, first at one and then at another. He then attempted twice or thrice to shoot himself, but it would not go off. Upon his laying it down, one took it up and blew out the priming. He was very angry, went and got fresh prime, came in again, sat down, beat the flint with his key; and about twelve, pulling off his hat and wig, said he would die like a gentleman, and shot himself through the head.[91]

Thur. 23. Returning from preaching at the Castle, I met once more with my old companion in affliction C[harles]

---

[88] Phil. 4:7.
[89] Cf. Wisd. 9:1, 4.
[90] *The Doctrine of Salvation, Faith, and Good Works*, (Oxford, 1738); *Bibliography*, No. 11; see Vol. 12 in this edn.
[91] In his *Works* (1774) this paragraph is prefixed with an asterisk, undoubtedly to emphasize the importance to him of this experience of what seemed to be telepathy.

D[elamotte],[92] who stayed with me till Monday. His last conversation with me was as follows:

> In this you are better than you was at Savannah. You know that you was then quite wrong. But you are not right yet. You know that you
> 5 was then blind. But you do not see now.
> I doubt not but God *will* bring you to the right foundation. But I have no hope for you while you are on your present foundation. It is as different from the true as the right hand from the left. You have all to begin anew.
> 10 I have observed all your words and actions, and I see you are of the same spirit still. You have a simplicity. But it is a simplicity of your own. It is not the simplicity of Christ. You think you do not trust in your own works. But you do trust in your own works. You do not yet believe in Christ.
> 15 You have a present freedom from sin. But it is only a temporary suspension of it, not a deliverance from it. And you have a peace. But it is not a true peace. If death were to approach, you would find all your fears return.
> But I am forbid to say any more. My heart sinks in me like a stone.

20 I was troubled. I begged of God an answer of peace and opened on those words, 'As many as walk according to this rule, peace be on them, and mercy, and upon the Israel of God.'[93] I was asking in the evening that God would fulfil all his promises in my soul, when I opened my Testament on those words, 'My hour is not yet 25 come.'[94]

Sun. Dec. 3. I began reading prayers at Bocardo (the city prison), which had been long discontinued. In the afternoon I received a letter earnestly desiring me to publish my account of Georgia, and another as earnestly dissuading me from it because 30 it would bring much trouble upon me. I consulted God in his Word and received two answers: the first Ezekiel 33:2-6;[95] the other, 'Thou therefore endure hardship, as a good soldier of Jesus Christ.'[96]

[92] Charles Delamotte stayed on in Savannah after JW left, giving devotional leadership to those whom JW had gathered together into a religious society. He also was attacked by Thomas Causton and returned to England, June 2, 1738. Cf. diary, p. 363 below.

[93] Gal. 6:16.

[94] John 2:4.

[95] The duty of a watchman in Israel: 'But if the watchman see the sword come, and blow not the trumpet, and the people be not warned [and any be killed], his blood will I require at the watchman's hand.'

[96] Cf. 2 Tim. 2:3.

Tues. 5. I began reading prayers and preaching in Gloucester Green workhouse, and on Thursday in that belonging to St. Thomas's Parish. On both days I preached at the Castle. At St. Thomas's was a young woman, raving mad, screaming and tormenting herself continually. I had a strong desire to 5 speak to her. The moment I began she was still. The tears ran down her cheeks all the time I was telling her, 'Jesus of Nazareth is able and willing to deliver you.' O where is faith upon earth? Why are these poor wretches left under the open bondage of Satan? Jesus, Master! Give thou medicine to heal their sick- 10 ness and deliver those who are now also vexed with unclean spirits![97]

About this time, being desirous to know how the work of God went on among our brethren at London, I wrote to many of them concerning the state of their souls. One or two of their answers I 15 have subjoined.

> *My Dear Friend, whom I love in the truth,*
> I know *my* Saviour's voice, and my heart burns with love and desire to follow him in the regeneration. I have no confidence in the flesh. I loathe myself and love him only. My dear brother, my spirit even at 20 this moment rejoices in God my Saviour, and the love which is shed abroad in my heart by the Holy Ghost, destroys all self-love, so that I could lay down my life for my brethren. I know that my Redeemer liveth, and have confidence towards God that through his blood my sins are forgiven. He hath begotten me of his own will and saves me 25 from sin so that it has no dominion over me. His Spirit bears witness with my spirit that I am his child by adoption and grace. And this is not for works of righteousness which I have done. For I am his workmanship, created in Christ Jesus unto good works: so that all boasting is excluded. It is now about eighteen years since Jesus took 30 possession of my heart. He then opened my eyes and said unto me, Be of good cheer, thy sins are forgiven thee. My dear friend, bear with my relating after what manner I was born of God. It was an *instantaneous* act. My whole heart was filled with a divine power, drawing all the faculties of my soul after Christ, which continued three or four nights 35 and days. It was as a mighty rushing wind coming into the soul, enabling me from that moment to be more than conqueror over those corruptions which before I was always a slave to. Since that time the whole bent of my will hath been towards him day and night, even in my dreams. I know that I dwell in Christ, and Christ in me; I am bone 40

[97] Luke 6:18; Acts 5:16.

of his bone and flesh of his flesh. That you, and all who wait for his
appearing, may find the consolation of Israel, is the earnest prayer of
                          Your affectionate brother in Christ,
                          W[illiam] F[ish][98]

5   *My most Dear and Honoured Father in Christ,*
     In the twentieth year of my age, 1737, God was pleased to open my
eyes and to let me see that I did not live as became a child of God. I
found my sins were great (though I was what they call a sober person)
and that God kept an account of them all. However, I thought if I
10 repented and led a good life, God would accept me. And so I went on
for about half a year and had sometimes great joy. But last winter I
began to find that whatever I did was nothing. My very tears I found
were sin, and the enemy of souls laid so many things to my charge that
sometimes I despaired of heaven. I continued in great doubts and
15 fears till April 9, when I went out of town. Here for a time I was greatly
transported, in meditating and seeing the glorious works of God, but
in about three weeks I was violently assaulted again. God then offered
a Saviour to me, but my self-righteousness kept me from laying hold
on him.
20   On Whitsunday I went to receive the blessed sacrament, but with a
heart as hard as a stone. Heavy laden I was indeed, when God was
pleased to let me see a crucified Saviour. I saw there was a fountain
opened in his side for me to wash in and be clean. But alas! I was
afraid to venture, fearing I should be too presumptuous. And I know,
25 and am sure, I at that time refused the atonement which I might then
have had. Yet I received great comfort. But in about nine days' time
my joy went out, as a lamp does for want of oil, and I fell into my old
state, into a state of damnation. Yet I was not without hope, for ever
after that time I could not despair of salvation: I had so clear a sight of
30 the fountain opened in the side of our Lord. But still when I thought
of death, or the day of judgment, it was a great terror to me. And yet I
was afraid to venture to lay all my sins upon Christ.
     This was not all. But whenever I retired to prayer I had a violent
pain in my head. This only seized me when I began to pray earnestly,
35 or to cry out aloud to Christ. But when I cried to him against this also,
he gave me ease. Well, I found God did love me and did draw me to
Christ. I hungered and thirsted after him and had an earnest desire to

[98] The original of this letter, dated Nov. 25, 1738, is in the Methodist Archives, John
Rylands University Library, Manchester. Wesley also includes part of a letter dated Dec.
5, 1738. For both letters see Henry Moore, *The Life of the Rev. John Wesley,* 2 vols.
(London, Kershaw, 1824–25), I.108-10. William Fish was connected with the Moravians.
In July 1738 he had accompanied Charles Wesley on a visit to Newgate, and on May 16,
1739 was to support lay preaching against him. CWJ, I.121; cf. JW to James Hutton,
Apr. 9, 1739.

be clothed with his righteousness. But I was still afraid to go boldly to Christ and to claim him as *my* Saviour.

July 3. My dear sister came down to see me. She had received the atonement on St. Peter's Day. I told her I thought Christ died for *me*, but as to the assurance she mentioned I could say nothing.   5

July 5. She went. That night I went into the garden, and considering what she had told me, I saw him by faith, whose eyes are as a flame of fire, him who justifieth the ungodly. I told him I was ungodly, and it was for *me* that he died. His blood did I plead with great faith, to blot out the handwriting that was against me. I told my 10 Saviour that he had promised to give rest to all that were heavy laden. This promise I claimed, and I saw him by faith stand condemned before God in my stead. I saw the fountain opened in his side. I found, as I hungered, he fed me: as my soul thirsted, he gave me out of that fountain to drink. And so strong was my faith that if I had had all the 15 sins of the whole world laid upon me, I knew and was sure one drop of his blood was sufficient to atone for all. Well, I clave unto him, and he did wash me in his blood. He hath clothed me with his righteousness and has presented me to his Father and my Father, to his God and my God, a pure, spotless virgin, as if I had never committed any sin. It is 20 on Jesus I stand, the Saviour of sinners. It is he that hath loved *me* and given himself for *me*. I cleave unto him as my surety, and he is bound to pay God the debt. While I stand on this rock I am sure the gates of hell cannot prevail against me. It is by faith that I am justified and have peace with God through him. His blood has made reconciliation to 25 God for me. It is by faith I have received the atonement. It is by faith that I have the Son of God and the Spirit of Christ dwelling in me. And what then shall separate me from the love of God which is in Christ Jesus my Lord?

You must think what a transport of joy I was then in, when I that 30 was lost and undone, dropping into hell, felt a Redeemer come, who is 'mighty to save',[99] 'to save unto the uttermost'.[1] Yet I did not receive the witness of the Spirit at that time. But in about half an hour the devil came with great power to tempt me. However, I minded him not, but went in and lay down pretty much composed in my mind. Now St. 35 Paul says, 'After ye believed, ye were sealed with the Spirit of promise.'[2] So it was with me. After I had believed on him that 'justifieth the ungodly',[3] I received that seal of the Spirit which is the 'earnest of our inheritance'.[4] But at that time I did not know anything of this. My sins were forgiven, but I knew I was not yet born of God. 40

[99] Isa. 63:1.
[1] Cf. Heb. 7:25.
[2] Cf. Eph. 1:13.
[3] Rom. 4:5.
[4] Eph. 1:14.

July 6. In the morning, being by myself, I found the work of the Spirit was very powerful upon me (although you know God does not deal with every soul in the same way). As my mother bore me with great pain, so did I feel great pain in my soul in being born of God.
5   Indeed I thought the pains of death were upon me, and that my soul was then taking leave of the body. I thought I was going to him whom I saw with strong faith standing ready to receive me. In this violent agony I continued about four hours, and then I began to feel 'the Spirit of God bearing witness with my spirit, that I was born of God'.[5]
10 'Because I was a child of God he sent forth the Spirit of his Son into me, crying, Abba, Father.'[6] For that is the cry of every newborn soul. O mighty, powerful, happy change! I who had nothing but devils ready to drag me to hell, now found I had angels to guard me to my reconciled Father; and my Judge, who just before stood ready to
15 condemn me, was now become my righteousness. But I cannot express what God hath done for my soul. No; this is to be my everlasting employment, when I have put off this frail, sinful body, this corrupt, hellish nature of mine; when I join with that great multitude which no man can number, in singing praises to the Lamb
20 that loved us and gave himself for us! O how powerful are the workings of the Almighty in a newborn soul! The love of God was shed abroad in my heart, and a flame kindled there, with pains so violent, yet so very ravishing, that my body was almost torn asunder. I loved. The Spirit cried strong in my heart. I sweated. I trembled. I
25 fainted. I sung. I joined my voice with those that excel in strength. My soul was got up into the holy mount. I had no thoughts of coming down again into the body. I who not long before had called to the rocks to fall on me, and the mountains to cover me, could now call for nothing else but, 'Come, Lord Jesus, come quickly.'[7] Then I could
30 cry out with great boldness, There, O God, is my surety! There, O death, is thy plague! There, O grave, is thy destruction! There, O serpent, is the seed that shall forever bruise thy head. O, I thought my head was a fountain of water! I was dissolved in love. 'My Beloved is mine, and I am his.'[8] He has all charms. He has ravished my heart. He
35 is my Comforter, my Friend, my All. He is now in his garden, feeding among the lilies. O, 'I am sick of love.'[9] He is altogether lovely, 'the chiefest among ten thousand'.[10] O how Jesus fills, Jesus extends, Jesus overwhelms the soul in which he dwells![11]

---

[5] Cf. Rom. 8:16.   [6] Cf. Gal. 4:6.
[7] Cf. Rev. 22:20.   [8] S. of S. 2:16.
[9] S. of S. 2:5; 5:8.   [10] S. of S. 5:10.
[11] This letter does not survive. Curnock (II.111, n. 1) allowed himself to be convinced by internal evidence that was hardly even circumstantial that the writer was William Delamotte, brother of Charles, who had given up his studies in Cambridge and was in touch with the earnest Henry Piers, vicar of Bexley.

Sun. 10. I administered the Lord's Supper at the Castle. At one I expounded at Mr. Fox's, as usual. The great power of God was with us, and one[12] who had been in despair several years received a witness that she was a child of God.

Mon. 11. Hearing Mr. Whitefield was arrived from Georgia,[13] I hastened to London, and on Tuesday 12 God gave us once more to take sweet counsel together.

Fri. 15. I preached at St. Antholin's.

Sat. 16. One who had examined himself by the reflections wrote October 14[14] made the following observations on the state of his own soul:

[I.] 1. I *judge* thus of myself. But I feel it not. Therefore there is in me still the old heart of stone.

2. I judge thus of happiness. But I still hanker after creature happiness. My soul is almost continually running out after one creature or another and *imagining* how happy should I be in such or such a condition. I have more pleasure in eating and drinking, and in the company of those I love, than I have in God. I have a relish for earthly happiness. I have not a relish for heavenly. 'I savour (φρονῶ) the things of men, not the things of God.'[15] Therefore there is in me still the carnal heart, the φρόνημα σαρκός.[16]

3. I *judge* thus of holiness. But I know it not. I know not (by experience) what the life of God means. Indeed I see neither myself, nor happiness, nor holiness, but by a natural light, acquired in a natural way, by conversing, reading, and meditation. I have not spiritual light. I have not the supernatural light. I am not taught of God.

I speculatively know what light is; and I see the light of faith, just as that man sees the light of the sun on whose closed eyes the sun shines. But I want the Holy Ghost to open my eyes, that I may see all things clearly.

Therefore the eyes of my understanding are not yet opened, but the old veil is still upon my heart.

II. 'This is the design of *my* life.' But a thousand little designs are daily stealing into my soul. This is my *ultimate* design; but *intermediate*

---

[12] Identified in JW's diary as Mrs. Hall. In 1741 JW addressed meetings in her house.

[13] Whitefield returned to England to obtain priest's orders and raise funds for his Orphan House in Georgia, landing on Nov. 30.

[14] In his diary for this date JW recorded, 'writ n', an entry which usually means that he wrote notes upon some significant event or development. His reflections, the substance of which presumably appears in the following entry in the *Journal*, like many such documents, including letters, were apparently often circulated among the societies.

[15] Cf. Matt. 16:23; Mark 8:33.

[16] Rom. 8:6, 7.

designs are continually creeping in upon me, designs (though often disguised) of pleasing myself, of doing my own will; designs wherein I do not eye God, at least not him singly.

Therefore my eye is not yet single, but I am still of a double
5   heart.[17]

III. Are my desires new? Not all. Some are new, some old. Not any properly; but partly new and partly old. My desires are like my designs. My *great* desire is to have 'Christ formed in my heart by faith'.[18] But little desires are daily stealing into my soul. And so my
10 great hopes and fears have respect to God. But a thousand little ones creep in between them.

Again, my desires, passions, and inclinations in general are mixed, having something of Christ and something of earth. I love you, for instance. But my love is only partly spiritual and partly natural.
15 Something of *my own* cleaves to that which is of God. Nor can I divide the earthly part from the heavenly.

Therefore I am not pure in heart. But herein manifestly appears that I am not a new creature.

Sun. 17. I preached in the afternoon at Islington; in the evening
20 at St. Swithun's,[19] for the last time. Sun. 24. I preached at Great St. Bartholomew's[20] in the morning and at Islington in the afternoon, where we had the blessed Sacrament every day this week and were comforted on every side.

Wed. 27. I preached at Basingshaw Church; Sunday 31, to
25 many thousands, in St. George's, Spitalfields.[21] And to a yet more

---

[17] *Works* (1774) reads, 'Therefore my eye is not yet single; at least, not always so.' It is unlikely that JW made this alternation from the original manuscript but made the change (like many others in this document as presented in the *Works)* with a view to its impact upon his readers rather than to its accuracy.

[18] Cf. Gal. 4:19; Eph. 3:17.

[19] Orig., 'Swithin's'. The church of St. Swithun's, London Stone, which stood at the SW. corner of St. Swithin's Lane, Cannon Street, no longer exists. Founded before 1330, it was destroyed in the Great Fire and replaced by a 'plain and substantial building erected by Sir Christopher Wren', which was a casualty of the Second World War (James Elmes, *A Topographical Dictionary of London* [London, 1831], p. 383). Some of its furnishings are in use in other city churches, and the parish is incorporated in St. Stephen's, Walbrook. The rector, 1729–65, was William Ayerst, D.D.

[20] St. Bartholomew-the-Great, Smithfield, began in the twelfth century as a thanksgiving offering of a pious monk in the shape of a priory and hospital ('Barts'). After the Dissolution the chancel was retained as a parish church but the nave was pulled down. Despite restorations at the end of the eighteenth century, parts of the church which were not wanted were let for secular uses including a blacksmith's shop. Much restoration was achieved at the end of the nineteenth century and in the early twentieth. The rector, 1738–61, was Richard Thomas Bateman (see below, May 31, 1747).

[21] 1742, 1748, 'Spittle-Fields'. The presumption is that this church was Christ Church, Spitalfields, built by Hawksmoor, 1714–29, and described as 'vast' though doubtless

crowded congregation at Whitechapel,[22] in the afternoon, I declared those glad tidings (O that they would know the things which make for their peace!)[23] 'I will heal their backsliding; I will love them freely.'[24]

Monday, January 1, 1739. Mr. Hall,[25] Kinchin,[26] Ingham, 5 Whitefield, Hutchings,[27] and my brother Charles were present at our love-feast in Fetter Lane, with about sixty of our brethren. About three in the morning, as we were continuing instant in prayer, the power of God came mightily upon us, insomuch that many cried out for exceeding joy, and many fell to the ground. As 10 soon as we were recovered a little from that awe and amazement at the presence of his majesty, we broke out with one voice, 'We praise thee, O God; we acknowledge thee to be the Lord.'[28]

Thur. 4. One who had had the form of godliness many years wrote the following reflections:[29] 15

My friends affirm *I am mad*, because I said 'I was not a Christian a year ago.' I affirm, I am not a Christian now. Indeed, what I might have been I know not, had I been faithful to the grace then given, when, expecting nothing less, I received such a sense of the forgiveness of my sins as till then I never knew. But that I am not a 20 Christian at this day I as assuredly know as that Jesus is the Christ.

hardly able to contain Wesley's 'many thousands'. The building, altogether beyond the resources of the depressed area which Spitalfields has become, was closed for worship as being dangerous in 1958, though the crypt is used as a rehabilitation centre for alcoholics. The rector, 1738–82, was John Prichard, M.A. The confusion in the entry probably arose from the fact that Sir George Wheler (see below, Feb. 18, 1739, n. 54) built the Wheler Chapel in Spital Square, which much later became St. Mary's.

[22] St. Mary's, Whitechapel, a casualty of the Second World War. Originating in the early fourteenth century, it stood at the beginning of the Mile End Road. It was originally a chapel of ease to the parish of Stepney and is supposed to have received its epithet 'White' from the colour of its walls. Becoming ruinous, it was taken down and rebuilt in 1673, and the patronage was purchased by Brasenose College, Oxford, in 1711. The rector, 1716–45, was Robert Shippen, D.D., master of Brasenose College, 1710–45, and vice-chancellor of Oxford, 1718–23.

[23] See Luke 19:42.

[24] Hos. 14:4.

[25] Rev. Westley Hall (see May 13, 1738, n. 9, 18:238-39 in this edn.).

[26] Rev. Charles Kinchin (see Mar. 10, 1738, n. 50, 18:228 in this edn.).

[27] Presumably John Hutchings of Pembroke College (see Apr. 29, 1738, n. 93, 18:235 in this edn.) who had written to JW on Feb. 6, 1737/38, welcoming him on his return from Georgia.

[28] BCP, Morning Prayer, Te Deum.

[29] JW notes in his diary under this date, 'Prayer, writ account of myself'. There is no doubt that he himself wrote these reflections and that the reference in the first sentence is to the embarrassing episode at Mr. Hutton's house briefly recorded in the *Journal*, May 28, 1738, and fully narrated above under that date, n. 90, 18:252 in this edn.

For a Christian is one who has the fruits of the Spirit of Christ, which (to mention no more) are love, peace, joy. But these I have not. I have not any love of God. I do not love either the Father or the Son. Do you ask, How do I know whether I love God? I answer by another question, How do you know whether you love me? Why, as you know whether you are hot or cold. You *feel* this moment that you do or do not love me. And I *feel* this moment I do not love God; which therefore I *know*, because I *feel* it. There is no word more proper, more clear, or more strong.

And I know it also by St. John's plain rule, 'If any man love the world, the love of the Father is not in him.'[30] For I love the world. I desire the things of the world, some or other of them, and have done all my life. I have always placed some part of my happiness in some or other of the things that are seen. Particularly in meat and drink, and in the company of those I loved. My desire, if not in a gross and lustful, yet in a more subtle and refined manner, has been almost continually running out towards this or that person.[31] For many years I have been, yea, and still am, hankering after a happiness in loving and in being loved by one or another. And in these I have from time to time taken more pleasure than in God. Nay, I do so at this day. I often ask my heart, when I am in company with one that I love, 'Do I take more delight in you or in God?' And cannot but answer, *In you*. For in truth I do not delight in God at all. Therefore I am so far from loving God with all my heart that whatever I love at all, I love more than God. So that all the love I have is flat idolatry.[32]

Again, joy in the Holy Ghost I have not. I have now and then some starts of joy in God: but it is not *that* joy. For it is not abiding. Neither is it greater than I have had on some worldly occasions. So that I can in no wise be said to 'rejoice evermore',[33] much less to 'rejoice with joy unspeakable and full of glory'.[34]

Yet again, I have not 'the peace of God';[35] *that* peace, peculiarly so called. The peace I have may be easily accounted for on natural principles. I have health, strength, friends, a competent fortune, and a composed, cheerful temper. Who would not have a sort of peace in such circumstances? But I have none which can with any truth or propriety be called a peace which passeth all understanding.

From hence I conclude (and let all the 'saints of the world'[36] hear,

---

[30] 1 John 2:15.
[31] 1774 omits 'My desire . . . that person'.
[32] 1774 omits the previous six sentences, from, 'Nay, I do . . .'.
[33] 1 Thess. 5:16.
[34] 1 Pet. 1:8.
[35] Phil. 4:7; Col. 3:15.
[36] I.e., formal or lukewarm Christians, a phrase adapted from Juan de Valdés, where it appears in Consideration 76 of *The Hundred and Ten Considerations*, which Wesley read in

that whereinsoever they boast they may be found even as I), though I have given and do give all my goods to feed the poor,[37] I am not a Christian. Though I have endured hardship, though I have in all things denied myself and taken up my cross, I am not a Christian. My works are nothing, my sufferings are nothing; I have not the fruits of the Spirit of Christ. Though I have constantly used all the means of grace for twenty years, I am not a Christian.[38] Yea, though I have all (other) faith, since I have not 'that faith' which 'purifieth the heart'.[39] Verily, verily I say unto you, I 'must be born again'.[40] For except I, and you, be born again, we 'cannot see the kingdom of God'.[41]

Wed. 10. I preached at Basingshaw Church. Sat. 13. I expounded to a large company at Beech Lane.[42] Sun. 14. After preaching at Islington, I expounded twice at Mr. Sims's[43] in the Minories.

Wed. 17. I was with two persons[44] who I doubt are properly *enthusiasts.* For, first, they think to attain the end without the means, which is *enthusiasm,* properly so called. Again, they think themselves inspired by God, and are not. But false, imaginary

October 1733, and took with him to Georgia in the translation by Nicholas Ferrar. Cf. Sermon 4, *Scriptural Christianity,* II.5 (1:167 in this edn.); the letter to his father, Dec. 10, 1734 *(Letters,* 25:400 in this edn.); and below, Mar. 28, 1739, n. 71.

[37] See 1 Cor. 13:3.
[38] 1774 omits the three following sentences and the entries for January 10-14.
[39] Cf. Acts 15:9.
[40] John 3:7.
[41] John 3:3.
[42] Orig., 'Beach-Lane'. In a letter to George Whitefield, Feb. 26, 1739, JW speaks of a society 'at Beech Lane where I usually expound to five or six hundred before I go to Mrs. Exall's society'.
[43] On Peter Sims, see above, Sept. 17, 1738, n. 33.
[44] According to the diary they were Mr. Hollis of High Wycombe, with whom Wesley usually stayed on journeys to Oxford, and one of the Seward family. In December 1739, Charles Wesley had a bad night lodging 'at Mr. Hollis's who entertained me with his French Prophets, equal, in his account, if not superior, to the Old Testament ones. While we were undressing, he fell into violent agitations, and gobbled like a turkey-cock. I was frightened and began exorcising him with, "Thou deaf and dumb devil" &c.' (CWJ, I.138). The four Seward brothers who were of gentry stock — Thomas, a clergyman of the Church of England; Benjamin, not yet converted; Henry, a violent opponent of the Methodists; and William — appear frequently in early Methodist history. The reference here is almost certainly to William (1711–40) who had made money as a stock-broker and had been active in assisting London charity schools. In November 1738 he was converted, and on Whitefield's return from America became devoted to him. 'So strong was his enthusiasm that he offered to place himself and his fortune at Whitefield's disposal and to accompany him wherever he might go' (A. Dallimore, *George Whitefield,* 2 vols. [London, Banner of Truth Trust, 1970], I.251). He became Whitefield's travelling companion and went to America to take over the business management of Whitefield's Orphan House and other ventures. He was also a benefactor of the Bristol New Room.

inspiration is *enthusiasm.* That theirs is only imaginary inspiration appears hence: it contradicts the law and the testimony.[45]

Sun. 21. We were greatly surprised in the evening while I was expounding in the Minories. A well-dressed, middle-aged 5 woman suddenly cried out as in the agonies of death. She continued so to do for some time, with all the signs of the sharpest anguish of spirit. When she was a little recovered I desired her to call upon me the next day.[46] She then told me that about three years before, she was under strong convictions of sin and in such 10 terror of mind that she had no comfort in anything, nor any rest, day or night; that she sent for the minister of her parish and told him the distress she was in; upon which he told her husband she was stark mad and advised him to send for a physician immediately. A physician was sent for accordingly, who ordered 15 her to be blooded, blistered, and so on. But this did not heal her wounded spirit. So that she continued much as she was before, till the last night he whose word she at first found to be 'sharper than any two-edged sword'[47] gave her a faint hope that he would undertake her cause and heal the soul which had sinned 20 against him.

Thur. 25. I baptized John Smith (late an Anabaptist) and four other adults at Islington. Of the adults I have known baptized lately, one only was at that time born again, in the higher sense of the word; that is, found a thorough, inward change, by the love of 25 God shed abroad in her heart.[48] Most of them were only born again in a lower sense, i.e., received the remission of their sins. And some (as it has since too plainly appeared) neither in one sense nor the other.

Sun. 28. I went (having been long importuned thereto) about 30 five in the evening, with four or five of my friends, to a house where was one of those commonly called 'French Prophets'.[49]

---

[45] Isa. 8:20.

[46] I.e., Mrs. Randal. The diary for Jan. 22, 1739, records: '1 At Bro. Sims's, religious talk with Mrs. Randal.' JW recalls this episode in the *Journal* under Sept. 5, 1739: 'I was glad to meet with Mrs. R.,' adding a reference to Whitefield's *Journal* of Mar. 1, 1739, which quotes a letter JW had himself written to Whitefield on Feb. 26, 1739 (misdated by Whitefield), describing the occasion in language closely resembling that of his own *Journal.*

[47] Heb. 4:12.

[48] See Rom. 5:5.

[49] Named in the diary as Mary Plewit. The French Prophets, who here make their first appearance in the *Journal*, had been notorious in the England of Queen Anne. A section of the French Huguenots, desperate at being deprived of inherited rights and at the brutal

After a time she came in. She seemed about four or five and twenty, of an agreeable speech and behaviour. She asked why we came. I said, 'To try the spirits, whether they be of God.'[50] Presently after she leaned back in her chair and seemed to have strong workings in her breast, with deep sighings intermixed. Her head, and hands, and by turns every part of her body, seemed also to be in a kind of a convulsive motion. This continued about ten minutes till (at six) she begun to speak (though the workings, sighings, and contortions of her body were so intermixed with her words that she seldom spoke half a sentence together) with a clear, strong voice, 'Father, thy will, thy will be done. Thus saith the Lord, If of any of you that is a father, his child ask bread, will he give him a stone? If he ask a fish, will he give him a scorpion? Ask bread of me, my children, and I will give you bread. I will not, will not give you a scorpion. By this judge of what ye shall now hear.'

She spoke much (all as in the person of God, and mostly in Scripture words) of the fulfilling of the prophecies, the coming of Christ now at hand, and the spreading of the gospel over all the earth. Then she exhorted us not to be in haste in judging her spirit to be or not to be of God, but to wait upon God, and he would teach us, if we conferred not with flesh and blood. She added, with many enforcements, that we must watch and pray, and take up our cross, and 'be still before God.'[51]

Two or three of our company were much affected and believed she spoke by the Spirit of God. But this was in no wise clear to me. The motion might be either hysterical or artificial. And the same words any person of a good understanding and well versed in the

treatment meted out by Louis XIV, succumbed to prophecies that the French church would collapse in 1690, and a school of several hundred child-prophets was trained to keep alive the apocalyptic spirit. Among them abnormal physical and psychical phenomena became common. When civil war broke out in the Cévennes in 1701, prophets were attached to each of the Protestant commandos, and trouble smouldered on till 1710. The prophecy was never accepted by leading sections of the Huguenot community in France or abroad, but military defeat added the French Prophets to the Protestant diaspora. In Germany, Holland, and England they obtained some following and, still surviving, operated within and on the fringes of Wesley's movement. They were also in the mind of Bishop Lavington in his attack on JW in *Enthusiasm of Methodists and Papists compared* (1749–51). The challenge they represented to English religious assumptions has been recently treated by Hillel Schwartz, *Knaves, Fools, Madmen, and that Subtile Effluvium* (Gainesville, Fla., 1978), and *The French Prophets. The history of a millenarian group in eighteenth-century England* (Berkeley, Calif., 1980).

[50] Cf. 1 John 4:1.
[51] Cf. Ps. 46:10.

Scriptures might have spoken. But I let the matter alone, knowing this, that 'if it be not of God, it will come to nought.'[52]

Sunday, February 4. I preached at St. Giles's, on 'Whosoever believeth on me, out of his belly shall flow rivers of living water.'[53] How was the power of God present with us! I am content to preach here no more.

Fri. 9. A note was given me at Wapping in (nearly) these words:

> Sir,
> Your prayers are desired for a child that is lunatic and sore vexed day and night, that our Lord would be pleased to heal him, as he did those in the days of his flesh, and that he would give his parents faith and patience till his time is come.

Tue. 13. I received the following note.

> Sir,
> I return you hearty thanks for your prayers on Friday for my tortured son. He grows worse and worse. I hope the nearer deliverance. I beg your prayers still to our Redeemer, who will cure him, or give us patience to bear the rod, hoping it is dipped in the blood of the Lamb.
> Sir, he is taken with grievous weeping, his heart beating as if it would beat through his ribs. He swells ready to burst, sweats great drops, runs about beating and tearing himself. He bites and pinches me, so that I carry his marks always on me. He lays his hands on the fire and sticks pins in his flesh. Thus he has been these five years. He is in his eleventh year, a wonder of affliction; I hope, of mercy also, and that I shall yet praise him who is my Redeemer and my God.

Sat. 17. A few of us prayed with him, and from that time (as his parents since informed us) he had more rest (although not a full deliverance) than he had had for two years before.

Sun. 18. I was desired to preach at Sir George Wheler's chapel[54] in Spitalfields morning and afternoon. I did so in the

---

[52] Cf. Acts 5:38.

[53] Cf. John 7:38.

[54] Sir George Wheler (1650–1723), son of Charles Wheler of Charing, Kent. He travelled in France and Italy, 1673–75, and in Greece and the Levant, 1675–76, collecting plants, coins, manuscripts, and marbles and publishing his *Journey into Greece*, 1682. Knighted in 1682, ordained in 1683, canon of Durham 1684, he held various other livings including finally the golden rectory of Houghton-le-Spring, Co. Durham, 1709–23. Possessed of considerable property at Spitalfields, he built the Wheler chapel, at which JW now preached, (later known as St. Mary's, Spital Square) for his tenants in 1693 and left an endowment for the minister in his will. He married Grace, daughter of Sir Thomas

morning, but was not suffered to conclude my subject (as I had designed) in the afternoon—a good remembrance that I should, if possible, declare at *every* time the *whole* counsel of God.

Sun. 25. I preached in the morning to a numerous congregation at St. Katherine's,[55] near the Tower; at Islington in 5 the afternoon. Many here were (as usual) deeply offended. But the counsel of the Lord it shall stand.[56]

Friday, March 2. It was the advice of all our brethren that I should spend a few days at Oxford, whither I accordingly went on Saturday 3. A few names I found here also who had not denied 10 the faith, neither been ashamed of their Lord, even in the midst of a perverse generation. And every day we were together we had convincing proof, such as it had not before entered into our hearts to conceive, that 'he is able to save unto the uttermost all that come unto God through him.'[57] 15

One of the most surprising instances of his power which I ever remember to have seen was on the Tuesday following, when I visited one[58] who was above measure enraged at 'this new way'[59] and zealous in opposing it. Finding argument to be of no other effect than to inflame her more and more, I broke off the dispute 20 and desired we might join in prayer, which she so far consented to as to kneel down. In a few minutes she fell into an extreme agony, both of body and soul, and soon after cried out with the utmost earnestness, 'Now I know, I am forgiven for Christ's sake.' Many other words she uttered to the same effect, witnessing a hope full 25 of immortality. And from that hour God hath set her face as a flint to declare the faith which before she persecuted.

Thur. 8. I called upon her and a few of her neighbours, who were met together in the evening, among whom I found a gentleman[60] of the same spirit she had been of, earnestly 30

Higgons. His third son, Granville, married Lady Catherine Hastings, the sister-in-law of the Countess of Huntingdon.

[55] St. Katherine Coleman, a church rebuilt in 1734 and pulled down in 1935. The parish is incorporated in St. Olave's, Hart Street.

[56] See Prov. 19:21. Wesley adds no punctuation.

[57] Cf. Heb. 7:25.

[58] The diary entry for Mar. 6, which is studded with exclamation marks indicating special blessing, indicates that this was Mrs. Compton of Oxford.

[59] Cf. Mark 1:27; Acts 17:19.

[60] According to the diary, one Washington, who had frequently appeared in the Oxford entries before. A fuller account of the episode is given in JW's letter to George Whitefield, Mar. 16, 1739 (*Letters*, 25:605-9 in this edn.), in which Washington is said to have 'read several passages out of Bishop Patrick's *Parable of the Pilgrim* to prove that we were all under a delusion, and that we were to be justified by faith and works. . . . [He was about]

labouring to pervert the truth of the gospel. To prevent his going on, as the less evil of the two, I entered directly into the controversy, touching both the cause and the fruits of justification. In the midst of the dispute one who sat at a small
5 distance[61] felt as it were the piercing of a sword, and before she could be brought to another house, whither I was going, could not avoid crying out aloud, even in the street. But no sooner had we made our request known to God than he sent her help from his holy place.

10   At my return from hence, I found Mr. Kinchin, just come from Dummer, who earnestly desired me, instead of setting out for London the next morning (as I designed), to go to Dummer and supply his church on Sunday. On Friday morning I set out, according to his desire, and in the evening came to Reading,
15 where I found a young man[a] who had in some measure known 'the powers of the world to come'.[62] I spent the evening with him and a few of his serious friends, and it pleased God much to strengthen and comfort them.

  Sat. 10. In the afternoon I came to Dummer, and on Sunday
20 morning had a large and attentive congregation. I was desired to expound in the evening at Basingstoke. The next day I returned to Reading, and thence on Tuesday to Oxford, where I found many more and more rejoicing in God their Saviour. Wednesday 14, I had an opportunity of preaching once again to the poor prisoners
25 in the Castle. Thursday 15, I set out early in the morning, and in the afternoon came to London.

[a] Mr. Cennick. [Footnote added in *Works*, 1774. John Cennick (1718–55), descendant of a Bohemian refugee called Kunnik and the son of a Quaker who conformed to the Church of England, suffered much from religious despondency. He had already been influenced by reading Whitefield's *Journal*, and was now induced to join JW, preaching and teaching at Kingswood School. After personal differences a few months later he joined Whitefield, toured among Moravians in Germany in 1745, and was ordained deacon in their London church in 1749. Many of his sermons were repeatedly reprinted, and he also published four small collections of hymns.]

to read Bishop Bull against the witness of the Spirit.' Henry Washington matriculated at Queen's College, Oxford, 1733, aged 16, and became a member of the Oxford Methodist group. Although during the summer of 1738 he rejected the possibility of a personal knowledge of salvation and of that salvation being based upon the imputed righteousness of Christ, he remained in friendly touch with the Wesleys until December 1738. He was now among their opponents.

[61] Mrs. James Mears, at whose house in St. Ebbe's JW had often held meetings. Cf. the letter of JW to George Whitefield, Mar. 16, 1739.

[62] Heb. 6:5.

During my stay here I was fully employed between our own society in Fetter Lane and many others, where I was continually desired to expound. So that I had no thought of leaving London when I received (after several others) a letter from Mr. Whitefield,[63] and another from Mr. Seward, entreating me in the most pressing manner to come to Bristol without delay. This I was not at all forward to do; and perhaps a little the less inclined to it (though I trust I do not count my life dear unto myself, so I may finish my course with joy[64]) because of the remarkable Scriptures which offered as often as we inquired, touching the consequence of this removal, though whether this was permitted only for the trial of our faith God knoweth, and the event will show. Till then, let me not be accounted superstitious if I barely recite them in the same order as they occurred.[65] 'And some of them would have taken him; but no man laid hands on him'[b] (not till the time was come). 'Because I tell you the truth, ye believe me not. Which of you convinceth me of sin? And if I say the truth, why do ye not believe me?'[c] 'Get thee up into this mountain . . . and die in the mount, whither thou goest up, and be gathered unto thy people.'[d] 'And the children of Israel wept for Moses in the plains of Moab thirty days.'[e] 'I will show him how great things he must suffer for my name's sake.'[f] 'And devout men carried Stephen to his burial and made great lamentation over him.'[g]

[b] John 7:44.
[c] [John] Chap. 8:45-46.
[d] Deut. 32:49-50.
[e] Deut. 34:8.
[f] Acts 9:16.
[g] Acts 8:2.

---

[63] This letter, written on March 22 and 23, is printed in Luke Tyerman, *The Life of the Rev. George Whitefield*, 2 vols. (London, Hodder and Stoughton, 1890), I.193-94. It urges '. . . Come, I beseech you; come quickly. I have promised not to leave this people till you or somebody come to supply my place.' Whitefield, who had gone to Bristol to collect money for the Orphan House in Georgia, had held very successful meetings in the area and in South Wales for six weeks, and now left for further preaching in South Wales, intending to work back to London and sail for America. For the connection between Whitefield and William Seward, see above, Jan. 17, 1739, n. 44.

[64] Cf. Acts 20:24. Charles Wesley and other London friends attempted to dissuade John from going to Bristol 'from an unaccountable fear that it would prove fatal to him' (CWJ, I.146). John's judgment was that 'as his constitution seemed not likely to support itself long under the great and continual labours he was engaged in . . . it [was] probable that his course was nearly finished' (Moore, *Wesley*, I.438).

[65] *Works* (1774) reads '. . . this removal: probably permitted for the trial of our faith', omitting the intervening comments and John 7:44; 8:45-46; and Deut. 32:49-50.

Wed. 28. My journey was proposed to our society in Fetter Lane.[66] But my brother Charles would scarce bear the mention of it; till, appealing to the oracles of God, he received those words as spoken to himself and answered not again: 'Son of man, behold, I
5 take from thee the desire of thine eyes with a stroke; yet shalt thou not mourn or weep, neither shall thy tears run down.'[67] Our other brethren, however, continuing the dispute without any probability of their coming to one conclusion, we at length all agreed to decide it by lot.[68] And by this it was determined I should go.
10 Several afterwards desiring we might open the Bible concerning the issue of this, we did so on the several portions of Scripture which I shall set down without any reflection upon them. 'Now there was a long war between the house of Saul and the house of David; but David waxed stronger and stronger, and the house of
15 Saul waxed weaker and weaker.'[h] 'When wicked men have slain a righteous person in his own house upon his bed, shall I not now require his blood at your hands and take you away from the earth?'[i] 'And Ahaz slept with his fathers, and they buried him in the city, even in Jerusalem.'[j]
20 Perhaps it may be a satisfaction to some if, before I enter upon this new period of my life, I give the reasons why I preferred for so many years an university life before any other. Then especially, when I was earnestly pressed by my father to accept of a cure of souls. I have here therefore subjoined the letter I wrote several
25 years ago on that occasion:[69]

---

[h] 2 Sam. 3:1.
[i] [Cf.] 2 Sam. 4:11.
[j] 2 Chron. 28:27.

---

[66] The rules of the Fetter Lane Society (of which only an abstract is given above under May 1, 1738) required 'That any person who desires or designs to take a journey, shall first, if it be possible, have the approbation of the bands' (Benham, *Hutton*, p. 31).

[67] Cf. Ezek. 24:16.

[68] On the twelve days of discussion culminating in the use of the lot and the rationale of the sortilege, cf. JW, *The Principles of a Methodist Farther Explained, Occasioned by the Rev. Mr. Church's Second Letter to Mr. Wesley* (1746), see 9:201-4 in this edn.

[69] This long and important letter is given here by JW in an edited and abridged form. For a reconstruction of the original from various sources see *Letters*, 25:397-409 in this edn., with fuller documentation of variants and references. For evidence that before his father's death on Apr. 25, 1735, JW unsuccessfully sought the succession in his living through the intervention of Bolingbroke, see Tyerman, *The Life and Times of John Wesley* (London, Hodder and Stoughton, 1870–71), I.102-4.

Oxon, Dec. 10, 1734

Dear Sir,

1. The authority of a parent and the call of providence are things of so sacred a nature that a question in which these are any way concerned deserves the most serious consideration. I am therefore 5 greatly obliged to you for the pains you have taken to set our question in a clear light; which I now intend to consider more at large with the utmost attention of which I am capable. And I shall the more cheerfully do it as being assured of your joining with me in imploring his guidance, who will not suffer those that trust in him to seek death 10 in the error of their life.

2. I entirely agree that 'the glory of God, and the different degrees of promoting it, are to be our sole consideration and direction in the choice of any course of life'; and consequently, that it must wholly turn upon this single point, which I ought to prefer, a college life, or 15 that of the rector of a parish. I do not say the glory of God is to be my *first* or my *principal* consideration, but my *only* one, since all that are not implied in this are absolutely of no weight. In presence of this they all vanish away: they are less than the small dust of the balance.

3. And indeed, till all other considerations were set aside, I could 20 never come to any clear determination: till my eye was single, my whole mind was full of darkness. Whereas so long as it is fixed on the glory of God, without any other consideration, I have no more doubt of the way wherein I should go, than of the shining of the midday sun.

4. Now that life tends most to the glory of God, wherein we most 25 promote holiness in ourselves and others. I say, in ourselves *and* others, as being fully persuaded that these can never be put asunder. And if not, then whatever state is best on either of these accounts is so on the other likewise. If it be, in the whole, best for others, it is so for ourselves. If it be best for ourselves, it is so for them. 30

5. However, when two ways of life are proposed, I would choose to consider first, 'Which, have I reason to believe, will be best *for my own soul?* Will most forward *me* in holiness? By holiness meaning, not fasting (as you seem to suppose) or bodily austerities, but the mind that was in Christ, a renewal of soul in the image of God. And I 35 believe the state wherein I am will most forward me in this, because of the peculiar advantages I now enjoy.

6. The first of these is, daily converse with my friends. I know no other place under heaven where I can have some always at hand of the same judgment and engaged in the same studies; persons who are 40 awakened into a full conviction that they have but one work to do upon earth; who see, at a distance, what that one work is, even the recovery of a single eye and a clean heart; who in order to this have, according to their power, absolutely devoted themselves to God and follow after their Lord, denying themselves and taking up their cross 45

daily. To have even a small number of such friends constantly watching over my soul and administering, as need is, reproof or advice with all plainness and gentleness, is a blessing I know not where to find in any other part of the kingdom.

5   7. Another blessing which I enjoy here in a greater degree than I could expect elsewhere is retirement. I have not only as much, but as little company as I please. Trifling visitants I have none. No one takes it into his head to come within my doors unless I desire him, or he has business with me. And even then, as soon as his business is done, he immediately goes away.

10   8. Both these blessings are greatly endeared to me when I spend but one week out of this place. The far greatest part of the conversation I meet with abroad, even with the better sort of men, turns on points that are quite wide of *my* purpose, that no way forward the end of *my* life. Now, if they have time to spare, I have not. 'Tis absolutely needful for such a one as me to follow with all possible care and vigilance that wise advice of Mr. Herbert:

> Still let thy mind be bent; still plotting how
> And when and where the business may be done.[70]

20   And this, I bless God, I can in some measure do while I avoid that bane of all religion, the company of 'good sort of men', as they are called, persons who have a *liking* to, but no *sense* of religion. But these insensibly undermine all my resolution and steal away what little zeal I have. So that I never come from among these saints of the world (as John Valdesso[71] terms them) faint, dissipated, and shorn of all my strength, but I say, 'God deliver me from a half-Christian.'

      9. Freedom from care is yet another invaluable blessing. And where could I enjoy this as I do now? I *hear* of such a thing as the cares of the world, but I *feel* them not. My income is ready for me on so many stated days; all I have to do is to carry it home. The grand article of my expense is food. And this too is provided without any care of mine. The servants I employ are always ready at quarter-day, so I have no trouble on their account. And what I occasionally need to buy I can immediately have, without any expense of thought. Here therefore I can be 'without carefulness'. I can 'attend upon the Lord without distraction'. And I know what a help this is to the being 'holy both in body and spirit'.[72]

      10. To quicken me in making a diligent and thankful use of these peculiar advantages, I have the opportunity of communicating weekly

---

[70] George Herbert, *The Temple*, 'The Church Porch', st. 57.
[71] Juan de Valdés (*c.* 1500–1541), Spanish humanist and religious writer, who raised a group of prominent men concerned for the reform and revival of the church at Naples.
[72] 1 Cor. 7:32, 35, 34.

and of public prayer twice a day. It would be easy to mention many more, as well as to show many disadvantages, which one of greater courage and skill than me could scarce separate from the way of life you speak of. But whatever others could do, I could not. I could not stand my ground one month against intemperance in sleep, 5 self-indulgence in food, irregularity in study; against a general lukewarmness in my affections and remissness in my actions; against a softness directly opposite to the character of a good soldier of Jesus Christ. And then, when my spirit was thus dissolved, I should be an easy prey to every temptation. Then might the cares of the world and 10 the desire of other things, roll back with a full tide upon me, and it would be no wonder if while I preached to others, I myself should be a castaway. I can't therefore but observe that the question does not relate barely to the *degrees* of holiness, but to the very *being of it*—

Agitur de vita et sanguine Turni.[73] 15

The point is, whether I shall or shall not work out my salvation? Whether I shall serve Christ or Belial?

11. What still heightens my fear of this untried state is that when I am once entered into it, I am entered irrecoverably, once for all:

Vestigia nulla retrorsum.[74] 20

If I should ever be weary of the way of life I am now in, I have frequent opportunities of quitting it: but whatever difficulties occur in that, foreseen or unforeseen, there is no return, any more than from the grave. When I have once launched out into the unknown sea, there's no recovering my harbour. I must on, through whatever whirl- 25 pools or rocks or sands, though all the waves and storms go over me.

12. Thus much as to myself. But I can't deny that 'we are not to consider ourselves alone; seeing God made us all for a social life, to which academical studies are only preparatory.' I allow, too, that 'he will take an exact account of every talent which he has lent us, not to 30 bury them, but to employ every mite we have received according to his will, whose stewards we are.' I own also that 'every follower of Christ is, in his proportion, the light of the world; that whosoever is such can no more be concealed than the sun in the midst of heaven; that if he is set as a light in a dark place, his shining must be the more 35 conspicuous; that to this very end was his light given, even to shine on all around him'; and indeed, that 'there is only one way to hide it, which is, to put it out.' I am obliged, likewise, unless I will lie against

---

[73] Virgil, *Aeneid*, xii.765; JW's paraphrase, in 'Latin Sentences Translated' in Vol. 32 of his *Works* (1774), was 'Life is at stake.'

[74] See Horace, *Epistles*, I.i.74-75. JW's translation *(Works*, Vol. 32, 1774), 'There is no going back.'

the truth, to grant that 'there is not a more contemptible animal upon earth than one that drones away life without ever labouring to promote either the glory of God, or the good of man; and that, whether he be young or old, learned or unlearned, *in* a college or *out*

5   of it.' Yet granting the superlative degree of contempt to be on all accounts due to a 'college-drone'; a wretch who has received ten talents and employs none; that is not only promised a reward hereafter, but is also paid beforehand for his work, and yet works not at all: but allowing all this, and whatever else you can say (for I own

10   you can never say enough) against the drowsy ingratitude, the lazy perjury of those who are commonly called 'harmless men', a fair proportion of whom I must, to our shame, confess are to be found in colleges; allowing this, I say, I do not apprehend it concludes against a college life in general. For the abuse of it does not destroy the use.

15   Though there are some here who are the mere lumber of the creation, it does not follow that others may not be of more service to the world in this station than they could be in any other.

13. That I in particular could, might (it seems) be inferred from what has been shown already, viz., that I may myself be holier here

20   than anywhere else, if I faithfully use the blessings I enjoy. But to waive this, I have other reasons so to judge. And the first is, the plenteousness of the harvest. Here is indeed a large scene of various action. Here is room for charity in all its forms. There is scarce any possible way of doing good for which here is not daily occasion. I can

25   now only touch on the several heads. Here are poor families to be relieved Here are children to be educated. Here are workhouses, wherein both young and old gladly receive the word of exhortation. Here are prisons, and therein a complication of all human wants. And, lastly, here are the schools of the prophets. Of these in particular

30   we must observe, that he who gains one does thereby do as much service to the world as he could do in a parish in his whole life. For his name is legion: in him are contained all those who shall be converted to God by him. He is not a single drop of the dew of heaven, but a river to make glad the city of God.

35   14. 'But Epworth', you say, 'is a larger sphere of action than this.' There I should 'have the care of two thousand souls.' Two thousand souls! I see not how it is possible for such a one as me to take care of one hundred. Because the weight that is now upon me is almost more than I can bear, shall I increase it tenfold?

40   . . . *imponere Pelio Ossam*
       Scilicet, atque Ossae frondosum involvere Olympum![75]

---

[75] Virgil, *Georgics*, i.281-82. JW's paraphrase *(Works*, Vol. 32, 1774), 'To heap mountain upon mountain, like the ancient giants, in order to scale heaven.'

Would this be the way to help either myself or others up to heaven? Nay, the mountains I reared would only crush my own soul and so make me utterly useless to others.

15. I need but just glance on several other reasons why I am more likely to be useful here than elsewhere. As, because I have the advice 5 of many friends in any difficulty and their encouragement in any danger; because we have the eyes of multitudes upon us, who even without designing it perform the most substantial office of friendship, apprising us if we have already done anything wrong and guarding us against doing so again; lastly, because we have a constant fund (which 10 I believe this year will amount to near eighty pounds) to supply the bodily wants of the poor, and thereby open a way for their souls to receive instruction.

16. If you say, 'The love of the people of Epworth' to me 'may balance these advantages,' I ask, How long will it last? Only till I come 15 to tell them plainly that their deeds are evil, and particularly to apply that general sentence, to say to each, Thou art the man! Alas, Sir, do not I know what love they had to you once? And how have many of them used you since? Why, just as everyone will be used whose business it is to bring light to them that love darkness. 20

17. Notwithstanding therefore their present prejudice in my favour, I cannot see that I am likely to do that good either at Epworth or any other place, which I may hope to do in Oxford. And yet one terrible objection lies in the way. 'Have you found it so in fact? What have you done there in fourteen years? Have not your very attempts to 25 do good there, for want either of a particular turn of mind for the business you engaged in, or of prudence to direct you in the right method of doing it, been always unsuccessful? Nay, and brought such contempt upon you as has in good measure disqualified you for any future success? And are there not men in Oxford who are not only 30 better and holier than you, but who, having preserved their reputation and being universally esteemed, are every way fitter to promote the glory of God in that place?'

18. I am not careful to answer in this matter. It is not *my* part to say whether God hath done good by *my* hands, whether I have a 35 particular turn of mind for this, or not; and whether want of success (where our attempts did not succeed) was owing to imprudence, or to other causes. But the latter part of the objection that 'one who is despised can do no good,' that 'without reputation a man cannot be useful,' being the stronghold of all the unbelieving, the vainglorious, 40 the cowardly Christians (so called), I will, by the grace of God, see what reason there is for this thus continually to exalt itself against the gospel of Christ.

19. With regard to contempt, then (under which word I include all the passions that border upon it, as hate, envy, etc., and all the fruits 45

that spring from it, such as calumny and persecution in all its forms),
my first position in defiance of worldly wisdom, is, *Every true Christian
is contemned wherever he lives, by all who are not so, and who know him to
be such,* that is, in effect, by all with whom he converses, since it is
5 impossible for light not to shine. This position I prove both from the
example of our Lord and from his express assertion. First from his
example. If 'the disciple is not above his Master, nor the servant above
his Lord,'[76] then, as our Master was 'despised and rejected of men',[77]
so will every one of his true disciples. But 'the disciple is not above
10 his Master, nor the servant above his Lord.' Therefore . . . the
consequence will not fail him a hair's breadth. I prove this, secondly,
from his own express assertion of this consequence. 'If they have
called the master of the house Beelzebub, how much more them of
his household?'[78] 'Remember' (ye that would fain forget or evade this)
15 'the word which I said unto you, the servant is not greater than the
Lord: if they have persecuted me, they will also persecute you.'[79] And
as for that vain hope that this belongs only to the first followers of
Christ, hear ye him: 'All these things will they do unto you, because
they know not him that sent me.'[80] And again, 'Because ye are not of
20 the world, therefore the world hateth you.'[81] Both the persons who are
hated, the persons who hate them, and the cause of their hating them,
are here set down. *The hated* are all that are not of the world, that know
and love God; *the haters* are all that are of the world, that know not,
love not God. *The cause of their hatred* is the entire irreconcilable
25 difference between their designs, judgments, and affections—because these know not God, and those are determined to know and
pursue nothing beside him. These esteem and love the world, and
those count it dung and dross, and singly desire the love of Christ.

20. My next position is this: *Till he is thus* despised, *no man is in a
30 state of salvation.* And this is a plain consequence of the former. For if
all that are 'not of the world' are therefore despised by those that are,
then till a man is despised he is 'of the world', that is, out of a state of
salvation. Nor is it possible for all the trimmers between God and the
world to elude the consequence, unless they can prove that a man may
35 be 'of the world' and yet be in a state of salvation. I must, therefore,
with or without the consent of these, keep close to my Saviour's
judgment and maintain that contempt is a part of the cross which
every man bears who follows him; that it is the badge of his discipleship, the stamp of his profession, the constant seal of his calling;

[76] Matt. 10:24.
[77] Isa. 53:3.
[78] Matt. 10:25.
[79] Cf. John 15:20.
[80] Cf. John 15:21.
[81] Cf. John 15:19.

insomuch that, though a man may be despised without being saved, yet he cannot be saved, without being despised.

21. I should not spend any more words on this great truth, but that it is at present voted out of the world. The masters in Israel, learned men, men of renown, seem absolutely to have forgotten it; nay, and censure those who have not forgotten the words of their Lord, as 'setters forth of strange doctrine'.[82] Yet they who hearken to God rather than man must lay down one strange position more: that *the being despised is absolutely necessary to our doing good in the world;* if not to our doing *some* good (for God *may* work by Judas), yet to our doing *so much good* as we otherwise might, seeing we must know God if we would fully teach others to know him. But if so we do, we must be despised of them that know him not. 'Where then is the scribe? Where is the wise? Where is the disputer of this world?'[83] Where is the replier against God with his sage maxims, 'He that is despised can do no good in the world? To be useful a man must be esteemed: to advance the glory of God you must have a fair reputation.' Saith the world so? Well, what saith the Scripture? Why, that God 'hath laughed' all this 'heathen' wisdom 'to scorn'.[84] It saith that twelve despised followers of a despised Master, all of whom were of *no reputation,* who were esteemed 'as the filth and offscouring of the world',[85] did more good in it than all the twelve tribes of Israel. It saith that their despised Master left an express declaration 'to us and to our children',[86] 'Blessed are ye' (not accursed with the heavy curse of doing no good, of being useless in the world) 'when men shall revile you and persecute you, and say all manner of evil of you falsely for my name's sake. Rejoice and be exceeding glad, for great is your reward in heaven.'[87]

22. These are a part of my reasons for choosing to abide as yet in the station wherein I now am. As to the flock committed to *your care,* whom you have many years fed with the sincere milk of the word, I trust in God your labour shall not be in vain. Some of them you have seen gathered into the garner. And for yourself, I doubt not, when your 'warfare is accomplished',[88] when you are 'made perfect through sufferings',[89] you shall follow the children whom God hath given you, full of years and victories. And he that took care of those poor sheep before you was born will not forget them when you are dead.

I am, etc.

[82] Cf. Acts 17:18.
[83] Cf. 1 Cor. 1:20.
[84] Cf. Pss. 2:1, 4; 64:8 (BCP).
[85] Cf. 1 Cor. 4:13.
[86] Cf. Matt. 27:25; Acts 2:39.
[87] Cf. Matt. 5:11-12.
[88] Isa. 40:2.
[89] Cf. Heb. 2:10.

Thursday, March 29. I left London and in the evening expounded to a small company at Basingstoke. Sat. 31. In the evening I reached Bristol and met Mr. Whitefield there. I could scarce reconcile myself at first to this *strange way* of preaching in
5 the fields, of which he set me an example on Sunday, having been all my life (till very lately) so tenacious of every point relating to decency and order that I should have thought the saving of souls *almost a sin* if it had not been done *in a church.*

April 1. In the evening (Mr. Whitefield being gone)[90] I begun
10 expounding our Lord's Sermon on the Mount (one pretty remarkable precedent of *field preaching,* though I suppose *there were churches* at that time also) to a little society which was accustomed to meet once or twice a week in Nicholas Street.

15 Mon. 2. At four in the afternoon I submitted to 'be more vile',[91] and proclaimed in the highways the glad tidings of salvation, speaking from a little eminence[92] in a ground adjoining to the city, to about three thousand people. The Scripture on which I spoke was this (is it possible anyone should
20 be ignorant that it is fulfilled in every true minister of Christ?): 'The Spirit of the Lord is upon me, because he hath anointed me to preach the gospel to the poor. He hath sent me to heal the broken-hearted, to preach deliverance to the captives and recovery of sight to the blind, to set at liberty them that are
25 bruised, to proclaim the acceptable year of the Lord.'[93]

At seven I began expounding the Acts of the Apostles to a society meeting in Baldwin Street. And the next day, the Gospel of St. John in the chapel at Newgate,[94] where I also daily read the Morning Service of the Church.
30 Wed. 4. At Baptist Mills (a sort of suburb or village about half a mile from Bristol) I offered the grace of God to about fifteen

[90] Whitefield did not in fact leave Bristol till April 2 but, while JW spoke to the Nicholas Street Society, was taking leave of the Baldwin Street Society.

[91] 2 Sam. 6:22, a phrase which quickly became one of the clichés of evangelical discourse. The reference is to David's dancing before the Ark of the Covenant to honour the Lord's choice of him as the leader of Israel.

[92] A brickyard, subsequently covered by railway sidings.

[93] Cf. Luke 4:18-19.

[94] Abel Dagge, the keeper of the Bristol Newgate, was an early convert of Whitefield during his ministry there in 1737 and opened the Newgate pulpit to him when he was excluded elsewhere. On his reforms in the jail, see JW's letter to the editor of the *London Chronicle,* Jan. 2, 1767; in A. C. H. Seymour, *The Life and Times of Selina, Countess of Huntingdon,* 2 vols. (London, Painter, 1840), II.357, 367-69.

hundred persons from these words, 'I will heal their backsliding, I will love them freely.'[95]

In the evening three women[96] agreed to meet together weekly, with the same intention as those at London, viz., 'To confess their faults one to another and pray one for another, that they may be 5 healed'.[97] At eight, four young men[98] agreed to meet in pursuance of the same design. How dare any man deny this to be (as to the substance of it) a means of grace, ordained by God? Unless he will affirm (with Luther in the fury of his solifidianism) that St. James's Epistle is 'an epistle of straw'?[99]   10

Thur. 5. At five in the evening I began at a society in Castle Street expounding the Epistle to the Romans; and the next evening, at a society in Gloucester Lane, the First Epistle of St. John. On Saturday evening at Weavers' Hall also I begun expounding the Epistle to the Romans and declared that gospel 15

[95] Hos. 14:4.

[96] Mrs. Norman, Mrs. Grevil, and Mrs. Panou (JW's letter to James Hutton, Apr. 9, 1739, *Letters,* 25:631 in this edn.). Elizabeth Grevil, a disputatious widow whose connexion with the society ended in 1740, was sister to George Whitefield. For a while JW lodged at her house, a grocer's in Wine Street, and for a time thereafter used it as a postal address. Mrs. Norman (1695–1779) was the daughter of a noted Mr. Oxford, and married Mr. Norman, a prosperous merchant *c.* 1716, who died, much afflicted by losses in business, 1744. She entertained Whitefield and JW who preached on Norman's land. Mrs. Norman is said to have borne her greatly reduced circumstances as a widow with exemplary patience and religious devotion (*Arminian Magazine* [1789], XII.240-45). Mrs. J. Panou was sister to two later members of the band, Esther Deschamps and Mary-Anne Page.

[97] Cf. Jas. 5:16.

[98] Samuel Wathen (surgeon), Richard Cross (upholsterer), Charles Bonner (distiller), and Thomas Westall (carpenter); see JW's letter to James Hutton, Apr. 9, 1739 (*Letters,* 25:626-37 in this edn.). On the Moravian pattern, their meeting was to be distinct from that of the women. Samuel Wathen, a leading member of the Baldwin Street Society, whose reading to the colliers on Hanham Mount furnished the first occasion for Cennick's preaching (WHS 6:107). He is probably to be identified with the Samuel Wathen who obtained medical qualifications from Aberdeen (1752) and the College of Physicians (1756). He settled in London, treated Charles Wesley there in 1750, and operated on JW's hydrocele in 1774. He died in 1777. Richard Cross was made a freeman of Bristol in 1740, and in the Bristol Society membership list of 1741 appears as a married man. Thomas Westall (or Westell) was admitted a freeman 1741, having already in 1740 become a lay preacher, the third to join JW, 'a pattern of Christian simplicity and humble love'. He died Apr. 20, 1794. *Large Minutes* Q. 27 (cf. Sermon 121, 'Prophets and Priests', §10, 4:79 in this edn.); Conference Minutes 1794, p. 296; Charles Atmore, *The Methodist Memorial; being an Impartial Sketch of the Preachers* (Bristol, Edwards, 1801), pp. 486-87.

[99] This phrase occurs in the comparison made by Luther of the Epistle of St. James with those New Testament scriptures he considered central to the gospel in his *Preface to the New Testament* (1545).

to all which is 'the power of God unto salvation to everyone that believeth'.[1]

Sun. 8. At seven in the morning I preached to about a thousand persons at Bristol, and afterwards to about fifteen hundred on the
5 top of Hanham Mount[2] in Kingswood. I called to them in the words of the evangelical prophet, 'Ho! every one that thirsteth, come ye to the waters; come and buy wine and milk without money and without price.'[3] About five thousand were in the afternoon at Rose Green (on the other side of Kingswood),
10 among whom I stood and cried, in the name of the Lord, 'If any man thirst, let him come unto me and drink. He that believeth on me, as the Scripture hath said, out of his belly shall flow rivers of living water.'[4]

Tue. 10. I was desired to go to Bath,[5] where I offered to about a
15 thousand souls the free grace of God to 'heal their backslidings',[6] and in the morning to (I believe) more than two thousand. I preached to about the same number at Baptist Mills in the afternoon, on 'Christ, made of God unto us wisdom, and righteousness, and sanctification, and redemption'.[7]

20 Sat. 14. I preached at the poorhouse.[8] Three or four hundred were within, and more than twice that number without, to whom I explained those comfortable words, 'When they had nothing to pay, he frankly forgave them both.'[9]

Sun. 15. I explained at seven, to five or six thousand persons,
25 the story of the Pharisee and the publican. About three thousand were present at Hanham Mount. I preached at Newgate after dinner to a crowded congregation. Between five and six we went to Rose Green. It rained hard at Bristol, but not a drop fell upon us while I declared to about five thousand, 'Christ our wisdom,
30 and righteousness, and sanctification, and redemption'.[10] I

---

[1] Rom. 1:16.
[2] Orig., 'Hannam-Mount', as usual in Wesley's day, a place described by him as 'at least four miles distant from the town' (JW to James Hutton, Apr. 9, 1739, *Letters*, 25:627-28 in this edn.).
[3] Cf. Isa. 55:1.
[4] John 7:37-38.
[5] For these events see JW's letter to James Hutton, Apr. 16, 1739, *Letters*, 25:631-33 in this edn.
[6] Hos. 14:4.
[7] Cf. 1 Cor. 1:30.
[8] JW regularly preached at the poorhouse 'without Lawford's gate' on Saturdays.
[9] Luke 7:42.
[10] Cf. 1 Cor. 1:30; cf. Apr. 10 above.

concluded the day by showing at the society in Baldwin Street that his 'blood cleanseth us from all sin'.[11]

Tue. 17. At five in the afternoon I was at a little society in the Back Lane. The room in which we were was propped beneath, but the weight of the people made the floor give way, so that in the beginning of the expounding the post which propped it fell down with a great noise. But the floor sunk no further, so that after a little surprise at first they quietly attended to the things that were spoken.

Thence I went to Baldwin Street and expounded, as it came in course,[12] the fourth chapter of the Acts. We then called upon God to confirm his word. Immediately one that stood by[13] (to our no small surprise) cried out aloud, with the utmost vehemence, even as in the agonies of death. But we continued in prayer, till 'a new song was put in her mouth, a thanksgiving unto our God.'[14] Soon after two other persons[15] (well known in this place, as labouring to live in all good conscience towards all men) were seized with strong pain and constrained to 'roar for the disquietness of their heart'.[16] But it was not long before they likewise burst forth into praise to God their saviour. The last who called upon God, as out of the belly of hell,[17] was J[ohn] E[llis],[18] a stranger in Bristol. And in a short space he also was overwhelmed with joy and love, knowing that God had healed his backslidings. So many living witnesses hath God given that 'his hand is *still* stretched out to heal, and that signs and wonders are even *now* wrought by his holy child Jesus'.[19]

Wed. 18. In the evening L[ucreti]a S[mith][20] (late a Quaker,

11 1 John 1:7.

12 I.e., in the Calendar of the BCP, where Acts 4 is the Second Lesson for Morning Prayer.

13 'A young woman (named [Hannah] Cornish)' (JW to James Hutton, Apr. 26, 1739, *Letters*, 25:636 in this edn.). In his diary under June 2, 1739 below, JW notes; '8.45 [a.m.] Religious talk to Miss Cornish, she in love with me!'

14 Cf. Ps. 40:3 (BCP).

15 Elizabeth Holder and Jane Worlock (JW to James Hutton, Apr. 26, 1739, *Letters*, 25:636 in this edn.). On Oct. 10 Betty Holder 'was still in grievous darkness' (see below). On Jenny Worlock's conversion see below, May 2, 1739. She became the leader of a band (see below, diary, Sept. 5, 1740).

16 Cf. Ps. 38:8 (BCP).

17 Jonah 2:2.

18 John Ellis. JW to James Hutton, Apr. 26, 1739, *Letters*, 25:636 in this edn.

19 Cf. Acts 4:30.

20 Lucretia Smith, a gentlewoman, who appears frequently in the journals and correspondence of the Wesley brothers as an estimable woman sadly prone to recurrent

but baptized the day before), R[ebecc]a M[organ],[21] and a few others, were admitted into the society. But R[ebecc]a M[organ] was scarcely able either to speak or look up. 'The sorrows of death compassed her about, the pains of hell got hold upon her.'[22] We
5 poured out our complaints before God and showed him of her trouble. And he soon showed he is a God 'that heareth prayer'.[23] She felt in herself that, 'being justified freely',[24] she had 'peace with God, through Jesus Christ'.[25] She 'rejoiced in hope of the glory of God',[26] 'and the love of God was shed abroad in her
10 heart.'[27]

April 20, being Good Friday, E[lizabe]th R[ya]n,[28] T[amage]l W[illiam]s,[29] and one or two others, first knew they had 'redemption in the blood of Christ, the remission of their sins'.[30]

Sat. 21. At Weavers' Hall a young man was suddenly seized
15 with violent trembling all over, and in a few minutes, 'the sorrows of his heart being enlarged',[31] sunk down to the ground. But we ceased not calling upon God, till he raised him up, full of 'peace and joy in the Holy Ghost'.[32]

On Easter Day, it being a thorough rain, I could only preach at
20 Newgate at eight in the morning and two in the afternoon, in a house near Hanham Mount at eleven, and in one near Rose Green at five. At the society in the evening many were cut to the heart and many comforted.

Mon. 23. On a repeated invitation I went to Pensford,[33] about

---

religious melancholia. She was chosen by lot to lead the women's band. JW to James Hutton, Apr. 26, 1739, *Letters*, 25:636 in this edn.

[21] Rebecca Morgan, 'deeply mourning . . . [who] received the promise of the Father', (JW to James Hutton, Apr. 26, 1736, *Letters*, 25:636 in this edn.).

[22] Cf. Ps. 116:3.

[23] Cf. Ps. 65:2.

[24] Rom. 3:24.

[25] Rom. 5:1.

[26] Rom. 5:2.

[27] Cf. Rom. 5:5.

[28] See JW to James Hutton, Apr. 16, 1739, *Letters*, 25:631 in this edn.

[29] Curnock's identification (II.181).

[30] Cf. Eph. 1:7.

[31] Cf. Ps. 25:16 (BCP).

[32] Rom. 14:17.

[33] '. . . Where a society is begun, five of whose members were with us at Baldwin Street the Tuesday before' (JW to James Hutton, Apr. 30, 1739, *Letters*, 25:637-41 in this edn.). Pensford was a small mining chapelry about 7 1/2 miles S. of Bristol in the parish of Stanton Drew. The curate was appointed by the vicar of Stanton Drew, Samuel Prigg, who at this time appointed himself his own curate. Prigg (c. 1657-1740) matriculated at St. Edmund Hall, Oxford, in 1675, graduated B.A. in 1679, and became vicar of Stanton Drew in 1680.

five miles from Bristol. I sent to the minister to ask leave to preach in the church, but having waited some time and received no answer, I called on many of the people who were gathered together in an open place, 'If any man thirst, let him come unto me and drink.'[34] At four in the afternoon there were above three thousand, in a convenient place near the city, to whom I declared, 'The hour is coming, and now is, when the dead shall hear the voice of the Son of God, and they that hear shall live.'[35]

I preached at Bath to about a thousand on Tuesday morning, and at four in the afternoon to the poor colliers, at a place about the middle of Kingswood called Two Mile Hill. In the evening at Baldwin Street a young man,[36] after a sharp (though short) agony, both of body and mind, found his soul filled with peace, 'knowing in whom he had believed'.[37]

Wed. 25. To above two thousand at Baptist Mills I explained that glorious Scripture (describing the state of every true believer in Christ, everyone who by faith is born of God), 'Ye have not received the spirit of bondage again unto fear, but ye have received the Spirit of adoption, whereby we cry Abba, Father.'[38]

Thur. 26. While I was preaching at Newgate on these words, 'He that believeth hath everlasting life,'[39] I was sensibly led, without any previous design, to declare strongly and explicitly that God 'willeth all men to be *thus* saved'[40] and to pray that if this were not the truth of God, he would not suffer the blind to go out of the way; but if it were, he would bear witness to his Word. Immediately one and another and another sunk to the earth: they dropped on every side as thunderstruck. One of them cried aloud. We besought God in her behalf, and he turned her heaviness into joy. A second being in the same agony, we called upon God for her also, and he spoke peace unto her soul.[41] In the evening I was again pressed in spirit to declare that Christ 'gave himself a

---

[34] John 7:37.

[35] John 5:25.

[36] John Bush, a member of the men's band created after the preaching at Bath that morning. JW to James Hutton, Apr. 30, 1739, *Letters*, 25:637-41 in this edn.

[37] Cf. 2 Tim. 1:12.

[38] Rom. 8:15.

[39] John 3:36.

[40] Cf. 1 Tim. 2:4.

[41] The diary indicates that one of these women was Ann ('Nanny') Davis, who became one of Charles Wesley's most intimate friends in Bristol. He wrote a hymn upon her death, Nov. 5, 1775 (CWJ, II.376-77).

ransom for all'.[42] And almost before we called upon him to set to
his seal, he answered. One was so wounded by the sword of the
Spirit that you would have imagined she could not live a moment.
But immediately his abundant kindness was showed, and she
5 loudly sang of his righteousness.[43]

Fri. 27. All Newgate rang with the cries of those whom the
Word of God cut to the heart, two of whom were in a moment
filled with joy, to the astonishment of those that beheld them.

Sun. 29. I declared the *free* grace of God to about four
10 thousand people, from those words, 'He that spared not his own
Son, but delivered him up for us all, how shall he not with him
also freely give us all things?'[44] At that hour it was that one who
had long continued in sin, from a despair of finding mercy,
received a full, clear sense of his pardoning love, and power to sin
15 no more. I then went to Clifton (a mile from Bristol) at the
minister's desire,[45] who was dangerously ill, and thence returned
to a little plain near Hanham Mount, where about three thousand
were present. After dinner I went to Clifton again. The church
was quite full at the prayers and sermon, as was the churchyard at
20 the burial which followed. From Clifton we went to Rose Green,
where were (by computation) near seven thousand, and thence to
Gloucester Lane Society. After which was our first love-feast in
Baldwin Street. O how has God renewed my strength! Who used
ten years ago to be faint and weary with preaching *twice* in *one* day!

25 Mon. 30. We understood that many were offended[46] at the
cries of those on whom the power of God came, among whom was
a physician, who was much afraid there might be fraud or
imposture in the case. Today one whom he had known many
years was the first (while I was preaching in Newgate) who broke
30 out into 'strong cries and tears'.[47] He could hardly believe his own
eyes and ears. He went and stood close to her, and observed every
symptom, till great drops of sweat ran down her face, and all her

---

[42] 1 Tim. 2:6.

[43] Probably Hannah Cox.

[44] Rom. 8:32. Or, as JW tersely put it in his letter to the Fetter Lane Society, 'On Sunday morning (being so directed again by lot) I declared openly for the first hour against "the horrible decree"' (JW to James Hutton, Apr. 30, 1739, *Letters*, 25:637-41 in this edn.).

[45] Rev. John Hodges, son of John Hodges of Clifton, gent.; matriculated at Balliol College, Oxford, Nov. 24, 1716, aged 18; died May 21, 1739.

[46] In particular Abel Dagge, the keeper of Newgate (JW to James Hutton, May 7, 1739, *Letters*, 25:641-45 in this edn.). The name of the physician is not known.

[47] Cf. Heb. 5:7.

bones shook. He then knew not what to think, being clearly convinced it was not fraud, nor yet any natural disorder. But when both her soul and body were healed in a moment, he acknowledged the finger of God.

Tuesday, May 1, many were offended again and, indeed, much more than before. For at Baldwin Street my voice could scarce be heard amidst the groanings of some and the cries of others, calling aloud to 'him that is mighty to save'.[48] I desired all that were sincere of heart to beseech with me 'the Prince exalted for us'[49] that he would 'proclaim deliverance to the captives'.[50] And he soon showed that he heard our voice. Many of those who had been long in darkness saw the dawn of a great light,[51] and ten persons (I afterwards found) then began to say in faith, 'My Lord and my God!'[52]

A Quaker who stood by was not a little displeased at 'the dissimulation of these creatures', and was biting his lips and knitting his brows, when he dropped down as thunderstruck. The agony he was in was even terrible to behold. We besought God not to lay folly to his charge. And he soon lifted up his head and cried aloud, 'Now I know, thou art a prophet of the Lord.'

Wed. 2. At Newgate another mourner was comforted. I was desired to step thence to a neighbouring house to see a letter wrote against me, as 'a deceiver of the people',[53] by teaching that God 'willeth *all men* to be saved'.[54] One who long had asserted the contrary was there, when a young woman came in (who could say before, 'I know that *my* Redeemer liveth') all in tears and in deep anguish of spirit.[55] She said she had been reasoning with herself how these things could be, till she was perplexed more and more, and she now found the Spirit of God was departed from her. We began to pray, and she cried out, 'He is come! He is come! I again rejoice in God *my* Saviour.' Just as we rose from giving thanks, another person reeled four or five steps and then dropped down. We prayed with her, and left her strongly convinced of sin and earnestly groaning for deliverance.

[48] Cf. Isa. 63:1.
[49] Cf. Acts 5:31.
[50] Cf. Luke 4:18.
[51] See Isa. 9:2.
[52] John 20:28.
[53] Cf. John 7:12.
[54] Cf. 1 Tim. 2:4.
[55] The diary notes: 'Jenny Worlock comforted.'

I did not mention one J[oh]n H[aydo]n,[56] a weaver, who was at Baldwin Street the night before. He was (I understood) a man of a regular life and conversation, one that constantly attended the public prayers and sacrament, and was zealous for the Church
5   and against Dissenters of every denomination. Being informed that 'people fell into strange fits at the societies', he came to see and judge for himself. But he was less satisfied than before, insomuch that he went about to his acquaintance one after another, till one in the morning, and laboured above measure to
10 convince them it was 'a delusion of the devil'. We were going home when one met us in the street and informed us that J[oh]n H[aydon] was fallen raving mad. It seems he had sat down to dinner, but had a mind first to end a sermon he had borrowed on *Salvation by Faith.*[57] In reading the last page he changed colour,
15 fell off his chair, and began screaming terribly and beating himself against the ground. The neighbours were alarmed and flocked together to the house. Between one and two I came in and found him on the floor, the room being full of people, whom his wife would have kept without; but he cried aloud, 'No; let them all
20 come, let all the world see the just judgment of God.' Two or three men were holding him as well as they could. He immediately fixed his eyes upon *me* and, stretching out his hand, cried, 'Ay, this is he, who I said was a deceiver of the people. But God has overtaken me. I said it was all a delusion. But this is no
25 delusion.' He then roared out, 'O thou devil! Thou cursed devil! Yea, thou legion of devils! Thou canst not stay. Christ will cast thee out. I know his work is begun. Tear me to pieces, if thou wilt, but thou canst not hurt me.' He then beat himself against the ground again, his breast heaving at the same time, as in the pangs
30 of death, and great drops of sweat trickling down his face. We all

---

[56] John Haydon (JW to James Hutton, May 7, 1739; to Samuel Wesley, May 10, 1739; *Letters*, 25:641-44, 645-47 in this edn.). He was subsequently taken on trial for membership. JW preached and met leaders at his house (JW to James Hutton, June 4, 1739, *Letters*, 25:654-56 in this edn.; diary, Aug. 8, Oct. 10, 1739). He may have been the John Haydon baptised at the church of St. Augustine the Less, Bristol on Nov. 5, 1694. *Register of the church of St. Augustine the Less, Bristol*, ed. A. Sabin (Bristol, 1956), p. 212.

[57] This sermon, No. 1 in the standard series (1:117-30 in this edn.), had been preached by JW before the University of Oxford in June 1738. The passage which struck home commences: 'For this reason the adversary so rages whenever "salvation by faith" is declared to the world. For this reason did he stir up earth and hell to destroy those who first preached it. And for the same reason, knowing that faith alone could overturn the foundations of his kingdom, did he call forth all his forces, and employ all his arts of lies and calumny, to affright . . . Martin Luther from reviving it' (III.9).

betook ourselves to prayer. His pangs ceased, and both his body and soul were set at liberty.

Thence I went to Baptist Mills and declared 'him whom God hath exalted to be a Prince and a Saviour, to give repentance unto Israel and remission of sins'.[58] Returning to J[oh]n H[aydon], we found his voice was lost and his body weak as that of an infant. But his soul was in peace, full of love, and 'rejoicing in hope of the glory of God'.[59]

The women of our society met at seven. During our prayer one of them[60] fell into a violent agony, but soon after began to cry out with confidence, 'My Lord and my God!'[61] Sat. 5. I preached, at the desire of an unknown correspondent, on those excellent words (if well understood as recommending faith, resignation, patience, meekness), 'Be still, and know that I am God.'[62]

Sun. 6. I preached in the morning to five or six thousand people on, 'Except ye be converted and become as little children, ye cannot enter into the kingdom of heaven'[63] (the same words on which I preached the next day and on Wednesday at Baptist Mills). On Hanham Mount I preached to about three thousand, on 'The Scripture hath concluded all under sin';[64] at two at Clifton Church, on Christ our 'wisdom, righteousness, . . . sanctification, and redemption';[65] and about five at Rose Green, on 'the promise by faith of Jesus Christ which is given to them that believe'.[66]

Mon. 7. I was preparing to set out for Pensford, having now had leave to preach in the church, when I received the following note:

Sir, Our minister,[67] having been informed you are beside yourself, does not care you should preach in any of his churches. . . .

I went, however, and on Priestdown, about half a mile from Pensford, preached Christ our 'wisdom, righteousness, sanctification, and redemption'.[68]

---

[58] Cf. Acts 5:31.
[59] Cf. Rom. 5:2.
[60] Mary Cutler, who was admitted as a member of the female band (*Letters*, 25:632, 636, 663). In *Letters*, 25:654, JW refers to her as Elizabeth Cutler; see also diary, May 2, 1739.
[61] John 20:28.   [62] Ps. 46:10.
[63] Cf. Matt. 18:3.   [64] Gal. 3:22.
[65] Cf. 1 Cor. 1:30.   [66] Cf. Gal. 3:22.
[67] See above, Apr. 23, 1739, n. 33.
[68] Cf. 1 Cor. 1:30.

Tue. 8. I went to Bath, but was not suffered to be in the meadow where I was before; which occasioned the offer of a much more convenient place, where I preached Christ to about a thousand souls.

5 Wed. 9. We took possession of a piece of ground, near St. James's churchyard, in the Horsefair, where it was designed to build a room large enough to contain both the societies of Nicholas and Baldwin Street and such of their acquaintance as might desire to be present with them at such times as the

10 Scripture was expounded.[69] And on Saturday 12 the first stone was laid, with the voice of praise and thanksgiving.

I had not at first the least apprehension or design of being personally engaged, either in the expense of this work or in the direction of it, having appointed eleven feoffees,[70] on whom I

15 supposed these burdens would fall of course. But I quickly found my mistake; first with regard to the expense. For the whole undertaking must have stood still had not I immediately taken upon myself the payment of all the workmen; so that before I knew where I was I had contracted a debt of more than an

20 hundred and fifty pounds. And this I was to discharge how I could, the subscriptions of both societies not amounting to one quarter of the sum. And as to the direction of the work, I presently received letters from my friends in London, Mr. Whitefield in particular, backed with a message by one just come from thence,

25 that neither he nor they would have anything to do with the building, neither contribute anything towards it, unless I would instantly discharge all feoffees and do everything in my own name. Many reasons they gave for this, but one was enough, viz., that such feoffees always would have it in their power to control

30 me, and if I preached not as they liked, to turn me out of the room I had built.[71] I accordingly yielded to their advice and, calling

---

[69] Though eventually enlarged and adopted as a preaching-house, the New Room was originally designed, as JW says, simply to enable two religious societies to meet together. In a polemical letter to George Whitefield, Apr. 27, 1741 (*Letters*, 26:58 in this edn.), JW reports: '"The Society-room at Bristol, you say, is adorned." How? Why, with a piece of green cloth, nailed to the desk, two sconces for eight candles each, in the middle, and — nay, I know no more. Now which of these could be spared I cannot tell. . . . "But lodgings are made for me or my brother." That is, in plain English, there is a little room, by the school, where I speak with the people that come to me, and a garret in which a bed is placed for me.'

[70] I.e., feoffees in trust, trustees of a freehold (rather than leasehold) estate in land, displaced in general usage (as in JW's apart from this instance) by the term 'trustee'.

[71] To provide against this danger the Model Deed was developed in the nineteenth

all the feoffees together, cancelled (no man opposing) the instrument made before, and took the whole management into my own hands. Money, it is true, I had not, nor any human prospect or probability of procuring it. But I knew, 'The earth is the Lord's, and the fullness thereof,'[72] and in his name set out, 5 nothing doubting.

In the evening, while I was declaring that Jesus Christ had 'given himself a ransom for all',[73] three persons almost at once sunk down as dead, having all their sins set in array before them. But in a short time they were raised up and knew that 'the Lamb 10 of God, who taketh away the sin of the world',[74] had taken away their sins.

Sun. 13. I began expounding in the morning the thirteenth chapter of the First Epistle to the Corinthians. At Hanham I farther explained the promise given by faith,[75] as I did also at Rose 15 Green. At Clifton it pleased God to assist me greatly in speaking on those words, 'He that drinketh of this water shall thirst again; but whoso drinketh of the water that I shall give him shall never thirst; but the water which I shall give him shall be in him a well of water, springing up into everlasting life.'[76] 20

My ordinary employment (in public) was now as follows. Every morning I read prayers and preached at Newgate. Every evening I expounded a portion of Scripture at one or more of the societies. On Monday in the afternoon I preached abroad near Bristol; on Tuesday at Bath and Two Mile Hill alternately; on Wednesday at 25 Baptist Mills; every other Thursday near Pensford; every other Friday in another part of Kingswood; on Saturday in the afternoon, and Sunday morning, in the Bowling Green (which lies near the middle of the city); on Sunday at eleven near Hanham Mount, at two at Clifton, and at five on Rose Green. 30 And hitherto, 'as my day is, so my strength hath been.'[77]

Tue. 15. As I was expounding in the Back Lane, on the righteousness of the scribes and Pharisees,[78] many who had before been righteous in their own eyes[79] abhorred themselves as

---

century. Thomas Jackson is said to have described the division of authority between Conference (to appoint the preachers) and the Trustees (to manage the property) in a memorably infelicitous epigram: 'The chapels are ours, and the debts are yours.' (R. Currie, *Methodism Divided* [London, 1968], p. 50.)

[72] Ps. 24:1.
[73] Cf. 1 Tim. 2:6.
[74] John 1:29.
[75] See Gal. 3:22; see above, May 6.
[76] Cf. John 4:13-14.
[77] Cf. Deut. 33:25.
[78] Matt. 5:20.
[79] See Job 32:1.

in dust and ashes.[80] But two, who seemed to be more deeply convinced than the rest, did not long sorrow as men without hope, but found in that hour that they had 'an advocate with the Father, Jesus Christ the righteous',[81] as did three others in Gloucester
5 Lane the evening before, and three at Baldwin Street this evening. About ten, two who after having seen a great light had again reasoned themselves into darkness,[82] came to us heavy laden. We cried to God, and they were again 'filled with peace and joy in believing'.[83]
10 Wed. 16. While I was declaring at Baptist Mills, 'He was wounded for our transgressions,'[84] a middle-aged man began violently beating his breast and crying to him 'by whose stripes we are healed'.[85] During our prayer God put a new song in his mouth. Some mocked and others owned the hand of God.
15 Particularly a woman of Baptist Mills, who was now convinced of her own want of an advocate with God and went home full of anguish, but was in a few hours filled with joy, knowing he had 'blotted out all her transgressions'.[86]

The Scripture which came in turn[87] at Newgate today was the
20 seventh of St. John. The words which I chiefly insisted on as applicable to every minister of Christ who in any wise follows the steps of his Master were these: 'The world cannot hate you; but me it hateth, because I testify of it that its deeds are evil. . . . There was a murmuring therefore concerning him among the
25 multitude; for some said, He is a good man; others said, Nay, but he deceiveth the people.'[88] After sermon I was informed the sheriffs had ordered I should preach here for the future 'but once a week'. Yea, and this is *once too often*, *if* 'he deceiveth the people'; but if otherwise, why not once a day?
30 Sat. 19. At Weavers' Hall a woman first, and then a boy (about fourteen years of age), was overwhelmed with sin and sorrow and fear. But we cried to God, and their souls were delivered.

Sun. 20. Seeing many of the rich at Clifton Church, my heart was much pained for them, and I was earnestly desirous that some

---

[80] See Job 42:6.   [81] 1 John 2:1.
[82] See Isa. 9:2.
[83] Cf. Rom. 15:13.
[84] Isa. 53:5.
[85] Ibid.
[86] Cf. Isa. 43:25.
[87] Not in the BCP Calendar, but possibly in some other course of Scripture reading.
[88] Cf. John 7:7, 12.

even of them might 'enter into the kingdom of heaven'.[89] But full as I was, I knew not where to begin in warning them to flee from the wrath to come, till my Testament opened on these words, 'I came not to call the righteous, but sinners to repentance';[90] in applying which my soul was so enlarged that methought I could 5 have cried out (in another sense than poor, vain Archimedes), 'Give me where to stand, and I will shake the earth.'[91] God's sending forth lightning with the rain did not hinder about fifteen hundred from staying at Rose Green. Our Scripture was, 'It is the glorious God that maketh the thunder. . . . The voice of the Lord 10 is mighty in operation, the voice of the Lord is a glorious voice.'[92] In the evening he spoke to three whose souls were all storm and tempest, and immediately there was a great calm.

During this whole time I was almost continually asked, either by those who purposely came to Bristol to inquire concerning this 15 strange work, or by my old or new correspondents, 'How can these things be?'[93] And innumerable cautions were given me (generally grounded on gross misrepresentations of things) not to regard visions or dreams; or to fancy people had remission of sins because of their cries or tears, or bare outward professions. To 20 one who had many times wrote to me on this head the sum of my answer was as follows:

The question between us turns chiefly, if not wholly, on matter of fact. You deny that God does *now* work *these* effects; at least, that he works them in *this* manner. I affirm both, because I have heard these 25 things with my own ears and seen them with my eyes. I have seen (as far as a thing of this kind can be seen) very many persons changed in a moment from the spirit of fear, horror, despair, to the spirit of love, joy, and peace; and from sinful desires till then reigning over them to a pure desire of doing the will of God. These are matters of fact, 30 whereof I have been, and almost daily am, an eye- or ear-witness. What I have to say touching visions or dreams is this: I know several persons in whom this great change was wrought, in a dream, or during a strong representation to the eye of their mind, of Christ either on the cross or in glory. This is the fact; let any judge of it as they please. 35 And that such a change was *then* wrought appears (not from their

[89] Matt. 5:20.
[90] Mark 2:17; Luke 5:32.
[91] For this reference to the lever by Archimedes (287–212 B.C.) see Pappus of Alexandria, *Collectio*, VIII.10.11.
[92] Ps. 29:3-4 (BCP).
[93] John 3:9.

shedding tears only, or falling into fits, or crying out: these are not the fruits, as you seem to suppose, whereby I judge, but) from the whole tenor of their life, *till then* many ways wicked; *from that time* holy, just, and good.

5 I will show you him that was a lion *till then,* and is now a lamb; him that *was* a drunkard, and *is* now exemplarily sober; the whoremonger that *was,* who now abhors the very garment spotted by the flesh. These are my living arguments for what I assert, viz., that God *does now, as aforetime, give remission of sins and the gift of the Holy Ghost, even*
10 *to us and to our children; yea, and that always suddenly, as far as I have known, and often in dreams or in the visions of God.* If it be not so, I am found a false witness before God. For these things I *do,* and by his grace *will* testify.[94]

Perhaps it might be because of the hardness of our hearts,
15 unready to receive anything unless we see it with our eyes and hear it with our ears, that God in tender condescension to our weakness suffered so many outward signs at[95] the very time when he wrought this inward change, to be continually seen and heard among us. But although they saw 'signs and wonders'[96] (for so I
20 must term them), yet many would not believe. They could not indeed *deny* the facts, but they could *explain* them away. Some said, 'These were purely *natural* effects; the people fainted away only because of the heat and closeness of the rooms.' And others[97] were sure 'It was all a cheat: they might help it if they would. Else
25 why were these things only in their private societies? Why were they not done in the face of the sun?' Today, Monday 21,[98] our Lord answered for himself. For while I was enforcing these words, 'Be still, and know that I am God,'[99] he began to make bare his arm, not in a close room, neither in private, but in the open
30 air,[1] and before more than two thousand witnesses. One and another and another was struck to the earth, exceedingly trembling at the presence of his power. Others cried with a loud and bitter cry, 'What must we do to be saved?'[2] And in less than an

---

[94] From a reply on Apr. 4, 1739, to his brother Samuel's letter of Mar. 26, 1739. For the full text see *Letters*, 25:622-23 in this edn.

[95] 1742, 1748, 'of'.

[96] John 4:48.

[97] E.g., Joseph Black who later was 'struck with death' only to rejoice with joy unspeakable. JWJ, Dec. 4, 1739; Jan. 15, 1741; CWJ, I.184.

[98] Date added 1748.

[99] Ps 46:10.

[1] At the Brickyard. Diary, May 21, 1739.   [2] Cf. Acts 16:30.

hour seven persons, wholly unknown to me till that time, were rejoicing and singing, and with all their might giving thanks to the God of their salvation.

In the evening I was interrupted at Nicholas Street, almost as soon as I had begun to speak, by the cries of one who was 'pricked 5 at the heart',³ and strongly groaned for pardon and peace. Yet I went on to declare what God had already done, in proof of that important truth that he is 'not willing *any* should perish, but that *all* should come to repentance'.⁴ Another person dropped down, close to one who was a strong asserter of the contrary doctrine. 10 While he stood astonished at the sight, a little boy near him was seized in the same manner. A young man who stood behind fixed his eyes on him and sunk down himself as one dead, but soon began to roar out and beat himself against the ground, so that six men could scarcely hold him. His name was Thomas Maxfield.⁵ 15 Except J[oh]n H[aydo]n, I never saw one so torn of the evil one. Meanwhile many others began to cry out to 'the Saviour of all',⁶ that he would come and help them, insomuch that all the house (and indeed all the street for some space) was in an uproar. But we continued in prayer, and before ten the greater part found rest to 20 their souls.

I was called from supper to one⁷ who, feeling in herself such a conviction as she never had known before, had run out of the society in all haste, *that she might not expose herself.* But the hand of God followed her still, so that after going a few steps she was 25 forced to be carried home, and when she was there grew worse and worse. She was in a violent agony when we came. We called upon God, and her soul found rest.

³ Cf. Acts 2:37.
⁴ 2 Pet. 3:9.
⁵ Thomas Maxfield (d. 1784) was soon travelling with Charles Wesley, and at the Conference of 1766 JW spoke of him as the first layman who 'desired to help him as a son in the gospel', which did not quite entitle him to be called the first lay preacher. In 1742 JW gave him charge of the Foundery Society and instructed him to pray with the people. He soon became a popular preacher, admired by Lady Huntingdon. In 1745 JW rescued him from being pressed for the navy in Cornwall but could not save him from being handed over to the army in which he served for several years before being ordained by the Bishop of Derry. Always a restless subordinate, Maxfield prophesied the end of the world and separated from JW in 1763. He then acted as an Independent minister in London. In 1778 he pamphleteered against JW, but in the following year there was talk of reunion, and JW visited him in his last illness and preached in his chapel, 1783. He married Elizabeth Branford, a lady of means, one of Whitefield's earliest followers.
⁶ 1 Tim. 4:10.
⁷ Noted in the diary simply as 'Mrs. _____', May 21, 1739.

About twelve I was greatly importuned to go and visit one person more. She had only one struggle after I came, and was then filled with peace and joy. I think twenty-nine in all had their heaviness turned into joy this day.

5 Tue. 22. I preached to about a thousand at Bath.[8] There were several fine, gay things among them, to whom especially I called, 'Awake, thou that sleepest, and arise from the dead, and Christ shall give thee light!'[9]

Sat. 26. One came[10] to us in deep despair, but after an hour
10 spent in prayer went away in peace. The next day, having observed in many a zeal which did not suit with the sweetness and gentleness of love, I preached at Rose Green on those words (to the largest congregation I ever had there, I believe upwards of ten thousand souls), 'Ye know not what manner of spirit ye are of. For
15 the Son of man is not come to destroy men's lives, but to save them.'[11] At the society in the evening, eleven were deeply convinced of sin, and soon after comforted.

Mon. 28. I began preaching at Weavers' Hall, at eleven in the forenoon, where two persons were enabled to cry out in faith, 'My
20 Lord and my God.'[12] As were seven during the sermon in the afternoon, before several thousand witnesses, and ten in the evening at Baldwin Street, of whom two were children.

Tue. 29. I was unknowingly engaged in conversation with a famous infidel, a confirmer of the unfaithful in these parts.[13] He
25 appeared a little surprised, and said he would pray to God to show him the true way of worshipping him.

On Ascension Day, in the morning, some of us went to Kings Weston Hill,[14] four or five miles from Bristol. Two gentlemen going by sent up to us in sport many persons from the

---

[8] '4 [p.m.] At the Ham' (diary, May 22, 1739).

[9] Eph. 5:14. This was the text of Charles Wesley's sermon preached before the University of Oxford, Apr. 4, 1742 (*Bibliography*, No. 59), and included by JW among his *Sermons on Several Occasions* (see Sermon 3, *'Awake, Thou That Sleepest'*, 1:142-58 in this edn.); JW's own sermon, however, has not survived.

[10] John Whitehead (diary, May 26, 1739). Not the doctor of the same name who was later JW's biographer.

[11] Luke 9:55-56.

[12] John 20:28.

[13] On the strength of a note in Seymour (*Countess of Huntingdon*, I.451 n.) that the Bath physician, William Oliver (1695–1764), was 'a most inveterate infidel till a short time before his death', Curnock conjectured (II.206 n.) that he was the infidel here encountered; the *DNB*, however, considered that this infidel reputation was 'probably an exaggeration', and the identification must be considered improbable.

[14] Kings Weston was a tything in the parish of Henbury, 4 1/2 miles NW. of Bristol.

neighbouring villages, to whom therefore I took occasion to explain those words, 'Thou art ascended up on high, thou hast led captivity captive, and received gifts for men, yea, even for the rebellious, that the Lord God might dwell among them.'[15]

Sun. June 3. In the morning, to about six thousand persons, in 5 concluding the thirteenth chapter of the First Epistle to the Corinthians, I described a truly charitable man. At Hanham I enforced these words, 'That every mouth may be stopped, and all the world become guilty before God.'[16] And again in the afternoon at Rose Green, to I believe eight or nine thousand. In 10 the evening, not being permitted to meet in Baldwin Street, we met in the shell of our new society room. The Scripture which came in course to be explained was, 'Marvel not if the world hate you.'[17] We sung,

> Arm of the Lord, awake, awake,   15
> Thine own immortal strength put on.[18]

'And God, even our own God, gave us his blessing.'[19]

Mon 4. Many came to me and earnestly advised me 'not to preach abroad in the afternoon, because there was a combination of several persons who threatened terrible things'. This report 20 being spread abroad brought many thither of 'the better sort of people' (so called) and added, I believe, more than a thousand to the ordinary congregation. The Scripture to which not my choice, but the providence of God directed me was, 'Fear not thou, for I am with thee: be not dismayed, for I am thy God. I will strengthen 25 thee, yea, I will help thee, yea, I will uphold thee with the right hand of my righteousness.'[20] The power of God came with his Word, so that none scoffed, or interrupted, or opened his mouth.

Tue. 5. There was great expectation at Bath of what a noted man was to do to me there, and I was much entreated 'not to 30 preach, because no one knew what might happen'. By this report also I[21] gained a much larger audience, among whom were many

---

15 Cf. Ps. 68:18.

16 Rom. 3:19.

17 1 John 3:13.

18 By Charles Wesley, from *Hymns and Sacred Poems* (1739), pp. 222-23, the first edition of which had been published in London a few weeks earlier (see *Bibliography*, No. 13). JW included the hymn as No. 375 in his *Collection of Hymns* (1780). See 7:547 in this edn.

19 Cf. Ps. 67:6 (BCP).

20 Isa. 41:10.

21 All eds. read 'I also'; cf. previous entry for implied reference.

of the rich and great. I told them plainly, the Scripture had
concluded them all under sin,[22] high and low, rich and poor, one
with another. Many of them seemed to be not a little surprised
and were sinking apace into seriousness, when their champion[23]
5 appeared and, coming close to me, asked by what authority I did
these things. I replied, 'By the authority of Jesus Christ, conveyed
to me by the (now) Archbishop of Canterbury,[24] when he laid his
hands upon me and said, "Take thou authority to preach the
gospel."' He said, 'This is contrary to Act of Parliament. This is a
10 conventicle.' I answered, 'Sir, the conventicles mentioned in that
Act (as the Preamble shows) are *seditious* meetings. But this is not
such. Here is no shadow of sedition. Therefore it is not contrary
to that Act.'[25] He replied, 'I say it is. And beside, your preaching
frightens people out of their wits.' 'Sir, did you ever hear me
15 preach?' 'No.' 'How then can you judge of what you never heard?'
'Sir, by common report. Common report is enough.'[26] 'Give me
leave, sir, to ask, Is not your name Nash?' 'My name is Nash.' 'Sir,
I dare not judge of you by common report. I think it is not enough
to judge by.' Here he paused awhile, and having recovered
20 himself asked, 'I desire to know what this people comes here for.'
On which one replied, 'Sir, leave him to me. Let an old woman
answer him.—You, Mr. Nash, take care of your body. We take
care of our souls, and for the food of our souls we come here.' He
replied not a word but walked away.[27]
25　　As I returned the street was full of people, hurrying to and fro
and speaking great words, but when any of them asked, 'Which is

[22] See Gal. 3:22.
[23] Richard ('Beau') Nash (1674–1762), who had made a false start in several
professions, was drawn to Bath by his addiction to gambling in 1705 and attained a great
celebrity by developing and civilizing the social life of the place. In 1738 he took a leading
part in the welcome given by the city to the Prince of Wales, but this was probably the peak
of his career. Legislation in the 1740s reduced his income from gambling, and he did not
sustain his popularity with the younger generation.
[24] John Potter, who as Bishop of Oxford had ordained JW deacon and priest in 1725 and
1728.
[25] The preamble of the second Conventicle Act of 1670 (22 Car. II, c.1) affirmed its
intention to provide 'further and more speedy remedies against the growing and
dangerous practices of seditious sectaries and other disloyal persons, who, under pretence
of tender consciences, have or may at their meetings contrive insurrections (as late
experience has shown) . . .'.
[26] The latter part of this dialogue was originally presented in alternating italic and
roman type. The alteration in 1774 and 1788 to 'Common report is not enough' ignores
this distinction, thus ascribing the sentence (surely incorrectly) to Wesley.
[27] In a letter to James Hutton, June 7, 1739, JW adds: 'We immediately began praying
for him and then for all the despisers' (*Letters*, 25:658 in this edn.).

he?' and I replied, 'I am he,' they were immediately silent. Several ladies following me into Mr. Merchant's[28] house, the servant told me there were some wanted to speak with me. I went to them and said, 'I believe, ladies, the maid mistook: you only wanted to look at me.' I added, 'I do not expect that the rich or great should want either to speak with *me* or to hear *me*. For I speak plain truth; a thing *you* hear little of and do not desire to hear.' A few more words passed between us, and I retired.

Thur. 7. I preached at Priestdown, on 'What must we do to be saved?'[29] In the midst of the prayer after sermon, two men (hired, as we afterwards understood, for that purpose) began singing a ballad. After a few mild words (for I saw none that were angry) used without effect, we all began singing a psalm, which put them utterly to silence. We then poured out our souls in prayer for them, and they appeared altogether confounded. O may this be a day much to be remembered by them, for the loving-kindness of the Lord!

Mon. 11. I received a pressing letter from London[30] (as I had several others before) to come thither as soon as possible, 'our brethren at Fetter Lane being in great confusion' for want of my 'presence and advice'. I therefore preached in the afternoon on these words, 'I take you to record this day, that I am pure from the blood of all men, for I have not shunned to declare unto you all the counsel of God.'[31] After sermon I commended them to the grace of God, in whom they had believed. Surely God hath yet a work to do in this place. I have not found such love, no, not in England; nor so childlike, artless, teachable a temper, as he hath given to this people.

Yet during this whole time I had many thoughts concerning the *unusual manner* of my ministering among them. But after

[28] 1742, 1748, 'Marchant'. See JW's letters of May 14 and June 7, 1739, to James Hutton, where he spells the name Merchant *(Letters*, 25:648, 658 in this edn.). Richard Marchant (*c.* 1666–1739) was the son of a Bath clothworker and himself a prominent member of the Society of Friends. His wife, Elizabeth Fry, was a prolific Quaker writer. JW had been a visitor at his house for the past month and had used his field as a central preaching station. The use of this field was withdrawn on July 17, 1739 (see below). *Journal of the Friends' Historical Society* 8 (1911), 82 n.

[29] Cf. Acts 16:30.

[30] From John Edmonds (1710–1803), at present highly esteemed by JW (cf. JW to John Edmonds, Apr. 9, 1739, *Letters*, 25:630 in this edn.) but increasingly suspect from this time on for his inclination to Moravianism. He was among the oldest surviving founder-members of the Fetter Lane Society.

[31] Acts 20:26-27. This sermon was preached in the Brickyard.

frequently laying it before the Lord and calmly weighing whatever objections I heard against it, I could not but adhere to what I had some time since wrote to a friend, who had freely spoken his sentiments concerning it.[32] An extract of that letter I
5 here subjoin, that the matter may be placed in a clear light.

Dear Sir,
    The best return I can make for the kind of freedom you use is to use the same to you. O may the God whom we serve sanctify it to us both and teach us the whole truth as it is in Jesus.
10   You say you cannot reconcile some parts of my behaviour with the character I have long supported. No, nor ever will. Therefore I have disclaimed that character on every possible occasion. I told all in our ship, all at Savannah, all at Frederica, and that over and over, in express terms, 'I am not a Christian; I only follow after, if haply I may
15 attain it.' When they urged my works and self-denial, I answered short, 'Though I give all my goods to feed the poor and my body to be burned, I am nothing.'[33] For I have not charity. I do not love God with all my heart. If they added, 'Nay, but you could not preach as you do if you was not a Christian,' I again confronted them with St. Paul,
20 'Though I speak with the tongue of men and angels, and have not charity, I am nothing.'[34] Most earnestly, therefore, both in public and private, did I inculcate this, 'Be not ye shaken however I may fall, for the foundation standeth sure.'[35]
    If you ask on what principle then I acted, it was this: a desire to be a
25 Christian and a conviction that whatever I judge conducive thereto, that I am bound to do; wherever I judge I can best answer this end, thither it is my duty to go. On this principle I set out for America; on this I visited the Moravian Church; and on the same am I ready now (God being my helper) to go to Abyssinia or China, or whithersoever
30 it shall please God by this conviction to call me.
    As to your advice that I should settle in college, I have no business there, having now no office and no pupils. And whether 'the other branch of your proposal be expedient for me, viz., to 'accept of a cure of souls', it will be time enough to consider when one is offered
35 me.
    But in the meantime, you think, I ought to sit still, because otherwise I should invade another's office if I interfered with other people's business and intermeddled with souls that did not belong to

---

[32] The date and recipient of this letter are not known. Wesley did write a letter to James Hervey on Mar. 20, 1739, but the original, now available, shows that earlier identifications with this letter are incorrect. See *Letters*, 25:609-10 in this edn.
[33] Cf. 1 Cor. 13:3.
[34] Cf. 1 Cor. 13:1-2.
[35] Cf. 2 Tim. 2:19.

me. You accordingly ask, how is it that I assemble Christians who are none of my charge to sing psalms and pray and hear the Scriptures expounded; and think it hard to justify doing this in other men's parishes, upon catholic principles.

Permit me to speak plainly. If by *catholic* principles you mean any 5 other than *scriptural*, they weigh nothing with *me:* I allow no other rule, whether of faith or practice, than the Holy Scriptures. But on scriptural principles I do not think it hard to justify whatever I do. God in Scripture commands me, according to my power, to instruct the ignorant, reform the wicked, confirm the virtuous. Man forbids 10 me to do this in another's parish; that is, in effect, to do it at all, seeing I have now no parish of my own, nor probably ever shall. Whom then shall I hear? God or man? 'If it be just to obey man rather than God, judge you.'[36] 'A dispensation of the gospel is committed to me, and woe is me if I preach not the gospel.'[37] But where shall I preach it 15 upon the principles you mention? Why, not in Europe, Asia, Africa, or America; not in any of the Christian parts, at least, of the habitable earth. For all these are, after a sort, divided into parishes. If it be said, 'Go back then to the heathens from whence you came,' nay, but neither could I now (on your principles) preach to them, for all the 20 heathens in Georgia belong to the parish either of Savannah or Frederica.

Suffer me now to tell you *my* principles in this matter. I look upon *all the world* as *my parish;* thus far I mean, that in whatever part of it I am, I judge it meet, right, and my bounden duty,[38] to declare unto all 25 that are willing to hear the glad tidings of salvation. This is the work which I know God has called me to. And sure I am that his blessing attends it. Great encouragement have I therefore to be faithful in fulfilling the work he hath given me to do. His servant I am, and as such am employed (glory be to him) day and night in his service. I am 30 employed according to the plain direction of his word, 'As I have opportunity, doing good unto all men'.[39] And his providence clearly concurs with his Word; which has disengaged me from all things else, that I might singly attend on this very thing, 'and go about doing good'.[40] 35

If you ask, 'How can this be? How can one do good, of whom men "say all manner of evil"?'[41] I will put you in mind (though you once knew this, yea, and much established me in that great truth) the more evil men say of me for my Lord's sake, the more good will he do by

---

[36] Cf. Acts 5:29.   [37] Cf. 1 Cor. 9:16-17.
[38] BCP, Communion, Exhortation 3.
[39] Cf. Gal. 6:10.
[40] Cf. Acts 10:38.
[41] Matt. 5:11.

me. That it is 'for his sake'[42] I know and he knoweth, and the event agreeth thereto; for he mightily confirms the words I speak, by the Holy Ghost given unto those that hear them. O my friend, my heart is moved toward you. I fear you have herein made shipwreck of the faith.

5 I fear, 'Satan, transformed into an angel of light',[43] hath assaulted you, and prevailed also. I fear that offspring of hell, *worldly* or *mystic prudence*, has drawn you away from the simplicity of the gospel. How else could you ever conceive that the being reviled and 'hated of all men',[44] should make us less fit for our Master's service? How else 10 could you ever think of 'saving yourself and them that hear you'[45] without being 'the filth and offscouring of the world'?[46] To this hour is this Scripture true. And I therein rejoice, yea, and *will* rejoice. Blessed be God, I enjoy the reproach of Christ! O may you also be vile, exceeding vile for his sake! God forbid that you should ever be 15 other than *generally* scandalous. I had almost said, *universally*. If any man tell you there is a new way of following Christ, 'he is a liar, and the truth is not in him.'[47]

I am, etc.

Wed. 13. In the morning I came to London, and after receiving 20 the Holy Communion at Islington, I had once more an opportunity of seeing my mother,[48] whom I had not seen since my return from Germany.

I can't but mention an odd circumstance here. I had read her a paper in June last year, containing a short account of what had 25 passed in my own soul till within a few days of that time.[49] She greatly approved it and said she heartily blessed God, who had brought me to so just a way of thinking. While I was in Germany a copy of that paper was sent (without my knowledge) to one of my relations.[50] He sent an account of it to my mother, whom I now 30 found under strange fears concerning me, being convinced by 'an account taken from one of my own papers' that I had greatly erred from the faith. I could not conceive what paper that should be, but

---

[42] Ibid.

[43] 2 Cor. 11:14.

[44] Matt. 10:22, etc.

[45] Cf. BCP, Consecration of Bishops, charge on delivering Bible.

[46] Cf. 1 Cor. 4:13.

[47] 1 John 2:4.

[48] Susanna Wesley was living with her daughter and son-in-law, the Rev. and Mrs. Westley Hall, who had lately moved from Salisbury to London.

[49] June 8, 1738. See the document under May 24, 1738, 18:241-42 in this edn.

[50] The paper was obtained by Samuel Wesley, probably from Mrs. Hutton. See above, June 8, 1738, n. 3, 18:254 in this edn. Samuel became estranged from his brother on the questions of religious experience and evangelism.

on inquiry found it was the same I had read her myself. . . . How hard is it to form a true judgment of any person or thing from the account of a prejudiced relater! Yea, though he be ever so honest a man: for he who gave this relation was one of unquestionable veracity. And yet by his *sincere* account of a writing which lay before his eyes was the truth so totally disguised that my mother knew not the paper she had heard from end to end, nor I that I had myself wrote.

At six I warned the women at Fetter Lane (knowing how they had been lately shaken), 'Not to believe every spirit, but to try the spirits whether they were of God'.[51] Our brethren met at eight, when it pleased God to remove many misunderstandings and offences that had crept in among them, and to restore in good measure 'the spirit of love and of a sound mind'.[52]

Thur. 14. I went with Mr. Whitefield to Blackheath, where were, I believe, twelve or fourteen thousand people. He a little surprised me by desiring me to preach in his stead, which I did (though nature recoiled) on my favourite subject, 'Jesus Christ, who of God is made unto us wisdom, righteousness, sanctification, and redemption'.[53]

I was greatly moved with compassion for the rich that were there, to whom I made a particular application. Some of them seemed to attend, while others drove away their coaches from so uncouth a preacher.

Fri. 15. I had much talk with one who is called a Quaker.[54] But he could not receive my saying. I was 'too strict' for him and

---

[51] Cf. 1 John 4:1. Charles Wesley noted that 'many of our friends have been pestered by the French Prophets' (see above, Jan. 28, 1739, n. 49) 'and such like *pretenders to* inspiration', collected information about the 'lewd life and conversation' of the Prophetess Lavington, and on the previous day, June 12, provoked a violent scene by confronting her and the society with it. On this occasion he records: 'June 13th. My brother returned. We had over the Prophetess's affair before the Society. Bray and Bowers [who had supported her] were much humbled. All agreed to disown the Prophetess'. Orthodoxy was further secured by expelling two Moravians (one of whom also claimed the spirit of prophecy) who disowned the Church of England. CWJ, I.152-53.

[52] 2 Tim. 1:7.

[53] Cf. 1 Cor. 1:30. JW included no sermon on this 'favourite subject' in his standard sermons.

[54] Anthony Purver (diary, June 15, 1739), with whom JW had conversed on occasions in April. Purver (1702–77), a farmer's son and shoemaker who took up the study of Hebrew, became a Quaker in his mid-twenties and devoted the rest of his life to the Quaker ministry, to teaching and translating the entire Bible — a work for which he failed to find a publisher but which was published by Dr. John Fothergill in 1764. J. Nichols, *Literary Anecdotes of the Eighteenth Century* (London, 1812–15), IX.739 n.

talked of 'such a perfection' as he could not think 'necessary', being persuaded 'there was no harm' in costly apparel, provided it was plain and grave, nor in putting scarlet or gold upon *our houses,* so it were not upon *our clothes.*

5   In the evening I went to a society at Wapping, weary in body and faint in spirit. I intended to speak on Romans 3:19, but could not tell how to open my mouth; and all the time we were singing my mind was full of some place, I knew not where, in the Epistle to the Hebrews. I begged God to direct, and opened the book on
10 Heb. 10:19, 'Having therefore, brethren, boldness to enter into the holiest, by the blood of Jesus; by a new and living way which he hath consecrated for us, through the veil, that is to say, his flesh . . . let us draw near with a true heart, in full assurance of faith, having our hearts sprinkled from an evil conscience, and our
15 bodies washed with pure water.'[55] While I was earnestly inviting all sinners 'to enter into the holiest' by this 'new and living way', many of those that heard begun to call upon God, with strong cries and tears. Some sunk down and there remained no strength in them; others exceedingly trembled and quaked; some were
20 torn with a kind of convulsive motion in every part of their bodies, and that so violently that often four or five persons could not hold one of them. I have seen many hysterical and many epileptic fits, but none of them were like these, in many respects. I immediately prayed that God would not suffer those who were weak to be
25 offended. But one woman was offended greatly, being sure 'they might help it' if they would—no one should persuade her to the contrary; and was got three or four yards when she also dropped down, in as violent an agony as the rest. Twenty-six of those who had been thus affected (most of whom during the prayers which
30 were made for them were in a moment filled with peace and joy) promised to call upon me the next day. But only eighteen came; by talking closely with whom I found reason to believe that some of them had gone home to their house justified. The rest seemed to be patiently waiting for it.

35   Sat. 16. We met at Fetter Lane to humble ourselves before God and own he had justly withdrawn his Spirit from us for our manifold unfaithfulness. We acknowledged our having grieved him by our divisions, 'one saying, I am of Paul, another, I am of Apollos';[56] by our leaning again to our own works and trusting in

[55] Heb. 10:19-22.
[56] Cf. 1 Cor. 3:4.

them instead of Christ; by our resting in those little beginnings of sanctification which it had pleased him to work in our souls; and above all by blaspheming his work among us, imputing it either to nature, to the force of imagination and animal spirits, or even to the delusion of the devil. In that hour we found God with us as at 5 the first. Some fell prostrate upon the ground. Others burst out, as with one consent, into loud praise and thanksgiving. And many openly testified, there had been no such day as this since January the first preceding.

Sun. 17. I preached at seven in Upper Moorfields[57] to (I 10 believe) six or seven thousand people, on, 'Ho! everyone that thirsteth, come ye to the waters.'[58] In the afternoon I saw poor R——d T——n,[59] who had left our society and the Church. We did not dispute, but pray; and in a short space the scales fell off from his eyes. He gladly returned to the Church and was in the 15 evening re-admitted into our society.

At five I preached on Kennington Common,[60] to about fifteen thousand people, on those words, 'Look unto him and be ye saved, all ye ends of the earth.'[61]

Mon. 18. I left London early in the morning, and the next 20 evening reached Bristol and preached (as I had appointed, if God should permit) to a numerous congregation. My text now also was, 'Look unto him and be ye saved, all ye ends of the earth.' Howell Harris[62] called upon me an hour or two after. He said he

[57] JW had been preceded in preaching in the open air in Moorfields and on Kennington Common by George Whitefield some six weeks before. Whitefield's meetings, which had also attracted vast crowds, marked his determination to disregard the parish system in a way that the preaching at Kingswood hardly had. Moorfields, an eighteen-acre park situated not far from the Fetter Lane and neighbouring societies (some of whose members had in turn preceded Whitefield in holding an open-air meeting there), was the scene of many of the coarse amusements of the period, which guaranteed the presence of large numbers of the public.

[58] Isa. 55:1.

[59] The same Richard Tompson, a founder-member of the Fetter Lane Society, who in 1755–56 carried on a considerable pseudonymous correspondence with JW on the doctrines of assurance and Christian perfection, which was published in 1760 as *Original letters between the Rev. Mr. John Wesley and M. Richard Tompson* (see *Letters*, 26:566–71, 574-80 in this edn.).

[60] An area of some 20 acres S. of the Thames with a permanent scaffold notable as a scene of hangings, and thronged by an even denser and rougher population than Moorfields.

[61] Cf. Isa. 45:22.

[62] Howell Harris (1714–73), third son of Howell Harris of Trevecca, Talgarth, Breconshire, and one of the leading founders of Welsh Calvinistic Methodism. He intended to seek ordination in the Established Church, but after a term in Oxford in 1735, he returned home and became an ardent and successful open-air evangelist. Early in 1739

had been much dissuaded from either hearing or seeing me by
many who said all manner of evil of me. 'But', said he, 'as soon as
I heard you preach, I quickly found what spirit you was of. And
before you had done I was so overpowered with joy and love that I
5 had much ado to walk home.'[63]

It is scarce credible what advantage Satan had gained during
my absence of only eight days. Disputes had crept into our little
society, so that the love of many was already waxed cold.[64] I
showed them the state they were in the next day (both at Newgate
10 and at Baptist Mills) from those words, 'Simon, Simon, behold
Satan hath desired to have you, that he may sift you as wheat.'[65]
And when we met in the evening, instead of reviving the dispute,[66]
we all betook ourselves to prayer. Our Lord was with us. Our
divisions were healed. Misunderstandings vanished away. And all
15 our hearts were sweetly drawn together and united as at the first.

Fri. 22. I called on one who 'did run well',[67] till he was hindered
by some of those called French Prophets.[68] 'Woe unto the
prophets, saith the Lord, who prophesy in my name, and I have
not sent them.'[69] At Weavers' Hall I endeavoured to point them
20 out, and earnestly exhorted all that followed after holiness to
avoid as fire all who do not speak according 'to the law and
the testimony'.[70]

Whitefield reckoned that Harris had gathered thirty societies in South Wales, and he then
extended his missions to the whole of the principality. After an open rupture with Daniel
Rowlands in 1751, he withdrew to Trevecca and established a religious settlement there.
Towards the end of his life he was warmly supported by the Countess of Huntingdon, who
set up a ministerial training college at Trevecca in 1768. Harris's elder brothers also
attained distinction: Joseph, as an assay master at the Mint and a writer on scientific
subjects; Thomas, as an army clothing contractor.

[63] George Whitefield wrote of Howell Harris: 'He is of a most catholic spirit, loves all
who love our Lord Jesus Christ, and therefore he is styled by bigots, a Dissenter' (*Journals*,
p. 229).

[64] See Matt. 24:12.

[65] Luke 22:31.

[66] Mrs. Grevil had forbidden the band access to her house. JW to James Hutton, July 2,
1739, *Letters*, 25:663 in this edn.

[67] Gal. 5:7.

[68] Thomas Whitehead, 'a professed Quaker about sixty years of age, who was convinced
of the necessity of being born of water as well as the Spirit', had been baptized by
Whitefield on Apr. 17, 1739 (*Journals*, p. 252), and had subsequently been much visited by
JW. He was probably the fifth child by the first marriage of Thomas Whitehead, clothier
and minister of Bruton meeting, who was born Jan. 5, 1670/71 (d. 1691). One of this name
was in the insurance business in 1761. W. E. Minchinton, *The Trade of Bristol in the 18th
Century* (Bristol, 1957), p. 186.

[69] Cf. Jer. 14:15.

[70] Isa. 8:20.

In the afternoon I preached at the Fishponds[71] but had no life
or spirit in me and was much in doubt whether God would not lay
me aside and send other labourers into his harvest. I came to the
society full of this thought, and began in much weakness to
explain, 'Beloved, believe not every spirit, but try the spirits 5
whether they be of God.'[72] I told them they were not to judge of
the Spirit whereby anyone spoke, either by *appearances*, or by
common report, or by their own *inward feelings*. No, nor by any
dreams, visions, or revelations supposed to be made to their souls,
any more than by their tears or any involuntary effects wrought 10
upon their bodies. I warned them all these were in themselves of a
doubtful, disputable nature: they *might* be from God and they
might not, and were therefore not simply to be relied on (any more
than simply to be condemned) but to be tried by a farther rule, to
be brought to the only certain test, 'the law and the testimony'. 15
While I was speaking one before me dropped down as dead, and
presently a second and a third. Five others sunk down in half an
hour, most of whom were in violent agonies. 'The pains as of hell
came about them; the snares of death overtook them.'[73] In their
trouble we called upon the Lord, and he gave us an answer of 20
peace. One indeed continued an hour in strong pain, and one or
two more for three days. But the rest were greatly comforted in
that hour and went away rejoicing and praising God.

Sat. 23. I spoke severally with those who had been so troubled
the night before. Some of them I found were only convinced of 25
sin; others had indeed found rest to their souls. This evening
another[74] was seized with strong pangs. But in a short time her
soul also was delivered.

Sun. 24. As I was riding to Rose Green, in a smooth, plain part
of the road, my horse suddenly pitched upon his head and rolled 30
over and over. I received no other hurt than a little bruise on one
side, which for the present I felt not, but preached without pain

---

[71] Described by JW as 'on the edge of Kingswood, about two miles from Bristol' (*Letters*,
25:654-55 in this edn.). See below, June 29, where Fishponds became a regular
preaching-station. Fishponds was a village in the parish of Stapleton 2 1/2 miles NE. by
N. from Bristol and derived its name from two extensive ponds which once existed there.

[72] 1 John 4:1. The text noted in JW's diary on this occasion was Isa. 65:22, 'They shall
not build, and another inherit; they shall not plant, and another eat,' from which he might
derive comfort at a moment of doubting his vocation.

[73] Cf. Ps. 18:4 (BCP).

[74] 'Ann Allin (a young woman)' (JW to James Hutton, July 2, 1739, *Letters*, 25:665 in this
edn.). It is clear from the diary that Ann Allin (otherwise Allen or Ayling) persevered in the
society over the next couple of years.

to six or seven thousand people on that important direction, 'Whether ye eat or drink, or whatever you do, do all to the glory of God.'[75] In the evening a girl of thirteen or fourteen,[76] and four or five other persons, some of whom had felt the power of God
5 before, were deeply convinced of sin and, with sighs and groans which could not be uttered,[77] called upon God for deliverance.

Mon. 25. About ten in the morning, J[ane] C[onno]r,[78] as she was sitting at work was suddenly seized with grievous terrors of mind, attended with strong trembling. Thus she continued all the
10 afternoon, but at the society in the evening God turned her heaviness into joy. Five or six others were also cut to the heart this day, and soon after found him whose 'hands make whole,'[79] as did one likewise who had been mourning many months, without any to comfort her.

15 Tue. 26. I preached near the house we had a few days before began to build for a school,[80] in the middle of Kingswood, under a little sycamore tree, during a violent storm of rain, on those words, 'As the rain cometh down from heaven and returneth not thither, but watereth the earth and maketh it bring forth and bud:
20 . . . so shall my word be that goeth out of my mouth: it shall not return unto me void. But it shall accomplish that which I please, and it shall prosper in the thing whereto I sent it.'[81]

Three persons terribly felt the wrath of God abiding on them at the society this evening. But upon prayer made in their behalf, he
25 was pleased soon to lift up the light of his countenance upon them.[82]

Fri. 29. I preached in a part of Kingswood where I never had been before. The places in Kingswood where I now usually preached were these: once a fortnight, a little above Conham, a
30 village on the south side of the wood; on Sunday morning, near Hanham Mount; once a fortnight, at the schoolhouse in the

---

[75] Cf. 1 Cor. 10:31.
[76] Sara Murray. See JW to James Hutton July 2, 1739, *Letters*, 25:665 in this edn.
[77] See Rom. 8:26.
[78] In his letter of July 2 to James Hutton *(Letters,* 25:665 in this edn.) JW speaks in similar terms of the experience of 'Mary Conway', probably an error discovered from his brother Charles, whose journal for Oct. 30, 1739, speaks of Jane Connor (or Mary Connor) of Baptist Mills, who recovered 'that unspeakable peace' which 'she first received some weeks ago' and then lost (CWJ, I.193).
[79] Job 5:18.
[80] The school for colliers' children, not the later school for preachers' children.
[81] Cf. Isa. 55:10-11.
[82] See Ps. 4:6.

middle of Kingswood; on Sunday in the evening at Rose Green; and once a fortnight near the Fishponds, on the north side of the wood.

Sat. 30. At Weavers' Hall seven or eight persons were constrained to roar aloud, while the sword of the Spirit was 5 'dividing asunder their souls and spirits and joints and marrow'.[83] But they were all relieved upon prayer, and sang 'praises unto our God, and unto the Lamb that liveth for ever and ever'.[84]

I gave a particular account, from time to time, of the manner wherein God here carried on his work to those whom I believed to 10 desire the increase of his kingdom, with whom I had any opportunity of corresponding.[85] Part of the answer which I received (some time after) from one of these I cannot but here subjoin:

> I desire to bless my Lord for the good and great news your letter 15 bears about the Lord's turning many souls 'from darkness to light, and from the power of Satan unto God',[86] and that such 'a great and effectual door is opened' among you as the 'many adversaries'[87] cannot shut. O may 'he that hath the keys of the house of David, that openeth and no man shutteth, and shutteth and no man openeth',[88] 20 set the door of faith more and more open among you, till his house be filled and till he gather together the outcasts of Israel. And may that prayer for the adversaries be heard, 'Fill their faces with shame, that they may seek thy name, O Lord.'[89]
>
> As to the outward manner you speak of, wherein most of them were 25 affected who were cut to the heart by the sword of the Spirit, no wonder that this was at first surprising to you, since they are indeed so very rare that have been thus pricked and wounded. Yet some of the

---

[83] Cf. Heb. 4:12.

[84] Cf. Rev. 5:13.

[85] A worldwide view of the movement of grace was part of the legacy of the pietist world to the evangelicals. Exchange of information of this kind was one of the ways in which expectations were created which were satisfied by the spread of the revival itself. In the 1740s John Erskine and other spokesmen for the Scots' revivals (Maclaurin, MacCulloch, Robe) exchanged correspondence and literature with Jonathan Edwards, Thomas Prince, and other American friends of Whitefield, from which developed an historical view that God's saving activity was not, as the hypercalvinists alleged, at an ebb, but at a flood tide, a view massively documented in standard works such as John Gillies, *Historical collections relating to remarkable periods of the success of the gospel* (4 vols., 1754–96), and its successors. Cf. W. R. Ward, 'The Baptists and the transformation of the Church, 1780-1830', *Baptist Quarterly* 25:170-71.

[86] Cf. Acts 26:18.

[87] Cf. 1 Cor. 16:9.

[88] Cf. Rev. 3:7.

[89] Ps. 83:16.

instances you give seem to be exemplified in the outward manner
wherein Paul and the jailer were at first affected, as also Peter's
hearers, Acts 2. The last instance you gave, of some struggling as in
the agonies of death and in such a manner as that four or five strong
5   men can hardly restrain a weak woman from hurting herself or others,
this is to me somewhat more inexplicable, if it do not resemble the
child spoke of, Mark 9:26, and Luke 9:42. Of whom it is said, that
while 'he was yet a coming, the devil threw him down and tore him.'[90]
Or what influence sudden and sharp awakenings may have upon the
10   body I pretend not to explain. But I make no question Satan, so far as
he gets power, may exert himself on such occasions, partly to hinder
the good work in the persons who are thus touched with the sharp
arrows of conviction, and partly to disparage the work of God, as if it
tended to lead people to distraction. . . . However, the merciful issue
15   of these conflicts in the conversion of the persons thus affected is the
main thing.

When they are brought by the saving arm of God to receive Christ
Jesus, to have joy and peace in believing, and then to walk in him and
give evidence that the work is a saving work at length, whether more
20   quickly or gradually accomplished, there is great matter of praise. . . .

All the outward appearances of people's being affected among us
may be reduced to these two sorts: one is hearing with a close, silent
attention, with gravity and greediness, discovered by fixed looks,
weeping eyes, and sorrowful or joyful countenances; another sort is
25   when they lift up their voice aloud, some more depressedly, and
others more highly, and at times the whole multitude in a flood of
tears, all as it were crying out at once, till their voice be ready to drown
the minister's, that he can scarce be heard from the weeping noise
that surrounds him. . . . The influence on some of these like a
30   land-flood dries up; we hear of no change wrought. But in others it
appears in the fruits of righteousness and the tract of a holy
conversation. . . .

May the Lord strengthen you to go on in his work! And in praying for
the coming of his kingdom with you and us, and I hope you shall not be
35   forgotten among us, in our joint applications to the throne of grace.

I am, Reverend and dear sir,
Your very affectionate brother
and servant in Christ,
Ralph Erskine[91]

[90] Luke 9:42.
[91] *Works* (1774) extends 'R. E.' to the complete name. Ralph Erskine (1685–1752),
Scottish divine and poet, supported his brother Ebenezer in the controversies over
doctrine and patronage which led to the formation of the Associate Presbytery, seceding
from the Kirk in 1737. Erskine was also in touch with Whitefield and invited him to
Scotland in 1741, failing, however, to tie him to the Associate Presbytery. The

Sunday, July 1. I preached to about five thousand, on that favourite advice of the infidel in Ecclesiastes (so zealously enforced by his brethren now) 'Be not righteous overmuch.'[92] At Hanham and at Rose Green I explained the latter part of the seventh of St. Luke, that verse especially, 'When they had nothing to pay, he frankly forgave them both.'[93]

A young woman sunk down at Rose Green, in a violent agony both of body and mind; as did five or six persons in the evening at the New Room, at whose cries many were greatly offended. The same offence was given in the morning by one at Weavers' Hall, and by eight or nine others at Gloucester Lane in the evening. The first that was deeply touched was L—— W——,[94] whose mother had been not a little displeased a day or two before when she was told how her daughter had 'exposed herself' before all the congregation. The mother herself was the next, who dropped down and lost her senses in a moment, but went home with her daughter full of joy, as did most of those that had been in pain.

Soon after the society I went to Mrs. T[hornhill]'s,[95] whose nearest relations were earnestly dissuading her from being 'righteous overmuch', and by the old motive, 'Why shouldst thou destroy thyself?'[96] She answered all they advanced with meekness and love, and continued steadfast and immovable. Endure hardship still, thou soldier of Christ! Persecuted, but not forsaken; torn with inward and encompassed with outward

Cambuslang Revival (1742), in which Whitefield participated, was regarded by the scholastic Calvinist Erskine as enthusiastic. Behind both Erskine's movement and the Cambuslang Revival lay the activities of the praying societies, not unlike the English religious societies. A. L. Drummond and James Bullock, *The Scottish Church 1688–1843* (Edinburgh, 1973), pp. 50–53; A. Fawcett, *The Cambuslang Revival* (London, 1971), pp. 183-89; Frank Baker, 'Wesley and the Erskines', *London Quarterly and Holborn Review* (Jan., 1958), 183:36-45.

[92] Eccles. 7:16. The reference to zealous enforcement was occasioned by the publication of a collection of anti-Methodist sermons by Joseph Trapp, *The Nature, Folly, Sin, and Danger of being Righteous Overmuch*. JW's sermon was a reply.

[93] Luke 7:42.

[94] Curnock (II.262, n. 2) conjectures one of the Quaker Wigginton family, the head of which was baptized by Charles Wesley on Oct. 26, 1739.

[95] Mrs. Thornhill, wife of William Thornhill, a member of the staff of Bristol Infirmary, 1735–65. Mrs. Thornhill was the mother of Rebecca Scudamore, whose *Life* by Sarah Young was abridged by JW for the *Arminian Magazine* (1793), XVI.211 *seq.*, and published posthumously. It is there stated (with confusion of dates) that she 'was endowed with an extraordinary good natural understanding, improved by education. She died when Rebecca (born 1729) was nine years of age. About four years before her death she was awakened and became truly religious' (S. Young, *Some Particulars relating to the Life and Death of Rebecca Scudamore* [Bristol, 1790], pp. 1-2).

[96] Eccles. 7:16.

temptations, but yielding to none. O may patience have its perfect work!

Tue. 3. I preached at Bath to the most attentive and serious audience I have ever seen there. On Wednesday I preached at
5 Newgate on those words, 'Because of the Pharisees, they durst not confess him. . . . For they loved the praise of men more than the praise of God.'[97] A message was delivered to me, when I had done, from the sheriffs, that I must preach there no more.[98]

Fri. 6. I pressed a serious Quaker[99] to tell me why he did not
10 come to hear me as formerly. He said, because he found we were not 'led by the Spirit',[1] for we fixed times of preaching beforehand; whereas we ought to do nothing unless we were 'sensibly moved thereto' by the Holy Ghost. I asked whether we ought not to do what God in Scripture commands when we have
15 opportunity. Whether the providence of God thus concurring with his Word were not a sufficient reason for our doing it, although we were not at that moment 'sensibly moved thereto' by the Holy Ghost. He answered, it was not a sufficient reason. This was to regard 'the letter that killeth'.[2] God grant that I may so
20 regard it all the days of my life!

In the afternoon I was with Mr. Whitefield, just come from London,[3] with whom I went to Baptist Mills, where he preached 'concerning the Holy Ghost, which all who believe are to receive';[4] not without a just, though severe, censure of those who
25 preach *as if* there were no Holy Ghost.

Sat. 7. I had an opportunity to talk with him of those outward signs which had so often accompanied the inward work of God. I found his objections were chiefly grounded on gross mis-

[97] John 12:42-43.
[98] Curnock conjectured that this prohibition was due to episcopal pressure; certainly opposition began to increase, and the bishop, Joseph Butler, concluded an interview with JW on August 16 with the advice, 'You have no business here. You are not commissioned to preach in this diocese. Therefore I advise you to go hence' (John Whitehead, *The Life of the Rev. John Wesley*, 2 vols. [London, Couchman, 1793-96], II.120). It is clear from an unpublished narrative fragment (see Frank Baker, 'John Wesley and Bishop Joseph Butler — a fragment of John Wesley's Manuscript Journal', WHS 42:93-100) that JW had three interviews with Butler, one on an unknown date in the summer, as well as two on August 16 and 18, each lasting more than an hour (see Appendix B below).
[99] Anthony Purver (diary, July 6, 1739); see above, June 15, 1739, n. 54.
[1] Rom. 8:14.
[2] 2 Cor. 3:6.
[3] Whitefield had been briefly in London on June 25 and 26, but had been travelling in Gloucestershire since that date.
[4] Cf. John 7:39.

representations of matter of fact. But the next day he had an opportunity of informing himself better. For no sooner had he begun (in the application of his sermon) to invite all sinners to believe in Christ, than four persons sunk down close to him, almost in the same moment. One of them lay without either sense or motion. A second trembled exceedingly. The third had strong convulsions all over his body but made no noise, unless by groans. The fourth, equally convulsed, called upon God with strong cries and tears.[5] From this time, I trust, we shall all suffer God to carry on his own work in the way that pleaseth him.

Thur. 13. I went to a gentleman[6] who is much troubled with what they call 'lowness of spirits'. Many such have I been with before, but in several of them it was no bodily distemper. They wanted something, they knew not what, and were therefore heavy, uneasy, and dissatisfied with everything. The plain truth is, they wanted God, they wanted Christ, they wanted faith, and God convinced them of their want in a way their physicians no more understood than themselves. Accordingly nothing availed till the Great Physician came. For, in spite of all natural means, he who made them for himself would not suffer them to rest till they rested in him.[7]

On Friday in the afternoon I left Bristol with Mr. Whitefield,[8] in the midst of heavy rain. But the clouds soon dispersed, so that we had a fair, calm evening and a serious congregation at Thornbury.

In the morning we breakfasted with a Quaker[9] who had been brought up in the Church of England, but being under strong conviction of inward sin and applying to several persons for

[5] Whitefield's *Journal* (p. 299) comments simply upon the reverent behaviour of the congregation, 'their loud and repeated Amens, which they put up to every petition, as well as the exemplariness of their conversation in common life'.

[6] Mr. Cutler, presumably the father of the Miss Cutler whom JW often visited in Bristol; he died May 9, 1740. Diary, July 12, 1739; May 9, 1740.

[7] See Augustine, *Confessions*, i.1, translated by JW, 'Thou hast made us for thyself; and our heart cannot rest, till it resteth in thee,' in his sermon on Mark 12:33, §9, and elsewhere (see Sermon 120, 'The Unity of the Divine Being', 4:64 in this edn.).

[8] Who had preached his 'farewell sermon, at seven in the morning, to a weeping and deeply affected audience' (*Journal*, pp. 303-4).

[9] Isaac Sharpless (diary, July 14, 1739). Sharpless (*c.* 1702–84) was born near Prescot, Lancs., of Quaker parents; but on the death of his mother in 1705, the family broke up, and he himself was baptized and confirmed to the Established Church. At the end of his apprenticeship he became a Friend by conviction and testified among them in Somerset in 1724. He married (1) Esther Thurston in 1735; she died in 1740; (2) in 1746 Mary Ransom of Hitchin, Herts., where they settled. She died 1798. After the death of his

advice; they all judged him to be under a disorder of body and gave advice accordingly. Some Quakers with whom he met about the same time told him it was the hand of God upon his soul, and advised him to seek another sort of relief than those miserable
5 comforters had recommended. 'Woe unto you, ye blind leaders of the blind!'[10] How long will ye pervert the right ways of the Lord?[11] Ye who tell the mourners in Zion, Much religion hath made you mad![12] Ye who send them whom God hath wounded to the devil for cure; to company, idle books, or diversions! Thus shall they
10 perish in their iniquity, but their blood shall God require of your hands![13]

We had an attentive congregation at Gloucester in the evening. In the morning, Mr. Whitefield being gone forward, I preached to about five thousand there, on 'Christ our wisdom, righteousness,
15 sanctification, and redemption'.[14] It rained violently at five in the evening, notwithstanding which two or three thousand people stayed, to whom I expounded that glorious vision of Ezekiel, of the resurrection of the dry bones.[15]

On Monday 16, after preaching to two or three thousand on
20 'What must I do to be saved?'[16] I returned to Bristol, and preached to about three thousand on those words of Job, 'There the wicked cease from troubling; there the weary are at rest.'[17]

Tue. 17. I rode to Bradford, five miles from Bath, whither I had been long invited to come. I waited on the minister,[18] and desired
25 leave to preach in his church. He said it was not usual to preach on the weekdays, but if I could come thither on a Sunday he should be glad of my assistance. Thence I went to a gentleman in the town[19] who had been present when I preached at Bath and,

first wife Sharpless became a diligent visitor of meetings throughout the United Kingdom, and also in Jersey and Holland, and he founded new meetings also. 'He was sometimes called the lazy preacher, because for a considerable time after standing up, his procedure was uncommonly slow, as if the subject matter was impeded in its flow, for his sentences were sometimes very short . . . .' Friends House Library, London.

10 Cf. Matt. 15:14; 23:16.
11 Acts 13:10.
12 See Acts 26:24.
13 See Ezek. 3:18, etc.
14 Cf. 1 Cor. 1:30.
15 See Ezek. 37:1-14.
16 Acts 16:30.
17 Job 3:17.
18 Doubtless the John Rogers of Bradford, Wilts., cler., whose son of the same name matriculated at Oriel College, Oxford, Mar. 13, 1734/35, aged 18.
19 The diary shows that the gentleman was Mr. Reed.

with the strongest marks of sincerity and affection, wished me 'good luck in the name of the Lord'.[20] But it was past. I found him now quite cold. He began disputing on several heads, and at last told me plainly one of our own college had informed him they always took me to be a little crack-brained at Oxford.

However, some persons who were not of his mind, having pitched on a convenient place (called Bearfield or Bury Field)[21] on the top of the hill under which the town lies, I there offered Christ to about a thousand people, for wisdom, righteousness, sanctification, and redemption.[22] Thence I returned to Bath, and preached on 'What must I do to be saved?'[23] to a larger audience than ever before. I was wondering the God of this world was so still, when at my return from the place of preaching, poor R[ichar]d Merchant[24] told me he could not let me preach any more in his ground. I asked him, 'Why?' He said the people hurt his trees and stole things out of his ground. 'And besides', added he, 'I have already, by letting thee be there, merited the displeasure of my neighbours.' O fear of man! Who is above thee, but they who indeed 'worship God in spirit and in truth'?[25] Not even those who have one foot in the grave! Not even those who dwell in rooms of cedar, and who have heaped up gold as the dust, and silver as the sand of the sea!

Sat. 21. I began expounding a second time[26] our Lord's Sermon upon the Mount. In the morning, Sunday 22, as I was explaining 'Blessed are the poor[27] in spirit'[28] to about three thousand people, we had a fair opportunity of showing all men what manner of spirit we were of; for in the middle of the sermon the press-gang came and seized on one of the hearers (Ye learned in the law, what becomes of Magna Charta, and of 'English liberty and property'? Are not these mere sounds, while, on any

[20] Cf. Ps. 129:8 (BCP).
[21] Orig., 'Bear Field'. Bearfield was just outside Bradford-on-Avon.
[22] See 1 Cor. 1:30.
[23] Acts 16:30.
[24] The separate contemporary editions read 'R—— M——', expanded in the *Works* (1774) to 'R——d M——l', corrected and filled out in the errata and in JW's own annotated copy to 'R——d Merchant'.
[25] Cf. John 4:23, 24.
[26] The previous occasion had been to the Nicholas Street Society on Apr. 1, 1739; JW now addressed 1200 in the open air at the Bowling Green. Diary, July 21, 1739.
[27] 1748 onwards, 'pure'.
[28] Matt. 5:3.

pretence, there is such a thing as a press-gang suffered in the land?); all the rest standing still, and none opening his mouth or lifting up his hand to resist them.[29]

Mon. 23. To guard young converts from fancying that they had
5 already attained or were already perfect, I preached on those words, 'So is the kingdom of God as when a man casteth seed into the ground; . . . and riseth day and night, and the seed buddeth forth and springeth up, he knoweth not how; . . . first the blade, then the ear, and then the full corn in the ear.'[30]

10 On several evenings this week, and particularly on Friday, many were deeply convinced, but none were delivered from that painful conviction. 'The children came to the birth, but there was not strength to bring forth.'[31] I fear we have grieved the Spirit of the jealous God, by questioning his work, and that therefore he is
15 withdrawn from us for a season. 'But he will return and abundantly pardon.'[32]

Mon. 30. Two more were in strong pain, both their souls and bodies being wellnigh torn asunder. But though we cried unto God, there was no answer, neither did he as yet deliver them
20 at all.

One of these[33] had been remarkably zealous against those that cried out and made a noise, being sure that 'any of them might help it if they would.' And the same opinion she was in still till the moment she was struck through as with a sword, and
25 fell trembling to the ground. She then cried aloud, though not articulately, her words being swallowed up. In this pain she continued twelve or fourteen hours, and then her soul was set at liberty. But her master (for she was a servant till that time, at a gentleman's in town) forbid her returning to him, saying he
30 would have none in his house 'who had received the Holy Ghost'.

Tue. 31. I preached at Bradford to above two thousand, many of whom were of the better rank, on 'What must I do to be saved?'[34] They all behaved with decency, and none went away till
35 all was ended. While I was preaching at Bath, in my return, some of the audience did not behave so well, being, I fear, a little too

[29] The press-gang was actively taking up landsmen as well as seamen against the emergency of war which was declared against Spain in October.
[30] Cf. Mark 4:26-28.
[31] Cf. Isa. 37:3.   [32] Cf. Isa. 55:7.
[33] Alice Philips, who was buried on Dec. 30, 1740 (see that date below).
[34] Acts 16:30.

nearly concerned when I came to the application of those words, 'Not only this our craft is in danger to be set at nought; but also that the temple of the great goddess Diana should be despised, ... whom all Asia and the world worshippeth.'[35]

Having *A Caution against Religious Delusion* put into my hands 5 about this time, I thought it my duty to write to the author of it,[36] which I accordingly did, in the following terms:

Reverend Sir,

1. You charge me (for I am called a 'Methodist', and consequently included within your charge) with 'vain and confident boastings, rash, 10 uncharitable censures, damning all who do not *feel* what I *feel*';[37] 'not allowing men to be in a salvable state unless they have experienced some *sudden* operation, which may be distinguished as the hand of God upon them, overpowering as it were the soul'.[38] with 'denying men the use of God's creatures, which he hath appointed to be 15 received with thanksgiving, and encouraging abstinence, prayer, and other religious exercises, to the neglect of the duties of our station'.[39] O sir, can you prove this charge upon me? The Lord shall judge in that day!

2. I do indeed go out into the highways and hedges to call poor 20 sinners to Christ. But not 'in a tumultuous manner',[40] not 'to the disturbance of the public peace' or 'the prejudice of families'.[41] Neither herein do I break any law which I know, much less 'set at nought all rule and authority'.[42] Nor can I be said to 'intrude into the labours'[43] of those who do not labour at all, but suffer thousands of 25 those for whom Christ died to 'perish for lack of knowledge'.[44]

---

[35] Acts 19:27.

[36] Henry Stebbing, *A Caution against Religious Delusion* (London, 1739; six edns. were published this year). Stebbing (1687–1763), a former fellow of St. Catherine Hall, Cambridge, was elected preacher to Gray's Inn, 1731; appointed chaplain to George II, 1732; archdeacon of Wiltshire, 1735; and chancellor of Sarum, 1739. He defended what he understood to be Anglican orthodoxy against Hoadly, Whitefield, and most of all, Warburton. He also wrote *An Earnest and Affectionate Address to the People called Methodists,* 2nd edn. (London, 1745).

[37] Stebbing, *Caution,* 3rd edn. (London, Gyles, 1739), p. 14. Wesley has added the emphasis upon 'feel'.

[38] Ibid.; cf. p. 8: 'But they will have it to be a *sensible* operation; an operation which may be *felt* and *distinguished* as the hand of God upon them; *overpowering,* as it were, the soul. And unless men are able to give account of their having at some time or other *experienced* some such sudden change within themselves, they will not allow him to be *regenerate,* nor therefore in a sa[l]vable state.' It seems likely that the emphasized 'sudden' in Wesley's rough quotation was intended as the word which Stebbing continually italicized — *sensible.*

[39] Ibid.; cf. p. 14.   [40] Cf. ibid., 'gathering tumultuous assemblies'.
[41] Ibid.   [42] Ibid.
[43] Cf. ibid., 'intruding into other men's labours'.   [44] Cf. Hos. 4:6.

3. They perish for want of knowing that *we* as well as the heathens are 'alienated from the life of God';[45] that *every one of us*, by the corruption of our inmost nature, 'is very far gone from original righteousness'; so far that 'every person born into the world,
5 deserveth God's wrath and damnation';[46] that we have by nature no power either to help ourselves, or even to call upon God to help us, all our tempers and works, in our natural state, being only evil continually. So that *our* coming to Christ, as well as *theirs*, 'must infer a great and mighty change'.[47] It must infer, not only an *outward change*,
10 from stealing, lying, and all corrupt communication; but a thorough *change of heart*, an *inward* renewal in the spirit of our mind. Accordingly 'the old man' implies infinitely more than *outward* 'evil conversation',[48] even 'an evil heart of unbelief',[49] corrupted by pride and a thousand deceitful lusts. Of consequence the 'new man' must
15 imply infinitely more than *outward* 'good conversation',[50] even 'a good heart',[51] 'which after God is created in righteousness and true holiness';[52] a heart full of that faith, which working by love, produces all holiness of conversation.

4. The change from the former of these states to the latter is what I
20 call 'the new birth'. But, you say, I am 'not content with this plain and easy notion of it, but fill myself and others with fantastical conceits'[53] about it. Alas, sir, how can you prove this? And if you cannot prove it, what amends can you make, either to God or to me or to the world, for publicly asserting a gross falsehood?

25 5. Perhaps you say you 'can prove this of Mr. Whitefield'.[54] What then? This is nothing to me. I am not accountable for *his* words. The *Journal*[55] you quote I never saw till it was in print. But indeed you wrong him as much as me. First, where you represent him as judging

[45] Eph. 4:18.
[46] Cf. BCP, Thirty-nine Articles, Art. IX, 'Of Original or Birth Sin'.
[47] Stebbing, *Caution*, p. 3.
[48] Ibid., p. 41, citing Eph. 4:22-29.
[49] Heb. 3:12.
[50] Jas. 3:13, etc.
[51] Cf. Luke 8:15; 1 Tim. 1:5.
[52] Eph. 4:24; cf. Stebbing, *Caution*, p. 4.
[53] Cf. Stebbing, *Caution*, p. 7.
[54] Stebbing does not in fact say this in so many words, but in three lengthy footnotes he does quote Whitefield's *Journal* (pp. 16, 19, 21), referring to Whitefield by name, though he never mentions Wesley.
[55] The passages in Whitefield's *Journal* to which Stebbing took particular exception are to be found on pp. 262, 248-49 (1960 edn.; pp. 91, 74 in the orig. edn.). Stebbing's sermon was forwarded to Whitefield by the Bishop of Gloucester with an admonition to preach only to the congregation to which he was appointed. Whitefield defended himself in a letter to the bishop, July 9, 1739 (*Journal*, pp. 300-302), which compares interestingly with JW's defence here.

the notions of the Quakers *in general* (concerning being led by the Spirit) to be right and good; whereas he speaks only of those *particular men* with whom he was then conversing.[56] And again where you say he 'supposes a person believing in Christ' to be without any 'saving knowledge' of him.[57] He *supposes* no such thing. 'To believe in Christ' was the very thing he 'supposed' wanting; as understanding that term 'believing' to imply, not only an assent to the articles of our Creed, but also, 'a true trust and confidence of the mercy of God through our Lord Jesus Christ'.[58]

6. Now this it is certain a man may want, although he can truly say, 'I am chaste, I am sober, I am just in my dealings, I help my neighbour, and use the ordinances of God.'[59] 'And however' such a man 'may have behaved in these respects, he is not to think well of his own state till he experiences something within himself which he has not yet experienced,' but 'which he may be beforehand assured he shall,'[60] if the promises of God are true. That 'something' is a living faith: 'a sure trust and confidence in God, that by the merits of Christ his sins are forgiven, and he reconciled to the favour of God'.[61] And from this will spring many other things which till then he experienced not, as the love of God, shed abroad in his heart,[62] that peace of God which passeth all understanding,[63] and joy in the Holy Ghost,[64] joy though not *unfelt*, yet *unspeakable* and full of glory.[65]

7. These are some of those *inward* 'fruits of the Spirit',[66] which must be *felt*, wheresoever they are. And without these I cannot learn from Holy Writ that any man is 'born of the Spirit'.[67] I beseech you, sir, by the mercies of God, that if as yet you 'know nothing of such inward feelings',[68] if you do not 'feel' in yourself these mighty workings of the Spirit of Christ',[69] at least you would not contradict and blaspheme. When the Holy Ghost hath fervently kindled *your*

[56] Stebbing, *Caution*, p. 19.
[57] Ibid., p. 16.
[58] Homilies, on the Passion, Pt. II.
[59] Cf. Stebbing, *Caution*, pp. 15-16: 'Am I sober, am I chaste; am I just and charitable to my neighbour; do I serve God in the use of his ordinances?'
[60] Cf. ibid., p. 16, introduced by Stebbing with 'But', with the last quoted clause beginning, 'and which', and continuing, 'this will lead him to cast off all hope in God, and to give himself up to despair'. Wesley affirms what Stebbing rejects.
[61] Homilies, Of Salvation, Pt. III — Wesley's favourite definition.
[62] See Rom. 5:5.
[63] Phil. 4:7.
[64] Rom. 14:17.
[65] 1 Pet. 1:8.
[66] Stebbing, *Caution*, p. 12; cf. Gal. 5:22.
[67] John 3:6, 8.
[68] Stebbing, *Caution*, p. 11.
[69] Cf. Thirty-nine Articles, Art. 17, 'Of Predestination and Election': '. . . such as feel in themselves the working of the Spirit of Christ'.

love towards God, you will know these to be very *sensible* operations. As you 'hear the wind, and feel it too', while it 'strikes upon your bodily organs',[70] you will know you are under the guidance of God's Spirit the same way, namely, by *feeling it in your soul:*[71] by the present
5 peace and joy and love which you feel within, as well as by its outward and more distant effects.

I am, etc.

I have often wished that all calm and impartial men would consider what is advanced by another writer, in a little discourse
10 concerning enthusiasm or religious delusion, published about this time.[72] His words are:

> A *minister* of our Church, who may look upon it as his duty to warn his *parishioners,* or an *author* who may think it necessary to caution his readers against *such preachers* or their doctrine (enthusiastic
> 15 preachers, I suppose, such as he takes it for granted the Methodist preachers are) ought to be very careful to act with a *Christian spirit,* and to advance nothing but with *temper, charity, and truth.* . . . Perhaps the following rules may be proper to be observed by them.
> 1. Not to *blame* persons for doing that now, which Scripture
> 20 records *holy men* of old to have practised, lest had they lived in those times they should have condemned them also.
> 2. Not to *censure* persons in *holy orders* for teaching the same doctrines which are taught in the *Scriptures* and by *our Church,* lest they should ignorantly *censure* what they profess to *defend.*
> 25 3. Not to censure any professed *members* of our Church, who live *good lives,* for resorting to *religious assemblies* in private houses, to perform in society acts of *divine worship;* when the same seems to have been practised by the primitive Christians; and when, alas! there are so many parishes where a person *piously* disposed has no opportunity
> 30 of joining in the Public Service of our Church more than *one hour and a half* in a week.
> 4. Not to *condemn* those who are constant attendants on the

---

[70] Stebbing, *Caution,* p. 12.

[71] Ibid., p. 12.

[72] Rev. Josiah Tucker, in Raikes's *Gloucester Journal* (No. 25 of 'Country Common Sense'). Tucker (1712-99), economist and divine, became curate of St. Stephen's, Bristol, 1737; and rector of All Saints, Bristol, 1739. Subsequently he became minor canon of Bristol and domestic chaplain to the bishop, Butler. In 1756 he became prebend of Bristol, and in 1758 dean of Gloucester. A notable writer on commercial matters, he advocated abandoning the colonies; and in 1771 he defended clerical subscription to the Thirty-nine Articles. He also published a *Brief History of the Principles of Methodism* (Oxford, 1742) to which JW replied with *The Principles of a Methodist* (1742). See also George Shelton, *Dean Tucker and Eighteenth-century Economic and Political Thought* (London, 1981).

Communion and *Service* of our Church if they sometimes use *other* prayers in private assemblies, since the *best divines* of our Church have composed and published many *prayers* that have not the sanction of public authority—which implies a general consent that our Church has not made provision for every private occasion. 5

5. Not to establish the power of *working miracles* as the great criterion of a divine mission, when Scripture teaches us that the agreement of doctrines with truth as taught in those Scriptures is the only infallible rule.

6. Not to drive any away from our *Church*, by opprobriously calling 10 them 'dissenters', or treating them as such, so long as they keep to her *communion*.

7. Not lightly to take up with *silly stories* that may be propagated to the discredit of persons of a general *good character.*

I do not lay down (says he) these *negative rules* so much for the sake 15 of any persons whom the unobservance of them would immediately injure, as of our *Church* and her professed *defenders.* For churchmen, however *well-meaning,* would lay themselves open to censure, and might do her *irretrievable damage* by a behaviour contrary to them. 20

Friday, August 3. I met with one who *did* run well, but Satan had hindered her. I was surprised at her ingenuous acknowledgment of the fear of man. O 'how hardly shall' even 'they who have rich' acquaintance 'enter into the kingdom of heaven'![73]

Sun. 5. Six persons at the New Room[74] were deeply *convinced of* 25 *sin,* three of whom were a little comforted by prayer but not yet *convinced of righteousness.*

Having frequently been invited to Wells, particularly by Mr. [Severs],[75] who begged me to make his house my home, on Thursday the 9th I went thither, and wrote him word the night 30 before, upon which he presently went to one of his friends and desired a messenger might be sent to meet me and beg me to turn back; 'Otherwise' (said he) 'we shall lose all our trade.' But this consideration did not weigh with him, so that he invited me to his own house. And at eleven I preached in his ground, on Christ our 35 'wisdom, righteousness, sanctification, and redemption',[76] to about two thousand persons. Some of them mocked at first,

[73] Cf. Matt. 19:23.
[74] The implication of this entry is that since JW conducted a service 'in the shell' of the New Room on June 3 (see above) the building had been completed.
[75] Diary, Aug. 9, 1739.
[76] Cf. 1 Cor. 1:30.

whom I reproved before all; and those of them who stayed were more serious. Several spoke to me after, who were for the present much affected. O let it not pass away as the morning dew!

Fri. 10. I had the satisfaction of conversing with a Quaker,[77] and afterward with an Anabaptist,[78] who, I trust, have had a large measure of the love of God shed abroad in their hearts.[79] O may those, in every persuasion, who are of this spirit increase a thousandfold, how many soever they be!

Sat. 11. In the evening two were seized with strong pangs, as were four the next evening, and the same number at Gloucester Lane on Monday, one of whom was greatly comforted.

Tue. 14. I preached at Bradford to about three thousand on 'One thing is needful.'[80] Returning through Bath, I preached to a small congregation suddenly gathered together at a little distance from the town[81] (not being permitted to be in R[ichard] M[erchant]'s ground any more) on 'The just shall live by faith.'[82] Three at the New Room this evening were cut to the heart. But their wound was not as yet healed.

Wed. 15. I endeavoured to guard those who were in their first love from falling into inordinate affection, by explaining those strange words at Baptist Mills, 'Henceforth know we no man after the flesh.'[83]

Fri. 17. Many of our society met, as we had appointed, at one in the afternoon and agreed that all the members of our society should obey the Church to which we belong by observing 'all Fridays in the year' as 'days of fasting or abstinence'.[84] We likewise agreed that as many as had opportunity should then meet to spend an hour together in prayer.

Mon. 20. I preached on those words (to a much larger congregation than usual) 'Oughtest not thou to have compassion on thy fellow servant, as I had pity on thee?'[85]

---

[77] Mr. (presumably Thomas) Whitehead; see above, June 22, 1739, n. 68; diary, Aug. 10, 1739.

[78] Probably Mrs. Padmore, at whose home JW had frequently visited. Diary, ibid.

[79] See Rom. 5:5.

[80] Luke 10:42.

[81] At John Feacham's (often referred to in the diary as 'Jo') where JW had preached since his earliest visits to Bath.

[82] Rom. 1:17, etc.

[83] 2 Cor. 5:16. For Wesley's interview with the Bishop of Bristol, and other details for Aug. 16-23, 1739, see Appendix B below.

[84] BCP, Tables and Rules.

[85] Cf. Matt. 18:33.

Wed. 22. I was with many that were in heaviness, two of whom[86] were soon filled with peace and joy. In the afternoon I endeavoured to guard the weak against what too often occasions heaviness, levity of temper or behaviour, from 'I said of laughter, It is mad; and of mirth, What doth it?'[87]

Mon. 27. For two hours I took up my cross, in arguing with a zealous man,[88] and labouring to convince him that I was not 'an enemy to the Church of England'. He allowed, I 'taught no other doctrines than those of the Church', but could not forgive my teaching them *out of the church walls*. He allowed too (which none indeed can deny who has either any regard to truth or sense of shame) that 'by this teaching many souls who till that time were perishing for lack of knowledge, have been, and are, brought from darkness to light, and from the power of Satan unto God.'[89] But he added, 'No one can tell what *may be hereafter;* and *therefore,* I say, these things ought not to be suffered.'

Indeed the report now current in Bristol was that I was 'a Papist, if not a Jesuit'. Some added that I was 'born and bred at Rome', which many cordially believed. O ye fools, when will ye understand that the preaching *justification by faith alone,* the allowing no meritorious cause of our justification but the death and righteousness of Christ, and no conditional or instrumental cause but faith, is overturning popery from the foundations? When will ye understand that the most destructive of all those errors which Rome, the mother of abominations, hath brought forth (compared to which transubstantiation and a hundred more are trifles light as air)[90] is that *we are justified by works* or (to express the same thing a little more decently) by faith *and* works. Now, do I preach *this?* I did for ten years: I was (fundamentally) a Papist, and knew it not. But I do now testify to all (and it is the very point for asserting which I have to this day been called in question) that 'no good works can be done before justification, none which have not in them the nature of sin.'[91]

---

[86] Mr. Bradshaw and Mrs. England (diary, Aug. 22, 1739). Both had been in touch with JW since his early days in Bristol, and Mrs. England had provided frequent hospitality for his meetings.

[87] Eccles. 2:2.

[88] Described in the diary as 'Th. Robins'. JW was at prayer 'at brother Robin's' at Bristol in 1785 (diary, Aug. 27, 1739; Mar. 19, 1785).

[89] See Acts 26:18.

[90] Shakespeare, *Othello,* III.iii.322.

[91] See the quotations in *A Farther Appeal to Men of Reason and Religion,* Pt. I, II.7, 11:114-15 in this edn.

I have often inquired who were the authors of this report, and have generally found they were either bigoted Dissenters or (I speak it without fear or favour) ministers of our own Church. I have frequently considered what possible ground or motive
5 they could have thus to speak, seeing few men in the world have had occasion so clearly and openly to declare their principles as I have done, both by preaching, printing, and conversation, for several years last past. And I can no otherwise think than that either they spoke thus (to put the most favourable construction
10 upon it) from gross ignorance—they knew not what popery was, they knew not what doctrines those are which the Papists teach —or they wilfully spoke what they knew to be false, probably 'thinking thereby to do God service'.[92] Now take this to yourselves, whosoever ye are, high or low, Dissenters or
15 Churchmen, clergy or laity, who have advanced this shameless charge, and digest it how ye can.

But how have ye not been afraid, if ye believe there is a God, and that he knoweth the secrets of your hearts (I speak now to you, preachers, more especially, of whatever denomination), to
20 declare so gross, palpable, a lie, in the name of the God of truth? I cite you all, before the Judge of all the earth, either publicly to prove your charge, or by publicly retracting it to make the best amends you can, to God, to me, and to the world.

For the full satisfaction of those who have been abused by these
25 shameless men, and almost brought to believe a lie, I will here add my serious judgment concerning the Church of Rome, wrote some time since to a priest of that communion:[93]

Sir,
  I return you thanks both for the favour of your letter, and for your
30 recommending my father's *Proposals* to the Sorbonne.[94]
  I have neither time nor inclination for controversy with any, but least of all with the Romanists. And that both because I can't trust any of their quotations without consulting every sentence they quote in the originals, and because the originals themselves can very hardly be
35 trusted in any of the points controverted between them and us. I am no stranger to their skill in *mending* those authors who did not at first speak home to their purpose, as also in *purging* them from[95] those

---

[92] Cf. John 16:2.
[93] Probably written in the summer of 1735. See *Letters*, 25:428-30 in this edn.
[94] I.e., Proposals to publish Samuel Wesley's book on *Job* which were printed in 1730, 1731, 1733, and 1734.
[95] I.e., 'of'.

passages which contradicted their emendations. And as they have not wanted opportunity to do this, so doubtless they have carefully used it with regard to a point that so nearly concerned them as the supremacy of the Bishop of Rome. I am not therefore surprised if the works of St. Cyprian (as they are called) do strenuously maintain it; but I am, that 5 they have not been better *corrected*—for they still contain passages that absolutely overthrow it. What gross negligence was it to leave his Seventy-fourth Epistle (to Pompeianus) out of the *Index Expurgatorius*, wherein Pope Cyprian so flatly charges Pope Stephen with 'pride and obstinacy, and with being a defender of the cause of 10 heretics and that against Christians and the very church of God'![96] He that can reconcile this with his believing Stephen the infallible head of the church may reconcile the Gospel with the Alcoran.

Yet I can by no means approve the scurrility and contempt with which the Romanists have often been treated. I dare not rail at or 15 despise any man, much less those who profess to believe in the same Master. But I pity them much, having the same assurance that Jesus is the Christ and that no Romanist can expect to be saved according to the terms of his covenant. For thus saith our Lord, 'Whosoever shall break one of the least of these commandments, and shall teach men 20 so, he shall be called the least in the kingdom of heaven.'[97] And, 'If any man shall add unto these things, God shall add unto him the plagues that are written in this book.'[98] But all Romanists, as such, do both. *Ergo.* . . .

The minor I prove, not from Protestant authors, or even from 25 particular writers of their own communion, but from the public, authentic records of the Church of Rome. Such are *The Canons and Decrees of the Council of Trent.* And the edition I use was printed at Cologne,[99] and approved by authority.

And, first, all Romanists, as such, do break and teach men to break 30 one (and not the least) of those commandments: the words of which, concerning images, are these: לֹא תִשְׁתַּחְוֶה לָהֶם.[1] Now שׁתח (as every smatterer in Hebrew knows) is *incurvare se—procumbere, honoris exhibendi causa*[k] (and is accordingly rendered by the Seventy in this very place by a Greek word of the very same import, προσκυνεῖν). 35 But the Council of Trent (and consequently all Romanists, as such, all who allow authority of that Council) teaches that it is *legitimus*

[k] To bow down before anyone, in token of honouring him.

---

[96] This is not a single quotation but a composite derived from 1, 7, 8. See *Ante-Nicene Fathers*, V.386-89, where Epistle 74 (in some edns.) is numbered as 73.
[97] Cf. Matt. 5:19.
[98] Rev. 22:18.
[99] Orig., 'Colen'.
[1] Exod. 20:5.

imaginum usus . . . eis honorem exhibere, procumbendo coram eis.[1]

Secondly, all Romanists, as such, do add to those things which are written in the Book of Life. For in the Bull of Pius IV,[2] subjoined to those *Canons and Decrees*, I find all the additions following: (1) seven
5 sacraments; (2) transubstantiation; (3) communion in one kind only; (4) purgatory, and praying for the dead therein; (5) praying to saints; (6) veneration of relics; (7) worship of images; (8) indulgences; (9) the priority and universality of the Roman Church; (10) the supremacy of the Bishop of Rome. All these things therefore do the Romanists add
10 to those which are written in the Book of Life.

I am, . . .

Tue. 28. My mouth was opened, and my heart enlarged, strongly to declare to above two thousand people at Bradford that 'the kingdom of God' (within us) 'is not meat and drink, but
15 righteousness, and peace, and joy in the Holy Ghost.'[3] At Bath I once more offered Christ to 'justify the ungodly'.[4] In the evening I met my brother, just come from London. 'The Lord hath' indeed 'done great things for us already.'[5] 'Not unto us, but unto thy name be the praise.'[6]
20 Wed. 29.[7] I rode with my brother to Wells and preached on 'What must I do to be saved?'[8] In the evening I summed up at the New Room, what I had said at many times from the beginning, of faith, holiness, and good works, as the root, the tree, and the fruit, which God has joined, and man ought not to put asunder.
25 Friday, August 31, I left Bristol and reached London about eight on Sunday morning. In the afternoon I heard a sermon[9] wherein it was asserted that our repentance was not sincere, but

---

[1] I.e., the proper use of images is to honour them, by bowing down before them (Session 25, para. 2).

[2] The summary of the doctrinal decisions of the Council of Trent by Pope Pius IV (1499–1565), the Bull *'Super forma juramenti professionis fidei'*, was appended to *Canones et Decreta* and imposed on all holders of ecclesiastical office.

[3] Rom. 14:17.

[4] Cf. Rom. 4:5.

[5] Ps. 126:4 (BCP). The particular cause for thanksgiving was that Charles Wesley, who had arrived in order to enable his brother to leave Bristol for a time, had lately found his preaching attended by unexampled power and effectiveness. CWJ, I.160-66 (Aug. 12-28, 1739).

[6] Ps. 115:1 (BCP).

[7] The diary makes it clear that this date should be Thursday, Aug. 30.

[8] Acts 16:30.

[9] Preached by Dr. Heylyn, rector of St. Mary-le-Strand. See above, May 19, 1738, n. 15, 18:241 in this edn.; diary, Sept. 2, 1739.

feigned and hypocritical, (1) if we relapsed into sin *soon after* repenting; especially if (2) we did not *avoid all occasions* of sin; or if (3) we *relapsed frequently;* and most of all if (4) our hearts were *hardened* thereby. O what a hypocrite have I been (if this be so) for near twice ten years! But I know it is not so. I know everyone 5 'under the law'[10] is even as I was. Everyone when he begins to see his fallen state and to feel the wrath of God abiding on him, relapses into the sin that most easily besets him, *soon after* repenting of it. Sometimes he avoids, and at many other times cannot persuade himself to *avoid the occasions* of it. Hence his 10 relapses are *frequent,* and of consequence his *heart is hardened* more and more. And yet all this time he is *sincerely* striving against sin. He can say 'unfeignedly, without hypocrisy',[11] 'The thing which I do, I approve not; the evil which I would not, that I do.'[12] 'To will is' even then 'present with' him; 'but how to perform that 15 which is good he finds not.'[13] Nor can he, with all his *sincerity,* avoid any one of these four marks of *hypocrisy,* till 'being justified by faith, he hath peace with God through Jesus Christ our Lord.'[14]

This helpless state I took occasion to describe at Kennington to 20 eight or ten thousand people, from those words of the Psalmist, 'Innumerable troubles are come about me; my sins have taken such hold upon me that I am not able to look up; yea, they are more in number than the hairs of my head, and my heart hath failed me.'[15]   25

Monday, September 3. I talked largely with my mother, who told me that till a short time since she had scarce heard such a thing mentioned as the having forgiveness of sins now, or God's Spirit bearing witness with our spirit; much less did she imagine that this was the common privilege of all true believers. 30 'Therefore' (said she) 'I never durst ask for it myself. But two or three weeks ago, while my son Hall[16] was pronouncing those words, in delivering the cup to me, "The blood of our Lord Jesus Christ, which was given for thee",[17] the words struck through my heart, and I knew God for Christ's sake had forgiven *me* all 35 *my* sins.'

---

[10] Rom. 3:19, etc.   [11] Cf. Jas. 3:17.   [12] Cf. Rom. 7:19.
[13] Cf. Rom. 7:18.   [14] Cf. Rom. 5:1.
[15] Ps. 40:15 (BCP). Wrongly referred to in the diary as Ps. 40:16.
[16] Her son-in-law, the Rev. Westley Hall, who had married JW's younger sister Martha and in whose household she was now resident.
[17] Cf. BCP, Communion.

I asked whether her father (Dr. Annesley)[18] had not the same faith. And whether she had not heard him preach it to others. She answered, 'He had it himself, and declared, a little before his death, that for more than forty years he had no darkness, no fear,
5　no doubt at all, of his being "accepted in the Beloved".'[19] But that nevertheless she did not remember to have heard him preach, no not once, explicitly upon it: whence she supposed he also looked upon it as the peculiar blessing of *a few*, not as promised to all the people of God.

10　[Tue. 4.] Both at Mr. B[ray]'s[20] at six, and at Dowgate Hill[21] at eight, were many more than the houses could contain. Several persons who were then convinced of sin came to me the next morning. One came also who had been mourning long, and earnestly desired us to pray with her.[22] We had scarce begun when
15　the enemy began to tear her, so that she screamed out as in the pangs of death. But his time was short, for within a quarter of an hour she was full of the peace that passeth all understanding.

I afterwards called on Mrs. E[uste]r,[23] with whom was one lately come from Bristol, in deep anguish of spirit. We cried to
20　God, and he soon declared his salvation, so that both their mouths were filled with his praise.

Thence I went to a poor woman who had been long in despair.[24] I was glad to meet with Mrs. R[andal][25] there—the

---

[18] Samuel Annesley (1620?–96), Puritan divine. In 1644 he became chaplain to the Earl of Warwick, admiral of the parliamentary fleet, and subsequently obtained preferment in the church. In 1648 he preached a first sermon before the Commons, was nominated by Cromwell to a lectureship at St. Paul's in 1657, and by Richard Cromwell to the vicarage of St. Giles's, Cripplegate, in 1658, from which he was ejected in 1662. He established a conventicle in Little St. Helen's. Susanna Wesley was his 25th and youngest child.

[19] Eph. 1:6.

[20] John Bray of Little Britain, with whom JW lived in London. One of the most important characters in the *Journal* of Charles Wesley, who described him as 'a poor ignorant mechanic, who knows nothing but Christ, yet by knowing him, knows and discerns all things' (I.86). Bray flirted with the French Prophets (see above, June 13, 1739, n. 51) and Moravians (CWJ, I.219, 228; but cf. 336) and in Apr. 1740 threatened to expel Charles Wesley from his band (ibid., I.210).

[21] 'At Mr. Crouch's' (diary, Sept. 4, 1739). A Thomas Crouch attended the Conference of 1747. *Wesley Historical Society,* Publication No. 1, p. 39.

[22] Hannah Knowles. Diary, Sept. 5, 1739.

[23] Mrs. Euster (whose name is spelled by JW variously as Euster, Ewster, and Eustace), a considerable favourite of Charles Wesley (CWJ, I.158). Her daughter Mary was among the first single women in the Moravian congregation in 1742. Benham, *Hutton,* p. 95.

[24] Mrs. S. Hamilton (diary, Sept. 5, 1739) whose son became the leader of a band.

[25] Mrs. Randal, mentioned anonymously by JW in a letter to George Whitefield, Feb. 26, 1739 (25:602-3 in this edn.): 'On Saturday se'ennight, a middle-aged, well-dressed woman at Beech Lane . . . was seized, as it appeared to several about her, with little less

person mentioned in Mr. Whitefield's *Journal,* who, after three years' madness (so called), was so deeply convinced of sin at Beech Lane, and soon after rejoiced in God *her* Saviour.[26]

Thur. 6. I was sent for by one who began to feel herself a sinner. But a fine lady unexpectedly coming in, there was scarce room for me to speak. The fourth person in the company was a poor, unbred girl; who beginning to tell what God had done for her soul, the others looked one at another as in amaze, but did not open their mouths. I then exhorted them not to cease from crying to God till they too could say, as she did, 'My Beloved is mine, and I am his.[27] I am as sure of it as that I am alive. For his Spirit bears witness with my spirit that I am a child of God.'[28]

Sun. 9. I declared to about ten thousand in Moorfields what they must do to be saved. My mother went with us about five to Kennington, where were supposed to be twenty thousand people. I again insisted on that foundation of all our hope, 'Believe in the Lord Jesus, and thou shalt be saved.'[29] From Kennington I went to a society at Lambeth.[30] The house being filled, the rest stood in the garden. The deep attention they showed gave me a good hope that they will not all be forgetful hearers.

Thence I went to our society at Fetter Lane and exhorted them to love one another. The want of love was a general complaint. We laid it open before our Lord. We soon found he had sent us an answer of peace. Evil surmisings vanished away. The flame kindled again as at the first, and our hearts were knit together.

Mon. 10. I accepted a pressing invitation to go to Plaistow.[31] At five in the evening I expounded there, and at eight again. But most of the hearers were very quiet and unconcerned. In the morning, therefore, I spoke stronger words. But it is only the voice of the Son of God which is able to wake the dead.

than the agonies of death. We prayed that God who had brought her to the birth, would give strength to bring forth, and that He would work speedily. . . . Five days she travailed and groaned, being in bondage. On Thursday evening our Lord got himself the victory, and from that moment, she has been full of life and joy. . . . Her friends have accounted her mad for these three years, and have accordingly bled, blistered her, and what not'.

[26] See Wesley's letter to Whitefield, Feb. 26, 1738/39, *Letters,* 25:601-3 in this edn.

[27] S. of S. 2:16.

[28] Cf. Rom. 8:16.

[29] Acts 16:31.

[30] Lambeth Marsh. Diary, Sept. 9, 1739.

[31] The implication of the diary (Sept. 10, 1739) is that this invitation was to a religious society.

Wed. 12. In the evening at Fetter Lane I described the life of faith, and many who had fancied themselves strong therein found they were no more than newborn babes. At eight I exhorted our brethren to keep close to the Church, and to all the ordinances of
5 God,[32] and to aim only at living 'a quiet and peaceable life, in all godliness and honesty'.[33]

Thur. 13. A serious clergyman[34] desired to know in what points we differed from the Church of England. I answered: 'To the best of my knowledge, in none. The doctrines we preach are the
10 doctrines of the Church of England; indeed, the fundamental doctrines of the Church, clearly laid down, both in her Prayers, Articles, and Homilies.'

He asked, 'In what points, then, do you differ from the other clergy of the Church of England?' I answered, 'In none from that
15 part of the clergy who adhere to the doctrines of the Church; but from that part of the clergy who dissent from the Church (though they own it not) I differ in the points following:

'First. They speak of justification either as the same thing as sanctification, or as something consequent upon it. I believe
20 justification to be wholly distinct from sanctification and necessarily antecedent to it.

'Secondly. They speak of our own holiness or good works as the *cause* of our justification, or that *for the sake of which, on account of which*, we are justified before God. I believe neither our own
25 holiness nor good works are any part of the cause of our justification; but that the death and righteousness of Christ are the whole and sole cause of it, or that *for the sake of which, on account of which*, we are justified before God.

'Thirdly. They speak of good works as a *condition* of
30 justification, necessarily previous to it. I believe no good work can be previous to justification, nor, consequently, a condition of it; but that we are justified (being till that hour ungodly, and therefore incapable of doing any good work) by faith alone, faith

[32] This proved a continuing embarrassment in London. Charles Wesley records in Apr. 1740: 'I asked Bray whether he denied the ordinances to be commands. He answered indirectly, "I grant them to be great privileges." (Edmunds confessed more honestly that he had cast them off.)' CWJ, I.209.

[33] 1 Tim. 2:2.

[34] The diary implies that this was 'Mr. Howard' (Sept. 13, 1739), 'the courteous Mr. Howard' of Charles Wesley's *Journal* (II.210). Perhaps Eden Howard, adm. Trinity Hall, Cambridge, 1726, aged 21. Chaplain to East India Company, 1732–45. Will proved 1781.

without works, faith (though producing all, yet) including no good work.

'Fourthly. They speak of *sanctification* (or holiness) as if it were an outward thing, as if it consisted chiefly, if not wholly, in these two points: (1) the doing no harm; (2) the doing good (as it is called), i.e., the using the means of grace, and helping our neighbour.

'I believe it to be an inward thing, namely, "the life of God in the soul of man",[35] a "participation of the divine nature",[36] "the mind that was in Christ";[37] or "the renewal of our heart after the image of him that created us."[38]

'Lastly. They speak of the *new birth* as an *outward* thing, as if it were no more than baptism; or at most a change from *outward wickedness* to *outward goodness;* from a *vicious* to (what is called) a *virtuous* life. I believe it to be an inward thing; a change from inward wickedness to inward goodness; an entire change of our inmost nature from the image of the devil (wherein we are born) to the image of God; a change from the love of the creature to the love of the Creator, from earthly and sensual to heavenly and holy affections—in a word, a change from the *tempers* of the spirits of darkness to those of the angels of God [as] they are in heaven.

'There is therefore a wide, essential, fundamental, irreconcilable difference between us: so that if they speak the truth as it is in Jesus, I am found a false witness before God. But if I teach the way of God in truth, they are blind leaders of the blind.'

Sun. 16. I preached at Moorfields to about ten thousand, and at Kennington Common to I believe near twenty thousand, on those words of the calmer Jews to St. Paul, 'We desire to hear of thee what thou thinkest, for as concerning this sect, we know that everywhere it is spoken against.'[39] At both places I described the real difference between what is generally called Christianity and the true *old Christianity*, which under the *new name* of 'Methodism' is now also 'everywhere spoken against'.

Mon. 17. I preached again at Plaistow, on 'Blessed are those that mourn.'[40] It pleased God to give us in that hour two living

---

[35] Apparently an allusion to the title of the well-known work by Henry Scougal, which Wesley read in 1732, and of which he published an abridged edition in 1744 (see *Bibliography*, No. 93).

[36] Cf. 2 Pet. 1:4.   [37] Cf. Phil. 2:5.

[38] Cf. Col. 3:10.

[39] Acts 28:22.

[40] Cf. Matt. 5:4.

instances of that piercing sense both of the guilt and power of sin, that dread of the wrath of God, and that full conviction of man's inability either to remove the power, or atone for the guilt of sin (called by the world despair) in which properly consist that
5 poverty of spirit and mourning which are the gate of Christian blessedness.

Tue. 18. A young woman[41] came to us at Islington, in such an agony as I have seldom seen. Her sorrow and fear were too big for utterance; so that after a few words, her strength as well as her
10 heart failing, she sunk down to the ground. Only her sighs and groans showed she was yet alive. We cried unto God in her behalf. We claimed the promises made to the weary and heavy laden; and he did not cast out our prayer. She saw her Saviour, as it were, crucified before her eyes. She laid hold on him by faith, and her
15 spirit revived.

At Mr. B[ray]'s at six, I was enabled earnestly to call all the weary and heavy laden; and at Mr. C[rouch]'s at eight, when many roared aloud, some of whom utterly refused to be comforted till they should feel their souls at rest in the blood of
20 the Lamb and have his love shed abroad in their hearts.

Thur. 20. Mrs. C[rouch], being in deep heaviness, had desired me to meet her this afternoon. She had long earnestly desired to receive the Holy Communion, having an unaccountably strong persuasion that God would manifest himself to her therein and
25 give rest to her soul. But her heaviness being now greatly increased, Mr. D[elamott]e[42] gave her that fatal advice not to communicate *till she had* living faith. This still added to her perplexity. Yet at length she resolved to obey God rather than man. And 'he was made known unto her in breaking of bread.'[43]
30 In that moment she felt her load removed; she knew she was accepted in the Beloved, and all the time I was expounding at Mr. B[ray]'s was full of that peace which cannot be uttered.

Fri. 21. Another of Dr. Monro's[44] patients came to desire my

---

41 Nanny Smith (diary, Sept. 18, 1739), to whom JW came to write much.
42 Probably Charles Delamotte who was now a Moravian.
43 Cf. Luke 24:35.
44 Dr. John Monro (1715–91), who studied insanity in Edinburgh and on the continent and in 1751 was appointed physician at Bethlehem Hospital ('Bedlam') in Moorfields, London. There are several references in the journals of the period to those who were deeply affected by evangelical preaching being sent to Monro: see above, Sept. 17, 1740; JW to William Warburton, Nov. 26, 1762 (Telford, IV.357-58); Whitefield, *Journal*, pp. 267-71; cf. CWJ, I.195-99.

advice. I found no reason to believe she had been any otherwise *mad* than everyone is who is deeply convinced of sin. And I cannot doubt but, if she will trust in the living God, he will 'give medicine to heal her sickness'.[45]

Sun. 23. I declared to about ten thousand in Moorfields, with great enlargement of spirit, 'The kingdom of God is not meat and drink, but righteousness, and peace, and joy in the Holy Ghost.'[46] At Kennington I enforced on about twenty thousand that great truth, 'one thing is needful.'[47] Thence I went to Lambeth and showed (to the amazement, it seemed, of many who were present) how 'he that is born of God doth not commit sin.'[48]

Mon. 24. I preached once more at Plaistow and took my leave of the people of that place. In my return a person galloping swiftly rode full against me, and overthrew both man and horse; but without any hurt to either. Glory be to him who 'saves both man and beast'![49]

Tue. 25. After dining with one of our brethren who was married this day,[50] I went (as usual) to the society at St. James's, weary and weak in body. But God strengthened me for his own work, as he did at six at Mr. B[ray]'s and at eight in Winchester Yard,[51] where it was believed were present eleven or twelve hundred persons, to whom I declared, 'If they had nothing to pay', God would 'frankly forgive them all'.[52]

Thur. 27. I went in the afternoon to a society at Deptford, and thence at six came to Turner's Hall;[53] which holds (by computation) two thousand persons. The press both within and without was very great. In the beginning of the expounding, there being a large vault beneath, the main beam which supported the

[45] Cf. Ps. 147:3 (BCP).
[46] Rom. 14:17.
[47] Luke 10:42.
[48] Cf. 1 John 3:9.
[49] Cf. Ps. 36:7 (BCP).
[50] Mr. Pattison (diary, Sept. 25, 1739).
[51] In Southwark; there was a meeting-house here at which a religious society met. WHS, 7:109.
[52] Cf. Luke 7:42.
[53] Turner's Hall, originally erected for the Company of Turners, had housed a succession of dissenting congregations since 1688. At the time of JW's visit it was occupied by a company of Independents under the pastoral care of William Bentley, a ruling elder. In the following year the congregation removed to larger premises at Crispin Street, Spitalfields. Some years later Turner's Hall was demolished. W. Wilson, *History and Antiquities of Dissenting Churches and Meeting-houses in London* (London, 1808–14), I.135, 146–48; IV.408.

floor broke. The floor immediately sunk, which occasioned much noise and confusion among the people. But, two or three days before, a man had filled the vault with hogsheads of tobacco. So that the floor, after sinking a foot or two, rested upon them, and I
5 went on without interruption.

Fri. 28. I met with a fresh proof that 'whatsoever ye shall ask, believing, ye shall receive.'[54] A middle-aged woman desired me to return thanks for her to God, who, as many witnesses then present testified, was a day or two before really distracted, and as
10 such tied down in her bed. But upon prayer made for her she was instantly relieved and restored to a sound mind.

Monday, October 1. I rode to Oxford and found a few[55] who had not yet forsaken the assembling themselves together; to whom I explained that 'holiness without which no man shall see
15 the Lord'.[56]

Tue. 2. I went to many who once heard the word with joy, but 'when the sun arose, the seed withered away.'[57] Yet some still *desired* to follow their Lord. But the world stood fawning or threatening between them.[58] In the evening I showed them the
20 tender mercies of God and his readiness still to receive them. The tears ran down many of their cheeks. O thou Lover of souls, seek and save that which is lost!

Wed. 3. I had a little leisure to take a view of the shattered condition of things here. The poor prisoners both in the Castle
25 and in the City Prison had now none that cared for their souls, none to instruct, advise, comfort, and build them up in the knowledge and love of the Lord Jesus. None was left to visit the workhouses, where also we used to meet with the most moving objects of compassion. Our little *school,* where about twenty poor
30 children at a time had been taught for many years, was on the point of being broke up, there being none now either to support or to attend it. And most of those *in the town,* who were once knit together, and strengthened one another's hands in God, were torn asunder and scattered abroad. 'It is time for thee, Lord, to lay
35 to thy hand!'[59]

---

[54] Matt. 21:22.
[55] 'At Mr. Fox's, many tarried' (diary, Oct. 1, 1739).
[56] Heb. 12:14.   [57] Cf. Matt. 13:6; Mark 4:6.
[58] One of JW's evening visits was to the rector of Lincoln, where they had religious talk; some of those led astray by the fawning or threatening of the world may have been college acquaintances. Diary, Oct. 2, 1739.
[59] Ps. 119:126 (BCP).

At eleven a little company of us met to entreat God 'for the remnant that was left'.[60] He immediately gave us a token for good. One who had been long in the gall of bitterness, full of wrath, strife, and envy,[61] particularly against one whom she had once tenderly loved,[62] rose up and showed the change God had wrought in her soul by falling upon her neck, and with many tears kissing her. The same spirit we found reviving in others also; so that we left them, not without hope that the seed which had been sown even here 'shall yet take root downward, and bear fruit upward'.[63]

About six in the evening I came to Burford; and at seven preached to, it was judged, twelve or fifteen hundred people, on Christ 'made unto us wisdom and righteousness and sanctification and redemption'.[64] Finding many *approved* of what they had heard, that they might not *rest in that approbation* I explained, an hour or two after, the holiness of a Christian; and in the morning I showed the way to this holiness, by giving both the false and the true answer to that important question, 'What must I do to be saved?'[65]

About three in the afternoon I came to Mr. Benjamin Seward's,[66] at Bengeworth near Evesham. At five I expounded in his house (part of the thirteenth chapter of the First of Corinthians), and at seven in the schoolhouse, where I invited all who 'had nothing to pay'[67] to come and accept of free forgiveness. In the morning I preached near Mr. Seward's house, to a small serious congregation, on those words, 'I came not to call the righteous, but sinners to repentance.'[68]

---

[60] Cf. 2 Kgs. 19:4; Isa. 37:4.

[61] Mrs. Clemenger, who had received peace in Mar. 1739.

[62] N. Fox (diary, Oct. 3, 1739), presumably Mrs. Fox, long esteemed by JW, at whose house his meetings often took place.

[63] Cf. 2 Kgs. 19:30; Isa. 37:31.

[64] 1 Cor. 1:30.

[65] Acts 16:30.

[66] 1742, 1748, 1788, 'Mr. B. S——'s'. Of the four Seward brothers (see above, Jan. 17, 1739, n. 44), Benjamin was the closest to the Wesley brothers. In March 1740 there was a fearful scene between Henry Seward, who interpreted his brother's religious attitude as madness, put him away accordingly, and cut off his correspondence, and Charles Wesley, whom he blamed for Benjamin's decline (CWJ, I.195-98, 201-5). He was with JW when he withdrew from the Fetter Lane Society (see below under July 20, 1740) and died about 1756. Bengeworth was a parish within the borough of Evesham, with which it was connected by a seven-arch bridge.

[67] Luke 7:42.

[68] Mark 2:17, etc.

In the evening I reached Gloucester. Sat. 6. At five in the evening I explained to about a thousand people the nature, the cause, and the condition or instrument of justification, from these words, 'To him that worketh not, but believeth on him
5 that justifieth the ungodly, his faith is counted to him for righteousness.'[69]

Sun. 7. A few, I trust, out of two or three thousand, were awakened by the explanation of those words, God 'hath not given unto you the spirit of bondage again, to fear; but he hath given
10 unto you the Spirit of adoption, whereby we cry, Abba, Father.'[70] About eleven I preached at Randwick, seven miles from Gloucester. The church was much crowded, though a thousand or upwards stayed in the churchyard. In the afternoon I explained further the same words, 'What must I do to be saved?'[71] I believe
15 some thousands were then present, more than had been in the morning. O what a harvest is here! When will it please our Lord to send more labourers into his harvest?

Between five and six I called on all who were present (about three thousand) at Stanley,[72] on a little green near the town, to
20 accept of Christ as their only 'wisdom, righteousness, sanctification, and redemption'.[73] I was strengthened to speak as I never did before, and continued speaking near two hours; the darkness of the night and a little lightning not lessening the number, but increasing the seriousness, of the hearers. I concluded the day by
25 expounding part of our Lord's Sermon on the Mount,[74] to a small serious company at Ebley.[75]

Mon. 8. About eight I reached Hampton Common, nine or ten miles from Gloucester. There were, it was computed, five or six thousand persons. I exhorted them all to come unto God, as
30 having nothing to pay.[76] I could gladly have stayed longer with this loving people, but I was now straitened for time. After sermon I therefore hastened away, and in the evening came to Bristol.

---

[69] Cf. Rom. 4:5 — apparently the sermon upon that text which was first published in 1746. See Sermon 5, 'Justification by Faith' (1:181-99 in this edn.).

[70] Cf. Rom. 8:15.

[71] Acts 16:30. JW spelled the town 'Runwick'.

[72] This was Stanley Borough near Stroud. See Diary, Oct. 7, 1739.

[73] Cf. 1 Cor. 1:30.

[74] Matt. 5:2, 3 'Blessed are the poor in spirit . . .' (diary, Oct. 7, 1739).

[75] Orig., 'Ebly'. Charles Wesley had been a frequent visitor at a devout Mr. Ellis's at Ebley. CWJ, I.165 (Aug. 26, 1739).

[76] Luke 7:42; cf. Oct. 4, 1739, n. 67, above.

Tue. 9. My brother and I rode to Bradford. Finding there had been a general misrepresentation of his last sermon, as if he had asserted reprobation therein, whereby many were greatly offended,[77] he was constrained to explain himself on that head and to show in plain and strong words that God 'willeth all men to 5 be saved'.[78] Some were equally offended at this. But whether men will hear or whether they will forbear,[79] we may not 'shun to declare' unto them 'all the counsel of God'.[80]

At our return in the evening, not being permitted to meet any longer at Weavers' Hall, we met in a large room[81] on Temple 10 Backs, where (having gone through the Sermon on the Mount and the Epistles of St. John) I began that of St. James, that those who had already learned the true nature of inward holiness might be more fully instructed in outward holiness, without which also we cannot see the Lord. 15

Wed. 10. Finding many to be in heaviness whom I had left full of peace and joy, I exhorted them at Baptist Mills to 'look unto Jesus, the author and finisher of our faith'.[82] We poured out our complaint before him in the evening and found that he was again with us of a truth. One came to us soon after I was gone home who 20 was still in grievous darkness.[83] But we commended her cause to God, and he immediately restored the light of his countenance.

Thur. 11. We were comforted by the coming in of one who *was* a notorious drunkard and common swearer. But he is washed, and old things are passed away. 'Such power belongeth unto 25 God.'[84] In the evening our Lord rose on many who were wounded, 'with healing in his wings';[85] and others who till then were careless and at ease felt the two-edged sword that cometh out of his mouth.[86]

One of these showed the agony of her soul by crying aloud to 30 God for help, to the great offence of many, who eagerly 'rebuked

---

[77] Charles Wesley records that 'the people were much exasperated against me, it being everywhere reported that I am . . . a strong Predestinarian. . . . We judged this a call for me to declare myself, if the weavers, who were to rise, would suffer me. . . . In much love I besought the dissenters not to lose their charity for me because I was of opinion God would have *all* men to be saved. For an hour and a half I strongly called all sinners to the Saviour of the world' (CWJ, I.188).

[78] Cf. 1 Tim. 2:4.　　　　　　　　　　　　[79] Ezek. 2:5, etc.
[80] Acts 20:27.　　　　　　　　　　[81] The Malt-house. Diary, Oct. 9, 1739.
[82] Cf. Heb. 12:2.　　　　　　　　　[83] Betty Holder. Diary, Oct. 10, 1739.
[84] Ps. 62:11.
[85] Mal. 4:2.
[86] See Rev. 1:16.

her that she should hold her peace'.[87] She continued in great torment all night, finding no rest either of soul or body. But while a few were praying for her in the morning, God delivered her out of her distress.

5   Fri. 12. We had fresh occasion to observe the darkness which was fallen on many who lately rejoiced in God. But he did not long hide his face from them. On Wednesday the spirit of many revived. On Thursday evening many more found him in whom they had believed to be 'a present help in time of trouble'.[88] And
10   never do I remember the power of God to have been more eminently present than this morning, when a cloud of witnesses declared his 'breaking the gates of brass, and smiting the bars of iron in sunder'.[89]

Yet I could not but be under some concern with regard to one
15   or two persons, who were tormented in an unaccountable manner, and seemed to be indeed 'lunatics' as well as 'sore vexed'.[90] But while I was musing what would be the issue of these things, the answer I received from the Word of God was, 'Glory to God in the highest, and on earth peace, goodwill towards
20   men.'[91]

Soon after I was sent for to one of these, who was so strangely torn by the devil[92] that I almost wondered her relations did not say, 'Much religion hath made thee mad.'[93] We prayed God to bruise Satan under her feet.[94] Immediately we had the petition we
25   asked of him. She cried out vehemently, 'He is gone, he is gone!' And was filled with the spirit of love and of a sound mind.[95] I have seen her many times since, strong in the Lord. When I asked abruptly, 'What do you desire now?' she answered, 'Heaven.' I asked, 'What is in your heart?' She replied, 'God.' I asked, 'But
30   how is your heart when anything provokes you?' She said, 'By the grace of God I am not provoked at anything. All the things of this world pass by me as shadows.' 'Ye have seen the end of the Lord.'[96] Is he not very pitiful and of tender mercy?

---

[87] Cf. Luke 18:39.
[88] Cf. Ps. 46:1.
[89] Cf. Ps. 107:16 (BCP).
[90] Matt. 17:15.
[91] Luke 2:14.
[92] Averel Spenser (diary, Oct. 12, 1739), who according to Charles Wesley received faith on Oct. 5, 1739. CWJ, I.186.
[93] Cf. Acts 26:24.
[94] See Rom. 16:20.
[95] 2 Tim. 1:7.   [96] Jas. 5:11.

We had a refreshing meeting at one, with many of our society who fail not to observe, as health permits, the weekly fast of our Church, and will do so, by God's help, as long as they call themselves members of it. And would to God all who contend for the rites and ceremonies of the Church (perhaps with more zeal than meekness and wisdom)[97] would first show their own regard for her discipline in this more important branch of it!

At four I preached near the Fishponds (at the desire of one who had long laboured under the apprehension of it) on the blasphemy against the Holy Ghost,[98] that is, according to the plain scriptural account, *the openly and maliciously asserting that the miracles of Christ were wrought by the power of the devil.*

Sat. 13. I was with one who, being in deep anguish of spirit, had been the day before to ask a clergyman's advice. He told her her head was out of order, and she must go and take physic. In the evening we called upon God for medicine to heal those that were 'broken in heart'.[99] And five who had long been in the shadow of death 'knew they were passed from death unto life'.[1]

The sharp frost in the morning, Sunday 14, did not prevent about fifteen hundred from being at Hanham, to whom I called, in the words of our gracious Master, 'Come unto me, all ye that are weary and heavy laden, and I will give you rest.'[2] In the evening we claimed and received the promise for several who were 'weary and heavy laden'.

Mon. 15. Upon a pressing invitation, some time since received,[3] I set out for Wales. About four in the afternoon I preached on a little green, at the foot of The Ddefauden[4] (a high hill, two or three miles beyond Chepstow), to three or four hundred plain people, on Christ 'our wisdom, righteousness, sanctification, and redemption'.[5] After sermon, one who, I trust, is an old disciple of Christ, willingly received us into his house;[6] whither many following, I showed them their need of a Saviour from these words, 'Blessed are the poor in spirit.'[7] In the morning

[97] See Jas. 3:13.
[98] Matt. 12:31. JW's exposition of the blasphemy against the Holy Ghost explains why (as the diary records) the text from which he preached was 'Matt. 12:22, etc.'.
[99] Ps. 147:3 (BCP).
[1] Cf. 1 John 3:14.
[2] Cf. Matt. 11:28.
[3] From Howell Harris, whom JW had met on June 18, 1739.
[4] Orig., 'the Devauden'.
[5] Cf. 1 Cor. 1:30.
[6] Mr. Nexey. Diary, Oct. 15, 1739.   [7] Matt. 5:3.

I described more fully the way to salvation, 'Believe in the Lord
Jesus, and thou shalt be saved';[8] and then, taking leave of my
friendly host, before two came to Abergavenny.

I felt in myself a strong aversion to preaching here. However,
5 I went to Mr. W[aters] (the person in whose ground Mr.
Whitefield preached)[9] to desire the use of it. He said, with all his
heart—if the minister[10] was not willing to let me have the use of
the church; after whose refusal (for I wrote a line to him
immediately), he invited me to his house. About a thousand
10 people stood patiently (though the frost was sharp, it being after
sunset) while from Acts 28:22 I simply described the plain old
religion of the Church of England, which is now almost
'everywhere' spoken against, under the new name of 'Methodism'. An hour after, I explained it a little more fully in a
15 neighbouring house,[11] showing how God 'had exalted Jesus to
be a Prince and a Saviour, to give repentance and remission
of sins'.[12]

Wed. 17. The frost was sharper than before. However five or
six hundred people stayed, while I explained the nature of that
20 salvation which is through faith, yea, faith alone; and the nature of
that living faith through which cometh this salvation. About noon
I came to Usk, where I preached to a small company of poor
people on those words, 'The Son of man is come, to save that
which is lost.'[13] One grey-headed man wept and trembled
25 exceedingly; and another who was there (I have since heard), as
well as two or three who were at The Ddefauden, 'are gone quite
distracted'—that is, they mourn and refuse to be comforted, till
they 'have redemption through his blood'.[14]

When I came to Pontypool in the afternoon, being unable to
30 procure any more convenient place, I stood in the street and cried
aloud to five or six hundred attentive hearers to 'believe in the
Lord Jesus', that they might 'be saved'.[15] In the evening I showed

[8] Cf. Acts 16:31.
[9] Mr. Waters, a Presbyterian author of religious pamphlets, who had invited
Whitefield to Abergavenny, and on Apr. 5, 1739, provided him with a preaching platform
in 'the backside of a garden' (diary, Oct. 16, 1739; Whitefield, *Journal*, p. 245).
[10] Rev. Evan Eustance, vicar of Abergavenny 1719–76. *John Wesley in Wales*, ed. A. H.
Williams (Cardiff, 1971), p. 2, n. 2.
[11] Belonging to Elizabeth James, a widow who befriended JW on a number of occasions
and unexpectedly married George Whitefield, Nov. 14, 1741. See below, Oct. 3, 1741,
n. 24.
[12] Cf. Acts 5:31.   [13] Cf. Matt. 18:11.
[14] Eph. 1:7; Col. 1:14.   [15] Cf. Acts 16:31.

his willingness to save all who desire to come unto God though him. Many were melted into tears. It may be that some will 'bring forth fruit with patience'.[16]

Thur. 18. I endeavoured to cut them off from all false supports and vain dependencies, by explaining and applying that 5 fundamental truth, 'To him that worketh not, but believeth on him that justifieth the ungodly, his faith is counted to him for righteousness.'[17]

When we were at The Ddefauden on Monday, a poor woman who lived six miles off came thither in great heaviness. She was 10 deeply convinced of sin and weary of it; but found no way to escape from it. She walked from thence to Abergavenny on Tuesday, and on Wednesday from Abergavenny to Usk. Thence in the afternoon she came to Pontypool; where between twelve and one in the morning, after a sharp contest in her soul, our Lord 15 got unto himself the victory; and the love of God was shed abroad in her heart,[18] testifying that her sins were forgiven her. She went on her way rejoicing to Cardiff; whither I came in the afternoon. And about five (the minister[19] not being willing I should preach in the church on a week-day) I preached in the Shire Hall (a large 20 convenient place) on 'Believe, and thou shalt be saved.'[20] Several were there who laboured much to make a disturbance. But our Lord suffered them not. At seven I explained to a much more numerous audience the blessedness of 'mourning' and 'poverty of spirit'.[21] Deep attention sat on the faces of the hearers, many of 25 whom, I trust, 'have believed our report'.[22]

Fri. 19. I preached in the morning at Newport, on 'What must I do to be saved?'[23] to the most insensible, ill-behaved people I have ever seen in Wales. One ancient man, during the great part of the sermon, cursed and swore almost incessantly; and towards the 30 conclusion took up a great stone, which he many times attempted to throw. But that he could not do. . . . Such the champions! Such the arms against field preaching!

[16] Luke 8:15.
[17] Cf. Rom. 4:5.
[18] See Rom. 5:5.
[19] Rev. Thomas Collrick (or Colerick), vicar of St. John's, Cardiff, 1718–61. In 1741 he forbade Charles Wesley the use of his pulpit on grounds of an episcopal prohibition. CWJ, I.290.
[20] Acts 16:31.
[21] Cf. Matt. 5:3, 4.
[22] Cf. Isa. 53:1.
[23] Acts 16:30.

At four I preached in the Shire Hall of Cardiff again, where many gentry, I found, were present. Such freedom of speech I have seldom had as was given me in explaining those words, 'The kingdom of God is not meat and drink, but righteousness, and
5 peace, and joy in the Holy Ghost.'[24] At six almost the whole town (I was informed) came together, to whom I explained the six last Beatitudes; but my heart was so enlarged I knew not how to give over, so that we continued there three hours. O may the seed they have received have its fruit unto holiness, and in the end,
10 everlasting life!

Sat. 20. I returned to Bristol. I have seen no part of England so pleasant for sixty or seventy miles together as those parts of Wales I have been in. And most of the inhabitants are indeed *ripe for the gospel.* I mean (if the expression appear strange), they are *earnestly*
15 *desirous* of being instructed in it; and as *utterly ignorant* of it they are as any Creek or Cherokee[25] Indian. I do not mean they are ignorant of the name of Christ. Many of them can say both the Lord's Prayer and the Belief.[26] Nay, and some, all the Catechism. But take them out of the road of what they have learned by rote,
20 and they know no more (nine in ten of those with whom I conversed) either of gospel salvation or of that faith whereby alone we can be saved, than Chicali or Tomochichi. Now, what spirit is he of, who had rather these poor creatures should perish for lack of knowledge than that they should be saved, even by the
25 exhortations of Howell Harris or an *itinerant* preacher?

Finding a slackness creeping in among them who had begun to run well, on Sunday 21, both in the morning and afternoon, I enforced those words, 'As ye have received the Lord Jesus Christ, so walk ye in him.'[27] In the evening I endeavoured to quicken
30 them farther, by describing 'pure and undefiled religion',[28] and the next day, to encourage them in pursuing it, by enforcing those words of our blessed Master, 'In the world ye shall have tribulation; but be of good cheer; I have overcome the world.'[29]

35 Tue. 23. In riding to Bradford I read over Mr. Law's[30] book

---

[24] Rom. 14:17.
[25] Orig., 'Cherikee'.
[26] An archaic term for the Apostles' Creed.
[27] Cf. Col. 2:6.
[28] Cf. Jas. 1:27.
[29] John 16:33.
[30] Name added in 1775 only.

on the new birth[31]—philosophical, speculative, precarious;
Behmenish, void, and vain!

O what a fall is there![32]

At eleven I preached at Bearfield to about three thousand on the
spirit of nature, of bondage, and of adoption.   5
Returning in the evening, I was exceedingly pressed to go back
to a young woman in Kingswood.[33] (The fact I nakedly relate and
leave every man to his own judgment of it.) I went. She was
nineteen or twenty years old, but (it seems) could not write or
read. I found her on the bed, two or three persons holding her. It 10
was a terrible sight. Anguish, horror, and despair, above all
description, appeared in her pale face. The thousand distortions
of her whole body showed how the dogs of hell were gnawing her
heart. The shrieks intermixed were scarce to be endured. But her
stony eyes could not weep. She screamed out, as soon as words 15
could find their way, 'I am damned, damned; lost for ever. Six
days ago you might have helped me. But it is past. I am the devil's
now. I have given myself to him. His I am. Him I must serve. With
him I must go to hell. I *will* be his. I *will* serve him. I *will* go with
him to hell. I cannot be saved. I *will* not be saved. I must, I *will*, I 20
will be damned.' She then began praying the devil. We began

Arm of the Lord, awake, awake![34]

She immediately sunk down as asleep; but as soon as we left off,
broke out again with unexpressible vehemence, 'Stony hearts,
break! I am a warning to *you*. Break, break, poor stony hearts! Will 25
you not break? What can be done more for stony hearts? I am
damned that you may be saved. Now break, now break, poor,
stony hearts! You need not be damned, though I must.' She then
fixed her eyes on the corner of the ceiling and said, 'There he is.
Ay, there he is. Come, good devil, come. Take me away. You said 30
you would dash my brains out. Come, do it quickly. I am yours. I
will be yours. Come just now. Take me away.' We interrupted her
by calling again upon God, on which she sunk down as before;

---

[31] *The Grounds and Reasons of Christian Regeneration; or, The New Birth, offered to the Consideration of Christians and Deists* (London, 1739).

[32] Cf. Shakespeare, *Julius Caesar*, III.ii.194.

[33] Sally Jones. Diary, Oct. 23, 1739.

[34] By Charles Wesley; see June 3, 1739. This hymn, one of the more popular at the time, was first published in *Hymns and Sacred Poems* (1739), p. 222.

and another young woman[35] began to roar out as loud as she had done. My brother now came in, it being about nine o'clock. We continued in prayer till past eleven; when God in a moment spoke peace into the soul, first of the first tormented, and then of the
5 other. And they both joined in singing praise to him who had stilled the enemy and the avenger.[36]

Wed. 24. I preached at Baptist Mills on those words of St. Paul, speaking in the person of one 'under the law'[37] (that is, still 'carnal and sold under sin',[38] though groaning for deliverance), 'I know
10 that in me dwelleth no good thing.'[39] A poor woman told me afterwards, 'I does hope as my husband won't hinder me any more. For I minded he did shiver every bone of him, and the tears ran down his cheeks like the rain.' I warned our little society in the evening to beware of levity, slackness in good works, and
15 despising little things; which had caused many to fall again into bondage.

Thur. 25. I was sent for to one in Bristol[40] who was taken ill the evening before. (This fact, too, I will simply relate, so far as I was an ear- or eye-witness of it.) She lay on the ground, furiously
20 gnashing her teeth, and after a while roared aloud. It was not easy for three or four persons to hold her, especially when the name of Jesus was named. We prayed; the violence of her symptoms ceased, though without a complete deliverance.

In the evening, being sent for to her again, I was unwilling,
25 indeed afraid, to go, thinking it would not avail unless some who were strong in faith were to wrestle with God for her. I opened my Testament on those words, 'I was afraid, and went and hid thy talent in the earth.'[41] I stood reproved, and went immediately. She began screaming before I came into the room; then broke out into
30 a horrid laughter, mixed with blasphemy, grievous to hear. One who from many circumstances apprehended a preternatural agent to be concerned in this, asking, 'How didst thou dare to enter into a Christian?' was answered, 'She is not a Christian. She is mine.' Q[uestion.] 'Dost thou not tremble at the name of
35 Jesus?' No words followed, but she shrunk back and trembled exceedingly. Q[uestion.] 'Art thou not increasing thy own damnation?' It was faintly answered, 'Ay, ay,' which was followed by fresh cursing and blaspheming.

---

35 Betty Somers. Diary, Oct. 23, 1739.   36 Ps. 44:16.
37 Rom. 3:19, etc.   38 Rom. 7:14.   39 Rom. 7:18.
40 N. Roberts. Diary, Oct. 25, 1739.   41 Matt. 25:25.

My brother coming in, she cried out, 'Preacher! Field preacher! I don't love field preaching.' This was repeated two hours together, with spitting and all the expressions of strong aversion.

We left her at twelve, but called again about noon on Friday 26. 5 And now it was that God showed he heareth the prayer. All her pangs ceased in a moment. She was filled with peace, and knew that the son of wickedness was departed from her.

Sat. 27. I was sent for to Kingswood again, to one of those who had been so ill before.[42] A violent rain began just as I set out, so 10 that I was thoroughly wet in a few minutes. Just at that time the woman (then three miles off) cried out, 'Yonder comes Wesley, galloping as fast as he can.' When I was come, I was quite cold and dead, and fitter for sleep than prayer. She burst out into a horrid laughter and said, 'No power, no power; no faith, no faith. She is 15 mine. Her soul is mine. I have her and will not let her go.'

We begged of God to increase our faith. Meanwhile her pangs increased more and more; so that one would have imagined, by the violence of the throes, her body must have been shattered to pieces. One who was clearly convinced this was no natural 20 disorder said, 'I think Satan is let loose. I fear he will not stop here,' and added, 'I command thee, in the name of the Lord Jesus, to tell if thou hast commission to torment any other soul?' It was immediately answered, 'I have. L[uc]y C[lea]r and S[ara]h J[one]s.'[43] (Two who lived at some distance and were then in 25 perfect health.)

We betook ourselves to prayer again and ceased not till she began, about six o'clock, with a clear voice and composed, cheerful look,

Praise God from whom all blessings flow.[44]   30

Sun. 28. I preached once more at Bradford at one in the afternoon. The violent rain did not hinder more, I believe, than

[42] Sally Jones. Diary, Oct. 27, 1739.

[43] Here JW may have made an error of transcription from his diary into the *Journal* or may have been the victim of one of his printer's frequent errors. The diary for Oct. 28 records: 'Betty Somers, Lucy Clear and S. Jones ill', the implication perhaps being that the two who lived at a distance were Lucy Clear and Betty Somers, who had been thought cured on Oct. 23. It is not, however, impossible that the entry is an error for Sally Robins, mentioned in the diary for Oct. 30 together with Sally Jones and Betty Somers, or for a second Sally Jones. Cf. the independent account in John Cennick's Journal, WHS, 6:109-10.

[44] Thomas Ken's doxology.

ten thousand from earnestly attending to what I spoke on those solemn words, 'I take you to record this day, that I am pure from the blood of all men. For I have not shunned to declare unto you all the counsel of God.'[45]

5   Returning in the evening I called at Mrs. J[ones]'s[46] in Kingswood. S[all]y J[one]s and L[uc]y C[lea]r were there. It was scarce a quarter of an hour before L[uc]y C[lea]r fell into a strange agony, and presently after S[all]y J[one]s. The violent convulsions all over their bodies were such as words cannot

10 describe. Their cries and groans were too horrid to be borne; till one of them in a tone not to be expressed, said, 'Where is your faith now? Come, go to prayers. I will pray with you. "Our Father, which art in heaven".' We took the advice, from whomsoever it came, and poured out our souls before God till L[uc]y C[lea]r's

15 agonies so increased that it seemed she was in the pangs of death. But in a moment God spoke; she knew his voice, and both her body and soul were healed.

We continued in prayer till near one, when S[all]y J[ones]'s voice was also changed, and she began strongly to call upon God.

20 This she did for the greatest part of the night. In the morning we renewed our prayers, while she was crying continually, 'I burn, I burn; O what shall I do? I have a fire within me. I cannot bear it, Lord Jesus! Help!' Amen, Lord Jesus! When thy time is come.

Wed. 31. I strongly enforced on those who imagine they *believe*

25 and do not, 'As the body without the spirit is dead, so faith without works is dead also.'[47] The power of God was in an unusual manner present at the meeting of the bands in the evening. Six or seven[48] were deeply convinced of their unfaithfulness to God, and two filled again with his love. But poor Mary W[otton] remained

30 as one without hope. Her soul refused comfort. She could neither pray herself, nor bear to hear us. At last she cried out, 'Give me the book, and I will sing.' She began giving out line by line (but with such an accent as art could never reach):

Why do these cares my soul divide,
35   If Thou indeed hast set me free?
Why am I thus, if God hath died,

---

[45] Acts 20:26-27.
[46] 'At Widow Jones's' (diary, Oct. 28, 1739), perhaps the mother of Sally Jones.
[47] Jas. 2:26.
[48] The names mentioned in the diary are: M. Wotton, B. Lin[ford], B. Oldfield, Margaret Evans, M. Smith, M. Lowman, B. Latcham.

> If God hath died to purchase me?
> Around me clouds of darkness roll;
> In deepest night I still walk on:
> Heavily moves my *damned* soul. . . .[49]

Here we were obliged to interrupt her. We again betook ourselves to prayer, and her heart was eased, though not set at liberty.

Thursday, November 1. I set out and the next evening came to Reading, where a little company of us met in the evening, at which the zealous mob was so enraged, they were ready to tear the house down. Therefore I hope God has a work to do in this place. In thy time let it be fulfilled!

About this time I received a letter from the author of those reflections which I mentioned July 31;[50] an extract of which I have subjoined:

Reverend Sir,

As I wrote the *Rules* and *Considerations* (in No. 25 of 'Country Common Sense') with an eye to Mr. *Whitefield, yourself,* and *your opposers,* from a sincere desire to do some service to Christianity, according to the *imperfect* notions I had at that time of the real merits of the cause, I at the same time resolved to take any opportunity that should offer for my *better* information.

On this principle it was that I made one of your audience, October 23, at Bradford. And because I thought I could form the best judgment of you and your doctrines from your sermon, I resolved to hear that first; which was the reason that, although by accident I was at the same house, and walked two miles with you to the place you preached at, I spoke little or nothing to you. I must confess, sir, that the discourse you made that day, wherein you pressed your hearers in the closest manner, and with the authority of a true minister of the gospel, not to stop at *faith* ONLY, but to add to it *all virtues,* and to show forth their *faith* by every kind of *good works,* convinced me of the great wrong done you by a public report, common in people's mouths, that you preach *faith* without *works.* For that is the only ground of *prejudice* which any true Christian can have, and is the sense in which your adversaries would take your words, when they censure them.

---

[49] 'In Desertion or Temptation', John and Charles Wesley, *Hymns and Sacred Poems* (1739), p. 148, vers. 2-3, closing,

> Heavily moves my fainting soul,
> My comfort and my God are gone.

[50] Rev. Josiah Tucker.

For that we are *justified* by faith ONLY is the doctrine of Jesus Christ, the doctrine of his apostles, and the doctrine of the Church of England. I am ashamed that, after having lived twenty-nine years since my baptism into this faith, I should speak of it in the lame,
5   unfaithful, I may say, *false* manner I have done in the paper above-mentioned! What mere *darkness* is man, when truth hideth her face from him!

Man is by nature a *sinner,* the child of the devil, under God's *wrath,* in a state of *damnation.* The Son of God took pity on this our
10 misery. He made himself *man,* he made himself *sin* for us; that is, he hath borne the *punishment* of our sin, the chastisement of *our* peace was upon him, and by his stripes we are healed. To receive this boundless mercy, this inestimable benefit, we must have faith in our Benefactor, and through him in God. . . . But then true faith is not a
15 lifeless principle, as your adversaries seem to understand it. They and you mean quite another thing by *faith.* They mean a bare believing that Jesus is the Christ. You mean a living, growing, purifying principle, which is the root both of inward and outward holiness; both of *purity* and *good works,* without which no man can have faith, at
20 least no other than a dead faith.

This, sir, you explained in your sermon at Bradford, Sunday, October 28, to near ten thousand people, who all stood to hear you, with awful silence and great attention. I have since reflected how much good the clergy might do if, instead of *shunning,* they would
25 come to hear and converse with you; and in their churches and parishes would farther enforce those *catholic doctrines* which you preach, and which I am glad to see have such a surprising *good effect* on great numbers of souls.

I think, indeed, too many clergymen are culpable in that they don't
30 inform themselves better of Mr. Wh[itefiel]d, yourself, and your doctrines, from your own mouths. I am persuaded if they did this with a Christian spirit the differences between you would soon be at an end. Nay, I think those whose *flocks* resort so much to hear you ought to do it out of their *pastoral duty* to them; that if you preach *good*
35 *doctrine* they may edify them on the impression so visibly made by your sermons, or, if *evil,* they may reclaim them from error.

I shall conclude this letter with putting you in mind, in all your sermons, writings, and practice, *nakedly* to follow the *naked* Jesus: I mean, to preach the *pure doctrines* of the gospel without respect of
40 persons or things. Many *preachers,* many *reformers,* many *missionaries,* have fallen by not observing this; by not having continually in mind, 'Whosoever shall break the least of these commandments, and teach men so, he shall be called the least in the kingdom of heaven.'[51]

---

[51] Cf. Matt. 5:19.

A N

EXTRACT

Of the REVEREND

Mr. *JOHN WESLEY*'s

JOURNAL,

FROM

NOVEMBER 1, 1739.

TO

SEPTEMBER 3, 1741.

---

*When I had waited (for they spake not, but stood still
and answered no more) I said, I will answer also
my Part, I also will shew my Opinion. Let me not,
I pray you, accept any Man's Person, neither let me
give flattering Titles unto Man. For I know not to
give flattering Titles, in so doing my Maker would
soon take me away.*

JOB xxxii. v. 16, 17, 21, 22.

L O N D O N:

Printed by W. STRAHAN; and sold by T. TRYE,
at *Gray's-Inn-Gate, Holbourn*; and at the *Foundery,*
near *Upper Moorfields.* 1744.

(Price One Shilling.)

To the
Moravian Church,[a]

More especially that part of it now or lately residing in England

5   1. I am constrained at length[1] to speak my present sentiments concerning you, according to the best light I have. And this, not only upon my own account, that if I judge amiss I may receive better information, but for the sake of all those who either love or seek the Lord Jesus in sincerity. Many of these have been utterly
10 at a loss how to judge; and the more so because they could not but observe (as I have often done with sorrow of heart) that scarce any have wrote concerning you (unless such as were extravagant in your commendation) who were not evidently prejudiced against you. Hence they either spoke *falsely*, laying to your charge things
15 which you knew not, or at least *unkindly*, putting the worst construction on things of a doubtful nature, and setting what perhaps was not strictly right in the very worst light it would bear. Whereas (in my apprehension) none is capable of judging right, or assisting others to judge right concerning you, unless he can
20 speak of you as he does of the friend who is as his own soul.
    2. Yet it is not wholly for their sake, but for your own also that I now write. It may be the Father of lights, the Giver of every good gift,[2] may even by a mean instrument speak to your hearts. My continual desire and prayer to God is, that you may clearly see
25 what is that good and perfect will of the Lord; and fully discern how to separate that which is precious among you from the vile.
    3. I have delayed thus long because I loved you, and was therefore unwilling to grieve you in anything; and likewise because I was afraid of creating another obstacle to that union
30 which (if I know my own heart in any degree) I desire above all things under heaven. But I dare no longer delay, lest my silence

---

[a] So called by themselves, though improperly [added in *Works* (1774) only].

[1] This introduction, dated almost three years after the last events narrated in the extract, is a commentary both upon the text chosen for the title-page and upon Wesley's intention, after a deliberate delay, to write with a controversial and apologetic purpose.
[2] See Jas. 1:17.

should be a snare to any others of the children of God; and lest
you yourselves should be more confirmed in what I cannot
reconcile to the law and the testimony. This would strengthen the
bar which I long to remove. And were that once taken out of the
way, I should rejoice to be a door-keeper in the house of God,[3] a 5
hewer of wood or drawer of water among you.[4] Surely I would
follow you to the ends of the earth, or remain with you in the
uttermost parts of the sea.[5]

4. What unites my heart to you is the excellency (in many
respects) of the doctrine taught among you: your laying the true 10
foundation, 'God was in Christ, reconciling the world to
himself';[6] your declaring the free grace of God the cause, and
faith the condition, of justification; your bearing witness to those
great fruits of faith, 'righteousness, and peace, and joy in the Holy
Ghost',[7] and that sure mark thereof, 'He that is born of God doth 15
not commit sin.'[8]

5. I magnify the grace of God which is in many among you,
enabling you to love him who hath first loved us; teaching you, in
whatsoever state you are, therewith to be content;[9] causing you to
trample under foot the lust of the flesh, the lust of the eye, and the 20
pride of life;[10] and above all giving you to love one another, in a
manner the world knoweth not of.

6. I praise God that he hath delivered and yet doth deliver you
from those outward sins that overspread the face of the earth. No
cursing, no light or false swearing, no profaning the name of 25
God is heard among you; no robbery or theft, no gluttony or
drunkenness, no whoredom or adultery, no quarrelling or
brawling (those scandals of the Christian name) are found within
your gates; no diversions but such as become saints, as may be
used in the name of the Lord Jesus. You regard not outward 30
adorning, but rather desire the ornament of a serious, meek, and
quiet spirit. You are not slothful in business,[11] but labour to eat
your own bread; and wisely manage the mammon of unrighteous-

---

[3] Ps. 84:10.
[4] See Deut. 29:11.
[5] See Ps. 139:8 (BCP).
[6] 2 Cor. 5:19.
[7] Rom. 14:17.
[8] Cf. 1 John 3:9.
[9] See Phil. 4:11.
[10] See 1 John 2:16.
[11] Rom. 12:11.

ness,[12] that ye may have to give to others also, to feed the hungry, and cover the naked with a garment.

7. I love and esteem you for your excellent discipline, scarce inferior to that of the apostolic age; for your due subordination of officers, every one knowing and keeping his proper rank; for your exact division of the people under your charge, so that each may be fed with food convenient for them; for your care that all who are employed in the service of the church should frequently and freely confer together; and, in consequence thereof, your exact and seasonable knowledge of the state of every member, and your ready distribution either of spiritual or temporal relief as every man hath need.

8. Perhaps then some of you will say, 'If you allow all this, what more can you desire?' The following extract will answer you at large, wherein I have first given a naked relation (among other things) of many facts and conversations that passed between us in the same order of time as they occurred; and then summed up what I cannot approve of yet, that it may be tried by the Word of God.

9. This I have endeavoured to do with a tender hand; relating no more than I believed absolutely needful; carefully avoiding all tart and unkind expressions, all that I could foresee would be disobliging to you, or any farther offensive than was implied in the very nature of the thing; labouring everywhere to speak consistently with that deep sense which is settled in my heart, that you are (though I cannot call you Rabbi—infallible) yet far, far better and wiser than me.

10. And if any of you will smite me friendly, and reprove me,[13] if you will show me wherein I have erred either in the matter or manner of the following relation, or any part thereof, I will, by the grace of God, confess it before angels and men, in whatsoever way you shall require.

Meanwhile do not cease to pray for,

Your weak,
But still affectionate brother,
John Wesley

London,
June 24, 1744

[12] Luke 16:9.
[13] Ps. 141:5 (BCP)

Journal

From November 1, 1739, to September 3, 1741

Thursday, November 1, 1739. I left Bristol, and on Saturday came to London. The first person I met with there was one whom I had left strong in faith and zealous of good works.[1] But she now 5 told me Mr. Molther[2] had fully convinced her she *'never had any faith at all'*, and had advised her, till she received faith, 'to be *still*, ceasing from outward works', which she had accordingly done and did not doubt but in a short time she should find the advantage of it. 10

In the evening Mr. Bray[3] also was highly commending 'the being *still* before the Lord'. He likewise spoke largely of 'the great danger that attended the doing of outward works', and of 'the folly of people that keep running about to Church and Sacrament, as I (said he) did till very lately'. 15

Sun. 4. Our society met at seven in the morning and continued *silent* till eight. One then spoke of 'looking unto Jesus'[4] and exhorted us all 'to lie *still* in his hand'.

In the evening I met the women of our society at Fetter Lane, where some of our brethren strongly intimated that none of them 20

---

[1] Titus 2:14.

[2] Philipp Heinrich Molther (1714–80), son of a Protestant pastor in Alsace, educated at Jena (1735) with a view to the ministry. Here he underwent a conversion experience, but resisting his father's wish that he should come home to accept a living, had to support himself by giving French lessons. Among his pupils in 1737 was Zinzendorf's son, Renatus. Through this connexion he became active in the service of the Moravian community, accompanying Zinzendorf on many of his journeys and in 1739 marrying Countess Johanna Sophia Seidewitz, companion to Countess Zinzendorf. Appointed to serve in Pennsylvania, he in fact travelled in France, Holland, Switzerland, and Britain, founding settlements in Switzerland and Germany. Faced with several months' delay in London waiting for a boat, Molther was introduced to the Fetter Lane Society by James Hutton and found the phenomena of popular religious enthusiasm abhorrent. In turn his quietist doctrines and depreciation of the formal means of grace proved very abhorrent to the Wesleys and very divisive to the religious societies in which they ministered. Molther was a noted composer of hymns and music, and translated many Moravian hymns into French. He was elected a bishop in 1775. The *Heft 11 Unitas Fratrum* (1982) was devoted to Molther.

[3] See above, June 13, 1739, n. 51; Sept. 4, 1739, n. 20.

[4] Heb. 12:2.

had any true faith; and then asserted in plain terms (1) that till they had true faith, they ought to be *still*, that is (as they explained themselves) 'to abstain from "the means of grace", as they are called—the Lord's Supper *in particular'*; (2) 'that *the ordinances*
5 *are not means of grace*, there being no other means than Christ'.

Wed. 7. Being greatly desirous to understand the ground of this matter, I had a long conference with Mr. Spangenberg. I agreed with all he said of the power of faith. I agreed that 'whosoever is' by faith 'born of God doth not commit sin.'[5] But I
10 could not agree, either that 'none has any faith so long as he is liable to any doubt or fear,' or that 'till we have it we ought to abstain from the Lord's Supper or the other ordinances of God.'

At eight our society met at Fetter Lane. We sat an hour without speaking. The rest of the time was spent in dispute; one having
15 proposed a question concerning the Lord's Supper, which many warmly affirmed 'none ought to receive till he had the full assurance of faith.'[6]

I observed every day more and more the advantage Satan had gained over us. Many of those who once 'knew in whom they had
20 believed'[7] were thrown into idle reasonings and thereby filled with doubts and fears, from which they now found no way to escape. Many were induced to deny the gift of God and affirm they never had any faith at all; especially those who had fallen again into sin, and of consequence into darkness. And almost all
25 these had *left off the means of grace*, saying they must now 'cease from their own works'; they must now 'trust in Christ alone'; they were 'poor sinners' and had 'nothing to do but to lie at his feet'.

Till Saturday the tenth, I think I did not meet with one woman of the society who had not been upon the point of casting away her
30 confidence in God.[8] I then indeed found one who, when many

[5] 1 John 3:9.   [6] Cf. Heb. 10:22.
[7] Cf. 2 Tim. 1:12.

[8] The role of the Wesleys and the part played by their attractiveness to the opposite sex (here merely alluded to) was unreservedly reported to Zinzendorf by Hutton: '*J. Wesley* having resolved to *do* all things himself and having told many souls that they were justified who have since discovered themselves to be otherwise and mixing the works of the Law with the Gospel as *means of grace*, is at enmity against the *Brethren*. Envy is not extinct in him. . . . But he will have the glory of doing all things. I fear by and by he will be an open enemy of Christ and his Church. *Chas. Wesley* is coming to London and determined to oppose all such as shall not use the means of grace. . . . *J. W. and C. Wesley*, both of them, are snares to many young women; several are in love with them. I wish they were married to some good sister, but I would not give them one of my sisters, if I had many' (Herrnhut MSS, R.13. A.7. R025). When the Fetter Lane Society divided, the Wesleys took the majority of the women, and the Moravians the majority of the men.

(according to their custom) laboured to persuade her she had no faith, replied, with a spirit they were not able to resist, 'I know that "the life which I now live, I live by faith in the Son of God, who loved *me*, and gave himself for *me*."⁹ And he has never left me one moment, since the hour he was made known to me *in the breaking 5 of bread.*'

What is to be inferred from this undeniable matter of fact—*one that had not faith received it in the Lord's Supper?* Why, (1) that there are 'means of grace', i.e., outward ordinances, whereby the inward grace of God is ordinarily conveyed to man, whereby the 10 faith that brings salvation is conveyed to them who before had it not; (2) that *one of these means is the Lord's Supper;* and (3) that *he who has not this faith ought to wait for it in the use both of this and of the other means which God hath ordained.*

Fri. 9. I showed how we are to 'examine ourselves, whether we 15 be in the faith',¹⁰ and afterwards recommended to all, though especially to them that believed, true stillness, that is, *a patient waiting upon God, by lowliness, meekness, and resignation, in all the ways of his holy law, and the works of his commandments.*

All this week I endeavoured also by private conversation 20 to 'comfort the feeble-minded'¹¹ and to bring back 'the lame which had been turned out of the way',¹² if haply it might be healed.

Mon. 12. I left London, and in the evening expounded at Wycombe, the story of the Pharisee and the publican. The next 25 morning a young gentleman overtook me on the road, and after a while asked me if I had seen Whitefield's *Journals.*¹³ I told him I had. 'And what do you think of them?' said he. 'Don't you think they are damned cant, enthusiasm from end to end? I think so.' I asked him, 'Why do you think so?' He replied, 'Why, he talks so 30 much about joy and stuff, and inward feelings. As I hope to be saved, I cannot tell what to make of it!' I asked, 'Did you ever feel the love of God in your heart? If not, how should you tell what to make of it? Whatever is spoke of the religion of the heart and of the inward workings of the Spirit of God *must* appear enthusiasm 35

⁹ Cf. Gal. 2:20.
¹⁰ Cf. 2 Cor. 13:5.
¹¹ 1 Thess. 5:14.
¹² Cf. Heb. 12:13.
¹³ Three parts of Whitefield's *Journal* of his journey to Georgia and back, and his subsequent stay in England had been published before the end of 1739 (in many edns., one with an address to the author in verse by Charles Wesley).

to those who have not felt them; that is, if they take upon them to judge of the things which they own they know not.'

At four in the afternoon I came to Oxford, and to a small company in the evening explained the nature and extent of that salvation wherewith 'by grace we are saved through faith.'[14] The next evening I showed what it is to believe; as well as more largely what are the fruits of true believing, from those words of the Apostle, 'This is the victory that overcometh the world, even our faith.'[15]

Thur. 15. My brother and I set out for Tiverton.[16] About eleven I preached at Burford.[17] On Saturday evening I explained at Bristol the nature and extent of *Christian perfection;* and at nine in the morning preached at Bath, on 'I know that in me dwelleth no good thing.'[18]

In the afternoon I exhorted four or five thousand people at Bristol neither to *neglect* nor *rest in* the means of grace. In the evening I endeavoured to 'lift up the hands that hung down',[19] by declaring, 'He will not break the bruised reed, nor quench the smoking flax.'[20]

Mon. 19. I earnestly exhorted those who had believed to beware of two opposite extremes: the one, the thinking while they were in light and joy *that the work was ended,* when it was but just begun; the other, the thinking when they were in heaviness *that it was not begun,* because they found it was not ended.

At eight I exhorted the society *to wait* upon God *in all his ordinances,* and in so doing *to be still* and suffer God to carry on his whole work in their souls. In that hour he was pleased to restore his light to many that sat in darkness; two of whom till then thought he had quite 'cast out their prayer, and turned his mercy from them'.[21]

[14] Cf. Eph. 2:8.

[15] 1 John 5:4.

[16] This journey was occasioned by the sudden death on Nov. 6, 1739, at the age of 48, of their eldest brother, Samuel Wesley, headmaster of Blundell's School, Tiverton. Tiverton was a substantial borough and market town 14 miles N. by E. from Exeter. Among the clothiers who had sustained the town's industrial past had been Peter Blundell, under whose will the school had been founded and endowed in 1604.

[17] Burford was a modest market town and parish on the main Oxford-Cheltenham road across the Cotswolds, 18 1/2 miles WNW. from Oxford.

[18] Rom. 7:18.

[19] Cf. Heb. 12:12.

[20] Cf. Matt. 12:20.

[21] Cf. Ps. 66:18 (BCP).

Tue. 20. We set out and on Wednesday 21, in the afternoon, came to Tiverton. My poor sister was sorrowing almost as one without hope.[22] Yet we could not but rejoice at hearing from one who had attended my brother in all his weakness that, several days before he went hence, God had given him a calm and full 5 assurance of his interest in Christ. O may everyone who opposes it be *thus* convinced that this doctrine is of God!

Sat. 24. We accepted an invitation to Exeter from one who came thence to comfort my sister in her affliction. And on Sunday 25 (Mr. D.[23] having desired the pulpit, which was readily granted 10 both for the morning and afternoon) I preached at St. Mary's on, 'The kingdom of God is not meat and drink, but righteousness, and peace, and joy in the Holy Ghost.'[24] Dr. W——[25] told me after sermon, 'Sir, you must not preach in the afternoon. Not', said he, 'that you preach any false doctrine. I allow all that you 15 have said is true. And it is the doctrine of the Church of England. But it is not *guarded*. It is dangerous. It may lead people into *enthusiasm* or *despair.*'

I did not readily see where the stress of this objection (so frequently started) lay. But upon a little reflection I saw it plain. 20 The real state of the case is this: *religion* is commonly thought to consist of three things—harmlessness, using the means of grace, and doing good (as it is called), that is, helping our neighbours, chiefly by giving alms. Accordingly by a 'religious man' is commonly meant one that is honest, just, and fair in his dealings; 25 that is constantly at church and Sacrament; and that gives much alms or (as it is usually termed) does much good.

Now in explaining those words of the Apostle, 'the kingdom of God' (or *true religion,* the consequence of God's dwelling and reigning in the soul) 'is not meat and drink,' I was necessarily led 30 to show that *religion* does not *properly consist* in any or all of these three things; but that a man might both be harmless, use the means of grace, and do much good, and yet have no true religion

---

[22] I.e., JW's sister-in-law, Ursula, daughter of John Berry, vicar of Wotton (1691–1730), who herself died in 1742.

[23] J. Wesley Thomas in *Wesleyan Methodist Magazine* (1871), 94:230, surmised that this might be 'Mr. Dunscombe, afterwards a zealous outdoor preacher in the neighbourhood and ultimately a Quaker'.

[24] Rom. 14:17.

[25] John Walker (c. 1674–1747), fellow of Exeter College, Oxford, 1696–1700; canon of Exeter, 1714; rector of St. Mary Major, Exeter, 1698; and of Upton Pyne, Devon, 1720. D.D. by diploma, 1714, for his book on *Sufferings of the clergy in the Grand Rebellion.*

at all. And sure it is, had God then impressed this great truth on any who before was ignorant of it, that impression would have occasioned such heaviness in his soul, as the world always terms *despair*.

5   Again, in explaining those words, 'the kingdom of God' (or true religion) 'is righteousness, and peace, and joy in the Holy Ghost,' I insisted that every follower of Christ ought to expect and pray for that 'peace of God which passeth all understanding';[26] that 'rejoicing in hope of the glory of God'[27] which is even now 10 'unspeakable and full of glory';[28] and above all (as being the very life and soul of religion, without which it is all dead show) 'the love of God, shed abroad in his heart by the Holy Ghost given unto him'.[29] But all this is 'enthusiasm from end to end' to those who have the form of godliness but not the power.[30]

15   I know indeed there is a way of *explaining* these texts so that they shall mean just nothing; so that they shall express far less of inward religion than the writings of Plato or Hierocles.[31] And whoever *guards* them thus (but God forbid I should do it) will undoubtedly avoid all *danger* of either driving people into *this* 20 despair or leading them into *this* enthusiasm.

Tue. 27. I writ Mr. D. (according to his request) a short account of what had been done in Kingswood and of our present undertaking there. The account was as follows:[32]

Few persons have lived long in the west of England who have not 25   heard of the colliers of Kingswood, a people famous from the beginning hitherto for neither fearing God nor regarding man; so ignorant of the things of God that they seemed but one remove from the beasts that perish; and therefore utterly without desire of instruction, as well as without the means of it.

30   Many last winter used tauntingly to say of Mr. Whitefield, 'If he *will* convert heathens, why does not he go to the colliers of Kingswood?' In the spring he did so. And as there were thousands who resorted to no place of public worship, he went after them into

---

[26] Phil. 4:7.
[27] Cf. Rom. 5:2.
[28] 1 Pet. 1:8.
[29] Cf. Rom. 5:5.
[30] See 2 Tim. 3:5.
[31] An older Stoic contemporary of Cicero (cf. his *On Oratory*, 2, 23, 95, and *Orations*, 69, 231).
[32] For a collation of this letter with a contemporary manuscript apparently written to another recipient, see *Letters*, 25:701-3 in this edn.

their own 'wilderness' to 'seek and save that which was lost'.[33] When he was called away, others went into 'the highways and hedges, to compel them to come in'.[34] And, by the grace of God, their labour was not in vain. The scene is already changed. Kingswood does not now, as a year ago, resound with cursing and blasphemy. It is no more filled with drunkenness and uncleanness, and the idle diversions that naturally lead thereto. It is no longer full of wars and fightings, of clamour and bitterness, of wrath and envyings. Peace and love are there. Great numbers of the people are mild, gentle, and easy to be entreated. They 'do not cry, neither strive', and hardly is 'their voice heard in the streets',[35] or indeed in their own wood, unless when they are at their usual evening diversion, singing praise unto God their Saviour.

That their children too might know the things which make for their peace, it was some time since proposed to build a house in Kingswood; and after many foreseen and unforeseen difficulties, in June last the foundation was laid. The ground made choice of was in the middle of the wood between the London and Bath roads, not far from that called Two Mile Hill, about three measured miles from Bristol.

Here a large room was begun for the school, having four small rooms at either end for the schoolmasters (and perhaps, if it should please God, some poor children) to lodge in. Two persons are ready to teach so soon as the house is fit to receive them; the shell of which is nearly finished, so that it is hoped the whole will be completed in spring or early in summer.

It is true, although the masters require no pay, yet this undertaking is attended with great expense. But let him that 'feedeth the young ravens'[36] see to that. He hath the hearts of all men in his hand. If he put it into your heart, or into that of any of your friends, to assist in bringing this his work to perfection, in this world look for no recompense; but it shall be remembered in that day when our Lord shall say, 'Inasmuch as ye did it unto the least of these my brethren, ye did it unto me.'[37]

Wed. Nov. 28. We left Tiverton, and the next day reached Bristol. On Friday many of us joined in prayer for one that was grievously tormented. She raged more and more for about two hours, and then our Lord gave her rest.

[33] Cf. Luke 15:4; 19:10.
[34] Luke 14:23.
[35] Cf. Matt. 12:19.
[36] Ps. 147:9 (BCP).
[37] Cf. Matt. 25:40.

Five were in the same agony in the evening. I ordered them to be removed to the door, that their cries might neither drown my voice nor interrupt the attention of the congregation. But after sermon they were brought into the room again, where a few of us
5 continued in prayer to God (being determined not to go till we had an answer of peace) till nine the next morning. Before that time three of them sang praise to God. And the others were eased, though not set at liberty.

Tuesday, December 4. I was violently attacked by some who
10 were exceedingly angry at those 'who cried out so', being sure (they said) 'It was all a cheat, and that anyone might help crying out, if he would.' J[oseph] Bl[ack][38] was one of those who were 'sure of this'. About eight the next morning, while he was alone in his chamber at private prayer, so horrible a dread overwhelmed
15 him that he began crying out with all his might. All the family was alarmed. Several of them came running up into his chamber; but he cried out so much the more, till his breath was utterly spent. God then rebuked the adversary; and he is now less wise in his own conceit.[39]

20   Thur. 6. I left Bristol, and (after preaching at Malmesbury[40] and Burford in the way) on Saturday 8 came into my old room at Oxford, from which I went to Georgia. Here, musing on the things that were past and reflecting how many that came after me were preferred before me, I opened my Testament on those
25 words (O may I never let them slip), 'What shall we say then? That the Gentiles, which followed not after righteousness, have attained to righteousness. . . . But Israel, which followed after the law of righteousness, have not attained to the law of righteousness.'[41]
30   'Wherefore? Because they sought it not by faith, but as it were by the works of the law.'[42]

Sun. 9. I expounded in the evening to a small but deeply serious company on 'There is one Mediator between God and man, even the man, Christ Jesus,'[43] and exhorted them earnestly
35 to go straight to him with all their miseries, follies, and sins.

---

[38] Joseph Black; cf. above, May 20, 1739, n. 97.
[39] Prov. 26:5, 12.
[40] Malmesbury was a substantial borough and market town with a declining textile trade.
[41] Rom. 9:30-31.
[42] Rom. 9:32.
[43] 1 Tim. 2:5.

Tue. 11. I visited Mrs. P[la]t,[44] one who, having long sought death in the error of her life,[45] was brought back to the great Shepherd of her soul the first time my brother preached faith in Oxford. In the midst of sickness and pain, and the deepest want, she was calmly rejoicing in God. By *this* faith may I be *thus* saved! 5 So as in the midst of heaviness through manifold temptations,[46] without raiment or food, or health or friends, to 'rejoice with joy unspeakable'.[47]

Thur. 13. I had some hours' conversation with a serious man who offered many considerations to show that there are no unholy 10 men on earth; and that there are no holy men; but that, in reality, all men are alike, there being no inward difference between them.

I was at first in doubt what could lead a man of learning and sense into so wonderful an opinion. But that doubt was soon 15 cleared. He had narrowly observed those whom the world calls good men, and could not but discern that the difference between them and others was merely external; their tempers, their desires, their springs of action, were the same. He clearly saw, although *one man* was a thief, a common swearer, a drunkard, and *another* 20 not; although *this woman* was a liar, a prostitute, a Sabbath-breaker, and *the other* clear of these things; yet they were both lovers of pleasure, lovers of praise, lovers of the present world. He saw self-will was the sole spring of action in both, though exerting itself in different ways; and that the love of God no more filled 25 and ruled the heart of *the one* than of *the other*. Hence therefore he inferred well, 'If these persons are holy, there are none unholy upon earth; seeing thieves and prostitutes have as good a heart as these "saints of the world".'[48] And whereas some of these said, 'Nay, but we have faith; we believe in and rely on Christ,' it was 30 easily replied, 'Yea, and *such* a faith in Christ, *such a reliance* on him to save them *in their* sins, have nine in ten of all the robbers and murderers of whom ye yourselves say, "Away with them from the earth."'

---

[44] The name is fully supplied in *Works* (1774). As the diary shows, JW frequently held meetings at her house in Oxford. CWJ does not record the occasion of Charles's preaching to her.

[45] See Wisd. 1:12.

[46] 1 Pet. 1:6. In 1760 Wesley published a sermon on this text with this title; see Sermon 47, 2:222-35 in this edn.

[47] 1 Pet. 1:8.

[48] See Jan. 4, 1738/39.

In the afternoon I was informed how many wise and learned men (who cannot, in terms, *deny* it, because our Articles and Homilies are not yet repealed) *explain* justification by faith. They say, (1) *justification is twofold; the first* in this life, *the second* at the 5 last day. (2) Both these are by *faith alone*, that is, by *objective faith*, or by the merits of Christ, which are the object of our faith. And this, they say, is all that St. Paul and the Church mean, by 'We are justified by faith only.' But they add, (3) we are not justified by *subjective faith alone*, that is, by the faith which is *in us*, but good 10 works[49] also must be added to this faith as a *joint condition* both of the *first* and *second justification*.

The sense of which hard words is plainly this: God accepts us both here and hereafter only for the sake of what Christ has done and suffered for us. This alone is the *cause* of our justification. But 15 the *condition* thereof is, not *faith alone*, but *faith and works* together.

In flat opposition to this I cannot but maintain (at least till I have a clearer light) (1) that the justification which is spoken of by St. Paul to the Romans, and in our Articles, is not twofold. It is one and no more. It is the present remission of our sins or our first 20 acceptance with God. (2) It is true that the merits of Christ are the 'sole cause' of this our justification. But it is not true that this is all which St. Paul and our Church mean by our being justified 'by faith only'; neither is it true that either St. Paul or the Church mean[s] by faith the merits of Christ. But (3) by our being justified 25 by faith only both St. Paul and the Church mean that the *condition* of our justification is *faith alone*, and *not good works;* inasmuch as 'all works done before justification have in them the nature of sin.'[50] Lastly, that faith which is the sole condition of justification is the faith which is *in us*[51] by the grace of God. It is 'a sure 30 trust which a man hath that Christ hath loved *him* and died for *him*'.[52]

During my short stay here, I received several unpleasing accounts of the state of things in London, a part of which I have subjoined:

---

[49] 'good' omitted 1749 onwards.

[50] See Art. XIII of Thirty-nine Articles, 'Of Works before Justification'.

[51] In JW's *Answer to Church's* Remarks, II.7, as presented in his *Works* (1772), he alters this quotation to 'wrought in us' (see n. 38, 9:99 in this edn.).

[52] See *Homilies*, 'Of Salvation', Pt. III, and Sermon on the Sacrament, Pt. I. For JW's discussion of the whole question, with similar quotations, see his Sermon 5, 'Justification by Faith', especially III.5 and IV.3, 1:192, 195 in this edn.

Many of our sisters are shaken: J[enn]y C[hamber]s[53] says that she never had faith. Betty and Esther H[opson][54] are grievously torn by reasonings; the former, I am told, is going to Germany. . . . On *Wednesday* night there are but few come to Fetter Lane till near nine o'clock. And then, after the names are called over, they presently 5 depart. It appears plain, our brethren here have neither wisdom enough to guide nor prudence enough to let it alone.

Mr. B——n[55] expounds much, and speaks so slightingly of the means of grace that many are much grieved to hear him; but others are greatly delighted with him. Ten or fourteen of them meet at our 10 Brother Clark's[56] with Mr. Molther,[57] and seem to consult about

[53] 'Jane Chambers, seamstress, born in Edinburgh, May 26, 1711; married Br. William Hammond, Jan. 22, 1750; went to Northampton' (Benham, *Hutton*, pp. 33, 95). JW had frequently been present at singing in her house. She was among the women of the Fetter Lane Society who went with the Moravians. WHS, 16:146.

[54] Esther Sutton Hopson (1714–94), 'a very remarkable woman' who married John West and with her husband joined the Moravians (WHS, 5:247; 16:146). 'She served the congregation for more than half a century, and . . . was buried at Chelsea' (Benham, *Hutton*, p. 92). 'Betty Hopson came, and prayed that today we might have a feast of fat things' (CWJ, I.145). Her father was an Anglican farmer at Ludgershall, Wilts., who, becoming embarrassed in circumstances, sent her to her grandfather Sutton in London at the age of eight. Discovering that he intended to marry her to his nephew, she left home and found employment as a silk dyer. She had contact with Hutton and Böhler during the Moravian awakening in London in the late 1730s but was converted through a vivid experience at Communion at St. Mary-le-Bow, Cheapside. After taking residence with an awakened group in Islington, she left them on grounds of principle and secured employment with George Stonehouse, vicar of Islington, becoming in effect companion to his wife. She lived with them till she was married on Apr. 11, 1741. She nursed Molther during his illness in England, and, becoming interested in the Brethren, she and her husband solicited help from Germany, to give which Töltschig and Spangenberg were sent. Becoming confirmed a Moravian at Little Wild Street in 1742, she became one of the London labourers, an office she sustained for fifty years. She and her husband visited Marienborn in 1746 and Herrnhaag in 1747. They had eight children of whom two survived. Moravian Church House, Benham Collection of Papers and Books, p. 425.

[55] Probably Richard Brampton, journeyman periwig-maker, born 1710 at Canon Frome in Herefordshire, an evangelist in the West of England (J. T. Hamilton, *History of the Moravian Church*, p. 130) who became a sick-waiter to the Moravian congregation established in London in 1742 and in the following year was in trouble for speaking against the Bishop of London. He went to Germany and then to the north of Ireland (Benham, *Hutton*, pp. 95, 97, 128). An identical phrase is used in *An Answer to the Rev Mr. Church's Remarks* (1745), quoting from the *Journal* of a Mr. Br——d, who was probably Abraham Louis Brandt *(c.* 1717–97), painter, brother of Mrs. James Hutton, and a Moravian leader in London who became one of the great international travellers and servants of the Moravian community. Benham, *Hutton*, p. 375 n.

[56] Curnock says 'almost certainly Matthew Clarke' (II.327, n. 3), one of the circle of the London devout at whose home innumerable visits are recorded in JW's diary from the autumn of 1738 onward. Though one of those who signed Hutton's letter to Zinzendorf, May 2, 1738, imploring the reappointment of Böhler to charge of the London society (Benham, *Hutton*, pp. 32-33, 154), he was one of the Fetter Lane members who stayed with JW.

[57] Cf. above, Nov. 1, 1739, n. 2. Molther professed to be shocked at the 'singing and

things as if they were the whole body. These make a mere jest of going to church or to the Sacrament. They have much confounded some of our sisters; and many of our brothers are much grieved.

In another letter, which I received a few days after this, were
5 these words:

Dec. 14, 1739
This day I was told, by one that does not belong to the bands, that the society would be divided. . . . I believe Brother Hutton,[58] Clark, Edmonds,[59] and Bray[60] are determined to go on, according to Mr.
10 Molther's directions, and to 'raise a church', as they term it; and I suppose above half our brethren are on their side. But they are so very confused they don't know how to go on; yet are unwilling to be taught, except by the Moravians.
We long to see you; nay, even those would be glad to see you who
15 will not be directed by you. I believe, indeed, things would be much better if you would come to town.

Wed. 19. I accordingly came to London, though with a heavy heart. Here I found every day the dreadful effects of our brethren's reasonings, and disputing with each other. Scarce one
20 in ten retained his first love, and most of the rest were in the utmost confusion, biting and devouring one another. I pray God ye be not consumed one of another!

shouting' in the Fetter Lane Society and formed a society of his own consisting at first of ten or fifteen persons meeting in a private house.

[58] James Hutton (1715–95), son of Rev. John Hutton, a Nonjuror, in whose house at Westminster he was converted by the preaching of JW, whom he wished to accompany to Georgia. A bookseller, he published Whitefield's journal in 1738 and 1739, but was already under Moravian influence. In 1739 he visited Germany and corresponded with Zinzendorf. The breach between JW and the Moravians, which involved the former's recruiting members of his Foundery Society from the Fetter Lane Society, led to a breach with Hutton also, he becoming the real founder of the Moravian Church in England. The two were, however, later reconciled.

[59] John Edmonds (1710–1803), poulterer and brewer, was one of the Fetter Lane Society who went with the Moravians (WHS, 16:146). A signatory of Hutton's letter to Zinzendorf in 1738 (see n. 56 above), he subsequently went with Spangenberg to the Yorkshire settlement and became a member of the committee of Hutton's second Society for the Furtherance of the Gospel, being involved in attempts to establish a mission to the Eskimos in Labrador. Benham, *Hutton*, pp. 33, 90, 411, 447, 474-75; Hamilton, *Moravian Church*, p. 286.

[60] John Bray, one of the signatories of Hutton's letter to Zinzendorf (see n. 56 above), in fact remained in connexion with JW after a period of claiming 'that it is impossible for anyone to be a true Christian out of the Moravian Church' (CWJ, I.219). He was a committee member of the first Society for the Furtherance of the Gospel and was regarded by Moravians as an informer against them to the Bishop of London, 1742. Benham, *Hutton*, pp. 33, 70, 109-10, 128.

Mon. 24. After spending part of the night at Fetter Lane, I went to a smaller company, where also we exhorted one another with hymns and spiritual songs and poured out our hearts to God in prayer. Toward morning, one of them was overwhelmed with joy and love, and could not help showing it by strong cries and tears. At this another was much displeased, saying it was 'only nature, imagination, and animal spirits'. O thou jealous God, lay not this sin to her charge![61] And let us not be wise above what is written![62]

Sun. 30. One came to me by whom I used to profit much. But her conversation was now too high for me. It was far above, out of my sight. My soul is sick of this *sublime* divinity! Let *me* think and speak as a little child! Let *my* religion be plain, artless, simple! Meekness, temperance, patience, faith, and love, be these *my* highest gifts; and let the highest words wherein I teach them be those I learn from the Book of God!

Mon. 31. I had a long and particular conversation with Mr. Molther himself. I weighed all his words with the utmost care; desired him to explain what I did not understand; asked him again and again, 'Do I not mistake what you say? Is this your meaning, or is it not?' So that I think, if God has given me any measure of understanding, I could not mistake him much.

As soon as I came home I besought God to assist me and not suffer 'the blind to go out of the way'.[63] I then wrote down what I conceived to be the difference between us, in the following words:[64]

As to *faith*, you believe,

1. There are *no degrees of faith*, and that no man has *any degree* of it before all things in him are become new, before he has the full assurance of faith, the abiding witness of the Spirit, or the clear perception that Christ dwelleth in him.

2. Accordingly you believe there is no *justifying faith*, or state of justification, short of this.

3. Therefore you believe our Brother Hutton, Edmonds, and others had *no justifying faith* before they saw you.

---

[61] See Acts 7:60.

[62] 'Wise above what is written' (i.e., in the Bible) was one of JW's favourite expressions, apparently based on 1 Cor. 4:6 and sometimes shown as a quotation. Cf. JWJ for Sept. 3, 6, 1740; Jan. 27, Dec. 15, 1748; Feb. 5, 1764.

[63] Cf. Deut. 27:18.

[64] For the many minor variants introduced into this document see Vol. 13 in this edn.,

4. And, in general, that that gift of God which many received since Peter Böhler came into England, viz., 'a sure confidence of the love of God to *them*', *was not justifying faith.*

5. And that the *joy and love* attending it were from *animal spirits*, from *nature*, or *imagination;* not 'joy in the Holy Ghost',[65] and the real 'love of God shed abroad in their hearts'.[66]

Whereas I believe,

1. There are *degrees of faith*, and that a man may have *some degree* of it before all things in him are become new; before he has the full assurance of faith, the abiding witness of the Spirit, or the clear perception that Christ dwelleth in him.

2. Accordingly I believe there is *a degree of justifying faith* (and consequently a state of justification) short of, and commonly antecedent to, this.

3. And I believe our Brother Hutton, with many others, had *justifying faith* long before they saw you.

4. And, in general, that that gift of God which many received since Peter Böhler came into England, viz., 'a sure confidence of the love of God to *them*', was *justifying faith.*

5. And that the *joy and love* attending it were *not* from *animal spirits*, from *nature*, or *imagination*, but a measure of 'joy in the Holy Ghost', and of 'the love of God shed abroad in their hearts'.

As to *the way to faith*, you believe,

That the way to attain it is to *wait* for Christ, and be *still*, i.e.,

Not to use (what *we* term) the 'means of grace';

Not to go to church;

Not to communicate;

Not to fast;

Not to use *so much* private prayer;

Not to read the Scripture;

(Because you believe these are *not* 'means of grace', i.e., do not ordinarily convey God's grace to unbelievers; and

That it is impossible for a man to *use* them without *trusting* in them);

Not to do temporal good;

Nor to attempt doing spiritual good;

Because, you believe, no fruit of the Spirit is given by those who have it not themselves;

And that those who have not faith are utterly blind, and therefore unable to guide other souls.

Whereas I believe,

A Short View of the Difference between the Moravian Brethren . . . and the Reverend Mr. John and Charles Wesley, 1745 (*Bibliography*, No. 100).

[65] Rom. 14:17.

[66] Cf. Rom. 5:5.

The way to attain faith is to *wait* for Christ and be *still*,
In using 'all the means of grace'.
Therefore I believe it right for him who knows he has not faith (i.e.,
that conquering faith),
To go to church; 5
To communicate;
To fast;
To use as much private prayer as he can, and
To read the Scripture;
(Because I believe these are 'means of grace', i.e., do ordinarily 10
convey God's grace to unbelievers; and
That it is possible for a man to *use* them, without *trusting* in them);
To do all the temporal good he can;
And to endeavour after doing spiritual good;
Because I know many fruits of the Spirit are given by those who 15
have them not themselves,
And that those who have not faith, or but in the lowest degree, may
have more light from God, more wisdom for the guiding of other
souls, than many that are strong in faith.
As to the *manner of propagating* the faith, you believe (as I have also 20
heard others affirm):
That we may, on some accounts, *use guile;*
By saying what we know will *deceive* the hearers, or lead them to
think the thing which is not;
By describing things a *little beyond the truth*, in order to their *coming* 25
up to it;
By speaking *as if* we meant what we do not.
But I believe,
That we may not *use guile* on any account whatsoever;
That we may not on any account say what we know will, and design 30
should, *deceive* the hearers;
That we may not describe things one jot *beyond the truth*, whether
they *come up to it* or no; and
That we may not speak, on any pretence, *as if* we meant what
indeed we do not. 35
Lastly, as to the fruits of your thus propagating the faith in England,
you believe,
Much good has been done by it;
Many unsettled from a false foundation;
Many brought into *true stillness*, in order to their coming to the true 40
foundation; and
Some, grounded thereon, who were wrong before, but are right
now.
On the contrary, I believe that very little good, but much hurt, has
been done by it; 45

Many who were beginning to build holiness and good works on the true foundation of faith in Jesus, being now wholly unsettled and lost in vain reasonings and doubtful disputations;

Many others being brought into a *false*, unscriptural *stillness;* so that
5 they are not likely to come to any true foundation;

And many being grounded on a faith which is without works; so that they who were right before, are wrong now.

Tuesday, January 1, 1740, I endeavoured to explain to our brethren the true, Christian, scriptural *stillness*, by largely
10 unfolding those solemn words, 'Be still, and know that I am God.'[67] Wed. 2. I earnestly besought them all to 'stand in the old paths'[68] and no longer to subvert one another's souls by idle controversies and strife of words. They all seemed convinced. We then cried to God to heal all our backslidings. And he sent forth
15 such a spirit of peace and love as we had not known for many months before.

Thur. 3. I left London, and the next evening came to Oxford, where I spent the two following days in looking over the letters which I had received for the sixteen or eighteen years last past.
20 How few traces of inward religion are here! I found but one among all my correspondents who declared (what I well remember, at that time I knew not how to understand) that 'God had shed abroad his love in his heart, and given him the peace that passeth all understanding.'[69] But, who believed his report?
25 Should I conceal a sad truth? Or declare it for the profit of others? He was expelled out of his society as a madman,[70] and being disowned by his friends and despised and forsaken of all men, lived obscure and unknown for a few months, and then went to him whom his soul loved.
30 Mon. 7. I left Oxford. In the evening I preached at Burford; the next evening at Malmesbury; and on Wednesday 9, I once more described the exceeding great and precious promises at Bristol.

Sat. 12. I explained the former part of Hebrews 6, and many were 'renewed again to repentance'.[71] Sunday 13, while the

67 Ps. 46:10.
68 Cf. Jer. 6:16.
69 Cf. Rom. 5:5; Phil. 4:7.
70 This may have been William Smith (*c.* 1705–65), elected fellow of Lincoln, 1731, who suffered a good deal of hostility in his college. Smith was at first very sympathetic to JW and kept in touch with him after they had both left Oxford. See *Letters*, 25:332, 354 in this edn.
71 Cf. Heb. 6:6.

Sacrament was administering at the house of a person that was sick in Kingswood, a woman who had been before much tempted of the devil sunk down as one dead. One could not perceive by any motion of her breast that she breathed, and her pulse was very hardly discernible. A strange sort of dissimulation this! I would 5 wish those who think it so only to stop their own breath and pulse one hour, and I will then subscribe to their opinion.

Mon. 14. I began expounding the Scriptures in order at the New Room at six in the morning; by which means many more attend the college prayers[72] (which immediately follow) than ever 10 before. In the afternoon I preached at Downend,[73] four miles from Bristol, on 'God hath given unto us eternal life, and this life is in his Son.'[74] Tue. 15. At Siston,[75] five miles from Bristol, on 'the blood' which 'cleanseth us from all sin'.[76] After preaching I visited a young man dangerously ill, who a day or two after cried 15 out aloud, 'Lord Jesus, thou knowest that I love thee! And I have thee and will never let thee go,' and died immediately.

Thur. 17. I preached at Kendalshire,[77] six miles from Bristol, on 'Whosoever is born of God doth not commit sin.'[78] Sun. 20. My heart was enlarged at Kingswood, in declaring, 'Ye are saved 20 through faith.'[79] And the woman who had been so torn of the devil last week was now made partaker of this salvation; being above measure filled with the love of God and with all peace and joy in believing.[80]

Mon. 21. I preached at Hanham,[81] four miles from Bristol. In 25 the evening I made a collection in our congregation for the relief of the poor, without Lawford's Gate;[82] who having no work (because of the severe frost) and no assistance from the parish

---

[72] I.e., Morning Prayer at the cathedral on College Green.
[73] Orig., 'Downing'. Downend was five miles NE. from Bristol, now in the district of Mangotsfield.
[74] 1 John 5:11.
[75] Orig., 'Sison'. Siston was a substantial pin-making parish 6 1/2 miles E. by N. from Bristol.
[76] Cf. 1 John 1:7.
[77] A group of cottages off the high road from Bristol to Yate, 7 miles NE. of Bristol. Cf. below, Sept. 8, 1784.
[78] 1 John 3:9.   [79] Cf. Eph. 2:8.
[80] See Rom. 15:13.
[81] Orig., 'Hannam'.
[82] 1744, 'La-fore Gate', as also in Wesley's original letter to James Hutton, Apr. 9, 1739 (*Letters*, 25:633 in this edn.). Lawford's Gate, which had been fortified as recently as 1643, became a nuisance to traffic in the eighteenth century and was removed by the Town Council in 1769.

wherein they lived, were reduced to the last extremity. I made another collection on Thursday, and a third on Sunday; by which we were enabled to feed a hundred, sometimes a hundred and fifty a day, of those whom we found to need it most.

5 Tue. 22. I preached at Bridge Gate, six miles from Bristol; Thursday 24 at Westerleigh,[83] eight miles from thence. In the evening at the New Room, I expounded Exodus 24. And we found that God's arm is not shortened, and 'rejoiced' before him 'with reverence'.[84] I was a little surprised in going out of the Room 10 at one who catched hold of me and said abruptly, 'I must speak with you, and will. I have sinned against light and against love. I have sinned beyond forgiveness. I have been cursing you in my heart and blaspheming God ever since I came here. I am damned. I know it. I feel it. I am in hell. I have hell in my heart.' I desired 15 two or three, who had confidence in God, to join in crying to him on her behalf. Immediately that horrible dread was taken away, and she began to see some dawnings of hope.

Fri. 25. Another was with me, who after having tasted the heavenly gift, was fallen into the depth of despair. But it was not 20 long before God heard the prayer and restored to her the light of his countenance.

One came to me in the evening to know if a man could not be saved without the faith of assurance. I answered, (1) I cannot approve of your terms because they are not scriptural. I find no 25 such phrase as either, 'faith of assurance' or 'faith of adherence' in the Bible. Beside, you speak as if there were *two faiths;* whereas St. Paul tells us there is but *one faith* in one Lord. (2) By 'ye are saved by faith'[85] I understand, ye are saved from your inward and outward sins. (3) I never yet knew one soul thus saved without 30 what you call 'the faith of assurance'; I mean, a sure confidence that, by the merits of Christ, *he* was reconciled to the favour of God.

Sat. 26. I was strongly convinced that if we asked of God, he would give light to all those that were in darkness.[86] About noon 35 we had a proof of it; one that was weary and heavy laden, upon prayer made for her, soon finding rest to her soul. In the

---

[83] Bridge Gate appears on the modern maps as Bridge Yate, W. of Bristol by the Chippenham Road. 1744, 'Westerly'. Westerleigh was a substantial parish 3 miles N. by W. from Chipping Sodbury and N. of Bridge Yate.
[84] Cf. Ps. 2:11 (BCP).
[85] Cf. Eph. 2:8.
[86] See Luke 1:79.

afternoon we had a second proof; another mourner being
speedily comforted. M[oll]y D[eaco]n[87] was a third, who about
five o'clock began again to rejoice in God her Saviour; as did
M——y H——y[88] about the same hour, after a long night of
doubts and fears.   5

Thur. 31. I went to one in Kingswood who was dangerously
ill—as was supposed, past recovery. But she was strong in the
Lord, longing to be dissolved and to be with Christ. Some of her
words were: 'I was long striving to come to my Saviour, and I then
thought he was afar off. But now I know he was nigh me all that 10
time; I know his arms were round me. For his arms are like the
rainbow. They go round heaven and earth.'

I had now determined, if it should please God, to spend some
time in Bristol. But quite contrary to my expectation I was called
away, in a manner I could not resist. A young man, who had no 15
thoughts of religion, had come to Bristol a few months before.[89]
One of his acquaintance brought him to me. He approved of what
he heard, and for a while behaved well. But soon after his
seriousness wore off. He returned to London and fell in with his
old acquaintance. By some of these he was induced to commit a 20
robbery on the highway; for which he was apprehended, tried,
and condemned. He had now a strong desire to speak with me;
and some of his words (in a letter to his friend) were: 'I adjure
him, by the living God, that he come and see me before I go
hence.'   25

Friday, February 1. I set out, and on Sunday 3 declared the
grace of God at Newbury[90] from those words of the prophet, 'I
will heal their backsliding. I will love them freely.'[91] And though
the church was full of (chiefly) genteel, well-dressed people, they
behaved as if they knew God was there.   30

Mon. 4. I came to Reading and met with a few still hungering
and thirsting after righteousness. A few more I found at Windsor
in the evening. The next afternoon I reached London.

---

[87] The leader of a band at Bristol. Diary, June 21, July 31, 1739; *Letters*, 25:664 in
this edn.

[88] Possibly Mary Hanney, of Bristol of whom Charles Wesley wrote in his Journal for
Sept. 28, 1739, that she had been beaten and turned out-of-doors by her father upon her
conversion.

[89] Gwillam Snowde; see below, Feb. 6, 12, 1740; and Jan. 11, 1742. The person who
brought him in was Robert Ramsey; see Snowde's letter of Feb. 12, 1740, below.

[90] Newbury was a large market town and parish, 17 miles W. by S. from Reading. By
this date, only industries directly dependent on agriculture persisted there.

[91] Hos. 14:4.

Wed. 6. I went to the poor young man, who lay under sentence of death. Of a truth God has begun a good work in his soul. O may it be brought to perfection.

I think it was the next time I was there that the Ordinary of
5 Newgate came to me and with much vehemence told me he was sorry I should turn Dissenter from the Church of England. I told him if it was so, I did not know it; at which he seemed a little surprised; and offered at something by way of proof, but which needed not a reply.

10   Our twentieth Article defines a true church, 'a congregation of faithful people, wherein the true Word of God is preached and the sacraments duly administered'.[92] According to this account, the Church of England is that body of faithful people (or holy believers) in England, among whom the pure Word of
15 God is preached and the sacraments duly administered. Who then are the worst dissenters from this church? (1) Unholy men of all kinds, swearers, sabbath-breakers, drunkards, fighters, whoremongers, liars, revilers, evil speakers; the passionate, the gay, the lovers of money, the lovers of dress, or of praise, the
20 lovers of pleasure more than lovers of God.[93] All these are dissenters of the highest sort, continually striking at the root of the Church; and themselves belonging in truth to no church, but to the synagogue of Satan. (2) Men unsound in the faith, those who deny the Scriptures of truth; those who deny the
25 Lord that bought them; those who deny justification by faith alone, or the present salvation which is by faith. These also are dissenters of a very high kind; for they likewise strike at the foundation, and were their principles universally to obtain there could be no true church upon earth. Lastly, those who unduly
30 administer the sacraments; who (to instance but in one point) administer the Lord's Supper to such as have neither the power nor the form of godliness.[94] These too are gross dissenters from the Church of England and should not cast the first stone at others.

35   Tue. 12. The young man who was to die the next day gave me a paper, part of which was as follows:

As I am to answer to the God of justice and truth, before whom I am to appear naked tomorrow.

92 Actually Article XIX, 'Of the Church'.
93 2 Tim. 3:4.   94 See 2 Tim. 3:5.

I came to Bristol with a design to go abroad, either as a surgeon, or in any other capacity that was suiting. It was there that I unfortunately saw Mr. Ramsey. He told me, after one or two interviews, that he was in the service of Mr. John Wesley; and that he would introduce me to him, which he did. I cannot but say I was always fond of the doctrine that I heard from him; however, unhappily I consented with Mr. Ramsey,[95] and I believe between us we might take more than thirty pounds out of the money collected for building the school in Kingswood.

I acknowledge the justice of God in overtaking me for my sacrilege, in taking that money which was devoted to God. But he, I trust, has forgiven me this and all my sins, washing them away in the blood of the Lamb.

Feb. 12, 1739/40 Gwillam Snowde[96]

I knew not in the morning whether to rejoice or grieve when they informed me he was reprieved for six weeks, and afterwards that he was ordered for transportation. But known unto God are all his works![97]

Wed. 20. I explained at Deptford the nature of Christian faith and salvation. Many seemed to receive the Word with joy. Others complained, 'Thou bringest strange things to our ears,'[98] though some of them had not patience to hear what this new doctrine was.

Thur. 21. I had a long conference with those whom I esteem very highly in love. But I could not yet understand them on one point, 'Christian openness and plainness of speech'. They pleaded for such a reservedness and closeness of conversation as I could in no wise reconcile with St. Paul's direction, 'by manifestation of the truth to commend ourselves to every man's conscience in the sight of God'.[99] Yet I scarce knew what to think, considering they had the practice of the whole Moravian Church on their side; till I opened my Testament on these words, 'What is that to thee? Follow thou me.'[1]

Tue. 26. Complaint was made again (as indeed had been done before, and that not once or twice only) that many of our brethren,

---

[95] For Robert Ramsay's subsequent fate see below, Jan. 11, 1742.
[96] 1745, 'Snowden'. The fuller original of this letter (in MA) is in fact signed 'Snowde'.
[97] Acts 15:18.
[98] Acts 17:20.
[99] Cf. 2 Cor. 4:2.
[1] John 21:22.

not content with leaving off the ordinances of God themselves, were continually troubling those that did not, and disputing with them, whether they would or no. The same complaint was made the next night also at the meeting of the society. I then
5 plainly set before them the things they had done, expostulated the case with them, and earnestly besought them not to 'trouble or perplex the minds of their brethren any more; but at least to *excuse* those who still waited for God in the ways of his own appointment'.[2]

10   Saturday, March 1. Many that were in heaviness being met together, we cried to God to comfort their souls. One of these soon found that God heareth the prayer. She had before been under the physician's hands; her relations taking it for granted she was *beside herself.* But the great Physician alone knew to heal
15 her sickness.

    Mon. 3. I rode by Windsor to Reading, where I had left two or three full of peace and love. But I now found some from London had been here, grievously troubling these souls also; labouring to persuade them (1) that they had *no faith* at all because they
20 sometimes felt doubt or fear. And (2) that they ought to *be still;* not to go to church, not to communicate, not to search the Scriptures—'because (say they) you can't do any of these things without trusting in them.'

    After confirming their souls we left Reading, and on
25 Wednesday 5 came to Bristol. It was easy to observe here in how different a manner God works now from what he did last spring. He then poured along like a rapid flood, overwhelming all before him. Whereas now

           He deigns his influence to infuse
30   Secret, refreshing as the silent dews.[3]

    Convictions sink deeper and deeper. Love and joy are more calm, even, and steady. And God in many is laying the axe to the root of the tree, who can have no rest in their spirits till they are

---

2 CWJ, I.222, describes how JW was soon putting this point much more strongly: 'My brother spoke after my own heart. . . . To the Society he demonstrated the ordinances to be both means of grace, and commands of God. . . . We trust the little flock, who were following their new leaders into ruin, will now, through grace, come back again.'

3 Mark Le Pla, *The Song of the Three Children Paraphrased*, ed. Samuel Wesley, M.A., 1728, st. XVI (p. 15); reprinted in John Wesley's *Collection of Moral and Sacred Poems* (1744), II.116, beginning, 'Bless God, who deigns. . .'.

fully renewed in the image of God, in righteousness and true holiness.[4]

Wed. 12. I found a little time (having been much importuned) to spend with the soldier in Bridewell who was under sentence of death. This I continued to do once a day; whereby there was also 5 an opportunity of declaring the gospel of peace to several desolate ones that were confined in the same place.

Tue. 18. In the evening, just after I had explained, as they came in course,[5] those comfortable words of God to St. Paul, 'Be not afraid, but speak, and hold not thy peace; for I am with thee, and 10 no man shall set on thee to hurt thee; for I have much people in this city,'[6] a person spoke aloud in the middle of the room, 'Sir, I am come to give you notice that at the next Quarter Sessions you will be prosecuted for holding a seditious conventicle.'

Tue. 25. The morning exposition began at five, as I hope it will 15 always for the time to come. Thur. 27, I had an interview with Joseph Chandler,[7] a young Quaker, who had sometimes spoke in their meeting; with whom I had never exchanged a word before, as indeed I knew him not either by face or name. But some had been at the pains of carrying him, as from me, a formal challenge 20 to dispute; and had afterward told him that I had declared in the open society, I challenged Joseph Chandler to dispute. And he promised to come; but broke his word. Joseph immediately sent to know from my own mouth if these things were so. If those who probably count themselves better Christians had but done like 25 this honest Quaker, how many idle tales, which they now potently believe, would like this have vanished into air?

Fri. 28. From these words, 'Then was Jesus led by the Spirit into the wilderness, to be tempted of the devil,'[8] I took occasion to describe that wilderness state, that state of doubts, and fears, and 30 strong temptation, which so many go through (though in different degrees) after they have received remission of sins.

Sat. 29. I spent another hour with one I had twice conversed with before; and with much the same effect. He asked wherein the doctrine I preached differed from the doctrine preached by 35

---

[4] See Col. 3:10; Eph. 4:24.

[5] Wesley's normal practice was to expound the lessons assigned for the day in the BCP. As Acts 18 did not appear in the Calendar for this month, JW may here refer to some additional 'course' of Scripture-reading.

[6] Acts 18:9-10.

[7] Joseph Chandler is not identifiable at Friends' House, London.

[8] Matt. 4:1.

other ministers of the Church. I told him, 'I hope, not at all from that which is preached by many other ministers. But from that which is preached by some it differs thus: I preach the doctrine of the Church, and they do not.' After he had long and zealously
5 laboured to prove that all ministers preached as I did, and there was no difference of doctrine at all, I was obliged to leave him abruptly; and should indeed have feared that my time had been spent to small purpose but for one piece of history which I then learned, *viz.*, that he had gone to the bishop,[9] before his lordship
10 left Bristol, and informed him that I said in the public congregation I had put them all to silence. Was his lordship so informed? And *could* he believe even this? O Joseph Chandler, Joseph Chandler!

I think it was about this time that the soldier was executed. For
15 some time I had visited him every day. But when 'the love of God was shed abroad in his heart'[10] I told him, 'Do not expect to see me any more. He who has now begun a good work in your soul will, I doubt not, preserve you to the end. But I believe Satan will separate us for a season.' Accordingly, the next day I was
20 informed that the commanding officer had given strict orders, neither Mr. Wesley nor any of his people should be admitted. For *they were all atheists*. But did that man die like an atheist? Let my last end be like his!

Tuesday, April 1. While I was expounding the former part of
25 the twenty-third chapter of the Acts (how wonderfully suited to the occasion, though not by my choice!) the flood began to lift up their voice. Some or other of the children of Belial had laboured to disturb us several nights before. But now it seemed as if all the hosts of the aliens were come together with one consent. Not only
30 the court and the alleys, but all the street, upwards and downwards, was filled with people, shouting, cursing, and swearing, and ready to swallow the ground with fierceness and rage. The mayor[11] sent order that they should disperse. But they set him at nought. The chief constable came next in person, who

---

9 Joseph Butler, the celebrated author of the *Analogy of Religion*, Bishop of Bristol, 1738–50, who had asked JW to cease preaching in his diocese the previous August (see above, July 4, 1739, n. 98). JW's account of this conversation is in Appendix B below.
10 Cf. Rom. 5:5.
11 Stephen Clutterbuck (d. 1746), before whom Captain Robert Williams swore the affidavit which led to the publication of JW's first *Journal*. Cf. above, Preface to *Journal*, Extract 1, ¶ 2, n. 5, 18:121-22 in this edn.

was till then sufficiently prejudiced against us. But they insulted him also in so gross a manner as, I believe, fully opened his eyes. At length the mayor sent several of his officers, who took the ringleaders into custody and did not go till all the rest were dispersed. Surely 'he hath been to us the minister of God for good.'[12]

Wed. 2. The rioters were brought up to the court, the Quarter Sessions being held that day. They began to excuse themselves by saying many things of me. But the mayor cut them all short, saying, 'What Mr. Wesley is is nothing to you. I will keep the peace. I will have no rioting in this city.'

Calling at Newgate in the afternoon, I was informed that the poor wretches under sentence of death[13] were earnestly desirous to speak with me; but that it could not be, Alderman Beacher[14] having just then sent an express order that they should not. I cite Alderman Beacher to answer for these souls at the judgment-seat of Christ.

Thur. 3. I went to the room weak and faint. The Scripture that came in course was, 'After the way that you call heresy, so worship I the God of my fathers.'[15] I know not whether God hath been so with us from the beginning hitherto. He proclaimed, as it were, a general deliverance to the captives. The chains fell off; they arose and followed him.[16] The cries of desire, joy, and love were on every side. Fear, sorrow, and doubt fled away. Verily, thou hast 'sent a gracious rain upon thine inheritance, and refreshed it when it was weary'.[17]

On Good Friday I was much comforted by Mr. T[ucker]'s[18] sermon at All Saints, which was according to the truth of the gospel; as well as by the affectionate seriousness wherewith he delivered the holy bread to a very large congregation. May the good Lord fill him with all the life of love, and with all 'spiritual blessings in Christ Jesus'.[19]

---

[12] Cf. Rom. 13:4.
[13] Benjamin Fletcher and William Lewis, executed at Gloucester, Apr. 14, for robberies on Durdham Down, Bristol.
[14] Michael Beacher, brother of Rev. Henry Beacher who repelled Charles Wesley and others from Communion at Temple Church, Bristol, July 27, 1740. He died Dec. 18, 1758. The name was also spelled 'Becher' and 'Beecher'. *Gentleman's Magazine* (Dec. 1758), XXVIII.612.
[15] Cf. Acts 24:14.   [16] See Acts 12:7, 9.
[17] Cf. Ps. 68:9 (BCP).
[18] Rev. Josiah Tucker; see above, July 31, 1739, n. 72.
[19] Cf. Eph. 1:3.

At five, preaching on John 19:34, 'A soldier pierced his side, and there came forth blood and water,'[20] I was enabled to speak strong words, both concerning the atoning blood and the living, sanctifying water. Many were deeply convinced of their want of
5 both; and others filled with strong consolation.

Mon. 7. At the pressing instance of Howell Harris[21] I again set out for Wales. In the evening I preached 'repentance and remission of sins'[22] at Llanvaches,[23] three miles from the New Passage. Tue. 8. I preached at Pontypool, on 'By grace ye are
10 saved through faith,'[24] and in the evening at Llanhithel,[25] three miles from thence, on 'I know that in me dwelleth no good thing.'[26]

Wed. 9. After reading prayers in Llanhithel church I preached on those words, 'I will heal their backsliding, I will love them
15 freely.'[27] In the afternoon Howell Harris told me how earnestly many had laboured to prejudice him against me; especially those who had gleaned up all the idle stories at Bristol and retailed them in their own country. And yet these were good Christians! These whisperers, talebearers, backbiters, evil-speakers! Just such
20 Christians as murderers or adulterers. 'Except ye repent, ye shall all likewise perish.'[28]

In the evening I expounded at Cardiff the story of the Pharisee and publican. The next day, Thursday 10, after preaching thrice, I rode to Watford,[29] five miles from Cardiff, where a few of us
25 joined together in prayer and in provoking one another to love and to good works.

---

[20] Cf. John 19:34.

[21] In a letter of Feb. 1, 1740, *Letters*, 26:5 in this edn.

[22] Cf. Mark 1:4; Luke 3:3.

[23] Orig., 'Lanvachas'. The New Passage (as distinct from the Old Passage between Beachley and Aust) plied between Black Rock, Sudbrook, and Chiswell Pill. It ceased operation in 1887. (Williams, *John Wesley in Wales*, p. 6, n. 5.) Llanvaches is 7 miles W. of Chepstow.

[24] Cf. Eph. 2:8.

[25] Orig., 'Lanhithel'. The living of Llanhilleth is said to have been vacant, 1661–1741. Llanhilleth is 2 miles S. of Abertillery.

[26] Rom. 7:18.

[27] Hos. 14:4.

[28] Luke 13:3, 5.

[29] Watford Fawr, the residence of Thomas Price, one of Howell Harris's converts, where Whitefield's wedding was held and where the first General Conference of the Calvinistic Methodist Church was held *(Wesleyan Methodist Magazine* [1902], 125:855). Price, a J.P., was one of the nine original partners of the Dowlais Iron Company founded in 1759.

Fri. 11. I preached in Llantarnam[30] church, on 'By grace ye are saved through faith.'[31] In the afternoon I preached at Penyrheol,[32] near Pontypool. A few were cut to the heart; particularly Mrs. A——d,[33] who had some time before given me up for a Papist; Mr. E[van]s,[34] the curate, having averred me to be such, upon his personal knowledge, at her house in Pontypool. I afterwards called, 'O ye dry bones, hear the word of the Lord.'[35] And there was a shaking indeed. Three or four came to me in such mourning as I had hardly seen; as did a poor drunkard between eleven and twelve, who was convinced by the word spoken on Tuesday.

Sat. 12. After preaching at Llanvaches in the way, in the afternoon I came to Bristol, and heard the melancholy news that ————, one of the chief of those who came to make the disturbance on the first instant, had hanged himself. He was cut down, it seems, alive, but died in less than an hour. A second of them had been for some days in strong pain and had many times sent to desire our prayers. A third came to me himself and confessed he was hired that night and made drunk on purpose; but when he came to the door he knew not what was the matter, he could not stir, nor open his mouth.

Mon. 14. I was explaining the *liberty* we have 'to enter into the holiest by the blood of Jesus'[36] when one cried out, as in an agony, 'Thou art a hypocrite, a devil, an enemy to the Church. This is false doctrine. It is not the doctrine of the Church. It is damnable doctrine. It is the doctrine of devils.' I did not perceive that any were hurt hereby; but rather strengthened by having such an opportunity of confirming their love toward him and returning good for evil.

Tue. 15. I received the following note:

Sir, This is to let you understand that the man which made the noise last night is named John Beon. He now goes by the name of

---

[30] Orig., 'Lantarnum'. Llantarnam is in the present district of Cwmbran.

[31] Cf. Eph. 2:8.

[32] Orig., 'Penreul'. Penyrheol, Gwent, is 1 mile SSW. of Pontypool.

[33] Williams, *John Wesley in Wales*, p. 6, n. 3, suggests the wife of Thomas Allgood at whose house JW had called on Oct. 17, 1739 (diary).

[34] On July 13, 1739, Rev. Edmund Jones, Independent minister at Pontypool, informed Howell Harris that 'Evans of Ponty Poole still continues to persecute and I am afraid will blast the hopeful beginnings there' (*Journal of the Historical Society of the Presbyterian Church of Wales*, Supplement 6, p. 193, quoted in Williams, *John Wesley in Wales*, p. 7, n. 4).

[35] Ezek. 37:4.　　　　　　　　　　　　　　　　[36] Heb. 10:19.

John Darsy. He is a Romish priest. We have people enough here in Bristol that know him.

Sat. 19. I received a letter from Mr. Simpson[37] and another from William Oxlee,[38] informing me that our poor brethren at
5 Fetter Lane were again in great confusion, and earnestly desiring that, if it were possible, I would come to London without delay.

Mon. 21. I set out and the next evening reached London. Wed. 23. I went to Mr. Simpson. He told me all the confusion was owing to my brother, who *'would preach up* the ordinances;
10 whereas believers (said he) are not "subject to ordinances";[39] and unbelievers *have nothing to do with them.* They ought to be *still;* otherwise they will be unbelievers all the days of their life.'

After a fruitless dispute of about two hours, I returned home with a heavy heart. Mr. Molther was taken ill this day. I believe it
15 was the hand of God that was upon him. In the evening our society met; but cold, weary, heartless, dead. I found nothing of brotherly love among them now, but a harsh, dry, heavy, stupid spirit. For two hours they looked one at another, when they looked up at all, as if one half of them was afraid of the other; yea,
20 as if a voice were sounding in their ears, 'Take ye heed every one of his neighbour; trust ye not in any brother. For every brother will utterly supplant, and every neighbour will walk with slanders.'[40]

I think not so few as thirty persons spoke to me in these two
25 days who had been strongly solicited (1) to deny what God had done for their souls, to own they never had living faith; (2) to be *still* till they had it, to leave off all the means of grace; not to go to

---

[37] John Simpson, son of Eli Simpson, of Lubbesthorpe, Leics., pleb. Matriculated at Lincoln College, Oxford, 1725, aged 18. Simpson is said (apparently inaccurately) to have been one of the early Oxford Methodists and was one of those who led part of the Fetter Lane Society into Moravianism and 'stillness'. Before joining the Moravians, he had held a living in Leicestershire and was regarded by the Countess of Huntingdon as one of the only two awakened clergy in the neighbourhood of her residence at Donington Park, preaching among the Inghamite societies of the Midlands. For his difficulties with the Moravians and his desire to return to the Church of England, see below, June 10, 1741, n. 83; August 1, 1757; and CWJ, I.205-41. In the 1750s he became a domestic chaplain to the Countess and was spoken of by Whitefield as a 'glorious monument of free grace' (Seymour, *Countess of Huntingdon*, I.47, 153).

[38] William Oxlee was one of the members of the Fetter Lane Society who signed Hutton's letter to Zinzendorf, May 2, 1738 (see above, Dec. 13, 1739, n. 56), joined the Moravians and, 'with the children at Buttermere', a congregation in Wiltshire, joined Spangenberg in his Yorkshire settlement. He was secretary to Hutton's second Society for the Futherance of the Gospel, 1766. Benham, *Hutton*, pp. 33, 229, 411.

[39] Col. 2:20.   [40] Cf. Jer. 9:4.

church, not to communicate, not to search the Scripture, not to use private prayer; at least, not *so much*, or not *vocally*, or not at any *stated times*.

Fri. 25. My brother and I went to Mr. Molther again and spent two hours in conversation with him. He now also explicitly affirmed (1) that there are *no degrees* in faith; that none has any faith who has ever any doubt or fear, and that none is justified till he has a clean heart, with the perpetual indwelling of Christ, and of the Holy Ghost; and (2) that everyone who has not this ought, till he has it, to be *still;* that is, as he explained it, not to use the ordinances, or 'means of grace',[41] so called. He also expressly asserted (1) that to those who have a clean heart the ordinances are not *matter of duty*. They are not *commanded* to use them; they are *free;* they *may* use them, or they *may not*. (2) That those who have not a clean heart *ought not* to use them, particularly not to communicate, because God neither *commands* nor *designs* they should (commanding them to none, designing them only for believers) and because they are not 'means of grace', there being no such thing as means of grace, but Christ only.

Ten or twelve persons spoke to me this day also, and many more the day following, who had been greatly troubled by this new gospel and thrown into the utmost heaviness; and indeed wherever I went I found more and more proofs of the grievous confusion it had occasioned; many coming to me, day by day, who were once full of peace and love, but were now again plunged into doubts and fears and driven even to their wit's end.

I was now utterly at a loss what course to take, finding no rest for the sole of my foot. These 'vain janglings'[42] pursued me wherever I went and were always sounding in my ears. Wed. 30. I went to my friend (that was!) Mr. St[onehouse], at Islington. But he also immediately entered upon the subject, telling me, now he was 'fully assured that no one has any degree of faith till he is "perfect as God is perfect"'.[43] I asked, 'Have *you* then *no degree* of faith?' He said, 'No; for I have not a clean heart.' I turned and asked his servant, 'Esther, have you a clean heart?' She said, 'No; my heart is desperately wicked. But I have no doubt or fear. I know my Saviour loves *me*. And I love him. I feel it every

41 BCP, Thanksgivings, 'A General Thanksgiving', 'for the means of grace, and for the hope of glory'.
42 Cf. 1 Tim. 1:6.
43 Cf. Matt. 5:48.

moment.' I then plainly told her master, 'Here is an end of your reasoning. This is the state, the existence of which you deny.'

Thence I went to the little society here, which had stood untainted from the beginning. But the plague was now spread to
5 them also. One of them who had been long full of joy in believing now denied she had any faith at all and said, till she had, she would communicate no more. Another, who said she had the 'faith that overcometh the world',[44] added, she had not communicated for some weeks, and it was all one to her whether she
10 did or no; for a believer was not 'subject to ordinances'.[45]

In the evening one of the first things started at Fetter Lane was the question concerning the ordinances. But I entreated we might not be always disputing; but rather give ourselves unto prayer.

I endeavoured all this time, both by explaining in public those
15 Scriptures which had been misunderstood and by private conversation, to bring back those who had been led out of the way; and having now delivered my own soul, on Friday, May 2, I left London; and lying at Hungerford that night, the next evening came to Bristol.

20 Sun. 4. I preached in the morning at the school, and in the afternoon at Rose Green, on 'I determined not to know anything among you, save Jesus Christ, and him crucified.'[46]

Mon. 5. I expounded those words, 'I write unto you, little children, because your sins are forgiven you,'[47] and described the
25 state of those who have forgiveness of sins but have not yet a clean heart.

Wed. 7. I prayed with a poor helpless sinner, who had been 'all his lifetime subject to bondage'.[48] But our Lord now proclaimed deliverance to the captive, and he rejoiced with joy unspeakable.
30 All the next day his mouth was filled with praise, and on Friday he fell asleep.

Thur. 8. I was greatly refreshed by conversing with several who were indeed as little children, not artful, not wise in their own eyes, not doting on controversy and 'strife of words',[49] but truly
35 'determined to know nothing save Jesus Christ and him crucified'.[50]

Fri. 9. I was a little surprised at some who were buffeted of Satan in an unusual manner, by such a spirit of laughter as they

44 Cf. 1 John 5:4.   45 Col. 2:20.   46 1 Cor. 2:2.
47 1 John 2:12.   48 Cf. Heb. 2:15.
49 Cf. 1 Tim. 6:4.   50 Cf. 1 Cor. 2:2.

could in no wise resist, though it was pain and grief unto them. I could scarce have believed the account they gave me, had I not known the same thing ten or eleven years ago. Part of Sunday my brother and I then used to spend in walking in the meadows and singing psalms. But one day, just as we were beginning to sing, he 5 burst out into a loud laughter. I asked him if he was distracted and began to be very angry, and presently after to laugh as loud as he. Nor could we possibly refrain, though we were ready to tear ourselves in pieces, but were forced to go home, without singing another line. 10

Tue. 13. In the evening I went to Upton, a little town five or six miles from Bristol, and offered to all those that had ears to hear, 'repentance and remission of sins'.[51] The devil knew his kingdom shook, and therefore stirred up his servants to ring bells and make all the noise they could. But my voice prevailed, so that most of 15 those that were present heard 'the word which is able to save their souls'.[52]

Wed. 14. I visited one of our colliers who was ill of the smallpox. His soul was full of peace, and a day or two after returned to God that gave it. 20

Sat. 17. I found more and more undeniable proofs that the Christian state is *a continual warfare*, and that we have need every moment to 'watch and pray, lest we enter into temptation'.[53] Outward trials indeed were now removed, and 'peace was in all our borders.'[54] But so much the more did inward trials abound; 25 and 'if one member suffered, all the members suffered with it.'[55] So strange a sympathy did I never observe before, whatever considerable temptation fell on anyone unaccountably spreading itself to the rest, so that exceeding few were able to escape it.

Sun. 18. I endeavoured to explain those important words of St. 30 Peter, 'Beloved, think it not strange concerning the fiery trial which is to try you, as if some strange thing happened unto you.'[56] Μὴ ξενίζεσθε τῇ ἐν ὑμῖν πυρώσει πρὸς πειρασμὸν ὑμῖν γινομένῃ, literally, 'Marvel not at the burning in you, which is for your trial.' 35

Wed. 21. In the evening such a spirit of laughter was among us that many were much offended. But the attention of all was soon fixed on poor L[ucreti]a S[mith], whom we all knew to be no

---

[51] Luke 24:47.
[52] Cf. Jas. 1:21.
[53] Cf. Matt. 26:41, etc.
[54] Cf. Ps. 147:14.
[55] Cf. 1 Cor. 12:26.
[56] Cf. 1 Pet. 4:12.

dissembler. One so violently and variously torn of the evil one did I never see before. Sometimes she laughed till almost strangled; then broke out into cursing and blaspheming; then stamped and struggled with incredible strength, so that four or five could
5 scarce hold her, then cried out, 'O eternity, eternity! O that I had no soul! O that I had never been born!' At last she faintly called on Christ to help her. And the violence of her pangs ceased.

Most of our brethren and sisters were now fully convinced that those who were under this strange temptation could not help it.
10 Only E[lizabe]th B[rown] and Anne H[olto]n[57] were of another mind; being still sure, 'Anyone might help laughing if she would.' This they declared to many on Thursday; but on Friday 23 God suffered Satan to teach them better. Both of them were suddenly seized in the same manner as the rest, and laughed whether they
15 would or no, almost without ceasing. Thus they continued for two days a spectacle to all; and were then, upon prayer made for them, delivered in a moment.

Mon. 26. S[usann]a H[ardin]g,[58] after she had calmly rejoiced several days in the midst of violent pain, found at once a return of
20 ease and health and strength; and arose and went to her common business.

Sunday, June 1. I explained 'the rest which remaineth here for the people of God',[59] in the morning at Kingswood School and in the evening at Rose Green to six or seven thousand people. I
25 afterwards exhorted our society (the time being come that I was to leave them for a season) to 'pray always',[60] that they might not faint in their minds, though they were 'wrestling not with flesh and blood, but with principalities and powers, and spiritual wickedness in high places'.[61]
30 Mon. 2. I left Bristol[62] and rode by Avon[63] and Malmesbury

[57] Anne Holton, a woman reported by Charles Wesley as being of immovable religious self-confidence. *Letters*, 25:41 in this edn.
[58] Susanna Harding is reported by Charles Wesley (CWJ, I.283) as a defender of Methodists and a servant in the household of Howell Harris's Bristol host.
[59] Cf. Heb. 4:9.
[60] Luke 21:36.
[61] Cf. Eph. 6:12.
[62] 'At a meeting held at Lady Huntingdon's house, it was unanimously agreed by Mr. Ingham, Mr. Stonehouse and others, that she should write an account of the proceedings [of the *still* Moravians] to Mr. Wesley, and urge his presence in London as speedily as possible' (Seymour, *Countess of Huntingdon*, I.36).
[63] Avon was a tiny chapelry in the parish of Christian Malford, 3 miles NE. from Chippenham.

(where I preached in the evening) to Oxford. Two or three even here had not yet been persuaded to cast away their confidence, one of whom was still full of her first love which she had received at the Lord's Table.

Thur. 5. I came to London, where finding a general temptation 5 prevail of leaving off *good works* in order to an increase of *faith*, I began on Friday 6 to expound the Epistle of St. James, the great antidote against this poison. I then went to Mr. S[tonehouse][64] once again, to try if we could yet come to any agreement. But oh, what an interview was there! He seriously told me he was going to 10 *sell his living*, only the purchaser did not seem quite willing to come up to *his price*. He would fain have *proved* to me the lawfulness of doing this, and in order thereto averred roundly, (1) that no honest man can officiate as a minister in the Church of England; (2) that no man can with a good conscience join in the 15 prayers of the Church, because (said he) 'they are all full of horrid lies.'

Mon. 9. A woman came to me from Deptford,[65] 'sent (as she said) from God'. I gave her the hearing, and she spoke great words and true. But I remembered, 'Judge nothing before the 20 time.'[66]

Wed. 11. I went with Mr. Ingham to Islington, purposely to talk with Mr. Molther. But they said he was so ill he could not be spoken to. In the evening I went to Fetter Lane and plainly told our poor, confused, shattered society wherein they had erred 25 from the faith. It was as I feared. They could not receive my saying. However, I am clear from the blood of these men.

Fri. 13. A great part of our society joined with us in prayer and kept, I trust, an acceptable fast unto the Lord.

Wed. 18. My brother set out for Bristol. At six I preached in 30 Marylebone[67] Fields (much against my will, but I believed it was the will of God), 'repentance and remission of sins'.[68] All were quiet, and the far greater part of the hearers seemed deeply attentive. Thence I went to our own society of Fetter Lane; before whom Mr. Ingham (being to leave London on the morrow) bore a 35

---

[64] Charles Wesley summarizes this interview thus: 'I went with my brother, and Howel Harris, and J. Purdy, to see Molther at Islington. I wished George Stonehouse joy of his good bargain; and left him to justify to my brother the selling of his living' (CWJ, I.237).

[65] Mrs. Jane Davis (see diary, June 9, 1740).

[66] 1 Cor. 4:5.

[67] Orig., 'Marybone'.

[68] Luke 24:47.

noble testimony for the *ordinances* of God and the reality of *weak faith*. But the short answer was, 'You are blind, and speak of the things you know not.'

Thur. 19. We discovered another snare of the devil. The woman of Deptford[69] had spoke plain to Mr. Humphreys,[70] ordering him 'not to preach, to leave off doing good, and, in a word, to be *still*'. We talked largely with her, and she was humbled in the dust, under a deep sense of the advantage Satan had gained over her.

In the evening Mr. Acourt[71] complained that Mr. Nowers[72] had hindered his going into our society. Mr. Nowers answered, It was by Mr. C. Wesley's order. 'What, (said Mr. A[court]) do you refuse admitting a person into your society, only because he differs from you in opinion?' I answered, 'No. But what opinion

---

[69] Mrs. Jane Davis; see n. 65 above.

[70] Joseph Humphreys (1720–?), erroneously referred to later by JW (JWJ, Sept. 9, 1790) as 'the first lay preacher that assisted me in England in the year 1738', the son of a Dissenting minister, himself trained for the Dissenting ministry at Deptford Academy (1733–39). In the summer of 1738 while at home at Burford he began to preach. In August 1739 he formed a religious society for Whitefield's converts at Deptford, which JW visited on September 27, 1739 (see Journal entry and diary of that date) and came to regard as a Methodist society. For these activities Humphreys was expelled from the academy on Dec. 25, 1739, but continued his studies for a year at John Eames's academy in Moorfields, London, where he became intimate with the Wesleys and assisted them first in the London area, and then in October 1740 at Bristol and Kingswood. With the increasingly militant Calvinism of Cennick threatening to disrupt these societies, JW thought of Humphreys as a possible replacement, but Humphreys declined responsibility there, and within a few months became estranged from JW on doctrinal grounds, joining Whitefield. He was among the founders of the Welsh Calvinistic Methodist Association in 1743, and continued lay preaching, especially in the Bristol area. He soon turned against them, however, and is said (in Richard Viney's diary, Aug. 15, 1744) to have been 'trying to form a Baptist congregation for himself'. He subsequently received both Presbyterian and episcopal ordination, and scoffed at inward religion, even at his own *Experience* (his autobiography of 1742) as 'one of the foolish things which I wrote in the time of my madness!' In 1762 Howell Harris found at Bath the 'Humphreys that had preached the faith, and is now fallen asleep and preaches dead morality and doctrine only as a Church minister, &c., but owning that much good is done by the Methodists and much error' (T. Beynon, *Howell Harris, Reformer and Soldier* [Caernarvon, Calvinistic Methodist Bookroom, 1958], p. 139). See also *Letters*, 26:57-58 in this edn.; *Wesleyan Methodist Magazine* (1884), 107:90-99, 193-201.

[71] As JW's letter (July 29, 1740, *Letters*, 26:22 in this edn.) makes clear, John Acourt was refused membership in the society not because of his Calvinist opinions but because he was determined to propagate them at whatever cost. He was perhaps from Barbados. WHS, 27:72.

[72] Edward Nowers, a former Moravian who had withdrawn from the Herrnhaag congregation, was said to have dissuaded Charles Wesley from going to Germany and was one of JW's propagandists against Moravianism. With his wife Margaret he became a member of the Foundery Society. Benham, *Hutton*, p. 47; George J. Stevenson, *City Road Chapel, London, and its Associations* (London [1872]), p. 33.

do you mean?' He said, 'That of election. I hold a certain number is elected from eternity. And these must and shall be saved. And the rest of mankind must and shall be damned. And many of your society hold the same.' I replied, 'I never asked whether they hold it or no. Only let them not trouble others by disputing about it.' 5 He said, 'Nay, but I *will* dispute about it.' 'What, wherever you come?' 'Yes, wherever I come.' 'Why then would you come among us, who you know are of another mind?' 'Because you are all wrong, and I am resolved to set you all right.' 'I fear your coming with this view would profit neither you nor us.' He 10 concluded, 'Then I will go and tell all the world that you and your brother are false prophets. And I tell you, in one fortnight you will all be in confusion.'

Fri. 20. I mentioned this to our society and without entering into the controversy besought all of them who were weak in the 15 faith not to 'receive one another to doubtful disputations',[73] but simply to follow after holiness and the things that make for peace.

Sun. 22. Finding there was no time to delay, without utterly destroying the cause of God, I began to execute what I had long 20 designed, to strike at the root of the grand delusion. Accordingly, from those words of Jeremiah, 'Stand ye in the way, ask for the old paths,'[74] I took occasion to give a plain account both of the work which God had begun among us and of the manner wherein the enemy had sown his tares among the good seed, to this effect:[75] 25

After we had wandered many years in the *new path* of *salvation by faith and works*, about two years ago it pleased God to show us the *old way* of *salvation by faith only*. And many soon tasted of this salvation, 'being justified' freely, 'having peace with God', 'rejoicing in hope of the glory of God', and having his 'love shed 30 abroad in their hearts'.[76] These now ran the way of his *commandments;* they performed all their *duty* to God and man. They walked in all the *ordinances* of the Lord, and through these

[73] Cf. Rom. 14:1.

[74] Cf. Jer. 6:16.

[75] On this and the following days of this week, JW devoted his early morning Bible expositions to expounding the basic Christian teaching as he understood it, in opposition to the quietist practices which seemed to be infecting many of those at Fetter Lane, chiefly under the influence of the Moravians. Summaries of his expositions are given in the *Journal.* These later formed a prominent part of his pamphlet, *A Short View of the Difference between the Moravian Brethren, lately in England, and the Reverend Mr. John and Charles Wesley,* 1745 *(Bibliography,* No. 100); see Vol. 13 in this edn.

[76] Cf. Rom. 5:1, 2, 5.

means which he had appointed for that end, received daily *grace* to help in time of need, and went on 'from faith to faith'.[77]

But eight or nine months ago certain men arose, speaking contrary to the doctrines we had received. They affirmed that we
5 were all in a wrong way still! That we had *no faith* at all; that faith admits of *no degrees*, and consequently *weak faith* is *no faith;* that none is justified till he has a clean heart and is incapable of any doubt or fear.

They affirmed also that there is *no commandment* in the New
10 Testament but *to believe;* that no other *duty* lies upon us; and that when a man does believe he is not *bound* or *obliged* to do anything which is commanded there: in particular, that he is not 'subject to ordinances',[78] that is (as they explained it), is not *bound* or *obliged* to pray, to communicate, to read or hear the Scriptures, but may
15 or may not use any of these things (being in *no bondage)* according as he finds *his heart free to it.*

They farther affirmed that a believer cannot use any of these *as a means of grace;* that indeed there is no such thing as any *means of grace,* this expression having no foundation in Scripture; and that
20 an unbeliever, or one who has not a clean heart, ought not to use them at all: ought not to pray, or search the Scriptures, or communicate, but to *be still,* i.e., leave off these *works of the law.* And then he will surely receive faith, which till he is *still* he cannot have.

25 All these assertions I propose to consider. The first was, that *weak faith* is *no faith.*

By 'weak faith' I understand, (1) that which is mixed with fear, particularly of not enduring to the end; (2) that which is mixed with doubt whether we have not deceived ourselves and whether
30 our sins be *indeed* forgiven; (3) that which has not yet *purified the heart,* at least not from all its idols. And thus *weak* I find the *faith* of almost all believers to be within a short time after they have first 'peace with God'.[79]

Yet that 'weak faith' *is faith* appears, (1) from St. Paul, 'Him
35 that is weak in the faith, receive';[80] (2) from St. John, speaking of believers who were 'little children', as well as of 'young men' and 'fathers';[81] (3) from our Lord's own words, 'Why are ye fearful, O ye of little faith?'[82] 'O thou of little faith, wherefore didst thou

[77] Rom. 1:17.   [78] Col. 2:20.
[79] Rom. 5:1.   [80] Rom. 14:1.
[81] 1 John 2:12, 13, 14.   [82] Matt. 8:26.

doubt?'[83] 'I have prayed for thee (Peter) that thy faith fail thee not.'[84] Therefore he then had faith. Yet so *weak* was that faith that not only *doubt* and *fear*, but gross *sin* in the same night prevailed over him.

Nevertheless he was 'clean, by the word Christ had spoken to him',[85] i.e., *justified*, though 'tis plain he had not *a clean heart*.

Therefore, there are *degrees in faith*, and *weak faith* may yet be *true faith*.

Mon. 23. I considered the second assertion, that there is but *one commandment* in the New Testament, viz., 'to believe'; that no other *duty* lies upon us, and that a believer is not obliged to do anything *as commanded.*

How gross, palpable a contradiction is this to the whole tenor of the New Testament! Every part of which is full of commandments, from St. Matthew to the Revelation! But it is enough to observe (1) that this bold affirmation is shamelessly contrary to our Lord's own words, 'Whosover shall break one of the least of *these commandments* shall be called the least in the kingdom of heaven.'[86] For nothing can be more evident than that he here speaks of *more than one*, of *several commandments*, which every soul, believer or not, is *obliged* to keep *as commanded;* (2) that this whole scheme is overturned from top to bottom by that other sentence of our Lord's, 'When ye have done all *that is commanded you*, say, We have done no more than it was *our duty* to do';[87] (3) that although to do what God commands is a believer's *privilege*, that does not affect the question—he does it nevertheless as his *bounden duty* and *as a command of God;* (4) that this is the surest evidence of his believing, according to our Lord's own words, 'If ye love me' (which cannot be unless ye believe), 'keep my commandments';[88] (5) that to desire to do what God commands, but not as a command, is to affect not freedom, but independency: such independency as St. Paul has not, for though 'the Son had made him free',[89] yet was he not without law to God, but 'under the law to Christ';[90] such as the holy angels have not, for they 'fulfill his commandments', and hearken to the voice of his words;[91] yea, such as Christ himself had not, for 'as the Father had given him commandment, so he spake.'[92]

[83] Matt. 14:31.　　[84] Luke 22:32.　　[85] Cf. John 15:3.
[86] Cf. Matt. 5:19.　　[87] Cf. Luke 17:10.　　[88] John 14:15.
[89] Cf. John 8:36.　　　　　　　　　　　　[90] 1 Cor. 9:21.
[91] Ps. 103:20 (BCP).　　　　　　　　　　[92] Cf. John 14:31.

Tue. 24. The substance of my exposition in the morning, on 'Why' yet 'are ye subject to ordinances?'[93] was:

From hence it has been inferred that 'Christians are not subject to the ordinances of Christ'; that believers *need not,* and unbelievers *may not,* use them; that these are not *obliged,* and those are not *permitted,* so to do; that these *do not sin* when they abstain from them, but those *do sin* when they do not abstain.

But with how little reason this has been inferred will sufficiently appear to all who consider:

(1) That the *ordinances* here spoken of by St. Paul are evidently *Jewish ordinances,* such as 'Touch not, taste not, handle not,'[94] and those mentioned a few verses before, concerning 'meats, and drinks, and new moons, and sabbaths'.[95] (2) That consequently this has no reference to the *ordinances of Christ,* such as prayer, communicating, and searching the Scriptures. (3) That Christ himself spake that 'Men *ought* always to pray,'[96] and commands 'not to forsake the assembling ourselves together',[97] to 'search the Scriptures',[98] and to eat bread and drink wine, 'in remembrance of him'.[99] (4) That the *commands* of Christ *oblige* all who are called by his name, whether (in strictness) believers or unbelievers, seeing 'whosoever breaketh the least of these commandments shall be called least in the kingdom of heaven.'[1]

In the evening I preached on 'Cast not away your confidence, which hath great recompense of reward.'[2]

Ye who have known and felt your sins forgiven, cast not away your confidence, (1) though your joy should die away, your love wax cold, and your peace itself be roughly assaulted; though, (2) you should find doubt or fear, or strong and uninterrupted temptation; yea, though, (3) you should find a body of sin still in you and thrusting sore at you that you might fall.

The first case may be only a fulfilling of your Lord's words, 'Yet a little while and ye shall not see me.'[3] But he 'will come unto you again, and your heart shall rejoice, and your joy no man taketh from you.'[4]

---

93 Col. 2:20.
95 Cf. Col. 2:16.
97 Cf. Heb. 10:25.
99 Cf. Luke 22:19; 1 Cor. 11:24, 25.
1 Cf. Matt. 5:19.
2 Heb. 10:35.
3 Cf. John 16:16, etc.
4 Cf. John 16:22.

94 Col. 2:21.
96 Luke 18:1.
98 John 5:39.

Your being in strong temptation, yea, though it should rise so high as to throw you into an agony or to make you fear that God had forgotten you, is no more a proof that you are not a believer than our Lord's agony and his crying, 'My God, my God, why hast thou forsaken me?'[5] was a proof that he was not the Son of God.

Your finding 'sin remaining'[6] in you still is no proof that you are not a believer. Sin does 'remain' in one that is justified, though 'it has not dominion'[7] over him. For he has not 'a clean heart'[8] at first, neither are all things as yet 'become new'.[9] But fear not, though you have an evil heart. Yet a little while, and you shall be endued with power from on high, whereby you may 'purify yourselves, even as he is pure',[10] and be 'holy, as he which hath called you is holy'.[11]

Wed. 25. From those words, 'All Scripture is given by inspiration of God,'[12] I took occasion to speak of *the ordinances of God*, as they are *means of grace.*

Although this expression of our Church, 'means of grace',[13] be not found in Scripture, yet if the sense of it undeniably is, to cavil at the term is a mere 'strife of words'.[14]

But the sense of it is undeniably found in Scripture. For God hath in Scripture ordained prayer, reading or hearing, and receiving the Lord's Supper, as the ordinary means of conveying his grace to man. And first, prayer. For thus saith the Lord, 'Ask, and it shall be given you.'[15] 'If any man lack wisdom, let him ask of God.'[16] Here God plainly ordains *prayer* as the *means* of receiving whatsoever *grace* we want, particularly that wisdom from above which is the chief fruit of the *grace* of God.

Here likewise God *commands* all to pray who desire to receive any *grace* from him. Here is no restriction as to *believers* or *unbelievers*, but least of all as to unbelievers, for such doubtless were most of those to whom he said, 'Ask, and it shall be given you.'

[5] Mark 15:34.
[6] Cf. John 9:41.
[7] Cf. Rom. 6:14.
[8] Pss. 51:10; 73:1.
[9] 2 Cor. 5:17.
[10] Cf. 1 John 3:3.
[11] Cf. 1 Pet. 1:15.
[12] 2 Tim. 3:16.
[13] BCP, Thanksgivings, 'A General Thanksgiving'; see n. 41 above.
[14] 1 Tim. 6:4.
[15] Matt. 7:7; Luke 11:9.
[16] Jas. 1:5.

We know indeed that the prayer of an unbeliever is full of sin.
Yet let him remember that which is written of one who could not
then believe, for he had not so much as heard the gospel:
'Cornelius, thy prayers and thine alms are come up for a
5 memorial before God.'[17]

Thur. 26. I showed concerning the Holy Scriptures, (1) that to
'search'[18] (i.e., read and hear them) is a *command* of God; (2) that
this *command* is given to *all, believers* or *unbelievers;* (3) that this is
commanded or ordained as 'a means of grace', a means of
10 conveying the grace of God to all, whether *unbelievers* (such as
those to whom he first gave this command, and those to whom
'faith cometh by hearing'),[19] or *believers*, who by experience know
that 'all Scripture is profitable,'[20] or a means to this end, 'that the
man of God may be perfect, thoroughly furnished to all good
15 works'.[21]

Fri. 27. I preached on 'Do this in remembrance of me.'[22]

In the ancient church everyone who was baptized communicated daily. So in the Acts we read, they 'all continued daily in the
breaking of bread and in prayer'.[23]

20 But in later times many have affirmed that the Lord's Supper is
not a *converting*, but a *confirming* ordinance.

And among us it has been diligently taught that none but those
who are converted, who 'have received the Holy Ghost',[24] who are
believers in the full sense, ought to communicate.

25 But experience shows the gross falsehood of that assertion that
the Lord's Supper is not a *converting* ordinance. Ye are the
witnesses. For many now present know, the very beginning of
your *conversion* to God (perhaps, in some, the first deep *conviction)*
was wrought at the Lord's Supper. Now one single instance of
30 this kind overthrows that whole assertion.

The falsehood of the other assertion appears both from
Scripture precept and example. Our Lord commanded those very
men who were then *unconverted*, who had *not* yet 'received the
Holy Ghost', who (in the full sense of the word) were not *believers*,
35 to 'do this in remembrance of him'. Here the precept is clear. And
to these he delivered the elements with his own hands. Here is
example, equally indisputable.

---

17 Cf. Acts 10:31.   18 John 5:39.
19 Rom. 10:17.   20 2 Tim. 3:16.
21 2 Tim. 3:17.   22 Cf. Luke 22:19; 1 Cor. 11:24.
23 Cf. Acts 2:42.   24 Acts 10:47; 19:2.

Sat. 28. I showed at large, (1) that the Lord's Supper was ordained by God to be a *means of conveying* to men either *preventing* or *justifying*, or *sanctifying grace*, according to their several necessities; (2) that the persons for whom it was ordained are all those who know and feel that they *want* the *grace* of God, either to 5 *restrain* them from sin, or to *show their sins forgiven*, or to *renew their souls* in the image of God; (3) that inasmuch as we come to his table, not to *give* him anything but to *receive* whatsoever he sees best for us, there is *no previous preparation* indispensably necessary, but *a desire* to receive whatsoever he pleases to give; 10 and (4) that *no fitness* is required at the time of communicating but *a sense of our state*, of our utter sinfulness and helplessness; every one who knows he is *fit for hell* being just *fit to come to Christ*, in this as well as all other ways of his appointment.

Sun. 29. I preached in the morning at Moorfields, and in the 15 evening at Kennington, on Titus 3:8, and endeavoured at both places to explain and enforce the Apostle's direction that those 'who have believed be careful to maintain good works'.[25] The works I particularly mentioned were praying, communicating, searching the Scriptures, feeding the hungry, clothing the naked, 20 assisting the stranger, and visiting or relieving those that are sick or in prison. Several of our brethren of Fetter Lane being met in the evening, Mr. Simpson told them I had been preaching up the works of the law, 'which (added Mr. V[iney])[26] we believers are no more bound to obey than the subjects of the King of England are 25 bound to obey the laws of the King of France.'

Wednesday, July 2. I went to the society. But I found their hearts were quite estranged. Fri. 4. I met a little handful of them who still stand in the old paths. But how long they may stand God

---

[25] Cf. Titus 3:8.

[26] Richard Viney, a ladies' stay-maker, who translated Böhler's addresses into English, was with JW at Heerendyck in 1738, and in May 1739 addressed a 'Letter from an English brother of the Moravian persuasion in Holland to the Methodists in England lamenting the irregularity of their present proceedings'. He was senior steward of the Fetter Lane Society, August 1741 (Benham, *Hutton*, p. 73). 'Having ministered for the Oxford society for so long a time, [he] afterwards left them' *(Letters*, 26:47 in this edn.). In 1742–43 he superintended the school of the Brethren at Broad Oaks, Essex, and on June 27, 1743, was appointed Warden of the Yorkshire societies (Benham, *Hutton*, pp. 140-46). In November 1743 he was excluded from the Moravian Church by Spangenberg and had hopes of reconciliation with JW, but he created havoc in the Birstall Society (CWJ, I.385), and JW's final comment was: 'Remember Richard Viney, a pillar of salt; not because he came out of Sodom, but because he looked *back!'* (JW to Francis Okely, Oct. 4, 1758). Excerpts from his diary were published in WHS, Vols. 13–15.

knoweth, the rest being continually pressing upon them. Wed. 9.
I came to an explanation once more, with them all together, but
with no effect at all. Tue. 15. We had yet another conference at
large. But in vain, for all continued in their own opinions.

5   Wed. 16. One desired me to look into an old book and give her
my judgment of it, particularly of what was added at the latter end.
This, I found, was *The Mystic Divinity of Dionysius*,[27] and several
extracts nearly allied thereto, full of the same 'super-essential
darkness'. I borrowed the book, and going in the evening to
10 Fetter Lane, read one of those extracts, to this effect:

> The Scriptures are good. Prayer is good. Communicating is good.
> Relieving our neighbour is good. But to one who is not born of God
> none of these are good, but all very evil. For him to read the
> Scriptures, or to pray, or to communicate, or to do any outward work,
> 15 is deadly poison. First, let him be born of God. Till then let him not
> do any of these things. For if he does, he destroys himself.[28]

After reading this twice or thrice over, as distinctly as I could, I
asked, 'My brethren, is this right, or is it wrong?' Mr. Bell[29]
answered immediately, 'It is right. It is all right. It is the truth, and
20 to this we must all come, or we never can come to Christ.' Mr.
Bray said, 'I believe our brother Bell did not hear what you read,
or did not rightly understand.' But Mr. Bell replied short, 'Yes, I
heard every word, and I understand it well. I say it is the truth. It is
the *very* truth. It is the *inward* truth.'

---

[27] An English translation of this work by John Everard was included in his *Some Gospel Treasures Opened* (London, 1653), pp. 767-79 (2nd edn., London, 1659, 2:415-27). The name of Dionysius the Pseudo-Areopagite (*c.* A.D. 500) is the name given to the author of a corpus of theological writings to which the Monophysites appealed at a colloquy at Constantinople in 533, attributing them to Dionysius of Athens. This attribution, though early challenged, was nominally accepted until the sixteenth century. The *Mystical Theology of Dionysius* describes the ascent of the soul to union with God.

[28] The passage of which Wesley conveys the 'effect' appears to come not from Dionysius the Areopagite, but from a passage from John Denqui appended by the English translator of Dionysius, John Everard, to his translation of the *Mystical Divinity (The Gospel-Treasury Opened*, London, 1659, 2:442): 'So it comes to pass, that to the wicked all things are deadly and forbidden; such as are good deeds, to make or hear sermons, to read the Scriptures, to do good to the poor, to pray, to fast, and such like, as is before said; for to the unclean all things are unclean and hurtful: so that it cannot be but the things that to the good are profitable, shall be to them unclean and deadly.'

[29] Richard Bell, a watch-case maker of Vine Court, Bishopsgate Street. An active Moravian in the Fetter Lane Society described by CW as 'more frank' and 'honest' for his forthrightness (CWJ, I.230-36); he became vice-elder of married men in 1744 but left the congregation. Benham, *Hutton*, p. 89.

Many then laboured to prove that my brother and I laid *too much stress* upon the ordinances. To put which matter beyond dispute, 'I (said Mr. Bowes)[30] used the ordinances twenty years, yet I found not Christ. But I left them off only for a few weeks, and I found him then. And I am now as close united to him as my arm is to my body.'

One asked whether they would 'suffer Mr. Wesley to preach at Fetter Lane'. After a short debate it was answered: 'No. This place is taken for the Germans.'[31] Some asked whether the Germans had converted any soul in England. Whether they had not done us much hurt, instead of good, raising a division of which we could see no end. And whether God did not many times use Mr. Wesley for the healing our divisions, when we were all in confusion. Several roundly replied: 'Confusion? What do you mean? We were never in any confusion at all.' I said, 'Brother Edmonds, you ought not to say so, because I have your letters now in my hands.' Mr. Edmonds replied, 'That is not the first time I have put darkness for light, and light for darkness.'

We continued in useless debate till about eleven. I then gave them up to God.

Fri. 18. A few of us joined with my mother in the great sacrifice of thanksgiving and then consulted how to proceed with regard to our poor brethren of Fetter Lane.[32] We all saw the thing was now come to a crisis, and were therefore unanimously agreed what to do.

Sun. 20. At Mr. Seward's[33] earnest request, I preached once more in Moorfields, on the 'work of faith' and the 'patience of hope' and the 'labour of love'.[34] A zealous man was so kind as to free us from most of the noisy, careless hearers (or spectators

---

[30] According to Benham *(Hutton,* pp. 89, 97, etc.), 'George Bowes [1691–1757], wholesale dealer in clokes or clocks, etc., in George Yard, Little Britain', was a leading Moravian in 1742. He is doubtless the 'Bowers' of JWJ, Sept. 8, 1746, and of CWJ, 1739–40, who uniformly spells the name thus (I.148, 151, 153, 156, 160, 209, supported in each instance by the manuscript original). A. C. Hasse's transcript of Hutton's list of the Fetter Lane bands and officers sent to Zinzendorf in June 1742, uses 'Bowers' and includes him among 'those who publicly keep meetings in Fetter Lane' along with Gambold, Holland, Richard Bellet, Brown, and Hutton himself. Moravian Archives, London, from the original at Herrnhut.

[31] The reference here is to the Fetter Lane chapel, which had been leased by James Hutton from Lady Day in 1740, and which was still not occupied by the society, which had hitherto met in a room off Fetter Lane.

[32] An account of this meeting is given in Seymour, *Countess of Huntingdon,* 1:36.

[33] William Seward, a supporter of Whitefield; see above, Jan. 17, 1739, n. 44.

[34] Cf. 1 Thess. 1:3.

rather) by reading meanwhile, at a small distance, a chapter in *The Whole Duty of Man.* I wish neither he nor they may ever read a worse book—though I can tell them of a better, the Bible.

In the evening I went with Mr. Seward to the love-feast in
5 Fetter Lane, at the conclusion of which, having said nothing till then, I read a paper, the substance whereof was as follows:

> About nine months ago, certain of you began to speak contrary to the doctrine we had till then received. The sum of what you asserted is this:
>
10 > 1. That there is no such thing as *weak faith;* that there is no justifying faith where there is ever any doubt or fear, or where there is not, in the full, proper sense, a new, a clean heart.
>
> 2. That a man ought not to use those *ordinances* of God which our Church terms 'means of grace', before he has such a faith as excludes
15 > all doubt and fear, and implies a new, a clean heart.
>
> 3. You have often affirmed that 'to search the Scriptures',[35] *to pray,* or *to communicate,* before we have this faith, is *to seek salvation by works,* and that till these works are laid aside no man can receive faith.
>
> I believe these assertions to be flatly contrary to the Word of God. I
20 > have warned you hereof again and again, and besought you to turn back to the law and the testimony. I have borne with you long, hoping you would return. But as I find you more and more confirmed in the error of your ways, nothing now remains but that I should give you up to God. You that are of the same judgment, follow me.

25 I then, without saying anything more, withdrew, as did eighteen or nineteen of the society.

Tue. 22. Mr. Chapman,[36] just come from Germany, gave me a letter from one of our (once) brethren there, wherein, after denying the gift of God which he received in England, he advised
30 my brother and me no longer 'to take upon us to teach and instruct poor souls, but to deliver them up to the care of the Moravians, who alone were able to instruct them'. You (said he) only instruct them 'in such errors that they will be damned at last', and added, 'St. Peter justly describes you, who "have eyes full of
35 adultery, and cannot cease from sin",[37] and take upon you to guide unstable souls and lead them in the way of damnation.'

---

[35] John 5:39.
[36] Probably George Chapman, butcher, born 1705, Lime Street, at whose house JW had often been entertained; he continued with the Moravians but later lapsed. Benham, *Hutton,* p. 90.
[37] Cf. 2 Pet. 2:14.

Wed. 23. Our little company met at the Foundery[38] instead of Fetter Lane. About twenty-five of our brethren God hath given us already, all of whom think and speak the same thing; seven or eight and forty likewise of the fifty women that were in band desired to cast in their lot with us. 5

Friday, August 1. I described that 'rest which remaineth for the people of God'.[39] Sun. 3. At St. Luke's, our parish church,[40] was such a sight as, I believe, was never seen there before: several hundred communicants, from whose very faces one might judge that they indeed sought him that was crucified. 10

Mon. 4. I dined with one[41] who told me, in all simplicity, 'Sir, I thought last week there could be no such rest as you describe; none in this world, wherein we should be so free as not to desire ease in pain. But God has taught me better. For on Friday and Saturday, when I was in the strongest pain, I never once had one 15 moment's desire of ease, but only that the will of God might be done.'

In the evening many were gathered together at Long Lane on purpose to make a disturbance, having procured a woman to begin, well known in those parts as neither fearing God nor 20 regarding man. The instant she broke out I turned full upon her and declared the love our Lord had for *her* soul. We then prayed that he would confirm the word of his grace. She was struck to the heart, and shame covered her face. From her I turned to the rest, who melted away like water and were as men that had no strength. 25 But surely some of them shall find who is their Rock and their strong Salvation.[42]

Sat. 9. Instead of the letters I had lately received, I read a few of those formerly received from our poor brethren who have since then denied the work of God and vilely cast away their shield.[43] O 30 who shall stand when the jealous God shall visit for these things?[44]

[38] JW had occupied the Foundery since Nov. 11, 1739, when the separation, one stage of which is here noted, began to seem inevitable.

[39] Cf. Heb. 4:9.

[40] St. Luke's, Old Street, was one of the fifty new churches built under the act of 1711, and is thought to have been designed by George Dance the Elder or John James. It was built of Portland stone, 1727–33. The building became dangerous, and in 1959 was closed and dismantled, leaving only the unusual obelisk-like steeple (Blatch, *London's Churches*, p. 178). A photograph of the church in its former state is given in Curnock, II.368. The rector, 1733–74, was William Nichols, D.D.

[41] Mr. William Standex; see diary, Aug. 4, 1740; May 8, 1741.

[42] See Ps. 62:2, 6.

[43] See 2 Sam. 1:21.   [44] See Jer. 5:9, 29; 9:9.

Sun. 10. From Galatians 6:3 I earnestly warned all who had tasted the grace of God (1) not to think they were justified before they had a clear assurance that God had forgiven their sins, bringing with it a calm peace, the love of God, and dominion over

5 all sin; (2) not to think themselves anything after they had this, but to press forward for the prize of their high calling, even a clean heart, thoroughly renewed after the image of God in righteousness and true holiness.

Mon. 11. Forty or fifty of those who were seeking salvation

10 desired leave to spend the night together at the society room in prayer and giving thanks. Before ten I left them and lay down. But I could have no quiet rest, being quite uneasy in my sleep, as I found others were, too, that were asleep in other parts of the house. Between two and three in the morning I was waked, and

15 desired to come downstairs. I immediately heard such a confused noise, as if a number of men were all putting to the sword. It increased when I came into the room and began to pray. One whom I particularly observed to be roaring aloud for pain was J—— W——,[45] who had been always till then very sure that 'none

20 cried out but hypocrites.' So had Mrs. S[i]ms also.[46] But she too now cried to God with a loud and bitter cry. It was not long before God heard from his holy place. He spake, and all our souls were comforted. He bruised Satan under our feet,[47] and sorrow and sighing fled away.[48]

25 Sat. 16. I called on one who, being at Long Lane on Monday the 4th instant, was exceeding angry at those that 'pretended to be in fits', particularly at one who dropped down just by her. She was just going 'to kick her out of the way' when she dropped down herself and continued in violent agonies for an hour. Being afraid,

30 when she came to herself, that her mother would judge of her as she herself had done of others, she resolved to hide it from her. But the moment she came into the house, she dropped down in as violent an agony as before. I left her weary and heavy laden, under a deep sense of the just judgment of God.

35 Sun. 17. I enforced that necessary caution, 'Let him that

---

45 Perhaps J. Wild, mentioned in CWJ, I.262.

46 Perhaps connected with (though not married to) Peter Sims, butcher; see above, Sept. 17, 1738, n. 33. He was one of the members of the first Moravian congregation in London and, marrying after 1742, went off to Northern Ireland. Benham, *Hutton*, p. 95.

47 See Rom. 16:20.

48 See Isa. 35:10.

standeth' (ὁ δοκῶν ἑστάναι, where δοκῶν seems expletive, as it is in many other places)[49] 'take heed lest he fall.'[50] Let him that is full of joy and love take heed lest he fall into *pride;* he that is in calm peace, lest he fall into *desire;* and he that is in heaviness through manifold temptations, lest he fall into *anger* or *impatience.* 5

I afterwards heard a sermon setting forth the *duty* of *getting a good estate* and *keeping a good reputation.* Is it possible to deny (supposing the Bible true) that such a preacher is 'a blind leader of the blind'?[51]

Tue. 19. I was desired to go and pray with one who had sent for 10 me several times before, lying in the New Prison under sentence of death, which was to be executed in a few days. I went, but the jailer said Mr. Wilson, the curate of the parish, had ordered I should not see him.

Wed. 20. I offered remission of sins to a small serious 15 congregation near Deptford. Toward the end a company of persons came in, dressed in habits fit for their work, and laboured greatly either to provoke or divert the attention of the hearers. But no man answering them a word, they were soon weary and went away. 20

Thur. 21. I was deeply considering those points wherein our German brethren affirm we err from the faith, and reflecting how much holier some of them were than me, or any people I had yet known. But I was cut short in the midst by those words of St. Paul, 'I charge thee before God, and the Lord Jesus Christ, and the 25 elect angels, that thou observe these things, without preferring one before another, doing nothing by partiality.'[a]

Fri. 22. I was desired to pray with an old, hardened sinner, supposed to be at the point of death. He knew not me, nor ever had heard me preach. I spoke much, but he opened not his 30 mouth. But no sooner did I name 'the Saviour of sinners' than he burst out, 'The Saviour of sinners indeed! I know it. For he has saved *me.* He told me so on Sunday morning. And he said I should not die yet, till I had heard his children preach his gospel and had told my old companions in sin that he is ready to save 35 them too.'

---

[a] 1 Tim. 5:21.

---

[49] *Works* (1774) omitted the parenthetic comment on the Greek.
[50] 1 Cor. 10:12.
[51] Cf. Matt. 15:14, etc.

Sat. 23. A gentlewoman (one Mrs. C——)[52] desired to speak with me and related a strange story. On Saturday the 16th instant (as she informed me) one Mrs G. of Northampton, deeply convinced of sin, and therefore an abomination to her husband, was by him put into Bedlam.[53] On Tuesday she slipped out of the gate with some other company, and after a while, not knowing whither to go, sat down at Mrs. C.'s door. Mrs. C., knowing nothing of her, advised her the next day to go to Bedlam again, and went with her, where she was then chained down and treated in the usual manner. This is the justice of men! A poor highwayman is hanged, and Mr. G. esteemed a very honest man!

Thur. 28. I desired one who had seen affliction herself to go and visit Mrs. G. in Bedlam, where it pleased God greatly to knit their hearts together and with his comforts to refresh their souls.

Disputes being now at an end and all things quiet and calm, on Monday, September 1, I left London and the next evening found my brother at Bristol, swiftly recovering from his fever.[54] At seven it pleased God to apply those words to the hearts of many backsliders, 'How shall I give thee up, Ephraim? How shall I deliver thee, Israel? How shall I make thee as Admah? How shall I set thee as Zeboim? Mine heart is turned within me; my repentings are kindled together.'[b]

Wed. 3. I met with one who, having been lifted up with the abundance of joy which God had given her, had fallen into such blasphemies and vain imaginations as are not common to men. In the afternoon I found another instance, nearly, I fear, of the same kind: one who, after much of the love of God shed abroad in her heart, was become wise, far above what is written, and set her *private revelations* (so called) on the selfsame foot with the written Word. She zealously maintained (1) that Christ had died for

[b] Hos. 11:8.

---

[52] Curnock (II.379, n. 1) surmises Mrs. Coventry, mentioned on Jan. 25 and Apr.28, 1763.

[53] The familiar name of Bethlehem Royal Hospital, the first asylum for the insane in England and the second in Europe. Founded in 1247 as a priory for the order of the Star of Bethlehem, it was handed over by Henry VIII with its revenues to the City of London as a hospital for the insane in 1547. In 1675 it was moved to Moorfields, the location here referred to. After further moves in the nineteenth and twentieth centuries, it is now at Shirley.

[54] On August 6, Charles Wesley, who had been preaching to the colliers at Kingswood, became dangerously ill of a fever. He was generously attended by Dr. Middleton with whom he formed a lifelong friendship. CWJ, I.248.

angels as well as men; (2) that none of the angels kept their first estate, but all sinned, less or more; (3) that by the death of Christ three things were effected: one part of the fallen spirits were *elected* and immediately confirmed in holiness and happiness, who are now the holy angels; another part of them, having more deeply 5 sinned, were *reprobated*, who are now devils; and the third part allowed a farther trial, and in order thereto sent down from heaven, and imprisoned in bodies of flesh and blood, who are now human souls. In the evening I earnestly besought them all to keep clear of vain speculations and seek only for the plain, practical 10 'truth,which is after godliness'.[55]

Thur. 4. A remarkable cause was tried. Some time since, several men made a great disturbance during the evening sermon here, behaving rudely to the women and striking the men who spake not to them. A constable standing by pulled out his staff and 15 commanded them to keep the peace. Upon this one of them swore he would be revenged, and going immediately to a justice, made oath that he (the constable) had picked his pocket, who was accordingly bound over to the next sessions. At these, not only the same man, but two of his companions, swore the same thing. But 20 there being eighteen or twenty witnesses on the other side, the jury easily saw through the whole proceeding and, without going out at all, or any demur, brought in the prisoner 'not guilty'.

Fri. 5. Our Lord brought home many of his banished ones. In the evening we cried mightily unto him, that brotherly love might 25 continue and increase. And it was according to our faith.

Sat. 6. I met the bands in Kingswood and warned them, with all authority, to beware of being 'wise above that is written'[56] and to desire 'to know nothing but Christ crucified'.[57]

Mon. 8. We set out early in the morning, and the next evening 30 came to London. Wed. 10. I visited one that was in violent pain and consumed away with pining sickness, but in everything giving thanks[58] and greatly rejoicing in hope of the glory of God.[59] From here we went to another dangerously ill of the smallpox, but desiring neither life nor ease, but only the holy will of God. If 35 these are unbelievers (as some of the *still brethren* have lately told them), I am content to be an unbeliever all my days.

[55] Titus 1:1.   [56] Cf. 1 Cor. 4:6.
[57] Cf. 1 Cor. 2:2.
[58] See 1 Thess. 5:18.
[59] See Rom. 5:2.

Thur. 11. I visited a poor woman who, lying ill between her two sick children, without either physic or food convenient for her, was mightily praising God her Saviour and testifying as often as she could speak her desire to be dissolved and to be with
5 Christ.

Sun. 14. As I returned home in the evening, I had no sooner stepped out of the coach than the mob, who were gathered in great numbers about my door, quite closed me in. I rejoiced and blessed God, knowing this was the time I had long been looking
10 for, and immediately spake to those that were next me of 'righteousness, and judgment to come'.[60] At first not many heard, the noise round about us being exceeding great. But the silence spread farther and farther, till I had a quiet, attentive congregation. And when I left them, they all showed much love
15 and dismissed me with a blessing.

Tue. 16. Many more, who came in among us as lions, in a short space became as lambs; the tears trickling apace down their cheeks, who at first most loudly contradicted and blasphemed. I wonder the devil has not wisdom enough to discern that he is
20 destroying his own kingdom. I believe he has never yet, any one time, caused this open opposition to the truth of God without losing one or more of his servants, who were found of God while they sought him not.

Wed. 17. A poor woman gave me an account of what I think
25 ought never to be forgotten. It was four years (she said) since her son, Peter Shaw, then nineteen or twenty years old, by hearing a sermon of Mr. Wh[eatle]y's,[61] fell into great uneasiness. She thought he was ill and would have sent for a physician, but he said, 'No, no. Send for Mr. Wh[eatley].' He was sent for, and came,
30 and after asking a few questions told her, 'The boy is mad. Get a coach and carry him to Dr. M[onro].[62] Use my name. I have sent several such to him.' Accordingly she got a coach and went with him immediately to Dr. M[onro]'s house. When the doctor came in the young man rose and said, 'Sir, Mr. Wh[eatley] has sent me
35 to you.' The doctor asked, 'Is Mr. Wh[eatley] your minister?' And

[60] Cf. Acts 24:25.
[61] Rev. Henry Wheatley (1689–1756), lecturer at St. Leonard's, Shoreditch, and Christ Church, Spitalfields, vicar of Shillington, Beds., 1710–56. The identification is made and the story retold in JW's *Letter to the Lord Bishop of Gloucester* (1763), I.26, 11:491 in this edn.
[62] Cf. Sept. 21, 1739, and note; also *An Answer to the Rev. Mr. Church's* Remarks, III.10, Vol. 9 in this edn.

bid him put out his tongue. Then, without asking any questions, he told his mother, 'Choose your apothecary, and I will prescribe.' According to his prescriptions, they the next day blooded him largely, confined him to a dark room, and put a strong blister on each of his arms, with another all over his head. 5 But still he was as mad as before, praying or singing, or giving thanks continually; of which having laboured to cure him for six weeks in vain, though he was now so weak he could not stand alone, his mother dismissed the doctor and apothecary and let him be *beside himself* in peace. 10

Thur. 18. The prince of the air made another attempt in defence of his tottering kingdom. A great number of men, having got into the middle of the Foundery, began to speak big, swelling words, so that my voice could hardly be heard while I was reading the eleventh chapter of Acts. But immediately after, the hammer 15 of the Word brake the rocks in pieces; all quietly heard the glad tidings of salvation, and some, I trust, not in vain.

Mon. 22. Wanting a little time for retirement, which it was almost impossible for me to have in London, I went to Mr. Piers's[63] at Bexley, where, in the mornings and evenings, I 20 expounded the Sermon on the Mount and had leisure during the rest of the day for business of other kinds. On Saturday 27, I returned.

Sun. 28. I began expounding the same Scripture at London. In the afternoon I described to a numerous congregation at 25 Kennington, 'the life of God in the soul'.[64] One person who stood on the mount made a little noise at first. But a gentleman (whom I knew not) walked up to him and, without saying one word, mildly took him by the hand and led him down. From that time he was quiet till he went away. 30

When I came home I found an innumerable mob round the door, who opened all their throats the moment they saw me. I

---

[63] Rev. Henry Piers (1694–1770), vicar of Bexley, 1736–70, son of Sir Henry Piers, third bart. Educated at Trinity College, Dublin, B.A. 1716, M.A. 1722. Inheriting an income from a plantation in Montserrat, Henry Piers found great difficulty in securing it and died indebted to James Hutton (on whose loan see Benham, *Hutton,* p. 180) and others. Piers was one of the four clergymen who joined the Wesleys at their first conference and was reckoned a member of the Fetter Lane Society. JW's sister Kezia was put under his care as a paying guest. Lady Huntingdon obtained him preferment in Ireland. Seymour, II.155; WHS, 5:225-27; *Wesleyan Methodist Magazine* (1902), 125:132-40.

[64] Cf. above, Sept. 13, 1739, n. 35.

desired my friends to go into the house, and then, walking into the midst of the people, 'proclaimed the name of the Lord',[65] 'gracious and merciful, and repenting him of the evil'.[66] They stood staring one at another. I told them they could not flee from
5 the face of this great God, and therefore besought them that we might all join together in crying to him for mercy. To this they readily agreed. I then commended them to his grace and went undisturbed to the little company within.

Tue. 30. As I was expounding the twelfth of the Acts, a young
10 man, with some others, rushed in cursing and swearing vehemently, and so disturbed all near him that after a time they put him out. I observed it and called to let him come in, that our Lord might bid his chains fall off. As soon as the sermon was over, he came and declared before us all that he was a smuggler then
15 going on that work, as his disguise and the great bag he had with him showed. But, he said, he must never do this more. For he was now resolved to have the Lord for his God.

Sun. 5. I explained the difference between *being called* a Christian and *being so*. And God overruled the madness of the
20 people, so that after I had spoke a few words they were quiet and attentive to the end.

Mon. 6. While I was preaching at Islington and rebuking sharply those that had made shipwreck of the faith, a woman dropped down, struck as was supposed with death, having the use
25 of all her limbs quite taken from her. But she knew the next day she should not die, but live, and declare the loving-kindness of the Lord.

Tue. 14. I met with a person[67] who was to be pitied indeed. He was once a zealous Papist, but being convinced he was wrong, cast
30 off popery and Christianity together. He told me at once, 'Sir, I scorn to deceive you, or any man living. Don't tell me of your Bible. I value it not. I don't believe a word of it.' I asked, 'Do you believe there is a God? And what do you believe concerning him?' He replied, 'I know there is a God. And I believe him to be the
35 soul of all, the *Anima mundi;* if he be not rather, as I sometimes think is more probable, the Τὸ Πᾶν the whole *compages* of body and spirit, everywhere diffused. But farther than this I know not. All is dark; my thought is lost. Whence I come, I know not; nor

---

[65] Exod. 34:5.
[66] Cf. Joel 2:13; Jonah 4:2.
[67] Mr. Mazine; see diary.

what or why I am; nor whither I am going. But this I know, I am unhappy. I am weary of life. I wish it were at an end.' I told him I would pray to the God in whom I believed to show him more light before he went hence, and to convince him how much advantage every way a believer in Christ had over an infidel.   5

Sun. 19. I found one[68] who was a fresh instance of that strange truth, *the servants of God suffer nothing.* His body was well-nigh torn asunder with pain. But God made all his bed in his sickness.[69] So that he was continually giving thanks to God and making his boast of his praise.   10

At five I besought all that were present to 'be followers of God, as dear children, and to walk in love, as Christ also loved us and gave himself for us'.[70] Many who were gathered together for that purpose endeavoured by shouting to drown my voice. But I turned upon them immediately and offered them deliverance 15 from their hard master. The word sunk deep into them, and they opened not their mouth. Satan, thy kingdom hath suffered loss. Thou fool! How long wilt thou contend with him that is mightier than thou?[71]

Mon. 20. I began declaring that 'gospel of Christ', which 'is the 20 power of God unto salvation',[72] in the midst of the publicans and sinners at Short's Gardens, Drury Lane.

Wed. 22. I spent an hour with Mr. St[onehouse]. O what πιθανολογία (persuasiveness of speech)[73] is here! Surely all the deceivableness of unrighteousness. Who can escape, except God 25 be with him?

Thur. 23. I was informed of an awful providence. A poor wretch who was here the last week, cursing and blaspheming and labouring with all his might to hinder the word of God, had afterwards boasted to many that he would come again on Sunday, 30 and no man should stop his mouth then. But on Friday, God laid his hand upon him, and on Sunday he was buried.

Yet on Sunday the 26th, while I was enforcing that great question, with an eye to the spiritual resurrection, 'Why should it

---

[68] Probably 'Bro. Ball' (see diary, Oct. 14, 1740), who appears to be one of the two men who pressed JW to open work at the Foundery. See *An Earnest Appeal*, 11:84-85 in this edn.

[69] See Ps. 41:3.

[70] Cf. Eph. 5:1-2.

[71] See Eccles. 6:10.

[72] Rom. 1:16.

[73] Col. 2:4 ('enticing words', AV).

be thought a thing incredible with you that God should raise the dead?'[74] the many-headed beast began to roar again. I again proclaimed deliverance to the captives. And their deep attention showed that the word sent to them did not return empty.

5   Mon. 27. The surprising news of poor Mr. S[ewar]d's death was confirmed.[75] Surely God will maintain his own cause. Righteous art thou, O Lord!

Saturday, November 1. While I was preaching at Long Lane the storm was so exceeding high that the house we were in shook 10 continually. But so much the more did many rejoice in him whom the winds and the seas obey, finding they were ready to obey his call, if he should then require their souls of them.

Mon. 3. We distributed, as everyone had need, among the numerous poor of our society, the clothes of several kinds which 15 many who could spare them had brought for that purpose.

Sun. 9. I had the comfort of finding all our brethren that are in band of one heart and of one mind.

Mon. 10. Early in the morning I set out, and the next evening came to Bristol.

20   I found my brother (to supply whose absence I came) had been in Wales for some days. The next morning I inquired particularly into the state of the little flock. In the afternoon we met together to pour out our souls before God and beseech him to bring back into the way those who had erred from his commandments.

25   I spent the rest of the week in speaking with as many as I could, either comforting the feeble-minded, or confirming the wavering, or endeavouring to find and save that which was lost.

Sun. 16. After communicating at St. James's, our parish church,[76] with a numerous congregation, I visited several of the 30 sick. Most of them were ill of the spotted fever, which, they informed me, had been extremely mortal, few persons recovering from it. But God said, 'Hitherto shalt thou come. . .'.[77] I believe there was not one with whom we were but recovered.

---

[74] Acts 26:8.

[75] William Seward (see above, Jan. 17, 1739, n. 44), 'the first Methodist martyr', who was itinerating with Howell Harris and who had just lost his sight after violence at Caerleon, died from head injuries received at Hay on Oct. 22, 1740.

[76] St. James's, Bristol, was consecrated as a priory church in 1130 and subsequently made parochial. The parishioners added a ninety-foot tower in 1374. It was a large church with galleries, 'a . . . noble organ, fine altarpiece with a capital painting of the transfiguration and several elegant monuments' (*A New History, Survey, and Description of Bristol* [Bristol, 1794]).

[77] Job 38:11.

Monday, Tuesday, and Wednesday, I visited many more, partly of those that were sick or weak, partly of the lame that had been turned out of the way, having confidence in God that he would yet return unto every one of these and leave a blessing behind him.

Thur. 20. My brother returned from Wales.[78] So, early on Friday 21, I left Bristol, and on Saturday in the afternoon came safe to London.

Tue. 25. After several methods proposed for employing those who were out of business, we determined to make a trial of one which several of our brethren recommended to us. Our aim was, with as little expense as possible, to keep them at once from want and idleness, in order to which we took twelve of the poorest and a teacher into the society room, where they were employed for four months, till spring came on, in carding and spinning of cotton. And the design answered: they were employed and maintained with very little more than the produce of their own labour.

Fri. 28. A gentleman[79] came to me full of goodwill to exhort me 'not to leave the Church' or (which was the same thing, in his account) 'to use extemporary prayer, which' (said he) 'I will prove to a demonstration to be no prayer at all. For you can't do two things at once. But thinking how to pray, and praying, are two things. *Ergo*, you can't both think and pray at once.' Now, may it not be proved by the selfsame demonstration that praying by a form is no prayer at all? e.g., 'You can't do two things at once. But reading and praying are two things. *Ergo*, you can't both read and pray at once.' *Q.E.D.*

In the afternoon I was with one of our sisters who for two days was believed to be in the agonies of death, being then in travail with her first child. But the pain, she declared, was as nothing to her, her soul being filled all that time with joy unspeakable.

Monday, December 1. Finding many of our brethren and sisters offended at each other, I appointed the several accusers to come and speak face to face with the accused. Some of them came almost every day this week. And most of the offences vanished away. Where any doubt remained I could only advise them each to

---

[78] CWJ, I.263, reports: 'I found my brother at the room, expounding Rom. 9. I confirmed his saying and gave some account of my success in Wales. A great power accompanied the word, and I prayed in the Spirit.'

[79] The implication of the diary is that this was 'Mr. Allen of Kettering' (cf. diary, June 19, 1741).

look to his own heart and to suspend their judgments of each other till God should bring to light the hidden things of darkness.[80]

Fri. 12. Having received many unpleasing accounts concern-
5 ing our little society in Kingswood,[81] I left London and, after some difficulty and danger by reason of much ice in the road, on Saturday evening came to my brother at Bristol, who confirmed to me what I did not desire to hear.

Sun. 14. I went to Kingswood, intending, if it should please
10 God, to spend some time there, if haply I might be an instrument in his hand of repairing the breaches which had been made; that we might again with one heart and one mouth glorify the Father of our Lord Jesus Christ.

Mon. 15. I began expounding, both in the morning and
15 evening, our Lord's Sermon upon the Mount. In the daytime I laboured to heal the jealousies and misunderstandings which had arisen, warning every man and exhorting every man, 'See that ye fall not out of the way.'[82]

Tue. 16. In the afternoon I preached on 'Let patience have her
20 perfect work.'[83] The next evening Mr. Cennick came back from a little journey into Wiltshire. I was greatly surprised when I went to receive him, as usual, with open arms, to observe him quite cold, so that a stranger would have judged he had scarce ever seen me before. However, for the present I said nothing, but did him
25 honour before the people.

Fri. 19. I pressed him to explain his behaviour. He told me many stories which he had heard of me. Yet it seemed to me something was still behind. So I desired we might meet again in the morning.

30 Sat. 20. A few of us had a long conference together. Mr. C[ennick] now told me plainly he could not agree with me, because I did not preach the truth, in particular with regard to

---

[80] 1 Cor. 4:5.
[81] On Sunday, Nov. 30, 1740, Charles Wesley warned the Kingswood Society against apostasy and noted that 'the strong ones were offended. The poison of Calvin has drunk up their spirit of love . . . . John Cennick never offered to stop them'. On Dec. 6, he wrote his brother 'a full account of the predestinarian party, their practices and designs, particularly "to have a Church within themselves, and to give themselves the sacrament in bread and water"' (CWJ, I.263-64; cf. Charles Wesley to JW, Dec. 3, 1740, *Letters*, 26:43-44 in this edn.). JW now took action.
[82] Gen. 45:24.
[83] Jas. 1:4.

election. We then entered a little into the controversy, but without effect.

Sun. 21. In the morning I enforced those words, 'Beloved, if God so loved us, we ought to love one another.'[84] Three of our sisters I saw in the afternoon, all supposed to be near death and calmly rejoicing in hope of speedily going to him whom their souls loved.

At the love-feast which we had in the evening at Bristol, seventy or eighty of our brethren and sisters from Kingswood were present, notwithstanding the heavy snow. We all walked home together, through the most violent storm of sleet and snow which I ever remember, the snow also lying above knee deep in many places. But our hearts were warmed, so that we went on rejoicing and praising God for the consolation.

Wed. 24. My brother set out for London. Thur. 25. I met with such a case as I do not remember either to have known or heard of before. L[ucreti]a Sm[ith],[85] after many years of mourning, was filled with peace and joy in believing. In the midst of this, without any discernible cause, such a cloud suddenly overwhelmed her that she could not believe her sins were ever forgiven at all nor that there was any such thing as forgiveness of sins. She could not believe that the Scriptures were true nor that there was any heaven or hell, or angel, or spirit, or any God. One more I have since found in the same state. So sure it is that all faith is the gift of God, which the moment he withdraws, the evil heart of unbelief will poison the whole soul.

Fri. 26. I returned early in the morning to Kingswood, in order to preach at the usual hour. But my congregation was gone to hear Mr. C[ennick], so that (except a few from Bristol) I had not above two or three men and as many women, the same number I had had once or twice before.

In the evening I read (nearly) through a treatise of Dr. John Edwards, on the *Deficiency of Human Knowledge and Learning.*[86] Surely never man wrote like this man! At least, none of all whom I have seen. I have not seen so haughty, overbearing, pedantic a

---

[84] Cf. 1 John 4:11.
[85] See above, Apr. 18, 1739.
[86] John Edwards (1637–1716), Fellow of St. John's College, Cambridge, 1659, one of the most celebrated Calvinist divines of his day and author of numerous polemical works, especially against Socianism, Arminianism, and Locke. The work here referred to is *Some new Discoveries of the Uncertainty, Deficiency, and Corruptions of human Knowledge and Learning* (London, 1714).

writer! Stiff and trifling in the same breath; positive and opiniated to the last degree; and of course treating others with no more good manners than justice. But above all, sour, ill-natured, morose, without a parallel, which indeed is his distinguishing
5 character. Be his opinion right or wrong, if Dr. Edwards's temper were the Christian temper, I would abjure Christianity for ever.

Tue. 30. I was sent for by one who had been a zealous opposer of 'this way'.[87] But the Lover of souls now opened her eyes and cut her off from trusting in the multitude of her good works; so that,
10 finding no other hope left, she fled, poor and naked, to the blood of the covenant and a few days after gladly gave up her soul into the hands of her faithful Redeemer.

At six, the body of Alice Philips being brought into the room, I explained, 'Today shalt thou be with me in paradise.'[88]This was
15 she whom her master turned away the last year 'for receiving the Holy Ghost'.[89] And she had then scarce where to lay her head. But she hath now an house of God, eternal in the heavens.[90]

Wed. 31. Many from Bristol came over to us, and our love was greatly confirmed toward each other. At half an hour after eight
20 the house[91] was filled from end to end, where we concluded the year, wrestling with God in prayer and praising him for the wonderful work which he had already wrought upon earth.

January 1, 1741. I explained, 'If any man be in Christ, he is a new creature.'[92] But many of our brethren, I found, had no ears to
25 hear, having *disputed away* both their faith and love. In the evening, out of the fullness that was given me, I expounded those words of St. Paul (indeed, of every true believer), 'To me to live is Christ, and to die is gain.'[93]

Sat. 3. The bodies of Anne Cole and Elizabeth Davis[94] were
30 buried. I preached before the burial, on 'Blessed are the dead which die in the Lord. Even so, saith the Spirit. For they rest from their labours, and their works do follow them.'[95] Sometime after Eliz[abeth] Davis was speechless, being desired to hold up her

[87] Acts 9:2, etc.
[88] Luke 23:43.
[89] See July 30, 1739.
[90] See 2 Cor. 5:1.
[91] I.e., the colliers' school-house.
[92] 2 Cor. 5:17.
[93] Phil. 1:21.
[94] Elizabeth Davis had been a member of one of the Bristol bands which had often met at her house since April 1739.
[95] Rev. 14:13, with changes introduced from BCP, Burial.

hand if she knew she was going to God, she looked up, and immediately held up both her hands. On Wednesday I had asked Anne Cole whether she chose to live or die. She said, 'I do not choose either, I *choose* nothing; I am in my Saviour's hands, and I have no will but his. Yet I know he will *restore* me soon.' And so he did, in a few hours, to the paradise of God.

Sun. 4. I showed the absolute necessity of 'forgetting the things that are behind', whether works, sufferings, or gifts, if we would 'press toward the mark of the prize of our high calling'.[96] In the evening, all the bands being present, both of Bristol and Kingswood, I simply related what God had done by me, for them of Kingswood in particular, and what return many of them had made for several months last past by their continual disputes, divisions, and offences, causing me to go heavily all the day long.

Wed. 7. I found another believer[97] patiently waiting for the salvation of God, desiring neither health, nor ease, nor life, nor death, but only that his will should be done.

Thur. 8. I expounded the twenty-third Psalm, and many were 'led forth by the waters of comfort';[98] two especially, who never knew till then that their iniquities were forgiven and their sin covered.[99]

Sun. 11. I met with a surprising instance of the power of the devil. While we were at the Room, Mrs. J[one]s,[1] sitting at home, took the Bible to read; but on a sudden threw it away, saying, 'I am good enough. I will never read or pray more.' She was in the same mind when I came, often repeating, 'I used to think I was full of sin, and that I sinned in everything I did. But now I know better. I am a good Christian. I never did any harm in my life. I don't desire to be any better than I am.' She spoke many things to the same effect, plainly showing that the spirit of pride and of lies had the full dominion over her. Mon. 12. I asked, 'Do you desire to be healed?' She said, '*I am* whole.' 'But do you desire to be saved?' She replied, 'I am saved. I ail nothing. I am happy.' Yet it was easy to discern she was in the most violent agony, both of body and mind: sweating exceedingly, notwithstanding the severe frost, and not continuing in the same posture a moment. Upon our

---

[96] Cf. Phil. 3:13-14.

[97] The implication of the diary is that this was Jenny Connor. See above, June 25, 1739, n. 78.

[98] Cf. Ps. 23:2 (BCP).

[99] See Rom. 4:7.

[1] The wife of John Jones, a member of the Bristol Society referred to below.

beginning to pray, she raged beyond measure but soon sunk down as dead. In a few minutes she revived and joined in prayer. We left her, for the present, in peace.

Mon. 12. In the evening our souls were so filled with the spirit of prayer and thanksgiving that I could scarce tell how to expound, till I found where it is written, 'My song shall be always of the loving-kindness of the Lord. With my mouth will I ever be showing thy truth, from one generation to another.'[2]

All this day Mrs. J[one]s was in a violent agony, till starting up in the evening she said, 'Now they have done. They have just done. C[ennick] prayed, and Humphreys preached. (And indeed, so they did.) And they are coming hither as fast as they can.' Quickly after they came in. She immediately cried out, 'Why, what do you come for? You can't pray. You know you can't.' And they could not open their mouths; so that, after a short time, they were constrained to leave her as she was.

Many came to see her on Tuesday; to every one of whom she spoke concerning either their actual or their heart sins, and that so closely that several of them went away in more haste than they came. In the afternoon Mr. J[ones] sent to Kingswood for me. She told him, 'Mr. Wesley won't come tonight. He will come in the morning. But God has begun, and he will end the work by himself. Before six in the morning I shall be well.' And about a quarter before six the next morning, after lying quiet awhile, she broke out, 'Peace be unto thee (her husband). Peace be unto this house. The peace of God is come to my soul. I know that my Redeemer liveth.'[3] And for several days her mouth was filled with his praise, and her talk was wholly of his wondrous works.

Thur. 15. I went to one of our brothers[4] who being (as was supposed) struck with death, was rejoicing with joy unspeakable. His mouth overflowed with praise, and his eyes with tears, in hope of going soon to him he loved.

Mon. 18. I found, from several accounts, it was absolutely necessary for me to be at London. I therefore desired the society to meet in the evening, and having settled things in the best manner I could, on Tuesday set out, and on Wednesday evening met our brethren at the Foundery.

Thur. 22. I began expounding where my brother had left off,

---

[2] Ps. 89:1 (BCP).
[3] Luke 10:5; Job 19:25.
[4] Joseph Black; see diary, Jan. 15, 1741.

viz., at the fourth chapter of the first Epistle of St. John. He had not preached the morning before, nor intended to do it any more.[5] 'The Philistines are upon thee, Samson.'[6] But the Lord is not 'departed from thee'.[7] He shall strengthen thee yet again, and thou shalt be 'avenged of them, for the loss of thy eyes'.[8]

Sun. 25. I enforced that great command, 'As we have opportunity let us do good unto all men';[9] and in the evening those solemn words, 'Take heed, brethren, that there be not in any of you an evil heart of unbelief, in departing from the living God.'[10]

Wed. 28. Our old friends, Mr. Gambold and Mr. Hall, came to see my brother and me. The conversation turned wholly on *silent prayer* and *quiet waiting* for God, which, they said, was the *only possible* way to attain living, saving faith.

Sirenum cantus, et Circes pocula nosti?[11]

Was there ever so pleasing a scheme! But where is it written? Not in any of those books which I account the oracles of God. I allow, if there is a better way to God than the scriptural way, this is it. But the prejudice of education so hangs upon me that I cannot think there is. I must therefore still 'wait' in the Bible way, from which this differs as light from darkness.

Fri. Jan. 30. I preached in the morning on, 'Then shall they fast in those days,'[12] and in the afternoon spent a sweet hour in prayer with some hundreds of our society.

Sunday, February 1. A private letter, wrote to me by Mr. Whitefield,[13] having been printed without either his leave or

---

[5] Notwithstanding the loss or destruction of the crucial portion of CWJ, it is clear that under a good deal of Moravian pressure he was briefly tempted to uphold the doctrines of 'stillness' he had fought for so long. For his return to old paths, see below, Feb. 12, 1741. For Lady Huntingdon's part in his recovery, see Lady Huntingdon to JW, *Letters*, 26:67-68 in this edn.

[6] Cf. Judg. 16:9, 12.

[7] Cf. Judg. 16:20.

[8] Cf. Judg. 16:28.

[9] Cf. Gal. 6:10.

[10] Cf. Heb. 3:12.

[11] Cf. Horace, *Epistles*, I.ii.23, 'Sirenum voces. . .'. In his *Works* (1774), Vol. 32, Wesley paraphrases, 'know'st thou th' enchanted cup, and Siren's song?'

[12] Mark 2:20; Luke 5:35.

[13] The breach between Whitefield and JW is here seen to be widening despite some goodwill on both sides. In April 1739 JW had preached and later published his sermon, *Free Grace*, with Charles Wesley's hymn on universal redemption appended, and distributed it in England and America (see Sermon 110, 3:542-63 in this edn.). The two

mine, great numbers of copies were given to our people, both at
the door and in the Foundery itself. Having procured one of
them, I related (after preaching) the naked fact to the congregation, and told them, 'I will do just what I believe Mr.
5 Whitefield would, were he here himself.' Upon which I tore it in
pieces before them all. Everyone who had received it did the
same. So that in two minutes there was not a whole copy left. Ah
poor Ahithophel![14]

Ibi omnis effusus labor![15]

10   Wed. 4. Being the general fast-day, I preached in the morning
on those words, 'Shall I not visit for these things, saith the Lord?
Shall not my soul be avenged on such a nation as this?'[16] Coming
from the service at St. Luke's I found our house so crowded that
the people were ready to tread one upon another. I had not
15 designed to preach, but seeing such a congregation I could not
think it right to send them empty away, and therefore expounded
the parable of the barren fig tree. O that it may at length bear fruit!

From hence I went to Deptford, where many poor wretches
were got together, utterly void both of common sense and
20 common decency. They cried aloud, as if just come from 'among
the tombs'.[17] But they could not prevail against the Holy One of
God. Many of them were altogether confounded, and I trust will
come again with a better mind.

Tuesday 10 (being Shrove Tuesday). Before I began to preach
25 many men of the baser sort, having mixed themselves with the
women, behaved so indecently as occasioned much disturbance.
A constable commanded them to 'keep the peace'. In answer to

corresponded on this matter several times in the course of the next eighteen months,
during many of which Whitefield was in America, and a pamphlet controversy
independent of the original protagonists was building up. The letter here referred to,
written from Boston, Sept. 25, 1740, was reprinted as a broadsheet and reproduced in
William Fleetwood, *The Perfectionist Examin'd* (London, Roberts, 1741), pp. 96-99; see
26:31-33 in this edn. JW's public challenge in tearing it up led Whitefield to publish a
reply he had written during the autumn and withheld while he took advice and hoped for a
better outcome: *A Letter to the Rev. Mr. John Wesley in Answer to his Sermon entitled 'Free
Grace'*, dated from Bethesda, Dec. 24, 1740, and printed by Strahan on Mar. 31, 1741.
The final upshot was the complete separation of the Arminian and Calvinist wings of the
revival, the latter being organized in Lady Huntingdon's Connexion and the Welsh
Calvinistic Methodist Church.

[14] See 2 Sam. 15:12.

[15] Cf. Virgil, *Georgics*, iv.491-92, translated by Wesley in his *Works* (1774), Vol. 32, 'So
all the labour's lost!'

[16] Jer. 5:29; 9:9.   [17] Mark 5:3.

which they knocked him down. Some who were near seized on two of them, and by shutting the doors prevented any farther contest. Those two were afterwards carried before a magistrate, and on their promise of better behaviour discharged.

Thur. 12. My brother returned from Oxford and preached on 5 'The true way of waiting for God,' thereby dispelling at once the fears of some and the vain hopes of others, who had confidently affirmed that Mr. Charles Wesley was *still* already and would come to London no more.

Mon. 16. While I was preaching in Long Lane, the host of the 10 aliens gathered together. And one large stone (many of which they threw) went just over my shoulder. But no one was hurt in any degree. For thy 'kingdom ruleth over all'.[18]

All things now being settled according to my wish, on Tuesday 17, I left London. In the afternoon I reached Oxford, and leaving 15 my horse there,[19] set out on foot for Stanton Harcourt. The night overtook me in about an hour, accompanied with heavy rain. Being wet and weary, and not well knowing my way, I could not help saying in my heart (though ashamed of my want of resignation to God's will), O that thou wouldst 'stay the bottles of 20 heaven'![20] or at least give me light, or an honest guide, or some help in the manner thou knowest! Presently the rain ceased; the moon broke out, and a friendly man overtook me, who set me on his own horse, and walked by my side till we came to Mr. Gambold's door.   25

Wed. 18. I walked on to Burford; on Thursday to Malmesbury; and the next day to Bristol. Sat. 21. I inquired as fully as I could concerning the divisions and offences which, notwithstanding the earnest cautions I had given, began afresh to break out in Kingswood. In the afternoon I met a few of the bands there, but it 30 was a cold, uncomfortable meeting. Sun. 22. I endeavoured to show them the ground of many of their mistakes, from those words, 'Ye need not that any man teach you, but as that same anointing teacheth you'[21]—a text which had been frequently brought in support of the rankest enthusiasm. Mr. Cennick[22] and 35

---

[18] Ps. 103:19.
[19] See *An Answer to the Rev. Mr. Church's* Remarks, III.8 (9:117-18 in this edn.), for a parenthetic insertion within a quotation of this passage: 'for he was tired, and the horse-road exceeding bad, and my business admitted of no delay.'
[20] Job 38:37.
[21] 1 John 2:27.
[22] 1744, 1749, 'Mr. C——'.

fifteen or twenty others came up to me after sermon. I told them they 'had not done right in speaking against me behind my back'. Mr. C[ennick], Ann A[llin],[23] and Thomas Bissicks,[24] as the mouth of the rest, replied, they had said no more of me behind my
5 back than they would say to my face, which was, that I did 'preach up man's faithfulness' and not the faithfulness of God.

In the evening was our love-feast at Bristol, in the conclusion of which, there being mention made that many of our brethren at Kingswood had formed themselves into a separate society, I
10 related to them at large the effects of the separations which had been made from time to time in London, and likewise the occasion of this, viz., Mr. C[ennick]'s preaching other doctrine than that they had before received. The natural consequence was that when my brother and I preached the same which we had
15 done from the beginning, many censured and spoke against us both, whence arose endless strife and confusion.

T[homas] B[issicks] replied, why, we preached false doctrine; we preached that there is righteousness in man. I said, 'So there is, after the righteousness of Christ is imputed to him through
20 faith. But who told you that what we preach was false doctrine? Who would you have believed this from, but Mr. C[ennick]?'[25] Mr. C[ennick] answered, 'You *do* preach righteousness in man. I did say this. And I say it still. However, we are willing to join with you. But we will also meet apart from you. For we meet to confirm
25 one another in those truths which you speak against.'

I replied, 'You should have told me of this before, and not have supplanted me in my own house, stealing the hearts of the people, and by private accusations separating very friends.' He said, 'I have never privately accused you.' I said, 'My brethren, judge,'
30 and read as follows:

Jan. 17, 1741

To the Reverend Mr. George Whitefield.
My dear Brother,

That you might come quickly, I have written a second time.
35 I sit solitary, like Eli, waiting what will become of the ark. And while

---

[23] 1744, 1749, 'A—— A——'; 1774 supplies 'Ann'; for Ann Allin or Ayling, see below, June 23, 1739, n. 74.
[24] 1744, 1749, 'T—— B——'.
[25] A view of this contretemps, in which Cennick was separated from Wesley not merely by theological differences, but by wishing to play down phenomena of abnormal

I wait and fear the carrying of it away from among my people, my trouble increases daily. How glorious did the gospel seem once to flourish in Kingswood! . . . I spake of the everlasting love of Christ with sweet power. . . . But now bro. Charles is suffered to open his mouth[26] against this truth, while the frighted sheep gaze and fly, as 5 if no shepherd was among them. . . . It is just as though Satan was now making war with the saints, in a more than common way. O pray for the distressed lambs yet left in this place, that they faint not. Surely they would, if preaching would do it. For they have nothing whereon to rest (who now attend on the sermons) but their own 10 faithfulness. . . .

  With universal redemption bro. Charles pleases the world. . . . Bro. John follows him in everything. I believe no atheist can more preach against predestination than they. And all who believe election are counted enemies to God, and called so. 15

  Fly, dear brother. I am as alone. . . . I am in the midst of the plague. . . . If God give thee leave, make haste.

Mr. C[ennick] stood up and said, 'That letter is mine. I sent it to Mr. Whitefield. And I do not retract anything in it, nor blame myself for sending it.'[27] 20

Perceiving some of our brethren began to speak with warmth, I desired he would meet me at Kingswood on Saturday, where each of us could speak more freely, and that all things might sleep till then.

  Tue. 24. The bands meeting at Bristol, I read over the names 25 of the United Society,[28] being determined that no disorderly walker should remain therein. Accordingly I took an account of every person (1) to whom any reasonable objection was made; (2) who was not known to and recommended by some on whose

psychology on which Wesley was insisting as tokens of the Spirit, and was condemned by a prearranged manoeuvre on charges that were never properly made clear to him, is given in J. E. Hutton, *John Cennick. A Sketch* (London, 1906), pp. 16-22.

[26] The reference is to the publication by the Wesley brothers of *Hymns on God's Everlasting Love. To which is added 'The Cry of a Reprobate' and the 'Horrible Decree'* (Bristol, 1741).

[27] Whitefield replied to Cennick, London, Mar. 25, 1741: 'Hasten hither with all speed, and then we shall see what God intends to do for and by us. . . . The Lord give us a due mixture of the lamb and the lion. . .'. Whitefield, *Works*, I.257-58.

[28] The 'Rules of the Society', with the commencement of JW's Foundery Society in mind, refer to the origin of the United Society at 'the latter end of the year 1739'. JW, however, first used the term in his diary for Oct. 30, 1739, referring to the union of the religious societies which had been meeting in Nicholas Street and Baldwin Street, Bristol, in their new premises at the New Room, Horsefair. The list of members JW here used survives in his own hand, headed, 'The United Society in Bristol, January 1, 1741'. See Curnock, 2:398, and cf. illustration facing p. 353 below.

veracity I could depend. To those who were sufficiently recommended, tickets[29] were given on the following days. Most of the rest I had face to face with their accusers, and such as either appeared to be innocent or confessed their faults and promised a
5 better behaviour were then received into the society. The others were put upon trial again, unless they voluntarily expelled themselves. About forty were by this means separated from us; I trust, only for a season.

Sat. 28. I met the Kingswood bands again and heard all who
10 desired it at large, after which I read the following paper:

By many witnesses it appears that several members of the band society in Kingswood have made it their common practice to scoff at the preaching of Mr. John and Charles Wesley; that they have censured and spoken evil of them behind their backs, at the very time
15 they professed love and esteem to their faces; that they have studiously endeavoured to prejudice other members of that society against them, and in order thereto have belied and slandered them in divers instances.

Therefore, not for their opinions, nor for any of them (whether
20 they be right or wrong), but for the causes above mentioned, viz., for their scoffing at the Word and ministers of God, for their talebearing, backbiting, and evil-speaking, for their dissembling, lying, and slandering,

I, John Wesley, by the consent and approbation of the band[30]
25 society in Kingswood, do declare the persons above mentioned to be no longer members thereof. Neither will they be so accounted until

---

[29] This is the first mention of membership tickets, an institution which seems not to have existed in the old religious societies. The tickets and their function were doubtless the same as those of the class tickets JW himself described for a slightly later date in *A Plain Account of the People Called Methodists* (1749): 'To each of those whose seriousness and good conversation I found no reason to doubt, I gave a testimony under my own hand, by writing their name on a *ticket* prepared for that purpose. . . . Those who bore these tickets (. . . being of just the same force with the συστατικαί, 'commendatory letters', mentioned by the Apostle) wherever they came, were acknowledged by their brethren and received with all cheerfulness. These were likewise of use in other respects. By these it was easily distinguished when the society were to meet apart, who were members of it and who not. These also supplied us with a quiet and inoffensive method of removing any disorderly member. He has no new ticket at the quarterly visitation (for so often are the tickets changed)' (9:265 in this edn.). None of these first tickets survives, but the earliest extant examples from 1742 onwards were wood and copperplate engravings printed on cardboard, floral devices and combinations of a dove, flowers, and crown. Illustrations of some of these early tickets are to be found in 9:76 in this edn.; see also WHS (1957), 31:2-9, 34-38, 70-73.
[30] 1774 omits 'band'.

they shall openly confess their fault, and thereby do what in them lies to remove the scandal they have given.

At this they seemed a little shocked at first, but Mr. C[ennick], T[homas] B[issicks], and A[nn] A[llin] soon recovered, and said they *had* heard both my brother and me many times preach popery. However they would join with us if we would. But they would not own they had done anything amiss.

I desired them to consider of it yet again, and give us their answer the next evening.

The next evening, March 1, they gave the same answer as before. However, I could not tell how to part, but exhorted them to wait yet a little longer and wrestle with God, that they might know his will concerning them.

Fri. 6. Being still fearful of doing anything rashly, or contrary to the great law of love, I consulted again with many of our brethren concerning the farther steps I should take. In consequence of which, on Saturday 7 all who could of the bands[31] being met together, I told them open dealing was best, and I would therefore tell them plainly what I thought (setting all opinions aside) had been wrong in many of them, viz.:

(1) Their despising the ministers of God and slighting his ordinances; (2) their not speaking or praying when met together, till they were sensibly moved thereto; and (3) their dividing themselves from their brethren and forming a separate society.

That we could not approve of delaying this matter because the confusion that was already increased daily.

That upon the whole we believed the only way to put a stop to these growing evils was for everyone now to take his choice, and quit one society or the other.

T[homas] B[issicks] replied, 'It is our holding election is the true cause of your separating from us.' I answered, 'You know in your conscience it is not. There are several predestinarians in our societies both at London and Bristol; nor did I ever yet put any one out of either because he held that opinion.'

He said, 'Well, we will break up our society, on condition you will receive and employ Mr. C[ennick] as you did before.'

I replied, 'My brother has wronged me much. But he doth not say, "I repent."'

---

[31] 1774, 'society'.

Mr. C[ennick] said, 'Unless in not speaking in your defence, I do not know that I have wronged you at all.'

I rejoined, 'It seems then nothing remains but for each to choose which society he pleases.'

5 Then, after a short time spent in prayer, Mr. C[ennick] went out and about half of those who were present with him.

Sun. 8. After preaching at Bristol on the abuse and the right use of the Lord's Supper, I earnestly besought them at Kingswood to beware of 'offending in tongue',[32] either against 10 justice, mercy, or truth. After sermon the remains of our society met and found we had great reason to bless God, for that after fifty-two were withdrawn, we had still upwards of ninety left. O may these, at least, hold the unity of the Spirit in the bond of peace!

15 I will shut up this melancholy subject with part of a letter wrote by my brother about this time.

If you think proper, you may show Brother C[ennick] what follows. (N.B. I did *not* think it proper then.)

My dearest brother John C[ennick], in much love and tenderness I
20 speak. You came to Kingswood upon my brother's sending for you. You served under him in the gospel as a son. I need not say how well he loved you. You used the authority he gave you to overthrow his doctrine. You everywhere contradicted it. (Whether true or false is not the question.) But you ought first to have fairly told him, 'I preach
25 contrary to you. Are you willing, notwithstanding, that I should continue *in your house*, gainsaying you? If you are not, I have no more place in these regions. You have a right to this open dealing. I now give you fair warning. Shall I stay here opposing you, or shall I depart?'

30 My brother, have you dealt thus honestly and openly with him? No. But you have stole away the people's heart from him. And when some of them *basely treated* their *best friend*, God only excepted, how patiently did you take it? When did you ever vindicate us, as we have you? Why did you not plainly tell them, 'You are eternally indebted to
35 these men. Think not that I will stay among you to head a party against my dearest friend—and brother, as he suffers me to call him, having humbled himself for my sake, and given me (no bishop, priest, or deacon) the right hand of fellowship. If I hear that one word more is spoken against him, I will leave you that moment, and never see your
40 face more.'

This had been just and honest, and *not more* than we have deserved

---

[32] Cf. Ps. 39:1 (BCP).

at your hands. I say *we*, for God is my witness how condescendingly loving I have been toward you. Yet did you so forget yourself as both openly and privately to contradict my doctrine, while in the meantime I was as a deaf man that heard not, neither answered a word, either in private or public. 5

Ah, my brother! I am distressed for you. I would—but you will not receive my saying. Therefore I can only commit you to him who hath commanded us to forgive one another, even as God, for Christ's sake, hath forgiven us.

Sun. 15. I preached twice at Kingswood, and twice at Bristol, 10 on those words of a troubled soul, 'O that I had wings like a dove, for then would I flee away and be at rest.'[33]

One of the notes I received today was as follows: 'A person whom God has visited with a fever, and has wonderfully preserved seven days in a hay-mow, without any sustenance but 15 now and then a little water out of a ditch, desires to return God thanks. The person is present and ready to declare what God has done both for his body and soul. For the three first days of his illness he felt nothing but the terrors of the Lord, greatly fearing lest he should drop into hell; till after long and earnest prayer he 20 felt himself given up to the will of God, and equally content to live or die. Then he fell into a refreshing slumber, and awaked full of peace and the love of God.'

Tue. 17. From these words, 'Shall not the Judge of all the earth do right,'[34] I preached a sermon (which I have not done before in 25 Kingswood School since it was built) directly on predestination.[35] On Wednesday (and so every Wednesday and Thursday) I saw the sick in Bristol, many of whom I found were blessing God for his seasonable visitation. In the evening I put those of the women who were grown slack into distinct bands by themselves, and 30 sharply reproved many for their unfaithfulness to the grace of God, who bore witness to his Word by pouring upon us all the spirit of mourning and supplication.

Thur. 19. I visited many of the sick, and among the rest J[udith] W[illiams],[36] who was in grievous pain both of body and mind. 35

---

[33] Ps. 55:6 (BCP).
[34] Gen. 18:25.
[35] The substance of this sermon (which as the diary shows JW preached also on the previous day) appeared in the published series as Sermon 58, *On Predestination*, 2:413-21 in this edn.
[36] For an account of her conversion, see CWJ, Oct. 1, 1739 (I.184).

After a short time spent in prayer, we left her. But her pain was gone, her soul being in full peace, and her body also so strengthened that she immediately rose and the next day went abroad.

5 Sat. 21. I explained in the evening the thirty-third chapter of Ezekiel, in applying which I was suddenly seized with such a pain in my side that I could not speak. I knew my remedy and immediately kneeled down. In a moment the pain was gone, and the voice of the Lord cried aloud to the sinners, 'Why will ye die,
10 O house of Israel?'[37]

Mon. 23. I visited the sick in Kingswood, one of whom surprised me much. Her husband died of the fever some days before. She was seized immediately after his death; then her eldest daughter; then another and another of her children, six of
15 whom were now sick round about her, without either physic, money, food, or any visible means of procuring it. Who but a Christian can at such a time say from the heart, 'Blessed be the name of the Lord'?[38]

Finding all things now, both at Kingswood and Bristol, far
20 more settled than I expected, I complied with my brother's request, and setting out on Wednesday 25, the next day came to London.

Sat. 28. Having heard much of Mr. Whitefield's unkind behaviour since his return from Georgia,[39] I went to him to hear
25 him speak for himself, that I might know how to judge. I much approved of his plainness of speech. He told me he and I preached two different gospels, and therefore he not only would not join with, or give me the right hand of fellowship, but was

[37] Ezek. 33:11.
[38] Job 1:21.
[39] Whitefield had landed in Falmouth on Mar. 11, 1741, and was soon afterwards examined before the Commons on Georgia affairs (on Apr. 14 the House voted £20,000 for the assistance of sufferers in a dreadful fire at Charleston, S.C.). He spent the next few weeks preaching in London, and one of his first acts was to publish a reply to JW's sermon on *Free Grace* (see above, Feb. 1, 1741, n. 13). Whitefield's affairs were now in a state of confusion; his relations with Elizabeth Delamotte again seemed critical; the death of William Seward exacerbated the financial difficulties confronting his Georgia orphanage; his London publisher, James Hutton the Moravian, declined to publish his tract against JW, 'on the principle which he uniformly maintained, that he ought not in his trade to publish that which he himself did not believe to be in accordance with the Divine Word' (Benham, *Hutton*, p. 69); and, apart from the crisis brought to a head by the Wesleys in the Kingswood School and society, there were other losses of support which Whitefield believed had been brought on by his own incautious expressions of anti-modernist views. Whitefield, *Works*, I.256-57.

resolved publicly to preach against me and my brother wheresoever he preached at all. Mr. Hall[40] (who went with me) put him in mind of the promise he had made but a few days before, that whatever his private opinion was, he would never publicly preach against us. He said that promise was only an effect 5 of human weakness, and he was now of another mind.

Mon. 30. I fixed an hour every day for speaking with each of the bands, that no disorderly walker might remain among them, nor any of a careless or contentious spirit. And the hours from ten to two, on every day but Saturday, I set apart for speaking with any 10 who should desire it.

Wednesday, April 1. At his earnest and repeated request I went to see one under sentence of death in the New Prison. But the keepers told me Mr. Wilson (the curate of the parish) had given charge I should not speak with him.[41] I am clear from the blood of 15 this man. Let Mr. Wilson answer for it to God.

Sat. 4. I believed both love and justice required that I should speak my sentiments freely to Mr. Wh[itefield] concerning the *Letter* he had published, said to be 'in answer to my sermon on free grace'. The sum of what I observed to him was this: (1) that it 20 was quite imprudent to publish it at all, as being only the putting of weapons into their hands who loved neither the one nor the other; (2) that if he was constrained to 'bear his testimony'[42] (as he termed it) against the error I was in, he might have done it by publishing a treatise on this head, without ever calling my name in 25 question; (3) that what he had published was a mere burlesque upon an answer, leaving four of my eight arguments untouched, and handling the other four in so *gentle* a manner as if he was afraid they would burn his fingers; however, that (4) he had said enough of what was wholly foreign to the question to make an 30 open (and probably irreparable) breach between him and me,[43]

---

[40] JW's brother-in-law, Westley Hall; see May 13, 1738, n. 9, 18:238-39 in this edn.
[41] Cf. Aug. 19, 1740.
[42] In his second paragraph Whitefield said, 'I think it my duty to bear an humble testimony. . .'.
[43] The one 'foreign' matter introduced by Whitefield, and the one which hurt, was that JW had determined to publish by drawing a lot. 'The answer was, *"preach and print"*. I have often questioned, as I do now, whether in so doing, you did not tempt the Lord. A due exercise of religious prudence, without a lot, would have directed you in that matter. Besides, I never heard that you enquired of God, whether or not election was a gospel doctrine? . . . At my desire you suppressed the publishing the sermon whilst I was in England; but soon sent it into the world after my departure. O that you had kept it in!' Whitefield, *Works*, IV.55-56.

seeing 'for a treacherous wound, and for the bewraying of secrets, every friend will depart.'[44]

Mon. 6. I had a long conversation with Peter Böhler. I marvel how I refrain from joining these men. I scarce ever see any of them but my heart burns within me. I long to be with them. And yet I am kept from them.

Tue. 7. I dined with one who had been a professed atheist[45] for upwards of twenty years. But coming some months since to make sport with the Word of God, it cut him to the heart. And he could have no rest day nor night till the God whom he had denied spoke peace to his soul.

In the evening, having desired all the bands to meet, I read over the names of the United Society and marked those who were of a doubtful character, that full inquiry might be made concerning them. On Thursday, at the meeting of that society, I read over the names of these and desired to speak with each of them the next day, or as soon as they had opportunity. Many of them afterwards gave sufficient proof that they were seeking Christ in sincerity. The rest I determined to keep on trial till the doubts concerning them were removed.

Fri. 10. In the evening, at Short's Gardens, I read over in order to expound the eighth chapter to the Romans. But thoughts and words crowded in so fast upon me that I could get no farther than the first verse; nor, indeed, than that single clause, 'Who walk not after the flesh, but after the Spirit'.[46]

Tue. 14. I was much concerned for one of our sisters, who having been but a few times with the 'still brethren', was on a sudden so much wiser than her teachers that I could neither understand her, nor she me. Nor could I help being a little surprised at the profound indifference she showed, who a few days before 'would have plucked out her eyes, had it been possible, and given them to me'.[47]

Wed. 15. I explained at Greyhound Lane the latter part of the fourth chapter to the Ephesians. I was so weak in body that I could hardly stand, but my spirit was much strengthened.

I found myself growing sensibly weaker all Thursday, so that on Friday 17, I could scarce get out of bed, and almost as soon as

---

[44] Cf. Ecclus. 22:22.
[45] 'Bro. Smethurst' (see diary, Apr. 7, 1741).
[46] Rom. 8:1.
[47] Cf. Gal. 4:15.

I was up was constrained to lie down again. Nevertheless, I made shift to drag myself on in the evening to Short's Gardens. Having, not without difficulty, got up the stairs, I read those words (though scarce intelligibly, for my voice too was almost gone), 'Whom he did foreknow, he did also predestinate.'[48] In a moment both my voice and strength returned. And from that time for some weeks I found such bodily strength as I had never done before, since my landing in America.

Mon. 20. Being greatly concerned for those who were tossed about with divers winds of doctrine,[49] many of whom were again entangled in sin, and carried away captive by Satan at his will, I besought God to show me where this would end, and opened my Bible on these words, 'And there was nothing lacking to them, neither small nor great, neither sons nor daughters, neither spoil nor anything that they had taken to them. David recovered all.'[50]

Tue. 21. I wrote to my brother, then at Bristol, in the following words:[51]

As yet I dare in no wise join with the Moravians: (1) because their general scheme is *mystical*, not *scriptural*, refined in every point above what is written, immeasurably beyond the plain gospel; (2) because there is darkness and closeness in all their behaviour, and guile in almost all their words; (3) because they not only do not practise, but utterly despise and decry self-denial and the daily cross; (4) because they conform to the world, in wearing gold and gay or costly apparel; (5) because they extend Christian liberty in many other respects also beyond all warrant of Holy Writ; and (6) because they are by no means zealous of good works, or at least only to their own people. For these reasons (chiefly) I will rather, God being my helper, stand quite alone than join with them; I mean, till I have full assurance that they are better acquainted with 'the truth as it is in Jesus'.[52]

Friday, May 1. I was with one who told me she had been hitherto taught of man, but now she was taught of God only. She added that God had told her not to partake of the Lord's Supper any more, since she fed upon Christ continually. O who is secure from Satan transforming himself into an angel of light![53]

[48] Cf. Rom. 8:29.
[49] See Heb. 13:9; see also list of London bands facing p. 353 below.
[50] 1 Sam. 30:19.
[51] For the complete letter from which this is an extract, see *Letters* 26:55-57 in this edn.
[52] Cf. Eph. 4:21.
[53] See 2 Cor. 11:14.

In the evening I went to a little love-feast which Peter Böhler made for those ten who joined together on this day three years, to 'confess our faults one to another'.[54] Seven of us were present, one being sick and two unwilling to come. Surely the time will
5 return when there shall be again,

Union of mind, as in us all one soul![55]

Sat. 2. I had a conversation of several hours with P. Böhler and Mr. Spangenberg. Our subject was, a new creature,[56] Mr. Spangenberg's account of which was this:

10   The moment we are justified *a new creature* is put into us. This is otherwise termed 'the new man'.[57]
    But notwithstanding, the 'old creature' or the 'old man' remains in us till the day of our death.
    And in this 'old man' there remains an 'old heart', corrupt and
15 abominable. For inward corruption remains in the soul, as long as the soul remains in the body.
    But the *heart* which is in the *new man* is *clean*. And the *new man* is stronger than the *old;* so that though corruption continually *strives*, yet while we look to Christ it cannot *prevail.*

20   I asked him, 'Is there still an *old man* in you?' He said, 'Yes, and will be as long as I live.' I said, 'Is there then corruption in your heart?' He replied, 'In the heart of my *old man* there is, but not in the heart of my *new man.*' I asked, 'Does the experience of your brethren agree with yours?' He answered, 'I know what I have
25 now spoken is the experience of all the brethren and sisters throughout our church.'
    A few of our brethren and sisters sitting by then spoke what *they* experienced. He told them (with great emotion, his hand trembling much), 'You all deceive your own souls. There is no
30 higher state than that I have described. You are in a very dangerous error. You know not your own hearts. You fancy your corruptions are taken away, whereas they are only covered. Inward corruption never can be taken away, till our bodies are in the dust.'
35   Was then inward corruption in our Lord? Or, cannot the servant be *as* his Master?

---

[54] Cf. Jas. 5:16.
[55] Cf. Milton, *Paradise Lost*, viii.604, 'Union of mind, or in us both one soul'.
[56] 2 Cor. 5:17; Gal. 6:15.   [57] Eph. 4:24; Col. 3:10.

Sun. 3. I gave the scriptural account of one who is 'in Christ a new creature', from whom 'old things are passed away', and in whom 'all things are become new'.[58] In the afternoon I explained at Marylebone[59] Fields, to a vast multitude of people, 'He hath showed thee, O man, what is good. And what doth the Lord require of thee, but to do justly, and to love mercy, and to walk humbly with thy God?'[60] The devil's children fought valiantly for their master, that his kingdom should not be destroyed. And many stones fell on my right hand and on my left. But when I began to examine them closely, what reward they were to have for their labour, they vanished away like smoke.

Wed. 6. Was a day on which we agreed to meet for prayer and humbling our souls before God, if haply he might show us his will concerning our reunion with our brethren of Fetter Lane. And to this intent all the men and women bands met, at one in the afternoon. Nor did our Lord cast out our prayer or leave himself without witness among us. But it was clear to all, even those who were before the most eagerly desirous of it, that the time was not come: (1) because they had not given up their most essentially erroneous doctrines; and (2) because many of us had found so much guile in their words that we could scarce tell what they really held, and what not.

Thur. 7. I reminded the United Society that many of our brethren and sisters had not needful food; many were destitute of convenient clothing; many were out of business, and that without their own fault; and many sick and ready to perish: that I had done what in me lay to feed the hungry, to clothe the naked, to employ the poor, and to visit the sick, but was not alone sufficient for these things; and therefore desired all whose hearts were as my heart,

1. To bring what clothes each could spare, to be distributed among those that wanted most.

2. To give weekly a penny, or what they would afford, for the relief of the poor and sick.[61]

'My design (I told them) is to employ for the present all the women who are out of business, and desire it, in knitting.[62]

[58] Cf. 2 Cor. 5:17.
[59] Orig. 'Marybone'.
[60] Mic. 6:8.
[61] From the beginning and throughout JW's lifetime, the London societies contributed far more to the assistance of the poor than to the support of the ministry.
[62] Among the polemics JW had to face at this time were charges of the peril to social

'To these we will first give the common price for what work they do, and then add, according as they need.

'Twelve persons are appointed to inspect these, and to visit and provide things needful for the sick.

5 'Each of these is to visit all the sick within their district, every other day, and to meet on Tuesday evening to give an account of what they have done, and consult what can be done farther.'

This week the Lord of the harvest began to put in his sickle among us. On Tuesday our brother Price, our sister Bowes on 10 Wednesday, today our sister Hawthorn, died.[63] They all went in full and certain hope to him whom their soul loved.

Fri. 8. I found myself much out of order. However I made shift to preach in the evening. But on Saturday my bodily strength quite failed, so that for several hours I could scarce lift up my 15 head. Sun. 10. I was obliged to lie down most part of the day, being easy only in that posture. Yet in the evening my weakness was suspended while I was calling sinners to repentance. But at our love-feast which followed, beside the pain in my back and head, and the fever which still continued upon me, just as I began 20 to pray I was seized with such a cough that I could hardly speak. At the same time came strongly into my mind, 'These signs shall follow them that believe. . . .'[64] I called on Jesus aloud to 'increase my faith',[65] and to 'confirm the word of his grace'.[66] While I was speaking my pain vanished away. The fever left me. My bodily 25 strength returned. And for many weeks I felt neither weakness nor pain. 'Unto thee, O Lord, do I give thanks.'[67]

Thur. 14. Hearing that one[68] was in a high fever of whom I had for some time stood in doubt, I went to her, and asked how she

discipline and morality involved in this industry (cf. *Scots Magazine*, 1741, p. 380). The winter of 1740–41 was a bad period of the business cycle, marked by high food prices, many bankruptcies, and a record demand for spirits. It was not only employment that suffered; Walpole's tenure of political power became increasingly precarious.

[63] The diary refers to S. Price (? an abbreviation for Sister Price). JW had been a frequent visitor at this house the previous August and as recently as April 8. Sister Bowes was probably the wife of George Bowes (see above, July 16, 1740, n. 30). Mrs. Hawthorn and her husband, who often provided hospitality for JW, kept a girls' school and were reported by Charles Wesley on Apr. 8, 1740 (CWJ, I.211), to be 'not far from the kingdom of God'. On May 4, in her last illness, JW took her Communion.

[64] Mark 16:17.

[65] Cf. Luke 17:5.

[66] Cf. Acts 14:3.

[67] Cf. Ps. 75:1.

[68] Nancy Morris (see diary, May 14, 1741). At this time JW was frequently a visitor at Nancy Morris's house for hospitality or worship.

did. She replied, 'I am very ill—but I am very well. Oh, I am happy, happy, happy, for my spirit continually rejoices in God *my* Saviour. All the angels in heaven rejoice in my Saviour. And I rejoice with them, for I am united to Jesus.'

She added, 'How the angels rejoice over an heir of salvation! 5 How they now rejoice over *me!* And I am partaker of their joy. O my Saviour, how happy am I in thee!'

Fri. 15. I called again. She was saying as I came in, 'My Beloved is mine. And he hath cleansed me from all sin. O how far is the heaven above the earth! So far hath he set my sins from me. O 10 how did he rejoice when he 'was heard in that he feared'.[69] He *was* heard, and he gained a possibility of salvation for me and all mankind. It is finished. His grace is free for all. I am a witness. I was the chief of sinners, a backsliding sinner, a sinner against light and love. But I am washed. I am cleansed.' 15

I asked, 'Do you expect to die now?' She said, 'It is not shown me that I shall. But life or death is all one to me. I shall not change my company. Yet I shall more abundantly rejoice when we stand before the Lord; you and I, and all the other children which he hath given you.' 20

In the evening I called upon her again, and found her weaker and her speech much altered. I asked her, 'Do you *now* believe? Do not you find your soul in temptation?' She answered, smiling and looking up, 'There is the Lamb. And where he is, what is temptation? I have no darkness, no cloud. The enemy may come. 25 But he hath no part in me.' I said, 'But does not your sickness hinder you?' She replied, 'Nothing hinders *me.* It is the Spirit of my Father that worketh in me. And nothing hinders that Spirit. My body indeed is weak and in pain. But my soul is all joy and praise.' 30

Sat. 16. I mentioned this to Peter Böhler. But he told me, 'There is no such state on earth. Sin *will* and *must* always remain in the soul. The *old man* will remain till death. The *old nature* is like an *old tooth.* You may break off one bit, and another, and another. But you can never get it all away. The stump of it will stay 35 as long as you live, and sometimes will *ache* too.'

Mon. 18. At the pressing instance of my brother I left London, and the next evening met him at Bristol. I was a little surprised when I came into the room, just after he had ended his sermon.

[69] Heb. 5:7.

Some wept aloud. Some clapped their hands, some shouted, and
the rest sang praise, with whom (having soon recovered
themselves) the whole congregation joined. So (I trust) if ever
God were pleased that we should suffer for the truth's sake, all
5 other sounds would soon be swallowed up in the voice of praise
and thanksgiving.

Wed. 20. I spent most of the morning in speaking with the new
members of the society. In the afternoon I saw the sick; but not
one in fear, neither repining against God.

10 Thur. 21. In the evening I published the great decree of God,
eternal, unchangeable (so miserably misunderstood and misrepresented by vain men that would be wise), 'He that believeth
shall be saved; he that believeth not shall be damned.'[70]

Sat. 23. At a meeting of the stewards of the society (who receive
15 and expend what is contributed weekly) it was found needful to
retrench the expenses, the contributions not answering thereto.
And it was accordingly agreed to discharge two of the schoolmasters at Bristol, the present fund being barely sufficient to
keep two masters and a mistress here, and one master and a
20 mistress at Kingswood.[71]

Mon. 25. Having settled all the business on which I came, I set
out early, and on Tuesday called at Windsor. I found here also a
few who have peace with God and are full of love both to him and
to one another. In the evening I preached at the Foundery yet
25 again, on 'Stand still, and see the salvation of the Lord.'[72]

Fri. 29. I spent an hour with poor Mr. M[acCun]e.[73] His usual
frown was vanished away. His look was clear, open, and
composed. He listened to the word of reconciliation with all
possible marks of deep attention, though he was too weak to
30 speak. Before I went we commended him to the grace of God in

[70] Cf. Mark 16:16.
[71] On Apr. 27, 1741, JW had written to Whitefield, resisting his charges of extravagance at Bristol and claiming that expenditure there had not been at the expense of Kingswood. See *Letters*, 26:58-61 in this edn.
[72] Exod. 14:13.
[73] In a letter to JW of Dec. 13, 1740 (Curnock, VIII.273), Susanna Wesley wrote: 'I am somewhat troubled at the case of poor Mr. McCune. I think his wife was ill-advised to send for that wretched fellow Monroe [the physician of Bedlam], for by what I hear, the man is not a lunatic, but rather under strong conviction of sin, and hath much more need of a spiritual than a bodily physician.' Curnock notes that he 'eventually joined the "Still Brethren"' (II.418). The Wesleys had been frequent visitors to the MacCunes' household up to this time.

confidence that our prayer was heard: to whom at two in the morning he resigned his spirit without any sign or groan.

Tuesday, June 2. I spoke plainly to Mr. Piers, who told me he had been much shaken by the 'still brethren'. But the snare is broken; I left him rejoicing in hope and praising God for the 5 consolation.

Thur. 4. I exhorted a crowded congregation 'not to receive the grace of God in vain'.[74] The same exhortation I enforced on the society (about nine hundred persons), and by their fruits it doth appear that they begin to love one another, 'not in word' only, 'but 10 in deed and in truth'.[75]

Fri. 5. Hearing that a deaf and dumb man near Marienborn had procured a remarkable letter to be wrote into England, I asked James Hutton if he knew of that letter, and what the purport of it was. He answered, yes, he had read the letter but had quite 15 forgot what it was about. I then asked Mr. V[iney], who replied, the letter was short, but he did not remember the purport of it.

Sun. 7. I preached in Charles Square[76] on, 'The hour is coming, and now is, when the dead shall hear the voice of the Son of God, and they that hear shall live.'[77] A violent storm of rain 20 began about the middle of the sermon. But these things move not those who seek the Lord. So much the more was his power present to heal, insomuch that many of our hearts danced for joy, praising 'the glorious God that maketh the thunder'.[78]

Mon. 8. I set out from Enfield Chase[79] for Leicestershire. In 25 the evening we came to Northampton, and the next afternoon to Mr. Ellis's[80] at Markfield, five or six miles beyond Leicester.

For these two days I had made an experiment which I had been so often and earnestly pressed to do, speaking to none concerning

[74] Cf. 2 Cor. 6:1.

[75] Cf. 1 John 3:18.

[76] Charles Square, Hoxton, came to be a place where great evangelical meetings were mustered. Cf. below, May 9, 1742, n. 60.

[77] John 5:25.

[78] Ps. 29:3 (BCP).

[79] Orig., 'Chace'. Enfield Chase was a residence of Lady Huntingdon, and it is probable that Wesley was moved to the Midlands by the desire to see the evangelistic work being undertaken in the neighbourhood of her seat at Donington.

[80] Ellis was the incumbent of Markfield and a firm friend of the Wesleys. Charles Wesley notes: 'I preached twice in Markfield church, and was much comforted with my brother Ellis, and his little increasing flock. I talked with several, and took knowledge of them that they have been with Jesus.' CWJ, Oct. 9, 1743 (I.337); *Wesleyan Methodist Magazine* (1856), 79:233.

the things of God, unless 'my heart was free' to it. And what was the event? Why, (1) that I spoke to none at all for fourscore miles together; no, not even to him that travelled with me in the chaise, unless a few words at first setting out; (2) that I had *no cross* either
5 to bear or to take up, and commonly in an hour or two fell fast asleep; (3) that I had much respect shown me wherever I came, everyone behaving to me as to a *civil, good-natured gentleman.* O how pleasing is all this to flesh and blood! Need ye 'compass sea and land'[81] to make proselytes to this!
10 Wed. 10. I preached in the morning, on 'The inward kingdom of God'. And many, I trust, found they were heathens in heart and Christians in name only.

In the afternoon we came to J[oseph] C[aladi]n's,[82] about ten miles beyond Markfield, a plain, open-hearted man, desirous to
15 know and do the will of God. I was a little surprised at what he said. 'A few months since there was a great awakening all round us. But since Mr. S[impson][83] came, three parts in four are fallen as fast asleep as ever.' I spoke to him of drawing people from the church and advising them to leave off prayer. He said there was
20 no Church of England left, and that there was no Scripture for family prayer nor for praying in private at any particular times, which a believer need not do. I asked what our Saviour then meant by saying, 'Enter into thy closet and pray'?[84] He said, 'Oh! that means, enter into the closet of your heart.' ·
25 Between five and six we came to Ockbrook,[85] where Mr. S[impso]n then was. I asked Mr. Greaves[86] what doctrine he taught here. He said: 'The sum of all is this: If you will believe, *be still.* Do not pretend to *do good* (which you can't do, till you believe), and leave off what you call the 'means of grace', such as
30 prayer and running to Church and Sacrament.'

About eight, Mr. Greaves offering me the use of his church, I

[81] Matt. 23:15.
[82] Joseph Caladin seems to have belonged to a family resident at Hemington near Castle Donington. WHS, 8:110-12.
[83] John Simpson, who had troubled the Wesleys so greatly at Fetter Lane (see above, Apr. 19, 1740, n. 37). For a time he was in charge of the Moravian society at Ockbrook, but was removed for forming a party and for erroneous teaching. For an example of Simpson's yielding to the direct leading of the Spirit at Ockbrook, see *Methodist Magazine* (1808), 31:315.
[84] Cf. Matt. 6:6.
[85] Orig., 'Ogbrook'. The society at Ockbrook had been founded by Benjamin Ingham and handed over to the United Brethren when he became a Moravian.
[86] William Greaves, vicar of Ockbrook, 1734-65.

explained the true gospel stillness; and in the morning, Thursday 11, to a large congregation, 'By grace ye are saved through faith.'[87]

In the afternoon we went on to Nottingham, where Mr. Howe[88] received us gladly. At eight the society met, as usual. I could not but observe (1) that the room was not half full, which used till very lately to be crowded within and without; (2) that not one person who came in used any prayer at all, but every one immediately sat down and began either talking to his neighbour or looking about to see who was there; (3) that when I began to pray there appeared a general surprise, none once offering to kneel down, and those who stood choosing the most easy indolent posture which they conveniently could. I afterward looked for one of our hymnbooks upon the desk (which I knew Mr. Howe had brought from London), but both that and the Bible were vanished away. And in the room lay the Moravian hymns and the Count's 'sermons'.

I expounded (but with a heavy heart), 'Believe in the Lord Jesus, and thou shalt be saved,'[89] and the next morning described (if haply some of the secure ones might awake from the sleep of death) the fruits of true faith, 'righteousness, and peace, and joy in the Holy Ghost'.[90]

In the evening we came to Markfield again, where the church was quite full while I explained, 'All we like sheep have gone astray, and God hath laid on him the iniquity of us all.'[91]

Sat. 13. In the morning I preached on those words, 'To him that worketh not, but believeth on him that justifieth the ungodly, his faith is counted to him for righteousness.'[92] We then set out for Melbourne, where finding the house too small to contain those who were come together, I stood under a large tree and

---

[87] Cf. Eph. 2:8.

[88] John How (Howe, Howes), a merchant hosier who had met JW in London, where How retained a room for personal use and the storage of merchandise, and who is said to have 'introduced Methodism into Nottingham' (G. H. Harwood, *History of Wesleyan Methodism in Nottingham* [Nottingham, 1872], p. 9); R. C. Swift, *Lively People — Methodism in Nottingham 1740–1929* [Nottingham, 1982], pp. 1-4). How seems in fact to have been the leader of a religious society gradually becoming Moravian, out of which Charles Wesley formed the first Methodist society on June 24, 1743 (CWJ, I.319; WHS, 5:167). He was doubtless the 'John How, Nottingham', enrolled among the Moravian Brethren when the first Moravian congregation was constituted at Fulneck in 1746. Benham, *Hutton*, p. 231 n.

[89] Cf. Acts 16:31.

[90] Rom. 14:17.

[91] Cf. Isa. 53:6.

[92] Cf. Rom. 4:5.

declared 'him whom God hath exalted to be a Prince and a Saviour, to give repentance unto Israel, and remission of sins'.[93]

Thence I went to Hemington,[94] where also, the house not being large enough to contain the people, they stood about the
5 door and at both the windows while I showed 'what we must do to be saved'.[95]

One of our company seemed a little offended when I had done, at 'a vile fellow, notorious all over the country for cursing, swearing, and drunkenness, though he was now grey-headed,
10 being near fourscore years of age'. He came to me, and catching me hold by the hands, said, 'Whether thou art a good or a bad man I know not. But I know the words thou speakest are good. I never heard the like in all my life. Oh, that God would set them home upon *my* poor soul!' He then burst into tears, so that he
15 could speak no more.

Sun. 14. I rode to Nottingham again, and at eight preached at the market-place to an immense multitude of people, on 'The dead shall hear the voice of the Son of God, and they that hear shall live.'[96] I saw only one or two who behaved lightly, whom I
20 immediately spoke to, and they stood reproved. Yet soon after a man behind me began aloud to contradict and blaspheme. But upon my turning to him, he stepped behind a pillar and in a few minutes disappeared.

In the afternoon we returned to Markfield. The church was so
25 excessive hot, being crowded in every corner, that I could not without difficulty read the evening service. Being afterwards informed that abundance of people were still without who could not possibly get into the church, I went out to them, and explained that great promise of our Lord, 'I will heal their backsliding; I will
30 love them freely.'[97] In the evening I expounded in the church on her who 'loved much, because she had had much forgiven'.[98]

Mon. 15. I set out for London and read over in the way that celebrated book, Martin Luther's Comment on the Epistle to the Galatians.[99] I was utterly ashamed. How have I esteemed this

---

[93] Cf. Acts 5:31.
[94] Hemington was a small township in the parish of Lockington, 8 miles NW. from Loughborough.
[95] Cf. Acts 16:30.   [96] John 5:25.
[97] Hos. 14:4.   [98] Cf. Luke 7:47.
[99] JW's revulsion against the work which had been instrumental in his brother's conversion is a measure both of his anxiety at the current situation and the degree to which his own mind was returning to old channels.

book, only because I had heard it commended by others! Or, at best, because I had read some excellent sentences occasionally quoted from it. But what shall I say, now I judge for myself? Now I see with my own eyes? Why, not only that the author makes nothing out, clears up not one considerable difficulty; that he is 5 quite shallow in his remarks on many passages, and muddy and confused almost on all; but that he is deeply tinctured with *mysticism* throughout, and hence often fundamentally[1] wrong. To instance only in one or two points. How does he (almost in the words of Tauler) decry *reason*, right or wrong, as an irreconcilable 10 enemy to the gospel of Christ! Whereas, what is *reason* (the faculty so called) but the power of apprehending, judging, and discoursing? Which power is no more to be condemned in the gross than seeing, hearing, or feeling. Again, how blasphemously does he speak of good works and of the law of God! Constantly 15 coupling the law with sin, death, hell, or the devil! And teaching that Christ 'delivers us from' them all alike. Whereas it can no more be proved by Scripture that Christ 'delivers us from the law of God' than that he delivers us *from holiness* or *from heaven*. Here (I apprehend) is the real spring of the grand error of the 20 Moravians. They follow Luther, for better, for worse. Hence their 'No works, no law, no commandments.' But who art thou that 'speaketh evil of the law, and judgest the law'?[2]

Tue. 16. In the evening I came to London and preached on those words, 'In Christ Jesus neither circumcision availeth 25 anything, nor uncircumcision, but faith which worketh by love.'[c] After reading Luther's miserable comment upon the text, I thought it my bounden duty openly to warn the congregation against that dangerous treatise and to retract whatever recommendation I might ignorantly have given of it. 30

Wed. 17. I set out and rode slowly toward Oxford. But before I came to Wycombe my horse tired. There I hired another, which tired also before I came to Tetsworth. I hired a third here and reached Oxford in the evening.

Thur. 18. I inquired concerning the exercises previous to the 35 degree of Bachelor in Divinity[3] and advised with Mr. Gambold

[c] Gal. 5:6.

---

[1] 1774, 'dangerously'.   [2] Cf. Jas. 4:11.
[3] Theological disputations had come to an end in Anne's reign, and the candidate for the B.D. degree now went through a farce of responding to standard questions with standard answers which he could purchase for five shillings. Early in the nineteenth

concerning the subject of my sermon before the University. But he seemed to think it of no moment:[4] 'For (said he) all here are so prejudiced that they will mind nothing you say.' I know not that. However, I am to deliver my own soul, whether they will hear, or
5 whether they will forbear.[5]

I found a great change among the poor people here. Out of twenty-five or thirty weekly communicants only two were left. Not one continued to attend the daily prayers of the Church. And those few that were once united together were now torn asunder
10 and scattered abroad.

Mon. 22. The words on which my book opened at the society in the evening were these, 'Ye have forsaken my ordinances, and have not kept them. Return unto me, and I will return unto you, saith the Lord of hosts. . . . Your words have been stout against
15 me, saith the Lord. But ye say, Wherein have we spoken against thee? Ye have said, It is vain that we worship God. And, What profit is it that we keep his ordinances?'[d]

Wed. 24. I read over and partly transcribed, Bishop Bull's *Harmonia Apostolica*.[6] The position with which he sets out is this,
20 'That *all good works*, and *not faith alone*, are the necessarily previous *condition of justification*,' or the forgiveness of our sins. But in the middle of the treatise he asserts that 'faith alone is the condition of justification'; 'For *faith*', says he, 'referred to justification, *means all* inward and outward *good works*.' In the
25 latter end he affirms that 'there are *two justifications*, and that *only*

[d] Mal. 3[:7, 13-14].

---

century this system was replaced by the requirement of a Latin thesis on a subject approved by the Regius Professor. The theses could also be bought, but the price went up to eight guineas. W. R. Ward, *Victorian Oxford* (London, 1965), p. 53.

[4] Following John Gambold's advice, JW wrote a savage attack on the doctrine and religious practice of the university, on Isa. 1:21: 'How is the faithful city become an harlot.' However, he scrapped this discourse and preached instead his famous sermon on *The Almost Christian*, which became No. 2 of the *Sermons* (see below, July 25, 1741, n. 24). The discarded sermon was published posthumously (see Sermon 150, 'Hypocrisy in Oxford', 4:392-407 in this edn.). The diary entry for June 28, 1741, lends support to Curnock's construction that it was Lady Huntingdon who persuaded JW not to preach his first thoughts.

[5] Ezek. 2:5, etc.

[6] George Bull (1634–1710), theologian and Bishop of St. David's (1705–10), sought in his first work, *Harmonia Apostolica* (London, 1670), to harmonize the views of Paul and James on the relationship of faith and works in justification, concluding that the former should be construed in the light of the latter on grounds that he (James) wrote later than Paul and might be presumed to be familiar with Paul's views.

inward good works necessarily precede the *former*, but both *inward and outward* the *latter*.'[7]

Sat. 27. I rode to London and enforced in the evening that solemn declaration of the great Apostle, 'Do we then make void the law through faith? God forbid. Yea, we establish the law.'[8]

Sun. 28. I showed in the morning at large, 'Where the Spirit of the Lord is, there is liberty';[9] liberty from sin, liberty to be, to do, and to suffer, according to the written Word. At five I preached at Charles Square to the largest congregation that, I believe, was ever seen there, on 'Almost thou persuadest me to be a Christian.'[10] As soon as I had done I quite lost my voice. But it was immediately restored when I came to our little flock with the blessing of the gospel of peace, and I spent an hour and half in exhortation and prayer, without any hoarseness, faintness, or weariness.[11]

Mon. 29. I preached in the morning on, 'Ye are saved through faith.'[12] In the afternoon I expounded at Windsor the story of the Pharisee and publican. I spent the evening at Wycombe, and the next morning, Tuesday 30, returned to Oxford.

Thursday, July 2, I met Mr. Gambold again, who honestly told me he was *ashamed* of my company, and *therefore* must be excused from going to the society with me. This is plain dealing at least!

Sat. 4. I had much talk with Mr. V[iney], who allowed (1) that *there are many* (not one only) *commands* of God, both to believers and unbelievers; and (2) that the Lord's Supper, the Scripture, and both public and private prayer, are God's ordinary *means* of conveying *grace* to man. But what will this private, oral confession avail, so long as the quite contrary is still declared in those *Sixteen Discourses* published to all the world and never yet either corrected or retracted?[13]

---

[7] JW's quotations from the three portions of the *Harmonia Apostolica* represent his very paraphrastic translations from a Latin text referring to the argument, especially in Diss. I, Ch.III. §4; IV. §9; Diss. II, IV. §4; V. §1; XVIII. §8. In George Bull, *Opera Omnia*, ed. J. E. Grabe (London, 1721), pp. 424, 444, 447, 514-15. An English translation was later published in the Library of Anglo-Catholic Theology (Oxford, 1842).

[8] Rom. 3:31.

[9] 2 Cor. 3:17.

[10] Acts 26:28. Cf. June 18, 1741, n. 4; July 25, 1741, n. 3.

[11] The diary shows that, despite weariness, JW went to Lady Huntingdon's at 10 p.m., continued discussing his sermon till 2 a.m., and, presumably after resting, took tea at 3.30 a.m., and preached at the Foundery at 5.30.

[12] Cf. Eph. 2:8.

[13] Count Zinzendorf, *Sixteen Discourses on the Redemption of Man by the Death of Christ. . . . Translated from the High Dutch* (London, for James Hutton, 1740).

Mon. 6. Looking for a book in our college library, I took down, by mistake, Episcopius,[14] the works of which, opening on an account of the Synod of Dort, I believed it might be useful to read it through. But what a scene is here disclosed! I wonder not at the
5 heavy curse of God, which so soon after fell on our Church and nation. What pity it is that the holy Synod of Trent and that of Dort did not sit at the same time! Nearly allied as they were, not only as to the *purity of doctrine* which each of them established, but also as to the *spirit* wherewith they acted! If the latter did not
10 exceed.

Thur. 9. Being in the Bodleian Library, I light on Mr. Calvin's account of the case of Michael Servetus,[15] several of whose letters he occasionally inserts, wherein Servetus often declares in terms, 'I believe the Father is God, the Son is God, and the Holy Ghost
15 is God.' Mr. Calvin, however, paints him such a monster as never was—an Arian, a blasphemer, and what not? Besides, strewing over him his flowers of *dog, devil, swine,* and so on, which are the usual appellations he gives to his opponents. But still he utterly denies his being the cause of Servetus's death. 'No', says he, 'I
20 *only advised* our magistrates, as having a right to restrain heretics by the sword, to seize upon and try that arch-heretic. But after he was condemned *I said not one word about his execution*'!

Fri. 10. I rode to London and preached at Short's Gardens on 'the name of Jesus Christ of Nazareth'.[16] Sun. 12. While I was
25 showing at Charles Square what it is 'to do justly, to love mercy, and to walk humbly with our God',[17] a great shout began. Many

14 Simon Episcopius (1583–1643), who was expelled by the Synod of Dort in 1618 from his position as professor of divinity at Leiden, being the leader of the Arminian party. The only work attributed to Episcopius in Lincoln College Library now, and almost certainly the one consulted by JW, *Confessio sive declaratio sententiae Pastorum qui in Foederato Belgio Remonstrantes vocantur super praecipuis articulis Religionis Christianae* (Horderwyck, 1622), is bound with another work, *Apologia pro Confessione sive Declaratione Sententiae eorum qui in Foederato Belgio vocantur Remonstrantes, super praecipuis Articulis Religionis Christianae, Contra Censuram Quatuor Professorum Leidensium* (1630). Hence, no doubt, JW's accidental discovery of Episcopius. I am indebted for this information to the kindness of Dr. V. H. H. Green.

15 *Defensio Orthodoxae Fidei*, 1554. For another unacknowledged reference by JW to this work see Sermon 55, *On the Trinity* (1775), §4 (2:378 in this edn.). Michael Servetus (1511–53), physician and theologian, born in Navarre, wrote extensively against the errors of the doctrine of the Trinity. After the anonymous publication of his principal work, *Christianismi Restitutio*, in 1553, he was denounced to the Catholic Inquisition by a friend of Calvin and imprisoned. However, he escaped to Geneva, where Calvin had him arrested. When he refused to recant, he was burnt as a heretic.

16 Acts 3:6; 4:10.
17 Cf. Mic. 6:8.

of the rabble had brought an ox, which they were vehemently labouring to drive in among the people. But their labour was in vain, for in spite of them all he ran round and round, one way and the other, and at length broke through the midst of them clear away, leaving us calmly rejoicing and praising God.   5

Mon. 13. I returned to Oxford, and on Wednesday rode to Bristol. My brother, I found, was already gone to Wales. So that I came just in season; and that, indeed, on another account also, for a spirit of enthusiasm was breaking in upon many, who charged their own *imaginations* on the 'will of God', and that not *written*,   10 but 'impressed on their hearts'. If these *impressions* be received as the rule of action instead of the *written Word*, I know nothing so wicked or absurd but we may fall into, and that without remedy.

Fri. 17. The school at Kingswood was thoroughly filled between eight and nine in the evening. I showed them from the   15 example of the Corinthians, what need we have to bear one with another, seeing we are not to expect 'many fathers in Christ',[18] no, nor young men among us as yet. We then poured out our souls in prayer and praise, and our Lord did not hide his face from us.

Sun. 19. After preaching twice at Bristol, and twice at   20 Kingswood, I earnestly exhorted the society to continue in the faith, 'enduring hardship as good soldiers of Jesus Christ'.[19] On Monday (my brother being now returned from Wales) I rode back to Oxford.

Wed. 22. At the repeated instance of some that were there I   25 went over to Abingdon. I preached on, 'What must I do to be saved?'[20] Both the yard and house were full. But so stupid, senseless a people, both in a spiritual and natural sense, I scarce ever saw before. Yet God is able of 'these stones to raise up children to Abraham'.[21]   30

Fri. 24. Several of our friends from London, and some from Kingswood and Bristol, came to Oxford. Alas! How long shall they 'come from the east and from the west and sit down in the kingdom of God',[22] while the children of the kingdom will not come in, but remain in utter darkness!   35

Sat. July 25. It being my turn (which comes about once in three years), I preached at St. Mary's before the university. The harvest

[18] Cf. 1 Cor. 4:15.   [19] Cf. 2 Tim. 2:3.
[20] Acts 16:30.
[21] Matt. 3:9.
[22] Cf. Luke 13:29.

truly is plenteous.[23] So numerous a congregation (from whatever motives they came) I have seldom seen at Oxford. My text was the confession of poor Agrippa, 'Almost thou persuadest me to be a Christian.'[24] I have 'cast my bread upon the waters'. Let me 'find
5 it again after many days'![25]

In the afternoon I set out (having no time to spare) and on Sunday 26 preached at the Foundery, on the *liberty* we have 'to enter into the holiest by the blood of Jesus'.[26]

Mon. 27. Finding notice had been given that I would preach in
10 the evening at Hackney, I went thither and openly declared those glad tidings, 'By grace ye are saved through faith.'[27] Many, we heard, had threatened terrible things. But no man opened his mouth. Perceive ye not yet that 'greater is he that is in us, than he that is in the world'?[28]

15 Tue. 28. I visited one[29] that was going heavily and in fear through the valley of the shadow of death.[30] But God heard the prayer, and soon lifted up the light of his countenance upon her. So that she immediately broke out into thanksgiving, and the next day quietly fell asleep.

20 Fri. 31. Hearing that one of our sisters (Jane Muncy)[31] was ill, I went to see her. She was [in] one of the first women['s] bands at Fetter Lane, and when the controversy concerning the *means of grace* began, stood in the gap and contended earnestly for the ordinances once delivered to the saints. When soon after it was
25 ordered that 'the unmarried men and women should have no conversation with each other,' she again withstood to the face those who were 'teaching for doctrines the commandments of

---

23 Matt. 9:37.
24 Acts 26:28. The sermon was published Aug. 16, 1741, as *The Almost Christian.* See Sermon 2, 1:131-41 in this edn. Cf. above, June 18, 1741, n. 4.
25 Cf. Eccles. 11:1.   26 Heb. 10:19.
27 Cf. Eph. 2:8.
28 Cf. 1 John 4:4.
29 As this was the last occasion that JW's diary records a visit to Nancy Morris, whose illness was reported in JWJ, May 14, 1741 (see also n. 68 under that date), it is probably her death that is here described.
30 Ps. 23:4.
31 The passage commencing with the next sentence and continuing for four paragraphs has a double interest. Jane Muncy was one of the women who followed JW when the Fetter Lane Society divided (WHS, 16:145), and her exemplary death has thus a dramatic appropriateness in JW's anti-Moravian polemic. Then, secondly, the passage was reprinted by JW in the *Arminian Magazine* (1781), IV.153, and accords with diary evidence that many of the accounts which Wesley there published were first prepared for reading in bands and contributed to the third of their three categories of spiritual pabulum, systematic Bible exposition, hymns, and religious experience.

men'.[32] Nor could all the sophistry of those who are, without controversy, of all men living the wisest in their generation, induce her either to deny the faith she had received, or to use less plainness of speech or to be less zealous in recommending, and careful in practising, good works. Insomuch that many times 5 when she had been employed in the labour of love till eight or nine in the evening, she then sat down and wrought with her hands till twelve or one in the morning; not that she wanted anything herself, but that she might have to give to others for necessary uses. 10

From the time that she was made leader of one or two bands she was more eminently a pattern to the flock: in self-denial of every kind, in openness of behaviour, in simplicity and godly sincerity, in steadfast faith, in constant attendance on all the public and all the private ordinances of God. And as she had 15 *laboured* more than they all, so God now called her forth to suffer. She was seized at first with a violent fever, in the beginning of which they removed her to another house. Here she had work to do which she knew not of. The master of the house was one who cared for none of these things. But he observed her, and was 20 convinced. So that he then began to understand and lay to heart the things that bring a man peace at the last.

In a few days the fever abated, or settled, as it seemed, into an inward impostume, so that she could not breathe without violent pain, which increased day and night. When I came in she 25 stretched out her hand and said, 'Art thou come, thou blessed of the Lord? Praised be the name of my Lord for this.' I asked, 'Do you faint, now you are chastened of him?' She said, 'O no, no, no. I faint not. I murmur not. I rejoice evermore.' I said, 'But can you in everything give thanks?'[33] She replied, 'Yes, I do, I do.' I said, 30 'God will make all your bed in your sickness.'[34] She cried out, 'He does, he does. I have nothing to desire. He is ever with me, and I have nothing to do but to praise him.'

In the same state of mind, though weaker and weaker in body, she continued till Tuesday following, when several of those who 35 had been in her band being present, she fixed her eyes upon them and fell into a kind of agonizing prayer, that God would keep them from the evil one. But in the afternoon when I came, she was

[32] Matt. 15:9; Mark 7:7.
[33] Cf. 1 Thess. 5:18.
[34] Cf. Ps. 41:3.

quite calm again, and all her words were prayer and praise. The same spirit she breathed when Mr. Maxfield called the next day. And soon after he went she slept in peace.—'A mother in Israel'[35] hast thou been, and 'thy works shall praise thee in the gates'![36]

5   Saturday, August 1. I had a long conversation with Mr. Ingham. We both agreed (1) that none shall finally be saved who have not, as they had opportunity, done all good works; and (2) that if a justified person does not do good as he has opportunity, he will lose the grace he has received, and if he 'repent' not 'and 10 do the former works',[37] will perish eternally. But with regard to the unjustified (if I understand him), we wholly disagreed. He believed it is not the will of God that they should wait for faith *in doing good.* I believe this is the will of God, and that they will never find him unless they seek him in this way.

15   Sun. 2. I went, after having been long importuned by Mr. Deleznot,[38] to the chapel in Great Hermitage Street, Wapping. Mr. Meriton[39] (a clergyman from the Isle of Man) read prayers. I then preached on those words in the former Lesson, 'Seest thou how Ahab humbleth himself? Because he hath humbled himself I 20 will not bring this evil in his days,'[40] and took occasion thence to exhort all unbelievers to use the grace God had already given

35 Judg. 5:7.

36 Cf. Prov. 31:31.

37 Cf. Rev. 2:5.

38 Rev. J. L. Deleznot, who in 1734–35 ministered at a Huguenot chapel in Swanfields. In the 1774 edn. 'Mr.' was changed to 'Dr.'. Part of JW's later apologetic for his position in relation to the Church of England was that although he administered Communion to members of his society, two hundred at a time, in Mr. Deleznot's chapel, he nevertheless advised 'those who had the Sacrament at their parish churches' to attend there. See 'Farther Thoughts on Separation from the Church' (1786; 9:538-40 in this edn.) and 'A Short History of the People called Methodists' (1781; 9:425-503 in this edn.). Even so, 'the rest communicated at St. Paul's, or at their several parish churches'. *Arminian Magazine* (1786), IX.676.

39 Rev. John Meriton (1698–1753), matriculated from Caius College, Cambridge, 1716, B.A., 1720, was an Englishman ordained by the Bishop of Norwich in 1723, who had met opposition to his evangelical preaching in the Isle of Man but found a welcome among the Methodists. He consulted Whitefield about going to Georgia, and it was Whitefield who secured him for the Methodists (Tyerman, *Whitefield*, I.558-60; II.39,44). He was invited by JW to the first Methodist Conference in 1744. Just before this event Charles Wesley reported him as 'longing to escape to us out of the hands of Calvin' (CWJ, May 10, 1744; I.365). He became the regular travelling companion of the Wesley brothers, is believed to have acted as amanuensis in 1748, and suffered a large share of the violence which accompanied the early Methodist preaching missions. Though his relations with the Wesleys cooled, Charles Wesley commemorated his death and sufferings by an elegy. CWJ, II.303-5; *Wesleyan Methodist Magazine* (1900), 123:495-501.

40 Cf. 1 Kgs. 21:29.

them, and in keeping his law according to the power they now had, to wait for the faith of the gospel.

Fri. 7. The body of our sister Muncy being brought to Short's Gardens, I preached on those words, 'Write! From henceforth, blessed are the dead which die in the Lord. Even so, saith the Spirit; for they rest from their labours, and their works do follow them.'[41] From thence we went with it to the grave, in St. Giles's Churchyard, where I performed the last office, in the presence of such an innumerable multitude of people as I never saw gathered together before. O what a sight will it be when God saith to the grave, 'Give back!' And all the dead, small and great, shall stand before him![42]

Wed. 12. I visited one whom God is purifying in the fire in answer to the prayers of his wife, whom he was just going to beat (which he frequently did) when God smote him in a moment, so that his hand dropped, and he fell down upon the ground, having no more strength than a newborn child. He has been confined to his bed ever since, but rejoices in hope of the glory of God.[43]

Fri. 14. Calling on a person near Grosvenor Square, I found there was but too much reason here for crying out of the increase of popery, many converts to it being continually made by the gentleman who preaches in Swallow Street three days in every week.[44]

Now why do not the champions who are continually crying out, 'Popery, popery', in Moorfields, come hither, that they may not always be fighting 'as one that beateth the air'?[45] Plainly because they have no mind to fight at all but to show their valour without an opponent. And they well know, they may defy popery at the Foundery without any danger of contradiction.

Wed. 19. The Scripture which came in turn to be expounded was the ninth chapter to the Romans. I was even constrained to speak an hour longer than usual, and am persuaded most, if not all who were present, saw that this chapter has no more to do

[41] Cf. Rev. 14:13. [42] See Rev. 20:12.
[43] See Rom. 5:2.
[44] No trace of this preacher has been found in the Westminster diocesan records. Many of the West End chapels favoured by the Catholic aristocracy originated in the embassy chapels of the foreign diplomatic corps. Despite JW's derogatory remarks, Moorfields was growing steadily into the principal centre of London Catholicism, and by the early nineteenth century it supported in St. Mary's a kind of cathedral for the London district. J. Bossy, *The English Catholic Community, 1570–1850* (New York, 1976), p. 311.
[45] 1 Cor. 9:26.

with personal, irrespective predestination than the ninth of Genesis.

Thur. 20. A clergyman having sent me word that if I would preach in the evening on the text he named he would come to hear
5 me, I preached on that text, Matt. 24:26. And strongly enforced the caution of our Lord to 'beware of false prophets',[46] i.e., all preachers who do not speak as the oracles of God.

Tue. 25. I explained at Chelsea[47] the nature and necessity of the new birth. One (who, I afterwards heard, was a Dissenting
10 teacher) asked me when I had done, 'Quid est tibi nomen?'[48] And on my not answering, turned in triumph to his companions and said, 'Ay, I told you he did not understand Latin!'

Wed. 26. I was informed of a remarkable conversation at which one of our sisters was present a day or two before; wherein a
15 gentleman was assuring his friends that he himself was in Charles Square when a person told Mr. Wesley to his face that he (Mr. Wesley) had paid twenty pounds already, on being convicted for selling Geneva,[49] and that he now kept two popish priests in his house. This gave occasion to another to mention what he had
20 himself heard at an eminent Dissenting teacher's, viz., That it was beyond dispute Mr. Wesley had large remittances from Spain in order to make a party among the poor, and that as soon as the Spaniards landed, he was to join them with twenty thousand men.[50]

25 Mon. 31. I began my course of preaching on the Common Prayer. Tuesday, September 1. I read over Mr. Whitefield's account of God's dealings with his soul.[51] Great part of this I

---

[46] Matt. 7:15.

[47] Zinzendorf lived at Chelsea and hoped to create a settlement there. In 1750 James Hutton acquired a long lease of a property in Chelsea from Sir Hans Sloane. A residence, chapel, and burial ground were created there and plans laid for a settlement on continental lines. Twenty years later a financial crisis forced the alienation of the property with the exception of the clergyhouse, chapel, and burial ground. Hamilton, *Moravian Church*, p. 146.

[48] 'What is your name?' — the opening question of the Catechism in the BCP.

[49] I.e., a spirit distilled from grain and flavoured with juniper berries.

[50] The spy mania and fears of internal treachery generated by the war years, 1739–48, brought anti-Methodist hysteria to its highest point. The closed meetings and national organisation of the Methodist movement evoked the same kind of charges as later became commonplace in anti-Catholic agitations in the United States; and, in time of war, allegations of covert popery could easily, as here, take on the colouring of political conspiracy. On this subject see John Walsh, 'Methodism and the mob in the eighteenth century', *Studies in Church History*, 8 (Cambridge, 1972), 213-27.

[51] Apparently a letter of which no trace has been found. Whitefield was engaged on an evangelistic tour in Scotland.

know to be true. 'O let not mercy and truth forsake thee! Bind them about thy neck! Write them upon the table of thy heart'![52]

Thur. 3. James Hutton having sent me word that Count Zinzendorf would meet me at three in the afternoon, I went at that time to Gray's Inn Walks. The most material part of our 5 conversation (which I dare not conceal) was as follows—to spare the dead I do not translate.[53]

Z. *Cur religionem tuam mutasti?*

W. *Nescio me religionem meam mutasse. Cur id sentis? Quis hoc tibi retulit?* 10

Z. *Plane tu. Id ex epistola tua ad nos video. Ibi, religione quam apud nos professus es, relicta, novam profiteris.*

W. *Qui sic? Non intelligo.*

Z. *Imo, istic dicis, vere Christianos non esse miseros peccatores. Falsissimum. Optimi hominum ad mortem usque miserabilissimi sunt* 15 *peccatores. Siqui aliud dicunt, vel penitus impostores sunt, vel diabolice seducti. Nostros fratres meliora docentes impugnasti. Et pacem volentibus, eam denegasti.*

W. *Nondum intelligo quid velis.*

Z. *Ego, cum ex Georgia ad me scripsisti, te dilexi plurimum. T[u]um* 20 *corde simplicem te agnovi. Iterum scripsisti. Agnovi corde simplicem, sed*

---

[52] Prov. 3:3.
[53] The closing sentence was added only in the errata sheet for JW's *Works* (1774), Zinzendorf having died in 1760. In fact JW had translated much of the conversation in *A Short View of the Difference between the Moravian Brethren, lately in England, and the Reverend Mr. John and Charles Wesley*, pp. 7-8. *(Bibliography*, No. 100; see Vol. 13 in this edn.). Henry Moore *(Wesley*, I.481-88) gave the following full literal translation:

Z. Why have you changed your religion?
W. I do not know that I have changed my religion. Why do you think so? Who has reported this to you?
Z. Plainly, yourself. I see it from your epistle to us. There, having departed from the religion which you professed among us, you have held out a new one.
W. How so? I do not understand you.
Z. Nay, you say there, that Christians are not miserable sinners. This is most false. The best of men are most miserable sinners, even unto death. If any speak otherwise, they are either manifest impostors, or diabolically seduced. Our brethren who taught better things, you have opposed; and when they desired peace, you have refused it.
W. I do not yet understand what you aim at.
Z. When you wrote to me from Georgia, I loved you very much. I perceived that you were simple in heart, but troubled in your ideas. You came to us. Your ideas were then still more troubled and confused. You returned to England. A little after, I heard that our brethren were contending with you. I sent Spangenberg to make peace between you. He wrote to me, that the Brethren had injured you. I wrote again, that they should

turbatis ideis. Ad nos venisti. Ideae tuae tum magis turbatae erant et confusae. In Angliam rediisti. Aliquandiu post, audivi fratres nostros tecum pugnare. Spangenbergium misi ad pacem inter vos conciliandam. Scripsit mihi, Fratres tibi iniuriam intulisse. Rescripsi, ne pergerent, sed et veniam a

5 *te peterent. Spangenberg scripsit iterum, Eos petiisse; sed te, gloriari de iis, pacem nolle. Iam adveniens, ideam audio.*

W. *Res in eo cardine minime vertitur. Fratres tui (verum hoc) me male tractarunt. Postea veniam petierunt. Respondi, Id supervacaneum; me nunquam iis succensuisse: sed vereri, (1) ne falsa docerunt; (2) ne prave*

10 *viverent. Ista unica est, et fuit, inter nos quaestio.*

Z. *Apertius loquaris.*

W. *Veritus sum, ne falsa docerent, (1) de sine fidei nostrae in hac vita, scil[icet,] Christiana perfectione; (2) de mediis gratiae, sic ab Ecclesia nostra dictis.*

15 Z. *Nullam inhaerentem perfectionem in hac vita agnosco. Est hic error errorum. Eum per totum orbem igne et gladio persequor, conculco, ad internecionem do. Christus est sola perfectio nostra. Qui perfectionem inhaerentem sequitur, Christum denegat.*

W. *Ego vero credo, spiritum Christi operari perfectionem in vere*

20 *Christianis.*

Z. *Nullimode. Omnis nostra perfectio est in Christo. Omnis Christiana perfectio est, fides in sanguine Christi. Est tota Christiana perfectio, imputata, non inhaerens. Perfecti sumus in Christo, in nobismet nunquam perfecti.*

---

not pursue the strife, but desire forgiveness of you. Spangenberg wrote again, that they had desired this, but that you, glorying over them, had refused peace. Now that I am come, I hear the same thing.

W. The matter does not at all turn on this point. Your Brethren, it is true, did not use me well. Afterward they desired forgiveness. I answered — that was superfluous, that I had never been offended with them; but I feared, (1) lest they should teach falsely; (2) lest they should live wickedly. This is, and was, the only question between us.

Z. Speak more fully [on that question].

W. I feared lest they should teach falsely; (1) Concerning the end of our faith in this life, to wit, Christian Perfection. (2) Concerning the means of grace, so termed by our church.

Z. I acknowledge no inherent perfection in this life. This is the error of errors. I pursue it through the world with fire and sword. I trample upon it: I devote it to utter destruction. Whoever follows inherent perfection, denies Christ.

W. But, I believe, that the spirit of Christ works this perfection in true Christians.

Z. By no means. All our perfection is in Christ. All Christian Perfection is, Faith in the blood of Christ. Our whole Christian Perfection is imputed, not inherent. We are perfect in Christ: In ourselves we are never perfect.

W. I think we strive about words. Is not every true believer holy?

Z. Highly so. But he is holy in Christ, not in himself.

W. *Pugnamus, opinor, de verbis. Nonne omnis vere credens sanctus est?*

Z. *Maxime. Sed sanctus in Christo, non in se.*

W. *Sed, nonne sancte vivit?*

Z. *Imo, sancte in omnibus vivit.*

W. *Nonne, et cor sanctum habet?* 5

Z. *Certissime.*

W. *Nonne, ex consequenti, sanctus est* in se?

Z. *Non, non. In Christo tantum. Non sanctus* in se. *Nullam omnino habet sanctitatem* in se.

W. *Nonne habet in corde suo* amorem Dei *et proximi, quin et totam* 10 *imaginem Dei?*

Z. *Habet. Sed haec sunt sanctitas legalis, non evangelica. Sanctitas evangelica est fides.*

W. *Omnino lis est de verbis. Concedis, credentis cor totum esse sanctum et vitam totam: Eum amare Deum toto corde, eique servire totis viribus.* 15 *Nihil ultra peto. Nil aliud volo per perfectio vel sanctitas Christiana.*

Z. *Sed haec non est sanctitas eius. Non magis sanctus est, si magis amat, neque minus sanctus, si minus amat.*

W. *Quid? Nonne credens, dum crescit in amore, crescit pariter in sanctitate?* 20

Z. *Nequaquam. Eo momento quo iustificatur, sanctificatur penitus. Exin, neque magis sanctus est, neque minus sanctus, ad mortem usque.*

W. *Nonne igitur pater in Christo sanctior est infante recens nato?*

W. But does he not live holy?

Z. Yes, he lives holy in all things.

W. And has he not a holy heart?

Z. Most certainly.

W. And is he not consequently holy *in himself?*

Z. No, no. In Christ only. He is not holy in himself: He hath no holiness at all in himself.

W. Hath he not the *love of God,* and his neighbour, in his heart? Yea, and the whole image of God?

Z. He hath. But these constitute legal holiness, not evangelical. Evangelical holiness is Faith.

W. The dispute is altogether about words. You grant that a believer is altogether holy in heart and life: That he loves God with all his heart, and serves him with all his powers. I desire nothing more. I mean nothing else [by the term] PERFECTION, OR CHRISTIAN HOLINESS.

Z. But this is not his holiness. He is not more holy if he loves more, or less holy, if he loves less.

W. What! Does not every believer, while he increases in love, increase equally in holiness?

Z. Not at all. In the moment he is justified, he is sanctified wholly. From that time he is neither more nor less holy, even unto death.

W. Is not therefore a father in Christ holier than a new-born babe?

Z. *Non. Sanctificatio totalis ac iustificatio in eodem sunt instanti; et neutra recipit maris aut minus.*

W. *Nonne vero credens crescit indies amore Dei? Num perfectus est amore, simulac iustificatur?*

5 Z. *Est. Non unquam crescit in amore Dei. Totaliter amat eo momento, sicut totaliter sanctificatur.*

W. *Quid itaque vult Apostolus Paulus, per, Renovamur de die in diem?*

Z. *Dicam. Plumbum si in aurum mutetur, est aurum primo die, et secundo, et tertio. Et sic renovatur de die in diem. Sed nunquam est magis*
10 *aurum, quam primo die.*

W. *Putavi, crescendum esse in gratia!*

Z. *Certe. Sed non in sanctitate. Simulac justificatur quis, Pater, Filius, et Spiritus Sanctus habitant in ipsius corde. Et cor eius eo momento aeque purum est ac unquam erit. Infans in Christo tam purus corde est quam pater*
15 *in Christo. Nulla est discrepantia.*

W. *Nonne iustificati erant apostoli ante Christi mortem?*

Z. *Erant.*

W. *Nonne vero sanctiores erant post diem Pentecostes, quam ante Christi mortem?*
20 Z. *Neutiquam.*

W. *Nonne eo die impleti sunt Spiritu Sancto?*

Z. *Erant.*[54] *Sed istud donum Spiritus, sanctitatem ipsorum non respexit. Fuit donum miraculorum tantum.*

---

[54] In Zinzendorf's version in the *Büdingische Sammlung*, 'Sunt'.

Z. No. Our whole justification, and sanctification, are in the same instant, and he receives neither more nor less.

W. Does not a true believer increase in love to God daily? Is he *perfected in love* when he is justified?

Z. He is. He never can increase in the love of God. He loves altogether in that moment, as he is sanctified wholly.

W. What therefore does the Apostle Paul mean by, *'We are renewed day by day?'*

Z. I will tell you. Lead, if it should be changed into gold, is gold the first day, and the second day, and the third: And so it is renewed day by day; but it is never more gold than in the first day.

W. I thought that we should grow in grace!

Z. Certainly; but not in holiness. Whenever anyone is justified, the Father, the Son, and the Holy Spirit, dwell in his heart; and from that moment his heart is as pure as it ever will be. A babe in Christ is as pure in heart as a father in Christ. There is no difference.

W. Were not the Apostles justified before the death of Christ?

Z. They were.

W. But were they not more holy after the day of Pentecost, than before Christ's death?

Z. By no means.

W. Were they not on that day *filled with the Holy Ghost?*

Z. They were. But that gift of the Spirit did not respect their holiness. It was a gift of miracles only.

W. Fortasse te non capio. Nonne nos ipsos abnegantes, magis magisque mundo morimur, ac Deo vivimus?

Z. Abnegationem omnem respuimus, conculcamus. Facimus credentes omne quod volumus et nihil ultra. Mortificationem omnem ridemus. Nulla purificatio praecedit perfectum amorem.   5

W. Quae dixisti, Deo adiuvante, perpendam.

The letter referred to by the Count was written August 8 preceding. It was as follows, excepting two or three paragraphs, which I have omitted as less material:[55]

John Wesley, a Presbyter of the Church of God in England, to the 10
Church of God at Herrnhut in Upper Lusatia.

1. It may seem strange that such an one as I am should take upon me to write to you. You, I believe to be 'dear children of God',[56] 'through faith which is in Jesus'.[57] Me you believe (as some of you have declared) to be a 'child of the devil',[58] 'a servant of corruption'.[59] 15
Yet whatsoever I am, or whatsoever you are, I beseech you to weigh the following words; if haply God, who 'sendeth by whom he will send',[60] may give *you* light thereby, although 'the mist of darkness'[61] (as one of you affirms) should be reserved for *me* for ever.

2. My design is freely and plainly to speak whatsoever I have seen 20 or heard among you, in any part of your church, which seems not agreeable to the gospel of Christ. And my hope is that the God whom you serve will give you thoroughly to weigh what is spoken, and if in anything 'ye have been otherwise minded than the truth is, will reveal even this unto you'.[62]   25

3. And first, with regard to Christian salvation, even the present salvation which is through faith, I have heard some of you affirm, (1) that it does not imply the proper *taking away* our sins, the cleansing

---

W. Perhaps I do not comprehend your meaning. Do we not while we deny ourselves, die more and more to the world and live to God?

Z. We reject all self-denial. We trample upon it. We do, as believers, whatsoever we will, and nothing more. We laugh at all mortification. No purification precedes perfect love.

W. What you have said I will thoroughly weigh, God being my helper.

The documents on Zinzendorf's side are given in *Büdingische Sammlung*, 3:337-40, 836-53 (cf. Telford, II.39-40), 1019-30; cf. also above, JW's Preface to *Journal* 4, 1-10.

[55] Cf. the fuller version of this letter in *Letters*, 26:24-31 in this edn., which includes in paragraphs 12 and 13 attacks upon the episcopacy of the Moravians and the overweening authority of Zinzendorf himself.

[56] Cf. Eph. 5:1.

[57] 2 Tim. 3:15.

[58] Acts 13:10.

[59] Cf. 2 Pet. 2:19.

[60] Cf. Exod. 4:13.

[61] 2 Pet. 2:17.

[62] Cf. Phil. 3:15.

our souls *from all sin,* but only *the tearing the system of sin* in pieces; (2) that it does not imply liberty from evil thoughts, neither from wanderings in prayer.

4. I have heard some of you affirm, on the other hand: (1) That it does imply liberty from the commandments of God, so that one who is saved through faith is not *obliged* or *bound* to obey them, does not do anything as a *commandment* or as a *duty.* To support which they have affirmed that there is *no command* in the New Testament but to believe;[e] that there is *no duty* required therein but that of believing, and that to a believer there is *no commandment* at all. (2) That it does imply liberty to conform to the world, by talking on useless, if not trifling subjects, by joining in worldly diversions in order to do good,[f] by putting on of gold and costly apparel,[63] by continuing in those professions, the gain of which depends on ministering hereto.[g] (3) That it does imply liberty to avoid persecution, by *not reproving* even those who sin in your sight;[h] by *not letting* your light shine before those men who love darkness rather than light; by *not using* plainness of speech, and *a frank, open carriage* to all men. Nay, by a close, dark, reserved conversation and behaviour, especially toward strangers.

---

[e] In the answer to this letter, which I received some weeks after, this is explained as follows: 'All things which are a *commandment* to the natural man are a *promise* to all that have been justified. . . . The *thing* itself is not lost, but the *notion* which people are wont to have of *commandments,* duties, etc.

I reply, (1), if this be all you mean, why do you not say so, explicitly to all men? (2), whether this be all, let any reasonable man judge, when he has read what is here subjoined.

[f] The Brethren answer to this, 'We believe it much better to discourse out of the newspapers than to chatter about holy things to no purpose.' Perhaps so. But what is this to the point? I believe both the one and the other to be useless, and therefore an abomination to the Lord.

This objection then stands in full force, the fact alleged being rather defended than denied.

The joining in worldly diversions in order to do good (another charge which cannot be denied) I think would admit of the same defence, viz., that 'there are other things as bad.'

[g] 'We wear (say the Brethren) neither gold nor silver.' You forget. I have seen it with my eyes. 'But we judge nobody that does.' How! Then you must judge both St. Peter and Paul false witnesses before God. 'And because those professions that minister thereto' (to sin, to what God has flatly forbidden) 'relate to trade, and trade is a thing relating to the magistrate, we therefore let all these things alone, entirely suspending our judgment concerning them.'

What miserable work is here! Because trade relates to the magistrate, am I not to consider whether my trade be innocent or sinful? Then the keeper of a Venetian brothel is clear. The magistrate shall answer for him to God!

[h] This fact also you grant, and defend thus: 'The power of reproving relates either to outward things or to the heart. Nobody has any right to the former but the magistrate.' (Alas! alas! what casuistry is this!) 'And if one will speak to the heart, he must be first sure that the Saviour has already got hold of it.' What then must become of all other men? O how pleasing is all this to flesh and blood!

---

[63] Cf. 1 Tim. 2:9; 1 Pet. 3:3.

And in many of you I have more than once found (what you called, 'being wise as serpents')[64] much subtlety, much evasion and disguise, much guile and dissimulation. You appeared to be what you were not, or not to be what you were. You so studied 'to become all things to all men'[65] as to take the colour and shape of any that were near you. So that your practice was indeed no proof of your judgment, but only an indication of your design, *nulli laedere os,*[66] and of your conformity to that (not scriptural) maxim, *Sinere mundum vadere ut vult; nam vult vadere.*[67]

5. Secondly, with regard to that faith through which we are saved, I have heard many of you say, 'A man may have justifying faith and not know it.' Others of you, who are now in England (particularly Mr. Molther) I have heard affirm that there is no such thing as *weak faith;* that there are *no degrees* in faith; that there is *no justifying faith* where there is ever any doubt; that there is no justifying faith without the *plerophory of faith,* the clear, abiding witness of the Spirit; that there is no justifying faith where there is not, in the full, proper sense, a new or clean heart; and, that those who have not these two gifts are only *awakened,* not *justified.*[i]

6. Thirdly, as to the way to faith, here are many among us whom your brethren have advised (what it is not to be supposed they would as yet speak to me, or in their public preaching) *not to use those ordinances* which our Church terms 'means of grace'[68] till they have such a faith as implies a clean heart and excludes all possibility of doubting. They have advised them, till then, *not to search the Scriptures, not to pray, not to communicate;* and have often affirmed that to do these things is seeking salvation by works; and that till these works are laid aside no man can receive faith, for 'No man (say they) can do these things without trusting in them. If he does not trust in them, why does he do them?'[j]

7. To those who answered, It is *our duty* to use the ordinances of God, they replied, There are *no ordinances* of Christ the use of which is now *bound* upon Christians as a *duty,* or which we are *commanded* to

---

[i] In the preface to the second *Journal* the Moravian Church is cleared from this mistake. [See §§9 and 10, 18:218-20 in this edn.]

[j] The substance of the answer to this and the following paragraph is: (1). That none ought to communicate till he has faith, i.e., a sure trust in the mercy of God through Christ. This is granting the charge. (2). That 'If the Methodists hold this Sacrament is a means of getting faith, they must act according to their persuasion.' We do hold it and know it to be so to many of those who are previously convinced of sin.

---

[64] Cf. Matt. 10:16.   [65] Cf. 1 Cor. 9:22.

[66] Terence, *Adelphi,* 864: 'to affront no man'.

[67] In Vol. 32 of his *Works* (1774) Wesley added the translation: 'To let the world go as it will; for it *will* go.'

[68] BCP, Thanksgivings, 'A General Thanksgiving'.

use. As to those you mention in particular (viz., prayer, communicating, and searching the Scripture), if a man have faith he *need* not; if he have not, he *must* not use them. A believer may use them, though not *as enjoined,* but an unbeliever (as before defined) *may not.*

5   8. To those who answered, 'I hope God will through these *means* convey his *grace* to my soul,' they replied, 'There is *no* such thing as 'means of grace'; Christ has *not ordained* any such in his church. But if there were they are nothing to you, for you are dead. You have no faith. And you cannot *work,* while you are *dead.* Therefore let these

10   things alone, *till* you have faith.'

9. And some of our English brethren, who are joined with yours, have said openly, 'You will never have faith till you leave running about to Church and Sacrament, and societies.' Another of them has said (in his public expounding), 'As many go to hell by praying as by

15   thieving.' Another, 'I knew one who, leaning over the back of a chair, received a great gift. But he must kneel down to give God thanks. So he lost it immediately. And I know not whether he will ever have it again.' And yet another, 'You have lost your first joy. Therefore you pray. That is the devil. You read the Bible. That is the devil. You

20   communicate. That is the devil.'

10. Let not any of you, my brethren, say, We are not chargeable with what *they* speak. Indeed you are. For you *can* hinder it, if you *will.* Therefore, if you do not, it must be charged upon *you.* If you do not use the power which is in your hands, and thereby prevent their

25   speaking thus, you do, in effect, speak thus yourselves. You make *their* words *your own,* and are accordingly chargeable with every ill consequence which may flow therefrom.

11. Fourthly, with regard to your *church* you greatly, yea, above measure, exalt yourselves and despise others.[k]

30   I have scarce heard one Moravian brother in my life own *his church* to be wrong in anything.

I have scarce heard any of you (I think not one in England) own *himself* to be wrong in anything.

Many of you I have heard speak of your church as if it were

---

[k] 'A *religion* (you say) and a *church* are not all one. A religion is an assembly wherein the Holy Scriptures are taught after a prescribed rule.' This is too narrow a definition. For there are many *pagan* (as well as *Mahometan)* religions. Rather, a religion is a method of worshipping God, whether in a right or a wrong manner.

'The Lord has such a peculiar hand in the several constitutions of religion that one ought to respect every one of them.' I cannot possibly: I cannot respect either the Jewish (as it is now) or the Romish religion. You add,

'A church' (I will not examine whether there are any in this present age, or whether there is no other beside ours) 'is a congregation of sinners who have obtained forgiveness of sins. . . . That such a congregation should be in an error cannot easily happen.'

I find no reason therefore to retract anything which is advanced on this or any of the following heads.

infallible, or so led by the Spirit that it was not possible for it to err in anything.

Some of you have set it up (as indeed you ought to do, if it be infallible) as the judge of all the earth, of all persons (as well as doctrines) therein; and you have accordingly passed sentence upon 5 them at once, by their agreement or disagreement with your church.

Some of you have said that there is *no* true *church* on earth *but yours;* yea, that there are *no true Christians out of it.* And your own members you require to have *implicit faith* in her decisions and to pay *implicit obedience* to her directions. 10

12. Fifthly, you receive not the *ancients* but the *modern mystics* as the best interpreters of Scripture, and in conformity to these you mix much of man's wisdom with the wisdom of God; you greatly refine the plain religion taught by the letter of Holy Writ and philosophize on almost every part of it to accommodate it to the *mystic* theory. Hence you talk 15 much, in a manner wholly unsupported by Scripture, against *mixing nature with grace,* against *imagination,* and concerning the *animal spirits,* mimicking the power of the Holy Ghost. Hence your brethren zealously caution us against *animal joy,* against *natural love* of one another, and against *selfish love* of God, against which (or any of them) there is no one 20 caution in all the Bible. And they have, in truth, greatly lessened, and had wellnigh destroyed brotherly love from among us.

13. In conformity to the *mystics* you likewise greatly check joy in the Holy Ghost by which cautions against *sensible comforts* as have no tittle of Scripture to support them. Hence also your brethren here 25 damp the zeal of babes in Christ, talking much of false zeal, forbidding them to declare what God hath done for their souls, even when their hearts burn within them to declare it, and comparing those to 'uncorked bottles' who simply and artlessly speak of the ability which God giveth. 30

14. Hence, lastly, it is that you undervalue good works (especially works of outward mercy), never publicly insisting on the necessity of them, nor declaring their weight and excellency. Hence, when some of your brethren have spoken of them they put them on a wrong foot, viz., *'If you find yourself moved,* if your heart *is free* to it, then reprove, 35 exhort, relieve.' By this means you wholly avoid the taking up your cross in order to do good, and also substitute an uncertain, precarious inward motion in the place of the plain written Word. Nay, one of your members has said of good works in general (whether works of piety or of charity), 'A believer is no more *obliged* to do *these* works of 40 the law than a subject of the King of England is obliged to obey the laws of the King of France.'

15. My brethren, whether ye will hear, or whether ye will forbear, I have now delivered my own soul. And this I have chosen to do in an artless manner, that if anything should come home to your hearts, the 45

effect might evidently flow not from the wisdom of man, but from the power of God.

Aug. 8, 1740.

5 Thus have I declared, and in the plainest manner I can, the real controversy between us and the Moravian Brethren: an unpleasing task, which I have delayed, at least as long as I could with a clear conscience. But I am constrained at length nakedly to speak the thing as it is, that I may not hinder the work of God.

10 I am very sensible of the objection which has so often been made, viz., 'You are inconsistent with yourself. You *did* tenderly love, highly esteem, and zealously recommend these very men. And now you *do* not love or esteem them at all. You not only do not recommend them, but are *bitter* against them; nay, and *rail* at them, before all the world.'

15 This is partly true and partly false. That the whole case may be better understood, it will be needful to give a short account of what has occurred between us from the beginning.

My first acquaintance with the Moravian Brethren began in my voyage to Georgia. Being then with many of them in the same 20 ship, I narrowly observed their whole behaviour. And I greatly approved of all I saw. Therefore I unbosomed myself to them without reserve.

From February 14, 1735 to December 2, 1737, being with them (except when I went to Frederica or Carolina) twice or 25 thrice every day, I loved and esteemed them more and more. Yet a few things I could not approve of. These I mentioned to them from time to time, and then commended the cause of God.

In February following I met with Peter Böhler. My heart clave to him as soon as he spoke. And the more we conversed, so much 30 the more did I esteem both him and all the Moravian Church. So that I had no rest in my spirit till I executed the design which I had formed long before; till, after a short stay in Holland, I hastened forward, first to Marienborn and then to Herrnhut.

In September 1738, soon after my return to England, I began 35 the following letter to the Moravian Church. But being fearful of trusting my own judgment, I determined to wait yet a little longer and so laid it by unfinished.

My dear Brethren,

I cannot but rejoice in your steadfast faith, in your love to our 40 blessed Redeemer, your deadness to the world; your meekness, temperance, chastity, and love of one another. I greatly approve of your conferences and bands, of your method of instructing children, and in general of your great care of the souls committed to your charge.

But of some other things I stand in doubt, which I will mention in love and meekness. And I wish that, in order to remove those doubts, you would on each of those heads, first, plainly answer whether the fact be as I suppose, and if so, secondly, consider whether it be right.

Do you not wholly neglect joint fasting?

Is not the Count all in all? Are not the rest mere shadows? Calling him 'Rabbi'? Almost implicitly both believing and obeying him?

Is there not something of levity in your behaviour? Are you, in general, serious enough?

Are you zealous and watchful to redeem time? Do you not sometimes fall into trifling conversation?

Do you not magnify your own church too much? Do you believe any who are not of it to be in gospel liberty?

Are you not straitened in your love? Do you love your enemies and wicked men as yourselves?

Do you not mix *human* wisdom with *divine?* Joining worldly prudence to heavenly?

Do you not use cunning, guile, or dissimulation in many cases?

Are you not of a close, dark, reserved temper and behaviour?

Is not the spirit of secrecy the spirit of your community?

Have you that childlike openness, frankness, and plainness of speech, so manifest to all in the apostles and first Christians?

It may easily be seen that my objections then were nearly the same as now. Yet I cannot say my affection was lessened at all till after September 1739, when certain men among us began to trouble their 'brethren' and 'subvert their souls'.[69] However, I cleared the Moravians still, and laid the whole blame on our English brethren.

But from November the first I could not but see (unwilling as I was to see them) more and more things which I could in no wise reconcile with the gospel of Christ. And these I have set down with all simplicity, as they occurred in order of time, believing myself indispensably obliged so to do, both in duty to God and man.

Yet do I this because I love them not? God knoweth; yea and in part I esteem them still. Because I verily believe they have a sincere desire to serve God; because many of them have tasted of

[69] Cf. Acts 15:23-24.

his love, and some retain it in simplicity; because they love one another; because they have *so much* of the truth of the gospel and *so far* abstain from outward sin; and lastly, because their discipline is, in most respects, so truly excellent.

5   'But why then are you *bitter* against them?' I do not know that I am. Let the impartial reader judge. And if any bitter word has escaped my notice, I here utterly retract it. 'But do not you *rail* at them?' I hope not. God forbid that I should *rail* at a Turk, infidel, or heretic. To one who advanced the most dangerous errors I durst
10 say no more than, 'The Lord rebuke thee!'[70] But I would point out what those errors were; and, I trust, in the spirit of meekness.

In this spirit, my brethren, I have read and endeavoured to consider all the books you have published in England, that I might inform myself whether on farther consideration you had retracted
15 the errors which were advanced before. But it does by no means appear that you have retracted any of them. For, waiving the odd and affected phrases therein, the weak, mean, silly, childish expressions; the crude, confused, and indigested notions, the whims, unsupported either by Scripture or sound reason; yea,
20 waiving these assertions, which, though contrary to Scripture and matter of fact, are however of no importance—those three grand errors run through almost all those books, viz., *universal salvation*, *antinomianism*, and a kind of new-reformed *quietism*.

1. Can *universal salvation* be more explicitly asserted than it is
25 in these words:

'By this his name *all* can and *shall* obtain life and salvation.'[1] This *must* include all men, at least, and *may* include all *devils* too.

Again, 'The name of the wicked will not be so much as mentioned on the great day.'[m] And if they are not so much as
30 *mentioned*, they cannot be *condemned*.

2. How can *antinomianism*,[n] i.e., 'making void the law through faith',[71] be more expressly taught then it is in those words:

---

[1] [Zinzendorf,] *Sixteen Discourses* [*on the Redemption of Man by the Death of Christ*, London, for James Hutton, 1740], p. 30. [Actually, pp. 33-34, the italics being added by JW. The title of the second English edn. (London, Bowyer, 1751) was changed to *Sixteen Discourses on Jesus Christ our Lord*, and many revisions made, including in this instance the alteration to 'by this his Name all can and ought to obtain life and salvation' (p. 25).]

[m] [Zinzendorf,] *Seven Discourses* [i.e., *Seven Sermons on the Godhead of the Lamb; or the Divinity of Jesus Christ*, London, for James Hutton, 1742], p. 22. [Orig., 'his name will not. . .'.]

[n] N.B. I speak of Antinomian doctrine abstracted from practice, good or bad.

---

[70] Jude 9.   [71] Cf. Rom. 3:31.

To believe certainly, that Christ suffered death for us. . . . This is the true means to be saved at once.

We want no more. For the history of Jesus's coming into the world is the power of God unto salvation to everyone that believeth[o]—the bare historical knowledge of this.   5

There is but *one duty*, which is that of believing.[p]

From any demand of the law, no man is obliged now to go one step, to give away one farthing, to eat or omit one morsel.[q]

What did our Lord do with the law? He abolished it.[r]

Here one may think, This is a fine sort of Christianity, where 10 nothing good is commanded, and nothing bad is forbid. But thus it is.[s]

So one ought to speak now. All commands and prohibitions are unfit for our times.[t]

3. Is not the very essence of *quietism* (though in a new shape) contained in those words: 15

The whole matter lies in this, that we should *suffer ourselves to be relieved.*[u]

One must *do nothing*, but *quietly attend* the voice of the Lord.[v]

To tell men who have not experienced the power of grace what they should do, and how they ought to behave, is as if you should send a 20 lame man upon an errand.[w]

The beginning is not to be made with doing what our Saviour has commanded. For whosoever will begin with doing, when he is dead he can do nothing at all; but whatever he doth *in his own activity* is but a cobweb, i.e., good for nothing.[x]   25

As soon as we *remain passive* before him as the wood which a table is to be made from, then something comes of us.[y]

O my brethren, let me conjure you yet again, in the name of our common Lord, 'If there be any consolation of love, if any bowels and mercies',[72] remove 'the fly' out of 'the pot of ointment',[73] 30

---

[o] *Sixteen Discourses*, p. 57. [JW has abridged and paraphrased slightly. The closing comment about 'the bare historical knowledge' is not in the original.]

[p] Ibid., p. 193. [JW's italics.]

[q] *Seven Discourses*, p. 11.   [r] Ibid., p. 33.

[s] Ibid., p. 34 [i.e., p. 33].

[t] Ibid. [i.e., p. 34.]

[u] *Sixteen Discourses*, p. 17.

[v] *Sixteen Discourses*, p. 29. [Wesley's italics.]

[w] Ibid., p. 70 [actually, pp. 69-70, abridged and slightly varied in expression].

[x] Ibid., pp. 72, 81 [i.e., p. 72 only, abridged slightly].

[y] *Seven Discourses*, p. 22. [JW adds the italics and omits an intervening passage.]

---

[72] Cf. Phil. 2:1.   [73] Cf. Job 41:31; Eccles. 10:1.

separate 'the precious from the vile'![74] Review, I beseech you,
your whole work and see if Satan hath gained no advantage over
you. 'Very excellent things' have been 'spoken of thee, O thou city
of God.'[75] But may not 'he which hath the sharp sword with two
5 edges' say, Yet 'I have a few things against thee.'[76] O that ye would
repent of these, that ye might be 'a glorious church, not having
spot, or wrinkle, or any such thing'![77]

   Three things above all permit *me*, even *me*, to press upon you,
with all earnestness of love. First, with regard to your doctrine,
10 that ye purge out from among you the leaven of *antinomianism*,
wherewith you are so deeply infected, and no longer 'make void
the law through faith'.[78] Secondly, with regard to your discipline,
that 'ye call no man Rabbi, Master,' Lord of your faith 'upon
earth'.[79] Subordination, I know, is needful, and I can show you
15 such a subordination as in fact answers all Christian purposes and
is yet as widely distant from that among *you* as the heavens are
from the earth. Thirdly, with regard to your practice, that ye
renounce all craft, cunning, subtlety, dissimulation—'wisdom',
falsely so called; that ye put away all disguise, all guile out of your
20 mouth; that in all 'simplicity and godly sincerity' ye 'have your
conversation in this world';[80] that ye use 'great plainness of
speech'[81] to all, whatever ye suffer thereby; seeking only, 'by
manifestation of the truth', to 'commend' yourselves 'to every
man's conscience in the sight of God'.[82]

25 June 24, 1744.[83]

[74] Jer. 15:19.
[75] Cf. Ps. 87:2 (BCP).
[76] Rev. 2:12, 14, 20.
[77] Eph. 5:27.
[78] Rom. 3:31.
[79] Cf. Matt. 23:8-9.
[80] Cf. 2 Cor. 1:12.
[81] 2 Cor. 3:12.
[82] Cf. 2 Cor. 4:2.
[83] The *Works* (1774) omitted the date (which underlines JW's asseveration that he had exercised due deliberation before publishing his polemic) as also two poems which are found in the original: 'The Means of Grace' (23 stanzas) and 'The Bloody Issue' (17 stanzas), for which see *Poet. Wks.*, I.233-36, and IV.451-54. 'The Means of Grace' had appeared in *Hymns and Sacred Poems* (1740); 'The Bloody Issue' appeared here for the first time. Both were by Charles Wesley.

AN

EXTRACT

OF THE

Rev^d. Mr. JOHN WESLEY's

JOURNAL,

From SEPT. 3, 1741.

TO OCTOBER 27, 1743.

BRISTOL.

Printed by FELIX FARLEY; and fold at the *School-Room* in the *Horfe-Fair:* Alfo by T. TRYE, near *Gray's-Inn Gate, Holborn;* and at the *Foundery* near *Upper-Moor-Fields,* LONDON. M.DCC.XLIX.

Journal

From September 6, 1741, to October 27, 1743

Sunday, September 6. Observing some who were beginning to 'use their liberty as a cloak for'[1] licentiousness, I enforced in the morning those words of St. Paul (worthy to be written in the heart of every believer), 'All things are lawful for me; but all things are not expedient';[2] and in the evening that necessary advice of our Lord, 'That men ought always to pray, and not to faint.'[3]

Mon. 7. I visited a young man in St. Thomas's Hospital,[4] who, in strong pain, was praising God continually. At the desire of many of the patients I spent a short time with them in exhortation and prayer. O what a harvest might there be, if any lover of souls who has time upon his hands would constantly attend these places of distress, and with tenderness and meekness of wisdom instruct and exhort those on whom God has laid his hands, to know and improve the day of their visitation!

Wed. 9. I expounded in Greyhound Lane, Whitechapel, part of the one hundred and seventh Psalm. And they did 'rejoice whom the Lord had redeemed and delivered from the hand of the enemy'.[5]

Sat. 12. I was greatly comforted by one whom God had lifted up from the gates of death, and who was continually telling, with tears of joy, what God had done for his soul. Sun. 13. I met about two hundred persons, with whom severally I had talked the week before at the French chapel in Hermitage Street, Wapping, where they gladly joined in the service of the Church, and particularly in the Lord's Supper, at which Mr. Hall[6] assisted. It was more than two years after this that he began so vehemently to declaim against my brother and me, as 'bigots to the church, and those "carnal ordinances"',[7] as he then loved to term them.

Fri. 18. I buried the only child of a tender parent, who, having

---

[1] Cf. 1 Pet. 2:16.   [2] 1 Cor. 10:23.   [3] Luke 18:1.
[4] Then on the east side of the borough of Southwark near London Bridge.
[5] Cf. Ps. 107:2.
[6] On Westley Hall's spiritual evolution, see May 13, 1738, n. 9, 18:238-39 in this edn.
[7] Heb. 9:10.

soon finished her course, after a short sickness went to him her soul loved, in the fifteenth year of her age.

Sun. 20. I preached in Charles Square, Hoxton, on these solemn words, 'This is life eternal, to know thee, the only true God, and Jesus Christ whom thou hast sent.'[8] I trust God 5 blessed his word. The scoffers stood abashed and opened not their mouth.

Mon. 21. I set out, and the next evening met my brother at Bristol, with Mr. Jones[9] of Fonmon Castle in Wales; now convinced of the truth as it is in Jesus[10] and labouring with his 10 might to 'redeem the time'[11] he had lost, to 'make his calling sure',[12] and to 'lay hold on eternal life'.[13]

Thur. 24. In the evening we went to Kingswood. The house was filled from end to end. And we continued in ministering the word of God, and in prayer and praise, till the morning. 15

Sun. 27. I expounded at Kingswood (morning and afternoon), at Bristol, and at Baptist Mills, the message of God to the church of Ephesus, particularly that way of recovering our first love which God hath prescribed and not man: 'Remember from whence thou art fallen, and repent and do the first works.'[14] 20

---

[8] Cf. John 17:3.

[9] Robert Jones (1706–42), son of Robert Jones (1681–1714) and Mary, daughter of Sir Humphrey Edwin, and great-grandson of Colonel Philip Jones (1618–74), Comptroller of Cromwell's Household, who bought Fonmon Castle. Robert Jones II matriculated from Christ Church, Oxford, 1724, and married Mary, daughter of Robert Forrest of Minehead, 1732. He took an active part in the public life of Glamorgan (WHS, 4:44) and had a reputation for piety and support of the religious societies. He was affected by the preaching of Howell Harris. In July 1741, Charles Wesley was in South Wales and, along with two other clergymen favourably disposed to Arminianism, Nathaniel Wells of Cardiff and John Hodges of Wenvoe, was invited to Fonmon by Jones. Satisfying himself that Charles Wesley was an Anglican, Jones made it possible for him to preach in Porthkerry church, and soon afterwards he formed a society at Fonmon. In September he accompanied Charles Wesley to Bristol, interceding with one of the local magistrates on his behalf and giving evidence of evangelical conversion. The prospect of his becoming a pillar of the cause was ended by his early death on June 8, 1742 (WHS, 26:56-59, 80-83; CWJ, I.287-302, *passim;* II.289-303; *Wesleyan Methodist Magazine* [1900], 123:26-33). The Countess of Huntingdon opposed the publication of an elegy written by Charles Wesley upon him. *Methodist Magazine* (1798), 21:531.

[10] See Eph. 4:21.

[11] Cf. Eph. 5:16; Col. 4:5.

[12] Cf. 2 Pet. 1:10.

[13] 1 Tim. 6:12, 19.

[14] Rev. 2:5. This sermon anticipated the panic-stricken letter by Charles Wesley on Sept. 28, 1741, exhorting his brother to take a strong line against the doctrine of predestination as taught by Whitefield. Tyerman, *Whitefield,* I.482.

Tue. 29. I was pressed to visit Nicholas Palmer,[15] one who had separated from us and behaved with great bitterness, till God laid his hand upon him. He had sent for me several times, saying he could not die in peace till he had seen me. I found him in great 5 weakness of body and heaviness of spirit. We wrestled with God on his behalf. And our labour was not in vain. His soul was comforted; and a few hours after he quietly fell asleep.

Thursday, October 1. We set out for Wales. But missing our passage over the Severn in the morning, it was sunset before we 10 could get to Newport. We inquired there if we could hire a guide to Cardiff. But there was none to be had. A lad coming in quickly after, who was going (he said) to Llanishen[16] (a little village two miles to the right of Cardiff), we resolved to go thither. At seven we set out. It rained pretty fast; and, there being neither moon nor 15 stars, we could neither see any road nor one another, nor our own horses' heads. But the promise of God did not fail. He gave his angels charge over us.[17] And soon after ten we came safe to Mr. Williams's[18] house at Llanishen.

Fri. 2. We rode to Fonmon Castle. We found Mr. Jones's 20 daughter[19] ill of the smallpox. But he could cheerfully leave her and all the rest in the hands of him in whom he now believed. In the evening I preached at Cardiff in the Shire Hall, a large and convenient place, on 'God hath given unto us eternal life, and this life is in his Son.'[20] There having been a feast in the town that day, I 25 believed it needful to add a few words upon intemperance. And while I was saying, 'As for you, drunkards, you have no part in *this* life; you abide in death; you choose death and hell,' a man cried out vehemently, 'I am one; and thither I am going.' But I trust God

[15] JW quoted this paragraph in his apologetic letter to Bishop Warburton, Nov. 26, 1762 (Telford, IV. 356), insisting that it was not evidence of an inexorable spirit in himself nor of damning men to perdition.

[16] Orig., 'Lanissan'. Llanishen was a small parish 3 1/2 miles N. of Cardiff.

[17] See Ps. 91:11; Luke 4:10.

[18] Not as Curnock (II.505, n. 3) conjectures, 'Thomas Williams of Blew House, Gent.', but Thomas Williams of Llanishen Fach farm, a member of a prominent family in the Vale of Glamorgan and for some years one of JW's exhorters. He died Apr. 19, 1783, aged 86. T. J. Hopkins in *Vale of History*, ed. Stewart Williams, pp. 110-12; *Bathafarn*, ix.44, quoted in Williams, *Wesley in Wales*, p. 8, n. 2. He was the father of Thomas Williams, who introduced Methodism into Ireland and urged Wesley to visit there; and possibly also of Jackie Williams, who absconded from Kingswood School in 1739. A. G. Ives, *Kingswood School in Wesley's Day and Since* (London, 1970), pp. 36, 38.

[19] Catherine Jones, aged five, who survived and eventually married John Coghlan of Bristol. *Bathafarn*, xxv.46.

[20] 1 John 5:11.

at that hour began to show him and others a more excellent way.[21]

Sat. 3. About noon we came to Pontypool. A clergyman[22] stopped me in the first street; and a few more found me out soon after, whose love I did not find to be cooled at all by the bitter adversaries who had been among them. True pains had been taken to set them against my brother and me by men who 'know not what manner of spirit they are of'.[23] But instead of disputing we betook ourselves to prayer. And all our hearts were knit together as at the first.

In the afternoon we came to Abergavenny. Those who are bitter of spirit had been here also. Yet Mrs. James (now Mrs. Whitefield)[24] received us gladly, as she had done aforetime. But we could not procure even two or three to join with us in the evening beside those of her own household. Sun. 4. I had an unexpected opportunity of receiving the Holy Communion. In the afternoon we had a plain, useful sermon on the Pharisee and the publican praying in the temple;[25] which I explained at large in the evening to the *best-dressed* congregation I have ever yet seen in Wales. Two persons came to me afterwards who were (it seemed) convinced of sin and groaning for deliverance.

Mon. 5. I preached in the morning at Pontypool, to a small but deeply attentive congregation. Mr. Price[26] conducted us from hence to his house at Watford. After resting here an hour, we hastened on and came to Fonmon, where I explained and enforced those words, 'What must I do to be saved?'[27] Many seemed quite amazed while I showed them the nature of salvation, and the gospel way of attaining it.

[21] 1 Cor. 12:31.
[22] Possibly Edmund Jones, a former critic of JW (Williams, *Wesley in Wales*, p. 9, n. 1). A year later the awakened of Pontypool were expecting a visit from Cennick.
[23] Cf. Luke 9:55.
[24] George Whitefield married Elizabeth James, widow *(c.* 1706-68), née Burnell, on Nov. 14, 1741, at St. Martin's Chapel, parish of Eglwysilan. He had never previously mentioned her in his letters, and his marriage (reported at the beginning, apparently erroneously, to be bringing him a fortune of £10,000 [*Gentleman's Magazine* (Nov. 1741), XI.608]) continued to attract spiteful comment, not least that of Berridge that 'matrimony has quite maimed poor Charles [Wesley], and might have spoiled John [Wesley] and George [Whitefield, as itinerant evangelists] if a wise master had not sent them a brace of ferrets' (Berridge to Lady Huntingdon, Mar. 23, 1770).
[25] Cf. Luke 18:10-14.
[26] Thomas Price, J.P. (cf. above, Apr. 10, 1740, n. 29). Charles Wesley had preached in this house on Nov. 15, 1740 (CWJ, I.257). Price tried to keep the temperature of controversy down, advising Harris on August 8 to beware of 'endless and drie disputings' (Williams, *Wesley in Wales*, p. 9, n. 4).
[27] Acts 16:30.

Tue. 6. I read prayers and preached in Porthkerry church.[28] My text was, 'By grace ye are saved through faith.'[29] In the evening at Cardiff I expounded Zechariah 4:7. 'Who art thou, O great mountain? Before Zerubbabel thou shalt become a plain.
5 And he shall bring forth the headstone thereof with shoutings, crying, Grace, grace unto it.' The next morning we set out, and in the evening praised God with our brethren in Bristol.

Thur. 8. I dined with C[aptain] T[urner],[30] greatly praising God for having done his own wise and holy will in taking away the
10 desire of his eyes. In the evening I preached on 'Looking unto Jesus'.[31] And many were filled with consolation.

Fri. 9. The same Spirit 'helped our infirmities'[32] at the hour of intercession; and again at Kingswood in the evening. I was just laid down when one came and told me Howell Harris desired to
15 speak with me at Bristol, being just come from London and having appointed to set out for Wales at three in the morning. I went, and found him with Mr. Humphreys and Mr. S[impson].[33] They immediately fell upon their favourite subject; on which, when we had disputed two hours and were just where we were at
20 first, I begged we might exchange controversy for prayer. We did so and then parted in much love, about two in the morning.

Sat. 10. His journey being deferred till Monday, H. Harris came to me at the New Room. He said, as to the decree of *reprobation*, he renounced and utterly abhorred it. And as to the
25 *not falling from grace*, (1) he believed that it ought not to be mentioned to the unjustified, or to any that were slack and careless, much less that lived in sin, but only to the earnest and disconsolate mourners; (2) he did himself believe it was possible for one to fall away who had been 'enlightened' with some
30 knowledge of God, who had 'tasted of the heavenly gift', and been

---

[28] A living in the gift of Robert Jones, Fonmon. The incumbent, 1728–57, was Rev. John Richards, whose suspicions of Methodism were dispelled after he had heard Charles Wesley preaching there on 15 July, 1741 (CWJ, I.287); Porthkerry was a small parish 9 miles SE. of Cowbridge.

[29] Cf. Eph. 2:8.

[30] Joseph Turner, mariner, a Methodist who, landing at St. Ives, Cornwall, in 1743, brought back news of the existence of a religious society there which led to a visit by Charles Wesley and others in July 1743. 'The desire of his eyes', his wife, was one of those whose professions of 'sinless perfection' distressed Cennick. *Moravian Messenger*, Apr. 12, 1906, p. 93.

[31] Heb. 12:2.

[32] Cf. Rom. 8:26.

[33] Joseph Humphreys (see above, June 19, 1740, n. 70) and John Simpson (see above, Apr. 19, 1740, n. 37).

'made partaker of the Holy Ghost',[34] and wished we could all agree to keep close in the controverted points to the very words of Holy Writ; (3) that he accounted no man so justified as not to fall till he was vitally united to Christ, till he had a thorough, abiding hatred to all sin and a continual hunger and thirst after all righteousness. Blessed be thou of the Lord, thou man of peace! Still follow after peace and holiness.

Thur. 15. I was preparing for another journey to Wales, which I had designed to begin on Friday, when I received a message from H. Harris, desiring me to set out immediately[35] and meet him near the New Passage. I accordingly set out at noon, but being obliged to wait at the water-side did not reach Wilcrick[36] (the place he had appointed for our meeting) till an hour or two after night. But this was soon enough. For he had not been there. Nor could we hear anything of him. So we went back to Magor,[37] and thence in the morning to Llanmarton, a village two miles off, where we heard Mr. Daniel Rowland[38] was to be, whom accordingly we found there. Evil surmisings presently vanished away, and our hearts were knit together in love. We rode together to Machen[39] (five miles beyond Newport) which we reached about twelve o'clock. In an hour after H. Harris came, and many of his friends from distant parts.[40] We had no dispute of any kind, but the spirit of peace and love was in the midst of us. At three we went to church. There was a vast congregation, though at only a few hours' warning. After prayers I preached first on those words in the Second Lesson, 'The life which I now live, I live by faith of

[34] Cf. Heb. 6:4.
[35] With a view to reuniting Arminian and Calvinistic Methodism.
[36] Orig., 'Will-creek'. The rector of Llanmartin and Wilcrick, 1740 until his death in 1795, was the Rev. John Powell, a friend of Methodism who attended the joint English and Welsh association at Watford in January 1743 (Williams, *Wesley in Wales*, p. 10, n. 3). Llanmartin was 5 miles NE. of Newport.
[37] Orig., 'Mather'. Magor is a village 8 miles SW. of Chepstow.
[38] Daniel Rowland (1713–90), a Welsh clergyman who became an itinerant preacher in addition to serving Welsh parishes about the same time that Howell Harris (a layman) was beginning to preach. Their eventual cooperation led to the founding of Welsh Calvinistic Methodism, which held its first 'association' (like the English Methodist Conference) in January 1743. Rowland was appointed deputy moderator of this body with power to act in George Whitefield's absence. The latter ceased to attend the body, and Rowland became chairman until his death. Suspended by Bishop Squire from his clerical functions in 1763, he preached with undiminished power at a new chapel in Llangeitho. JW often spelled his name 'Rowlands'.
[39] Orig., 'Machan'. Machen was a village 4 miles E. of Caerphilly.
[40] Including Herbert Jenkins, Thomas Price, and Mrs. Elizabeth James. *Bathafarn*, x.43, quoted in Williams, *Wesley in Wales*, p. 11, n. 3.

the Son of God, who loved *me* and gave himself for *me*.'[41] Mr.
Rowlands then preached in Welsh on Matthew 28:8. 'Fear ye not;
for ye seek Him that was crucified.'[42]
We rode afterwards to St. Bride's in the moors,[43] where Mr.
5 Rowlands preached again. Here we were met by Mr. Humphreys
and Thomas Bissicks of Kingswood. About eleven a few of us
retired in order to provoke one another to love and to good
works.[44] But T. Bissicks immediately introduced the dispute, and
others seconded him. This H. Harris and Mr. Rowlands strongly
10 withstood; but finding it profited nothing Mr. Rowlands soon
withdrew. H. Harris kept them at a bay till about one o'clock in
the morning. I then left them and Capt[ain] T[urner] together.
About three they left off just where they began.
Sat. 17. Going to a neighbouring house, I found Mr.
15 H[umphreys] and T. Bissicks tearing open the sore with all their
might. On my coming in all was hushed. But Mrs. James of
Abergavenny[45] (a woman of candour and humanity) insisted that
those things should be said to my face. There followed a lame
piece of work. But although the accusations brought were easily
20 answered, yet I found they left a soreness on many spirits. When
H. Harris heard of what had passed, he hasted to stand in the gap
once more and with tears besought them all to 'follow after the
things that make for peace'.[46] And God blessed the healing words
which he spoke, so that we parted in much love, being all
25 determined to let controversy alone and to preach Jesus Christ
and him crucified.[47]
I preached at Cardiff at three, and about five set out thence for
Fonmon Castle. Notwithstanding the great darkness of the night,
and our being unacquainted with the road, before eight we came
30 safe to the congregation, which had been some time waiting for
us. I preached on our Lord's words to the rich young man, 'If thou
wilt enter into life, keep the commandments.'[48] Blessed be God
that we have a better covenant, established upon better promises.

---

[41] Cf. Gal. 2:20.
[42] Cf. Matt. 28:5.
[43] St. Bride's Wentlloog, a village 4 miles S. of Newport.
[44] See Heb. 10:24. Joseph Humphreys had broken with Wesley in April; Thomas
Bissicks had sided with Cennick when he broke away from Wesley at Kingswood on
March 7.
[45] See above, Oct. 3, n. 24.
[46] Rom. 14:19.
[47] 1 Cor. 2:2.
[48] Matt. 19:17.

Sun. 18. I rode to Wenvoe.[49] The church was thoroughly filled with attentive hearers, while I preached on those words, 'Whom ye ignorantly worship, him declare I unto you.'[50] In the afternoon I read prayers and preached at Porthkerry. In the evening there was a great concourse of people at the Castle[51] to whom I strongly declared 'the hope of righteousness' which is 'through faith'.[52]

Mon. 19. I preached once more at Porthkerry, and in the afternoon returned to Cardiff and explained to a large congregation, 'When they had nothing to pay, he frankly forgave them both.'[53]

Tue. 20. At eleven I preached at the prison, on 'I came not to call the righteous, but sinners to repentance.'[54] In the afternoon I was desired to meet one of the 'honourable women';[55] whom I found a *mere sinner*, groaning under the mighty hand of God. About six, at Mr. W's[56] desire, I preached once more on those words, 'Whom ye ignorantly worship, him declare I unto you.'

Wed. 21. I set out soon after preaching, and about nine came to Newport. A clergyman,[57] soon after I was set down, came into the next room and asked aloud, with a tone unusually sharp, where those vagabond fellows were. Capt[ain] T[urner], without any ceremony, took him in hand. But he soon quitted the field and walked out of the house. Just as I was taking horse he returned and said, 'Sir, I am afraid you are in a wrong way. But if you are right, I pray God to be with you, and prosper your undertakings.'

About one I came to Caldicot[58] and preached to a small, attentive company of people, on 'Blessed are they which do

[49] The home of the rector of the parish, John Hodges (1700–1777), one of the Welsh clergy most sympathetic to JW, who attended the first three Conferences. He was said about this time to have administered Holy Communion every Sunday, catechized every Sunday afternoon, and kept a society in his church every Sunday evening. Later in life he lost interest in Methodism in favour of mysticism. (Williams, *Wesley in Wales*, p. 12, n. 2, with references.) Wenvoe was a small parish 6 miles SW. by W. from Cardiff.

[50] Acts 17:23.

[51] I.e., at Fonmon.

[52] Cf. Gal. 5:5.

[53] Luke 7:42.

[54] Mark 2:17; Luke 5:32.

[55] Acts 13:50; 17:12. The woman in this instance has been supposed to be Susan Young, who had been mortified by a rebuke from Charles Wesley on Nov. 10, 1740. CWJ, II.256.

[56] Williams (*Wesley in Wales*, p. 13, n. 1) suggests Rev. Nathaniel Wells, rector of St. Andrew's, Dinas Powys, who had first invited CW to Cardiff in November 1740.

[57] Possibly Rev. Thomas Mills Hoare, M.A., incumbent of St. Woollo's, 1726–59. Williams, *Wesley in Wales*, p. 13, n. 2.

[58] Orig., 'Callicut'. Caldicot was a parish of modest size 6 miles SW. of Chepstow.

hunger and thirst after righteousness; for they shall be filled.'[59]
Between seven and eight we reached Bristol.

Thur. 22. I called upon Edward W——, who had been ill for
several days. I found him in deep despair. Since he had left off
prayer, 'all the waves and storms were gone over him.'[60] We cried
unto God, and his soul revived. A little light shone upon him and,
just as we sung,

> Be Thou his strength and righteousness,
> His Jesus and his all,[61]

his spirit returned to God.

Fri. 23. I saw several others who were ill of the same distemper.
Surely our Lord will do much work by this sickness. I do not find
that it comes to any house without leaving a blessing behind it. In
the evening I went to Kingswood and found Ann Steed[62] also
praising God in the fires and testifying that all her weakness and
pain wrought together for good.

Sat. 24. I visited more of the sick, both in Kingswood and
Bristol. And it was pleasant work, for I found none of them
'sorrowing as men without hope'.[63] At six I expounded, 'God is
light, and in him is no darkness at all.'[64] And his light broke in
upon us in such a manner that we were even lost in praise and
thanksgiving.

Sun. 25. After the Sacrament at All Saints' I took horse for
Kingswood. But before I came to Lawrence Hill my horse fell,
and attempting to rise, fell down again upon me. One or two
women ran out of a neighbouring house, and when I rose, helped
me in. I adore the wisdom of God. In this house were three
persons who began to run well, but Satan had hindered them.[65]

---

[59] Matt. 5:6.
[60] Cf. Ps. 42:9 (BCP).
[61] See Watts, *Hymns and Spiritual Songs*, ii.90, 'How sad our state by nature is,' ver. 6:

> Be thou my strength and righteousness,
> My Jesus, and my all.

Wesley included this hymn in his 1737 Charlestown *Collection*, p. 52, from which it
came into the 1741 *Collection of Psalms and Hymns* (pp. 18-19), doubtless in use on this
occasion.
[62] JW had conversed with Ann Steed privately (see diary, July 18, 1741) and was to
preach her funeral sermon (see JWJ, Oct. 28, 1762), commending her as 'the first witness
in Bristol of the great salvation', i.e., of sanctification.
[63] Cf. BCP, Burial, Collect.
[64] 1 John 1:5.
[65] See 1 Thess. 2:18.

But they resolved to set out again. And not one of them has looked back since.

Notwithstanding this delay I got to Kingswood by two. The words God enabled me to speak there, and afterwards at Bristol (so I must express myself still; for I dare not ascribe them to my own wisdom), were as a hammer and a flame. And the same blessing we found at the meeting of the society. But more abundantly at the love-feast which followed. I remember nothing like it for many months. A cry was heard from one end of the congregation to the other; not of grief, but of overflowing joy and love. 'O continue forth thy loving-kindness unto them that know thee; and thy mercy to them that are true of heart!'[66]

The great comfort I found both in public and private, almost every day of the ensuing week, I apprehend was to prepare me for what followed; a short account of which I sent to London soon after in a letter, the copy of which I have subjoined,[67] although I am not insensible there are several circumstances therein which some may set down for mere enthusiasm and extravagance.

Dear Brother,

All last week I found hanging upon me the effects of the violent cold I had contracted in Wales; not, I think (as Mr. Turner and Walcam[68] supposed), by lying in a damp bed at St. Bride's, but rather by riding continually in the cold and wet nights, and preaching immediately after. But I believed it would pass off, and so took little notice of it till Friday morning. I then found myself exceeding sick, and as I walked to Baptist Mills (to pray with Susanna Basil, who was ill of a fever), felt the wind pierce me, as it were, through. At my return I found myself something better. Only I could not eat anything at all. Yet I felt no want of strength at the hour of intercession, nor at six in the evening, while I was opening and applying those words, 'Sun, stand thou still in Gibeon, and thou, moon, in the valley of Ajalon.'[69] I was afterwards refreshed and slept well, so that I apprehended no farther disorder, but rose in the morning as usual and declared with a strong voice and an enlarged heart, 'Neither circumcision availeth anything, nor uncircumcision, but faith that worketh by love.'[70] About

[66] Cf. Ps. 36:10 (BCP).
[67] This letter was almost certainly written to his brother Charles and most probably on Nov. 7, 1741.
[68] John Walcam, broker and teaman, Castle Precincts, Bristol, a member of the Methodist society. For JW's account of the death of his daughter, see JWJ, June 1, 1751.
[69] Josh. 10:12.
[70] Gal. 5:6.

two in the afternoon, just as I was set down to dinner, a shivering came
upon me and a little pain in my back, but no sickness at all, so that I eat
[ate] a little, and then, growing warm, went to see some that were sick.
Finding myself worse about four I would willingly have lain down. But
5   having promised to see Mrs. G——, who had been out of order for
some days, I went thither first, and thence to Weavers' Hall. A man
gave me a token for good as I went along: 'Ay', said he, '*he* will be a
martyr too by and by.' The Scripture I enforced was, 'My little
children, these things I write unto you, that ye sin not. But if any man
10   sin, we have an advocate with the Father, Jesus Christ the
righteous.'[71] I found no want either of inward or outward strength.
But afterwards, finding my fever increased, I called on Dr.
Middleton.[72] By his advice I went home and took my bed—a strange
thing for me, who had not kept my bed a day (for five and thirty years)
15   ever since I had the smallpox. I immediately fell into a profuse sweat,
which continued till one or two in the morning. God then gave me
refreshing sleep, and afterwards such tranquillity of mind that this
day, Sunday, November 1, seemed the shortest day to me I had ever
known in my life.

20   I think a little circumstance ought not to be omitted, although I
know there may be an ill construction put upon it. Those words
were now so strongly impressed upon my mind that for a
considerable time I could not put them out of my thoughts:
'Blessed is the man that provideth for the poor and needy; the
25   Lord shall deliver him in the time of trouble. The Lord shall
strengthen him when he lieth sick upon his bed; make thou all his
bed in his sickness.'[73]

On Sunday night likewise I slept well and was easy all Monday
morning. But about three in the afternoon the shivering returned,
30   much more violent than before. It continued till I was put to bed. I was
then immediately as in a fiery furnace. In a little space I began
sweating, but the sweating seemed to increase rather than allay the
burning heat. Thus I remained till about eight o'clock, when I
suddenly awaked out of a kind of doze, in such a sort of disorder
35   (whether of body or mind, or both) as I know not how to describe. My
heart and lungs and all that was within me, and my soul too, seemed to

---

[71] Cf. 1 John 2:1.

[72] Dr. John Middleton (perhaps matriculated at Edinburgh, 1699), who died December
1760, was on intimate terms with both the Wesley brothers (cf. above, Sept. 1, 1740, n. 54)
and sustained a reputation for 'great natural and acquired abilities in his profession, . . .
unaffected piety, diffusive benevolence and untainted morals'.

[73] Cf. Ps. 41:1, 3 (BCP).

be in perfect uproar. But I cried unto the Lord in my trouble, and he delivered me out of my distress.[74]

I continued in a moderate sweat till near midnight, and then slept pretty well till morning. On Tuesday, November 3, about noon, I was removed to Mr. Hooper's.[75] Here I enjoyed a blessed calm for several 5 hours, the fit not returning till six in the evening, and then in such a manner as I never heard or read of. I had a quick pulse, attended with violent heat; but no pain either in my head or back or limbs; no sickness, no stitch, no thirst. Surely God is a present help in time of trouble. And he does make all my bed in my sickness. 10

Wed. 4. Many of our brethren agreed to seek God today by fasting and prayer. About twelve my fever began to rage. At two I dozed a little, and suddenly awaked in such disorder (only more violent) as that on Monday. The silver cord appeared to be just then loosing, and the wheel breaking at the cistern.[76] The blood whirled to and fro, as if 15 it would immediately force its way through all its vessels, especially in the breast; and excessive, burning heat parched up my whole body, both within and without. About three, in a moment, the commotion ceased, the heat was over, and the pain gone. Soon after it made another attack, but not near so violent as the former. This lasted till 20 half an hour past four and then vanished away at once. I grew better and better till nine. Then I fell asleep, and scarce awaked at all till morning.

Thur. 5. The noisy joy of the people in the streets[77] did not agree with me very well; though I am afraid it disordered their poor souls 25 much more than it did my body. About five in the evening my cough returned, and soon after the heat and other symptoms; but with this remarkable circumstance, that for fourteen or fifteen hours following I had more or less sleep in every hour. This was one cause why I was never light-headed at all, but had the use of my understanding, from 30 the first hour of my illness to the last, as fully as when in perfect health.

Fri. 6. Between ten and twelve the main shock began. I can give but a faint account of this, not for want of memory, but of words. I felt in my body nothing but storm and tempest, hailstones and coals of fire. 35 But I do not remember that I felt any fear (such was the mercy of God!) nor any murmuring. And yet I found but a dull, heavy kind of patience, which I knew was not what it ought to be. The fever came

---

[74] See Ps. 107:6.
[75] Mr. Hooper was a maltster in Old Market Street, to whose home letters for JW were addressed. Charles Wesley had also been nursed in this home when sick and had written an elegy on Mrs. Hooper when she died, May 6, 1741. Cf. CWJ, I.270-72; *Poet. Wks.*, II.183-84.
[76] See Eccles. 12:6.
[77] It being Guy Fawkes Day.

rushing upon me as a lion, ready to break all my bones in pieces. My body grew weaker every moment; but I did not feel my soul put on strength. Then it came into my mind, 'Be still, and see the salvation of the Lord. I will not stir hand or foot; but let him do with me what is good in his own eyes.'[78] At once my heart was at ease. My mouth was filled with laughter and my tongue with joy.[79] My eyes overflowed with tears, and I began to sing aloud. One who stood by said, 'Now he is light-headed.' I told her, 'O no. I am not light-headed, but I am praising God. God is come to my help, and pain is nothing. Glory be to God on high.' I now found why it was not expedient for me to recover my health sooner; because then I should have lost this experimental proof how little everything is which can befall the body, so long as God carries the soul aloft, as it were on the wings of an eagle.

An hour after, I had one more grapple with the enemy, who then seemed to collect all his strength. I essayed to shake myself and praise God as before. But I was not able: the power was departed from me. I was shorn of my strength, and become weak and like another man. Then I said, 'Yet here I hold. Lo, I come to bear thy will, O God.' Immediately he returned to my soul, and lifted up the light of his countenance. And I felt, 'He rideth easily enough whom the grace of God carrieth.'[80]

I supposed the fit was now over, it being about five in the afternoon, and began to compose myself for sleep, when I felt first a chill and then a burning all over, attended with such an universal faintness and weariness and utter loss of strength, as if the whole frame of nature had been dissolved. Just then my nurse, I know not why, took me out of bed and placed me in a chair. Presently a purging began, which I believe saved my life. I grew easier from that hour and had such a night's rest as I have not had before, since it pleased God to lay his hand upon me.

From Saturday November 7 to Sunday 15 I found my strength gradually increasing, and was able to read Turretin's history of the church[81] (a dry, heavy, barren treatise) and the life of that truly

---

[78] Cf. Exod. 14:13; 2 Kgs. 10:5.

[79] See Ps. 126:2 (BCP).

[80] Kempis, *Christian's Pattern*, ed. JW, 1735 (*Bibliography*, No. 4), II.ix.1.

[81] John Alphonse Turretini, *Historiae Ecclesiasticae Compendium a Christo nato usque ad annum MDCC* (Geneva, 1734). Turretini (1671–1737), rector of the Academy at Geneva (1701–11), was professor of church history there (1697–1705) and then professor of systematic theology. With Ostervald and Werenfels he presided over the transition from high orthodoxy to slightly more liberal views in Swiss Protestantism, and hoped for a union of the Reformed, Lutheran, and Anglican churches.

good and great man, Mr. Philip Henry.[82] On Monday and Tuesday I read over the life of Mr. Matthew Henry,[83] a man not to be despised, either as a scholar or a Christian, though (I think) not equal to his father. On Wednesday I read over once again *Theologia Germanica.*[84] O how was it that I could ever so admire 5 the affected obscurity of this unscriptural writer! Glory be to God that I now prefer the plain apostles and prophets before him and all his *mystic* followers.

Thur. 19. I read again, with great surprise, part of the ecclesiastical history of Eusebius.[85] But so weak, credulous, 10 thoroughly injudicious[86] a writer have I seldom found. Fri. 20. I began Mr. Laval's history of the reformed churches in France,[87] full of the most amazing instances of the wickedness of men and of the goodness and power of God. About noon the next day I went out in a coach as far as the school in Kingswood; where one 15 of the mistresses lay (as was believed) near death, having found no help from all the medicines she had taken. We determined to try one remedy more. So we poured out our souls in prayer to God. From that hour she began to recover strength, and in a few days was out of danger. 20

Sun. 22. Being not suffered to go to church as yet, I communicated at home. I was advised to stay at home some time

[82] Matthew Henry, *An Account of the Life and Death of the Rev. Philip Henry* (np. 1698). Philip Henry (1631–96) was one of the Puritan ministers who lost his benefice at the Restoration but retained such scruples against acting to the detriment of the establishment that 'he would never call himself a pastor' to those who attached themselves to his ministry *(Life of Philip Henry,* ed. J. B. Williams, 2nd edn., Edinburgh, 1974, pp. 131-33). JW included extracts from the *Life* in his *Christian Library,* Vol. L.

[83] W. Tong, *An Account of the Life and Death of Matthew Henry* (London, 1716). Matthew Henry, the son and biographer of Philip, was for generations greatly prized as an exegete by that evangelical tradition which derived from Baxter, and his expository works were used by JW himself.

[84] *Theologia Germanica* was the title of a mystical work of the late fourteenth or early fifteenth century written by a regular priest in Sachsenhausen, edited by Luther in 1516 and 1518, and studied by JW in Georgia. Stressing the need for simplicity and self-denial, the text was much prized among Lutheran pietists.

[85] Eusebius's *Ecclesiastical History* (final edn. by the author, A.D. 323), esteemed mostly as a collection of source materials, compiled but not critically assessed, was available even in JW's day in numerous editions. The most recent English version had been published in London, 1729.

[86] The original in all contemporary editions has 'throughly-injudicious', a usage not recorded by *OED.*

[87] Stephen Abel Laval, *A compendious History of the Reformation in France, and of the Reformed Churches in that Kingdom. From the first Beginnings of the Reformation to the Repealing of the Edict of Nantz* (3 vols. in 4, London, 1737–43). Laval was one of the ministers of the United Chapels of Castle Street and Berwick Street.

longer. But I could not apprehend it necessary; and therefore, on Monday 23, went to the New Room, where we praised God for all his mercies. And I expounded (for about an hour, without any faintness or weariness), on 'What reward shall I give unto the Lord for all the benefits that he hath done unto me? I will receive the cup of salvation, and call upon the name of the Lord.'[88]

I preached once every day this week and found no inconvenience by it. Sun. 29. I thought I might go a little farther. So I preached both at Kingswood and Bristol; and afterwards spent near an hour with the society, and about two hours at the love-feast. But my body could not yet keep pace with my mind. I had another fit of my fever the next day. But it lasted not long, and I continued slowly to recover my strength.

On Thursday December 3, I was able to preach again, on 'by their fruits ye shall know them';[89] and Friday evening on 'Cast thy bread upon the waters, and after many days thou shalt find it again.'[90]

Mon. 7. I preached on 'Trust ye in the Lord Jehovah, for in the Lord is everlasting strength.'[91] I was showing what cause we had to trust in the Captain of our salvation when one in the midst of the room cried out, 'Who was *your* captain the other day, when you hanged yourself? I know the man who saw you when you was cut down.' This wise story, it seems, had been diligently spread abroad and cordially believed by many in Bristol. I desired they would make room for the man to come nearer. But the moment he saw the way open he ran away with all possible speed, not so much as once looking behind him.

Wed. 9. God humbled us in the evening by the loss of more than thirty of our little company, who I was obliged to exclude as no longer adorning the gospel of Christ. I believed it best openly to declare both their names and the reasons why they were excluded.[92] We then all cried to God that this might be for their edification and not for destruction.

Fri. 11. I went to Bath. I had often reasoned with myself concerning this place, 'Hath God left himself without witness'?[93]

[88] Ps. 116:11-12 (BCP).
[89] Matt. 7:20.
[90] Cf. Eccles. 11:1.
[91] Cf. Isa. 26:4.
[92] Cf. below, Dec. 27, 1741, in London.
[93] Cf. Acts 14:17.

Did he never raise up such as might be shining lights, even in the midst of this sinful generation? Doubtless he has; but they are either gone 'to the desert'[94] or hid under the bushel of *prudence*. Some of the most serious persons I have known at Bath are either *solitary Christians*,[95] scarce known to each other, unless by name; or *prudent Christians*, as careful not to give offence as if that were the unpardonable sin, and as zealous to 'keep their religion to themselves' as they should be to 'let it shine before men'.[96]

I returned to Bristol the next day. In the evening one desired to speak with me. I perceived him to be in the utmost confusion, so that for a while he could not speak. At length he said, 'I am he that interrupted you at the New Room on Monday. I have had no rest since, day or night, nor could have till I had spoken to you. I hope you will forgive me, and that it will be a warning to me all the days of my life.'

Tue. 15. It being a hard frost I walked over to Bath and had a conversation of several hours with one who had lived above seventy, and 'studied' divinity above thirty, years.[97] Yet remission of sins was quite a new doctrine to him. But I trust God will write it or his heart.

In the evening I took down the names of some who desired to strengthen each other's hands in God. Thus the 'bread' we have 'cast upon the waters' is 'found again after many days'.[98]

I returned to Bristol the next day. Thur. 17. We had a night of solemn joy, occasioned by the funeral of one of our brethren, who died with a hope full of immortality.[99]

Fri. 18. Being disappointed of my horse, I set out on foot in the

---

[94] An allusion to the mystics. See *Hymns and Sacred Poems* (1739), preface, §3 pp. v–vi (Vol. 12 in this edn.): 'They advise, "To the desert, to the desert, and God will build you up." Numberless are the commendations that occur in all their writings, not of retirement intermixed with conversation, but of an entire seclusion from men (perhaps for months or years) in order to purify the soul.'

[95] Cf. ibid., §5, p. viii: ' "holy solitaries" is a phrase no more consistent with the gospel than holy adulterers. The gospel of Christ knows of no religion but social; no holiness but social holiness.'

[96] Cf. Matt. 5:16.

[97] Probably Dr. George Cheyne (1671–1743), two of whose works Wesley had studied in Oxford, and who continued to be an important influence upon Wesley's thought and practice (cf. Mar. 12, 1742 below, etc.). A physical and moral crisis led Cheyne to 'more serious views of things and a deeper sense of religion' *(DNB)* and to adopt a regimen of winter courses of Bath waters and summer professional practice in London. He was the brother-in-law of Dr. John Middleton (see above, Oct. 25, 1741, n. 72).

[98] Cf. Eccles. 11:1.

[99] Wisd. 3:4.

evening for Kingswood. I catched no cold, nor received any hurt, though it was very wet, and cold, and dark. Mr. Jones of Fonmon met me there, and we poured out our souls before God together. I found no weariness, till a little before one, God gave me
5 refreshing sleep.

Sun. 20. I preached once more at Bristol, on 'Little children, keep yourselves from idols';[1] immediately after which I forced myself away from those to whom my heart was now more united than ever. And I believe their hearts were even as my heart. O
10 what poor words are those, 'You abate the *reverence* and *respect* which the people owe to their pastors.' Love is all in all, and all who are alive to God *must* pay this to every true pastor. Wherever a flock is duly fed with the pure milk of the word, they will be ready (were it possible) to pluck out their eyes and give them to
15 those that are over them in the Lord.

I took coach on Monday 21, and on Wednesday came to London. Thur. 24. I found it was good for me to be here; particularly while I was preaching in the evening. The society afterwards met; but we scarce knew how to part, our hearts were
20 so enlarged toward each other.

Sat. 26. The morning congregation was increased to above thrice the usual number, while I explained, 'Grace be unto you, and peace, from God the Father and from our Lord Jesus Christ.'[2] At Long Lane likewise in the evening I had a crowded
25 audience, to whom I spoke from those words, 'O the depth of the riches both of the wisdom and knowledge of God! How unsearchable are his judgments, and his ways past finding out!'[3]

Sun. 27. After diligent inquiry made, I removed all those from
30 the congregation of the faithful whose behaviour or spirit was not agreeable to the gospel of Christ; openly declaring the objections I had to each, that others might fear and cry to God for them.[4]

Thur. 31. By the unusual overflowing of peace and love to all which I felt, I was inclined to believe some trial was at hand. At
35 three in the afternoon my fever came. But finding it was not violent, I would not break my word, and therefore went at four and committed to the earth the remains of one who had died in

[1] 1 John 5:21.
[2] Cf. 1 Cor. 1:3, etc.
[3] Rom. 11:33.
[4] Cf. below, Dec. 9, 1741, in Bristol. This paragraph was omitted from *Works* (1774).

the Lord a few days before; neither could I refrain from exhorting the almost innumerable multitude of people, who were gathered together round her grave, to cry to God that they might die the death of the righteous, and their last end be like hers. I then designed to lie down, but Sir John G[anson][5] coming and sending to speak with me, I went to him, and from him into the pulpit, knowing God could renew my strength. I preached, according to her request who was now with God, on those words with which her soul had been so refreshed a little before she went hence, after a long night of doubts and fears: 'Thy sun shall no more go down, neither shall thy moon withdraw itself. For the Lord shall be thine everlasting light, and the days of thy mourning shall be ended.'[6]

At the society which followed many cried after God with a loud and bitter cry. About ten I left them and committed myself into his hands, to do with me what seemed him good.

Friday, January 1, 1742. After a night of quiet sleep I waked in a strong fever, but without any sickness or thirst or pain. I consented, however, to keep my bed; but on condition that everyone who desired it should have liberty to speak with me. I believe fifty or sixty persons did so this day, nor did I find any inconvenience from it. In the evening I sent for all of the bands who were in the house,[7] that we might magnify our Lord together. A near relation[8] being with me when they came, I asked her afterwards if she was not offended. 'Offended!' said she: 'I wish I could be always among you. I thought I was in heaven.'

---

[5] Sir John Ganson (who appears neither in the *Book of Knights* nor the *Complete Baronetage*), a Middlesex magistrate who extended legal protection to the Methodists (cf. May 31, 1740, CWJ, I.236, where the name is spelled 'Gunson'). As the diary shows, JW had been in touch with him at intervals for over a year and visited him affectionately as a nonagenarian (see JWJ, Dec. 8, 1764). In 'A Short History of the People called Methodists' (1781) JW recalled that on the present occasion, 'Sir John Ganson called upon me, and informed me, "Sir, you have no need to suffer these riotous mobs to molest you, as they have done long. I and all the other Middlesex magistrates have orders from above to do you justice whenever you apply to us." Two or three weeks after, we did apply. Justice was done, though not with rigour. And from that time we had peace in London' (9:433 in this edn.). The 'orders from above' were a personal intervention of George II in Council; for the story of his motives see Moore, *Wesley*, II.2-3; J. S. Simon, *John Wesley and the Methodist Societies* (London, Epworth, 1921), pp. 39-40.

[6] Isa. 60:20.

[7] I.e., in the Foundery.

[8] Probably JW's sister Anne, Mrs. Lambert (born 1702), with whom, as the diary shows, he was often in contact in London. But unmarried sisters of his mother also lived in London.

This night also, by the blessing of God, I slept well, to the utter astonishment of those about me, the apothecary in particular, who said he had never seen such a fever in his life. I had a clear remission in the morning, but about two in the afternoon a 5 stronger fit than any before. Otherwise I had determined to have been at the meeting of the bands. But good is the will of the Lord.

Sun. 3. Finding myself quite free from pain, I met the leaders, morning and afternoon, and joined with a little company of them in the great sacrifice of thanksgiving.[9] In the evening, it being the 10 men's love-feast, I desired they would all come up. Those whom the room would not contain stood without, while we all with one mouth sang praise to God.

Mon. 4. I waked in perfect health. Does not God both kill and make alive? This day (I understand) poor Charles Kinchin died![10]

15   . . . *Cui Pudor, et Justitiae soror,*
        Incorrupta Fides, nudaque Veritas,
        Quando ullum invenient parem?[11]

I preached morning and evening every day, for the remaining part of the week. On Saturday, while I was preaching at Long 20 Lane, a rude rout lift up their voice on high. I fell upon them without delay. Some pulled off their hats and opened their mouth no more. The rest stole out, one after another. All that remained were quiet and attentive.

Sun. 10. I got a little time to see Mr. Dolman.[12] Two 25 years ago he seemed to be dying of an asthma, being hardly able to rise at eight o'clock in a morning, after struggling, as it were, for life. But from the time he came thither first, he rarely failed to be at the Foundery by five o'clock. Nor was he at all the worse, his distemper being suspended till within a very few 30 days. I found him just on the wing, and full of love and peace and joy in believing. And in the same spirit (as I afterwards

---

[9] The Eucharist.

[10] See above, Mar. 10, 1738, n. 50 (18:228 in this edn.). Kinchin's widow continued a very active Moravian, marrying Ernst Ludolf Schlicht.

[11] Horace, *Odes*, I.xxiv.6–8, on the death of Virgil. (The original has 'inveniet'.) In the 'Latin sentences translated', appended to Vol. 32 of his *Works* JW included a paraphrase:

> When will his like be found, for Modesty,
> Unblemished Faithfulness, and naked Truth?

[12] The diary shows that JW had been a frequent visitor at Dolman's house over the two years in question.

understood) he continued, till God took himself to himself.

Mon. 11. I went twice to Newgate, at the request of poor R[obert] R[amsey],[13] who lay there under sentence of death, but was refused admittance. Receiving a few lines from him on the day he was to die, I desired Mr. Richards[14] to try if he could be 5 admitted then. But he came back with a fresh refusal.

It was above two years before that, being destitute and in distress, he applied to me at Bristol for relief. I took him in and employed him for the present in writing and keeping accounts for me. Not long after I placed him in the little school which was kept 10 by the United Society. There were many suspicions of him during that time, as well as of his companion Gwillim Snowde.[15] But no proof appeared, so that, after three or four months, they quietly returned to London. But they did not deceive God nor escape his hand. Gwillim Snowde was soon apprehended for a robbery, and 15 when condemned sent for me and said nothing lay heavier upon him than his having thus returned evil for good. I believe it was now the desire of poor R[amsey], too, to tell me all that he had done. But the hour was past! I could not now be permitted to see or speak with him. So that he who before would not receive the 20 word of God from my mouth, now desired what he could not obtain. And on Wednesday he fell a sacrifice to the justice of a long-offended God. O consider this, ye that *now* forget God, and know not the day of your visitation!

In the afternoon I buried the body of James St. Angel,[16] who 25 having long been tried in the fire, on Monday, in the full triumph of faith, gave up his spirit to God.

I heard of several today who began to run well but did not endure to the end. Men fond of their own opinions tore them from their brethren and could not keep them when they had 30

[13] Robert Ramsey had stolen money from Kingswood School. See above, Jan. 31, 1740, n. 90.

[14] Thomas Richards was one of the first masters at Kingswood (where he would have known Ramsey) and was regarded by JW as 'rough' (see JWJ, June 21, 1751). He attended the Conferences of 1744 and 1745 (Wesley Historical Society, Publication No. 1, pp. 7, 19), but obtained episcopal ordination through Lady Huntingdon (Seymour, *Countess of Huntingdon*, I.446 n.). On Nov. 15, 1749, he married Mary Davie, widow, at Hayes, Middlesex (WHS, 4:34).

[15] Cf. above, Feb. 12, 1740, where Snowde spells his name 'Gwillam', 1769 has 'Gwilliam'.

[16] The extant band-lists of the Foundery Society do not begin until Apr. 17, 1742, and no one with this surname appears in the first; it is probable that James St. Angel was a single man or a widower.

done; but they soon fell back into the world, and are now swallowed up in its pleasures or cares. I fear those zealots who took these souls out of my hands will give but a poor account of them to God.

5   On Thursday and Friday I visited the sick, by many of whom I was greatly refreshed. Mon. 18. We greatly rejoiced in the Lord at Long Lane, even in the midst of those that contradicted and blasphemed. Nor was it long before many of them also were touched, and blasphemies were turned to praise.

10   Thur. 21. I again visited many that were sick, but I found no fear either of pain or death among them. One (Mary Whittle) said, 'I shall go to my Lord tomorrow. But before I go, he will finish his work.' The next day she lay quiet for about two hours, and then opening her eyes, cried out, 'It is done, it is done! Christ

15 liveth in me! He lives in me!' And died in a moment.

Fri. 22. I met the society at Short's Gardens, Drury Lane, for the first time. Sat. 23. I called on another, who was believed to be near death, and greatly triumphing over it. 'I know', said she, 'that my redeemer liveth, and will stand at the latter day upon the

20 earth. I fear not death. It hath no sting for me. I shall live for evermore.'

Mon. 25. While I was explaining at Long Lane, 'He that committeth sin is of the devil,'[17] his servants were above measure enraged: they not only made all possible noise (although, as I had

25 desired before, no man stirred from his place or answered them a word), but violently thrust many persons to and fro, struck others, and brake down part of the house. At length they began throwing large stones upon the house, which, forcing their way wherever they came, fell down together with the tiles among the people, so

30 that they were in danger of their lives. I then told them, 'You must not go on thus. I am ordered by the magistrate, who is in this respect to us the minister of God, to inform him of those who break the laws of God and the king. And I must do it, if you persist herein, otherwise I am a partaker of your sin.' When I ceased

35 speaking they were more outrageous than before. Upon this I said, 'Let three or four calm men take hold of the foremost and charge a constable with him, that the law may take its course.' They did so, and brought him into the house, cursing and blaspheming in a dreadful manner. I desired five or six to go with

---

[17] 1 John 3:8.

him to Justice Copeland,[18] to whom they nakedly related the fact. The Justice immediately bound him over to the next Sessions at Guildford.

I observed, when the man was brought into the house, that many of his companions were loudly crying out, 'Richard Smith! Richard Smith!' Who, as it afterward appeared, was one of their stoutest champions. But Richard Smith answered not; he was fallen into the hands of One higher than they. God had struck him to the heart, as also a woman, who was speaking words not fit to be repeated and throwing whatever came to hand, whom he overtook in the very act. She came into the house with Richard Smith, fell upon her knees before us all, and strongly exhorted him never to turn back, never to forget the mercy which God had now shown to his soul. From this time we had never any considerable interruption or disturbance at Long Lane, although we withdrew our prosecution, upon the offender's submission and promise of better behaviour.

Tue. 26. I explained at Chelsea[19] the faith which worketh by love. I was very weak when I went into the room. But the more 'the beasts of the people'[20] increased in madness and rage, the more was I strengthened, both in body and soul; so that I believe few in the house, which was exceeding full, lost one sentence of what I spoke. Indeed they could not see me nor one another at a few yards' distance by reason of the exceeding thick smoke, which was occasioned by the wild-fire and things of that kind, continually thrown into the room. But they who could praise God in the midst of the fires were not to be affrighted by a little smoke.

Wed. 27. I buried the body of Sarah Whiskin,[21] a young woman late of Cambridge: a short account of whom follows, in the words of one that was with her during her last struggle for eternity.

The first time she went, intending to hear Mr. Wesley, was January 3. But he was then ill. She went again Tuesday 5 and was not

---

[18] Probably John Copeland of Peckham, who died Aug. 22, 1761, aged 87. *Gentleman's Magazine* (Sept. 1761), XXXI.430.
[19] Chelsea was a London suburb, still a single parish on the north bank of the Thames, with its palmiest days as a suburb still to come.
[20] Cf. Ps. 68:30 (BCP).
[21] Sarah Whiskin, died Jan. 27, 1742. A full account of 'her last struggle for eternity', finally victorious, is given in *Arminian Magazine* (1781), IV.198-201. She was probably connected with James Whiskin, Mayor of Cambridge in 1717, 1727, and 1736, who died on Jan. 16, 1741. F. Blomefield, *Collectanea Cantabrigiensia* (Norwich, 1751), pp. 227-28; *Gentleman's Magazine* (Jan. 1741), XI.50.

disappointed. From that time she seemed quite taken up with the things above, and could willingly have been always hearing, or praying, or singing hymns. Wednesday 13 she was sent for into the country; at which news she cried violently, being afraid to go, lest she

5   should be again conformable to the world. With tears in her eyes she asked me, 'What shall I do? I am in a great strait.' And being advised to commit her cause to God and pray that his will might be done, not her own, she said she would defer her journey three days, to wait upon God, that he might show his will concerning her. The next day

10 she was taken ill of a fever. But being something better on Friday, she sent and took a place in the Cambridge coach for the Tuesday following. Her sister asking her if she thought it was the will of God she should go, she answered, 'I leave it to the Lord; and am sure he will find a way to prevent it, if it is not for my good.' Sun. 17. She was

15 ill again, and desired me to write a note that she might be prayed for. I asked what I should write. She answered, 'You know what I want, a lively faith.' Being better on Monday 18, she got up to prepare for her journey, though still desiring God to put a stop to it, if it was not according to his will. As soon as she rose from prayer she fainted

20 away. When she came to herself she said, 'Where is that Scripture of Balaam journeying, and the angel of the Lord standing in the way? I can bring this home to myself. I was just going this morning, and see, God has taken away all my strength.'

From this hour she was almost continually praying to God that he

25 would reveal himself to her soul. On Tuesday 19, being in tears, she was asked what was the matter. She answered, 'The devil is very busy with me.' One asking, 'Who condemns you?' she pointed to her heart and said, 'This; and God is greater than my heart.' On Thursday, after Mr. Richards had prayed with her, she was much cheerfuller

30 and said she could not doubt but God would fulfil the desire which he had given her.

Fri. 22. One of her sisters coming out of the country to see her, she said, 'If I had come to you, evil would have befallen me. But I am snatched out of the hands of the devil. Though God has not yet

35 revealed himself unto me, yet I believe, were I to die this night, before tomorrow I should be in heaven.' Her sister saying, 'I hope God will restore you to health,' she replied, 'Let him do what seemeth him good.'

Sat. 23. She said, 'I saw my mother and brother and sister in my

40 sleep, and they all received a blessing in a moment.' I asked if she thought she should die. And whether she believed the Lord would receive her soul. Looking very earnestly, she said, 'I have not seen the Lord yet. But I believe I shall see him and live. Although these are bold words for a sinner to say. Are they not?'

45 Sun. 24. I asked her, 'How have you rested?' She answered, 'Very

well. Though I have had no sleep, and I wanted none, for I have had the Lord with me. O let us not be ashamed of him, but proclaim him upon the house-top. And I know, whatever I ask in the name of Jesus, according to his will, I shall have.' Soon after she called hastily to me and said, 'I fear I have deceived myself. I thought the "amen" was 5 sealed in my heart, but I fear it is not. Go down and pray for me, and let him not go till he has given my heart's desire.' Soon after she broke out into singing and said, 'I was soon delivered of my fears. I was only afraid of a flattering hope, but if it had been so I would not have let him go.' 10

Her sister that was come to see her was much upon her mind. 'You', said she, 'are in pain for her. But I have faith for this little child. God has a favour unto her.' In the afternoon she desired me to write a bill for her. I asked, 'What shall I write?' She said, 'Return thanks for what God has done for me, and pray that he would manifest himself to 15 my relations also. Go to the preaching. Leave but one with me.' Soon after we were gone she rose up, called to the person that was with her and said, 'Now it is done. I am assured my sins are forgiven.' The person answering, 'Death is a little thing to them that die in the Lord,' she replied with vehemence, 'A little thing! It is nothing.' The person 20 then desiring she would pray for her, she answered, 'I do: I pray for all. I pray for all I know, and for them I do not know. And the Lord will hear the prayer of faith.' At our return, her sister kneeling by the bedside, she said, 'Are you not comforted, my dear, for me?' Her speech then failing, she made signs for her to be by her, and kissed 25 her and smiled upon her. She then lay about an hour without speaking or stirring; till about three o'clock on Monday morning she cried out, 'My Lord and my God!' fetched a double sigh, and died.

Fri. 29. Hearing of one who had been drawn away by those who prophesy smooth things, I went to her house. But she was 30 purposely gone abroad. Perceiving there was no human help, I desired the congregation at Short's Gardens to join with me in prayer to God that he would suffer her to have no rest in her spirit till she returned into the way of truth. Two days after she came to me of her own accord and confessed, in the bitterness of her soul, 35 that she had no rest, day or night, while she remained with them out of whose hands God had now delivered her.

There was something remarkable in the manner of their love-feast, at which she was present, Sunday 31. For above an hour all were silent; no singing, no prayer, no word of exhortation. 40 Then Mr. S—— said, 'My sisters, I was thinking in my heart how many Scripture-names there are among you.' (Might he not as well have been thinking how many barley-corns would reach

from London to Edinburgh?) 'There are three Marthas'; so he went on, telling with great exactness how many there were of every name. Then silence ensued. After a while he spake again. 'Seven of our sisters are going to Pennsylvania. But my Saviour
5 will give us as many more.' One replied, 'See, he has given us one already.' 'It is in my heart', said Mr. S——, 'to give him thanks for it': on which he spoke a few words of thanksgiving. Just before they broke up Mrs. H——[22] said, 'My Saviour puts it into my heart to pray.' She then spoke five or six sentences, and the
10 company was dismissed.

Monday, February 1. I found, after the exclusion of some who did not walk according to the gospel, about eleven hundred (who are, I trust, of a more excellent spirit) remained in the society.[23]

Thur. 4. A clergyman lately come from America,[24] who was at
15 the preaching last night, called upon me, appeared full of good desires, and seemed willing to cast in his lot with us. But I cannot suddenly answer in this matter. I must first know what spirit he is of. For none can labour with us unless he 'count all things dung and dross that he may win Christ'.[25]

20 Fri. 5. I set out and with some difficulty reached Chippenham on Saturday evening, the weather being so extremely rough and boisterous that I had much ado to sit my horse. On Sunday about noon I came to Kingswood, where were many of our friends from Bath, Bristol, and Wales. O that we may ever thus love one
25 another, with a pure heart fervently!

Mon. 8. I rode to Bath and in the evening explained the latter part of the seventh of St. Luke. Observing many noisy persons at the end of the room, I went and stood in the midst of them. But the greater part slipped away to that end from which I came, and
30 then took heart and cried aloud again. I paused, to give them their full scope, and then began a particular application to them. They were very quiet in a short time, and I trust will not forget it so soon as some of them may desire.

---

[22] Mr. S—— and Mrs. H—— have not been identified.

[23] The eleven hundred members included the Foundery, Short's Gardens, Greyhound Lane, and Wapping. JW's handwritten lists are preserved in the Colman Collection now housed at the John Rylands Library, Manchester.

[24] The identity of this clergyman remains obscure, as does that of the Dr. Andrews conjectured by Curnock (II.527, n. 1). Curnock's alternative conjecture that it was George Thompson of St. Gennys is unacceptable, being based on a confusion of George Thompson with Thomas Thompson, rector of St. Bartholomew's, Ponpon, whom JW had met in America.

[25] Cf. Phil. 3:8.

Wednesday 10, and the following days of this week, I spoke severally with all those who desired to remain in the United Society and to watch over each other in love.

Mon. 15. Many met together to consult on a proper method for discharging the public debt.[26] And it was at length agreed (1) that every member of the society who was able should contribute a penny a week; (2) that the whole society should be divided into little companies or classes, about twelve in each class; and (3) that one person in each class should receive the contribution of the rest and bring it in to the stewards weekly.

Fri. 19. I went to Bath. Many threatened great things. But I knew the strength of them and their god. I preached on, 'He shall save their people from their sins,'[27] none disturbing or interrupting me.

Sat. 20. I preached at Weavers' Hall. It was a glorious time. Several dropped to the ground as if struck by lightning. Some cried out in bitterness of soul. I knew not where to end, being constrained to begin anew, again and again. In this acceptable time we begged of God to restore our brethren who are departed from us for a season: and to teach us all to 'follow after the things that make for peace' and the 'things whereby one may edify another'.[28]

Sun. 21. In the evening I explained the 'exceeding great and precious promises'[29] which are given us, a strong confirmation whereof I read in a plain, artless account of a child whose body then lay before us. The substance of this was as follows:

John Woolley[30] was for some time in your school. But was turned out for his ill behaviour. Soon after he ran away from his parents, lurking about for several days and nights together, and hiding himself

---

[26] How JW assumed personal responsibility for the expenses of building the room in the Horsefair at Bristol is described above under May 12, 1739. In *Thoughts upon Methodism* (1786), he gave a fuller account of the way in which the Methodist class-meeting thus originated as a fund-raising device, and Capt. Foy undertook to pay the class-monies of the poorer members. See §5, 9:528 in this edn.

[27] Cf. Matt. 1:21.

[28] Cf. Rom. 14:19.

[29] 2 Pet. 1:4.

[30] John Woolley, who died Feb. 13, 1742, aged 13, had been turned out from Kingswood School for bad behaviour and then absconded from home. Appearing one night at the New Room, he was converted by a sermon of JW on disobedience to parents and returned home a model child, notwithstanding temptations to suicide. Taken ill, he sought the conversion of his father and sister and died in peace. *Arminian Magazine* (1781), IV.259-63.

in holes and corners, that his mother might not find him. During this
time he suffered both hunger and cold. Once he was three whole days
without sustenance, sometimes weeping and praying by himself, and
sometimes playing with other loose boys.

5 One night he came to the New Room. Mr. Wesley was then
speaking of disobedience to parents. He was quite confounded, and
thought there never was in the world so wicked a child as himself. He
went home, and never ran away any more. His mother saw the change
in his whole behaviour, but knew not the cause. He would often get

10 upstairs by himself to prayer, and often go alone into the fields, having
done with all his idle companions.

And now the devil began to set upon him with all his might,
continually tempting him to self-murder. Sometimes he was
vehemently pressed to hang himself, sometimes to leap into the river.

15 But this only made him the more earnest in prayer; in which after he
had been one day wrestling with God he saw himself, he said,
surrounded on a sudden with an inexpressible light, and was so filled
with joy and the love of God that he scarce knew where he was, and
with such love to all mankind that he could have laid himself on the

20 ground for his worst enemies to trample upon.

From this time his father and mother were surprised at him, he was
so diligent to help them in all things. When they went to the
preaching, he was careful to give their supper to the other children;
and when he had put them to bed hurried away to the Room, to light

25 his father or mother home. Meantime he lost no opportunity of
hearing the preaching himself or of doing any good he could, either at
home or in any place where he was.

One day, walking in the fields, he fell into talk with a farmer, who
spoke very slightly[31] of religion. John told him he ought not to talk so

30 and enlarged upon that word of the apostle (which he begged him to
consider deeply), 'Without holiness no man shall see the Lord.'[32] The
man was amazed, caught the child in his arms, and knew not how to
part with him.

His father and mother, once hearing him speak pretty loud in the

35 next room, listened to hear what he said. He was praying thus: 'Lord,
I do not expect to be heard for my much speaking. Thou knowest my
heart. Thou knowest my wants.' He then descended to particulars.
Afterward he prayed very earnestly for his parents and for his
brothers and sisters by name; then for Mr. John and Charles Wesley,

40 that God would set their faces as a flint and give them to go on,
conquering and to conquer; then for all the other ministers he could

---

[31] Apparently 'disparagingly' or 'slightingly' rather than 'carelessly' or 'lightly'. Other
examples of both these usages may be seen in *OED*.
[32] Cf. Heb. 12:14.

remember by name, and for all that were, or desired to be, true ministers of Christ.

In the beginning of his illness his mother asked him if he wanted anything. He answered, 'Nothing but Christ, and I am as sure of him as if I had him already.' He often said, 'O mother, if all the world 5 believed in Christ, what a happy world would it be! And they may. For Christ died for every soul of man. I was the worst of sinners, and he died for *me*. O Thou that callest the worst of sinners, call *me*. O, it is a free gift, I am sure I have done nothing to deserve it.'

On Wednesday he said to his mother, 'I am in very great trouble for 10 my father. He has always taken an honest care of his family. But he does not know God; if he dies in the state he is in now, he cannot be saved. I have prayed for him, and will pray for him.[a] If God should give him the true faith and then take him to himself, do not you fear. Do not you be troubled. God has promised to be a father to the 15 fatherless and a husband to the widow. I will pray for him and you in heaven; and I hope we shall sing hallelujah in heaven together.'

To his eldest sister he said, 'Do not puff yourself up with pride. When you receive your wages, which is not much, lay it out in plain necessaries. And if you are inclined to be merry, do not sing songs; 20 that is the devil's diversion. There are many lies and ill things in those idle songs. Do you sing psalms and hymns? Remember your Creator in the days of your youth. When you are at work, you may lift up your heart to God. And be sure never to rise or go to bed without asking his blessing.' 25

He added, 'I shall die. But do not cry for me. Why should you cry for me? Consider what a joyful thing it is to have a brother go to heaven. I am not a man. I am but a boy. But is it not in the Bible, "Out of the mouth of babes and sucklings thou hast ordained strength"? I know where I am going. I would not be without this knowledge for a 30 thousand worlds. For though I am not in heaven yet, I am as sure of it as if I was.'

On Wednesday night he wrestled much with God in prayer. At last, throwing his arms open, he cried, 'Come, come, Lord Jesus! I am thine. Amen and Amen.' He said, 'God answers me in my heart, Be of 35 good cheer, thou hast overcome the world'; and that immediately after he was filled with love and joy unspeakable.

He said to his mother, 'That school was the saving of my soul, for there I began to seek the Lord. But how is it that a person no sooner begins to seek the Lord but Satan straight stirs up all his instruments 40 against him?'

When he was in agony of pain he cried out, 'O Saviour, give me patience. Thou hast given me patience. But give me more. Give me

[a]N.B. His father died not long after.

thy love, and pain is nothing. I have deserved all this, and a thousand times more. For there is no sin but I have been guilty of.'

A while after he said, 'O mother, how is this? If a man does not do his work, the masters in the world will not pay him his wages. But it is not so with God. He gives me good wages, and yet I am sure I have done nothing to gain them. O, it is a free gift. It is free for every soul. For Christ has died for all.'

On Thursday morning his mother asked him how he did. He said, 'I have had much struggling tonight. But my Saviour is so loving to me I do not mind it; it is no more than nothing to me.'

Then he said, 'I desire to be buried from the Room, and I desire Mr. Wesley would preach a sermon over me, on those words of David (unless he thinks any other to be more fit), "Before I was afflicted I went astray, but now I have kept thy word." '[33]

I asked him, How do you find yourself now? He said, 'In great pain, but full of love.' I asked, But does not the love of God overcome pain? He answered, 'Yes; pain is nothing to me. I did sing praises to the Lord in the midst of my greatest pain. And I could not help it.' I asked him if he was willing to die. He replied, 'O yes, with all my heart.' I said, But if life and death were set before you, what would you choose then? He answered, 'To die and to be with Christ. I long to be out of this wicked world.'

On Thursday night he slept much sweeter than he had done for some time before. In the morning he begged to see Mr. John Wesley. When Mr. Wesley came, and after some other questions asked him what he should pray for, he said, that God would give him a clean heart and renew a right spirit within him. When prayer was ended he seemed much enlivened, and said, 'I thought I should have died today. But I must not be in haste. I am content to stay. I will tarry the Lord's leisure.'

On Saturday one asked if he still chose to die. He said, 'I have no will; my will is resigned to the will of God. But I shall die. Mother, be not troubled. I shall go away like a lamb.'

On Sunday he spoke exceeding little. On Monday his speech began to falter. On Tuesday it was gone; but he was fully in his senses, almost continually lifting up his eyes to heaven. On Wednesday, his speech being restored, his mother said, 'Jacky, you have not been with your Saviour tonight.' He replied, 'Yes, I have.' She asked, 'What did he say?' He answered, 'He bid me not be afraid of the devil. For he had no power to hurt me at all, but I should tread him under my feet.' He lay very quiet on Wednesday night. The next morning he spent in continual prayer; often repeating the Lord's Prayer and earnestly commending his soul into the hands of God.

[33] Ps. 119:67.

He then called for his little brother and sister, to kiss them, and for his mother, whom he desired to kiss him. Then (between nine and ten) he said, 'Now let me kiss *you,*' which he did, and immediately fell asleep.

He lived some months above thirteen years. 5

Sun. 28. In the evening I set out for Wales. I lay that night about six miles from Bristol, and preached in the morning, March 1, to a few of the neighbours. We then hastened to the passage, but the boat was gone, half an hour before the usual time. So I was obliged to wait till five in the afternoon. We then set out with a fair 10 breeze. But when we were nearly half over the river the wind entirely failed. The boat could not bear up against the ebbing tide, but was driven down among the rocks, on one of which we made shift to scrabble up, whence about seven we got to land.

That night I went forward about five miles, and the next 15 morning came to Cardiff. There I had the pleasure of meeting Mr. Jones of Fonmon, still pressing on into all the fullness of God. I rode with him to Wenvoe. The church was thoroughly filled, while I explained the former part of the Second Lesson, concerning the barren fig tree;[34] and the power of the Lord was 20 present, both to wound and to heal.

I explained in the evening at Fonmon, though in weakness and pain, how 'Jesus saveth us from our sins.'[35] The next morning at eight I preached at Bonvilston,[36] a little town four miles from Fonmon. Thence I rode to Llantrisant[37] and sent to the minister[38] 25 to desire the use of his church. His answer was, he should have been very willing; but the bishop had forbidden him. By what law? I am not legally convict, either of *heresy* or any other crime.

---

[34] Luke 13:6-9; the BCP Calendar prescribed Luke 13 for Mar. 2.

[35] Cf. Matt. 1:21.

[36] Orig., 'Bolston'; a tiny parish, 4 miles E. from Cowbridge.

[37] Orig., 'Lantrissent' (a spelling still in use in the nineteenth century). Llantrisant was a borough and market town 10 miles NW. by W. from Cardiff.

[38] The same fate had almost befallen Charles Wesley who reports on Nov. 17, 1740 (CWJ, I.258): 'Again my mouth was opened to preach the law and the Gospel at Llantrisant. Mr. Harris, the minister, was exceedingly civil. He had been dealt with to refuse me the pulpit, but would not break his word.' Richard Harris was vicar of Llantrisant, 1728–66. The bishop, John Gilbert (1693–1761), who ruled the diocese of Llandaff 1740–48 and was later Archbishop of York, left a reputation for haughtiness and refused to ordain the evangelical John Newton (C. J. Abbey, *The English Church and its Bishops* [London, 1887], 2:47). He is said to have introduced the practice of laying hands on each candidate at confirmation.

By what authority then am I suspended from preaching? By barefaced arbitrary power.

Another clergyman immediately offered me his church. But it being too far off I preached in a large room, spent a little time
5 with the society[39] in prayer and exhortation, and then took horse for Cardiff.

Thur. 4. About noon I preached at Llanishen, and was afterward much refreshed in meeting the little, earnest society.[40] I preached at Cardiff at seven, on 'Be not righteous overmuch,'[41] to
10 a larger congregation than before; and then exhorted the society to fear only the being over-wicked, or the falling short of the full image of God.

Fri. 5. I talked with one[42] who used frequently to say, 'I pray God I may never have this *new faith*. I desire that I may not know
15 my sins forgiven, till I come to die.' But as she was some weeks since reading the Bible at home, the clear light broke in upon her soul. She knew all *her* sins were blotted out and cried aloud, '*My* Lord and *my* God.'[43]

In the evening I expounded, 'This is the victory that
20 overcometh the world, even our faith.'[44] We afterwards admitted several new members into the society, and were greatly comforted together. Sat. 6. I left Cardiff, and about eight in the evening[45] came to Bristol.

Wed. 10. I was with a gentlewoman whose distemper has
25 puzzled the most eminent physicians for many years; it being such as they could neither give any *rational* account of nor find any remedy for. The plain case is, she is tormented by an evil spirit, following her day and night. Yea, try all your drugs over and over; but at length it will plainly appear that 'this kind goeth not out, but
30 by prayer and fasting.'[46]

Fri. 12. I read part of Dr. Cheyne's *Natural Method of Curing Diseases;* of which I cannot but observe it is one of the most ingenious books which I ever saw. But what epicure will ever

---

[39] Probably a Calvinistic Methodist society, Llantrisant being an important centre of such societies. Williams, *Wesley in Wales*, p. 14, n. 4.

[40] An ambiguous notice in CWJ, I.287, suggests that this society to which Charles Wesley had preached on July 16, 1741, may also have been a Calvinistic Methodist society.

[41] Eccles. 7:16.

[42] Perhaps Susan Young; see above, Oct. 20, 1741, n. 55.

[43] John 20:28.

[44] 1 John 5:4.

[45] 1749, 'I left Cardiff about eight, and in the evening . . .'.

[46] Matt. 17:21.

regard it? For 'the man talks against good eating and drinking'![47]

Our Lord was gloriously present with us at the watch-night, so that my voice was lost in the cries of the people. After midnight about an hundred of us walked home together, singing and rejoicing and praising God.

Fri. 19. I rode once more to Pensford, at the earnest request of several serious people. The place where they desired me to preach was a little green spot near the town. But I had no sooner begun than a great company of rabble, hired (as we afterwards found) for that purpose, came furiously upon us, bringing a bull which they had been baiting, and now strove to drive in among the people. But the beast was wiser than his drivers, and continually ran, either on one side of us or the other, while we quietly sang praise to God and prayed for about an hour. The poor wretches, finding themselves disappointed, at length seized upon the bull, now weak and tired, after having been so long torn and beaten both by dogs and men, and by main strength partly dragged and partly thrust him in among the people. When they had forced their way to the little table on which I stood, they strove several times to throw it down, by thrusting the helpless beast against it, who of himself stirred no more than a log of wood. I once or twice put aside his head with my hand, that the blood might not drop upon my clothes, intending to go on as soon as the hurry should be a little over. But the table falling down, some of our friends caught me in their arms and carried me right away on their shoulders; while the rabble wreaked their vengeance on the table, which they tore bit from bit. We went a little way off, where I finished my discourse without any noise or interruption.

Sun. 21. In the evening I rode to Marshfield,[48] and on

---

[47] *The Natural Method of Curing the Diseases of the Body and Disorders of the Mind Depending on the Body* (London, 1742), was the last major work of George Cheyne (1671–1743), a notable medical writer who did not shrink from mixing medical, theological, and mathematical speculations in unstable proportions and presenting them to the general public. What impressed JW (who had been a reader of Cheyne from his Oxford days) was the way he had overcome the disabilities occasioned by weighing thirty-two stones [i.e., 448 pounds] by a diet of milk and vegetables. How his psychosomatic doctrines entered popular Methodism is illustrated by a communication to the *Arminian Magazine* (1779), II.433: 'The ingenious Dr. Cheyne reckons all gloomy wrong-headedness, and spurious free-thinking, so many symptoms of bodily diseases; and, I think, says, the human organs in some nervous distempers may be rendered fit for the actuation of demons: and advises religion as an excellent remedy.' Cf. above, Dec. 15, 1741, n. 97.

[48] Marshfield was a modest market town and parish 1 1/2 miles E. of Bristol and on the main road to Chippenham.

Tuesday, in the afternoon, came to London. Wed. 24. I preached for the last time in the French chapel at Wapping, on, 'If ye continue in my word, then are ye my disciples indeed.'[49]

Thur. 25. I appointed several earnest and sensible men to meet
5 me, to whom I showed the great difficulty I had long found of knowing the people who desired to be under my care. After much discourse, they all agreed there could be no better way to come to a sure, thorough knowledge of each person, than to divide them into classes like those at Bristol, under the inspection of those in
10 whom I could most confide. This was the origin of our classes at London, for which I can never sufficiently praise God; the unspeakable usefulness of the institution having ever since been more and more manifest.

Wed. 31. My brother set out for Oxford. In the evening I called
15 upon Ann Calcut. She had been speechless for some time. But almost as soon as we began to pray God restored her speech. She then witnessed a good confession indeed. I expected to see her no more; but from that hour the fever left her, and in a few days she arose and walked, glorifying God.
20 Sunday, April 4. About two in the afternoon, being the time my brother was preaching at Oxford before the university, I desired a few persons to meet with me and join in prayer. We continued herein much longer than we at first designed, and believed we had the petition we asked of God.
25 Fri. 9. We had the first watch-night in London.[50] We commonly choose for this solemn service the Friday night nearest the full moon, either before or after, that those of the congregation who live at a distance may have light to their several homes. The service begins at half an hour past eight and
30 continues till a little after midnight. We have often found a

---

[49] John 8:31. See above, Aug. 2, 1741.

[50] In *A Plain Account of the People called Methodists* (1749) JW describes a substitute found by Kingswood colliers for Saturday night at the ale-house, viz., spending 'the greater part of the night in prayer, and praise and thanksgiving' (9:264 in this edn.). Being advised to put an end to the practice, he concluded on reflection that it had primitive sanction and that he should take charge of it. The first watch-night meeting began after eight, finished a little after midnight, and, because it proved a popular observance, watch-night meetings were extended to the major centres of Bristol, London, and Newcastle, and were regularly planned by the early Conferences. Special hymns were written for these occasions, and in a celebrated riposte to an Irish clergyman who reproached him with holding 'midnight assemblies', JW asked, 'Sir, did you never see the word 'vigil' in your Common Prayer Book? Do you know what it means?' (*A Letter to the Rev. Mr. Baily of Corke* [1750], 9:305 in this edn.).

peculiar blessing at these seasons. There is generally a deep awe upon the congregation, perhaps in some measure owing to the silence of the night; particularly in singing the hymn with which we commonly conclude:

> Hearken to the solemn voice! 5
> The awful midnight cry!
> Waiting souls, rejoice, rejoice,
> And feel the Bridegroom nigh.[51]

April 16. Being Good Friday, I was desired to call on one that was ill at Islington. I found there several of my old acquaintance, 10 who loved me once as the apple of their eye. By staying with them but a little I was clearly convinced that was I to stay but one week among them (unless the providence of God plainly called me so to do), I should be as *still* as poor Mr. St[onehouse]. I felt their words as it were thrilling through my veins. So soft! So pleasing to 15 nature! It seemed *our* religion was but a heavy, coarse thing; nothing so delicate, so refined as *theirs*. I wonder any person of taste (that has not faith) can stand before them!

Sun. 18. In the afternoon one who had tasted the love of God, but had turned again to folly, was deeply convinced and torn, as it 20 were, in pieces by guilt and remorse and fear. And even after the sermon was ended she continued in the same agony, it seemed both of body and soul. Many of us were then met together in another part of the house; but her cries were so piercing, though at a distance, that I could not pray, nor hardly speak, being quite 25 chilled every time I heard them. I asked whether it were best to bring her in, or send her out of the house. It being the general voice, she was brought in, and we cried to God to heal her backsliding. We soon found we were asking according to his will. He not only had her 'depart in peace',[52] but filled many others, till 30 then heavy of heart, with peace and joy in believing.

Mon. 19. At noon I preached at Brentford,[53] and again about seven in the evening. Many who had threatened to do terrible things were present; but they made no disturbance at all.

Tue. 20. Was the day on which our noisy neighbours had 35

---

[51] John and Charles Wesley, *Hymns and Sacred Poems* (1742), p. 131, entitled, 'A Midnight Hymn' *(Poet. Wks.*, II.191), included in the 1780 hymnbook as No. 53 (7:146 in this edn.). The original reads, 'And see the Bridegroom nigh.'

[52] Luke 2:29.

[53] Brentford was a market town on the Great West Road, 7 miles W. of Hyde Park Corner.

agreed to summon all their forces together; a great number of whom came early in the evening and planted themselves as near the desk as possible. But he that sitteth in heaven laughed them to scorn.[54] The greater part soon vanished away; and to some of the
5 rest I trust his word came with the demonstration of his Spirit.

Fri. 23. I spent an agreeable hour with Mr. Wh[itefield]. I believe he is sincere in all he says concerning his earnest desire of joining hand in hand with all that love the Lord Jesus Christ.[55] But if (as some would persuade me) he is not, the loss is all on his own
10 side. I am just as I was. I go on my way, whether he goes with me or stays behind.

Sun. 25. At five I preached in Ratcliff Square, near Stepney, on, 'I came not to call the righteous, but sinners to repentance.'[56] A multitude of them were gathered together before I came home,
15 and filled the street above and below the Foundery. Some who apprehended we should have but homely treatment begged me to go in as soon as possible. But I told them, 'No. Provide you for yourselves. But I have a message to deliver first.' I told them, after a few words, 'Friends, let every man do as he pleases. But it is *my*
20 manner when I speak of the things of God, or when another does, to uncover my head'; which I accordingly did, and many of them did the same. I then exhorted them to repent and believe the gospel. Not a few of them appeared to be deeply affected. Now, Satan, count thy gains.

25 Mon. 26. I called on one who was sorrowing as without hope, for her son who was turned again to folly. I advised her to wrestle with God for his soul. And in two days he brought home the wandering sheep, fully convinced of the error of his ways and determined to choose the better part.

30 Saturday, May 1. One called whom I had often advised 'not to hear them that preach smooth things'. But she could not believe there was any danger therein, 'seeing we were all' (she said) 'children of God'. The effects of it which now appeared in her were these: (1) She was grown above measure wise in her own
35 eyes. She knew everything as well as any could tell her and needed not to be 'taught of man'. (2) She utterly despised all her brethren, saying they were all in the dark; they knew not what

---

[54] Cf. Ps. 2:4.
[55] In the summer of 1742 Whitefield reciprocated these kindly sentiments and, like JW, coupled them with the determination to act independently. Whitefield, *Works*, I.438, 449.
[56] Mark 2:17; Luke 5:32.

faith meant. (3) She despised her teachers as much, if not more than them, saying they knew nothing of the gospel; they preached nothing but the law, and brought all into bondage who minded what they said. 'Indeed', said she, 'after I had heard Mr. Sp[angenberg] I was amazed; for I never since heard you preach 5 one good sermon. And I said to my husband, "My dear, did Mr. Wesley always preach so?" And he said, "Yes, my dear; but your eyes were not opened."'

Thur. 6. I described that falling away, spoken of by St. Paul to the Thessalonians, which we so terribly feel to be already come 10 and to have overspread the (so called) Christian world. One of my hearers was highly offended at my supposing any of the Church of England to be concerned in this. But his speech soon bewrayed him to be of no church at all, zealous and orthodox as he was. So that after I had appealed to his own heart, as well as to all that 15 heard him, he retired with confusion of face.

Sat. 8. One of Fetter Lane mentioning a letter he had received from a poor man in Lincolnshire, I read and desired a copy of it; part of which is as follows:

May 3, 1742 20

Samuel Meggot[57] *to Richard Ridley*[58]

Brother,

I have now much communion with thee, and desire to have more. . . . But till now I found a great gulf between us, so that we could not one pass to the other. Therefore thy letters were very death to me, and 25 thou wast to me as a branch broke off and thrown by to wither. . . . Yet I waited, if the Lord should please to let us into the same union we had before. So the Lord hath given it. And in the same I write, desiring it may continue until death.

I wrote before to thee and John Harrison,[59] 'Be not afraid to be 30

---

[57] Samuel Meggot (died *c.* 1764) was spoken to seriously by JW on June 10 (see below), and though never one of JW's preachers, he became a notable revivalist in Weardale. See JWJ, June 17, 19, 1763; JW's letter to John Cricket, Feb. 10, 1783 (Telford, VII.166); JW's 'A Short History of the People called Methodists' (1781), §122, 9:425 in this edn.; also Thomas Jackson ed., *Lives of Early Methodist Preachers*, 4th edn., 6 vols. (London, Wesleyan Conference Office, 1871), V.239; VI.155-56.

[58] Though not appearing in the lists of members of the Fetter Lane Society, Richard Ridley had given Charles Wesley much trouble at the time of the division of that society between the Moravians and those who accepted the authority of the Wesleys, and, as appears below under June 6, 1742, had propagated doctrines of 'stillness' and opposition to 'the ordinances' in the Epworth district (Apr. 30, 1740, CWJ, I.223).

[59] John Harrison accompanied Ridley on his mission to Epworth; see below, June 6, 1742.

found sinners,' hoping you would not separate the law from the Spirit, until the flesh was found dead. For I think our hearts are discovered by the law, yea, every tittle, and condemned by the same. Then we are quickened in the Spirit. Justice cannot be separated from mercy;

5 neither can they be one greater than the other. 'Keep the commandments and I will pray the Father, and he shall give you another comforter.' Mark that! 'Thy sins be forgiven thee. Arise, take up thy bed and walk.' Here is work before mercy, and mercy before work. . . . So then, through the law by faith our heart is pure. . . .

10 Beware therefore of them who, while they promise you liberty, are themselves the servants of corruption. O dead faith, that cannot always live pure! Treacherous Judas, that thus betrayest thy master! . . .

Let the law arraign you, till Jesus Christ bring forth judgment in

15 your hearts unto victory. Yea, let your hearts be open wide, receiving both, that the one may confirm the other. So thou livest so much in the Son's righteousness that the law saith, I have nought against thee. . . . This is faith, that thus conquers the old man, in putting him off and putting on Christ. Purify your hearts by faith: so shall the

20 temple of God be holy and the altar therein, that spiritual sacrifices may be offered, acceptable to the Lord. Now if any man be otherwise minded let him be ashamed. For if there lives any of our self in us, that one branch of nature, that one member, shall cause the whole man to burn everlastingly. Let as many as know not this perfection, which is

25 by Jesus Christ, press forward by faith till they come to the experimental knowledge of it.

But how many souls have I seen washed, and turned again to the wallowing in their sins. . . . O that Lamb! How is he put to an open shame again, who had once reconciled them to the Father!

30 Now I would write a little of the travail of my own soul. I thought myself right long since. But when the light of life came, I saw myself ready to die in my sins. . . . I had faith; but I had it by knowledge and not in power. Yet by this faith I had great liberty. . . . Nevertheless this faith kept my heart corrupt, and the whole man of sin alive. . . .

35 My way of proceeding was thus. Sometimes I was overtaken in a fault, and so was put to a stand a little. But as soon as I could I would wipe myself by knowledge, saying, 'Christ died for sinners.' I was right so far and no farther. He died for sinners, but not to save him that continues in his sins. For whomsoever he cleanses, they are clean

40 indeed; first sinners, then saints, and so they remain. By and by I was overtaken again; and the oftener I was overtaken the stronger I thought myself in the Lord. Yea, for my corruption's sake I was forced to get more knowledge, or else I should have been condemned. So I arrived at such a pitch of knowledge (i.e., of notional faith) that I could

45 crucify Christ with one hand and take pardon with the other; so that I

was always happy. . . . Here was the mystery of iniquity, conceived in my heart. For it led me to this: if I was to take of any man's goods, I would say or think, 'I am a sinner of myself; but Christ died for *me;* so his righteousness is mine.' And farther, I could not see but if I was to kill a man, yet I should be pure. So great a friend to sin and the devil 5 was I, that I would have made sin and the devil to become the righteousness of God in Christ; yea, that I began to love him whom the Lord hath reserved for everlasting fire. . . .

So I held Christ without and the devil within. This is a mystery, that I should feel myself safe and pure, and yet the devil to be in me. Judge 10 who gave me this purity and taught me to be *thus* perfect in Christ! But ere long that began to break forth in action which I had conceived in my heart. But it was the Lord's will I should not go far before I was again brought under the law. Then did I stand stripped and naked of that knowledge. I wish all who are so deceived as I was were brought 15 under the law, that they might learn what it is to come to Jesus Christ. And I wish them not to pass from under the law till they clearly see the end of the law come into their hearts.

The law being mixed with faith makes it quick and powerful. For as the law will not leave one hair of our heads uncondemned, so faith will 20 not leave one unreconciled. And blessed is he who lives in the same reconciliation and turns not as a dog to his vomit. Then shall he be called the child of God, which cannot sin, because his seed remaineth in him. . . .

Thou writest, 'Jesus makes it manifest to thee that thou art a great 25 sinner.' That is well; and if more, it would be better for thee. Again thou sayst, 'since thou first receivedst a full and free pardon for all thy sins, thou hast received so many fresh pardons that they are quite out of count.' And this, thou sayst, is spoken 'to thy own shame and thy Saviour's praise'. Come, my brother, let us both be more ashamed. 30 Let us see where we are, and what we are doing to the Lamb. We are not glorifying him (let us not mistake ourselves thus); we are crucifying him afresh. We are putting him to an open shame and bringing swift damnation on our own heads.

Again thou sayst, 'Though thy sins be great and many, yet thy 35 Saviour's grace is greater.' Thou sayst right; or else, how should we have been cleansed? But his great cleansing power does not design that we should become foul again; lest he call us away in our uncleanness, and we perish forever. For it will not profit us that we were once cleansed, if we be found in uncleanness. 40

Take heed to thyself, that the knowledge that is in thee deceive thee not. For thou writest so to my experience that I can tell thee as plain how thou art, or plainer, than thou canst thyself. Thou sayst, 'After thou hast done something amiss, thou needest not to be unhappy one moment, if thou wilt but go to thy Saviour.' Is not this the very state I 45 have mentioned? O that that knowledge was cast out! So shouldst thou always do the things that please the Father. O my dear brother, how art thou bewitched by the deceiver of thy soul! Thou art a stranger to the Saviour, who is gone to heaven to give repentance to his people and remission of sins. I am afraid the devil is thy saviour: more of him is manifest in thee than of Christ. He tells thee thou art pure and washed; but he cozens thee; yea, his deceitfulness cries out for vengeance. Yet he would be a Christ or a God.

Thou sayst thou hast 'need of remission of sins every day'. Yes, so thou hast, and more. Thou hast need every moment; so shouldst thou be clean; for this *every moment* should be eternity to thy soul. Thou thankest God that 'he hath provided such an high priest for thee.' Let him be thine; so shalt thou be ruled by him every moment. What? Is he such a Saviour as can cleanse us from sin and not keep us in the same? Judge where thou art. Thou and I and many more were once made pure. And we were pure while we believed the same, and were kept by the Father for his own name's sake. But how long did we *thus* believe? Let every man judge himself.

Now, my brother, answer for thyself. Dost thou believe that thou must always have this thy heart, which is corrupted through and through with sin? I say, Dost thou believe thy heart must be thus unpure? If thou dost, the same doctrine must be preached to thee which was at first, 'Ye must receive the Holy Ghost'; that is, thou must be brought to the first remission, and there thou wilt see Jesus laid slain in thy heart. This thy first purity I will acknowledge, and none else. I believe the foundation of life was once in thee. But many together with thee have fallen away. Thou hearest how I acknowledge thee and where and nowhere else. And herein I have communion with thee in my spirit, and hope it will continue to the end. . . .

And is poor Samuel Meggot himself now fallen into the very same snare against which he so earnestly warned his friend? Lord, what is man!

Sun. 9. I preached in Charles Square[60] to the largest congregation I have ever seen there. Many of the baser people would fain have interrupted. But they found after a time it was lost labour. One who was more serious was (as she afterward confessed) exceeding angry at them. But she was quickly rebuked by a stone which light upon her head and struck her down to the

[60] Charles Square, Hoxton, was one of the places where the evangelicals were holding spectacular meetings at this time; Whitefield had been announced to preach there on the previous day (Tyerman, *Whitefield*, 1.558 and n. 2). Whitefield's successes here, at Moorfields and elsewhere (Whitefield, *Works*, I.383-86) form the immediate background for the visit to the Primate recorded in the next paragraph.

ground. In that moment her anger was at an end, and love only
filled her heart.

Wed. 12. I waited on the Archbishop of Canterbury[61] with Mr.
Whitefield, and again on Friday; as also on the Bishop of
London.[62] I trust if we should be called to appear before princes 5
we should not be ashamed.

Mon. 17. I had designed this morning to set out for Bristol, but
was unexpectedly prevented. In the afternoon I received a letter
from Leicestershire,[63] pressing me to come without delay and pay
the last office of friendship to one whose soul was on the wing for 10
eternity. On Thursday 20, I set out. The next afternoon I stopped
a little at Newport Pagnell, and then rode on till I overtook a
serious man, with whom I immediately fell into conversation. He
presently gave me to know what his opinions were; therefore I
said nothing to contradict them. But that did not content him. He 15
was quite uneasy to know whether I held the doctrine of the
decrees as he did. But I told him over and over, 'We had better
keep to practical things, lest we should be angry at one another.'
And so we did for two miles, till he caught me unawares and
dragged me into the dispute before I knew where I was. He then 20
grew warmer and warmer, told me I was rotten at heart, and

[61] John Potter, Archbishop of Canterbury, 1737–47 (see JW's Preface to *Journal*,
Extract, ¶4, n. 26, 18:126 in this edn. What passed between the archbishop and JW is not
known, but the latter's subsequent references to Potter are marked by warm affection and
respect. 'Archbishop Potter once said, "These gentlemen are irregular; but they have
done good and I pray God to bless them"' (Letter to the printer of the *Dublin Chronicle*,
June 2, 1789 [Telford, VIII.141]). 'Near fifty years ago, a great and good man, Dr. Potter,
then Archbishop of Canterbury, gave me an advice for which I have ever since had
occasion to bless God: "If you desire to be extensively useful, do not spend your time and
strength in contending for or against such things as are of a disputable nature; but in
testifying against open, notorious vice, and in promoting real, essential holiness." Let us
keep to this' (Sermon 104, 'On Attending the Church Service', §33, 3:478 in this edn.

[62] Edmund Gibson (1669–1748), Bishop of Lincoln 1716–20; Bishop of London
1720–48. Long expected to succeed William Wake as Primate, Gibson fell from political
favour in the mid-1730s and was passed over in favour of Potter in 1737; he declined an
offer of the primacy on Potter's death in 1747.

[63] I.e., from the Countess of Huntingdon, giving the news that Frances Cowper was
dying and wished to see one of the Wesley brothers before the end. This summons caused
JW to cancel a promised preaching tour to Bristol, which would enable him to exchange
headquarters with Charles. Lady Huntingdon sent her servant to JW with a horse, and the
pair subsequently went together to the North of England (see JW's letter to Charles
Wesley, May 17, 1742, *Letters*, 26:77-78 in this edn.; Seymour, *Countess of Huntingdon*,
I.52-53; *Methodist Magazine* [1798], 21:531-34; and *Wesleyan Methodist Magazine* [1908],
131:687). Fanny Cowper, who is frequently mentioned in the Countess of Huntingdon's
letters to JW, was the daughter of William Cowper, Esq., of Enfield Chase; she was buried
on May 30. WHS, 7:39.

supposed I was one of John Wesley's followers. I told him, 'No, I am John Wesley himself.' Upon which,

> *Improvisum aspris veluti qui sentibus anguem*
> *Pressit*—[64]

5 he would gladly have run away outright. But being the better mounted of the two I kept close to his side and endeavoured to show him his heart, till we came into the street of Northampton. Sat. 22. About five in the afternoon, I reached Donington Park. Miss Cowper was just alive. But as soon as we came in her spirit 10 greatly revived. For three days we rejoiced in the grace of God, whereby she was filled with a 'hope full of immortality';[65] with meekness and gentleness, patience and humble love, knowing in whom she had believed.

Tue. 25. I set out early in the morning with John Taylor[66] (since 15 settled in London), and Wednesday 26, at eight or nine o'clock,[67] reached Birstall,[68] six miles beyond Wakefield.

John Nelson had wrote to me some time before; but at that time I had little thought of seeing him. Hearing he was at home, I sent for him to our inn; whence he immediately carried me to his 20 house and gave me an account of the strange manner wherein he had been led on, from the time of our parting at London.[69]

[64] Virgil, *Aeneid*, ii.381-82, trans. Wesley, *Works* (1774), Vol. 32, 'as one that has unawares trodden upon a snake'.

[65] Wisd. 3:4.

[66] John Taylor, like his elder brother David, the preacher, was a servant of the Countess of Huntingdon who had been pressing JW to visit 'the colliers in the north'. The Countess hoped to make him 'a schoolmaster among those people who are awakened'.

[67] 1774, 'Wednesday 26 in the evening'.

[68] Birstall was a populous parish 7 1/2 miles SW. of Leeds.

[69] John Nelson (1707–74) was born at Birstall and raised to his father's trade of stonemason. Troubled by religious perplexities from childhood, he found peace only under the preaching of JW at Moorfields in 1739 and returned to preach in his native district, opening a work which JW now joined. He continued evangelism in many parts of the country and published a journal which went through several editions. He was impressed into the army, but after some months Charles Wesley secured his release by finding a substitute. He served as a Methodist preacher from 1750 till his death. JW summarized what he found on this first visit to Nelson in his 'A Short History of the People called Methodists' (1781), §20: 'In May [1742], on the repeated invitation of John Nelson, who had been for some time calling sinners to repentance at Birstall and the adjoining towns in the West Riding of Yorkshire, I went to Birstall, and found his labour had not been in vain. . . . Many of the most abandoned drunkards were now sober; many sabbath-breakers remembered the sabbath to keep it holy. The whole town wore a new face, such a change did God work by the artless testimony of one plain man. And from thence his word sounded forth to Leeds, Wakefield, Halifax, and all the West Riding of Yorkshire' (9:434 in this edn.).

He had full business there and large wages. But from the time of his finding peace with God it was continually upon his mind that he must return (though he knew not why) to his native place. He did so about Christmas, in the year 1740. His relations and acquaintance soon began to inquire what he thought of this new 5 faith; and whether he believed there was any such thing as a man's knowing that his sins were forgiven. John told them point blank that this new faith, as they called it, was the old faith of the gospel; and that he himself was as sure his sins were forgiven as he could be of the shining of the sun. This was soon noised abroad. More 10 and more came to inquire concerning these strange things. Some put him upon the proof of the great truths which such inquiries naturally led him to mention. And thus he was brought unawares to quote, explain, compare, and enforce several parts of Scripture. This he did at first sitting in his house, till the company 15 increased so that the house could not contain them. Then he stood at the door, which he was commonly obliged to do in the evening, as soon as he came from work. God immediately set his seal to what was spoken, and several believed, and therefore declared that God was merciful also to their unrighteousness and 20 had forgiven all their sins.

Mr. Ingham hearing of this came to Birstall, inquired into the facts, talked with John himself, and examined him with the closest exactness, both touching his knowledge and spiritual experience. After which he encouraged him to proceed, and pressed him, 25 as often as he had opportunity, to come to any of the places where himself had been and speak to the people as God should enable him.

But he soon gave offence, both by his plainness of speech and by advising people to go to church and Sacrament. Mr. Ingham 30 reproved him; but finding him incorrigible, forbade any that were in his societies to hear him. But being persuaded this is the will of God concerning him, he continues to this hour working in the day, that he may be burdensome to no man, and in the evening 'testifying the truth as it is in Jesus'.[70] 35

I preached at noon on the top of Birstall Hill to several hundreds of plain people, and spent the afternoon in talking severally with those who had tasted of the grace of God. All of these, I found, had been vehemently pressed not to 'run about to

---

[70] Cf. Eph. 4:21.

church and sacrament', and to keep their religion to themselves; to be still, not to talk about what they had experienced. At eight I preached on the side of Dewsbury Moor, about two miles from Birstall, and earnestly exhorted all who believed to wait upon God 5 in his own ways and to let their light shine before men.[71]

Thur. 27. We left Birstall, and on Friday 28 came to Newcastle upon Tyne. I read with great expectation, yesterday and today, Xenophon's *Memorable Things of Socrates*.[72] I was utterly amazed at his want of judgment. How many of these things would Plato 10 never have mentioned! But it may be well that we see the shades too of the brightest picture in all heathen antiquity.

We came to Newcastle about six, and after a short refreshment walked into the town. I was surprised: so much drunkenness, cursing, and swearing (even from the mouths of little children), 15 do I never remember to have seen and heard before in so small a compass of time. Surely this place is ripe for him who 'came not to call the righteous but sinners to repentance'.[73]

Sat. 29. I was informed that one Mr. Hall had been there about a year before and had preached several times;[74] but I could not 20 learn that there was the least fruit of his labour. Nor could I find any that desired to hear him again nor any that appeared to care for such matters.

Sun. 30. At seven I walked down to Sandgate,[75] the poorest and

---

[71] See Matt. 5:16.

[72] The *Memorabilia* was the title by which Xenophon's *Apomnemoneamata* was known from 1659. In the first part of it he replied to the actual indictment against Socrates, so far as he knew it, but more especially refuted replies to the growing body of literature produced by the posthumous cult of Socrates. Of this literature Plato's *Apology* was part, but it seems only to have been used by Xenophon in his later sections (Xenophon, *Memorabilia and Oeconomicus*, ed. E. C. Marchant [Loeb edn., London, 1965], pp. vii-xiii). The difference between the Socrates of Xenophon and that of Plato is summarized by Albin Lesky (*A History of Greek Thought* [London, 1966], p. 494) as 'roughly that Xenophon presents Socrates the virtuous citizen who, through his life, refutes all the reproaches which led to his death, while Plato shows us the thinker who struggles with the classification of basic conceptions and . . . develops the theory of ideas'.

[73] Mark 2:17; Luke 5:32.

[74] An autobiographical manuscript of Westley Hall, JW's brother-in-law, indicates that in 1740 he made a preaching visit to Newcastle 'with Tho. Keene & his daughter-in-law' (WHS, 5:148).

[75] Henry Bourne reported at the time that Sandgate, so called from having been built on the common shore outside and to the east of the wall, 'has in it a vast number of lanes on the east side of it which are crowded with houses. It is chiefly inhabited by people that work upon the water, particularly the keelmen. The number of souls in this street and the lanes belonging to it is computed to several thousands' (*The History of Newcastle-upon-Tyne* [Newcastle, 1736]). A century later the *Wesleyan Methodist Magazine* (1848), 71:91, reported that Sandgate was 'still one of the strongholds of Satan', and at this time

most contemptible part of the town, and standing at the end of the street with John Taylor, began to sing the hundredth psalm. Three or four people came out to see what was the matter, who soon increased to four or five hundred. I suppose there might be twelve or fifteen hundred before I had done preaching; to whom 5 I applied those solemn words, 'He was wounded for our transgressions, he was bruised for our iniquities; the chastisement of our peace was upon him, and by his stripes we are healed.'[76]

Observing the people when I had done to stand gaping and 10 staring upon me, with the most profound astonishment, I told them, 'If you desire to know who I am, my name is John Wesley. At five in the evening, with God's help, I design to preach here again.'

At five the hill on which I designed to preach was covered from 15 the top to the bottom. I never saw so large a number of people together, either in Moorfields or at Kennington Common. I knew it was not possible for the one half to hear, although my voice was then strong and clear, and I stood so as to have them all in view, as they were ranged on the side of the hill. The word of God which I 20 set before them was, 'I will heal their backsliding, I will love them freely.'[77] After preaching, the poor people were ready to tread me underfoot, out of pure love and kindness. It was some time before I could possibly get out of the press. I then went back another way than I came. But several were got to our inn before me, by whom I 25 was vehemently importuned to stay with them, at least a few days; or, however, one day more. But I could not consent, having given my word to be at Birstall, with God's leave, on Tuesday night.

Some of these told me they were members of a Religious Society which had subsisted for many years, and had always gone 30 on in a prudent, regular manner, and been well spoken of by all men. They likewise informed me what a fine library they had, and that the steward read a sermon every Sunday. And yet how many

resembled 'for filth and wretchedness the liberties of Dublin, . . . constantly pouring forth its hoards of men and women, like fiends newly arrived from the bottomless pit, and speaking, in the nervous style of old Christopher Hopper, who visited it soon after Mr. Wesley, "the language of hell as though they had received a liberal education in the regions of woe"'.

[76] Isa. 53:5.
[77] Hos. 14:4.

of 'the publicans and harlots' will go into the kingdom of heaven before these![78]

Mon. 31. About three I left Newcastle. I read over today the famous Dr. Pitcairn's works.[79] But I was utterly disappointed by
5 that dry, sour, controversial book! We came in the evening to Boroughbridge, where to my great surprise the mistress of the house, though much of a gentlewoman, desired she and her family might join with us in prayer. They did so likewise between four and five in the morning. Perhaps even this seed may bring
10 forth fruit.

Tuesday, June 1. As we were riding through Knaresborough, not intending to stop there, a young man stopped me in the street and earnestly desired me to go to his house. I did so. He told me our talking with a man as we went through the town before had set
15 many in a flame, and that the sermon we gave him had travelled from one end of the town to the other. While I was with him a woman came and desired to speak with me. I went to her house, whither five or six of her friends came, one of whom had been long under deep convictions. We spent an hour in prayer, and all
20 our spirits were refreshed.

About one we came to Mr. Moore's, at Beeston,[80] near Leeds. His son rode with me after dinner to Birstall, where (a multitude of people being gathered from all parts) I explained to them the spirit of bondage and adoption.[81] I began about seven but could
25 not conclude till half an hour past nine.

Wed. 2. I was invited to Mrs. Holmes's,[82] near Halifax; where I

---

[78] See Matt. 21:31.

[79] Alexander Pitcarne (Pitcairn, according to the catalogue of the Edinburgh Advocates' Library) (1622?–95), a Scottish Presbyterian polemical divine who was ejected from his parish and in 1685 took refuge in Holland, where he published his *Harmonia Evangelica Apostolorum Pauli et Jacobi in doctrina Justificatione* (Rotterdam, 1685). Restored to his parish in 1690, he became principal of St. Mary's College, St. Andrews, in 1693. His best-known work was his first, *The Spiritual Sacrifice or a Treatise . . . concerning the Saint's Communion with God in Prayer* (Edinburgh, 1664).

[80] Beeston was a populous chapelry and mining and textile community within the parish and borough of Leeds and 2 1/4 miles SW. by S. from that town.

[81] See Rom. 8:15.

[82] Smith House, Lightcliffe, the residence of John Holmes and his wife Elizabeth, afforded accommodation to both Methodists and Moravians, a large party of whom, invited from London by Ingham to support the Yorkshire work on May 20, 1742, took up their residence in a tall building specially erected at the place. It was nevertheless John rather than Elizabeth Holmes (who inclined to the Methodists) who favoured the Moravians, and upon his death *c.* 1742, they moved their headquarters to another part of Lightcliffe. Thus the contemporaneous separation between Moravianism and Methodism

preached at noon on 'Ask, and ye shall receive.'[83] Thence I rode to Dr. Legh's, the Vicar of Halifax,[84] a candid inquirer after truth. I called again upon Mrs. Holmes in my return, when her sister a little surprised me by asking, 'Ought not a minister of Christ to do three things: first to preach his law in order to convince of sin; then to offer free pardon through faith in his blood to all convinced sinners; and in the third place to preach his law again as a rule for those that believe? I think if anyone does otherwise he is no true minister of Christ. He divides what God has joined, and cannot be said to preach the whole gospel.'

I preached at eight near Dewsbury Moor, and at eight the next morning, Thursday 3, at Mirfield,[85] where I found Mr. Ingham had been an hour before. Great part of the day I spent in speaking with those who have tasted the powers of the world to come,[86] by whose concurrent testimony I find that Mr. I[ngham]'s method to this day is (1) to endeavour to persuade them that they are in a delusion and have indeed no faith at all; if this cannot be done, then (2) to make them keep it to themselves; and (3) to prevent their going to the church or sacrament, at least to guard them from having any reverence or expecting to find any blessing in those ordinances of God.

In the evening I preached at Adwalton,[87] a mile from Birstall, in a broad part of the highway, the people being too numerous to be contained in any house in the town. After preaching, and the next day, I spoke with more, who had, or sought, for redemption through Christ; all of whom I perceived had been advised also to

in this part of Yorkshire was illustrated in Smith House itself. For JW's continued affection for Mrs. Holmes (who died 1781), see Apr. 19, 1776.

[83] John 16:24.

[84] George Legh (c. 1694–1775) received LL.D. at Trinity Hall, Cambridge, 1728; vicar of Halifax, 1731–75; prebendary of York, 1732–75. For JW's hospitable reception in Legh's church and household, see Apr. 17, 1774. Legh is described by Dr. Whitaker (J. U. Walker, *History of Wesleyan Methodism in Halifax* [Halifax, 1836], p. 32) as 'a low churchman, and popular among the dissenters, a disciple of Bishop Hoadley, and his co-adjutor in what was called 'the Bangorian controversy', about which he seems to have been more in earnest than his duty as a preacher, which he is said to have performed in a very careless and languid manner. He was a man of great singularity of character, subject to fits of absence and forgetfulness which not infrequently exposed him to ridicule.' By the mid-1740s, Legh was a confidential correspondent of Zinzendorf, to whom he admitted that he was under pressure from the Archbishop of York to exclude Methodist and other similar delusions from his parish (Herrnhut Archiv, MSS R.13. A.18. nos. 27-34).

[85] Mirfield was a parish 2 3/4 miles W. by S. from Dewsbury.

[86] See Heb. 6:5.

[87] 1749, 1769, 'Atherton', apparently a misprint. Adwalton was a hamlet in the chapelry of Drighlington, Birstall parish, 5 1/2 miles SE. by E. from Bradford.

put their light under a bushel or to forsake the ordinances of God
in order to find Christ.

Fri. 4. At noon I preached at Birstall once more. All the hearers
were deeply attentive, whom I now confidently and cheerfully
committed to 'the great Shepherd and Bishop of souls'.[88]

Hence I rode to Beeston. Here I met once more with the works
of a celebrated author, of whom many great men cannot speak
without rapture and the strongest expressions of admiration. I
mean Jacob Boehme.[89] The book I now opened was his *Mysterium
Magnum*, or the exposition of Genesis. Being conscious of my
ignorance, I earnestly besought God to enlighten my understanding. I seriously considered what I read, and endeavoured to
weigh it in the balance of the sanctuary.[90] And what can I say
concerning the part I read? I can and must say thus much (and
that with as full evidence as I can say that two and two make four):
it is most sublime nonsense; inimitable bombast; fustian not to be
paralleled! All of a piece with his inspired interpretation of the
word 'tetragrammaton', on which (mistaking it for the unutter-
able name itself, whereas it means only a word consisting of four
letters) he comments with exquisite gravity and solemnity, telling
you the meaning of *every syllable* of it.

Sat. 5. I rode for Epworth. Before we came thither I made an
end of Madam Guyon's *Short Method of Prayer* and *Les Torrents
Spirituelles*.[91] Ah, my brethren; I can answer your riddle, now I

---

[88] Cf. 1 Pet. 2:25.

[89] For Jacob Boehme, see above, Feb. 18, 1738, n. 30, 18:225 in this edn. His *Mysterium
Magnum sive Expositio Geneseos Germanica* was first published in 1623. For JW's later
repudiation of Boehme and of William Law's attempt to give currency to his views in
England, see his *Thoughts on Jacob Behmen* (1780) and *A Specimen of the divinity and
philosophy of the highly illuminated Jacob Behmen*, in Jackson, IX.509-18.

[90] Cf. Sermon 10, 'The Witness of the Spirit, I', II.8 and n., 1:281 in this edn.

[91] Madame Guyon (1648–1717), French mystical writer, born Jeanne Marie Bouvier
de la Mothe. Neurotic and inclined to mysticism from her youth, she devoted herself
increasingly to mysticism after her unhappy marriage in 1664 to Jacques Guyon, an invalid
twenty-two years older than herself. On his death in 1676 she entered upon a life of
religious devotion. Attracted by the works of the quietist, Molinos, she and her spiritual
director, Lacombe, began to propagate them about the country. Despite the support of
Madame de Maintenon at court and defence by Fénélon, the pair encountered great legal
and political trouble and spent long periods in prison. Lacombe died in prison insane in
1699, and Madame Guyon was released on her submission in 1702. Her works (and those
of her disciple and editor, Pierre Poiret) enjoyed considerable respect in religiously
awakened Protestant circles in the early eighteenth century. The *Short Method of Prayer*
(1688) and *Torrents Spirituelles* were not published in English till late in JW's lifetime; he
himself published a *Life* of Madame Guyon (1776).

have ploughed with your heifer. The very words I have so often heard some of you use are not your own, no more than they are God's. They are only retailed from this poor quietist, and that with the utmost faithfulness. O that ye knew how much God is wiser than man! Then would you drop quietists and mystics ⁵ together, and at all hazards keep to the plain, practical, written Word of God.

It being many years since I had been in Epworth before, I went to an inn in the middle of the town,⁹² not knowing whether there were any left in it now who would not be ashamed of my 10 acquaintance. But an old servant of my father's, with two or three poor women, presently found me out. I asked her, 'Do you know any in Epworth who are in earnest to be saved?' She answered, 'I am, by the grace of God; and I know I am saved through faith.' I asked, 'Have you then the peace of God? Do you know that he has 15 forgiven your sins?' She replied, 'I thank God, I know it well. And many here can say the same thing.'

Sun. 6. A little before the service began I went to Mr. Romley,⁹³ the curate, and offered to assist him either by preaching or reading prayers. But he did not care to accept of my assistance. 20 The church was exceeding full in the afternoon, a rumour being spread that I was to preach. But the sermon on 'Quench not the Spirit'⁹⁴ was not suitable to the expectation of many of the hearers. Mr. Romley told them one of the most dangerous ways of quenching the Spirit was by enthusiasm, and enlarged on the 25 character of an enthusiast in a very florid and oratorical manner. After sermon John Taylor stood in the churchyard and gave notice as the people were coming out, 'Mr. Wesley not being permitted to preach in the church, designs to preach here at six o'clock.' 30

Accordingly at six I came, and found such a congregation as I believe Epworth never saw before. I stood near the east end of the church, upon my father's tombstone, and cried, 'The kingdom of

⁹² The Red Lion.
⁹³ John Romley (*c.* 1711–51), educated at Lincoln College, Oxford, studied divinity under Samuel Wesley, the father of JW, became his curate at Epworth, and in his later years assisted him as an amanuensis with his work on the book of Job. In 1733 he courted JW's sister Martha (who later married Westley Hall). Later he was a schoolmaster at Wroot. JW described him as a drunkard *(Works,* 11:76 in this edn.), and in 1751 he became mad and died. Tyerman, *Samuel Wesley,* pp. 323, 373.
⁹⁴ 1 Thess. 5:19.

heaven is not meats and drinks, but righteousness, and peace, and joy in the Holy Ghost.'[95]

At eight I went to Edward Smith's,[96] where were many not only of Epworth, but of Burnham, Haxey, Owston, Belton, and other villages round about, who greatly desired that I would come over to them and help them. I was now in a strait between two, desiring to hasten forward in my journey, and yet not knowing how to leave these poor bruised reeds in the confusion wherein I found them. John Harrison,[97] it seems, and Richard Ridley,[98] had told them in express terms, 'All the ordinances are man's inventions; and if you go to church or sacrament you will be damned.' Many hereupon wholly forsook the church, and others knew not what to do. At last I determined to spend some days here, that I might have time both to preach in each town and to speak severally with those in every place who had found or waited for salvation.

Mon. 7. I preached at Burnham,[99] a mile from Epworth, on, 'The Son of man hath power on earth to forgive sins.'[1] At eight in the evening I stood again on my father's tomb (as I did every evening this week) and cried aloud to the earnestly attentive congregation, 'By grace ye are saved through faith.'[2]

Tue. 8. I walked to Hibaldstow[3] (about twelve miles from Epworth) to see my brother and sister.[4] The minister of Owston[5] (two miles from Epworth) having sent me word I was welcome to preach in his church, I called there in my return; but his mind being changed I went to another place in the town and there explained, 'Thou shalt call his name Jesus; for he shall save his people from their sins.'[6] At eight I largely enforced at Epworth

---

[95] Cf. Rom. 14:17, and Sermon 7, 'The Way to the Kingdom', 1:217-32 in this edn.
[96] Charles Wesley preached in Edward Smith's yard a year later. CWJ, I.318.
[97] See above, May 8, 1742, n. 59.
[98] Ibid. n. 58.
[99] Low Burnham was a hamlet 1 mile S. of Epworth.
[1] Matt. 9:6; Mark 2:10.
[2] Cf. Eph. 2:8.
[3] Hibaldstow was a parish 3 miles SW. of Brigg.
[4] The identity of these relatives is entirely uncertain. Against Foster's surmise that the sister was Susanna Wesley (Mrs. Richard Ellison) is the fact that she had been separated from her husband for some years. Adam Clarke's conjecture that it was Anne Wesley and her husband, John Lambert, is possible; very shortly afterwards Anne is known to have been in London, nursing her mother during her last illness.
[5] The vicar of Owston, a substantial parish 7 1/2 miles N. of Gainsborough, 1721-57, was John Wardell. W. B. Stonehouse, *History and Topography of the Isle of Axholme* (London, 1839), p. 239.
[6] Matt. 1:21.

the great truth (so little understood in what is called a Christian country), 'Unto him that worketh not, but believeth on him that justifieth the ungodly, his faith is counted to him for righteousness.'[7] I went thence to the place where the little society met, which was sufficiently thronged both within and without. Here I found some from Hainton (a town twenty miles off) who informed us that God had begun a work there also, and constrained several to cry out in the bitterness of their soul, What must I do to be saved?[8]

Wed. 9. I rode over to a neighbouring town to wait upon a Justice of Peace, a man of candour and understanding;[9] before whom (I was informed) their angry neighbours had carried a whole waggon-load of these new heretics. But when he asked what they had done, there was a deep silence, for that was a point their conductors had forgot. At length one said, 'Why, they pretended to be better than other people. And besides, they prayed from morning to night.' Mr. S[tovin] asked, 'But have they done nothing besides?' 'Yes, sir', said an old man, 'an't please your worship, they have *converted* my wife. Till she went among them she had such a tongue! And now she is as quiet as a lamb.' 'Carry them back, carry them back', replied the justice, 'and let them convert all the scolds in the town.'

I went from hence to Belton to H[enry] F[oste]r's,[10] a young man who did once run well, but now said he saw the devil in every corner of the church and in the face of everyone who had been there. But he was easily brought to a better mind. I preached under a shady oak, on, 'The Son of man hath power upon earth to forgive sins.'[11] At Epworth, in the evening, I explained the story of the Pharisee and the publican. And I believe many began in that hour to cry out, 'God be merciful to me a sinner.'[12]

Thur. 10. I spoke severally with all who desired it. In the

---

[7] Cf. Rom. 4:5.

[8] Acts 16:30.

[9] George Stovin of Crowle (*c.* 1695–1780), antiquarian and friend of Samuel Wesley, rector of Epworth (*Gentleman's Magazine* [Jan. 1747], XVII.23), later resident at Winterton (WHS, 5:198-200; Stonehouse, *Axholme*, pp. 428-29). The Stovins were numerous in Lincolnshire, and another Methodist branch is discussed in Cornelius Stovin, *Journals of a Methodist Farmer 1871–1875*, ed. Jean Stovin (London, 1982), Appendix III.

[10] The will of Henry Foster, cordwainer, was proved in 1761 (Lincoln Record Office, Stow Wills, 1761, No. 148). Belton was a substantial parish 1 3/4 miles N. of Epworth.

[11] Luke 5:24.

[12] Luke 18:13.

evening I explained, 'Ye have not received the spirit of bondage again unto fear, but . . . the Spirit of adoption, whereby we cry, Abba Father.'[13] I had afterwards an hour's calm conversation with Samuel Meggot and James Herbury. What good did God do by
5 these for a time! O let not their latter end be worse than the first!

Fri. 11. I visited the sick and those who desired but were not able to come to me. At six I preached at Upperthorpe[14] near Haxey (a little village about two miles from Epworth), on that comfortable Scripture, 'When they had nothing to pay, he frankly
10 forgave them both.'[15] I preached at Epworth about eight, on Ezekiel's vision of the resurrection of the dry bones.[16] And great indeed was the shaking among them. Lamentation and great mourning were heard, God bowing their hearts so that on every side, as with one accord, they lift up their voice and wept aloud.
15 Surely he who sent his Spirit to breathe upon them will hear their cry and will help them.

Sat. 12. I preached on the righteousness of the law and the righteousness of faith.[17] While I was speaking several dropped down as dead; and among the rest such a cry was heard of sinners
20 groaning for the righteousness of faith as almost drowned my voice. But many of these soon lifted up their heads with joy and broke out into thanksgiving, being assured they now had the desire of their soul, the forgiveness of their sins.

I observed a gentleman there who was remarkable for not
25 pretending to be of any religion at all. I was informed he had not been at public worship of any kind for upwards of thirty years. Seeing him stand as motionless as a statue, I asked him abruptly, 'Sir, are you a sinner?' He replied with a deep and broken voice, 'Sinner enough', and continued staring upwards till his wife and a
30 servant or two, who were all in tears, put him into his chaise and carried him home.

Sun. 13. At seven I preached at Haxey, on 'What must I do to be saved?'[18] Thence I went to Wroot,[19] of which (as well as Epworth) my father was rector for several years. Mr. Whitelamb[20]

---

13 Rom. 8:15.
14 Orig., 'Overthorp'; 1 kilometer W. of Haxey.
15 Luke 7:42.   16 See Ezek. 37:1-14.
17 See below, June 13, 1742.   18 Acts 16:30.
19 Orig., 'Wroote'. Wroot was a tiny parish 8 miles NE. by N. from Bawtry.
20 John Whitelamb (1710–69) was born near Wroot and educated at an endowed school there under John Romley (see above, June 6, 1742, n. 93), who recommended him to Samuel Wesley, rector of Epworth. The latter employed him as successor to Romley, as an

offering me the church, I preached in the morning, on 'Ask, and it shall be given you';[21] in the afternoon on the difference between 'the righteousness of the law and the righteousness of faith'.[22] But the church could not contain the people, many of whom came from far. And, I trust, not in vain.

At six I preached for the last time in Epworth churchyard (being to leave the town the next morning) to a vast multitude gathered together from all parts, on the beginning of our Lord's Sermon on the Mount. I continued among them for near three hours, and yet we scarce knew how to part. O let none think his labour of love is lost because the fruit does not immediately appear. Near forty years did my father labour here. But he saw little fruit of all his labour. I took some pains among this people too,[23] and my strength also seemed spent in vain. But now the fruit appeared. There were scarce any in the town on whom either my father or I had taken any pains formerly but the seed sown so long since now sprung up, bringing forth repentance and remission of sins.

Mon. 14. Having a great desire to see David Taylor,[24] whom God had made an instrument of good to many souls, I rode to Sheffield; but not finding him there, I was minded to go forward immediately. However, the importunity of the people constrained

amanuensis on his book on Job, educated him, got him to Lincoln College, Oxford, in 1731, where JW was his tutor. In 1733 Whitelamb became Samuel Wesley's curate and married his daughter Mary. She died a year later, and overwhelmed with grief, Whitelamb wished to go to Georgia with JW. However, Samuel Wesley resigned the rectory of Wroot in his favour in 1734. After Whitelamb's death, JW published his letter of June 11, 1742 (*Letters*, 26:80 in this edn.), accompanied by his offer of the use of his church with the warmest expressions of personal regard and gratitude for past favours; and another to Charles Wesley of Sept. 2, 1742, explaining that the outcry occasioned by Wesley's visit might cause him trouble at the next visitation and that he considered the Wesleys' 'doctrines as of ill consequence' and their followers' 'testimony of the Spirit . . . merely the effect of a heated fancy' (*Arminian Magazine* [1788], XI.183-86; Tyerman, *Samuel Wesley*, pp. 374-76).

[21] Matt. 7:7; Luke 11:9.
[22] Cf. Rom. 10:5-6. Apparently the basis of Sermon 6, 'The Righteousness of Faith' (1:200-16 in this edn.).
[23] JW's pastoral work in Wroot, undertaken to assist his father during a period of ill health, is described in his diary for the summer of 1726.
[24] David Taylor (died *c.* 1780), like his brother John (see above, May 25, 1742, n. 66), had been a servant in the household of the Countess of Huntingdon and had been employed by her as an itinerant evangelist with great effect, first in the villages round Donington Park, then further afield in Cheshire, the Peak, and around Birstall, where he generated considerable response before the arrival of John Nelson (see above, May 25, 1742, n. 69). His marriage and his cooperation with Benjamin Ingham, however, made him suspect to the Countess, who wrote to Wesley on Mar. 25, 1742, that she suspected

me to stay and preach both in the evening and in the morning.[25]
Tue. 15. He came. I found he had occasionally exhorted multitudes of people in various parts. But after that he had taken
no thought about them. So that the greater part were fallen
5 asleep again.

In the evening I preached on the inward kingdom of God; in
the morning, Wednesday 16, on the spirit of fear and the Spirit of
adoption.[26] It was now first I felt that God was here also; though
not so much as at Barley Hall (five miles from Sheffield),[27] where
10 I preached in the afternoon. Many were here melted down and
filled with love toward him whom 'God hath exalted to be a Prince
and a Saviour'.[28]

I talked with one here who for about six months (from the hour
that she knew the pardoning love of God) has been all peace and
15 love. She rejoices evermore and prays without ceasing. God gives
her whatever petitions she asks of him, and enables her in
everything to give thanks.[29] She has the witness in herself that
whatsoever she does, it is all done to the glory of God. Her heart
never wanders from him, no, not for a moment, but is continually
20 before the throne. Yet whether she was sanctified throughout or
not I had not light to determine.

Thur. 17. I began preaching about five, on 'the righteousness
of faith'.[30] But I had not half finished my discourse when I was
constrained to break off in the midst—our hearts were so filled

him of building a chapel for himself and would support him no further unless he delivered
all his societies to the control of the Wesleys *(Wesleyan Methodist Magazine* [1845],
68:1072-73). In May 1743 he was still battling at Charles Wesley's side in the Sheffield
riots (CWJ, I.309), but he failed to find a place in the Moravian or Quaker communities,
and when he ultimately returned to Methodism, his preaching gifts were gone. Atmore,
Methodist Memorial, pp. 412-13.

[25] At the first Methodist chapel in Sheffield, built the previous year at Cheney-square.

[26] See Rom. 8:15; cf. Sermon 9, 'The Spirit of Bondage and of Adoption' (1:248-66 in
this edn.).

[27] Barley Hall was a farmhouse near Thorp Hesley, first visited by JW with his father in
1733. Charles Wesley and David Taylor were mobbed there on May 27, 1743 (CWJ,
I.311). Preaching continued at Barley Hall until the present century.

[28] Cf. Acts 5:31.

[29] See 1 Thess. 5:16-18. Everett was informed that this was Miss Johnson, the daughter
of the owner of Barley Hall (J. Everett, *Methodism in Sheffield* [1823], 1:22). But it has also
been conjectured to be Jane Holmes (b. 1723), later Mrs. Green of Rotherham, one of the
first Methodists in Sheffield, who was converted under the influence of her aunt, Mrs.
Bagley. Overcoming the opposition of her Anglican relatives to her Methodist connexions,
she made her home in Rotherham, a centre of Methodist influence. J. Guest, *Historic
Notices of Rotherham* (Worksop, 1879), p. 473.

[30] Rom. 10:5-6; cf. above, June 13, n. 22.

with a sense of the love of God, and our mouths with prayer and thanksgiving. When we were somewhat satisfied herewith, I went on to call sinners to the salvation ready to be revealed.

The same blessing from God we found in the evening, while I was showing how he justifies the ungodly. Among the hearers was one who some time before had been deeply convinced of her ungodliness; insomuch that she cried out day and night, 'Lord, save, or I perish.'[31] All the neighbours agreeing that she was stark mad, her husband put her into a physician's hands, who blooded her largely, gave her a strong vomit, and laid on several blisters. But all this proving without success, she was in a short time judged to be incurable. He thought however he would speak to one person more, who had done much good in the neighbourhood. When Mrs. Johnson[32] came, she soon saw the nature of the disease, having herself gone through the same. She ordered all the medicines to be thrown away and exhorted the patient to 'look unto Jesus',[33] which this evening she was enabled to do by faith. And he healed the broken in heart.

Fri. 18. I left Sheffield, and after preaching at Ripley, by the way, hastened on to Donington Park. But Miss Cowper, I found, was gone to rest, having finished her course near three weeks before.[34]

Sun. 20. I read prayers at Ockbrook[35] and preached on Acts 17:23: 'Whom ye ignorantly worship, him declare I unto you.' At six in the evening I preached at Melbourne. There were many hearers. But I see little fruit.

Tue. 22. I had a long conversation with Mr. Simpson. And of this I am fully persuaded, that whatever he does is in the uprightness of his heart. But he is led into a thousand mistakes by one wrong principle (the same which many either ignorantly or wickedly ascribe to the body of the people called Methodists), the making *inward impressions* his rule of action, and not the *written Word.*

About eight I left Donington Park and before noon came to Markfield. We lay at Coventry, and the next day, Wednesday 23,

---

[31] Cf. Matt. 8:25.
[32] Mrs. Johnson was the wife of the owner of Barley Hall.
[33] Cf. Heb. 12:2.
[34] See above, May 17, 1742, n. 63.
[35] Orig., 'Ogbrook'.

in the afternoon came to Evesham.[36] At eight I preached. There were many who came with a design to disturb the rest. But they opened not their mouth.

Thur. 24. I spent great part of the day in speaking with the members of the society, whom in the evening I earnestly besought no more to tear each other in pieces by disputing but to 'follow after holiness'[37] and 'provoke one another to love and to good works.'[38]

Fri. 25. I rode to Painswick,[39] where in the evening I declared to all those who had been fighting and troubling one another, from the beginning hitherto, about rites and ceremonies, and modes of worship, and opinions, 'The kingdom of God is not meats and drinks, but righteousness and peace and joy in the Holy Ghost.'[40]

Sat. 26. I was desired to call upon Mr. Walker,[41] 'the pillar of the church'[42] in these parts. As soon as I came in he fell upon me with might and main for saying people might *know* their sins were forgiven. And brought a great book to confute me at once. I asked if it was the Bible. And upon his answering, 'No,' inquired no farther, but laid it quietly down. This made him warmer still, upon which I held it best to shake him by the hand and take my leave.

I had appointed to preach in Stroud at noon. But about ten, observing it to rain faster and faster, I was afraid the poor people would not be able to come, many of whom lived some miles off. But in a quarter of an hour the rain ceased, and we had a fair, pleasant day; so that many were at the market-place while I applied the story of the Pharisee and publican, the hard rain in the morning having disengaged them from their work in the grounds. There would probably have been more disturbance, but that a drunken man began too soon, and was so senselessly impertinent that even his comrades were quite ashamed of him.

---

[36] Evesham was a modest borough and market town situated 15 miles SE. of Worcester, in one of JW's favourite countrysides.

[37] Cf. Heb. 12:14.

[38] Cf. Heb. 10:24.

[39] Painswick was a substantial market town and parish 6 1/2 miles SSE. from Gloucester.

[40] Cf. Rom. 14:17.

[41] The full name replaces 'Mr. W——' in the errata and Wesley's own copy of the *Works* (1774).

[42] Cf. Rev. 3:12.

In the evening I preached on Minchinhampton Common.[43] Many of Mr. Whitefield's society were there, to whom, as well as to all the other sinners (without meddling with any of their opinions), I declared, in the name of the Great Physician, 'I will heal their backsliding, I will love them freely.'[44]

Sun. 27. I preached in Painswick at seven, on 'The spirit of fear and the Spirit of adoption'.[45] I went to church at ten and heard a remarkable discourse, asserting that we are justified by faith alone; but that this faith, which is the previous condition of justification, is the complex of all Christian virtues, including all holiness and good works, in the very idea of it.

Alas! How little is the difference between asserting either, (1) that we are justified by works, which is popery barefaced (and indeed so gross that the sober Papists, those of the Council of Trent in particular, are ashamed of it); or (2) that we are justified by faith and works, which is popery refined or veiled (but with so thin a veil that every attentive observer must discern it is the same still); or (3) that we are justified by faith alone, but by such a faith as includes all good works. What a poor shift is this! 'I will not say, we are justified by works, nor yet by faith and works, because I have subscribed Articles and Homilies which maintain just the contrary. No, I say, We are justified by faith alone—but then by faith I *mean* works!'

When the afternoon service was ended at Randwick[46] I stood and cried to a vast multitude of people, 'Unto him that worketh not, but believeth, his faith is counted for righteousness.'[47] I concluded the day on Minchinhampton Common, by explaining to a large congregation the essential difference between the righteousness of the law and the righteousness of faith.[48]

Mon. 28. I rode to Bristol. I soon found disputing had done much mischief here also. I preached on those words, 'From that time many of his disciples went back and walked no more with him. Then said Jesus unto the twelve, Will ye also go away?'[49] Many were cut to the heart. A cry went forth; and great was the company of the mourners. But God did not leave them

---

[43] Orig., 'Hampton Common'; a large market town and parish 14 miles S. of Gloucester.
[44] Hos. 14:4.
[45] Cf. Rom. 8:15.
[46] Orig., 'Runwick'. Randwick was a populous parish 2 miles NW. by W. from Stroud.
[47] Rom. 4:5.
[48] See June 13, 1742, above.
[49] John 6:66-67.

comfortless; some knew, in the same hour, that he had the words of eternal life.

Tue. 29. I was desired to visit one in Newgate. As I was coming out, poor Benjamin Rutter[50] stood in my way and poured out such a flood of cursing and bitterness as I scarce thought was to be found out of hell.

From Thursday, July 1, till Monday, I endeavoured to compose the little differences which had arisen. On Monday I rode to Cardiff and found much peace and love in the little society there. Tue. 6. I rode over to Fonmon and found Mrs. Jones thoroughly resigned to God, although *feeling* what it was to lose an husband, and *such* an husband, in the strength of his years![51]

Wed. 7. I returned, and at five in the afternoon preached to a small attentive congregation near Henbury.[52] Before eight I reached Bristol and had a comfortable meeting with many who knew in whom they had believed.

Now at length I spent a week in peace, all disputes being laid aside. Thur. 15. I was desired to meet one who was ill of a very uncommon disorder. She said, 'For several years I have heard, wherever I am, a voice continually speaking to me, cursing, swearing, and blaspheming in the most horrid manner, and inciting me to all manner of wickedness. I have applied to physicians and taken all sorts of medicines, but am never the better.' No, nor ever will, till a better physician than these bruises Satan under her feet.

I left Bristol in the evening of Sunday 18, and on Tuesday came to London. I found my mother on the borders of eternity. But she had no doubt or fear, nor any desire but (as soon as God should call), 'to depart, and to be with Christ'.[53]

Fri. 30. About three in the afternoon I went to my mother and found her change was near. I sat down on the bedside. She was in her last conflict, unable to speak, but I believe quite sensible. Her

---

[50] Benjamin Rutter, encountered by Charles Wesley as 'a drunken Quaker' (Aug. 28, Sept. 4, 1739; CWJ, I.166, 168), a bellows-maker, Castle Precincts. He was the father of Esther Moxham (1730–98).

[51] On Robert Jones (who died June 8, 1742) and his wife, see above, Sept. 21, 1741, n. 9. On July 11 Howell Harris heard how 'dear Mr. [Robert] Jones . . . had desired to have his corpse to be encompassed with Methodists' (*Bathafarn*, vi. 58-59, quoted in Williams, *Wesley in Wales*, p. 16, n. 2).

[52] Henbury was a small township and substantial parish 4 1/4 miles WNW. from Bristol.

[53] Phil. 1:23.

look was calm and serene, and her eyes fixed upward, while we commended her soul to God. From three to four the silver cord was loosing, and the wheel breaking at the cistern;[54] and then, without any struggle or sign or groan, the soul was set at liberty. We stood round the bed and fulfilled her last request, uttered a little before she lost her speech, 'Children, as soon as I am released, sing a psalm of praise to God.'[55]

Sunday, August 1. Almost an innumerable company of people being gathered together, about five in the afternoon I committed to the earth the body of my mother, to sleep with her fathers. The portion of Scripture from which I afterwards spoke was, 'I saw a great white throne, and him that sat on it; from whose face the earth and the heaven fled away, and there was found no place for them. And I saw the dead, small and great, stand before God, and the books were opened. . . . And the dead were judged out of those things which were written in the books, according to their works.'[56] It was one of the most solemn assemblies I ever saw, or expect to see on this side eternity.

We set up a plain stone at the head of her grave, inscribed with the following words:

Here lies the body of Mrs. Susannah[57] Wesley, the youngest and last surviving daughter of Dr. Samuel Annesley.

In sure and steadfast hope to rise
And claim her mansion in the skies,
A Christian here her flesh laid down,
The cross exchanging for a crown.

True daughter of affliction she,
Inured to pain and misery,
Mourned a long night of griefs and fears,
A legal night of seventy years.

The Father then revealed his Son,
Him in the broken bread made known.

---

[54] See Eccles. 12:6.

[55] JW gave a fuller account of his mother's death in letters to his brother Charles, July 31, 1742, and to Howell Harris, Aug. 6, 1742, *Letters*, 26:82, 86 in this edn.

[56] Rev. 20:11-12.

[57] Mrs. Wesley herself spelled her name without the final 'h', as did Charles Wesley in the surviving manuscript versions of the poem. A new headstone with a different inscription was erected by the Wesleyan Book Committee *c.* 1828; George J. Stevenson, *Memorials of the Wesley Family* (London [1876]), p. 228. The interment took place in the Dissenters' burial ground at Bunhill Fields. Cf. Moore, *Wesley*, I.563; *Arminian Magazine* (1781), IV.312-13.

She knew and felt her sins forgiven,
And found the earnest of her heaven.[58]

Meet for the fellowship above,
She heard the call, 'Arise, my love.'
5   'I come,' her dying looks replied,
And lamb-like, as her Lord, she died.[59]

I cannot but farther observe that even she (as well as her father
and grandfather, her husband, and her three sons) had been, in
her measure and degree, a preacher of righteousness.[60] This I
10 learned from a letter, wrote long since to my father, part of which
I have here subjoined:

Feb. 6, 1711/12
. . . As I am a woman, so I am also mistress of a large family. And
though the superior charge of the souls contained in it lies upon you,
15 . . . yet in your absence I cannot but look upon every soul you leave
under my care as a talent committed to me under a trust by the great
Lord of all the families, both of heaven and earth. And if I am
unfaithful to him or you, in neglecting to improve these talents, how
shall I answer unto him when he shall command me to render an
20 account of my stewardship?
As these and other such like thoughts made me at first take a more
than ordinary care of the souls of my children and servants, so
knowing our religion requires a strict observation of the Lord's day,
and not thinking that we fully answered the end of the institution by
25 going to church, unless we filled up the intermediate spaces of time by
other acts of piety and devotion, I thought it my duty to spend some
part of the day in reading to and instructing my family. . . . And such
time I esteemed spent in a way more acceptable to God than if I had
retired to my own private devotions.
30 This was the beginning of my present practice. Other people's
coming in and joining with us was merely accidental. Our lad told his
parents; they first desired to be admitted; then others that heard of it
begged leave also. So our company increased to about thirty, and it
seldom exceeded forty last winter. . . .

[58] While receiving Holy Communion in 1739, Mrs. Wesley experienced an assurance
of her own acceptance with God.
[59] The poem was published in Charles Wesley's *Hymns and Sacred Poems* (1749), I.282.
[60] In a letter to his brother Charles, Jan. 15, 1768 (Telford, V.76), JW commented still
more emphatically on this succession, claiming that 'such a thing has scarce been for three
thousand years before'. What was in his mind was, not to deny the historicity of a clerical
succession which became a post-Reformation commonplace, but to stress his sense of
continuity with a Puritan past, a sense also exemplified in his choice of titles for his
Christian Library.

But soon after you went to London last I light on the account of the Danish missionaries.[61] I was, I think, never more affected with anything. . . .[62] I could not forbear spending good part of that evening in praising and adoring the divine goodness for inspiring them with such ardent zeal for his glory. . . . For several days I could think or speak of little else. At last it came into my mind, though I am not a man, nor a minister, yet if my heart were sincerely devoted to God, and I was inspired with a true zeal for his glory, I might do somewhat more than I do. I thought I might pray more for them, and might speak to those with whom I converse with more warmth of affection. I resolved to begin with my own children; in which I observe the following method. I take such a proportion of time as I can spare every night to discourse with each child apart. On Monday I talk with Molly; on Tuesday with Hetty; Wednesday with Nancy; Thursday with Jacky; Friday with Patty; Saturday with Charles; and with Emily and Suky together on Sunday.

With those few neighbours that then came to me I discoursed more freely and affectionately. I chose the best and most awakening sermons we have. And I spent somewhat more time with them in such exercises, without being careful about the success of my undertaking.

Since this our company increased every night, for I dare deny none that ask admittance. Last Sunday I believe we had above two hundred. And yet many went away for want of room to stand.

We banish all temporal concerns from our society. None is suffered to mingle any discourse about them with our reading or singing. We keep close to the business of the day, and when 'tis over, all go home.

---

[61] A pamphlet entitled *Propagation of the Gospel in the East: Part II containing a further account of the progress made by some missionaries to Tranquebar upon the coast of Coromandel for the conversion of the barbarians* was published at London, 1710.

[62] The ellipses (shown by dashes in Wesley's transcription) are at least partly filled in, and the remainder filled out, by the version preserved by Dr. John Whitehead *(Wesley,* I.46-54), to whom the original was also available: 'Soon after you went to London, Emily found in your study the account of the Danish missionaries, which, having never seen, I ordered her to read to me. I was never, I think, more affected with anything than with the relation of their travels; and was exceeding pleased with the noble design they were engaged in. Their labours refreshed my soul beyond measure; and I could not forbear spending a good part of that evening in praising and adoring the divine goodness for inspiring those good men with such an ardent zeal for his glory that they were willing to hazard their lives and all that is esteemed dear to men in this world, to advance the honour of their Master, Jesus. For several days I could think or speak of little else. At last it came into my mind, though I am not a man, nor a minister of the gospel, and so cannot be employed in such a worthy employment as they were; yet, if my heart were sincerely devoted to God, and if I were inspired with a true zeal for his glory, and did really desire the salvation of souls, I might do somewhat more than I do. I thought I might live in a more exemplary *manner in some things;* I might pray more for *the people,* and speak with more warmth to those with whom I have an opportunity of conversing. However, I resolved to begin with my own children.'

I cannot conceive why any should reflect upon *you,* because your wife endeavours to draw people to church, and to restrain them from profaning the Lord's day by reading to them, and other persuasions. For my part, I value no censure upon this account. I have long since shook hands with the world. And I heartily wish I had never given them more reason to speak against me.

As to its looking particular, I grant it does. And so does almost anything that is serious, or that may any way advance the glory of God, or the salvation of souls. . . .

As for your proposal of letting some other person read—Alas! you don't consider what a people these are. I don't think one man among them could read a sermon, without spelling a good part of it. Nor has any of our family a voice strong enough to be heard by such a number of people. . . .

But there is one thing about which I am much dissatisfied; that is, their being present at family prayers. I don't speak of any concern I am under barely because so *many* are present—for those who have the honour of speaking to the great and holy God need not be ashamed to speak before the whole world—but because of my sex I doubt if it is proper for *me* to present the prayers of the people to God. Last Sunday I would fain have dismissed them before prayers; but they begged so earnestly to stay I durst not deny them. . . .

To the Rev. Mr. Wesley, in St. Margaret's Churchyard, Westminster.

For the benefit of those who are entrusted, as she was, with the care of a numerous family, I cannot but add one letter more, which I received from her many years ago:

July 24, 1732

Dear Son,

According to your desire I have collected the principal rules I observed in educating my family; which I now send you as they occurred to my mind, and you may (if you think they can be of use to any) dispose of them in what order you please.

The children were always put into a regular method of living, in such things as they were capable of, from their birth; as in dressing, undressing, changing their linen, etc. The first quarter commonly passes in sleep. After that they were, if possible, laid into their cradles awake, and rocked to sleep; and so they were kept rocking till it was time for them to awake. This was done to bring them to a regular course of sleeping; which at first was three hours in the morning, and three in the afternoon; afterward two hours, till they needed none at all.

When turned a year old (and some before) they were taught to fear the rod, and to cry softly; by which means they escaped abundance of correction they might otherwise have had; and that most odious noise of the crying of children was rarely heard in the house; but the family usually lived in as much quietness as if there had not been a child among them. 5

As soon as they were grown pretty strong they were confined to three meals a day. At dinner their little table and chairs were set by ours, where they could be overlooked; and they were suffered to eat and drink (small beer) as much as they would, but not to call for anything. If they wanted aught they used to whisper to the maid which 10 attended them, who came and spake to me; and as soon as they could handle a knife and fork were set to our table. They were never suffered to choose their meat, but always made to eat such things as were provided for the family.

Mornings they had always spoon-meat; sometimes on nights. But 15 whatever they had, they were never permitted to eat at those meals of more than one thing, and of that sparingly enough. Drinking or eating between meals was never allowed, unless in case of sickness, which seldom happened. Nor were they suffered to go into the kitchen to ask anything of the servants, when they were at meat; if it was known they 20 did they were certainly beat, and the servants severely reprimanded.

At six, as soon as family prayers was over, they had their supper; at seven the maid washed them, and beginning at the youngest she undressed and got them all to bed by eight; at which time she left them in their several rooms awake, for there was no such thing 25 allowed of in our house as sitting by a child till it fell asleep.

They were so constantly used to eat and drink what was given them that when any of them was ill there was no difficulty in making them take the most unpleasant medicine; for they durst not refuse it, though some of them would presently throw it up. This I mention to 30 show that a person may be taught to take anything, though it be never so much against his stomach.

In order to form the minds of children, the first thing to be done is to conquer their will, and bring them to an obedient temper. To inform the understanding is a work of time, and must with children 35 proceed by slow degrees as they are able to bear it; but the subjecting the will is a thing which must be done at once—and the sooner the better. For by neglecting timely correction they will contract a stubbornness and obstinacy, which is hardly ever after conquered, and never without using such severity as would be as painful to me as 40 to the child. In the esteem of the world they pass for kind and indulgent whom I call cruel parents, who permit their children to get habits which they know must be afterwards broken. Nay, some are so stupidly fond as in sport to teach their children to do things which in a while after they have severely beaten them for doing. 45

Whenever a child is corrected it must be conquered, and this will be no hard matter to do, if it be not grown headstrong by too much indulgence. And when the will of a child is totally subdued, and it is brought to revere and stand in awe of the parents, then a great many

5 childish follies and inadvertencies may be passed by. Some should be overlooked and taken no notice of, and others mildly reproved; but no wilful transgression ought ever to be forgiven children without chastisement, less or more, as the nature and circumstances of the offence require.

10 I insist upon conquering the will of children betimes, because this is the only strong and rational foundation of a religious education, without which both precept and example will be ineffectual. But when this is thoroughly done, then a child is capable of being governed by the reason and piety of its parents, till its own understanding

15 comes to maturity, and the principles of religion have taken root in the mind.

I cannot yet dismiss this subject. As self-will is the root of all sin and misery, so whatever cherishes this in children ensures their after wretchedness and irreligion; whatever checks and mortifies it

20 promotes their future happiness and piety. This is still more evident if we farther consider that religion is nothing else than the doing the will of God, and not our own; that the one grand impediment to our temporal and eternal happiness being this self-will, no indulgences of it can be trivial, no denial unprofitable. Heaven or hell depends on

25 this alone. So that the parent who studies to subdue it in his child works together with God in the renewing and saving a soul; the parent who indulges it does the devil's work, makes religion impracticable, salvation unattainable, and does all that in him lies to damn his child, soul and body, for ever.

30 The children of this family were taught, as soon as they could speak, the Lord's prayer, which they were made to say at rising and bedtime constantly; to which, as they grew bigger, were added a short prayer for their parents, and some collects; a short catechism, and some portions of Scripture, as their memories could bear.

35 They were very early made to distinguish the sabbath from other days; before they could well speak, or go. They were as soon taught to be still at family prayers, and to ask a blessing immediately after, which they used to do by signs before they would kneel or speak.

They were quickly made to understand they might have nothing

40 they cried for, and instructed to speak handsomely for what they wanted. They were not suffered to ask even the lowest servant for aught without saying, 'Pray give me such a thing'; and the servant was chid if she ever let them omit that word. Taking God's name in vain, cursing and swearing, profaneness, obscenity, rude, ill-bred names,

45 were never heard among them. Nor were they ever permitted to call

each other by their proper names without the addition of brother or sister.

None of them were taught to read till five years old, except Kezzy, in whose case I was overruled; and she was more years learning than any of the rest had been months. The way of teaching was this. The 5 day before a child began to learn, the house was set in order, every one's work appointed them, and a charge given that none should come into the room from nine till twelve, or from two till five, which, you know, were our school hours. One day was allowed the child wherein to learn its letters, and each of them did in that time know all 10 its letters, great and small, except Molly and Nancy, who were a day and a half before they knew them perfectly; for which I then thought them very dull; but since I have observed how long many children are learning the hornbook I have changed my opinion. But the reason why I thought them so then was because the rest learned so readily, 15 and your Brother Samuel, who was the first child I ever taught, learned the alphabet in a few hours. He was five years old on the 10th of February; the next day he began to learn, and as soon as he knew the letters began at the first chapter of Genesis. He was taught to spell the first verse, then to read it over and over, till he could read it 20 offhand without any hesitation; so on to the second, etc., till he took ten verses for a lesson, which he quickly did. Easter fell low that year, and by Whitsuntide he could read a chapter very well; for he read continually, and had such a prodigious memory that I cannot remember ever to have told him the same word twice. 25

What was yet stranger, any word he had learned in his lesson he knew wherever he saw it, either in his Bible or any other book; by which means he learned very soon to read any English author well.

The same method was observed with them all. As soon as they knew the letters they were put first to spell; and read one line, then a 30 verse, never leaving till perfect in their lesson, were it shorter or longer. So one or other continued reading at school-time, without any intermission, and before we left school each child read what he had learned that morning; and ere we parted in the afternoon, what they had learned that day. 35

There was no such thing as loud talking or playing allowed of; but everyone was kept close to their business for the six hours of school. And it is almost incredible what a child may be taught in a quarter of a year, by a vigorous application, if it have but a tolerable capacity, and good health. Every one of these, Kezzy excepted, could read better in 40 that time than the most of women can do as long as they live.

Rising out of their places, or going out of the room, was not permitted unless for good cause, and running into the yard, garden, or street, without leave, was always esteemed a capital offence.

For some years we went on very well. Never were children in better 45

order. Never were children better disposed to piety, or in more
subjection to their parents, till that fatal dispersion of them after the
fire into several families. In these they were left at full liberty to
converse with servants, which before they had always been restrained
from; and to run abroad and play with any children, good or bad.
They soon learned to neglect a strict observation of the sabbath, and
got knowledge of several songs and bad things which before they had
no notion of. That civil behaviour which had made them admired
when at home by all which saw them was in great measure lost, and a
clownish accent and many rude ways were learned, which were not
reformed without some difficulty.

When the house was rebuilt, and the children all brought home, we
entered upon a strict reform; and then was begun the custom of
singing Psalms at beginning and leaving school, morning and
evening. Then also that of a general retirement at five o'clock was
entered upon, when the oldest took the youngest that could speak,
and the second the next, to whom they read the Psalms for the day,
and a chapter in the New Testament; as in the morning they were
directed to read the Psalms and a chapter in the Old, after which
they went to their private prayers, before they got their breakfast or
came into the family. And I thank God this custom is still preserved
among us.

There were several by-laws observed among us, which slipped my
memory, or else they had been inserted in their proper place; but I
mention them here, because I think them useful.

1. It had been observed that cowardice and fear of punishment
often leads children into lying, till they get a custom of it, which they
cannot leave. To prevent this, a law was made that whoever was
charged with a fault, of which they were guilty, if they would
ingenuously confess it, and promise to amend, should not be beaten.
This rule prevented a great deal of lying, and would have done more if
one in the family[63] would have observed it. But he could not be
prevailed on, and therefore was often imposed on by false colours and
equivocations, which none would have used (except one) had they
been kindly dealt with. And some, in spite of all, would always speak
truth plainly.

2. That no sinful action, as lying, pilfering, playing at church, or
on the Lord's day, disobedience, quarrelling, etc., should ever pass
unpunished.

3. That no child should ever be chid or beat twice for the same

---

[63] Probably Samuel Wesley, Sen., of whom his wife had remarked in a letter to JW
on Feb. 23, 1725: 'It is an unhappiness almost peculiar to our family, that your father
and I seldom think alike' (Tyerman, *Samuel Wesley*, p. 392; *Letters*, 25:159-60 in
this edn).

fault, and that if they amended they should never be upbraided with it afterwards.

4. That every signal act of obedience, especially when it crossed upon their own inclinations, should be always commended, and frequently rewarded, according to the merits of the cause.   5

5. That if ever any child performed an act of obedience, or did anything with an intention to please, though the performance was not well, yet the obedience and intention should be kindly accepted, and the child with sweetness directed how to do better for the future.

6. That propriety be inviolably preserved, and none suffered to 10 invade the property of another in the smallest matter, though it were but of the value of a farthing, or a pin; which they might not take from the owner without, much less against his consent. This rule can never be too much inculcated on the minds of children, and from the want of parents or governors doing it as they ought proceeds that shameful 15 neglect of justice which we may observe in the world.

7. That promises be strictly observed; and a gift once bestowed, and so the right passed away from the donor, be not resumed, but left to the disposal of him to whom it was given; unless it were conditional, and the condition of the obligation not performed.   20

8. That no girl be taught to work till she can read very well; and then that she be kept to her work with the same application, and for the same time, that she was held to in reading. This rule also is much to be observed; for the putting children to learn sewing before they can read perfectly is the very reason why so few women can read fit to 25 be heard, and never to be well understood.

Sun. 8. I cried aloud, in Radcliff Square, 'Why will ye die, O house of Israel?'[64] Only one poor man was exceeding noisy and turbulent. But in a moment God touched his heart. He hung down his head. Tears covered his face; and his voice was heard 30 no more.

I was constrained this evening to separate from the believers some who did not 'show their faith by their works'.[65] One of these, Samuel Prig,[66] was deeply displeased, spoke many very bitter words, and went abruptly away. The next morning he called, told 35 me, neither my brother nor I preached the gospel or knew what it meant. I asked, 'What do we preach, then?' He said, 'Heathen morality: Tully's *Offices*,[67] and no more. So I wash my hands of

---

[64] Ezek. 18:31; 33:11.

[65] Cf. Jas. 2:18.

[66] JW's diary records his taking tea with Samuel Prig (or his wife) on Mar. 23, 1741. Elizabeth Prig was still a member at the Foundery in 1745.

[67] I.e., Marcus Tullius Cicero, to whom Wesley in fact did frequently refer.

you both. We shall see what you will come to in a little time.'

Wed. 11. He sent me a note demanding the payment of one hundred pounds, which he had lent me about a year before to pay the workmen at the Foundery. On Friday morning at eight he
5 came and said he wanted his money and could stay no longer. I told him I would endeavour to borrow it, and desired him to call in the evening. But he said he could not stay so long and must have it at twelve o'clock. Where to get it I knew not. Between nine and ten one came and offered me the use of an hundred pounds for a
10 year. But two others had been with me before to make the same offer. I accepted the bank note which one of them brought, and saw that God is over all!

Mon. 16. I rode to Oxford, and the next day to Evesham. On Wednesday and Thursday, in riding from Evesham to Bristol, I
15 read over that surprising book, the life of Ignatius Loyola[68]— surely one of the greatest men that ever was engaged in the support of so bad a cause! I wonder any man should judge him to be an enthusiast. No; but he knew the people with whom he had to do. And setting out (like Count Z[inzendorf]) with a full
20 persuasion that he might *use guile* to promote the glory of God or (which he thought the same thing) the interest of his church, he acts in all things consistent with his principles.

In the evening I met my brother and Mr. Graves,[69] who being able to delay it no longer, at length sent the following letter to the
25 fellows of St. Mary Magdalen College in Oxford:

Bristol, Aug. 20, 1742

Gentlemen,

In December, 1740, I signed a paper containing the following words:

---

[68] A *Life of B. Father Ignatius of Loyola* by Pedro de Ribadeneira had been translated into English in 1616 and 1622.

[69] Charles Caspar Graves (*c.* 1717–87), son of Richard Graves of Mickleton, Glos., gent., demy of Magdalen College, Oxford, 1736–41; B.A. 1740. In 1737 his friends removed him from the college as 'stark mad', but Charles Wesley, denying that he had made him mad, took him to Stanton Harcourt, where he remained some time (July 25, Oct. 2, 10, 1737; CWJ, I.73, 76, 77). He was converted in 1738 and became a zealous field-preacher and one of the two 'awakened' clergy in the neighbourhood of the Countess of Huntingdon's estate at Donington Park. In 1740 he was pressed to sign the paper here given disclaiming Methodist principles and practices; but within two years he was active with the Wesleys again (ibid., I.135, 160, 205, 320, 395, 422). His father was Richard Graves the antiquary; his brother Richard Graves the poet, rector of Tissington, Derbys., 1759–87.

'I, Charles Caspar Graves, do hereby declare that I do renounce the modern practice and principles of the persons commonly called Methodists, namely, of preaching in fields, of assembling together and expounding the Holy Scriptures in private houses, and elsewhere than in churches, in an irregular and disorderly manner, and their 5 pretensions to an extraordinary inspiration and inward feeling of the Holy Spirit.

'I do farther declare my conformity to the Liturgy of the Church of England, and my unfeigned assent and consent to the Articles thereof, commonly called the Thirty-nine Articles. 10

'Lastly, I do declare that I am heartily sorry that I have given offence and scandal by frequenting the meetings and attending the expositions of the persons commonly called Methodists, and that I will not frequent their meetings nor attend their expositions for the future, nor take upon me to preach and expound the Scriptures in the 15 manner preached by them.

Charles Caspar Graves'

I believe myself indispensably obliged openly to declare before God and the world that the motives whereby I was induced to sign that paper were partly a sinful fear of man, partly an improper 20 deference to the judgment of those whom I accounted wiser than myself, and lastly a resolution that if my own judgment should at any time be better informed, I would then openly retract, in the presence of God and man, whatever I should be convinced I had said or done amiss. 25

Accordingly, having now had (besides a strong conviction immediately consequent thereon) many opportunities of informing my judgment better, and being fully convinced of my fault, I do hereby declare my sincere repentance for my wicked compliance with those oppressive men, who, without any colour of law, divine or 30 human, imposed such a condition of receiving a testimonial upon me.

I do farther declare that I know no *principles* of the Methodists (so called) which are contrary to the Word of God; nor any practices of them but what are agreeable both to Scripture and to the laws of the Church of England; that I believe, in particular, their 'preaching' the 35 gospel 'in the fields' (being first forbid so to do in churches, although 'a dispensation of the gospel is committed to them', and 'woe unto them if they preach not the gospel'[70]) or in 'private houses', or in any part of his dominion who filleth heaven and earth, can never be proved to be contrary to any written law, either of God or man; that I 40 am not apprised or their preaching anywhere in 'an irregular, disorderly manner'; neither of their 'pretending' to any 'extraordinary' inspiration or 'extraordinary' feelings of the Holy Spirit; but to

[70] Cf. 1 Cor. 9:16-17.

those *ordinary* ones only which, if a man have not, he is 'without hope and without God in the world'.[71]

I do yet farther declare that (whatever indiscretion I may in other respects have been guilty of) I know of no just 'offence or scandal' which I ever gave by 'frequenting the meetings or attending the expositions of the persons commonly called Methodists'; and that I verily believe no offence was ever taken thereat, unless either by persons loaded with prejudice, or by those who enter not into the kingdom of heaven themselves, and if others would enter in, suffer them not.

I do, lastly, declare that I look upon myself to be under no kind of obligation (except only that I do still assent and consent to the Articles and Liturgy of the Church) to observe anything contained in that scandalous paper, so unchristianly imposed upon me.

Witness my hand,

Charles Caspar Graves

After having regulated the society here and in Kingswood, I set out again for London. On Monday 30, I read over that excellent tract, Mr. Middleton's *Essay on Church Government*,[72] so nicely avoiding the two extremes of either exalting or depressing the regal power. Tue. 31. I read once more the life of that good and wise (though much mistaken man) Gregory Lopez.[73] Surely it must be a compliment made him by the biographer (of which Gregory himself was in no wise worthy) that 'he ascribed all his virtues to the merits and mediation of the Queen of heaven.'

We reached London in the afternoon. Friday, September 3, I preached on Phil. 1:9, 'This I pray, that your love may abound more and more, in knowledge, and in all judgment'—or rather *feeling*, as it is in the margin. It pleased God to make this discourse

[71] Cf. Eph. 2:12.

[72] Patrick Middleton, *A dissertation upon the power of the church: in a middle way, betwixt those who screw it up to the highest, with the Papists and Scottish Presbyterians on the one hand, and the Erastians and followers of Hugo Grotius, who, on the other hand, do wholly reject the intrinsic spiritual authority wherewith Jesus Christ hath vested the rulers of the church* (London, 1733). Patrick Middleton (1661–1736), a Scots nonjuring divine, minister of Leslie, 1684, was deprived of his clerical functions after the Revolution for his open Jacobitism, and, having obtained a meeting-house in Edinburgh in 1716, he was prosecuted in 1717 for not praying for George I in the terms of the Toleration Act, and forbidden to preach or exercise any ministerial function.

[73] Gregory Lopez (1542–96) was born in Madrid but went to South America at the age of twenty and ultimately died there. The book here referred to (which JW highly esteemed, took with him to Georgia, and abridged in 1755) was *The holy life, pilgrimage and blessed death of Gregory Lopez, a Spanish hermit in the West Indies*, trans. Abraham Woodhead (London, 1675). Lopez and de Renty stood side by side in JW's view as models of practical godliness, and Lopez's *Life* was serialized in the *Arminian Magazine* in 1780.

an occasion of discovering such wiles of Satan as it never entered into my heart to conceive.

Sat. 4. I was pressed to visit a poor murderer in Newgate, who was much afflicted both in body and soul. I objected, it could not be; for all the turnkeys, as well as the keeper, were *so good* Christians they abhorred the name of a Methodist, and had absolutely refused to admit *me* even to one who earnestly begged it the morning he was to die. However I went, and found, by a surprising turn, that all the doors were now open to me. I exhorted the sick malefactor to cry unto God with all his might for grace to repent and believe the gospel. It was not long before the rest of the felons flocked round, to whom I spoke strong words concerning the Friend of sinners, which they received with as great signs of amazement as if it had been a voice from heaven. When I came down into the common hall (I think they called it), one of the prisoners there asking me a question gave me occasion to speak among them also; more and more still running together while I declared, God was not willing any of them should perish, but that all should come to repentance.[74]

Mon. 6. Finding many had been offended at the sermon I preached on Friday night, especially those who were supposed to be strong in faith, I determined to examine the matter thoroughly. Accordingly I desired M. C., M. F., E. H., and A. G., and a few others, to meet me with Sarah Cl[avel], Jane J[ackso]n, and Ann P[ye], to whom they had said most concerning the point in question.[75] I then heard each of them relate her experience at large. I afterwards examined them severally touching the circumstances which I did not understand; on which I then talked with several others also. And thus far I approved of their

[74] 2 Pet. 3:9.

[75] The presumption is that JW here summoned members of the London societies (whose initials he gives) who had complained of his doctrine, together with their class leaders. There is no difficulty in completing the names of the class leaders from manuscript and other sources, but there were several members (all women) whose initials fit those here given (see Curnock, III.43, n. 1). The point in question was how far the working of the Spirit of God was to be detected in physical abnormalities rather than in an abundance of graces of character. Characteristically, JW keeps an open mind upon the former, but leans heavily towards the latter. In a letter to Thomas Rutherforth, Mar. 28, 1768, he said, 'I was so disgusted at them for those dreams that I expelled them out of the society' (9:384 in this edn.). It may be noteworthy that JW did not publish a sermon on this text [Phil. 1:9], although more than half of the fourteen occasions on which he recorded preaching on it in his sermon register, 1747–61, were remembered as attended with special blessing.

experience (because agreeable to the written Word) as to their *feeling* the working of the Spirit of God, in peace and joy and love. But as to what some of them said farther concerning feeling the blood of Christ running upon their arms, or going down their
5 throat, or poured like warm water upon their breast or heart, I plainly told them, the utmost I could allow, without renouncing both Scripture and reason, was that *some* of these circumstances might be from God (though I could not affirm they were), working in an unusual manner, no way essential either to
10 justification or sanctification; but that all the rest I must believe to be the mere, empty dreams of an heated imagination.

Wed. 8. I observed that the leaven of stillness is not yet purged out from among us. One of our brethren saying he was uneasy because he had wilfully neglected the Lord's Supper, another
15 replied, then his faith was weak, else his peace could not be shaken by such little things. Yea, but I think such little things as these will shake the peace of any true believer, viz., a wilful breach of any commandment of God. If it does *not* shake us, we are asleep in the devil's arms.

20   Thur. 9. I buried the body of Lucy Godshall, one of the first women [in] bands at Fetter Lane. After pressing toward the mark for more than two years, since she had known the pardoning love of God, she was for some time weary and faint in her mind, till I put her out of the bands. God blessed this greatly to her soul, so
25 that in a short time she was admitted again. Soon after, being at home, she felt the love of God in an unusual manner poured into her heart.[76] She fell down upon her knees and delivered up her soul and body into the hands of God. In the instant the use of all her limbs was taken away, and she was in a burning fever. For
30 three days she mightily praised God and rejoiced in him all the day long. She then cried out, 'Now Satan hath desired to have me, that he may sift me as wheat.' Immediately darkness and heaviness fell upon her, which continued till Saturday the fourth instant. On Sunday the light shone again upon her heart. About
35 ten in the evening one said to her, 'Jesus is ready to receive your soul.' She said, 'Amen! Amen!' closed her eyes, and died.

[76] Notwithstanding JW's reservations about unusual physical accompaniments to religious phenomena, forcibly expressed under September 6, his description of the experience of Lucy Godshall involved him in later controversy with those (especially Bishop Warburton and Thomas Rutherforth) who wished to convict him of enthusiasm (see 11:467-538 and 9:374-88 in this edn.).

Sun. 12. I was desired to preach in an open place, commonly called 'the Great Gardens', laying between Whitechapel and Coverlet's Fields, where I found a vast multitude gathered together. Taking knowledge that a great part of them were little acquainted with the things of God, I called upon them in the words of our Lord, 'Repent ye, and believe the gospel.'[77] Many of the beasts of the people laboured much to disturb those who were of a better mind. They endeavoured to drive in a herd of cows among them; but the brutes were wiser than their masters. They then threw whole showers of stones, one of which struck me just between the eyes. But I felt no pain at all, and when I had wiped away the blood went on testifying with a loud voice that God hath given to them that believe, 'not the spirit of fear, but of power and love and of a sound mind'.[78] And by the spirit which now appeared through the whole congregation I plainly saw what a blessing it is when it is given us, even in the lowest degree, to suffer for his name's sake.

Mon. 13. I preached about nine at Windsor,[79] and the next evening came to Bristol. I spent the remainder of this and the following week in examining those of the society; speaking severally to each, that I might more perfectly know the state of their souls to Godward.

Thur. 23. In the evening, almost as soon as I began to pray in the society, a voice of lamentation and bitter mourning was heard from the whole congregation. But in a while loud thanksgivings were mixed therewith, which in a short space spread over all, so that nothing was to be heard on every side but 'Praise to God and to the Lamb for ever and ever!'[80]

Fri. 24. I had notes from nineteen persons, desiring to return God thanks. Some of them follow.

John Merriman, a blind man, desires to return thanks to Almighty God for the discovery of his love to him, an old sinner.

One desires to return God thanks for giving her a token of his love, in removing all prejudices, and giving her love to all mankind.

Edith W—— desires to return thanks for great and unspeakable mercies which the Lord was pleased to reveal to her heart; even telling me, I am he that blotteth out thy transgressions, and thy sins I

---

[77] Mark 1:15.   [78] Cf. 2 Tim. 1:7.
[79] Windsor was a borough, market town, and parish and royal residence, 22 1/2 miles W. by S. from London.
[80] Cf. Rev. 5:13.

will remember no more. And I desire that the praise of the Lord may be ever in my heart.

Ann Simmonds desires to return hearty thanks to God for the great mercies she received last night. For she has a full assurance of her redemption in the blood of Christ.

Mary K—— desires to return thanks to God for giving her a fresh sense of her forgiveness.

Mary F—— desires to return thanks for that the Lord hath made her triumph over sin, earth, and hell.

Mary W——n desires to return thanks to Almighty God for a fresh sense of forgiveness.

Sir, I desire to return humble thanks to Almighty God for the comfortable assurance of his pardoning love. E. C——.

Many others took an opportunity of speaking to me and declaring what God had done for their souls. But one came to me, Mrs. Sp——,[81] who was still torn in pieces with sorrow and doubts and fears. Her chief fear, she said, was that we were all Papists. I asked her how she came to fear this, after she had heard us preach for near three years, and been more than a twelvemonth in the society! She said, 'Why, it is not long since I met with a gentleman who told me he was a Roman Catholic. And when I asked him if Mr. Wesley was a Papist he would not say yes or no, but only 'Mr. W. is a very good man, and you do well to hear him.' Besides, it is but two or three nights since, as I was just setting out to come to the Room, Miss Gr——[82] met me and said, 'My dear friend, you shan't go. Indeed you shan't. You don't know what you do. I assure you Mr. W. is a Papist, and so am I; he converted *me*. You know how I used to pray to saints and to the Virgin Mary. It was Mr. W. taught me when I was in the bands. And I saw him rock the cradle on Christmas Eve. You know I scorn to tell a lie.' 'Well, but', said I, 'how comes it that none of the rest who are in the bands have found this out as well as you?' 'Oh', replied she, 'they are not let into the secret yet. Perhaps if you was in the bands you might not hear a word of it for a year or more. Oh! you can't

---

[81] Probably Mrs. Sparrow of Lewisham (and printed thus in the excerpt from his Journal quoted by JW in his letter to Warburton, Nov. 26, 1762, 11:493 in this edn.), a great friend not only of Whitefield but also of Charles Wesley, who described her as 'a martyr to worldly civility'. She died May 1748, leaving him a small legacy. CWJ, I.363.

[82] Probably Miss Gregory whom JW, as his diary shows, frequently visited in Bristol. This passage was another on which JW had to defend himself against Warburton (11:493 in this edn.).

imagine the depth of the design.' The maid at her back then fell a crying and said, 'Indeed, madam! Miss Gr—— talks so fine! Do, madam, mind what she says.' So between one and the other, poor Mrs. Sp—— was utterly confounded.

Perhaps I need observe no more upon this than that the popish priest knew well how much it would be for the interest of *his* church to have *me* accounted a member of it. And that Miss Gr—— had lately been raving mad (in consequence of a fever); that, as such, she was tied down in bed, and as soon as she was suffered to go abroad went to Mr. Whitefield to inquire of *him* whether *she* was not a Papist. But he quickly perceived she was only a lunatic, the nature of her disorder soon betraying itself. O that all who advance the same assertion with her had as good a plea to urge in their excuse!

Sun. 26. In the evening I rode to Marshfield. The next evening I reached Whitchurch.[83] Tue. 28. In the morning I preached at Great Marlow,[84] on the Pharisee and the publican. Many were surprised, and perhaps in some measure convinced (but how short-lived are most of these convictions!), that 'tis very possible a man may be a Pharisee *now*—yea, though he be not a Methodist.

A little before twelve I came to Windsor. I was soon informed that a large number of the rabble had combined together and declared again and again, there should be no preaching there that day. In order to make all sure they had provided gunpowder enough, and other things, some days before. But Burnham Fair coming between, they agreed to go thither first and have a little diversion there. Accordingly they went, and bestowed a few of their crackers upon their brother mob at Burnham.[85] But these, not being Methodists, did not take it well, turned upon them, and gave them chase. They took shelter in an house. But that would not serve. For those without soon forced a way in and seized on as many as they could find, who, upon information made, were sent to jail. The rest run away, so that when I came, none hindered or interrupted. In the evening I came to London; I proposed spending a fortnight there and then returning to Bristol.

I spent this time partly in speaking severally to all the members

[83] Probably Whitchurch, a parish 6 1/2 miles NW. of Reading on the N. bank of the Thames opposite Pangbourne.
[84] Great Marlow was a substantial borough, market town, and parish situated on the Thames 31 miles W. by N. from London.
[85] Burnham was a substantial village and parish 3 1/2 miles NW. by N. from Eton.

of the society, partly in making a full inquiry into those devices of Satan whereof I had scarce ever heard or read before. And I believe they were now thoroughly discovered and brought to nought. O may they never more deceive the hearts of the simple!

5 Monday, Oct. 11. I had designed to leave London. But Mr. Richards being taken ill, I put off my journey. He was much better on Tuesday; so I set out the next morning, and before seven in the evening reached the half-way house, four miles short of Hungerford.

10 I now found it was well I did not set out on Monday in order to be at Bristol on Tuesday night as usual. For all the travellers who went that way on Tuesday were robbed. But on Thursday the road was clear, so that I came safe to Kingswood in the afternoon, and in the evening preached at Bristol.

15 My chief business now was to examine thoroughly the society in Kingswood. This found me full employment for several days. On Wednesday 27, having finished my work, I set out very early, and (though my horse fell lame) on Thursday evening came to London.

20 Fri. 29. I largely explained, 'Where the spirit of the Lord is, there is liberty';[86] namely, liberty to obey the whole will of God, to *be* and *do* whatsoever he hath commanded—in a word, to love God with all our heart and to serve him with all our strength.

Sun. 31. Several of the *leaders* desired to have an hour's 25 conversation with me. I found they were greatly perplexed about 'want of management, ill husbandry, encouraging idleness, improper distribution of money', 'being imposed upon by fair pretences', and 'men who talked well, but had no grace in their hearts'. I asked who those men were. But that they could not tell. 30 Who encouraged idleness? When and how? What money had been improperly distributed? By whom and to whom? In what instances *I* had been imposed on (as I presumed they meant *me),* and what were the particulars of that ill husbandry and mismanagement of which they complained? They stared at one 35 another, as men in amaze. I began to be amazed too, not being able to imagine what was the matter, till one dropped a word by which all came out. They had been talking with Mr. Hall,[87] who had started so many objections against all I said or did that they

---

[86] 2 Cor. 3:17.
[87] Apparently Rev. Westley Hall.

were in the utmost consternation, till the fire thus broke out, which then at once vanished away.

Wednesday, November 3. Two of those who are called 'prophets' desired to speak with me. They told me they were sent from God with a message to me, which was that very shortly I should be 'borned' again. One of them added that they would stay in the house till it was done, unless I turned them out. I answered gravely, 'I will not turn you out,' and showed them down into the society room. It was tolerably cold, and they had neither meat nor drink. However, there they sat from morning to evening. They then went quietly away, and I have heard nothing from them since.

Sun. 7. I concluded the Epistle to the Hebrews, that strong barrier against the too prevailing imagination that the privileges of Christian believers are to be measured by those of the Jews. Not so: that Christians are under 'a better covenant',[88] established upon *better* promises; that although 'the law made nothing perfect', made none perfect either in holiness or happiness, yet 'the bringing in of a better hope did, by which we' now 'draw nigh unto God'[89]—this is the great truth continually inculcated herein, and running through this whole Epistle.

Mon. 8. I set out at four, reached Northampton that night, and the next evening, Donington Park. Wed. 10. I rode on to Rusworth Inn,[90] and on Saturday 13 reached Newcastle.

My brother had been here for some weeks before and was but just returned to London. At eight I met the wild, staring, loving society. But not them alone, as I had designed. For we could not persuade the strangers to leave us. So that we only spent about an hour in prayer.

Sun. 14. I began preaching at five o'clock (a thing never heard of before in these parts), on, 'I came not to call the righteous, but sinners to repentance.'[91] And the victorious sweetness of the grace of God was present with his word. At ten we went to All Saints', where was such a number of communicants as I have scarce seen but at Bristol or London. At four I preached in the square of the Keelman's Hospital,[92] on, 'By grace ye are saved,

---

[88] Heb. 8:6.

[89] Heb. 7:19.

[90] Apparently an inn on the main road near Retford, which a little later fell into obscurity, being remembered this century only as 'Rushey Inn'.

[91] Mark 2:17; Luke 5:32.

[92] The keelmen of Newcastle worked the barges which brought coal from the

through faith.'⁹³ It rained and hailed hard, both before and after; but there were only some scattering drops⁹⁴ while I preached, which frightened away a few careless hearers. I met the society at six, and exhorted all who had 'set their hand to the plough' not to
5 'look back'.⁹⁵

Mon. 15. I began at five expounding the Acts of the Apostles. In the afternoon (and every afternoon this week) I spoke severally with the members of the society. On Tuesday evening I began the Epistle to the Romans. After sermon the society met. I reproved
10 some among them who walked disorderly, and earnestly besought them all to beware lest, by reason of their sins, the way of truth should be evil spoken of.⁹⁶

Thur. 18. I could not but observe the different manner wherein God is pleased to work in different places. The grace of God
15 flows here with a wider stream than it did at first either in Bristol or Kingswood. But it does not sink so deep as it did there. Few are thoroughly convinced of sin, and scarce any can witness that the Lamb of God has taken away their sins.

Fri. 19. I found the first witness of this good confession.
20 Margaret H—— (O how fallen since then!) told me that the night before her sight (an odd circumstance) and her strength were taken away at once. At the same time the love of God so overflowed her soul that she could not speak or move.

James R—— also gave me an account today that in going home
25 the day before he lost his sight in a moment, and was forced to catch hold of some rails for fear of falling. He continues under strong conviction, longing for the salvation of God.

Sun. 21. After preaching in the room at five, I began preaching about eight at the hospital. It rained all the time; but that did not
30 disturb either me or the congregation while I explained, 'Thou shalt call his name Jesus; for he shall save his people from their sins.'⁹⁷

Tue. 23. There seemed in the evening to be a deeper work in many souls than I had observed before. Many trembled ex-
35 ceedingly; six or seven (both men and women) dropped down as dead. Some cried unto God out of the deep; others would have

coal-drops on the Tyne down to the sea-going colliers. Their hospital stood above Sandgate to the east of the town wall.
⁹³ Cf. Eph. 2:8.
⁹⁴ Cf. June 20, 1761, a rare usage noted by *OED* (1774, 'scattered').
⁹⁵ Cf. Luke 9:62.
⁹⁶ See 2 Pet. 2:2.   ⁹⁷ Matt. 1:21.

cried, but their voice was lost. And some have found that the Lord is 'gracious and merciful, forgiving iniquity and transgression and sin'.[98]

Thur. 25. In the evening God was pleased to wound many more who were quiet and at ease. And I could not but observe that *here* the very *best people*, so called, were as deeply convinced as open sinners. Several of these were now constrained to roar aloud for the disquietness of their hearts; and these generally not young (as in most other places), but either middle-aged or well stricken in years.

I never saw a work of God, in any other place, so evenly and gradually carried on. It continually rises step by step. Not so much seems to be done at any one time as hath frequently been at Bristol or London; but something at every time. It is the same with particular souls. I saw none in that triumph of faith which has been so common in other places. But the believers go on, calm and steady. Let God do as seemeth him good.

Fri. 26. Between twelve and one I preached in a convenient ground at Whickham,[99] two or three miles from Newcastle. I spoke strong, rough words; but I did not perceive that any regarded what was spoken. The people indeed were exceeding quiet, and the cold kept them from falling asleep, till (before two) I left them, very well satisfied with the preacher and with themselves.

Sun. 28. I preached both at five in the room, and at eight in the hospital, on 'Him hath God exalted to be a Prince and a Saviour, to give repentance and remission of sins.'[1] We then walked over to Tanfield Lea,[2] about seven miles from Newcastle. Here a large company of people were gathered together from all the country round about, to whom I expounded the former part of the fifth chapter to the Romans. But so dead, senseless, unaffected a congregation have I scarce seen, except at Whickham. Whether gospel or law, or English or Greek, seemed all one to them!

Yet the seed sown even here was not quite lost. For on Thursday morning, between four and five, John Brown,[3] then of

---

[98] Cf. Num. 14:18.

[99] Whickham was a modest township and large parish 3 1/2 miles WSW. from Gateshead.

[1] Cf. Acts 5:31.

[2] Orig., 'Tanfield Leigh'. Tanfield was a chapelry in the parish of Chester-le-Street, 6 3/4 miles SW. of Gateshead.

[3] John Brown (*c.* 1717–1808), farmer, speedily became a notable evangelist in this area, gathering societies at Lower Spa, Newlands, and Blanchland, and assisting in the

Tanfield Lea, was waked out of sleep by the voice that raiseth the dead. And ever since he has been full of love and peace and joy in the Holy Ghost.

At four I preached in the Hospital Square to the largest
5 congregation I had seen since we left London, on Jesus Christ 'our wisdom, righteousness, sanctification and redemption'.[4]

Wednesday, December 1. We had several places offered on which to build a room for the society. But none was such as we wanted. And perhaps there was a providence in our not finding
10 any as yet. For by this means I was kept at Newcastle, whether I would or no.

Sat. 4. I was both surprised and grieved at a genuine instance of enthusiasm. J[ohn] B[rown] of Tanfield Lea, who had received a sense of the love of God a few days before, came riding through
15 the town, hollowing[5] and shouting and driving all the people before him, telling them God had told him he should be a king, and should tread all his enemies under his feet. I sent him home immediately to his work, and advised him to cry day and night to God that he might be lowly in heart, lest Satan should again get an
20 advantage over him.

Today a gentleman[6] called and offered me a piece of ground. On Monday an article was drawn, wherein he agreed to put me into possession on Thursday, upon payment of thirty pounds.[7]

Tue. 7. I was so ill in the morning that I was obliged to send Mr.
25 Williams[8] to the Room. He afterward went to Mr. Stephenson,[9] a

---

missioning of Weardale. Brown later suffered criticism from his family for neglecting his farm, and in 1759 JW found him in despair at Newlands, having ceased to preach. However, he recovered and resumed his labours. See June 13, 1759, June 4, 1772; and *Methodist Magazine* (1809), 32:481.

[4] Cf. 1 Cor. 1:30.

[5] All eds. read the same. Cf. Mar. 2, 1744, for the use of 'Halloo'd' as a near synonym.

[6] Mr. Riddell.

[7] After the erection of the Orphan House the property was described in the trust deed as 'all that lately erected messuage, house or tenement, with the yard and garden thereunto belonging . . . being without Pilgrim-street Gate . . . on a yard and house lately belonging to Phillis Gibson and others, on the north-west; on a garden belonging to John Stephenson, Esq. on the southwest, and a piece of ground or passage belonging to the said John Stephenson, on the southeast' (W. W. Stamp, *Orphan House of Wesley* [London, 1863], p. 268).

[8] Probably 'one Mr. Williams an Ingineer who now makes Fire Ingines to draw water from Colepits' (WHS, 14:193), of State's Hall near Jesmond Dene, Newcastle, with whom Charles Wesley stayed the following year (June 15, 1743; CWJ, I.316).

[9] John Stephenson, merchant and common councillor of Newcastle. It was Stephenson's hesitation to complete the conveyance which delayed the vesting of the property in trust till 1745. Stamp, *Orphan House*, p. 23.

merchant in the town, who had a passage through the ground we intended to buy. I was willing to purchase that passage. Mr. Stephenson told him, 'Sir, I don't want money. But if Mr. Wesley wants ground he may have a piece of my garden, adjoining to the place you mention. I am at a word. For *forty pounds* he shall have 5 sixteen yards in breadth, and thirty in length.'

Wed. 8. Mr. Stephenson and I signed an article, and I took possession of the ground. But I could not fairly go back from my agreement with Mr. Riddell.[10] So I entered on his ground at the same time. The whole is about forty yards in length; in the middle 10 of which we determined to build the house, leaving room for a small courtyard before and a little garden behind the building.

Sun. 12. I expounded at five the former part of the parable of the sower. At eight I preached in the Square on, 'I am the good Shepherd: the good Shepherd layeth down his life for the 15 sheep.'[11] The effect of what had been spoken in the morning now evidently appeared. For one could not observe any in the congregation to stir hand or foot. When the sermon was done, they divided to the right and left, none offering to go till I was past. And then they walked quietly and silently away, lest Satan should 20 catch the seed out of their hearts.

Mon. 13. I removed into a lodging adjoining to the ground where we were preparing to build. But the violent frost obliged us to delay the work. I never felt so intense cold before. In a room where a constant fire was kept, though my desk was fixed within a 25 yard of the chimney, I could not write for a quarter of an hour together without my hands being quite benumbed.

Wed. 15. I preached at Horsley[12] upon Tyne, eight (computed) miles from Newcastle. It was about two in the afternoon. The house not containing the people, we stood in the open air in spite 30 of the frost. I preached again in the evening, and in the morning. We then chose to *walk* home, having each of us catched a violent cold by *riding* the day before. Mine gradually wore off. But Mr. Meyrick's[13] increased, so that on Friday he took his bed. I advised him to bleed, but he imagined he should be well without it in 35 a few days.

---

[10] Orig., 'Riddel'.

[11] Cf. John 10:11.

[12] Here, as usually, JW spells the name 'Horseley'. Horsley was a small township in the parish of Ovingham 9 3/4 miles W. by N. from Newcastle.

[13] Thomas Meyrick (or Merrick), a Cornishman trained for the law, seems to have been

Sun. 19. I cried to all who felt themselves lost, 'Believe in the Lord Jesus Christ and thou shalt be saved';[14] and in the afternoon, 'Ho! everyone that thirsteth, come ye to the waters.'[15] At that hour one who was bitterly mourning after Christ (Mary Emerson) was
5 filled with joy unspeakable.

Mon. 20. We laid the first stone of the house.[16] Many were gathered from all parts to see it; but none scoffed or interrupted while we praised God and prayed that he would prosper the work of our hands upon us. Three or four times in the evening I was
10 forced to break off preaching that we might pray and give thanks to God.

When I came home they told me the physician said he did not expect Mr. Meyrick would live till the morning. I went to him, but his pulse was gone. He had been speechless and senseless for
15 some time. A few of us immediately joined in prayer. (I relate the naked fact.) Before we had done his sense and his speech returned. Now he that will account for this by *natural causes* has my free leave. But I choose to say, This is the power of God.

Thur. 23. It being computed that such a house as was proposed
20 could not be finished under seven hundred pounds, many were positive it would never be finished at all; others, that I should not live to see it covered. I was of another mind, nothing doubting but as it was begun for God's sake, he would provide what was needful for the finishing it.[17]

25 Sat. Dec. 25. The physician told me he could do no more: Mr. Meyrick could not live over the night. I went up and found them all crying about him, his legs being cold and (as it seemed) dead already. We all kneeled down and called upon God with strong cries and tears. He opened his eyes and called for me. And from
30 that hour he continued to recover his strength, till he was restored to perfect health.[18] I wait to hear who will either disprove this fact or philosophically account for it.

one of JW's business managers at the Foundery and then became an itinerant preacher. In 1750, having secured episcopal ordination, he became curate of St. Anne's, Halifax, where he died about 1770, according to JW, 'not in peace' *(Arminian Magazine* [1789], XII.23; Atmore, *Methodist Memorial*, pp. 270-72).

   [14] Acts 16:31.   [15] Isa. 55:1.

   [16] The preaching-house at Newcastle.

   [17] Henry Moore relates that when JW resolved to build this, his fourth and largest, preaching-place, he had £1.6s., but shortly afterwards received a note for £100 from a pious Quaker. Moore, *Wesley*, I.550.

   [18] The following conversation, jotted down by JW upon a blank portion of a letter which he had received from Mary Bainton of Bristol, dated Oct. 3, 1742, probably refers to his

Sun. 26. From those words, 'Sing we merrily unto God our strength; make a cheerful noise unto the God of Jacob,'[19] I took occasion to show the usual way of keeping these days holy in honour of the birth of our Lord; namely, by an extraordinary degree of gluttony and drunkenness; by heathen, and worse than 5 heathen, diversions (with their constant attendants, passion and strife, cursing, swearing, and blasphemy); and by dancing and card-playing, equally conducive to the glory of God. I then described the right way of keeping a day holy to the Lord: by extraordinary prayer, public and private; by thanksgiving; by 10 hearing, reading, and meditating on his Word, and by talking of all his wondrous works.

Mon. 27. I rode to Horsley. The house being too small, I was obliged again to preach in the open air. But so furious a storm have I seldom known. The wind drove upon us like a torrent, 15 coming by turns from east, west, north, and south. The straw and thatch flew round our heads, so that one would have imagined it could not be long before the house must follow; but scarce anyone stirred, much less went away, till I dismissed them with the peace of God. 20

Tue. 28. I preached in an open place at Swalwell,[20] two or three miles from Newcastle. The wind was high and extremely sharp; but I saw none go away till I went. Yet I observed none that seemed to be much convinced; only stunned, as if cut in the head.

Wed. 29. After preaching (as usual) in the square, I took horse 25 for Tanfield. More than once I was only not blown off my horse. However at three I reached the Lea and explained to a multitude of people the salvation which is through faith. Afterwards I met the society in a large upper room, which rocked to and fro with the violence of the storm. But all was calm within, and we rejoiced 30 together in hope of a kingdom which cannot be moved.[21]

conversation with Thomas Meyrick on his supposed deathbed. It is in severely abridged longhand, which is here extended:

Christmas Day

'Are you afraid to die?' No. 'Do you know God loves you?' Yes, yes. O what would I not go through, to come to Thee. Let me come now. Dear Father, let me not stay here. Thou knowest I could die this moment to be with Thee. O let me come now.—The devil! Twenty devils. 'Are you afraid of him?' No. No. He knows that. He knows he cannot hurt me. But he will trouble me as long as he can. (Original in Methodist Archives)

[19] Ps. 81:1 (BCP).
[20] Swalwell, a township in the parish of Whickham, 4 3/4 miles W. by S. from Gateshead and the site of the famous Crawley ironworks.
[21] Heb. 12:28.

Thur. 30. I carefully examined those who had lately *cried out* in the congregation.[22] Some of these, I found, could give no account at all how or wherefore they had done so, only that of a sudden they dropped down they knew not how; and what they afterwards
5 said or did they knew not. Others could just remember they were in fear; but could not tell what they were in fear of. Several said they were afraid of the devil, and this was all they knew. But a few gave a more intelligible account of the piercing sense they then had of their sins, both inward and outward, which were set in
10 array against them round about; of the dread they were in of the wrath of God and the punishment they had deserved, into which they seemed to be just falling, without any way to escape. One of them told me: 'I was as if I was just falling down, from the highest place I had ever seen. I thought the devil was pushing me off, and
15 that God had forsaken me.' Another said, 'I felt the very fire of hell already kindled in my breast, and all my body was in as much pain as if I had been in a burning fiery furnace.' What wisdom is that which rebuketh these, that 'they should hold their peace'?[23] Nay, let such an one cry after Jesus of Nazareth, till he saith, 'Thy
20 faith hath made thee whole!'[24]

At eleven I preached my farewell sermon in the Hospital Square. I never saw such a congregation there before; nor did I ever speak so searchingly. I could not conclude till one, and then both men, women, and children hung upon me, so that I knew not
25 which way to disengage myself. After some time I got to the gate and took horse; but even then 'a muckle woman' (as one called her in great anger) kept her hold and ran by the horse's side, through thick and thin, down to Sandgate. Jonathan Reeves[25] rode with me. We reached Darlington that night, and
30 Boroughbridge[26] the next day.

---

[22] Six months later Charles Wesley was conducting a similar but more severe examination in the north, exposing 'many counterfeits' and having the innocent carried out of his meetings. From this he observed two good effects, a great reduction in the incidence of abnormal phenomena and 'that many more of the gentry come now the stumbling-block of the fits is taken out of their way' (June 4, 15, 1743; CWJ, I.314, 316).

[23] Matt. 20:31.   [24] Mark 10:52.

[25] Jonathan Reeves (*d.* May 13, 1787) was one of the earliest itinerant preachers. He obtained episcopal ordination and became the first chaplain of Magdalen Hospital, London (1758–64), where the Trustees required him, instead of preaching, to read Tillotson's sermons. For the last eighteen years of his life he was lecturer in the parish of West Ham; he was also joint lecturer at Whitechapel. Thomas Jackson, *Early Methodist Preachers*, I.68, 143, 187; H. F. B. Compton, *The Magdalen Hospital* (London, 1917), pp. 63-64; Stamp, *Orphan House*, p. 42; and Atmore, *Methodist Memorial*, pp. 345-46.

[26] Boroughbridge, a market town and chapelry in the parish of Aldborough, 17 1/2

What encouragement have we to speak for God! At our inn we met an ancient man, who seemed by his conversation never to have thought whether he had any soul or no. Before we set out I spoke a few words concerning his cursing and idle conversation. The man appeared quite broken in pieces. The tears started into 5 his eyes. And he acknowledged (with abundance of thanks to *me*) his own guilt and the goodness of God.

Saturday, January 1, 1743. Between Doncaster and Epworth I overtook one who immediately accosted me with so many and so impertinent questions that I was quite amazed. In the midst of 10 some of them concerning my travels and my journey, I interrupted him and asked, 'Are you aware that we are on a longer journey? That we are travelling toward eternity?' He replied instantly, 'Oh, I find you, I find you! I know where you are. Is not your name Wesley? 'Tis pity! 'Tis great pity! Why could not your 15 father's religion serve *you*? Why must you have a *new* religion?' I was going to reply, but he cut me short by crying out in triumph, 'I am a Christian! I am a Christian! I am a Churchman! I am a Churchman! I am none of your *Culamites*';[27] as plain as he could speak—for he was so drunk he could but just keep his seat. 20 Having then clearly won the day, or as his phrase was, 'put them all down', he began kicking his horse on both sides and rode off as fast as he could.

In the evening I reached Epworth. Sun. 2. At five, I preached on, 'So is everyone who is born of the Spirit.'[28] About eight I 25 preached from my father's tomb, on Hebrews 8:11. Many from the neighbouring towns asked if it would not be well, as it was Sacrament Sunday, for them to receive it. I told them, 'By all means. But it would be more respectful first to ask Mr. Romley, the curate's, leave.' One did so, in the name of the rest. To whom 30 he said, 'Pray tell Mr. Wesley I shall not give *him* the Sacrament. For he is not *fit*.'

How wise a God is our God! There could not have been so *fit* a

---

miles NW. by W. from York, which outstripped its mother parish in importance by virtue of its situation at a bridge over the river Ure on the Great North Road.

[27] The Culamites were a small body of high-Calvinist Baptists raised up in the neighbourhood of Wisbech in Lincolnshire by David Culy (who died *c.* 1725). They were said already to have declined to a few families, though reported by Thomas Blanshard in an unsatisfactory note of 1802 *(Methodist Magazine* [1802], 25:463) still to consist of two congregations. It is clear that Methodists were often abused as, or confused with, Culamites. WHS, 2:116; 7:137.

[28] John 3:8.

place under heaven where this should befall me first as my father's house, the place of my nativity, and the very place where, 'according to the straitest sect of our religion', I had so long 'lived a Pharisee'![29] It was also *fit*, in the highest degree, that he who 5 repelled me from that very table where I had myself so often distributed the bread of life, should be one who owed his all in this world to the tender love which *my* father had shown to *his*, as well as personally to *himself.*

Mon. 3. I rode to Birstall, where John Nelson gave a 10 melancholy account of many that *did* run well. I told him I was as willing they should be with the Germans as with *us*, if they did but grow in grace. He said, 'But that is not the case. They grow worse instead of better. They are changed both in their tempers and lives. But not for the better at all. They now do things without 15 scruple which they could not do before. They are light and trifling in their behaviour. They are easy and thoughtless, having now no holy fear, no earnest care to work out their own salvation.'

Wed. 5. I came wet and weary to Sheffield, and on Friday to Donington Park, which I left before eight the next morning, in 20 order to go to Wednesbury in Staffordshire. I was immediately met by a vehement shower of rain, driven full in my face by a strong wind. But in an hour the day was clear and calm. About four in the afternoon I came to Wednesbury. At seven I preached in the Town Hall. It was filled from end to end; and all appeared 25 to be deeply attentive while I explained, 'This is the covenant which I will make after those days, saith the Lord. . . .'[30]

Sun. 9. The hall was filled again at five; and I proclaimed 'the name of the Lord; . . . The Lord, the Lord God, merciful and gracious, long-suffering, and abundant in goodness and truth'.[31] 30 At eight we met in the place where my brother preached, made, as it were, for the great congregation.[32] It is a large hollow, scarcely a mile from the town, capable of containing four or five thousand people. They stood in a half circle one above another, and seemed all to receive with joy that great truth, 'the kingdom of God is not 35 meats and drinks, but righteousness and peace and joy in the Holy Ghost.'[33]

---

[29] Cf. Acts 26:5.
[30] Heb. 10:16.
[31] Exod. 34:5-6.
[32] A natural amphitheatre in the Coalpit Field, destroyed eighty years later when Telford put the Holyhead road through Wednesbury.
[33] Cf. Rom. 14:17.

In the afternoon Mr. Egginton[34] preached a plain, useful sermon. Almost the whole congregation then went down to the place, where abundance of people were already waiting for us, so that the hollow could not contain them, but was edged round with those who came from all parts. My subject was, 'By grace ye are 5 saved, through faith.'[35] O that all who heard might experience this salvation!

Mon. 10. I preached at five, at eight, and at three. In the intervals of preaching I spoke to all who desired it. Last night twenty-nine of them were joined together, Tuesday 11, about an 10 hundred. O that none of these may 'draw back to perdition'! Let these 'believe, unto the saving of the soul'![36]

Wed. 12. I took my leave of them in the morning by showing the difference between the righteousness of the law and that of faith; and in the evening explained to a large congregation at Evesham, 15 'So is everyone that is born of the Spirit.'[37]

Thur. 13. I rode to Stratford-upon-Avon. I had scarce sat down before I was informed that Mrs. K——, a middle-aged woman of Shottery,[38] half a mile from Stratford, had been for many weeks last past in a way which nobody could understand; 20 that she had sent for a minister, but almost as soon as he came began roaring in so strange a manner (her tongue at the same time hanging out of her mouth, and her face distorted into a most terrible form) that he cried out, 'It *is* the devil, doubtless! It is the devil!' And immediately went away. 25

I suppose this was some unphilosophical minister. Else he would have said, 'Stark mad! Send her to Bedlam.'

I asked, 'What good do you think I can do?' One answered, 'We cannot tell. But Mrs. K. (I just relate what was spoken to me, without passing any judgment upon it) earnestly desired you 30 might come, if you was anywhere near, saying she had seen you in a dream and should know you immediately. "But the devil said" (those were her own expressions), "I will tear thy throat out before he comes." But "afterwards" (she said) "his words were,

---

[34] Edward Egginton, son of Thomas Egginton of Doverdale, Warwicks., pleb. Matriculated at St. Alban Hall, Oxford, 1709, aged 16. Rector of Doverdale, 1716; vicar of Wednesbury, 1719.

[35] Cf. Eph. 2:8.

[36] Cf. Heb. 10:39.

[37] John 3:8.

[38] Orig., 'Shattery'. Shottery is in the W. part of Stratford-upon-Avon and contains Anne Hathaway's cottage.

'If he does come, I will let thee be quiet, and thou shalt be as if nothing ailed thee, till he is gone away.'"'

A very odd kind of madness this! I walked over about noon; but when we came to the house desired all those who came with me to
5 stay below. One showing me the way, I went up straight to her room. As soon as I came to the bedside she fixed her eyes and said, 'You are Mr. Wesley. I am very well now, I thank God. Nothing ails me, only I am weak.' I called them up, and we began to sing,

10
> Jesu, thou hast bid us pray,
>   Pray always and not faint;
> With the Word, a power convey
>   To utter our complaint. . . .³⁹

After singing a verse or two we kneeled down to prayer. I had
15 but just begun (my eyes being shut) when I felt as if I had been plunged into cold water. And immediately there was such a roar that my voice was quite drowned, though I spoke as loud as I usually do to three or four thousand people. However, I prayed on. She was then reared up in the bed, her whole body moving at
20 once without bending one joint or limb, just as if it were one piece of stone. Immediately after it was writhed into all kind of postures, the same horrid yell continuing still. But we left her not till all the symptoms ceased, and she was (for the present, at least) rejoicing and praising God.

25   Between one and two I preached at Stratford, on, 'The Son of man hath power on earth to forgive sins.'⁴⁰ Most of the hearers stood like posts. But some mocked. Others blasphemed. And a few believed.

I preached at Evesham in the evening, rode to Painswick the
30 next day, and on Saturday 15 to Bristol; where the following week I spoke to each member of the society and rejoiced over them, finding they had not been 'barren or unfruitful in the knowledge of our Lord Jesus Christ'.⁴¹

Mon. 24. I preached at Bath. Some of the rich and great were
35 present, to whom, as to the rest, I declared with all plainness of speech, (1) that by nature, they were all children of wrath; (2) that

---

³⁹ John and Charles Wesley, *Hymns and Sacred Poems* (1742), p. 202 *(Poet. Wks.*, II.255; and Hymn 290 in the 1780 *Collection*, 7:442-44 in this edn.).
⁴⁰ Matt. 9:6; Mark 2:10.
⁴¹ 2 Pet. 1:8.

all their natural tempers were corrupt and abominable; and (3) all their words and works, which could never be any better but by faith; and that (4) a natural man has no more faith than a devil, if so much. One of them, my Lord ——, stayed very patiently till I came to the middle of the fourth head. Then starting up he said, ''Tis hot! 'Tis very hot,' and got downstairs as fast as he could.

Several of the gentry desired to stay at the meeting of the society; to whom I explained the nature of inward religion, words flowing upon me faster than I could speak. One of them (a noted infidel)[42] hung over the next seat in an attitude not to be described; and when he went left half a guinea with Mary Naylor[43] for the use of the poor.

On the following days I spoke with each member of the society in Kingswood. I can't understand how any minister can hope ever to give up his account with joy unless (as Ignatius advised) he 'know all his flock by name, not overlooking the men-servants and maid-servants'.[44]

I left Bristol on Friday 28, came to Reading on Saturday, and to Windsor on Sunday morning. Thence I walked over to Egham,[45] where Mr. —— preached one of the most miserable sermons I ever heard: stuffed so full of dull, senseless, improbable lies of those he complimented with the title of 'false prophets'.

I preached at one and endeavoured to rescue the poor text (Matt. 7:16 [i.e., 15])[46] out of so bad hands. About four I left Egham, and at eight in the evening met a joyful congregation at the Foundery.

Mon. 31. One writing to desire that I would preach on Isaiah 58, I willingly complied with his request in the evening. A day or two after I received a letter from a girl of sixteen or seventeen, whom I had often observed as being in an eminent degree of a

---

[42] Cf. the journal entry for May 29, 1739, above.

[43] Mrs. Mary Naylor, who died on Mar. 21, 1757, was regarded by JW (who buried her) as 'a most eminent pattern of truly Christian courage, plainness of speech and plainness of apparel' (see under Mar. 25, 1757) and was a great friend of Charles Wesley with whom she went through the Devizes riots. He wrote a series of hymns on her death. CWJ, II.338-48.

[44] This is probably a reminiscence of Ignatius's *Epistle to Polycarp*, IV.2-3, trans. Kirsopp Lake, 'Seek out all by their name. Do not be haughty to slaves, either men or women.' *Apostolic Fathers* (London, 1925), 1:272-73.

[45] Egham was a large parish 20 miles W. by S. from London.

[46] A sermon on this text came to form Sermon 32, 'Upon our Lord's Sermon on the Mount, Discourse XII' (1:675-86 in this edn.). It was also published in 1750 (together with Sermon 31) as a pamphlet entitled *A Caution Againt False Prophets* (see 4:461-62 in this edn.).

meek and lowly spirit. Some of her words were: 'I do not think there were above six or seven words of the true gospel in your whole sermon. I think nothing ought to concern *you* but the errand which the Lord gave you. But how far are you from this!
5 You preach more the law than the gospel!' Ah, my poor *still* sister! Thou art an apt scholar indeed! I did not expect this quite so soon.

Wednesday, February 2. My brother and I began visiting the society together, which employed us from six in the morning
10 every day till near six in the evening.[47] Sun. 6. I preached in the morning, on 'While we have opportunity, let us do good unto all men,'[48] and in the afternoon, on 'By manifestation of the truth, commending ourselves to every man's conscience in the sight of God'.[49] So rough a charity sermon was scarce ever heard. But
15 God gave it his blessing, insomuch that fifty pounds were contributed toward finishing the house at Newcastle.

Fri. 11. I called on poor Joseph Hodges,[50] who after so long withstanding all the wiles of the enemy has been at last induced, by his fatal regard for Mr. Hall, to renounce my brother and me in
20 form. But he had perfectly learned the exercise of his arms. He was so *happy*, so *poor* a sinner, that to produce either Scripture or reason against him was mere beating the air.

Mon. 14. I left London, and (riding early and late) the next evening came to Newark.[51] Here I met with a few who had tasted
25 the good word; one of whom received me gladly and desired me whenever I came to Newark to make his house my home.

Wed. 16. I reached Epworth. I was to preach at six. But the house not being able to contain half the congregation I went out and declared, 'We love him, because he first loved us.'[52] In the
30 morning, Thursday 17, I largely explained 'the Spirit of adoption, whereby we cry, Abba, Father'.[53] And it was high time, for I soon found the spirit of delusion was gone abroad here also, and some

---

[47] This visitation is described Feb. 4, 5, 1743; CWJ, I.305.
[48] Cf. Gal. 6:10.
[49] 2 Cor. 4:2.
[50] Joseph Hodges (1710–78), smith, was one of the members of the Fetter Lane Society who went with the Moravians, becoming a committee member of the Society for the Furtherance of the Gospel and a 'much valued' member of the congregation. Benham, *Hutton*, pp. 93, 411.
[51] Newark was a large borough, market town, and parish on the Great North Road, 20 miles NE. of Nottingham and 124 miles from London.
[52] 1 John 4:19.
[53] Rom. 8:15.

began to boast that Christ had 'made them free' who were still the
'servants of sin'.[54] In the evening I preached on that bold assertion
of St. John (indeed of all who have the true Spirit of adoption),
'We know that we are of God, and the whole world lieth in
wickedness.'[55]

Fri. 18. I rode forward for Newcastle. We inquired at
Poppleton,[56] a little town three miles beyond York, and hearing
there was no other town near, thought it best to call there. A Bible
lying in the window, my fellow-traveller[57] asked the woman of the
house if she read that book. She said, 'Sir, I can't read, the worse
is my luck. But that great girl is a rare scholar. And yet she cares
not if she never looks in a book. She minds *nout*[58] but play.' I
began soon after to speak to our landlord, while the old woman
drew closer and closer to me. The girl spun on. But all on a
sudden she stopped her wheel, burst out into tears, and, with all
that were in the house, so devoured our words that we scarce
knew how to go away.

In the evening we came to Boroughbridge, and Saturday 19 to
Newcastle.

Sun. 20. I went on in expounding the Acts of the Apostles and
St. Paul's Epistle to the Romans. In the following week I
diligently inquired who they were that did not walk according to
the gospel. In consequence of which I was obliged to put away
above fifty persons. There remained about[59] eight hundred in
the society.

Sat. 26. I visited those that were sick. One of these had kept her
room for many months, so that she had never heard the voice or
seen the face of any preacher of 'this way'.[60] But God had taught
her in the school of affliction. She gave a plain and distinct
account of the manner wherein she had received a sense of her
acceptance with God, more than a year before; and of a fuller
manifestation of his love, of which she never after doubted for
a moment.

[54] Cf. Rom. 6:20, 22.
[55] 1 John 5:19.
[56] Orig., 'Poplington'. Nether Poppleton was a small parish 4 miles NW. from York;
Upper Poppleton was a small chapelry 4 1/2 miles NW. by W. from York.
[57] Said by Curnock (III.67, n. 1) to be Thomas Dixon.
[58] JW clearly wished to reproduce the dialect form, using the obsolete spelling 'nout'.
Works (1774) changed this to the formal 'nought'.
[59] 1769, 1774, 'above'.
[60] Acts 9:2, etc.

Mon. 28. I preached again at Horsley and spoke severally with
those of the society. The world now begins to take the alarm and
to cast out their name as evil. After a *very good* woman (so called)
had used abundance of arguments to hinder her neighbour from
5 going near these people, she told her at length, 'Why, none but
the wickedest people upon earth go there.' 'Nay then', replied
she, 'I will go immediately. For I am sure none upon earth is
wickeder than *me.*' Such be the event of all worldly wisdom!

Tuesday, March 1. I preached at two in Pelton,[61] five miles
10 south of Newcastle. A multitude of people were gathered
together from all the neighbouring towns, and (which I rejoiced at
much more) from all the neighbouring pits. In riding home I
observed a little village called Chowdean,[62] which they told me
consisted of colliers only. I resolved to preach there as soon as
15 possible; for these *are* sinners and *need* repentance.

Sun. 6. I read over in the society the rules[63] which all our
members are to observe, and desired everyone seriously to
consider whether he was willing to conform thereto or no. That
this would shake many of them I knew well; and therefore on
20 Monday 7, I began visiting the classes again, lest 'that which is
lame should be turned out of the way'.[64]

Tue. 8. In the afternoon I preached on a smooth part of the Fell
(or Common) near Chowdean. I found we were got into the very
Kingswood of the north. Twenty or thirty wild children ran round
25 us as soon as we came, staring as in amaze. They could not
properly be said to be either clothed or naked. One of the largest
(a girl, about fifteen) had a piece of a ragged, dirty blanket, some
way hung about her, and a kind of cap on her head of the same
cloth and colour. My heart was exceedingly enlarged towards
30 them. And they looked as if they would have swallowed me up;
especially while I was applying those words, 'Be it known unto
you, men and brethren, that through this man is preached unto
you the forgiveness of sins.'[65]

---

61 Pelton was a small township in the parish of Chester-le-Street, 8 miles N. by W. from
Durham.
62 Orig., 'Chowden'. Chowdean borders on Low Fell, some 2 1/2 miles S. of
Gateshead.
63 It was only on Feb. 23, 1742/43, three years after the first United Societies had
begun in London, that JW published *The Nature, Design, and General Rules of the United
Societies in London, Bristol, Kingswood, and Newcastle upon Tyne.* See *Bibliography*, No. 73,
and Vol. 9:69-75 of this edn.
64 Cf. Heb. 12:13.
65 Acts 13:38.

Sat. 12. I concluded my second course of visiting, in which I inquired particularly into two things: (1) the case of those who had almost every night the last week cried out aloud during the preaching, (2) the number of those who were separated from us, and the reason and occasion of it.

As to the former I found,

(1) That all of them (I think, not one excepted) were persons in perfect health and had not been subject to fits of any kind, till they were thus affected.

(2) That this had come upon every one of them in a moment, without any previous notice, while they were either hearing the Word of God or thinking on what they had heard.

(3) That in that moment they dropped down, lost all their strength, and were seized with violent pain.

This they expressed in different manners. Some said they felt just as if a sword was running through them; others, that they thought a great weight lay upon them, as if it would squeeze them into the earth. Some said they were quite choked, so that they could not breathe; others, that their hearts swelled ready to burst; and others, that it was as if their heart, as if all their inside, as if their whole body, was tearing all to pieces.

These symptoms I can no more impute to any natural cause than to the Spirit of God. I can make no doubt but it was Satan 'tearing' them, as they were 'coming' to Christ.[66] And hence proceeded those grievous cries, whereby he might design both to discredit the work of God and to affright fearful people from hearing that Word whereby their souls might be saved.

I found, (4) that their minds had been as variously affected as their bodies. Of this some could give scarce any account at all, which also I impute to that wise spirit, purposely stunning and confounding as many as he could that they might not be able to bewray his devices. Others gave a very clear and particular account from the beginning to the end. The Word of God pierced their souls and convinced them of inward, as well as outward, sin. They saw and felt the wrath of God abiding on them and were afraid of his judgments. And here the accuser came with great power, telling them there was no hope, they were lost forever. The pains of body then seized them in a moment and extorted those loud and bitter cries.

[66] Cf. Luke 9:42.

As to the latter, I observed the number of those who had left the society since December 30 was seventy-six:

Fourteen of these (chiefly Dissenters) said they left it because otherwise their ministers would not give them the Sacrament.

5 Nine more, because their husbands or wives were not willing they should stay in it.

Twelve, because their parents were not willing.

Five, because their master and mistress would not let them come.

10 Seven, because their acquaintance persuaded them to leave it.

Five, because people said such bad things of the society.

Nine, because they would not be laughed at.

Three, because they would not lose the poor's allowance.

Three more, because they could not spare time to come.

15 Two, because it was too far off.

One, because she was afraid of falling into fits.

One, because people were so rude in the street.

Two, because Thomas Naisbit was in the society.

One, because he would not turn his back on his baptism.

20 One, because we were *mere* Church of England men. And

One, because it was time enough to serve God yet.

The number of those who were expelled the society was sixty-four:

Two, for cursing and swearing.

25 Two, for habitual sabbath-breaking.

Seventeen, for drunkenness.

Two, for retailing spirituous liquors.

Three, for quarrelling and brawling.

One, for beating his wife.

30 Three, for habitual, wilful lying.

Four, for railing and evil-speaking.

One, for idleness and laziness. And

Nine and twenty, for lightness and carelessness.

Sun. 13. I went in the morning in order to speak severally with

35 the members of the society at Tanfield. From the terrible instances I met with here (and indeed in all parts of England) I am more and more convinced that the devil himself desires nothing more than this, that the people of any place should be half-awakened and then left to themselves to fall asleep again.

40 Therefore I determine, by the grace of God, not to strike one stroke in any place where I cannot follow the blow.

Mon. 14. I preached again near Chowdean; and this I continued to do weekly, as well as at all the other places round Newcastle (except Swalwell) where I had preached once.

Thur. 17. As I was preaching at Pelton, one of the old colliers, not much accustomed to things of this kind, in the middle of the sermon began shouting amain for mere satisfaction and joy of heart. But their usual token of approbation (which somewhat surprised me at first) was clapping me on the back.

Fri. 18. As I was meeting the leaders, a company of young men, having prepared themselves by strong drink, broke open the door, and came rushing in with the utmost fury. I began praying for them immediately. Not one opened his mouth or lifted up a finger against us. And after half an hour we all went away together in great quietness and love.

Tue. 22. I went to South Biddick,[67] a village of colliers, seven miles south-east of Newcastle. The spot where I stood was just at the bottom of a semicircular hill, on the rising sides of which many hundreds stood; but far more on the plain beneath. I cried to them in the words of the prophet, 'O ye dry bones, hear the word of the Lord.'[68] Deep attention sat on every face. So that here also I believed it would be well to preach weekly.

Wed. 23. I met a gentleman in the streets, cursing and swearing in so dreadful a manner that I could not but stop him. He soon grew calmer, told me he *must* treat me with a glass of wine and that he would come and *hear* me, only he was afraid I should say something against *fighting of cocks*.

Fri. 25. At the pressing instance of a cursing, swearing, drunken Papist, who would needs bring me into a state of salvation, I spent some hours in reading an artful book entitled *The Grounds of the Old Religion*.[69] In the first thirty pages the

[67] Biddick was a village now incorporated in the new town of Washington; South Biddick, a hamlet adjacent to Shiney Row and Penshaw.

[68] Ezek. 37:4.

[69] Richard Challoner, *The Grounds of the Old Religion: or some general arguments in favour of the Catholick, Apostolick, Roman Communion. Collected from both ancient and modern controversialists, and modestly proposed to the consideration of his countrymen, by a convert* (August, 1742). Richard Challoner (1691–1781), a Dissenter by baptism, was befriended by a family of Catholic gentry in his youth, embraced their faith, and was educated by the English College at Douai, becoming professor of philosophy there 1713–20, vice-president and professor of divinity, 1720–30. In 1730 he joined the English mission and engaged in controversy with Conyers Middleton. In 1741 he became a bishop *in partibus* and coadjutor to the vicar-apostolic, becoming himself vicar-apostolic of the London district in 1758. He wrote a *Caveat against Methodists* in 1760.

author heaps up Scriptures concerning the privileges of the church. But all this is beating the air till he proves the Romanists to be the church, i.e., that a part is the whole. In the second chapter he brings many arguments to show that 'the Scripture is
5 not the sole rule of faith; at least, not if interpreted by private judgment, because private judgment has no place in matters of religion'! Why, at this moment you are appealing to *my* private judgment; and you cannot possibly avoid it. The foundation of *your*, as well as *my*, religion must necessarily rest here. First you
10 (as well as I) must judge for yourself whether you are implicitly to follow the church or no. And also which is the true church. Else it is not possible to move one step forward.

This evening I preached in the shell of the new house, on the rich man and Lazarus. A great multitude were gathered together
15 there, most of whom stayed with us and *watched*[70] unto the Lord.

Sat. 26. I preached at Birtley,[71] a village four miles south of Newcastle, surrounded by colliers on every side. The greater part of the congregation earnestly attended to those solemn words, 'The Spirit of the Lord is upon me; because he hath anointed me
20 to preach the gospel to the poor.'[72]

Mon. 28. I was astonished to find it was real fact (what I would not believe before) that three of the dissenting ministers (Mr. A——rs, Mr. A——ns, and Mr. B——)[73] had agreed together to exclude all those from the Holy Communion who would not
25 refrain from hearing us. Mr. A——ns publicly affirmed we were all Papists, and our doctrine was mere popery. And Mr. B[ruce],

---

[70] The italicizing is present in all the early edns. and seems to imply that JW conducted a vigil in connection with the opening, after the normal preaching service.

[71] Orig., 'Burtley'. Birtley was a mining township in the parish of Chester-le-Street, 5 1/4 miles S. by E. from Gateshead.

[72] Luke 4:18.

[73] Apparently Rev. William Arthur, first minister of the Groat Market Presbyterian Meeting-House, 1715–59. Probably graduated at Edinburgh, 1698. Rev. Edward Aitken, Scotch Relief, minister of Castle Garth Meeting-House, 1736–62; graduated at Edinburgh, 1721. Rev. George Bruce, M.A., first minister of a Presbyterian meeting-house in Sandgate. He published a sermon, *Personal religion a necessary qualification in a minister of the gospel* (2nd edn., Newcastle, 1744). He later removed to Dunbar (E. Mackenzie, *Descriptive and historical account of Newcastle-upon-Tyne* [Newcastle upon Tyne, 1827], pp. 386, 391, 384). At the end of the eighteenth century Newcastle possessed 'six congregations of Presbyterians, properly so called, united in doctrine, discipline and communion with the church of Scotland; and one of each of the classes of the secession from that church, stiled Burghers and Antiburghers. . .' (*Monthly Magazine*, 11:310, quoted in John Baillie, *An Impartial History of Newcastle-upon-Tyne and its Vicinity* [Newcastle upon Tyne, 1801], p. 275).

in the conclusion of a course of sermons, which he preached professedly against us, went a step farther still: for after he had confessed, 'Many texts in the Bible are *for them,*' he added, 'but you ought not to mind these texts; for the Papists have put them in!' 5

Wed. 30. While I was *reasoning* (from the twenty-fourth chapter of the Acts) on 'righteousness, temperance, and judgment to come', God constrained many of the stout-hearted sinners to tremble. O that they may not put him off to 'a more convenient season'![74] 10

April 1. Being Good Friday, I had a great desire to visit a little village called Plessey,[75] about ten measured miles north of Newcastle. It is inhabited by colliers only, and such as had been always in the first rank for savage ignorance and wickedness of every kind. Their grand assembly used to be on the Lord's day, on 15 which men, women, and children met together to dance, fight, curse and swear, and play at chuck,[76] ball, span-farthing,[77] or whatever came next to hand. I felt great compassion for these poor creatures, from the time I heard of them first; and the more because all men seemed to despair of them. Between seven and 20 eight I set out with John Heally,[78] my guide. The north wind, being unusually high, drove the sleet full in our face, which froze as it fell, and cased us over presently. When we came to Plessey we could very hardly stand. As soon as we were a little recovered I went into the square and declared him who 'was bruised for our 25 sins, and wounded for our iniquities'.[79] The poor sinners were quickly gathered together, and gave earnest heed to the things

[74] Cf. Acts 24:25.

[75] Orig., 'Placey'. Plessey was a joint township with Shotton in the parish of Stannington, 6 miles S. by E. from Morpeth.

[76] Short for chuck-farthing, and extended to other games like pitch-and-toss (see *OED*).

[77] 'A play at which money is thrown within a span, or mark' (Johnson). The *OED* defines the game as similar in principle to span-counter, a game in which the object of one player was to throw his counters so close to those of his opponents that the distance between them could be spanned with the hand.

[78] John Heally, who had to be sent away from Newcastle 'that he might not be torn to pieces by the mob, some of whom he has struck', and who had a reputation for returning blows in kind, attained celebrity in the Methodist community for astutely circumventing charges of Jacobitism made against him at Nottingham in 1744; but in 1749 Charles Wesley disowned him 'before the Society, for beating the poor old madman' (Feb. 19, Mar. 10, 1744; May 8, July 6, 1749; CWJ, I.352, 355; II.58, 62).

[79] Cf. Isa. 53:5.

which were spoken.[80] And so they did in the afternoon again, in spite of the wind and snow, when I besought them to receive him for their King; to 'repent and believe the gospel'.[81]

On Easter Monday and Tuesday I preached there again, the
5 congregation continually increasing. And as most of these had never in their lives pretended to any religion of any kind, they were the more ready to cry to God as *mere sinners* for the free 'redemption which is in Jesus'.[82]

Thur. 7. Having settled all things according to my desire, I
10 cheerfully took leave of my friends at Newcastle and rode that day to Sand Hutton.[83] At our inn I found a good-natured man sitting and drinking in the chimney corner; with whom I began a discourse, suspecting nothing less than that he was the minister of the parish. Before we parted I spoke exceeding plain. And he
15 received it in love, begging he might see me when I came that way again. But before I came he was gone into eternity.

Fri. 8. I preached at Knaresborough and at Leeds, on, 'By grace ye are saved through faith.'[84] The three following days I divided between Leeds and Birstall, and on Tuesday rode to
20 Sheffield.

I found the society both here and at Barley Hall earnestly pressing on toward the mark, although there had not been wanting here also those who by fair speeches deceive the hearts of the simple.

25 Fri. 15. I rode in two days to Wednesbury. I found things surprisingly altered here. The inexcusable folly of Mr. W[illiam]s[85] had so provoked Mr. E[gginto]n that his former love was turned into bitter hatred.[86] But he had not yet had time to

---

[80] For religious impressions made on this occasion, see *Arminian Magazine* (1779), II.590.

[81] Cf. Mark 1:15.   [82] Cf. Rom. 3:24.

[83] Sand Hutton, a small chapelry in the parish of Thirsk, 4 miles W. by S. of that town (not the chapelry 8 miles NE. of York). Here he would probably lodge at the Sign of the Crown kept by John Pickering, a Quaker, as did John Bennet (see his diary, May 2, 1743). Wesley always spells the name 'Sandhutton'.

[84] Cf. Eph. 2:8.

[85] Robert Williams was frequently in trouble for attacks upon the Established Church both in England and Ireland, he being a member of the Irish Conference, 1766–69. JW is said to have often left his name out of the Minutes. In 1769 he preceded Boardman and Pilmoor to America where he did valiant work, especially in Maryland and Virginia, where he died Sept. 26, 1775. His funeral sermon was preached by Francis Asbury. He was the first publisher of Wesley literature in America.

[86] Egginton apparently believed that he had been publicly charged with drunkenness. See JW's letter to 'John Smith', June 25, 1746, 26:204-5 in this edn.

work up the poor people into the rage and madness which afterwards appeared; so that they were extremely quiet both this and the following days, while I improved the present opportunity and exhorted them, morning and evening, to believe on the Lord Jesus and to work out their salvation with fear and trembling.[87]

Yet on Sunday 17 the scene began to open. I think I never heard so wicked a sermon, and delivered with such bitterness of voice and manner, as that which Mr. E[gginton] preached in the afternoon. I knew what effect this must have in a little time and therefore judged it expedient to prepare the poor people for what was to follow, that when it came they might not be offended. Accordingly on Tuesday 19, I strongly enforced those words of our Lord, 'If any man come after me, and hate not his father and mother . . . , yea, and his own life, he cannot be my disciple. And whosoever doth not bear his cross and come after me cannot be my disciple.'[88]

While I was speaking a gentleman rode up, very drunk, and after many unseemly and bitter words laboured much to ride over some of the people. I was surprised to hear he was a neighbouring clergyman. And this too is a man zealous for the Church! Ah, poor Church! If it stood in need of such defenders!

Thur. 21. I spent an hour with some of my old friends whom I had not seen for many years. I rejoiced to find them still loving and open of heart, just as they were before I went to Georgia. In the afternoon I called at Berkswell,[89] near Coventry, where I had formerly spent many pleasant hours.[90] And here likewise I found friendship and openness still. But the master of the house was under heavy affliction; and such affliction as I believe will never be removed till he is filled with peace and joy in the Holy Ghost.[91]

Fri. 22. I rode to Painswick, and on Saturday 23 through heavy rain to Bristol.

I had now a week of rest and peace, which was refreshing both to my soul and body. Sun. May 1. I had an opportunity of receiving the Lord's Supper at St. James's, our parish church. We had another comfortable hour in the afternoon, while I was

[87] See Phil. 2:12.
[88] Luke 14:26-27.
[89] Orig., 'Barkswell'. Berkswell was a parish 6 1/4 miles W. by N. from Coventry.
[90] The Boyces of Berkswell had often entertained the Wesley brothers in the 1730s, had been their guests in Oxford, and mixed with them at Stanton Harcourt. In the early 1730s JW corresponded with Serena, the daughter of the house.
[91] Rom. 14:17.

explaining, 'This is the covenant which I will make, saith the Lord; I will put my laws in their minds, and write them in their hearts, and I will be unto them a God, and they shall be unto me a people.'[92]

5   Tuesday, May 3. I set out for Wales, in company with one who was my pupil at Oxford. We could get that night no farther than the Bull,[93] five Welsh miles beyond Abergavenny.[94] The next morning we came to Builth, just as the church prayers began. Mr. Phillips,[95] the rector of Maesmynys[96] (at whose invitation I

10   came), soon took knowledge of me, and we began a friendship which I trust shall never end. I preached on a tomb at the east end of the church at four, and again at seven.[97] Mr. Gwynne[98] and Mr. Prothero[99] (Justices of Peace) stood on either hand of me; and all the people before, catching every word, with the most serious and

15   eager attention.[1]

Thur. 5. I rode over such rugged mountains as I never saw before to Cardiff. But it was late before we came in, so that I could not preach that night. Friday 6, I preached at eleven in the new room[2] which the society had just built in the heart of the town.

---

[92] Cf. Heb. 8:10.

[93] Possibly an error for the Bell, Llangrwyne. Williams, *Wesley in Wales*, p. 16, n. 3.

[94] 1749, 1769, 'Aberga'ny', and so Sept. 26, 1743, although when JW first visited the place, Oct. 3, 1741, he used its full name in all three edns. rather than the local abbreviation.

[95] Edward Phillips (1716–*c.* 1776), born at Llanvareth, Radnor; educated at Jesus College, Oxford, 1734–38; ordained priest 1740, and instituted curate (later rector) at Maesmynys, where he worked till his death. The Wesley brothers visited him some eight times each, 1744–48 (WHS, 12:174-76), and he retained Methodist sympathies to the end.

[96] Orig., 'Maesmennys'. Maesmynys was a tiny parish 1 1/2 miles SW. of Builth.

[97] Thomas James, the Calvinist exhorter at Crickadarn, states that JW 'kept a society' at Builth after preaching twice, and 'prayed with great power for Brother Harris' *(The Christian History*, iii.70-71).

[98] Marmaduke Gwynne (*c.* 1694–1769) of Garth, Breconshire, magistrate and local notability, was converted under the preaching of Howell Harris at a meeting he had gone prepared to suppress under the Riot Act, and became a pillar of evangelicalism in that area. The Wesleys were frequently received with innumerable others into his great household (nine children, twenty servants, and a chaplain), and in 1749 Charles Wesley married his daughter Sarah. He attended the second Conference.

[99] Marmaduke Prothero, J.P., of Builth, whose daughter married John Jones, Llanfaredd, a member for a time of the Moravian society at Rhos Goch, Radnorshire, and of their congregation at Leominster. Williams, *Wesley in Wales*, p. 16, n. 6 (with refs.).

[1] 'I believe the Lord blessed you much to young Mr. Philips, the minister when you were here,' wrote Harris to Wesley on May 27. *Selected Trevecka Letters (1742–47)*, p. 97; *The Christian History*, iii.82.

[2] In Church Street, the first Methodist chapel in Wales. It had been built since JW's last visit on July 6, 1742.

And our souls were sweetly comforted together. About two I preached at Llantrisant;[3] and at Fonmon Castle in the evening, to a loving and serious congregation.[4]

Sat. 7. I was desired to preach at Cowbridge. We came into the town about eleven. And many people seemed very desirous to hear for themselves concerning the way which is everywhere spoken against. But it could not be. The sons of Belial gathered themselves together, headed by one or two wretches, called gentlemen; and continued shouting, cursing, blaspheming, and throwing showers of stones, almost without intermission. So that after some time spent in prayer for them, I judged it best to dismiss the congregation.

Sun. 8. I preached in the Castle yard at Cardiff [5] at five in the morning and seven in the evening; in the afternoon at Wenvoe, where the church was quite filled with those who came from many miles round. And God answered many of them in the joy of their hearts. It was a solemn and refreshing season.

Mon. 9. I returned to Bristol. Most of the week I spent in visiting the society in Kingswood; whom I now found quite clear of those vain janglings which had for a time well-nigh torn them in pieces.

Tue. 17. My brother set out for Cornwall,[6] where (according to the accounts we had frequently received) abundance of those who before neither feared God, nor regarded man, began to inquire what they must do to be saved. But the same imprudence which had laid the foundation for all the disturbances in Staffordshire had broke out here also and turned many of our friends into bitter and implacable enemies. Violent persecution was a natural

---

[3] Orig., 'Lantrissent'.

[4] This congregation was reported to be increasing daily, and had lately attracted two hundred hearers.

[5] The scene is described in a letter of Howell Harris to George Whitefield, May 12, 1743: 'Last Sunday I heard Bro. John Wesley preach upon the seventh of Romans. He was very sweet and loving, and seemed to have his heart honestly bent on drawing the poor souls to Christ. The persecutors at Cardiff said if he would preach anywhere but at the New Room they would not disturb him, but would come and hear him; whereupon he preached at the Castle Green, concluding it was God's call out of the house to the streets, etc. He was disturbed and hindered preaching at Cowbridge.' Printed in *Account of the Progress of the Gospel*, in *The Christian History*, Vol. 3, no. 2, pp. 79-80.

[6] This is an error arising from the writing up of the journal at a later date. CWJ notes: 'May 17th [1743]. I set out for the north with Mr. Gurney,' and he continued eventually as far as Newcastle. His first journey to Cornwall in the second half of July had much the results reported here.

consequence of this, but the power of God triumphed over all.

May 22, being Whitsunday, I preached both at Kingswood and Bristol, on those solemn words, 'Jesus stood and cried, If any man thirst, let him come unto me and drink. He that believeth on me, as the Scripture hath said, out of his belly shall flow rivers of living water.'[7]

Tue. 24. I rode to Cirencester[8] and preached on a green place at a little distance from the town, on 'The kingdom of God is not meats and drinks, but righteousness and peace and joy in the Holy Ghost.'[9] Wed. 25. I preached to a little company at Oxford. Thur. 26. I had a large congregation at Wycombe;[10] from whence I hastened to London and concluded the day by enforcing those awful words at the Foundery, 'The Lord hath proclaimed unto the end of the world, Say ye to the daughters of Zion, Behold thy salvation cometh! Behold his reward is with him, and his work before him.'[11]

Sun. 29. Being Trinity Sunday, I began officiating at the chapel in West Street, near the Seven Dials, of which (by a strange chain of providences) we have a lease for several years.[12] I preached on the Gospel for the day, part of the third chapter of St. John, and afterwards administered the Lord's Supper to some hundreds of communicants. I was a little afraid at first that my strength would not suffice for the business of the day, when a service of five hours (for it lasted from ten to three) was added to my usual employment. But God looked to that. So I must think, and they that will call it enthusiasm, may. I preached at the Great Gardens at five, to an immense congregation, on 'Ye must be born again.'[13] Then the leaders met (who filled all the time that I was not speaking in public), and after them the bands. At ten at night I was less weary than at six in the morning.

---

[7] John 7:37-38.

[8] Cirencester was a large parish and borough 17 miles SE. of Gloucester.

[9] Cf. Rom. 14:17.

[10] High Wycombe was a substantial borough, market town, and parish 29 miles W. by N. from London.

[11] Isa. 62:11.

[12] West Street Chapel was opened in 1700 for French Protestants (on the site of an episcopal chapel where services had been conducted in Erse), one of a group of eight in and about Soho (William Maitland, *History of London* [London, 1756–57], II.1190). It was purchased in 1728 with the proceeds of a benefaction for poor widows of St. Clement Dane's parish and rented out. It was probably offered to JW by the rector, Thomas Blackwell. John Telford, *Two West-End Chapels* (London, 1886), pp. 8-10.

[13] John 3:7. 'A Short History of the People called Methodists', §26, adds, 'the Great Gardens in Whitechapel', 9:437 in this edn.

The following week I spent in visiting the society. On Sunday, June 5, the service at the chapel lasted till near four in the afternoon; so that I found it needful, for the time to come, to divide the communicants into three parts, that we might not have above six hundred at once.   5

Wed. 8. I ended my course of visiting; throughout which I found great cause to bless God, so very few having 'drawn back to perdition',[14] out of nineteen hundred and fifty souls.

Sat. 18. I received a full account of the terrible riots which had been in Staffordshire.[15] I was not surprised at all; neither should I   10 have wondered if, after the advices they had so often heard from the pulpit, as well as from the episcopal chair, the zealous High-Churchmen had rose and cut all that were called Methodists in pieces.

Mon. 20. Resolving to assist them as far as I could, I set out   15 early in the morning, and after preaching at Wycombe about noon, in the evening came to Oxford. Tue. 21. We rode to Birmingham; and in the morning, Wednesday 22, to Francis Ward's[16] at Wednesbury.[17]

Although I knew all that had been done here was as contrary to   20 law as it was to justice and mercy, yet I knew not how to advise the poor sufferers or to procure them any redress. I was then little acquainted with the English course of law, having long had scruples concerning it. But, as many of these were now removed, I thought it best to inquire whether there could be any help from   25 the laws of the land. I therefore rode over to Counsellor Littleton[18] at Tamworth, who assured us we might have an easy remedy if we resolutely prosecuted, in the manner the law directed, those rebels against God and the king.

Thur. 23. I left Wednesbury, and in the evening preached at   30 Melbourne in Derbyshire. I preached at Nottingham (where I

---

[14] Cf. Heb. 10:39.

[15] The chief trouble had been at Walsall (see May 21, 1743; CWJ, I.307-8).

[16] Francis Ward (1707–82), of 92 Bridge Street, Wednesbury, underground manager in John Wood's colliery and churchwarden, became famous in the Methodist community for the assistance he gave JW later in the year during the Wednesbury riots (see below under Oct. 20, 1743, and subsequently), his bravery being the more striking since his employer and the vicar were prominent instigators of trouble.

[17] Wednesbury was a market town and parish 19 miles SSE. from Stafford.

[18] Edward Littleton, son of Sir Edward Littleton of Moat House, Tamworth. Littleton's advice encouraged Ward and John Griffiths to apply for protection to another magistrate but without success.

met my brother coming from the north) on Friday, and on Saturday and Sunday at Epworth.

Mon. 27. I preached at Alkborough,[19] on the Trent side, to a stupidly attentive congregation. We then crossed over and rode to 5 Sykehouse;[20] on Tuesday at Smeaton,[21] and on Wednesday to Newcastle.

Thur. 30. I immediately inquired into the state of those whom I left here striving for the mastery. And some of them I found were grown faint in their minds; others had turned back as a dog to the 10 vomit.[22] But about six hundred still continued, striving together for the hope of the gospel.

Monday, July 4, and the following days I had time to finish the *Instructions for Children.*[23] Sun. 10. I preached at eight on Chowdean Fell, on 'Why will ye die, O house of Israel?'[24] Ever 15 since I came to Newcastle the first time, my spirit had been moved within me at the crowds of poor wretches who were every Sunday in the afternoon sauntering to and fro, on the Sandhill. I resolved, if possible, to find them a better employ, and as soon as the service at All Saints was over, walked straight from the church to the 20 Sandhill and gave out a verse of a psalm. In a few minutes I had company enough, thousands upon thousands crowding together. But the prince of this world fought with all his might, lest his kingdom should be overthrown. Indeed the very mob of Newcastle, in the height of their rudeness, have commonly some 25 humanity left. I scarce observed that they threw anything at all; neither did I receive the least personal hurt. But they continued thrusting one another to and fro, and making such a noise that my voice could not be heard; so that after spending near an hour in singing and prayer, I thought it best to adjourn to our own house.

30 Mon. 11. I had almost such another congregation in the High Street at Sunderland. But the tumult subsided in a short time; so that I explained, without any interruption, the one true religion, 'Righteousness and peace and joy in the Holy Ghost'.[25]

---

[19] Orig., 'Awkborough'. Alkborough was a village 7 miles N. of Scunthorpe.
[20] Sykehouse was a chapelry in the parish of Fishlake, Yorks., 5 1/2 miles NW. by W. from Thorne.
[21] Orig., 'Smeton'. Great Smeaton was a parish 6 1/2 miles N. by W. from Northallerton, bordering on the Tees.
[22] See Prov. 26:11; 2 Pet. 2:22.
[23] See *Bibliography*, No. 101. The work was not published until 1745.
[24] Ezek. 18:31; 33:11.
[25] Rom. 14:17.

Thur. 14. I preached at the Lower Spen,[26] seven or eight (northern) miles from Newcastle. John Brown had been obliged to remove hither from Tanfield Lea (I believe by the peculiar providence of God). By his rough and strong, though artless words, many of his neighbours had been much convinced, and began to search the Scriptures as they never had done before; so that they did not seem at all surprised when I declared, 'He that believeth, hath everlasting life.'[27]

Sun. 17. I preached (as I had done the Wednesday before) to my favourite congregation at Plessey, on 'Him hath God exalted with his own right hand to be a Prince and a Saviour.'[28] I then joined a little company of them together, who desire 'repentance and remission of sins'.[29]

Mon. 18. I set out from Newcastle with John Downes[30] of Horsley. We were four hours riding to Ferryhill,[31] about twenty measured miles. After resting there an hour we rode softly on, and at two o'clock came to Darlington. I thought my horse was not well. He thought the same of his; though they were both young, and very well the day before. We ordered the hostler to fetch a farrier, which he did without delay. But before the men could determine what was the matter, both the horses laid down and died.

I hired a horse to Sand Hutton and rode on, desiring John Downes to follow me. Thence I rode to Boroughbridge on Tuesday morning, and then walked on to Leeds.

Wed. 20. I preached at Birstall and Hightown. After I had visited all the societies in these parts and preached at as many of the little towns as I could, on Monday 25, I rode to Barley Hall. Many from Sheffield were there. We rejoiced greatly together in 'him who justifieth the ungodly'.[32] On Tuesday night and

---

[26] Lower Spen was about 1/2 mile SE. of High Spen and 2 miles W. of Rowlands Gill. The site of the hamlet is now occupied by Hookergate School, and a reminiscence of its name is preserved in Low Spen Farm.

[27] Cf. John 3:36; 6:47.

[28] Acts 5:31.

[29] Luke 24:47.

[30] John Downes (*c.* 1723–74), one of JW's most trusted preachers from 1743. In the panegyric he wrote after Downes died while preaching, JW declared, 'he was by nature full as great a genius as Sir Isaac Newton' (see Nov. 4, 1774). Among Downes's accomplishments was engraving, a celebrated portrait of JW being his work. Atmore, *Methodist Memorial*, pp. 109-10.

[31] Orig. 'Ferry Hill'. Ferryhill was a mining chapelry in the parish of Merrington, 5 3/4 miles ENE. of Bishop Auckland.

[32] Rom. 4:5.

Wednesday morning I preached at Nottingham; on Wednesday evening at Markfield. Friday 28 we rode to Newport Pagnell, and Saturday 29 to London.

Saturday, August 6. A convenient chapel was offered me in
5 Snowsfield[s], on the other side of the water. It was built on purpose, it seems, by a poor Arian misbeliever for the defence and propagation of her bad faith.[33] But the wisdom of God brought that device to nought and ordered by his overruling providence that it should be employed, not for 'crucifying the Son of God
10 afresh',[34] but for calling all to believe on his name.

Mon. 8. Upon mention made of my design to preach here, a zealous woman warmly replied, 'What! At Snowsfields! Will Mr. W[esley] preach at Snowsfields? Surely he will not do it! Why, there is not such another place in all the town. The people there
15 are not men but devils.' However, I resolved to try if God was not stronger than them. So this evening I preached there on that Scripture, Jesus said, 'They that be whole need not a physician, but they that are sick. I came, not to call the righteous, but sinners to repentance.'[35]
20 Sun. 14. Mr. G[arden][36] assisted me at the chapel, one who had *then* a deep sense of the goodness of God, in lifting him up from the gates of death and delivering him out of all his troubles.

Mon. 22. After a few of us had joined in prayer, about four I set out and rode softly to Snow Hill, where the saddle slipping quite
25 upon my mare's neck, I fell over her head, and she ran back into Smithfield. Some boys caught her and brought her to me again, cursing and swearing all the way. I spoke plainly to them, and they promised to amend. I was setting forward when a man cried, 'Sir, you have lost your saddle-cloth.' Two or three more would needs
30 help me to put it on; but these two swore at almost every word. I turned to one and another and spoke in love. They all took it well

---

[33] The Snowsfields Chapel was built in 1736 by Mrs. Ginn, a zealous Baptist seceder from the Maze Pond Chapel looking for a more liberal religion. She installed Sayer Rudd, a pastor of Unitarian opinions, who served for six years. Suffering friction with the congregation because of his theological views, Rudd converted to the Church of England and received the living of Walmer, Kent. The Snowsfields congregation then dissolved, and JW acquired the building, his third, for the Long Lane Society. Wilson, *Dissenting Meeting Houses*, IV.279-84.

[34] Cf. Heb. 6:6.

[35] Cf. Mark 2:17; Luke 5:31-32.

[36] James Garden, rector of Slingsby, Yorks., and curate of Hovingham, Mar. 1739/40, till his death *c.* 1772.

and thanked me much. I gave them two or three little books, which they promised to read over carefully.

Before I reached Kensington[37] I found my mare had lost a shoe. This gave me opportunity of talking closely for near half an hour, both to the smith and his servant. I mention these little 5 circumstances to show how easy it is to redeem every fragment of time (if I may so speak) when we feel any love to those souls for which Christ died.

Tue. 23. I came to Kingswood in the afternoon, and in the evening preached at Bristol. Wed. 24. I made it my business to 10 inquire concerning the truth of a strange relation which had been given me. And I found there was no possibility of doubting it. The plain fact was this.

The Rev. Mr. [Weston][38] (I use the words of a gentleman of Bristol, whose manuscript lies by me) preached at two or three churches on 15 these words, 'Having the form of godliness, but denying the power thereof'.[39] After showing the different sorts of Dissenters from the Church of England, who (as he said) had only the form of godliness, he inveighed very much against the 'novel sect', the 'upstart Methodists' (as he termed them), which indeed he was accustomed to 20 do, more or less, in almost all his sermons. 'These are the men', said he, 'whom St. Paul foretold, who have the form, the outside show of holiness, but not the power, for they are ravening wolves, full of hypocrisy within.'[40] He then alleged many grievous things against them, but without all colour of truth, and warned his flock to 'turn 25 away from' them, and not to bid them God speed, lest they should be partakers of their evil deeds.

Shortly after he was to preach at St. Nicholas Church. He had named the above-mentioned text twice, when he was suddenly seized with a rattling in his throat, attended with an hideous groaning. He 30 fell backward against the door of the pulpit; burst it open, and would have fallen down the stairs but that some people caught him and carried him away, as it seemed dead, into the vestry. In two or three days he recovered his senses, and the Sunday following, died!

In the evening, the word of God was indeed quick and 35 powerful. Afterwards I desired the men as well as women to meet.

---

[37] Kensington was a parish and royal residence 2 miles W. by S. from London.

[38] Rev. Mr. Weston, curate of St. Peter's, Bristol, died July 11, 1743. He may have been John Weston, son of Paul Weston, of Bristol, gent., matriculated at Balliol College, Oxford, 1725/26, aged 16; M.A., 1732.

[39] 2 Tim. 3:5. [40] Cf. Matt. 7:15.

But I could not speak to them. The spirit of prayer was so poured upon us all that we could only speak to God.

Having found for some time a strong desire to unite with Mr. Whitefield as far as possible to cut off needless dispute,[41] I wrote 5 down my sentiments, as plain as I could, in the following terms:

> There are three points in debate: (1) unconditional election; (2) irresistible grace; (3) final perseverance.
> With regard to the first, unconditional election, I believe,
> That God, before the foundation of the world, did *unconditionally*
> 10 *elect* certain persons to do certain works, as Paul to preach the gospel;
> That he has *unconditionally elected* some nations to receive peculiar privileges, the Jewish nation in particular;
> That he has *unconditionally elected* some nations to hear the gospel, as England and Scotland now, and many others in past ages;
> 15 That he has *unconditionally elected* some persons to many peculiar advantages, both with regard to temporal and spiritual things;
> And I do not deny (though I cannot prove it is so),
> That he has *unconditionally elected* some persons, thence eminently styled, the elect, to eternal glory.
> 20 But I cannot believe,
> That all those who are *not* thus *elected* to glory *must* perish everlastingly; or
> That there is one soul on earth who had not nor ever had *a possibility* of escaping eternal damnation.
> 25 With regard to the second, irresistible grace, I believe,
> That the grace which brings faith, and thereby salvation into the soul, is irresistible *at that moment;*
> That most believers may remember some time when God did *irresistibly* convince them of sin;
> 30 That most believers do at some other times find God *irresistibly* acting upon their souls;
> Yet I believe that the grace of God both before and after those moments, may be, and hath been, resisted; and
> That, in general, it does not act *irresistibly,* but we *may* comply
> 35 therewith or *may not.*
> And I do not deny,
> That in those eminently styled 'the elect' (if such there be) the

---

[41] What was in view was a conference to resolve the differences between the Wesleys and their friends, and Whitefield, the Countess of Huntingdon, their friends, and the Moravians. The Moravians, however, withdrew (Aug. 12, 1743; CWJ, I.334), still hoping, it seems, for a special arrangement with the Church of England. This was the last attempt at union in the evangelical camp.

grace of God is so far *irresistible* that they cannot but believe and be finally saved.

But I cannot believe,

That all those *must* be damned in whom it does not *thus irresistibly* work; or, 5

That there is one soul on earth who has not, and never had, any other grace than such as does in fact increase his damnation, and was designed of God so to do.

With regard to the third, final perseverance, I incline to believe,[42]

That there is a state attainable in this life, from which a man cannot 10 finally fall; and

That he has attained this who is, according to St. Paul's account, 'a new creature'; that is, who can say, 'Old things are passed away; all things' in me 'are become new.'[43]

And I do not deny, 15

That all those eminently styled the elect will infallibly persevere to the end.[44]

Thur. 25. My subject in the evening was, 'As ye have received the Lord Jesus Christ, so walk ye in him.'[45] O what a season was this! I scarce remember such an hour since the first stone of the 20 house was laid.

Fri. 26. I set out for Cornwall. In the evening I preached at the cross in Taunton, on 'The kingdom of God is not meats and drinks, but righteousness and peace and joy in the Holy Ghost.'[46] A poor man had posted himself behind in order to make some 25 disturbance. But the time was not come. The zealous wretches who 'deny the Lord that bought them'[47] had not yet stirred up the people. Many cried out, 'Throw down that rascal there! Knock him down! Beat out his brains!' So that I was obliged to entreat for him more than once, or he would have been but roughly 30 handled.

Sat. 27. I reached Exeter in the afternoon; but as no one knew of my coming I did not preach that night, only to one poor sinner at the inn; who, after listening to our conversation for a while, looked earnestly at us and asked whether it was possible for one 35 who had in some measure known 'the powers of the world to come' and was 'fallen away' (which she said was the case) to be

---

[42] 1749, 1769, 'I believe'.
[43] Cf. 2 Cor. 5:17.
[44] *Works* (1774) omits the last sentence.
[45] Cf. Col. 2:6.
[46] Cf. Rom. 14:17.   [47] Cf. 2 Pet. 2:1.

'renewed again to repentance'.[48] We besought God in her behalf and left her sorrowing; yet not without hope.

Sun. 28. I preached at seven to a handful of people. The sermon we heard at church was quite innocent of meaning; what 5 that in the afternoon was, I know not; for I could not hear a single sentence.

From church I went to the Castle,[49] where were gathered together (as some imagined) half the grown persons in the city. It was an awful sight. So vast a congregation in that solemn 10 amphitheatre! And all silent and still, while I explained at large and enforced that glorious truth, 'Happy are they whose iniquities are forgiven, and whose sins are covered.'[50]

I went thence to poor Mr. V—— the clergyman,[51] lying under sentence of death. He had for some time acted the lunatic, but I 15 soon put him out of his play, and he appeared to have wit enough in his anger. I designed to close in with him immediately; but two cruelly-impertinent gentlemen would needs come into the room, so that I could say no more, but was obliged to leave him in their hands.

20 The lad who was to die the next day was quite of another spirit. He appeared deeply affected while we were speaking, and yet more during our prayer. And no sooner were we gone than he broke out into a bitter cry. Who knows but he might be heard by him that made him?

25 Mon. 29. We rode forward.[52] About sunset we were in the middle of the first, great, pathless moor beyond Launceston. About eight we were got quite out of our way. But we had not gone far before we heard Bodmin bell. Directed by this, we turned to the left and came to the town before nine.

30 Tue. 30. In the evening we reached St. Ives.[53] About seven I

48 Cf. Heb. 6:5-6.

49 Rougemont Castle, built by William the Conquerer in 1068; the main gateway, the curtain wall, and one tower survive. W. G. Hoskins, *A New Survey of England: Devon* (London, 1954), p. 394.

50 Cf. Rom. 4:7.

51 Rev. Peter Vine, hanged at Exeter for rape, Oct. 5, 1743 (*Gentleman's Magazine* [Oct. 1743], XIII.551). He was probably the son of Richard Vine, of Hartland Devon, pleb.; matriculated from Exeter College, Oxford, 1736, aged 19; B.A., 1739.

52 The party consisted of JW and William Shepherd, together with John Nelson and John Downes, who, having only one horse between them, usually set out first. Thomas Jackson, *Early Methodist Preachers*, I.73-75.

53 St. Ives was a flourishing seaport, borough, and parish 9 miles NE. by N. from Penzance.

invited all guilty, helpless sinners who were conscious they 'had nothing to pay',[54] to accept of free forgiveness. The room was crowded both within and without. But all were quiet and attentive.

Wed. 31. I spoke severally with those of the society, who were about one hundred and twenty. Near an hundred of these had found peace with God. Such is the blessing of being persecuted for righteousness' sake![55] As we were going to church at eleven, a large company at the market-place welcomed us with a loud huzza—wit as harmless as the ditty sung under my window (composed, one assured me, by a gentlewoman of *their own town):*

> Charley[56] Wesley is come to town,
> To try if he can pull the churches down.

In the evening I explained 'the promise of the Father'.[57] After preaching, many began to be turbulent. But John Nelson went into the midst of them and spoke a little to the loudest, who answered not again but went quietly away.

Thursday, September 1. We had a day of peace. Fri. 2. I preached at Morvah,[58] about eight miles west of St. Ives, on the north sea. My text was, 'The land of Zabulon and the land of Nephthalim, by the way of the sea. . . . The people which sat in darkness saw great light, and to them which sat in the region and shadow of death light is sprung up.'[59]

I observed an earnest, stupid attention in the hearers, many of whom appeared to have good desires, but I did not find one who was *convinced of sin,* much less who knew the pardoning love of God.

Sat. 3. I rode to the Three-cornered Down[60] (so called) nine or ten miles east of St. Ives, where we found two or three hundred tinners, who had been some time waiting for us. They all appeared quite pleased and unconcerned, and many of them ran after us to Gwennap[61] (two miles east), where their number was

---

[54] Luke 7:42.
[55] See Matt. 5:10.
[56] 1774, 'Charles'.
[57] Acts 1:4.
[58] Morvah was a cliff-top parish 6 miles NW. of Penzance.
[59] Matt. 4:15-16.
[60] Possibly Illogan Downs (WHS, 4:185).
[61] 1749, 1769, 'Gwynap'; 1774, 'Gwenap'. Gwennap was a copper-mining parish 3 1/2 miles E. by S. from Redruth.

quickly increased to four or five hundred. I had much comfort here in applying those words, 'He hath anointed me to preach the gospel to the poor.'[62] One who lived near invited us to lodge at his house and conducted us back to the green in the morning. We came thither just as the day dawned, and I strongly applied those gracious words, 'I will heal their backsliding, I will love them freely,'[63] to five or six hundred serious people. At Treswithian Downs,[64] five miles nearer St. Ives, we found seven or eight hundred waiting, to whom I cried aloud, 'Cast away all your transgressions; for why will ye die, O house of Israel?'[65] After dinner I preached again to about a thousand people, on 'Him whom God hath exalted to be a Prince and a Saviour'.[66] It was here first I observed a little impression made on two or three of the hearers; the rest (as usual) showing huge approbation and absolute unconcern.

At seven I met the society at St. Ives, where two women who came from Penzance fell down as dead and soon after cried out in the bitterness of their souls. But we continued crying to God in their behalf, till he put a new song in their mouths.[67] At the same time a young man of the same place, who had once known the peace of God but had sinned it away, had a fresh and clear manifestation of the love of God.

Tue. 6. I preached at Morvah, on 'Righteousness and peace and joy in the Holy Ghost'.[68] But still I could not find the way into the hearts of the hearers, although they were earnest to hear what they understood not.

Wed. 7. I preached to two or three hundred people at Zennor[69] (four miles west of St. Ives) and found much goodwill in them, but no life. It was much the same on Thursday 8, while I preached at Kenneggy[70] Downs, five miles south of St. Ives, on 'the resurrection of the dry bones'.[71] There is not yet so much as a shaking among them, much less is there any breath in them.

Fri. 9. I rode in quest of St. Hilary Downs,[72] ten or twelve miles

[62] Luke 4:18.   [63] Hos. 14:4.
[64] Orig., 'Trezuthan Downs'. Treswithian was a village 1 mile W. of Camborne.
[65] Cf. Ezek. 18:31.
[66] Cf. Acts 5:31.
[67] See Ps. 40:3; 1749, 'mouth'.
[68] Rom. 14:17.
[69] 1749, 1769, 'Zunnor'. Zennor was a mining parish 5 miles WSW. from St. Ives.
[70] Orig., 'Cannegy'. Kenneggy Downs is 6 miles W. of Helston.
[71] Cf. Ezek. 37:1-14.
[72] St. Hilary was a parish comprising the market town of Marazion.

south-east of St. Ives. And the Downs I found, but no congregation, neither man, woman, nor child. But by that [time] I had put on my gown and cassock about an hundred gathered themselves together, whom I earnestly called 'to repent and believe the gospel'.[73] And if but one heard, it was worth all 5 the labour.

Sat. 10. There were prayers at St. Just in the afternoon, which did not end till four. I then preached at the cross to, I believe, a thousand people, who all behaved in a quiet and serious manner.

At six I preached in Sennen,[74] near the Land's End, and 10 appointed the little congregation (consisting chiefly of old grey-headed men) to meet me again at five in the morning. But on Sunday 11, great part of them were got together between three and four o'clock. So between four and five we began praising God; and I largely explained and applied, 'I will heal their 15 backslidings; I will love them freely.'[75]

We went afterwards down, as far as we could go safely, toward the point of the rocks at the Land's End. It was an awful sight! But how will these melt away when God ariseth to judgment! The sea between does indeed 'boil like a pot'. 'One would think the deep 20 to be hoary.'[76] But 'though they swell, yet can they not prevail; he hath set their bounds which they cannot pass.'[77]

Between eight and nine I preached at St. Just, on the green plain near the town, to the largest congregation (I was informed) that ever had been seen in these parts. I cried out with all the 25 authority of love, 'Why will ye die, O house of Israel?'[78] The people trembled and were still. I had not known such an hour before in Cornwall.

Soon after one we had such another congregation on the north side of the Morvah church. The Spirit of the Great King was in 30 the midst. And I was filled both with matter and words, even more abundantly than at St. Just. 'My strength will I ascribe unto thee.'[79]

At Zennor I preached about five, and then hastened to St. Ives, where we concluded the day in praising God with joyful lips. 35

---

[73] Cf. Mark 1:15.
[74] Orig., 'Sennan'. Sennen was a fishing parish which included Land's End, 8 1/4 miles WSW. from Penzance.
[75] Hos. 14:4.   [76] Job 41:31-32.
[77] Cf. Jer. 5:22.
[78] Ezek. 18:31; 33:11.
[79] Ps. 59:9 (BCP).

Mon. 12. I preached at one on Treswithian Downs, and in the
evening at St. Ives. The dread of God fell upon us while I was
speaking, so that I could hardly utter a word; but most of all in
prayer, wherein I was so carried out as scarce ever before in
5 my life.
I had *had* for some time a great desire to go and publish the love
of God our Saviour, if it were but for one day, in the Isles of Scilly.
And I had occasionally mentioned it to several. This evening
three of our brethren came and offered to carry me thither, if I
10 could procure the mayor's boat, which (they said) was 'the best
sailor of any in the town'. I sent, and he lent it me immediately.
So the next morning, Tuesday 13, John Nelson, Mr. Shepherd,[80]
and I, with three men and a pilot, sailed from St. Ives. It seemed
strange to me to attempt going in a fisher boat fifteen leagues
15 upon the main ocean, especially when the waves began to swell
and hang over our heads. But I called to my companions, and we
all joined together in singing lustily and with a good courage:

> When passing through the watery deep,
> I ask in faith his promised aid,
20 The waves an awful distance keep,
> And shrink from my devoted head.
> Fearless their violence I dare:
> They cannot harm, for God is [t]here.[81]

About half an hour after one we landed on St. Mary's,[82] the chief
25 of the inhabited islands.
We immediately waited upon the governor,[83] with the usual
present, viz., a newspaper. I desired him likewise to accept of an
Earnest Appeal.[84] The minister[85] not being willing I should preach
in the church, I preached at six in the streets to almost all the

80 Probably William Shepherd, an itinerant preacher, 1743–48 (when he ceased to
travel). See JWJ, July 4, 1747, and *Wesleyan Methodist Magazine* (1852), 75:785.
81 John and Charles Wesley, *Hymns and Sacred Poems* (1739), p. 153 *(Poet. Wks.,* I.136).
Wesley reproduced this hymn, 'Peace, doubting heart, my God's I am,' in his 1780
Collection, No. 264 (7:406-8 in this edn.). It seems likely that the alteration from the
original rhyming 'there' to 'here' was not a misprint but deliberate for this special occasion.
82 St. Mary's is about 30 miles W. of Land's End. JW's estimate of the distance from St.
Ives was near the mark.
83 Francis Godolphin, 2nd Earl Godolphin (1678–1766), Lord Warden of the
Stannaries, 1705-8, and governor of the Scilly Isles, 1733–36.
84 John Wesley *An Earnest Appeal to Men of Reason and Religion,* which had been
published that spring (see *Bibliography,* No. 74, and Vol. 11 in this edn.).
85 Ralph Hathaway, minister of St. Mary's, Scilly, 1737–45.

town, and many soldiers, sailors, and workmen, on, 'Why will ye die, O house of Israel?'[86] It was a blessed time, so that I scarce knew how to conclude. After sermon I gave them some little books and hymns, which they were so eager to receive that they were ready to tear both them and me to pieces.

For what *political reason* such a number of workmen were gathered together and employed at so large an expense, to fortify a few barren rocks, which whosoever would take deserves to have them for his pains, I could not possibly devise; but a *providential reason* was easy to be discovered. God might call them together to hear the gospel, which perhaps otherwise they might never have thought of.

At five in the morning I preached again, on, 'I will heal their backsliding, I will love them freely.'[87] And between nine and ten, having talked with many in private and distributed both to them and others between two and three hundred hymns and little books, we left this barren, dreary place and set sail for St. Ives, though the wind was strong and blew directly in our teeth. Our pilot said we should have good luck if we reached the land; but he knew not him whom the wind and seas obey. Soon after three we were even with the Land's End, and about nine we reached St. Ives.

Fri. 16. I preached to four or five hundred on St. Hilary Downs. And many seemed amazed. But I could find none as yet who had any deep or lasting conviction.

In the evening, as I was preaching at St. Ives, Satan began to fight for his kingdom. The mob of the town burst into the room and created much disturbance, roaring and striking those that stood in their way as though Legion himself possessed them. I would fain have persuaded our people to stand still, but the zeal of some and the fear of others had no ears, so that finding the uproar increase, I went into the midst and brought the head of the mob up with me to the desk. I received but one blow on the side of the head, after which we reasoned the case, till he grew milder and milder, and at length undertook to quiet his companions.

Sat. 17. I preached at St. Just,[88] and at the Land's End, where in the morning, Sunday 18, I largely declared (what many shall

---

[86] Ezek. 18:31; 33:11.
[87] Hos. 14:4.
[88] St. Just was a large tin-mining parish 7 miles W. by N. from Penzance.

witness in due time), 'By grace ye are saved through faith.'[89]

The congregation at St. Just was greatly increased, while I proclaimed to every convicted sinner, 'Believe in the Lord Jesus Christ, and thou shalt be saved.'[90]

5 About one I preached at Morvah on Romans 8:15, to the largest congregation I had seen in Cornwall. The society afterwards met, consisting of above an hundred members. Which of these will endure to the end?

At Zennor I preached on Isaiah the fifty-third, feeling no 10 weariness at all, and concluded the day with our brethren at St. Ives, rejoicing and praising God.

Mon. 19. We were informed the rabble had designed to make their general assault in the evening. But one of the aldermen came, at the request of the mayor,[91] and stayed with us the whole 15 time of the service. So that no man opened his mouth while I explained, 'None is like unto the God of Jeshurun, who rideth upon the heavens unto thy help, and in his excellency upon the sky.'[92]

Tue. 20. I concluded my preaching here by exhorting all who 20 had 'escaped the corruption that is in the world' to 'add to' their 'faith, courage, knowledge, temperance, patience, godliness, brotherly kindness, and charity'.[93] At eleven I spent some time with our brethren in prayer and commended them to the grace of God.

25 At Treswithian Downs I preached to two or three thousand people, on 'the highway of the Lord, the way of holiness'.[94] We reached Gwennap a little before six and found the plain covered from end to end. It was supposed there were ten thousand people, to whom I preached Christ our 'wisdom, righteousness, 30 sanctification, and redemption'.[95] I could not conclude till it was so dark we could scarce see one another. And there was on all sides the deepest attention, none speaking, stirring, or scarce looking aside. Surely here, though in a temple not made with hands, was God 'worshipped in the beauty of holiness'![96]

[89] Cf. Eph. 2:8.
[90] Acts 16:31.
[91] John Stevens, already found by Charles Wesley to be 'an honest Presbyterian', and 'our deliverer from the hands of unrighteous and cruel men' (July 17, Aug. 5, 1743; CWJ, I.321, 331).
[92] Cf. Deut. 33:26.
[93] Cf. 2 Pet. 1:4-7.
[94] Cf. Isa. 35:8.
[95] Cf. 1 Cor. 1:30.
[96] Cf. Ps. 29:2, etc.

One of those who were present was Mr. P——, once a violent adversary. Before sermon began he whispered one of his acquaintance, 'Captain, stand by me; don't stir from me.' He soon burst out into a flood of tears, and quickly after, sunk down. His friend caught him and prevented his falling to the ground. O may the Friend of sinners lift him up!

Wed. 21. I was waked between three and four by a large company of tinners, who fearing they should be too late had gathered round the house and were singing and praising God. At five I preached once more, on 'Believe in the Lord Jesus Christ, and thou shalt be saved.'[97] They all devoured the word. O may it be health to their soul and marrow unto their bones![98]

We rode to Launceston that day. Thursday 22, as we were riding through a village called Sticklepath,[99] one stopped me in the street and asked abruptly,[1] 'Is not thy name John Wesley?' Immediately two or three more came up and told me I *must* stop there. I did so, and before we had spoke many words our souls took acquaintance with each other. I found they were called Quakers; but that hurt not *me*, seeing the love of God was in their hearts.[2]

In the evening I came to Exeter and preached in the Castle; and again at five in the morning to such a people as I have rarely seen, void both of anger, fear, and love.

We went by Axminster[3] at the request of a few there that feared God, and had joined themselves together some years since.[4] I exhorted them so to seek after the power as not to despise the form of godliness, and then rode on to Taunton, where we were gladly received by a little company of our brethren from Bristol.

I had designed to preach in the yard of our inn, but before I had named my text, having uttered only two words, 'Jesus Christ', a tradesman of the town (who it seems was mayor *elect*)[5] made so

---

[97] Acts 16:31.

[98] See Prov. 3:8.

[99] Sticklepath was a Devon village 4 miles E. of Okehampton.

[1] 1749, 1769, 'abrupt'.

[2] Charles Wesley enjoyed a similar friendly encounter with the Quakers of Sticklepath (July 13, 1744; CWJ, I.369), a colony which had migrated there from Exeter early in the eighteenth century. *Wesleyan Methodist Magazine* (1908), 131:523.

[3] Axminster was a small market town and parish 25 miles E. by N. from Exeter.

[4] This sounds like a reference to a religious society, but Methodism is said to have been already introduced to Axminster by a former army non-commissioned officer, who had seen service in Ireland, been converted under the Methodist ministry, and retired to the town. *Wesleyan Methodist Magazine* (1840), 63:891.

[5] For additional information, including the reading of the Riot Act, see WHS,

much noise and uproar that we thought it best to give him the ground. But many of the people followed me up into a large room, where I preached unto them Jesus. The next evening, Saturday 24, we arrived safe at Bristol.

5   Sun. 25. I preached at Bristol in the morning, and at Kingswood in the afternoon on 'Jesus Christ, the same yesterday and today and for ever'.[6] A vast congregation in the evening were quite serious and attentive.

Mon. 26. I had a great desire to speak plain to a young man who
10 went with us over the New Passage. To that end I rode with him three miles out of my way, but I could fix nothing upon him. Just as we parted, walking over Caerleon bridge,[7] he stumbled and was like to fall. I caught him and began to speak of God's care over us. Immediately the tears stood in his eyes, and he appeared
15 to *feel* every word which was said; so I spoke, and spared not. The same I did to a poor man[8] who led my horse over the bridge, to our landlord and his wife, and to one who occasionally came in. And they all expressed a surprising thankfulness.

About seven in the evening we reached Crickhowell,[9] four
20 miles beyond Abergavenny. Tuesday 27 we came to Mr. Gwynne's at Garth. It brought fresh to my mind our first visit to Mr. Jones at Fonmon. How soon may the master of this great house too be called away into an everlasting habitation!

Having so little time to stay, I had none to lose. So the same
25 afternoon, about four o'clock, I read prayers and preached to a small congregation on the 'faith' which 'is counted' to us 'for righteousness'.[10]

Very early in the morning I was obliged to set out in order to reach Cardiff before it was dark. I found a large congregation
30 waiting there, to whom I explained Zech. 9:11: 'By the blood of thy covenant I have sent forth thy prisoners out of the pit wherein is no water.'

30:186–87. See also *Gentleman's Magazine* (Jan. 1744), XIV.51: 'Tuesday 24. Mr. Westley beginning to preach to a very numerous auditory in the court of the Three Cups Inn at Taunton, had scarce named his text, when the Mayor came in formality and ordered the Proclamation to be read, which immediately silenced the preacher.'

    [6] Heb. 13:8.

    [7] Caerleon was a small market town situated on the river Usk in the parish of Llangattock, 20 1/2 miles SW. from Monmouth.

    [8] 1774, 'woman'.

    [9] Orig., 'Kirk-howell'. Crickhowell was a small market town and parish 13 miles SE. from Brecon.

    [10] Rom. 4:5.

Thur. 29. I preached at the Castle of Fonmon to a loving, simple people. Friday 30, it being a fair, still evening, I preached in the Castle yard at Cardiff; and the whole congregation, rich and poor, behaved as in the presence of God. Saturday, October 1. I preached at Caerphilly[11] in the morning, Llantrisant at 5 noon, and Cardiff at night.

Sun. 2. Fearing my strength would not suffice for preaching more than four times in the day, I only spent half an hour in prayer with the society in the morning. At seven, and in the evening, I preached in the Castle, at eleven in Wenvoe church, and in the 10 afternoon in Porthkerry church,[12] on, 'Repent ye, and believe the gospel.'[13]

Mon. 3. I returned to Bristol and employed several days in examining and purging the society, which still consisted (after many were put away) of more than seven hundred persons. The 15 next week I examined the society in Kingswood, in which I found but a few things to reprove.

Sat. 15. The leaders brought in what had been contributed in their several classes toward the public debt. And we found it was sufficient to discharge it, which was therefore done without delay. 20

Mon. 17. I left Bristol, and preached in the evening to a very *civil* congregation at Painswick. Tuesday 18, I preached to a little earnest company at Gotherington[14] near Tewkesbury, and in the evening at Evesham, on the happiness of him 'whose iniquities are forgiven, and his sins covered'.[15] 25

Wed. 19. I called on Mr. Taylor[16] at Quinton, six or seven miles north of Evesham. About eleven I preached in his church to a thin, dull congregation, and then rode on to Birmingham.

Thur. 20. After preaching to a small, attentive congregation, I rode to Wednesbury. At twelve I preached in a ground near the 30 middle of the town to a far larger congregation than was expected,

[11] Orig., 'Carphilly'. Caerphilly was a market town and chapelry in the parish of Eglwysilan, 7 miles N. by W. from Cardiff.

[12] Porthkerry was a tiny parish 9 miles SE. from Cowbridge. The church of St. Curig, in early English style, seated one hundred persons.

[13] Mark 1:15.

[14] Orig., 'Gutherton', and so May 8, 1744. Gotherington was a hamlet in the parish of Bishop's Cleeve, 4 miles W. by N. from Winchcombe.

[15] Cf. Rom. 4:7.

[16] Rev. Samuel Taylor (1711–72), vicar of Quinton 1738–72. Matriculated from Merton College, Oxford, 1729; B.A. from University College, 1737. He was present at the first and third Conferences in 1744 and 1746, and was associated with the Wesleys, 1743–46. See *Wesleyan Methodist Magazine* (1850), 73:386–88.

on 'Jesus Christ, the same yesterday and today and for ever'.[17] I believe everyone present felt the power of God. And no creature offered to molest us, either going or coming: but 'the Lord fought for' us, and we 'held our peace'.[18]

5   I was writing at Francis Ward's in the afternoon when the cry arose that the mob had beset the house.[19] We prayed that God would disperse them. And it was so: one went this way and another that; so that in half an hour not a man was left. I told our brethren, 'Now is the time for us to go.' But they pressed me
10 exceedingly to stay. So that I might not offend them, I sat down, though I foresaw what would follow. Before five the mob surrounded the house again, in greater numbers than ever. The cry of one and all was, 'Bring out the minister; we *will* have the minister.' I desired one to take their captain by the hand and bring
15 him into the house. After a few sentences interchanged between us, the lion was become a lamb.[20] I desired him to go and bring one or two more of the most angry of his companions. He brought in two, who were ready to swallow the ground with rage, but in two minutes they were as calm as he. I then bade[21] them make
20 way, that I might go out among the people. As soon as I was in the midst of them I called for a chair, and standing up asked, 'What do any of you want with me?' Some said, 'We want you to go with us to the justice.' I replied, 'That I will with all my heart.' I then spoke a few words, which God applied, so that they cried out with
25 might and main, 'The gentleman is an honest gentleman, and we will spill our blood in his defence.' I asked, 'Shall we go to the justice tonight or in the morning?' Most of them cried, 'Tonight, tonight.' On which I went before, and two or three hundred followed, the rest returning whence they came.
30   The night came on before we had walked a mile, together with heavy rain. However on we went to Bentley Hall, two miles from

---

[17] Heb. 13:8.

[18] Cf. Exod. 14:14.

[19] For another version of this account by Wesley, somewhat fuller, and with many variants, see *Modern Christianity; exemplified at Wednesbury* (1745), 9:132-58 in this edn., and *Bibliography*, No. 110. For a briefer version, see *A Farther Appeal*, Pt. III, II.14, 11:288-89 in this edn. For Francis Ward, see above, June 22, 1743, n. 16.

[20] The theme of lions becoming lambs, possibly based on Isa. 11:6-7, became almost proverbial with Wesley, and examples are frequent in the *Journal;* cf. Apr. 7, 1744; Aug. 16, 1755; Sept. 5, 1755; June 24, 1759; Aug. 22, 1768; Apr. 15, 1774; Sept. 1, 1774; May 30, 1787. (The vast majority of these instances occurred in Cornwall.)

[21] Wesley usually spells this 'bad', as here—a clue to his pronunciation.

Wednesbury.[22] One or two ran before to tell Mr. Lane[23] they had brought Mr. Wesley before his worship. Mr. Lane replied, 'What have I to do with Mr. Wesley? Go and carry him back again.' By this time the main body came up and began knocking at the door. A servant told them Mr. Lane was in bed. His son followed and 5 asked what was the matter. One replied, 'Why, an't please you, they sing psalms all day; nay, and make folks rise at five in the morning. And what would your worship advise us to do?' 'To go home', said Mr. Lane, 'and be quiet.'

Here they were at a full stop, till one advised to go to Justice 10 Persehouse[24] at Walsall. All agreed to this. So we hastened on, and about seven came to his house. But Mr. P[ersehouse] likewise sent word that he was in bed. Now they were at a stand again; but at last they all thought it the wisest course to make the best of their way home. About fifty of them undertook to convey 15 me. But we had not gone a hundred yards when the mob of Walsall came, pouring in like a flood, and bore down all before them. The Darlaston mob made what defence they could; but they were weary, as well as outnumbered. So that in a short time, many being knocked down, the rest ran away and left me in 20 their hands.

To attempt speaking was vain, for the noise on every side was like the roaring of the sea. So they dragged me along till we came to the town; where, seeing the door of a large house open, I attempted to go in; but a man catching me by the hair pulled me 25 back into the middle of the mob. They made no more stop till they had carried me through the main street from one end of the town to the other. I continued speaking all the time to those within hearing, feeling no pain or weariness. At the west end of the town, seeing a door half open, I made toward it and would have gone in. 30 But a gentleman in the shop would not suffer me, saying they would 'pull the house down to the ground'. However, I stood at the door and asked, 'Are you willing to hear me speak?' Many cried out, 'No, no! Knock his brains out, down with him, kill him at once.' Others said, 'Nay, but we will hear him first.' I began 35

---

[22] Orig., 'Wensbury'.

[23] John Lane (1699–1748), grandson of the Colonel Lane who sheltered Charles II at Bentley Hall after the battle of Worcester.

[24] William Persehouse (1691–1749), of Reynolds Hall, Walsall, a member of an old Staffordshire family *(Gentleman's Magazine* [Mar. 1749], XIX.141), a burgess, and later Mayor of Walsall. *Victoria County History, Staffordshire,* 17:216.

asking, 'What evil have I done? Which of you all have I wronged in word or deed?' And continued speaking for above a quarter of an hour, till my voice suddenly failed. Then the floods began to lift up their voice again, many crying out, 'Bring him away, bring
5 him away.'

In the meantime my strength and my voice returned, and I broke out aloud into prayer. And now the man who just before headed the mob turned and said, 'Sir, I will spend my life for you. Follow *me*, and not one soul here shall touch a hair of your head.'
10 Two or three of his fellows confirmed his words and got close to me immediately. At the same time the gentleman in the shop cried out, 'For shame, for shame, let him go.' An honest butcher, who was a little farther off, said it *was* a shame they should do thus, and pulled back four or five, one after another, who were
15 running on the most fiercely. The people then, as if it had been by common consent, fell back to the right and left, while those three or four men took me between them and carried me through them all. But on the bridge the mob rallied again. We therefore went on one side, over the mill dam, and thence through the meadows, till,
20 a little before ten, God brought me safe to Wednesbury,[25] having lost only one flap of my waistcoat and a little skin from one of my hands.

I never saw such a chain of providences before; so many convincing proofs that the hand of God is on every person and
25 thing, overruling all as it seemeth him good.

The poor woman of Darlaston who had headed that mob and sworn that none should touch me, when she saw her fellows[26] give way, ran into the thickest of the throng and knocked down three or four men, one after another. But many assaulting her at once,
30 she was soon overpowered, and had probably been killed in a few minutes (three men keeping her down and beating her with all their might), had not a man called to one of them, 'Hold, Tom, hold!' 'Who is there?' said Tom. 'What, honest Munchin?[27] Nay then let her go.' So they held their hand, and let her get up and
35 crawl home as well as she could.

From the beginning to the end I found the same presence of mind as if I had been sitting in my own study. But I took no

[25] 1749, 1769, 'Wensbury'.
[26] 1774, 'followers'.
[27] A nickname for George Clifton, who was buried in 1789, aged 85, in St. Paul's churchyard, Birmingham.

thought for one moment before another; only once it came into my mind that if they should throw me into the river it would spoil the papers that were in my pocket. For myself, I did not doubt but I should swim across, having but a thin coat and a light pair of boots.

The circumstances that follow I thought were particularly remarkable: (1) That many endeavoured to throw me down while we were going downhill on a slippery path to the town, as well judging, that if I was once on the ground, I should hardly rise any more. But I made no stumble at all, nor the least slip till I was entirely out of their hands. (2) That although many strove to lay hold on my collar or clothes to pull me down, they could not fasten at all; only one got fast hold of the flap of my waistcoat, which was soon left in his hand. The other flap, in the pocket of which was a bank-note, was torn but half off. (3) That a lusty man just behind struck at me several times with a large oaken stick; with which if he had struck me once on the back part of my head, it would have saved him all farther trouble. But every time the blow was turned aside, I know not how; for I could not move to the right hand or left. (4) That another came rushing through the press, and raising his arm to strike, on a sudden let it drop and only stroked my head, saying, 'What soft hair he has!' (5) That I stopped exactly at the mayor's[28] door, as if I had known it (which the mob doubtless thought I did), and found him standing in the shop, which gave the first check to the madness of the people. (6) That the very first men whose hearts were turned were the heroes of the town, the captains of the rabble on all occasions, one of them having been a prize-fighter at the bear-garden. (7) That from first to last I heard none give a *reviling* word or call me by any *opprobrious* name whatever. But the cry of one and all was, 'The preacher! The preacher! The parson! The minister!' (8) That no creature, at least within my hearing, laid anything to my charge, either true or false; having in the hurry quite forgot to provide themselves with an accusation of any kind. And, lastly, that they were as utterly at a loss what they should do with me; none proposing any determinate thing, only, 'Away with him; kill him at once!'

By how gentle degrees does God prepare us for his will! Two years ago a piece of a brick grazed my shoulders. It was a year after

---

[28] William Haslewood, chandler, Mayor of Wednesbury, Michaelmas 1743.

that the stone struck me between the eyes. Last month I received one blow, and this evening, two: one before we came into the town, and one after we were gone out. But both were as nothing, for though one man struck me on the breast with all his might, and the other on the mouth with such a force that the blood gushed out immediately, I felt no more pain from either of the blows than if they had touched me with a straw.

It ought not to be forgotten that when the rest of the society made all haste to escape for their lives, four only would not stir, William Sitch,[29] Edward Slater,[30] John Griffiths, and Joan Parks;[31] these kept with me, resolving to live or die together. And none of them received one blow but William Sitch, who held me by the arm from one end of the town to the other. He was then dragged away and knocked down; but he soon rose and got to me again. I afterwards asked him what he expected when the mob came upon us. He said, 'To die for him who had died for us'; and he felt no hurry or fear, but calmly waited till God should require his soul of him.

I asked J. P[arks] if she was not afraid when they tore her away from me. She said, 'No, no more than I am now. I could trust God for you as well as for myself. From the beginning I had a full persuasion that God would deliver you. I knew not how; but I left that to him, and was as sure as if it were already done.' I asked if the report was true that she had *fought* for me. She said, 'No; I knew God would fight for his children.' And shall these souls perish at the last?

When I came back to Francis Ward's I found many of our brethren waiting upon God. Many also whom I had never seen before came to rejoice with us. And the next morning, as I rode through the town in my way to Nottingham, everyone I met expressed such a cordial affection that I could scarce believe what I saw and heard.

I cannot close this head without inserting as great a curiosity in its kind as I believe was ever yet seen in England, which had its birth within a very few days of this remarkable occurrence at Walsall:

[29] William Sitch came from Mares Green, West Bromwich. J. H. Waddy, *The Bitter Sacred Cup* (London, 1976), pp. 20, 34.
[30] Edward Slater was brother-in-law of John Griffiths.
[31] Joan Parks of Darlaston, later a class-leader in Wednesbury.

To all high-constables, petty-constables, and other of his Majesty's peace-officers, within the said county, and particularly to the constable of Tipton (near Walsall):

Whereas we, his Majesty's Justices of the Peace, for the said county 5 of Stafford, have received information that several disorderly persons, styling themselves Methodist preachers, go about raising routs and riots, to the great damage of his Majesty's leige people, and against the peace of our Sovereign Lord the King:

These are in his Majesty's name to command you and every one of 10 you, within your respective districts, to make diligent search after the said Methodist preachers, and to bring him or them before some of us his said Majesty's Justices of the Peace, to be examined concerning their unlawful doings.

Given under our hands and seals, this [12th] day of October, 1743. 15

J. Lane

W. Persehouse

N.B. The very justices to whose houses I was carried, and who severally refused to see me!

Sat. 22. I rode from Nottingham to Epworth, and on Monday 20 set out for Grimsby. But at Ferry[32] we were at a full stop; the boatmen telling us we could not pass the Trent. It was as much as our lives were worth to put from shore before the storm abated. We waited an hour. But being afraid it would do much hurt if I should disappoint the congregation at Grimsby, I asked the men 25 if they did not think it possible to get to the other shore. They said they could not tell, but if we would venture our lives, they would venture theirs. So we put off, having six men, two women, and three horses in the boat. Many stood looking after us on the riverside; in the middle of which we were, when in an instant, the 30 side of the boat was under water, and the horses and men rolling one over another. We expected the boat to sink every moment, but I did not doubt of being able to swim ashore. The boatmen were amazed as well as the rest, but they quickly recovered and rowed for life. And soon after our horses leaping overboard 35 lightened the boat, and we all came unhurt to land.

They wondered what was the matter, I did not rise (for I lay along in the bottom of the boat); and I wondered too, till upon

---

[32] The crossing between Owston Ferry and East Ferry, 7 1/2 miles S. of Scunthorpe.

examination we found that a large iron crow,[33] which the boatmen
sometimes used, was (none knew how) run through the string of
my boot, which pinned me down that I could not stir. So that if the
boat had sunk, I should have been safe enough from swimming
5 any further.

The same day, and as near as we could judge the same hour,
the boat in which my brother was crossing the Severn at the New
Passage was carried away by the wind and in the utmost danger of
splitting upon the rocks. But the same God, when all human hope
10 was past, delivered them as well as us.

In the evening, the house at Grimsby not being able to contain
one fourth of the congregation, I stood in the street and exhorted
every prodigal to 'arise and go to his father'.[34] One or two
endeavoured to interrupt, but they were soon stilled by their own
15 companions. The next day, Tuesday 25, one in the town
promised us the use of a large room. But he was prevailed upon to
retract his promise before the hour of preaching came. I then
designed going to the Cross, but the rain prevented, so that we
were a little at a loss till we were offered a very convenient place by
20 'a woman which was a sinner'.[35] I there declared 'him' (about one
o'clock) whom 'God hath exalted, to give repentance and
remission of sins'.[36] And God so confirmed the word of his grace
that I marvelled any one could withstand him.

However *the prodigal*[37] held out till the evening, when I
25 enlarged upon *her* sins and faith, who 'washed' our Lord's 'feet
with tears and wiped them with the hairs of her head'.[38] She was
then utterly broken in pieces (as indeed, was well-nigh the whole
congregation) and came after me to my lodging, crying out, 'O sir!
"What must I do to be saved?" '[39] Being now informed of her case,
30 I said, 'Escape for your life. Return instantly to your husband.'
She said, 'But how can it be? Which way can I go? He is above an
hundred miles off. I have just received a letter from him; and he is
at Newcastle upon Tyne.' I told her, 'I am going for Newcastle in
the morning. You may go with me. William Blow[40] shall take you

---

[33] A grappling-hook (now obsolete).   [34] Cf. Luke 15:18.
[35] Cf. Luke 7:37.
[36] Cf. Acts 5:31.
[37] I.e., the 'woman which was a sinner', Mrs. S. (see Oct. 26, below).
[38] Luke 7:44.
[39] Acts 16:30.
[40] William Blow, cordwainer of Grimsby, one of the first to receive John Nelson there.
Thomas Jackson, *Early Methodist Preachers*, I.68, 70, 80, 81.

behind him.' And so he did. Glory be to the Friend of sinners! He hath plucked one more brand out of the fire. Thou poor sinner, thou hast received a prophet in the name of a prophet, and thou art found of him that sent him.

Wed. 26. I enlarged upon those deep words, 'Repent, and believe the gospel.'[41] When I had done a man stood forth in the midst, one who had exceedingly troubled his brethren, vehemently maintaining (for the plague had spread hither also) that they ought not to pray, to sing, to communicate, to search the Scriptures, or to trouble themselves about works, but only to believe and 'be still',[42] and said with a loud voice, 'Mr. Wesley! Let *me* speak a few words. Is it not said, "A certain man had two sons. And he said unto the younger, Go and work in my vineyard. And he answered, I will not; but afterwards he repented and went"? I am he. I said yesterday, "I will not go to hear him, I will have nothing to do with him." But I repent. Here is my hand. By the grace of God, I will not leave you as long as I live.'

William Blow, Mrs. S., and I set out at six. During our whole journey to Newcastle I scarce observed her to laugh or even smile once. Nor did she ever complain of anything or appear moved in the least with those trying circumstances which many times occurred in our way. A steady seriousness or sadness rather appeared in her whole behaviour and conversation, as became one that felt the burden of sin and was groaning after salvation. In the same spirit, by all I could observe or learn, she continued during her stay at Newcastle. Not long after, her husband removed from thence and wrote to her to follow him. She set out in a ship bound for Hull. A storm met them by the way. The ship sprung a leak. But though it was near the shore, on which many people flocked together, yet the sea ran so exceeding high that it was impossible to make any help. Mrs. S. was seen standing on the deck as the ship gradually sunk, and afterwards hanging by her hands on the ropes till the masts likewise disappeared. Even then for some moments they could observe her, floating upon the waves, till her clothes, which buoyed her up, being thoroughly wet, she sunk—I trust into the ocean of God's mercy.

[41] Mark 1:15.
[42] Ps. 46:10, etc.

April 17. 1742.

1. Jos. Hodges	6. Saml Milburn
. Walter Jones	Jo Burridge
. Tho. Scalefield	Walter Loyd s.
Richd Langman	Birch Batchcomb
Saml Tiler	Jos. Webb
Stephen Gibbs 6	Tho. Andrews 6
2. Will. Osgood	7. Geo. Jos. Ashton
Chas Morgan	Will. Taylor W. Holt.
Robt Lane	Tho. Loveluck
Geo. Broadmead	Saml Butcher
Geo. Orrell 5	Will. Arnold 5.
3. Will. Sander	8. Jos. Carter
Jo Tenant	Jo Harlay
Tho. Pike	John Erwin tr
Jo Creak	Danl Garnault tr
Richd Wadd 2	Edw. Rowison tr W. Bishop
Jo Marks 6	Will. Kendrick S tr
4 Jos. Swain	9. Will. Davis
Jo Meredith	Stephen Dupee
Simon Wood	Abr. Smagg tr
2 Wm Hollingworth W. Loyd	Jo Wilac. W. Chad tr
Tho. Smith s 5	Digby Trim tr 6
5 Robt Oliver tr	10. Tho. Hay
. Henry Thornton	Robert Holt
. Jo Parker	John Head
Will. Barber	James Flemit
Jo Vanderslet tr	Jo Hooper tr
Abr. Williams. 6	Tho. Pollard 6

APPENDIX A

LONDON DIARIES,

September 17, 1738–August 8, 1741

EDITORIAL INTRODUCTION

This edition of Wesley's Works is primarily intended to reproduce the writings which Wesley himself prepared and published for the public. Both for literary and historical purposes, however, it is important to present at least some of the material which lies behind the published work. Wesley's Oxford diaries and memoranda (1725–35) will be published in Volume 32 of this edition; the remainder are presented in association with the published *Journals* for the corresponding periods.

The diaries for 1738–41 are printed in this Appendix; appropriate annotations will be found at the proper place with the published *Journal*. An essay describing the nature, design, and editorial styling of Wesley's private diaries appears in the editorial introduction to the appendix in Volume 18 of this edition (pp. 299-310).

The diary material used in this volume can be described briefly as follows:

London Diary 1, April 1, 1738–October 14, 1739 (with gaps from May 1–September 16, and November 10-21, 1738); on eighty-eight mostly unnumbered leaves, and not in consecutive order; additional notes at front and back in Wesley's hand; Vol. XVII in the Colman Collection, MA.

London Diary 2, October 15, 1739–August 8, 1741 (with gap from November 11, 1739–May 31, 1740); on one-hundred-sixty-one numbered pages; additional notes in back in Wesley's hand; Vol. XIII in the Colman Collection, MA.

Fragment, April 13–May 29, 1740; on nineteen mostly numbered pages in a notebook bound similarly to Georgia Diaries 1 and 3; in the Osborn Collection, Drew University Library, Madison, New Jersey.

For a glossary of terms used in the diary, see 18:308-10 in this edition. The entry, 'con', represents a symbol that probably means 'convinced' or 'convincing'. The equal sign (=) apparently indicates a positive blessing of some sort, associated with various religious activities; it virtually disappears from use after Christmas 1738.

LONDON DIARY 1 (cont.)
17 September 1738—14 October 1739

SUNDAY [SEPTEMBER] 17 [1738]. 5 Dressed; necessary talk (religious); prayed. 6 St Ann's, read Prayers, Sermon, Communion. 8 At Mr Bray's, prayed, sang. 9 Tea, religious talk, sang. 10 St Bennet's, Grace-Church Street, read Prayers. 11 Charles preached. 12.45 Mr Bray's; sang; dinner. 1.30 Meditated upon sermon. 3 St Bennet's, read Prayers, preached. 4 Mrs Sims'. 5 Minories, preached; sang; prayed. 7 At home; supper, read account of Herrnhut; read; religious talk; prayed. 9.15.

MONDAY, SEPTEMBER 18. 6 Dressed; sang; prayed. 8 James Hutton, etc; prayed. 8.30 Mrs Delamotte's, sang. 9 Prayed; tea, religious talk; sang; prayed. 10.30 At home; heard Charles' sermon; writ diary. 11 Religious talk to Mr Fox. 11.45 Walked; met Mr Broughton, religious talk. 1.15 At home; dinner. 2 James Hutton, read of Herrnhut; sang; prayed. 5 Read Prayers; tea; read. 7 Richter's, religious talk; prayed; sang. 8.30 James Hutton's. 9 The band there; sang, etc. 10 At home; supper, religious talk; writ diary. 11.

TUESDAY, SEPTEMBER 19. 6 James Hutton, etc; read of Herrnhut, religious talk. 8 Sang; tea. 9 Transcribed account of Herrnhut. 11 At Newgate, read Prayers; religious talk to the condemned. 12.30 At home; writ account. 1.30 Mr Claggett's, dinner; sang; prayed. 3.30 Mrs Heath's, religious talk; prayed. 5 Mr Clark's, Mr Hollis of Wycombe there, religious talk; tea. 6 He went; religious talk, sang, prayed. 7.30 Bear-yard, prayed, etc. 9.30 Mr Bray's, sang. 10 Supper, religious talk; prayed. 11 Religious talk. 11.15.

WEDNESDAY, SEPTEMBER 20. 6 Sang; writ account of Herrnhut. 8 Tea, religious talk. 9 Writ account. 11 At Newgate, read Prayers, spoke. 12.30 Writ account. 1 Dinner. 2 Account. 3.15 Read Prayers. 4.15 At James Hutton's; shaved. 5 Tea. 5.15 At Mrs Thornbury's, Miss Claggett there; con[vinced?]. 6 At James Hutton's, Mrs Claggett, etc; sang; religious talk; prayed. 8 At Mr Harris', prayed; sang, etc. 9.30 At home; supper, religious talk; prayed. 11.15.

THURSDAY, SEPTEMBER 21. 6 Sang; writ account. 7.15 Read Prayers; Communion. 9 James Hutton's, prayed. 10 At home; tea; account. 11 Mrs Delamotte and Miss H——; sang; religious talk; read account; sang. 1 Account. 1.30 Dinner; account. 3.15 Read Prayers. 4 account. 5.15 Religious talk. 5.30 Mrs Smith's, Mr Wogan, Morgan, etc; tea; useful and necessary talk; prayed, etc (lively zeal, con[vinced]). 7.45 At the Savoy; prayed, etc. 10 At home; eat [ate]; religious talk; prayed. 11.30.

FRIDAY [SEPTEMBER] 22. 6.30 Sang; James Hutton, etc; prayed; religious talk. 8.30 Tea, religious talk; prayed. 9.30 Read my sermon and Mr Bedford's. 3.15 Prayed. 4 At home; at Mr Burton's, Mr Hollis, religious talk; tea. 6 Mrs Sims', Mrs Hind's, religious talk. 6.30 Mrs Capel's, religious talk. 9 Ate; religious talk. 10.30 At home; religious talk; prayed. 11.30.

SATURDAY [SEPTEMBER] 23. 6 Sang; account. 9 Tea; account. 10.45 Newgate; read with Bryan. 11 Read Prayers, preached (lively zeal). 12.30 At Charles Rivington's, religious talk (=). 1 At home; religious talk. 1.30 dinner. 2.30 Charles read letters. 3.15 Read Prayers. 4 At Mr Fish's, necessary talk (religious). 5.30 At home; Henry Delamotte, etc; tea, religious talk; Charles read his sermon. 6.30 Writ diary; Mr Exall's; sang; prayed; preached; prayed (lively zeal). 9.30 At home; supper, religious talk; prayed. 11.

SUNDAY [SEPTEMBER] 24. 5.45 Sang; dressed; St Ann's, read Prayers, Sermon, Communion. 8.30 At home; sang; prayed. 9 Tea, religious talk. 10 St John's Chapel; read Prayers, preached. 1.15 Mrs Metcalf's; sang, religious talk; dinner. 3 St John's, read Prayers, preached. 5.30 Mr Sims', tea, religious talk. 6 In the Minories; sang; prayed; preached. 7.30 At home; sang; Bible; religious talk. 9 Supper, religious talk. 11.

MONDAY [SEPTEMBER] 25. 6.30 Sang; writ to Mr Bedford. 8 Claggett's, religious talk; tea, sang. 9.30 At home; Charles read his journal. 11 Newgate, with Bryan, religious talk; prayed; read Prayers, preached. 1 Charles read journal. 1.30 Mr Claggett's, sang; dinner, religious talk; prayed. 3.30 Charterhouse, religious talk with Mr Agutter. 4 Read Prayers; meditated. 4.45 Religious talk. 5.15 Mr Lyne's; tea, religious talk; sang. 6 James Hutton's, necessary talk (religious). 7 The bands met, prayed, religious talk; sang; prayed for Mrs Claggett; (=). 9.45.

TUESDAY [SEPTEMBER] 26. 3.30 Sang; dressed; prayed. 4.15 Walked; with James Hutton, etc; sang; religious talk. 7.15 Hounslow; sang; tea, religious talk. 8.45 Walked; religious talk; sang. 1 Windsor; Mr Thorold's; prayed; religious talk. 2.30 Dinner. 3 Read account of Herrnhut. 5.15 Mr Michener's; tea; sang; prayed; preached. 8 Read Prayers; Mr Fish's, religious talk; supper. 10.15 Michener's, prayed.

WEDNESDAY [SEPTEMBER] 27. 3.30 Prayed. 4 Walked; sang; religious talk. 6 Longford; tea. 7 Walked; religious talk; sang. 10 Turnham Green; tea. 11 Walked; sang; religious. 1 Mr Wolf's; shaved; religious talk. 2 James Hutton's; dinner. 3.15 At home; religious talk; writ diary. 4 Writ letter. 4.30 Tea. 5 Bow [St Mary-le-Bow]; read Prayers, Mr Hu[tton?] preached! 7 At home; religious talk; supper. 8 Mr Harris'. 9 Prayed, etc; all agreed! 10 Religious talk. 11 Tempted; (=).

THURSDAY [SEPTEMBER] 28. 7 Sang; letter. 8.15 Tea, religious talk. 9 Letter. 11 Newgate; read Prayers. 12 Preached. 1 Mr Lyne's; dinner, religious talk. 2 At home; letter. 4 Writ diary; Mrs and Miss Claggett came; sang; religious talk! 6 Mr Brockmer's; sang; prayed; read, etc. 8.30 At the Savoy; sang, etc. 10.15 At home; supper, religious talk; prayed. 11 Religious talk. 11.30.

FRIDAY [SEPTEMBER] 29. 6.30 Sang; dressed. 7.15 St Dunstan's; read Prayers, Communion. 9 James Hutton's; sang. 10 Prayed; tea, religious talk; letter. 12.30 Met Mr Snowball, religious talk. 1 At home; necessary business. 2 Dinner. 3 Account of Herrnhut. 3.15 Read Prayers. 4 At Mr Fish's, necessary talk (religious). 5.30 Mr Wolf's, religious talk of the band; tea; (=). 6.30 Religious talk with Mrs Jenkins; prayed. 7.15 At home; writ diary. 7.30 Supper. 8 Prayed, etc. 10.15 Religious talk; prayed. 11.30.

SATURDAY [SEPTEMBER] 30. 6 Sang; account of Herrnhut. 8 Mrs Prat's; tea, religious talk; sang. 10 At home; account; writ diary. 11 With Nat Philips at Newgate; read Prayers. 12 Preached; prayed with Bryan. 1 At Mr Philips'; dinner, religious talk. 3 Mrs Bray's, religious and necessary talk. 3.45 Mr Jennings', he in despair, religious talk; prayed. 4 He received! ((faith)). 4.30 Mrs Claggett; sang; prayed; tea; (=). 6.15 Mr Burton's, religious talk. 6.45 Walked. 8 Mr Exall's, prayed, etc. 10 Prayed with Mrs Jenkins. 10.30 At home; religious talk; prayed. 11.

SUNDAY, OCTOBER 1. 6 Religious talk with Charles; sang. 7 Writ diary; Charles read letters. 8 Walked; at Mr Parker's; tea, religious talk. 10 St George's, read Prayers, preached. 12 Communion. 1.30 Mrs H[utton?]'s; dinner, religious talk. 2.45 St George's, read Prayers, preached, baptized. 4.30 Mrs Ironmonger's; many there; tea, religious talk; prayed. 5.30 Mr Sims'; sang, etc. 7.15 Mrs Sims'; sang; supper, prayed. 8.45 At home; sang, etc. 11 Prayed; religious talk. 12.

MONDAY [OCTOBER] 2. 7 Prayed; Charles read letters. 8.15 Tea, religious talk; read Prayers. 9 Charles read letters. 10.30 Writ diary; dressed. 11 Newgate; read Prayers; preached. 1 Necessary business. 1.30 Mr Brockmer's; sang; dinner; sang. 2.30 At home; Charles read. 3 Read Prayers; Mrs C[laggett]'s; sang; religious talk. 5 Mrs Heath's; religious talk; Communion. 6 Mrs Sims', religious talk; tea; sang; prayed. 7.15 Mrs C[laggett]'s; sang. 8 James Hutton's; sang, etc. 9.15 Mrs C[laggett]'s; supper; sang; Bible. 11 Religious talk; sang. 12.30.

TUESDAY [OCTOBER] 3. 6.15 Dressed; read Bible to Miss C[laggett]; sang; Will Delamotte; sang; prayed. 8.15 At Mrs Delamotte's; sang; tea, necessary talk (religious); prayed. 9.45 Necessary and religious talk. 11 At the Society. 1 At home; writ diary; dinner; slept. 3 Read Prayers; at Mrs West's. 4 Tea, religious talk, sang, prayed. 5.45 At Mrs Sims', she not there. 6.15 At home; necessary talk; at Mr Thacker's, necessary talk (religious); Mr and Mrs Bride, religious talk, prayed. 8 The Bear-yard; prayed, etc (=). 10 At home; prayed; religious talk; prayed. 11.

WEDNESDAY [OCTOBER] 4. 6.30 Sang; writ Account. 8 Mrs Sisson's; tea, religious talk. 9 Read verses with Charles. 11 Newgate; read Prayers, preached. 1.30 At Dr Watts', religious talk. 2.30 Walked; sang; religious talk. 3 Islington; read Prayers. 4 At Mr Stonehouse's, (=); sang, religious talk, prayed, tea, religious talk. 5.45 Walked, religious talk. 7 At home; religious talk; supper. 8 Mr Harris', sang, etc (=); religious talk. 11 Prayed.

THURSDAY [OCTOBER] 5. 6 Dressed; necessary talk (religious). 7 Mr Delamotte's, necessary talk (religious). 7.30 In the boat; read; sang. 9 Greenwich; tea, religious talk. 10 Walked with Mr Bray and Will Delamotte; prayed; rain stopped. 11.30 Blendon; sang; prayed. 12.30 Religious talk. 1 Sister Kezzy came; sang; religious talk. 2 Dinner, religious talk with sister Kezzy (=); tea; sang; prayed. 4 Set out; sang, religious talk with Will Delamotte. 5.30 He went. 7.15 At home; supper, religious talk. 8 Mr Brockmer's; read, sang, religious talk. 11.

FRIDAY [OCTOBER] 6. 6.15 Dressed; necessary talk (religious); meditated. 7 St Antholin's; read Prayers, preached. 9 At Mr Hall's, tea, religious talk. 10.15

Mr Mason's, religious talk, sang. 10.30 At home; read with Charles. 11.30 Newgate, preached. 12.45 At home; religious talk with Mrs Musgrove. 1 Set out; read verse. 2.45 At Hoxton, religious talk with Mr Bedford (=). 4 Walked; read. 4.30 Mr Stonehouse's, berrying; dinner, religious talk (=). 5.15 Mrs——'s, religious talk; prayed. 6 Walked. 7 Mr Bray's, necessary talk (religious). 8 Mr Parker's, Wapping; read; sang; prayed. 9.30 Supper. 10 Religious talk; prayed. 11.

SATURDAY [OCTOBER] 7. 6.15 Walked; meditated. 7 Meditated; at home; necessary business. 8 Mrs Claggett, etc; tea, religious talk. 9 Sang; prayed. 10 Religious talk. 11 At James Hutton's, necessary talk (religious). 12 Mr Summers', sang, prayed, etc. 2 Dinner. 3 Sang; prayed, etc. 5.30 Tea, religious talk. 6 Sang, prayed, etc. 8 Mr Exall's, sang, prayed, etc. 10 At home; supper, religious talk. 10.30 Prayed. 11.15.

SUNDAY [OCTOBER 8]. 5 Dressed; prayed. 6 St Lawrence's, read Prayers, Sermon, Communion. 8.45 At home. 9 Tea, religious talk; prayer. 10 At the Savoy; meditated. 10.30 Read Prayers, preached. 1 Mr Jones', dinner, religious talk; writ; prayed. 3 Bridewell, Mr Hutchings preached. 4.15 Mrs Claggett's, sang, tea, religious talk. 5.15 At Mr Sims', sang, etc. 7.30 At home; supper, sang, etc. 11.

MONDAY [OCTOBER 9]. 6.15 Dressed; prayed. 7 Mrs Claggett's, tea, sang, religious talk. 8 Mr Jennings', tea, sang, religious talk. 9.30 Walked with Mr Bray, Jennings, and Shaw, religious talk, sang, prayed. 11.30 They went, religious talk with Mr Shaw, sang. 2 Uxbridge; dinner. 3 Walked, religious talk, sang. 7 Wycombe; Mr Hollis not [there]. 7.30 Mr Crouch's. 8 Tea, religious talk, prayed, religious talk. 11.

TUESDAY [OCTOBER 10]. 6.15 Tea, religious talk, prayed. 8 Shaw went; walked; verses; sang. 10.30 At the Hut, religious talk. 11.45 Walked; read account of New England. 12.15 Tetsworth; dinner. I Walked; read; meditated. 4.30 Mr Sarney's, necessary talk (religious). 5.30 Read Prayers. 6 At Mr Evans', tea, necessary talk (religious). 8 Washington and Combes, sang, prayed. 9 Mr Fox, sang, prayed. 10.45 At Mr Combes', religious talk. 11.

WEDNESDAY [OCTOBER] 11. 6 Dressed; prayed. 7 At College; meditated; necessary talk; read Prayers. 8 At Mr Vesey's, tea, mostly religious talk. 9 Mr Combes', Mrs Ford, etc. 10 Necessary business. 11 Mrs Fox's, prayed. 11.30 Necessary business; necessary talk. 12 At home; meditated; writ diary; necessary business. 1.45 Writ notes. 3 At Mr Combes' tea, religious talk. 4 Sang; writ notes. 5.15 Meditated; read Prayers. 6 Mrs Fox's, Mrs Ford, etc, sang, prayed. 7 At Mr Watson's, Greek Testament, religious talk, prayed. 9 Mr Combes'; supper; prayed. 10.30.

THURSDAY [OCTOBER] 12. 6.30 Prayed; necessary business. 7 Meditated; read Prayers; necessary business. 8.30 Mr Evans', prayed. 9 Tea; writ. 10 At home; writ to brother Samuel, my mother, Charles Kinchin. 12 Mr Gambold, dinner, religious talk. 1.30 At Mr Wells', religious talk. 2 At Mr Evans Cl——, religious talk, tea. 4 Writ diary; Garden, Greek Testament; meditated; prayed. 5.30 Read Prayers. 6 Common Room, good talk (necessary); supper. 7 Mrs Ford's, sang, etc, Mrs Plat comforted. 8.15 Necessary business. 9 Mrs Fox's, Mrs Cleminger, etc, sang, prayed. 11.45.

FRIDAY [OCTOBER] 13. 6.30 Prayed; meditated; Greek Testament. 7.30 Read Prayers. 8 Mrs Ford's, Mr Sarney, etc. 9 Tea, religious talk, sang, prayed. 9.45 At home; writ to Dr Koker, to Ingham. 12 Garden, corrected prayers. 1 Writ verses. 2.45 Mr Sarney's, prayed, tea, religious talk. 4 At Mr Wells', religious talk, prayed. 5 At home; Mr Evans, religious talk. 5.30 Read Prayers. 6 Mr Fox's, Mrs Ford, etc, sang, prayed. 7 Mr Washington's, Turner, etc, prayed, religious talk, prayed. 9 At home; writ notes. 11.15.

SATURDAY [OCTOBER] 14. 6.30 Sang; writ. 7.30 Mrs Fox's, Mrs Hall, etc, tea, religious talk. 8.15 Read Prayers; writ to Count Zinzendorf, to Herrnhut. 11 Garden; read notes. 12 Dinner, good talk. 12.45 Writ diary; sang. 1 Mrs Fox's, read Bible, sang, prayed. 2 Writ notes. 3 Garden; Mr Hutchins, good talk. 3.30 Greek Testament. 4 Read Prayers; Mrs Perkins, religious talk, prayed. 5 Greek Testament; meditated; prayed. 6 Mrs Ford's, tea, religious talk, sang. 7 Mrs Mears, religious talk, prayed. 7.30 At home; writ notes; writ to Allicock. 10 Greek Testament. 11.

SUNDAY [OCTOBER] 15. 6.15 Sang; dressed. 7 Prayed. 7.30 Mrs Fox's, sang, tea, prayed. 8.30 Meditated. 9 At the Castle, read Prayers, preached, Communion. 12 Mr Evans', dinner, religious talk, prayed, 1 Mrs Fox's, sang, etc. 2 Sermon. 3 At the Castle, read Prayers, preached. 4.30 Mr Sarney's, tea. 5 At home; prayed, meditated, 6 Mrs Fox's, sang, etc. 7 Mrs Mears', sang, etc. 8 Mrs Ford's, ate. 8.15 At Mr Jones', Bible, prayed. 9.15 Writ diary; writ. 11.

MONDAY, OCTOBER 16. 6 Meditated. 6.30 Walked with Watson, religious talk, sang. 8.30 Stanton Harcourt. 10 Sang, tea, religious talk, prayed. 12 Walked, religious talk, sang. 2 Fox's, prayed, sang. 3 Tea, religious talk. 4 Walked with Watson, religious talk. 4.30 Mr Hurst's, religious talk, prayed (=). 5.30 Mrs West's, religious talk. 6.15 Mrs Ford's, sang, etc. 7 St Ole's, sang, etc. 8 Mr Sarney's, Greek Testament. 9 Supper, religious talk. 10 At home; necessary business. 10.30 Writ diary.

TUESDAY [OCTOBER] 17. 6 Dressed; prayed. 6.30 Mrs Fox's, sang, tea, religious talk, prayed. 8.15 Walked, prayed. 10 Greek Testament. 12 Ate, Greek Testament. 5 Wycombe, at Mr Hollis', religious talk; tea. 8 Prayed. 9 Supper, religious talk, prayed. 11.15.

WEDNESDAY [OCTOBER] 18. 6 Prayed, religious talk, tea. 8.30 Walked, sang, prayed, Greek Testament. 12.30 Ate, Greek Testament. 6 At Mr Bray's, religious talk, supper. 7 James Hutton, etc, prayed, religious talk, sang. 8 Religious talk, prayed. 10.

THURSDAY [OCTOBER] 19. 6 Prayed, religious talk with Hutchings, tea, sang. 8.30 James Hutton's, religious talk, sang. 9 He went; at the Room, necessary talk. 10.30 At Mr Fish's, necessary talk. 11 At Mrs Sims' with Charles, necessary talk (religious), prayed, sang. 1 At Mrs Hind's with James Hutton and Charles. 2 Mrs Sims', dinner. 3 Mr Clark's, prayed; at Mr Bedford's, necessary talk (religious). 4.15 Read Prayers; necessary talk (religious). 6.15 At home; religious talk, tea. 7 James Hutton's, religious talk. 8 Savoy, prayed, etc. 11.15 At home; prayed. 11.30.

FRIDAY [OCTOBER] 20. 6.15 Sang, prayed, writ verse. 8.15 At Mr Easy's, religious talk, tea. 9.45 At the Bishop of London's, prayed with Charles. 10.15 Necessary talk (religious) with the Bishop (=). 11 At Mr Hutton's, he not [there]; prayed. 12.15 At James Hutton's, necessary talk. 12.45 At home; writ diary. 1 Writ notes. 3 Walked. 3.30 Islington, read Prayers. 4 Mr Stonehouse's; ate, religious talk, sang. 5 Visited, religious talk, prayed. 6 Walked, religious talk, prayed. 7 James Hutton's, tea. 7.30 Westminster with the Society, prayed, etc. 10 At home; Mr Piers, etc; religious talk, prayed. 11 Writ diary.

SATURDAY, OCTOBER 21. 6.30 Sang. 7 Writ account of Herrnhut. 8.30 Tea, religious talk, prayed. 9.15 Account. 11 Newgate Prison, preached. 12.30 At Mrs Claggett's. 1 Mr Piers, etc, dinner. 2 Religious talk, sang, prayed. 2.30 At home; account. 3.30 James Hutton, tea, religious talk; account. 5.15 James Hutton's; shaved. 6.15 Mr Exall's. 7 Tea, religious talk. 8 Sang, etc. 10.30 At home; necessary business; necessary talk (religious); prayed. 11.15.

SUNDAY [OCTOBER] 22. 5.45 Dressed; St Ann's, read Prayers, Sermon, Communion. 8.30 Prayed, sang. 9 At Mr Hodges', sang, tea, religious talk, sang, prayed. 10.30 St George's, read Prayers, preached. 12.30 Mrs Metcalf's, sang. 1 Dinner. 2.45 Shadwell, read Prayers, preached. 4.30 At Mrs Ironmonger's, sang, tea, religious talk, sang. 5.15 Mr Sims', sang, etc. 7 At home; supper, sang, etc. 10.45.

MONDAY [OCTOBER] 23. 6 Sang, prepared hymns. 8.30 At Mrs Duzzy's, tea, religious talk. 9.30 Mr P Sims', necessary talk. 10 Mrs. Sims', religious talk with Mrs Loyd. 10 Necessary talk with Charles. 10.30 At home; hymns. 12.15 Writ diary; account of Herrnhut. 1 Dinner; carried letters. 3.30 At sister [Hetty] Wright's, tea, mostly religious talk; at Mr Fish's, necessary talk. 5.45 At Mrs West's, sang, etc. 7 Tea, religious talk. 8 At James Hutton's, sang, religious talk, prayed. 10.30 At Mrs West's, religious talk, prayed. 11.15.

TUESDAY [OCTOBER] 24. 5.45 Dressed, prayed, tea. 6.45 Walked with West, sang, religious talk, read Jennings upon preaching. 10 Blendon, religious talk, sang, prayed. 11 Bexley, sang, religious talk. 12 Read account of Herrnhut. 2 Mrs Delamotte, Miss Hetty, etc; dinner. 2.45 Explained Bible, prayed. 3.30 Set out; Mr Wright. 6.30 At home; supper. 7 Sang, etc. 8 Bear-yard, sang, etc. 10.30 At home; religious talk, prayed. 11.

WEDNESDAY [OCTOBER] 25. 5.45 Account of Herrnhut. 8 James Hutton, went to Mr Dubart's, prayed. 9 Tea, religious talk, prayed. 10.30 Mr Claggett's, he convinced. 11.30 Newgate, religious talk, prayed, preached. 12.30 At home; religious talk with Mrs Woods. 1 Walked. 1.15 At Stonehouse's, sang, religious talk, dinner, sang, religious talk. 4 At home; tea, meditated. 4.30 At Mr Holland's. 5 Basingshaw, read Prayers, preached. 7 At home; sang, prayed, supper, religious talk. 8 James Ha——'s, sang, etc. 10.15 At home; religious talk. 11 Prayed, read Mr Wh[itefield]'s journal. 12.

THURSDAY, OCTOBER 26. 6.30 Sang; Account of Herrnhut. 8.30 At Mr Easy's, tea, religious talk, prayed. 9.15 Account of Herrnhut. 11 Newgate, prayed with Bryan. 11.15 Read Prayers, preached. 12.45 Writ diary; dinner, religious talk. 2 Account of Herrnhut. 3.15 Read Prayers. 4 At Mr Rivington's, religious talk (necessary). 5 Mr Bray's, tea; Mrs Claggett's, etc, religious talk. 6 Account of

Herrnhut. 7.30 James Hutton's, religious talk, tea. 8 Savoy. 10.15 At home; religious talk. 11 Prayed.

F RIDAY [OCTOBER] 27. 6 Account of Herrnhut. 7 St Antholin's, read Prayers, preached. 8.45 Necessary talk. 9 Mrs Claggett's, sang, tea, sang, read Account of Herrnnut. 11 Account of Herrnhut. 11.30 Newgate, read Prayers, preached. 12.30 With Bryan, religious talk (=), prayed. 1 Dressed; writ diary. 1.30 Walked with Mr Bray. 2.30 At Mr. Stonehouse's, sang, religious talk. 3.15 Read Prayers. 4 Dinner, religious talk, prayed. 5.30 Visited, prayed. 6.30 At home; religious talk, tea. 8 At Wapping, sang, etc. 10 Supper, prayed. 11.15.

S ATURDAY [O CTOBER] 28. 6.15 Dressed, walked. 7.15 St Dunstan's, read Prayers, Communion; necessary talk. 9 James Hutton's, prayed, sang, tea, religious talk. 10.45 At home; religious talk with ——. 11.15 Account of Herrnhut. 12.15 Writ diary, necessary talk. 12.30 Walked. 1 Mrs May's, religious talk. 2 Dinner, sang, prayed. 4 At home; tea, religious talk. 4.30 Writ letters. 6.30 Mr. Exall's, tea, religious talk. 7 Mr Goole's, religious talk with me (?). 8 Sang, etc. 10.15 At home; ate, prayed. 11.15.

S UNDAY [OCTOBER] 29. 6 Dressed. 6.15 St Ann's, read Prayers, Sermon, Communion. 8.15 Sang, prayed, dressed. 9 At Mrs Metcalf's, tea; walked, meditated. 10 Islington, read Prayers, preached. 12.15 Mr Stonehouse's, sang, dinner, sang, prayed. 3 At London Wall, read Prayers, preached. 4.30 Mr Savage's, tea, sang, prayed. 5.30 St Bride's, prayed, sang, Bible, sang, prayed. 7.45 At home; supper, religious talk. 8.30 Sang, etc. 10 Religious talk. 10.30 (=).

Προσεδέχετο καὶ αὐτὸς τὴν βασιλείαν τοῦ θεοῦ. Luke 23:51 ('Who also himself waited for the kingdom of God').

ἐκ τῶν ἔργων ἡ πίστις ἐτελειώθη. James 2:22 ('By works was faith made perfect').

M ONDAY, O CTOBER 30. 5.30 Sang, writ to brother Samuel. 8.30 Mrs Hind's, tea, religious talk with Mr Broughton, prayed. 10.30 Mrs Sims', religious talk with Mrs Loyd, etc. 11.30 Religious talk with James Hutton; at Newgate, read Prayers, preached, visited. 12.30 At home; writ diary; necessary business. 1.30 Dinner, religious talk. 2.45 Transcribed letters. 4.30 W[illiam] D[elamotte]; at Mrs Claggett's, religious talk. 5.45 At Mrs West's. 6 Sang, etc; tea. 7.30 Necessary talk (religious) with Mrs Manwaring. 8.15 James Hutton's, necessary talk (religious). 9 Mr Bray's, the bands met, sang, prayed, necessary talk (religious), sang, prayed. 10.30 Prayed. 10.45.

T UESDAY [O CTOBER] 31. 5.15 Sang; letters. 8.15 Mr Easy's, with Mrs Musgrove, tea, religious talk, prayed. 9.30 Transcribed letters. 11 Writ diary; Newgate, read Prayers, preached. 12.30 At home; letters. 1.15 At Mr Jennings' with Charles, sang, religious talk. 2 Dinner. 2.30 At Mr Sherman's, religious talk. 2.15 Read Prayers. 4 Necessary talk; with Mr Ingham, religious talk, at James Hutton's. 6.15 At home; supper, religious talk. 7 Sang, etc. 8.15 Bear-yard, sang, etc (=). 10.15 Religious talk with Goole (=). 10.30 At home; necessary talk (religious) with Charles, prayed. 11.15.

Gal. 3:8, 9 Προϊδοῦσα [δὲ] ἡ γραφή. ('The Scripture foreseeing [that God would justify the heathen through faith . . .]')

Why art Thou so heavy, O my soul, etc [cf. Ps. 42:5].

WEDNESDAY, NOVEMBER 1. 5.30 Sang, prayed. 6 Letter. 7.15 Read Prayers, Communion. 9 James Hutton's, prayed. 9.30 At Mr Clark's, tea, religious talk. 11 At home; necessary business; writ diary; walked; necessary business; necessary talk. 12.30 Newgate. 1.30 Mr Stonehouse's with Ingham, etc, sang, dinner. 2 Religious talk, sang. 3.15 Read Prayers. 4 Religious talk with Ingham (=). 5.15 Sang, tea, religious talk. 6.30 At home; with the bands. 7 Tea; Southwark, sang (=). 8 Bible, etc (=). 10.15 James Hutton's, religious talk with Ingham, etc, prayed. 12.

THURSDAY [NOVEMBER] 2. 5 Prayed, religious talk, walked with Mr Ingham and James Hutton, religious talk. 6.30 At Mr Cox's, religious talk, prayed. 7.30 At home; necessary talk (religious); writ diary. 8.30 At Mr Hall's. 9 Prayed, tea, religious talk, prayed. 11.15 At home; writ diary; writ. 12.15 Religious talk. 1 At Mr Clark's, Mr Stonehouse, etc, dinner, sang, religious talk. 4.15 Meditated; at home. 5 Transcribed letters. 6 Gutter Lane, Mr Wogan, etc. 7 At home; letter. 8.15 Savoy, sang, etc. 10.15 At home. 10.45.

FRIDAY, NOVEMBER 3. 5.45 Sang, meditated, dressed. 7 St Antholin's, read Prayers, preached. 9 At Mrs Sisson's, prayed, tea, religious talk. 10.15 At home; religious talk with Mr Stonehouse. 11 Newgate, read Prayers; Mr Gu[?] and Mr Rawlins preached. 1.30 At home; writ diary; writ notes. 3 At Mrs May's, sang, prayed, religious talk. 4 Dinner, sang, prayed. 5.45 At Mr Clark's, religious talk, prayed. 7.30 At Mr Parker's, Bible, sang. 8.15 Read Prayers. 9.15 At Mr Parker's, supper, religious talk, Bible, sang, prayed. 11.15.

SATURDAY [NOVEMBER] 4. 6.30 Sang, prayed. 7.30 At home; writ diary. 8 Necessary talk; at Mr Easy's, tea, religious talk, prayed. 9.30 At home; writ to sister Emily. 10.45 Newgate, prayed, with Bryan. 11.15 With James Hill, religious talk, prayed. 12 At Mr Summers', sang, etc. 2 Dinner; at the Room. 3 At Mr Summers', sang, etc. 5 Religious talk, tea, James Hutton came. 6 Sang, etc. 7.15 At Mr Exall's, tea, religious talk. 8 Sang, etc. 10.30 At home; religious talk, prayed. 11.15.

SUNDAY [NOVEMBER] 5. 6.30 Sang; the bands met; chose leaders by lot, sang, prayed. 8.30 Tea, religious talk. 9.15 Meditated upon sermon. 10 St Botolph's, read Prayers, preached, Communion. 2.30 Islington, dinner, sang. 2.45 Read Prayers, preached. 5.15 At Mr Sherman's, sang, tea. 6 St Clement's, read Prayers. 8 At Mr Bray's, supper. 8.30 Sang, prayed (=, +). 11.15.

MONDAY [NOVEMBER] 6. 6 Sang, writ diary, necessary business. 7 Prepared. 8 James Hutton, etc, necessary talk (religious). 9 Tea, Richter and Pisch, religious talk. 10.15 At the Room. 11 Newgate with Charles, Ingham, etc, read Prayers, preached. 12 At Mr Chapman's with Ingham, etc, sang, religious talk. 2 Dinner, religious talk. 3 Religious talk with Mrs Loyd, Harper, and Mary Hanson. 4 Prayed. 4.30 At Mr Cook's, religious talk (=). 5.45 At Mrs West's, sang, etc. 6.45 Tea, religious talk. 8 James Hutton's, religious talk, Mr Seward. 8.45 At Mr Tolley's, he read, etc. 10.15 At home; ate, religious talk, prayed. 11. Mrs Drewit.

TUESDAY, NOVEMBER 7. 6 Sang, writ. 7.30 Walked. 8 At Mrs Duzzy's, tea, religious talk, sang, prayed. 10 At Mrs Ironmonger's, religious talk, sang. 11 At

Mr Sims', necessary talk. 11.45 Newgate. 12 Religious talk with Bryan, prayed. 1 At Mrs Claggett's, religious talk, sang. 1.30 At home; dinner. 2.30 In Whitecross Street, religious talk, prayed. 3.15 Writ diary. 4 Newgate, read Prayers, preached. 5.15 At home; tea, religious talk. 7 Sang, etc. 8 At Bear-yard, sang, etc (=). 10.30 At home; religious talk, prayed. 11.

WEDNESDAY [NOVEMBER] 8. 5.45 Sang, dressed, necessary talk. 6.30 Newgate with Charles, all believed (=). 7 Communion, read Prayers, preached. 9 In the coach, meditated, sang. 10 At St Giles', tea. 10.30 Tyburn; meditated. 11 In the cart, prayed. 12 Sang, prayed, all cheerful. 12 They died; prayed. 1 Preached to the mob. 1 At St Giles', walked. 1.45 At home; necessary talk; Islington. 2 Religious talk, dinner, prayed. 4 Tea, religious talk. 5.15 Basingshaw, preached. 7 At Mr Richter's, at the Love-feast, ate, religious talk, sang. 8.15 At J Harris', sang, etc. 10.15 At home; religious talk, prayed. 11.

THURSDAY [NOVEMBER] 9. Sang; meditated. 7 St Antholin's, read Prayers, preached. 9 At Mr Clark's. 10 Tea, religious talk. 11 James Hutton's, religious talk with Ingham. 12.15 At home.

[No entries until November 22, six and one-half pages later, originally blank allowing for two days' entry per page, later filled in with entries for October 1739.]

WEDNESDAY, NOVEMBER 22. 4 Writ to Dr. Koker, Viney, Lelong, Moscheros, Töltschig. 7 Religious talk (necessary) with Watson; he very heavy! 8 Read Prayers. 8.15 Writ hymns. 2 Tea; Charles Kinchin, religious talk. 2.30 Bocardo, religious talk, prayed. 3.15 Writ hymns. 3.45 At Mr Carter's, religious talk. 4.30 Hymns. 5.15 Prayed, private prayer. 6 At Mrs Fox's, sang, prayed. 7.30 Washington's, religious talk, prayed. 9.30.

THURSDAY [NOVEMBER] 23. 4 Hymns. 7.15 Read Prayers; writ to R. Aldworth. 8.30 At Mrs Mears'. 9 Tea, sang. 10 Hymns. 11 Meditated. 12 Dinner, read notes. 1.30 Hymns. 3.15 At the Castle, read Prayers, preached. 4.45 At home; Charles and Charles Delamotte! prayed, religious talk. 5.15 At Mrs Ford's, supper, sang. 6 With Charles, necessary talk. 7 At Mrs Ford's, sang, etc. 8 At home; necessary talk (religious); prayed, sang. 10.

FRIDAY [NOVEMBER] 24. 4 Sang, religious talk, hymns. 6 Sang with Charles Delamotte, prayed, religious talk. 7.30 Read Prayers. 8 At Mrs H[utton]'s, sang, tea; Charles, Charles Kinchin, and Charles Delamotte, religious talk. 9 At Mr Sarney's. 10 At home with him, prayed, religious talk (necessary). 11.30 Necessary business. 12 Writ to brother Ingham and James Hutton. 1 Dressed; at Mrs Townsend's. 2 Castle, sang. 2.30 At Mrs Fox's, religious talk. 3 Tea, sang, religious talk. 3.30 Writ to Mr Fox. 4.15 Necessary talk (religious) with Charles and Charles Delamotte. 5 Read verse. 5.30 Read Prayers. 6 At Mrs Fox's, prayed. 7 At Mrs Ford's, supper. 7.30 Washington's, Bible. 9.30.

SATURDAY [NOVEMBER] 25. 4 Sang; writ notes; Bible; sang. 6 Read History of the French Prophets. 7 Religious talk; Turner came, tea. 8 Read Prayers; Watson, religious talk, prayed. 9.30 Religious talk, sang. 11 Charles Kinchin, religious talk. 12 Dinner, slept. 1 At Mrs Fox's, sang, etc. 2 Bocardo, religious talk, prayed. 3 Visited, religious talk, prayed. 4 Read Prayers, religious talk. 6 At Mrs Fox's, tea, religious talk. 7 At home; Jeffrys and Turner, began the Acts. 9.15 Prayed, religious talk. 10.

SUNDAY [NOVEMBER] 26. 4.45 Sang, prayed, religious talk. 6.30 At Mrs Fox's, prayed, tea, religious talk, sang, prayed. 7.30 Read Prayers, Communion. 9 Writ to James Hutton. 10 Religious talk with Charles Delamotte. 11.30 Meditated. 12 Dinner, religious talk. 1 At Mrs Fox's, sang, etc. 2 At Sermon. 3 At Castle, read Prayers, preached. 4.45 At Mrs Fox's, writ for her, tea, religious talk. 6 Sang, etc. 7 At Mears', sang, etc. 8 At home; Turner and Charles Delamotte, sang, religious talk. 9.30.

MONDAY, NOVEMBER 27. 4 Prayed; writ to Mr Fish, Summers, J Harris, James Hutton. 6 Tea, religious talk. 7 Charles Delamotte went; read Prayers. 8 At Mrs Fox's, necessary talk (religious). 8.45 Walked, meditated. 10.30 At Mr Gambold's, Charles Kinchin and Charles, religious talk, sang. 1.30 Communion. 2 Dinner, sang. 3 Walked, meditated. 5.15 At home; meditated; read Prayers. 6 At Mrs Fox's, tea, religious talk. 7 At N Reeves', sang, etc. 8 At home; necessary business; meditated. 8.30 Charles and Charles Kinchin, necessary talk (religious), prayed. 9.30.

Gal. 6:14-16. Ἐμοὶ [δὲ] μὴ γένοιτο καυχᾶσθαι . . .
Acts 4:11. Οὗτός ἐστιν ὁ λίθος ὁ ἐξουθενηθεὶς . . .
Luke 2:40. Τὸ δὲ παιδίον ηὔξανε, καὶ ἐκραταιοῦτο πνεύματι, . . .
John 2:3, 4. Οὔπω ἥκει ἡ ὥρα μου.

Charles Delamotte

In this you are better than you was at Savannah: you know that you was then quite wrong. But you are not yet right. You know that you was then blind. But you do not yet see.

I doubt not but God will bring you to the right foundation. But I have no hope for you on your present foundation. It is as different from the true, as the right hand from the left. You have all to begin anew.

I have observed all your words and actions, and I see you are of the same spirit still. You have a simplicity. But it is a simplicity of your own. It is not the simplicity of Christ. You think you do not trust in your own works. But you do trust in your own works and your own righteousness. You do not yet believe in, or build on, the rock Christ.

Your present freedom from sin is only a temporary suspension of, not a deliverance from it. And your peace is not a true peace. If death were to approach, you would find all your fears return.

But I am forbid to say any more. My heart sinks in me like a stone.

TUESDAY, NOVEMBER 28. 4 Sang, prayed; writ sermon. 5 Slept. 7 Necessary talk (religious); read Prayers. 8 Charles Kinchin, tea, religious talk. 9 Mr Chickley, good talk (religious), tea. 10.45 Necessary talk; dressed. 11.15 Garden, meditated. 12 Dinner; writ notes. 1 Charles, read the Homily. 1.45 At Mrs Fox's, religious talk, prayed. 2.30 With Charles Kinchin at Mr Watson's, religious talk, prayed for him (=). 3.30 At Mrs Stanton's, her son dead, religious talk, prayed. 4 At home; Watson, Charles, and Charles Kinchin, prayed (=). 4.30 At Mrs Fox's, religious talk. 5 At home; meditated, sang. 5.30 Read Prayers. 6 At Mrs Fox's, supper. 6.45 Sang, etc. 8 At Mr Evans', sang, etc. 9.30.

WEDNESDAY [NOVEMBER] 29. 4 Sang; sermon; Garden. 5 Prayed, sang, Spanish, sermon. 7.15 Read Prayers. 8 At Charles Kinchin's. 9 Mr Watson, Washington, Jeffrys, Charles, tea, religious talk and prayed. 9.30 At home; sermon; necessary business. 12 Sermon. 12.45 Mr Carter of London and [Mr] King, religious talk. 1.30 Tea, Watson came, prayed. 2.30 Walked; meditated. 3.15 At Sarah Hurst's, religious talk, ate, prayed; John Bray's letter, prayed. 4.30 Walked; meditated. 5 At home; necessary business; writ; meditated. 5.45 At Mrs Fox's, religious talk, sang. 6 Charles and Charles Kinchin, prayed. 7 At Charles Kinchin's, supper, Watson, etc. 8 Greek Testament. 9.15 At home; prayed. 9.45.

THURSDAY [NOVEMBER] 30. 4.45 Sang, prayed. 6 Writ to brother Samuel. 6.45 Watson came, tea, religious talk, sang, prayed. 7.30 Letter. 8.15 Read Prayers. 9 Letter. 10 St Mary's. 11 Letter. 11.30 Writ notes. 12 Necessary talk with Mr Sarney. 12.15 At Mrs Ford's. 1 Charles Kinchin, dinner, sang, religious talk. 1.15 At home; Charles Kinchin and Mrs Fox. 2 Read Mr Bedford's sermon, tea. 3.30 Castle, read Prayers, preached. 5 At home; Mr Chickley, necessary talk (religious). 5.30 At Mrs Fox's, religious talk, sang, supper. 6.45 At Mrs Ford's, sang, etc. 8 St Clement's, sang, etc. 9.15 At home; prayed.

FRIDAY, DECEMBER 1. 4.30 Prayed, sang, writ to Hutchins. 6 Watson, Greek Testament. 7.30 Read Prayers; at Mrs Fox's, Charles Kinchin, etc, tea, sang, prayed. 10.30 At Mr Sarney's, religious talk; prayed with Charles Kinchin. 11 Writ to my mother. 11.15 Necessary business; read Newcomb. 12 Garden, prayed. 1 Prayed with Charles. 2 At M—n Jervas', religious talk. At Mr Watson's, tea, prayed, religious talk, prayed. 4.15 At home; writ to James Hutton. 5.30 Read Prayers. 6 At Mrs Fox's, prayed; Mrs Ford (Fox?) sick of love (life?)! 7 At home; Jeffrys, etc, Greek Testament. 9 Prayed. 9.30.

SATURDAY, DECEMBER 2. 4.30 Sang, writ to sister Emily. 6 Necessary business; Watson, Greek Testament. 7.15 Jeffrys, religious talk, tea. 8.15 Read Prayers; hymns. 11.45 Garden, meditated. 12 Dinner, sang; hymns. 1 At Mrs Fox's, sang, etc. 2.30 Bocardo; at Mr Evans', religious talk, prayed. 3.15 At the Castle, read Prayers. 4.15 At home; prayed, letters, writ to Charles Delamotte. 5.15 Prayed with Charles. 5.30 At Mrs Fox's, sang, religious talk, tea; Charles came, sang, religious talk. 7 At Washington's, religious talk, Greek Testament, prayed. 9 Writ diary, sang, necessary talk. 9.30.

SUNDAY [DECEMBER] 3. 4 Sang, prayed, Greek Testament. 5.45 Writ to Stonehouse. 6.30 At Mrs Fox's, tea, sang. 7.30 Read Prayers, Communion. 9 Sang; writ to Sympson, to Marshall at Jena. 10.30 Bocardo, read Prayers. 11.15 Garden, meditated, writ diary. 12 Dinner, prayed. 1 At Mrs Fox's, sang, etc. 2 Sermon. 3 At the Castle, read Prayers, preached. 4.30 At home; read letter. 4.45 Meditated, sang. 5.30 Tea. 6 At Mears', sang, etc. 7.30 At home; Washington, etc, Greek Testament, prayed. 9.45.

Ezekiel [33] verse 2 etc.

Σὺ οὖν κακοπάθησον, ὡς καλὸς στρατιώ της Ἰησοῦ Χριστοῦ. [2 Timothy 2:3]

MONDAY [DECEMBER] 4. 4 Read Prayers, sang, German, Spanish, Italian. 6.15 Watson, Greek Testament. 7.30 Read Prayers. 8 Tea with Charles, religious talk. 9.15 Writ to Gottschalck, etc. 11 Garden, meditated, read, religious talk with Hughes and J Mears. 12 Dinner; Mrs Fox, religious talk, sang, prayed. 1 Watson and Washington, prayed, read Account of Georgia. 3 Set out, prayed. 3.45 Cowley, religious talk with S[arah] H[urst]. 4.15 Prayed. 4.30 Walked, meditated. 5.30 At home; tea, religious talk. 6.30 Writ diary; at N Reeves', sang, etc. 8 At home; Watson and Washington, religious talk, sang. 9.30.

TUESDAY [DECEMBER] 5. 4 Sang; necessary business; prayed. 5.15 Charles, read. 6.15 Watson, Greek Testament. 6.45 Chickley, tea, religious talk. 7.30 Read Prayers. 8 Sermon. 11.30 Mrs Fox, religious talk. 12 Dinner. 12.30 Sang, religious talk. 1.15 At the Workhouse, religious talk with Mears, prayed. 1.30 Prayed with all. 2 Convocation. 2.45 At the Castle, read Prayers. 4 At Mrs Plat's, religious talk, he came, religious talk, prayed. 4.45 At Mrs Fox's, religious talk, sang. 5.30 Read Prayers. 6 Tea with Charles. 6.30 At Mrs Fox's, sang, etc. 8 At Mrs Evans', sang, etc. 9.15 At home; sang. 9.30.

WEDNESDAY, DECEMBER 6. 4.30 Sang, prayed. 5.30 Writ sermon. 7.30 Read Prayers. 8 At Mrs Fox's, sang. 9 Tea, sang, prayed. 9.30 At Home; sermon. 1.15 Read; Greek Testament. 2 At Bocardo, read Prayers, spoke. 3.15 At Sarah Jervas', religious talk. 4.15 At home; Mr Wells, tea, religious talk. 5.15 Sang, prayed. 5.30 Read Prayers. 6 At Mrs Fox's, sang, prayed. 7 At home; necessary talk (religious); Watson, etc, Greek Testament, sang, prayed. 9.15.

THURSDAY [DECEMBER] 7. 4 Sang; sermon. 6.15 Prayed. 6.30 Watson, Greek Testament. 7.30 Read Prayers. 8 Mr Checkley [Chickley?], tea, religious talk. 9.15 Sermon. 1.15 With Watson to St Thomas's Workhouse, read Prayers, spoke. 3 Castle, read Prayers, preached. 4.30 At home; Mr Wells, tea, religious talk. 5.30 Mrs Ford's, tea, religious talk. 6.30 Sang, etc. 8 St Clement's, sang, etc. 9 At Mrs Fox's, religious talk, sang. 9.45.

FRIDAY [DECEMBER] 8. 4 Sang; sermon; prayed. 5 Sermon. 6.30 Watson, Greek Testament. 7.30 Read Prayers; sermon. 8.30 At Mr Evans', tea, prayed. 9.45 At home; sermon. 1.30 Writ diary; sins!!!; sermon. 2 Bocardo, read Prayers. 3 At home; Watson, etc, prayed, tea, religious talk. 4 Transcribed sermon. 4.45 At Mrs Fox's, religious talk, sang. 5.30 Read Prayers. 6 At Mrs Fox's, prayed. 7 At home; sermon. 7.30 With the poisoned woman. 8.45 At Mr Fox's, he there, supper, sang, religious talk. 9.45.

SATURDAY [DECEMBER] 9. 4 Sang; sermon. 5 Sang, prayed; sermon. 8 Read letters. 8.15 Read Prayers; at Mr Wells', coffee, religious talk. 10 Garden, read letters. 11 Meditated. 12 Dinner; necessary business. 1 At Mr Fox's, sang, etc. 2 Read account of Georgia and journal. 4 Read Prayers; Mr Wells, tea, religious talk. 5.45 At Mr Fox's. 6 Sang, read journal, tea, religious talk. 7.15 At home; Watson and Washington. 8 Religious talk, read letters, sang, prayed. 9.30.

SUNDAY, DECEMBER 10. 5.15 Prayed, sang. 6.15 Read Prayers. 7 At Mrs Cleminger's, Mr Easy, Charles, and Mrs Fox. 8.15 Necessary business. 9 At the Castle, read Prayers, Charles preached. 11 Communion (thirty-eight there). 12 Dinner; necessary business, sang. 12.45 Necessary business. 1 At Mr Fox's, sang, prayed, Mrs Hall received [the witness of the Spirit]! 2.45 At home; Garden. 4 Read Prayers; meditated. 5 At Mrs Ford's, tea, religious talk, tea. 6 At Mrs Mears', prayed, etc. 7.45 At home; Watson, etc, religious talk, sang. 9.30.

Monday [December] 11. 4 Prayed; necessary business. 5 At Mrs Fox's, sang, prayed, religious talk, sang, prayed. 7 Walked with Mr Easy and Hitchman, religious talk, sang, prayed. 9 Hitchman went, prayed. 11 Tetsworth, dinner. 11.30 Walked, religious talk, prayed. 4 At Mr Crouch's, religious talk, tea. 6.30 At Mr King's, Mr Pierce, religious talk. 8 At Mr Crouch's, supper, religious talk, sang. 11.

Tuesday [December] 12. 5.15 Sang, tea, religious talk, prayed. 6.45 At Mr Pierce's, religious talk. 7 Walked. 9 Prayed. 11.15 Uxbridge, tea, religious talk. 12 Walked, prayed, religious talk. 2 At the Green Man, dinner. 3.30 Walked, religious talk, prayed. 5 At James Hutton's; brother Ingham and Shaw, prayed, religious talk. 5.30 At brother Clark's, tea, religious talk, sang; (success in temporal affairs). 7.45 At Mr Bray's, religious talk (necessary). 8.30 George Whitefield, religious talk, prayed, James Hutton. 9.30 Supper, necessary talk (religious). 11.30 Prayed, religious talk with brother Ingham and George Whitefield. 1.30.

Wednesday [December] 13. 6.45 Prayed, writ notes. 8.30 Tea, necessary talk (religious). 9.30 Religious talk with Mr Bray. 11.15 Read Prayers. 12 Read my sermon to John Bray, religious talk. 1.15 At Mr Wells', religious talk. 2 Dinner. 3.15 At Mr Thelkeld's funeral. 4 Spoke; prayed. 5.15 At Mr Bray's, James Hutton, etc, tea, religious talk. 7 The leaders, religious talk, sang. 8 Religious talk, read Mr Whitefield's sermon. 9.45 Religious talk, supper, George Whitefield, religious talk, prayed. 12.

Thursday [December] 14. 6.45 Sang, dressed, prayed with George Whitefield. 8 Necessary talk (religious), tea. 9.30 Writ to Mr Griffin, Mrs Griffin, Mrs Vanderplank. 11.15 At Newgate, read prayers, preached. 1.30 At Mr Stonehouse's, James Hutton, Ingham, etc, sang, Mr Stonehouse read his sermon. 2.15 Dinner, sang, religious talk. 3.30 Read Prayers. 4 Mrs Vaughan, etc, sang, prayed, tea, religious talk. 5.30 At home; religious talk, read George Whitefield's sermon. 8 At Blackfriars', sang, prayed, etc. 10 At home; supper, sang, prayed, religious talk. 11.45.

Friday [December] 15. 6.45 Dressed; St Antholin's, read Prayers, preached. 9 At Mr Rimer's, tea, religious talk. 10 At home; writ to Hird, Mr Tolly; religious talk. 2.30 Writ diary. 3 Newgate, read Prayers, spoke. 4 At home; tea. 4.45 With Esther Hopson, religious talk. 7 In Southwark, prayed, sang, etc. 9.15 At Bartholomew's Hospital, religious talk, prayed. 10 At home; supper, religious talk, prayed. 12.

Saturday [December] 16. 6.30 Sang, prayed. 7.30 Writ to John Lindal; tea, religious talk; writ notes [see JWJ]. 10.30 At the Hospital, religious talk, prayed. 11.15 At Mr Clark's, necessary talk (religious); shaved. 12.30 At James Hutton's, religious talk, dinner, sang, read letters. 2 At home: prayed, writ to Mr Burnside. 3 At Mr Easy's, writ, read Prayers. 4 Writ diary, read letters. 5 Sang, religious talk. 6.30 At Mr Exall's, Mr Gould, religious talk, tea. 7.45 Sang, etc. 10 At home; prayed, religious talk, sang. 12.

Sunday [December] 17. 5.30 Sang, prayed, dressed. 6.15 At St Michael's, Crooked Lane. 7 Meditated, read Prayers, Communion. 8.30 At Mrs Hind's, George Whitefield, etc, tea, sang, religious talk. 9.45 At Mr Crouther's, religious talk. 10.15 St Katherine's, read Prayers, George Whitefield preached. 12.45 At Mr Crouther's, dinner, religious talk. 2.45 Islington, read Prayers, preached. 4.15 At Mr Stonehouse's, sang, religious talk. 5.30 At St Swithin's. 7.30 At Mrs West's, Esther and Betty Hopson, tea, religious talk. 8.30 Prayed, sang. 10 At home; religious talk, prayed. 11.15.

MONDAY [DECEMBER] 18. 6.30 Prayed, writ ((to Habersham)). 8 At Mrs Duzzy's, prayed, tea, sang, religious talk, prayed. 10 At home; writ to Habersham and Mr Garden. 12.30 At Mr Clark's, religious talk. 1 Dinner, religious talk, prayed. 2.30 At Mrs Howman's, religious talk, prayed. 3.30 At the Hospital, religious talk. 4 At Mr Brockmer's, Richter, etc., religious talk, sang, tea. 5.30 James Hutton's, religious talk. 6 Visited Betty. 6.30 At Mrs Wolf's, in the band, sang, religious talk, tea. 8 James Hutton's, in our band. 10.15 At home; George Whitefield, read letters. 11.15 Prayed. 11.30.

TUESDAY, DECEMBER 19. 5.45 Sang, prayed; writ to sister Kezzy. 7 At brother Clark's, Oxlee, Wolf, Shaw, Brown, Hartlee, religious talk, prayed. 8 Tea, religious talk. 9 At Mrs Humberstone's, religious talk prayed. 10 At home; George Whitefield read his journal. 12 At our Society. 1 At Mrs Claggett's, religious talk, prayed. 1.30 At home; writ diary; meditated. 3 At Mr Stonehouse's, sang, read Prayers. 4 Prayed. 5 Tea, sang, Betty Hopson, etc. 6.30 Religious talk with Betty Hopson. 7.45 At Exall's, tea, religious talk. 8.15 Sang, etc. 10.30 At home; supper, religious talk, prayed, religious talk. 11.30.

WEDNESDAY [DECEMBER] 20. 6.45 Sang, prayed, George Whitefield read his journal. 8.15 At Mr Oswald's, religious talk (necessary). 9 At Mrs Heathfield's, religious talk, tea, prayed. 10.30 At Mr ——'s, religious talk. 11 At home; writ diary; at James Hutton's, necessary talk (religious); at brother Clark's, shaved. 1 At home; necessary talk (religious). 1.30 At Mr Dubart's, many there, religious talk. 2 Dinner, religious talk, sang. 3.45 At Mrs Howman's, religious talk, prayed. 5.15 At Mrs West's, Esther and Betty Hopson, tea, sang, prayed. 7.45 At Mr Hodges', tea, religious talk. 8.15 Sang, etc. 10.15 At home; religious talk, prayed. 11.15.

THURSDAY [DECEMBER] 21. 6 Sang, prayed, religious talk. 7.15 At St Dunstan's, read Prayers, Communion; religious talk with Esther and Betty Hopson. 9 At brother Clark's, tea, religious talk, sang, prayed. 10.15 At home; religious talk, sang. 11.45 Read papers. 12.30 Writ diary; necessary talk (religious). 1 At Mr Oswald's, religious talk. 2 Dinner, religious talk, prayed. 5 At Mr Burton's, tea, religious talk. 6 At Mr Brockmer's, sang, etc; Mr Dobree there! 8 Savoy, sang, etc. 10 At home; supper, religious talk, prayed. 12.

FRIDAY [DECEMBER] 22. 6 Sang, prayed, George Whitefield read his journal, tea, religious talk. 8.30 Corrected his sermon. 11 At Mr Jones', Goodman Fields, prayed, religious talk. 12.15 At Bloomsbury, religious talk, Communion, religious talk. 1.30 At home; corrected. 3 Writ diary; at Mr Bell's, sang, etc. 5.15 At Mr Parker's, tea. 6 Sang, etc. 8 Sang, etc; Garden; (con[vinced], lively zeal, +). 10.15 Supper, religious talk. 11.45.

SATURDAY [DECEMBER] 23. 7.15 Prayed, religious talk. 7.45 With Mrs Butts, Communion, prayed. 8.15 At Mr Parker's, tea, religious talk. 9.45 At home; prayed; writ. 11 George Whitefield read journal. 12 Writ verse. 12.15 Writ. 1 At

Mrs West's, George Whitefield, etc, sang, dinner, sang. 3 Religious talk, tea, sang. 5 At Esther Hopson's, religious talk. 5.45 At Mr Hopson's, religious talk. 7 At Mr Exall's, tea, religious talk. 8 Sang, etc. 10.30 At home; religious talk, prayed. 12.

SUNDAY [DECEMBER] 24. 5.30 Sang, dressed; St Lawrence, read Prayers, Sermon, Communion. 8.15 At home; prayed, sang. 9 At Mrs Taylor's, tea, religious talk. 10 Great St Bartholomew's, read Prayers, preached. 1 At home; dinner, religious talk. 2.30 At Islington, prayed. 3 Read Prayers, preached, 5 At home; tea, religious talk. 5.30 St Bride's, sang, etc. 7 At home; many there, sang, etc; (+, lively zeal). 9.15 Supper, sang, prayed. 3.

[MONDAY, DECEMBER 25] Christmas Day. 5.30 Sang, prayed, sang. 8.30 Tea, religious talk, sang. 10.30 Read Prayers for Dr More (+, lively zeal, =). 1.30 At Mr Summers', dinner, religious talk. 4.30 At St James's, sang, etc. 6 At Mrs West's, sang, etc. 7 Tea, religious talk. 8 Bridgewater Square, sang, etc. 10.30 At home; prayed. 11.

TUESDAY [DECEMBER] 26. 7 Sang, writ diary, writ notes. 8.15 Tea, religious talk. 9.30 Walked, religious talk. 10 Islington, religious talk, sang. 11 Read Prayers, sermon George Whitefield, Communion. 1.45 Sang, prayed. 2.30 Dinner, religious talk, sang. 3.45 At Mrs May's, religious talk. 4 At Mr Clark's, Bell there, religious talk, tea, sang. 5.30 At Mrs May's, religious talk, sang, etc. 7 Supper, religious talk. 8.15 At our Room. 8.45 At Mr Exall's, sang, etc. 10 At the Room, religious talk, prayed, 11 At home; religious talk, prayed. 12.

WEDNESDAY [DECEMBER] 27. 7 Prayed, necessary talk, tea. 8.30 Religious talk with Mrs Goldwire, necessary talk (religious); corrected for George Whitefield. 10.30 Islington, sang, religious talk. 10.45 Read Prayers, Sermon, Communion. 2 Prayed with Mrs Vaughan. 3.30 Dinner, sang, religious talk. 4.30 At Mrs Loyd's, Mary Hanson and Nanny, sang, religious talk. 5 At Basingshaw, read Prayers, preached. 6.45 The leaders met, sang, religious talk, prayed. 10.15 At home; religious talk with Esther Hopson, 11 Supper, religious talk, prayed. 12.

THURSDAY [DECEMBER] 28. 7 Prayed, necessary talk (religious). 8 Tea, religious talk, prayed. 9.30 At brother Clark's, shaved, religious talk, meditated. 11 Islington, read Prayers, preached, Communion; (+). 2.30 Sang, religious talk, dinner. 4.30 At Mr Exall's, J Loyd and Nanny, tea, sang, religious talk. 5.30 At Mr Sherman's, religious talk. 6 James Hutton's, at band. 7 At brother Summers', tea, religious talk. 7.30 Bible. 8 Savoy, sang, etc. 10 At home; religious talk. 11.30 Prayed, religious talk. 12.30.

FRIDAY [DECEMBER] 29. 7 Prayed, religious talk, tea. 8.30 At Mr Claggett's, religious talk. 10 At home; writ preface to Haliburton. 11 Islington, read Prayers, preached, Communion, sang, prayed. 3 At Mr Bell's, sang, etc. 5 At Mr Birnham's, tea, religious talk, prayed. 6.30 At Esther Hopson's, many there, could not speak! 8 At St Ann's Lane, sang, etc. 10 At home; supper. 11 Prayed, writ diary. 11.30.

SATURDAY [DECEMBER] 30. 6.30 William Delamotte, sang, dressed. 7.15 At St Dunstan's. 9 At Miss Delamotte's, tea, sang, prayed with George Whitefield, etc. 11 At home; religious talk with many. 12.15 Fetter Lane, sang, religious talk, prayed. 2.15 At brother Clark's, dinner. 3.30 Fetter Lane, sang, prayed. 5

At brother Clark's, tea, religious talk. 6 Fetter Lane, sang, etc. 7.45 At Mr Exall's, tea, sang, etc. 10 At home; necessary talk (religious). 11 Prayed.

SUNDAY [DECEMBER] 31. 6 Sang; Crooked Lane, prayed, Communion. 8 At brother Chapman's, prayed, sang, tea, religious talk. 10.15 Spittlefields, read Prayers, preached (con)! 12.30 At Mr Russel's, dinner, religious talk. 2.45 Whitechapel, read Prayers, preached. 5.15 At Mr Sims', sang, etc. 7.30 At home; Esther Hopson, prayed, sang. 9.30 Ate, religious talk with Esther Hopson, etc, sang. 11.45.

[MONDAY] JANUARY 1, 1739. 7.15 Sang; necessary business. 8.30 At Mrs Duzzy's, sang, tea, religious talk, prayed. 11 Islington, Robson preached, Communion. 1 Sang, prayed. 2.15 At Mr Claggett's, dinner. 3.30 At Mrs May's, sang, etc. 5 At Mrs West's, tea, prayed. 5.30 Sang, etc. 7.30 At Deadman's Fields, sang, etc. 9.30 At Fetter Lane. 10 All the brethren, Love-feast, sang, religious talk. 3 Prayed. 4 Sang, prayed! (lively zeal). 6.30.

TUESDAY [JANUARY] 2. 9 Tea, religious talk; necessary business; letters. 12.30 Corrected Haliburton. 1.30 Dinner. 3 At Mr Ripley's, religious talk, tea, prayed. 4.45 At Mr Hastings', sang, etc. 6.45 At Mr Exall's, tea, religious talk. 10 At home; religious talk. 10.45.

WEDNESDAY [JANUARY] 3. 7.30 Sang, necessary talk (religious). 8.30 At Mr Mason's, George Whitefield, Ingham, etc, tea, religious talk, prayed. 10.30 At home; George Whitefield, Ingham, Hutchins, Kinchin, etc, read Account of Georgia. 1 Religious talk; with Oswald; necessary talk. 2 At James Hutton's, Thorold, Ingham, etc, dinner. 3.45 At Dr Newton's, tea, religious talk. 5 Basingshaw, read Prayers, preached. 6.30 At home; the leaders, sang, religious talk, prayed, tea. 8 Fetter Lane, prayed, sang, religious talk, sang, prayed. 11.15 At home; prayed. 11.30.

THURSDAY [JANUARY] 4. 7 Prayed, writ account of myself [see JWJ and 1/7, 1/8, 1/11, 1/21]. 9 George Whitefield, Hutchins, etc, tea, religious talk. 10.15 Writ for our Society. 1 At Mr Merrit's, religious talk with George Whitefield. 2.15 Dinner, religious talk. 3.30 At Mrs Burton's, religious talk, prayed. 4.15 At Mrs West's, necessary talk (religious talk), tea, religious talk. 6 Religious talk with Esther Hopson. 6.30 At Mr Brockmer's, sang. 7 At brother Summers', tea, sang, etc. 8 Savoy, sang, etc. 10 At home; religious talk, prayed, writ diary. 11 Writ our orders. 12.15.

FRIDAY [JANUARY] 5. 7.30 Dressed, necessary talk (religious). 8.30 Islington, George Whitefield, Hutchins, Hall, Ingham, Kinchin, and Charles, prayed, religious talk, sang. 2.30 Tea, religious talk. 345 At Mr Bell's, sang, etc, tea. 6.15 With Mr Jennings, religious talk. 7.15 At Mr Exall's, tea, religious talk. 7.45 At St Anne's Lane, Westminster, sang, etc. 10 At Fetter Lane, prayed, sang. 11.30 At home; supper, religious talk, prayed. 12.45.

SATURDAY [JANUARY] 6. Sang, dressed. 7.15 St Dunstan's, read Prayers, Communion. 9 James Hutton's, tea, religious talk. 10.30 At home; writ orders. 12.30 At brother Sims', prayed for his child. 1.15 Writ to sister Kezzy. 1.30 At Mrs Lewin's, dinner, religious talk. 3.15 At St Paul's, read Prayers. 4 At Mr Easy's, tea, religious talk. 5 At home; religious talk; visited Jacky Storer, religious talk. 6.30 At Mr Exall's, religious talk, tea. 8 Sang, etc. 9.45 Betty

Hopson, religious talk. 10.45 At home with her and Esther. 11 Religious talk, sang, prayed. 3.15.

SUNDAY [JANUARY] 7. 6 Sang; writ account of myself. 8.30 Tea, religious talk. 9.30 At Mr Sparkes', prayed. 10 At St Mary Somerset, read Prayers, Dr Croxall preached. 1 At brother Hodges', reconciled Arthur and Tom Hodges; dinner, sang, prayed. 3 At home; sang, prayed. 3.30 St Paul's, read Prayers, Sermon. 4.45 At home; religious talk. 5.15 At Creed Church Society [St Katherine Cree], read Prayers, sang, etc. 7 At Mr Bell's, tea, ((religious talk,)) sang, etc. 9.45 Fetter Lane, religious talk, sang, prayed. 7 At home; slept.

MONDAY [JANUARY] 8. 9.15 Tea, religious talk. 10.15 Writ account of myself. 12.45 At Dr Newton's, religious talk. 2 Dinner, religious talk. 3.45 At Mrs Sellars' with George Whitefield, etc, religious talk, prayed. 5 George Whitefield went, religious talk, prayed; (lively zeal). 6.30 At Mr Dean's, religious talk, prayed. 8 At James Hutton's. 9 With our band. 9.30 Tea, religious talk. 10.30 At home; Hill there ((etc, religious talk)), religious talk, prayed. 11.

TUESDAY [JANUARY] 9. 7.45 Dressed, religious talk, sang. 9 At Mrs Claggett's, religious talk, tea, prayed. 11 At Mr Brockmer's, religious talk. 1.30 At home; dinner, sang. 2.30 Religious talk. 3.15 At Mrs Hind's with George Whitefield, etc, necessary talk (religious). 5 Prayed, Bible, sang. 6.15 At the door, gathered for the Saltzburghers. 7.45 At Mr Exall's, tea, sang, etc. 10.30 At home; religious talk, prayed. 11.

WEDNESDAY [JANUARY] 10. 6 Religious talk with Charles Kinchin, etc, prayed. 7 At the inn, with Charles Kinchin, prayed, sang. 8.30 At Islington with Hutchins, etc, prayed, religious talk, sang. 11 Read Prayers, religious talk. 2 At Mrs Duzzy's, prayed; with Thompson, religious talk. 3 At Jenny's, Loyd's, sang, religious talk. 4.45 At Mary Hanson's, Mrs Sellars, etc, sang, prayed, religious talk. 5 Basingshaw, read Prayers, preached. 7 With the leaders, sang, etc. 8 Fetter Lane, sang, etc, religious talk. 10.45 At home; supper, religious talk, prayed. 12.

THURSDAY, JANUARY 11. 5 Prayed, necessary talk (religious), tea, prayed. 7 George Whitefield and Hutchins went; writ notes. 8.30 At Miss Delamotte's, Ingham and James Hutton and Miss Claggett, sang, tea, religious talk, read Betty Hopson's letter, prayed. 12 James Hutton at brother Clark's, necessary talk (religious). 1 James Hutton's, dinner, religious talk. 3.30 At Mary Hanson's, she sick, prayed. 4.15 At Jenny Loyd's, religious talk, prayed, sang. 5.45 At home; religious talk. 6.15 At James Hutton's, religious talk. 7 Tea, religious talk. 8 Savoy, sang, etc. 10.30 At home; religious talk, prayed. 11.

FRIDAY [JANUARY] 12. 6.45 Dressed, read Prayers. 7.45 Writ diary, necessary talk. 8.45 Islington, necessary talk (religious), sang, tea, religious talk. 12 At home; religious talk. 12.30 At Mr Burton's, Esther Hopson there, necessary talk (religious), prayed. 2.45 At home; necessary talk (religious). 3 With Miss Claggett, at Mrs Sellars', prayed, religious talk, prayed. 4 At home; John Lilly, Holland, religious talk, coffee. 5.30 Writ diary; writ account of Esther Hopson. 6 Hollis came and John Bray, prayed. 7.30 Westminster, sang, etc. 9.15 At Mr Exall's, tea, religious talk. 10.30 At home; religious talk, prayed. 11 Necessary talk (religious) with Brown. 11.45.

SATURDAY [JANUARY] 13. 6 Sang; writ account of Esther Hopson. 7 Read Prayers; walked. 8.15 At Mr Burton's. 9 Esther Hopson there, tea, religious talk, prayed; Charles came, prayed, sang. 11.30 At brother Thompson's, religious talk, Communion. 12.30 With Esther Hopson and Charles, prayed, sang. 1.30 At home; dinner, religious talk. 2.30 Charterhouse, Wildern, prayed, Greek Testament. 5 At home; Mrs Claggett, etc, Charles read his sermon. 6 At Beech Lane. 7 Sang, etc. 8.15 At Mrs West's, tea, Esther and Betty Hopson, prayed, sang. 11 At home; prayed, necessary talk (religious). 11.45.

SUNDAY [JANUARY] 14. 5 Dressed, sang, St Lawrence's, read Prayers, Sermon, Communion. 8.30 At home; sang, prayed. 9.30 Tea, religious talk. 10 St Paul's, read Prayers, Sermon, Communion. 12.30 At Mrs West's. 1 James Hutton, etc, dinner; Esther and Betty Hopson, religious talk, sang. 2.30 Islington, read Prayers, preached. 5.45 At Mr Sims', sang, etc, twice. 8.15 At home; supper. 9 Prayed with Esther, etc. 11.15.

MONDAY, JANUARY 15. 6.30 Dressed, sang. 7 Read Prayers, religious talk with Hanson. 8 At Mrs Storer's, tea, religious talk, prayed, sang. 10 At home; corrected Haliburton; sins!! 1 Mr Palmer came! Haliburton. 2 Dinner, religious talk. 2.45 With Mrs Easy, religious talk. 3.15 At St Paul's, read Prayers. 4 At J Loyd's band, religious talk, prayed. 5 At Mary Hanson's, Esther there, prayed. 6 At Mrs West's, sang, etc. 7.30 Tea, religious talk. 8 At our band. 10.30 At home; prayed. 11 Writ diary.

Ἕτερον ἀνίστασθαι ἱερέα, etc. ['another priest should rise', Hebrews 7:11].

Though ye fight against the Chaldeans, ye shall not prosper [Jeremiah 32:5].

TUESDAY [JANUARY] 16. 6 Corrected sermon. 7 Read Prayers; tea, religious talk, prayed. 8.15 Corrected Haliburton. 11 With Mary Hanson, prayed, religious talk. 12.15 John Bray, etc, Communion, prayed. 2.30 At Islington with Esther, etc, prayed, sang. 3.15 Read Prayers. 4 Tea, religious talk. 5 Prayed. 6.15 At Exall's with Esther, etc, tea, religious talk. 7.30 Sang, etc. 10 At home; supper, religious talk. 11.30.

WEDNESDAY [JANUARY] 17. 6.30 Prayed, dressed. 7 Read Prayers; tea, religious talk. 8.15 Prayed; At Mr Agutter's. 9 Writ sermon. 11.15 At home; religious talk (necessary). 11.45 Prayed with Seward, Hollis, etc. 1.15 Dinner, religious talk. 3.15 Read Prayers. 4 Clerkenwell with Betty S——, religious talk. 5.30 At Mrs West's, religious talk, tea, prayed, sang. 6.15 With the leaders. 8 Ate. 8.15 Fetter Lane. 10.30 At Mary Hanson's, Esther there, prayed, religious talk. 12.

THURSDAY [JANUARY] 18. 12 [midnight] Prayed, religious talk. 1.15 Slept. 3.15 Prayer, religious talk. 4 Slept. 6 Prayed, religious talk, tea. 7 Read Prayers, religious talk with Betty Hopson. 8 At home; tea. 8.45 At Mr Agutter's, writ sermon. 10 Mr Herdson, religious talk, prayed. 11 Meditated, religious talk. 12.15 At home; Miss Hutton, prayed for her. 1 Religious talk, read. 1.30 Dinner, religious talk. 3.15 Read Prayers. 4 Slept. 5 At Mary Hanson's, she better; prayed. 6 At James Hutton's band. 7.30 Tea, religious talk. 8 Savoy, sang, etc. 10 James Hutton's, religious talk with brother Ingham. 10.30 At home; religious talk, prayed. 11.30.

FRIDAY [JANUARY] 19. 6 Prayed with Mrs Plat, religious talk. 7 Read Prayers; tea, religious talk. 8.30 At Mr Agutter's, writ sermon. 2 At Mrs Sellars', religious talk. 2.30 Miss Claggett came, religious talk, prayed. 3.15 Read Prayers. 4 At James Hutton's, tea, religious talk. 5 At brother Oxlee's, Mrs Stoleday there, religious talk, prayed. 6 Mary Hanson's, Esther there. 7 Religious talk, prayed, tea. 8 Fetter Lane, sang, etc. 10.15 At home; supper, religious talk, prayed. 11.30.

SATURDAY [JANUARY] 20. 6 Necessary business; sang. 7 Necessary business. 8.15 At Mr Agutter's, sermon. 9 At Mr Herdson's, tea, religious talk, prayed. 10 Writ sermon. 1 At home; writ to sister Kezzy. 2.30 Dinner, religious talk. 3 At James Hutton's, Cossart there, religious talk. 4 At Mr Clark's, shaved. 5 At Mr Burton's, George Whitefield there, tea, religious talk. 7 At Mary Hanson's, Esther and Betty Hopson, prayed, religious talk, read my sermon, prayed. 10 Walked with Betty, religious talk. 10.30 At home; ate, religious talk, prayed. 11.30.

SUNDAY [JANUARY] 21. 5.15 Sang; necessary business. 6 St Lawrence's, read Prayers, Sermon, Communion. 8.45 At home; prayed, sang. 9.15 Tea, religious talk with brother Roberts. 10.15 Writ account of myself. 12 Walked, meditated. 1 At Mr Parker's, dinner, religious talk. 2 Sang; at Mrs Butts', prayed. 2.30 Wapping Church, read Prayers, preached. 4.15 At Mr Parker's, prayed; at Hill's, tea, religious talk. 5 At Mr Sims', sang, etc. 7 Sang, etc. 8.30 Walked, religious talk. 9 At Mrs Modcing's[?], supper. 9.30 Walked, religious talk. 10 At home; prayed, sang. 11.30 Religious talk of the prophets, prayed, religious talk. 12.

MONDAY [JANUARY] 22. 6 Sang; necessary business. 7 Read Prayers; at Mary Hanson's, Esther there, prayed, tea, religious talk, prayed. 9.15 At home; necessary business; necessary talk (religious). 10 At Agutter's, corrected hymns. 1 At brother Sims', religious talk with Mrs Randal. 2.30 Dinner, religious talk. 3 At Mrs Duzzy's, Mrs Robinson, etc, sang, tea, religious talk, prayed. 5 At Mary Hanson's, religious talk, prayed. 6 At Mrs West's, sang, etc. 7.15 Tea, religious talk, sang, prayed. 8.15 James Hutton's, sang, religious talk, prayed. 10.15 At Mary Hanson's, Mrs Sellars, prayed, religious talk, prayed. 11 At Mrs Burton's, sang, prayed, sang. 12.30 At home.

TUESDAY [JANUARY] 23. 6.45 Betty Hopson, sang, prayed, religious talk. 8.45 At Mrs Delamotte's, sang, tea, religious talk. 11 Charterhouse, walked, meditated. 12 At home; writ orders. 1 At Mr Driver's, Mr Samuel there, dinner, religious talk. 3 At Mr Fish's, religious talk, tea. 4.30 At Mary Hanson's, prayed, religious talk with Esther Hopson. 5.15 Walked with her. 6 At Mrs Wolf's band, religious talk. 7 At Mr Exall's, Mr John Smith, tea, religious talk. 8 Sang, etc. 10 At home; religious talk, prayed. 12.

WEDNESDAY [JANUARY] 24. 6.30 Sang; necessary business. 7 Read Prayers, tea; George Whitefield, brother Ingham,, read letters. 10 Necessary talk; with Charles, necessary talk (religious). 11 Read letters, etc. 12.30 Corrected verse. 3.15 Read Prayers. 4 At Mary Hanson's, prayed; at brother Burton's, religious talk, he cold. 5 At Mrs West's, Betty Hopson, etc, tea, religious talk. 6 Sang, prayed. 7 At home; with the leaders. 8 Fetter Lane, prayed, etc. 10 At home; necessary talk (religious), ((prayed)). 10.30.

THURSDAY [JANUARY] 25. 5.15 Prayed with brother Patterson; writ rules for the women. 7 Tea, religious talk. 7.30 Betty Hopson, religious talk. 8.30 The catechumens came, sang, prayed. 9.30 Set out, religious talk, sang. 10 Islington, religious talk. 10.15 Read Prayers, baptized five adults, preached, Communion. 1.30 Prayed, sang, dinner. 2.15 In the kitchen, sang, prayed. 3 At Spittlefields, George Whitefield preached, for the orphan house. 5 At Mr Slade's, necessary talk (religious). At Mary Hanson's, sang, prayed. 6.30 At our band. 7.30 At Mr. Clark's, tea, religious talk. 8 At the Savoy, sang, etc. 10 At home; ate, religious talk, prayed. 11.15.

FRIDAY [JANUARY] 26. 6 Writ. 7 Read Prayers; at Mr Bowes', prayed, Bible. 8.30 Tea, religious talk. 10 Corrected verse. 2 At Mr Slath's, religious talk with a papist. 3 At Mrs Sellars' with Miss Claggett, religious talk, prayed. 4 At Mary Hanson's, Communion, tea, religious talk. 5.15 At Mr Abbott's, sang, etc. 6.30 At Mr Parker's, sang, etc. 8.30 Religious talk. 8.45 Sang, etc. 11 Supper, religious talk, prayed. 12.15.

SATURDAY [JANUARY] 27. 6.30 Sang, religious talk. 7.30 Visited. 8.15 Tea, prayed. 9 Prayed with Mrs Butts. 10 At Mrs Mills', Communion; at Mrs Special's, prayed; at Mrs Duzzy's, sang, religious talk. 12 Fetter Lane, sang, etc. 2 At brother Clark's, dinner, religious talk. 3 Fetter Lane, sang, etc. 5 At home; buried; at Mr Easy's, tea. 6 Fetter Lane, sang, etc. 8 At Mr Agutter's, Betty, Esther Hopson, Shaw, Patterson, Bray, etc, tea, sang, religious talk, prayed, sang. 11 At home; religious talk, prayed. 12.

SUNDAY, JANUARY 28. 7 Sang, necessary talk (religious); necessary business. 8 Tea, prayed, sang. 9.30 At St. Paul's, meditated. 10.30 Read Prayers, Sermon, Communion. 1.15 At home; dinner. 2.30 Islington, read Prayers, preached. 5 With Margaret Plewit, Betty, Esther Hopson, Mr Bray, Edmunds, Brown, and Mrs Sellars there, prayed, sang. 6 She spoke!! 7 At Mr Bray's, tea, sang, etc. 10.15 Ate, religious talk. 10.45 Prayed. 11.30.

　　Acts 10:17-20—'While Peter yet doubted'.

MONDAY [JANUARY] 29. 6.30 Sang, writ. 7 Read Prayers; at Mr Lyne's, prayed, tea, religious talk. 8.45 At Mr Agutter's, writ account of the prophets. 1.15 At home; necessary business. 1.45 Dinner. 2 Necessary business. 3.15 Read Prayers. 4 At Mr Rivington's, religious talk, coffee. 5.15 At Jenny Loyd's band, sang, tea, religious talk. 7 At Mrs West's, sang, etc. 8.30 at Mr Dobree's, Mr Venn, Berriman, etc, religious talk. 10 Supper, religious talk. 12.30 At Mr Wathen's, religious talk, prayed. 1.30.

TUESDAY [JANUARY] 30. 7.45 Prayed. 8.15 At home; sorted papers; tea, prayed. 11 Read Prayers; sorted papers. 3.15 Read Prayers; at home; tea, religious talk. 4.45 At Mary Hanson's, prayed, many there. 6.15 At home; prayed, sang, etc. 8 At Mr Blake's, sang, etc (+, lively zeal). 10 At home; with Esther, etc, prayed, supper, religious talk. 11.30.

WEDNESDAY [JANUARY] 31. 6.15 Sang, prayed. 7 Read Prayers, religious talk. 8 Corrected proof, tea. 9 Communion with Esther Hopson, Mrs Claggett, Mrs Metcalf, etc, prayed. 10.15 At Mr Agutter's with brother Bray and Esther, prayed; writ our conversation with Mr Venn. 1 At brother Bell's, Mrs Pierce there, dinner, religious talk. 3 At Mrs Preston's, religious talk, prayed. 3.45 At Mrs May's, religious talk, prayed. 4.30 At Mr Clark's, religious talk. 5 At Mrs

West's, religious talk, prayed. 6.30 With the leaders, supper. 8 Fetter Lane. 10.30 At home; prayed, writ diary. 10.45 Religious talk. 11.

THURSDAY, FEBRUARY 1. 6.15 Sang, religious talk with Charles. 7 Read Prayers; necessary talk (religious). 8 At Mary Hanson's, tea, prayed. 9 Religious talk with Esther. 10.30 James Hutton's, religious talk. 12 Cossart came, went to his inn; (w4/1); Richter, James Hutton, etc. 1.45 At Mrs Sims'. 2 Dinner, religious talk, sang. 3.30 At Mr Xere's, religious talk, tea. 5.15 At Mr Savage's, religious talk, tea. 6.30 At James Hutton's, our band, sang, religious talk, prayed. 8 Savoy. 10.15 At home; religious talk, supper, prayed. 11.30.

FRIDAY [FEBRUARY] 2. 6.15 Sang; writ. 6.30 Betty Hopson, religious talk, prayed. 7.30 Tea; prayed. 9.30 Necessary talk (religious). 10 Islington, religious talk; visited. 11 Read Prayers, George Whitefield preached. 1 Communion. 2.45 At Mrs Dyer's with sister Kezzy, etc, religious talk, tea. 5 At sister Hetty's, tea, religious talk. 6.30 At Mrs Wolf's, Mrs Soane, tea, religious talk. 8 At Fetter Lane, sang, etc. 10 At James Hutton's, Shaw, supper, religious talk, prayed. 12.

SATURDAY [FEBRUARY] 3. 6.15 Dressed; meditated. 7 Read Prayers; tea, religious talk, prayed. 8.30 At Mr Agutter's, writ to my mother, Mr Fox, brother Samuel. 1 At home; necessary talk (religious); dinner. 2.15 At Mrs Burton's, religious talk. 4 At Mrs Duzzy's, James Hutton and Shaw there, religious talk, prayed, tea. 5 At Mary Hanson's, Esther and Miss Claggett there, religious talk. 5.45 At brother Clark's, religious talk with Mrs Small, prayed. 6.15 Fetter Lane, sang, etc. 8.30 Agutter's, Esther, Betty, Brown, Patterson, religious talk, sang, prayed. 10.30 At home; religious talk, prayed. 11.45 Writ diary.

SUNDAY [FEBRUARY] 4. 7 Sang; dressed; tea, religious talk; Betty Hopson, prayed, sang. 10 At St George's, read Prayers, George Whitefield preached, Communion (one thousand there!). 3 At St Giles', read Prayers, preached. 5 At Mr Gibbs', sang, religious talk, tea. 6.15 At Mr Sims', sang, etc. 7.30 Sang, etc. 9 Fetter Lane, religious talk, Love-feast, prayed. 3.

MONDAY [FEBRUARY] 5. 3 At Mrs Thornbury's, Communion. 4.30 Slept. 8 Sang, tea, religious talk; necessary business. 9.45 At Agutter's, writ to Mr Hutchins, to Sally's mother. 1 At home; dinner, religious talk. 2.30 At Mr Bell's, with Esther, religious talk. 3.30 With Mrs Preston, etc., religious talk, Communion, prayed. 4.15 At Mrs May's, sang, etc. 5.30 At Mary Hanson's band, religious talk. 6.15 At Mrs West's, sang, etc. 7.30 Tea, religious talk. 8.15 At our band. 10 At home; religious talk, prayed. 11.15.

TUESDAY [FEBRUARY] 6. 6.30 Necessary business. 7 Read Prayers; tea, religious talk. 9 At Mr Agutter's, writ letters. 1.15 Dinner, necessary talk (religious). 2.45 James Hutton, religious talk, tea. 3.30 At Mr Summers', sang, religious talk. 4.45 At Mrs Wolf's, religious talk, sang. 5.30 At Mr Hastings', sang, etc. 7 At Mr Exall's, tea, religious talk. 8 Sang, etc. 10 At home; religious talk, prayed. 12.

WEDNESDAY [FEBRUARY] 7. 6.30 Sang; necessary business. 7 Read Prayers; tea, religious talk. 9.45 At Mr Agutter's, writ preface to Haliburton. 12 At home; prayed; George Whitefield went; dinner, Dr Byrom, religious talk; Mr Hall went. 1.30 Walked. 2 With sister Kezzy, religious talk, tea. 3.30 Read Prayers; Mrs Dymox christened. 4.30 Prayed. 5.15 At Mrs Claggett's, religious talk. 6 Fetter Lane. 10.15 Supper, religious talk, prayed. 11.30.

THURSDAY [FEBRUARY] 8. 6.30 Necessary business. 7 Read Prayers; at James Hutton's, tea, religious talk. 9.30 At brother Clark's, prayed with Mrs Small. 10 At James Hutton's, necessary talk (religious). 12 Agutter's, writ notes. 1.30 At Mr Evans', religious talk, dinner, prayed, sang. 3.15 At Mary Hanson's, Communion, religious talk with Levi, prayed. 4.30 At Mr Burton's, religious talk. 5 At Mrs Sims', sang, etc. 6 At Mrs West's, Betty Hopson, etc, tea, religious talk, prayed. 8 Savoy, sang, etc. 10 At home; supper, religious talk, prayed; necessary business. 12.

FRIDAY [FEBRUARY] 9. 6.30 Betty Hopson, prayed. 8.15 At Mr Bowes', tea, religious talk, prayed, sang. 9.30 At Mr Agutter's, writ preface to Haliburton. 1.30 At home; writ diary. 2 Necessary talk (religious). 1.30 At Mrs Claggett's. 3 At Mrs Mills', religious talk, tea, sang, prayed. 4.45 At Mr Abbott's. 5 Sang, etc. 7 At Mr Parker's, sang, etc. 8.30 Sang, etc. 10 Supper, religious talk, prayed. 11.30.

SATURDAY [FEBRUARY] 10. 7 Prayed, religious talk, tea. 9 With Mrs ——, in despair. 10 At Mrs Mudge's, religious talk, prayed. 11 At Mr Sims', religious talk, prayed. 12 At home; James Hutton, religious talk. 1.15 At Mr Brooks', Spittlefields, Mr Evans, etc, prayed. 2 Dinner, Bible, prayed. 3.15 At home; writ diary; necessary business. 4.30 Walked, religious talk. 5 Religious talk with Betty Hopson. 5.30 At home; necessary talk (religious). 6 Fetter Lane; at James Hutton's, prayed with Okeley. 8 At Exall's, tea, sang, etc. 9.30 With Nanny Hopson, religious talk. 10.30 At home; prayed; corrected proof. 11.30.

SUNDAY, FEBRUARY 11. 6.30 Prayed. 7 Tea, religious talk. 8 Betty Hopson, Esther, Mrs Chambers, etc, prayed, sang. 10 At Islington, read Prayers, preached, Communion; prayed. 1 At Lady Crisp's, dinner, religious talk, sang. 3 At Aldersgate, read Prayers, Sermon. 4.45 At Mary Hanson's, prayed. 5 Mr Sims', sang, etc. 6.30 Tea; at brother Bell's, sang, etc. 8.30 At home; supper, sang, etc. 11.

MONDAY [FEBRUARY] 12. 6.15 Religious talk (necessary) with Charles, sang. 7 Read Prayers; Suky Claggett, Horn, Richter, Pisch, etc, tea, religious talk. 9 At Agutter's, writ answer to Mr Hooker. 12.30 At Mrs Thornbury's, Mrs Prat, etc, religious talk, Communion, sang. 1.30 Religious talk with Mr Mosely. 1.45 At Mr Oswald's, Mason, etc, dinner, Bible, prayed, sang. 4 At Mrs May's, sang, etc. 5.15 At Mary Hanson's, religious talk, prayed. 6 At Mrs West's, sang, etc, tea, religious talk. 8 Gravel Lane, sang, etc. 10.15 At home; prayed. 10.30 Writ diary; meditated. 11.

TUESDAY [FEBRUARY 13]. 6 Sang, prayed. 6.40 Religious talk with Charles. 7 Read Prayers; tea, religious talk. 9 Agutter's, hymns. 11.15 Newgate, read Prayers, preached. 1.30 At Mr Hastings' with Brown and Metcalf, Mrs Chambers, dinner, religious talk, sang. 4 Sang, etc. 6 At Mrs Wolf's, tea, religious talk, sang. 7.30 At Dowgate Hill, sang, etc; tea. 9.15 At Mrs Hind's, necessary talk. 9.45 At Mrs Sellars', Hanson, etc, religious talk (necessary) of her and him. 11.15 At Mrs Metcalf's, religious talk. 12.30.

WEDNESDAY [FEBRUARY] 14. 6.45 Necessary talk (religious). 7 Read Prayers; necessary business; tea, religious talk; at Mrs Hind's with Mr Broughton. 10 At James Hutton's, necessary talk (religious). 12 At home; necessary business;

read. 1 At Mr Bell's, dinner, religious talk. 2 At Mrs Preston's, religious talk, Communion, sang. 3.45 At Mrs West's; at Mr Berriman's, religious talk (necessary) of all objections. 6.15 Fetter Lane. 10.30 At James Hutton's, religious talk, ate, religious talk. 12.30.

THURSDAY [FEBRUARY] 15. 6.45 Dressed; necessary business. 7.30 At home; necessary talk (religious); tea. 9 Agutter's, writ to Mr Barnard. 10 Read, religious talk. 11.15 Newgate, read Prayers, preached. 1 At James Hutton's, religious talk, dinner. 3.30 Islington, read Prayers; at sister Kezzy's, necessary talk (religious), tea. 5.15 At Mrs Sims', sang, etc. 6 At Mary Hanson's, religious talk. 7 At brother Chapman's, tea, religious talk. 8 Fetter Lane. 10 At home; supper, religious talk, prayed. 12.

FRIDAY, FEBRUARY 16. 6.30 Betty Hopson, sang, prayed. 8 At Mr Bowes', brother Bray, etc, tea, religious talk, prayed. 9.30 At Agutter's, sang, writ notes. 12 Wildern, Greek Testament; meditated. 2 At Mrs Sellars', religious talk, prayed. 3.30 At Mrs Mills', religious talk, tea, prayed. 5 At Mr Abbott's, sang, etc. 6.45 At Mr Parker's, sang, etc. 8.30 Sang, etc. 9.45 Supper, religious talk, prayed. 11.15.

SATURDAY [FEBRUARY] 17. 6.30 Prayed. 7.15 Walked; at Mrs Blackburn's, necessary talk (religious). 8 Prayed, religious talk. 9.30 With a sick person, religious talk, prayed. 11.30 At home; necessary talk. 12 Wildern, meditated, Greek Testament. 1.30 At home; dinner, religious talk. 2.30 At brother Clark's, necessary talk (religious), shaved. 3.45 At brother Thacker's, Mrs Chambers, etc, settled her band. 4.30 Tea, sang, religious talk. 5.15 At brother Clark's with them, religious talk, prayed. 6 Beech Lane, sang, etc. 8.15 At Mrs Exall's, tea, sang, etc. 10.30 At home; religious talk, prayed. 11.30.

SUNDAY [FEBRUARY] 18. 6.30 Meditated; prayed. 7 Necessary business; tea, religious talk. 8 Prayed, sang. 10 At Sir George Wheler's Chapel, read Prayers, preached. 12.15 At Mr London's, sang, religious talk, dinner. 2.30 At the Chapel, read Prayers, forbidden to preach. 4.15 At Mr Duthoit's, tea, religious talk, sang. 5.15 At Southwark, sang, etc. 7 Prayed with ——. 7.30 Fetter Lane, the Love-feast of the women; tea, sang, prayed. 10.30 At home; prayed, religious talk. 12.

MONDAY [FEBRUARY] 19. 6.45 Dressed; read Prayers; necessary business; tea, religious talk. 9 At Agutter's, read Cole's book. 11.30 At James Hutton's; Mrs Okeley, religious talk (necessary). 12 Summers, religious talk. 12.45 At Mrs Thornbury's, Communion, sang. 1.15 James Hutton's, dinner, sang. 1 Palmer, religious talk. 3.15 With brother Payne, religious talk, prayed. 4 At Mrs May's, sang, etc. 5.15 At Mary Hanson's, religious talk, prayed. 6 At Mrs West's, sang, etc. 7.15 Tea, religious talk. 8 Gravel Lane, sang, etc. 10.15 At home; prayed, religious talk. 11.30.

TUESDAY [FEBRUARY 20]. 6.45 Sang, read Prayers; tea, religious talk. 8.45 Necessary business; writ diary, walked. 9.30 At Mr Johnson's, religious talk. 11.30 At James Hutton's, necessary talk; at home; sins! 12 Writ to Morgan, to Mr Wragg. 12.30 Necessary talk (religious), meditated. 1.30 Dinner. 2.30 Prayed; at Mrs Eustace's [Ewster's?], religious talk, prayed. 4 At Mrs Hastings', sang, etc. 5.45 With one sick, prayed. 6.30 At Mr Savage's. 7 Esther, etc, sang, prayed, etc; tea. 8 Dowgate Hill, sang, etc. 9.45 Tea, religious talk. 10.15 At Charles Metcalf's, religious talk. 11.45.

WEDNESDAY [FEBRUARY 21]. 6.30 Necessary talk (religious); at home; dressed. 7.30 Tea, religious talk. 8 At Furnival's Inn, Communion, sang. 9.15 At the Archbishop's, religious talk with him. 10 At the Bishop of London's with Charles, religious talk. 11 Agutter's, corrected verses. 12.30 Wildern, verse; Agutter's, read Martin Luther. 2.45 At home; writ diary. 3 Read. 3.30 Religious talk with man. 5 At Mrs West's, the band. 6.45 With the leaders. 8 Fetter Lane. 10.30 Supper, religious talk, prayed. 11.45.

THURSDAY [FEBRUARY] 22. 6 Prayed. 6.30 Esther, religious talk, prayed. 7.30 At Agutter's, writ to H Hatfield. 8 Tea; writ to Mr Simpson, sister Emily, Mr Hutchins. 10 Brother Ridley, prayed, sang. 10.30 At James Hutton's, read Bishop Bull upon the witness of the spirit. 11 Mrs Nichols, religious talk. 12 Mrs Hopson, religious talk. 1 At home; writ diary; dinner, religious talk. 2.30 Walked; at brother Clark's. 3 At Mrs Thacker's, sang, Bible. 4.30 Betty Hopson, religious talk, tea. 5 At Mrs Sims', sang, etc. 6.30 At home; religious talk with Mr Johnson. 7 At Mr Brockmer's, sang, etc. 8 At Mrs Claggett's, prayed. 8.30 At the Savoy, sang, etc. 10 At James Hutton's, supper, religious talk, sang, religious talk. 12.15.

FRIDAY [FEBRUARY] 23. 6 Dressed; prayed. 7 At Mrs Mills', religious talk, tea, sang. 8.15 At Mrs Blackburn's, prayed. 9.15 At home; dressed. 10 Islington, read Prayers, preached, Communion. 1 Fetter Lane, sang, prayed. 2 At brother Clark's, tea. 3 Fetter Lane, sang; letters. 5 Visited Miss Suky Claggett, she sick! 6 Fetter Lane, sang, etc. 7 Beech Lane, sang, etc. 8.45 At Mr Exall's, tea, he sick! I sang, etc. 10.30 At home; religious talk, prayed; corrected. 11.45.

SATURDAY [FEBRUARY] 24. 6.45 Dressed; read Prayers. 7.45 Visited Mr Randal, religious talk, prayed. 8.30 Agutter's, tea, answered Dr Webster. 12 Bray and Fish, prayed, religious talk. 2.15 Visited. 3.15 At Mrs Mills', tea, religious talk, prayed. 5 At Mr Abbott's, sang, etc. 6.45 At Mr Parker's, sang, etc. 8.45 Sang, etc. 10.30 Supper, religious talk. 11.30 Prayed.

SUNDAY, FEBRUARY 25. 6 Sang; meditated; dressed; writ diary. 7 Esther and Betty Hopson, prayed. 7.30 At Suky Claggett's, Communion, prayed. 8 At home; prayed, sang. 8.45 Tea, religious talk. 10 At St Katherine's, walked, meditated. 10.15 Read Prayers, preached (con). 12.15 At Mr Bisset's, dinner, mostly religious talk. 2.30 Islington, read Prayers, preached (con). 5 At Mr Sims', sang, etc. 6 Tea. 6.30 At Mr Bell's, sang, etc. 8.15 At Fetter Lane. 9 At Mr Bray's, prayed, sang. 10 Supper, prayed. 11.

MONDAY [FEBRUARY] 26. 6 Sang; necessary business. 7 Read Prayers; visited Suky Claggett, prayed. 8.15 At Agutter's, tea, religious talk. 9 Writ to Mr Seward and George Whitefield. 11 Newgate, read Prayers, preached. 12.45 At Mrs Thornbury's, Communion. 1.30 Religious talk with Mrs Mosely. 2 Dinner, religious talk, sang; with Mr Okeley. 4 At Mrs May's, sang, etc. 5 At Mary Hanson's, with Nanny, religious talk. 5.30 With her band. 6.30 At Mrs West's, sang, etc. 7.30 Tea, religious talk. 8.15 Gravel Lane, sang, etc. 10 At home. 10.15 In bed; sins!!

TUESDAY [FEBRUARY] 27. 6.45 Dressed; read Prayers; with Suky Claggett, Communion. 8.30 Chocolate. 9 At Robert Westley's, necessary talk. 9.30 At Agutter's, writ to Viney. 11 [Read] Jenks of the righteousness of Christ. 1 Necessary talk (religious); at home. 1.30 Dinner, religious talk. 3 At James Hutton's, tea, religious talk. 4 At Mr Hastings', sang, etc. 5.15 At Mrs Ripley's, religious talk, sang. 6 At Mr Seagrave's, necessary talk (religious); necessary talk (religious) with brother Payne, religious talk. 7.15 At Betty Hopson's, tea, religious talk, prayed. 8 At Mr Crouch's, sang, etc. 10 At Metcalf's, supper, religious talk. 11.30.

WEDNESDAY [FEBRUARY] 28. 6.30 Dressed; at home; ill of the flux; read Luther; chocolate. 1 Read Erskine; religious talk with many. 5.30 Tea, religious talk. 7 The leaders, sang, etc. 8 Fetter Lane. 10 At home; Betty Hopson, supper, religious talk, prayed. 11.30 Corrected proof. 12.15.

THURSDAY, MARCH 1. 6 Prayed. 7 Chocolate; at Suky Claggett's, religious talk, prayed. 8.30 At Payne's, prayed. 9.45 At Betty Hopson's, brother Shaw, etc, prayed, sang, tea, religious talk. 10 At Mary Hanson's, religious talk; at brother Burton's, necessary talk (religious). 11 Newgate, read Prayers, preached, prayed. 12.45 Writ diary; necessary talk (religious). 1.15 Dinner; necessary business. 3.30 At Mrs Nichols', religious talk. 4.30 With her at Mrs West's; tea, religious talk. 6 At Mr Brockmer's, sang, etc. 7.30 Islington, sang, etc. 9.45 At home; supper, religious talk, prayed. 11.

FRIDAY [MARCH] 2. 6 Prayed. 6.45 Necessary business. 7.15 Tea, religious talk. 8 At Mrs Claggett's, religious talk, prayed. 9 At James Hutton's, necessary talk (religious); at brother Clark's, necessary talk (religious). 10 At Mrs Ripley's, religious talk. 11 At Mr Brockmer's, necessary talk. 11.30 Newgate, read Prayers, preached. 1 At Mrs Sellars', religious talk. 2.45 At home; Miss Delamotte, religious talk. 3 At Mrs Mills', Thompson, etc, tea, religious talk, prayed. 4.45 At Mr Abbott's, sang, etc. 6.30 At Mr Parker's, sang, etc. 8 Sang, etc. 9.30 Supper. 10.30 At home; necessary talk (religious), prayed. 11 Writ diary.

SATURDAY [MARCH] 3. 3.30 Chocolate, religious talk. 4 Set out with Mr Franklin, etc, mostly religious talk. 8.30 Uxbridge, tea, read *Life of a Private Gentleman*. 12.30 At Wycombe, dinner. 1.30 Set out, mostly religious talk, read *Life*. 7 At Mrs Fox's, Metcalf, Mrs Ford, etc, sang, religious talk. 8 Read Prayers. 8.45 At Mrs Fox's, two students, etc, sang, prayed, sang. 9.30 Religious talk, sang. 11.15.

SUNDAY [MARCH] 4. 6 Sang, dressed, prayed, tea; Mrs Ford. 7.30 Walked; Jenks. 9 Meditated. 10 Castle, read Prayers, preached, Communion (twenty-seven there). 12.30 At Mr Franklin's, mostly religious talk. 1 Dinner, mostly religious talk. 1.45 At Mrs Fox's, Washington there. 2 St Mary's. 3.15 Castle, read Prayers, preached. 5 With Hutchins, necessary talk. 5.30 At Mrs Fox's. 6 Sang, etc; many gownsmen. 7 At Mears', Washington, read Burkitt. 8 At Mrs Fox's, Sarah Hurst, etc, sang, tea, sang, prayed. 9.45 Sarah Hurst went; religious talk with Mrs Plat. 10.15 Religious talk with Mrs Fox. 11 Writ diary.

MONDAY, MARCH 5. 6 Sang; meditated; dressed. 7.30 Read Prayers. 8 Religious talk with ——. 8.45 At Mrs Fox's, Mrs Ford, etc, tea, sang. 10 Prayed. 11.30

Religious talk with Mrs Hamilton. 12 Religious talk with Patty Thurston and Betty Hughes. 1.15 At Mr Evans', religious talk, tea, sang, prayed. 3.15 At Mrs Fox's, Shaw there; at Mr Wells' with him, religious talk. 5.30 Read Prayers. 6 At Mr Hughes', religious talk, sang. 6.15 At Thomas Collins' with James Mears, religious talk, prayed. 7 At Mrs Ford's, sang, etc. 8 At Mr Stephens'. 9 Supper, religious talk, prayed. 9.30 At Mrs Fox's, Patty Thurston and Betty Hughes, religious talk, sang, prayed. 11.30.

TUESDAY [MARCH] 6. 6.30 Dressed, sang. 7 Garden with Shaw and Metcalf, read Prayers. 8 At Mrs Compton's, many there, tea, religious talk, sang. 10.30 With Shaw and Metcalf. 11 Walked; went by Mr Gambold. 1.45 At home; Mrs Compton called us in, dinner, religious talk, prayed; Mrs Compton j[ustified]! sang. 3.15 At home; religious talk. 4 At the Castle, read Prayers, preached. 6 At home; tea. 6.30 Sang, etc. 7.15 At Mrs Compton's, sang, etc. 8.15 At Mrs Shrieves', sang, etc. 10 At home; Betty Hughes, etc, prayed, sang!! 11.15 Writ diary.

WEDNESDAY [MARCH] 7. 6.30 Sang; dressed; religious talk with James Mears. 7.30 Mrs Matthews, religious talk. 8.45 At Mr Evans', religious talk, tea, sang, prayed. 10.15 Castle, read Prayers, preached, Communion (forty-seven there). 1 At home; necessary business. 1.30 Sang, prayed. 2 At Mr Bannister's, Patty Pricket, etc, religious talk, sang, prayed. 3 At Mrs Compton's, Mrs Bully, etc, tea, religious talk, prayed. 5 Read Prayers, read letters. 6 At home; necessary business; tea. 6.45 Prayed; Mrs Forest, etc, came, sang, prayed. 8 Prayed with Nanny [Hopson]!! 8.30 At Mr Wells', Score, Shaw, Gambold there, religious talk. 9.30 At home; Sarah Hurst, etc, sang, religious talk, prayed. 11.45.

THURSDAY [MARCH] 8. 6.30 Sang; dressed; religious talk. 7.30 Read Prayers; at Mr Score's, Gambold, Shaw, Metcalf, prayed, tea, religious talk, prayed. 10 At Mrs Compton's, religious talk, sang, prayed. 11 Washington and Gibbs, he read Bishop Patrick against Faith *[Parable of the Pilgrim].* 12 He went, religious talk, prayed. 1.30 At Mr Score's, religious talk with Gibbs. 1 Writ to George Whitefield. 3.30 At Mrs Ford's, necessary talk (religious). 4 At Mrs Bully's, Washington, Watson, Mrs Mears, etc, religious talk, tea. 5.15 Prayed, religious talk with Mr Hughes. 6 At Mrs Ford's, sang, etc. 7 At Mrs Mears', Washington there, disputed. 8 He went; religious talk, prayed. 8.30 At Mrs Shrieves', Mrs Mears, etc!! [See letter to George Whitefield, Mar. 16, 1741.] 10 At home; Charles Kinchin, religious talk, prayed, sang, religious talk, prayed. 12 Writ diary.

FRIDAY [MARCH] 9. 6.30 Sang, religious talk, read Prayers. 8 At Mrs Compton's, Metcalf, etc, religious talk, prayed. 10.30 At home; Charles came, read his sermon. 1 Writ notes; tea, religious talk. 2.30 Set out with Mr Fox, religious talk; meditated. 5 Prayed. 7 Reading; at Mr Cennick's [MS reads Senwick's], Kezzy, Sally, Mr Laycock, etc, tea, religious talk, sang, prayed. 11.45.

SATURDAY [MARCH] 10. 6 Religious talk, read Prayers. 7 Religious talk, prayed, tea, sang. 10 Set out with Cennick, religious talk. 12 Prayed. 1 Religious talk. 3.30 At Dummer; Molly Kinchin and G Field, prayed, religious talk. 4.30 Tea, religious talk, sang, religious talk, sang. 7.15 Prayed. 8 Miss Kezzy went to bed. 8.45 Read Prayers. 8.30 Supper, religious talk with Mrs Cleminger, prayed, sang. 10.15.

SUNDAY [MARCH] 11. 6.15 Prayed, sang, tea, sang. 9 Miss Molly came, religious talk, sang, prayed. 11 Read Prayers, preached. 1 Sang; dinner, religious talk, sang. 2.30 Read Prayers. 3.30 Religious talk, sang, tea. 4.30 Set out; meditated. 6 Basingstoke, religious talk. 6.15 Sang, etc. 8.15 Set out with Cennick and John Field. 9 At home; sang, supper, prayed. 10.30.

MONDAY [MARCH] 12. 7 Sang, prayed; read Prayers. 8 Tea, religious talk. 9 Writ for Miss Molly. 10.30 Prayed with Mrs Cleminger, sang. 12 Dinner, with Miss Molly, religious talk, prayed, sang. 2 Set out with Cennick, prayed, sang. 6.15 At Reading, Kezzy and Sally. 7 Lost group; meditated, religious talk. 8 Tea, religious talk, sang, prayed. 11.15.

TUESDAY [MARCH] 13. 5.45 Sang, religious talk, tea, sang, prayed. 7.30 Religious talk with Kezzy and Sally. 8 Set out; meditated, prayed. 9 Sang. 1.15 Oxford; at Mr Fox's, religious talk, tea, sang. 3 At Mrs Compton's, religious talk, sang, prayed. 4 At Mr Hughes', religious talk, prayed. 4.30 At Mr Score's, Gibbs there, tea, religious talk. 6 At Mrs Fox's, sang, etc. 7 At Mrs Compton's, sang, etc. 8 At Mrs Fox's, necessary talk (religious); supper. 9 With Mr Fox's band, sang, prayed. 9.15 With Patty Thompson's band, sang, prayed. 9.30 With Charles Kinchin and Charles Graves! religious talk, sang, prayed. 11.15.

WEDNESDAY [MARCH] 14. 6.30 Sang, prayed, writ. 8 At Mr Score's, Charles Graves and Charles Kinchin, prayed. 9 Tea, religious talk. 9.30 At home; writ; sins of thought. 2 Walked with Mr Score, religious talk. 3 At Mrs Compton's, Charles Kinchin, etc, tea, religious talk, prayed. 4 Castle, read Prayers, preached. 5 At Patty Pricket's, religious talk. 6 At Mrs Fox's, tea, religious talk, prayed. 7.30 At Mr Gibbs', Washington, etc, religious talk, prayed. 8.30 At Mr Fox's, religious talk. 9 Sang, prayed, religious talk. 11.

THURSDAY, MARCH 15. 2.30 Sang, religious talk, tea. 3.30 In the coach, mostly religious talk. 6 Read. 7.15 Tetsworth, tea. 8 Set out, mostly religious talk, read. 11 Wycombe, dinner. 12.15 Set out, religious talk, read. 7 At Mr Bray's, tea, religious talk. 8 At James Hutton's, religious talk (necessary), sang. 10 At home; supper, religious talk, prayed. 11.

FRIDAY [MARCH] 16. 6 Sang, necessary talk (religious) with Charles. 7 Read Prayers; chocolate; at Agutter's, religious talk; writ to Mrs Fox, Perkins, Compton, Patty Thurston, Charles Kinchin, sister Emily, Mr Simpson, brother Hall; writ diary. 1 Writ to George Whitefield. 4 At Mrs Mills', tea, prayed, sang. 6 Wapping Room, sang, etc. 9 At home; mostly religious talk; supper, religious talk, prayed. 11.

SATURDAY [MARCH] 17. 6 Sang, prayed. 7 Read Prayers; Mr Boschi, tea, religious talk. 8.15 At Agutter's, writ the preface. 2 James Hutton, he read letters. 3.15 At home; necessary talk (religious) with Charles; tea. 4 At Mrs Mason's, with a sick woman, prayed, religious talk. 5.30 At brother Clark's, tea, shaved. 6 Fetter Lane, sang, etc. 8 At Exall's, sang, etc. 10.15 At home; supper, religious talk, prayed. 11.15.

SUNDAY [MARCH] 18. 6 Sang, meditated, religious talk. 6.45 Mary Hanson, etc, prayed, sang. 7.30 Tea, religious talk, prayed. 9.15 Walked; Islington, read Prayers, preached, Communion. 1 At Stonehouse's, sang, prayed; dinner. 3.15

Read Prayers at St Paul's. 5 Southwark, sang, etc. 7 Fetter Lane, the women's [Love-] feast, tea, sang, etc. 10.30 At home; many there, prayed, sang. 11.15.

MONDAY [MARCH] 19. 6 Sang, prayed, religious talk. 7 Read Prayers; religious talk; chocolate. 8.15 At Agutter's, religious talk, preface. 1 Read Luther. 2 Charles came, religious talk (necessary). 2.45 With Nanny, necessary talk (religious). 3.15 At Mrs May's, tea, religious talk. 4.15 Sang, etc. 5 At Mary Hanson's band, religious talk, sang. 6.15 At Mrs West's, sang, etc, tea, religious talk. 8 At Gravel Lane, sang, etc. 10.30 At Jewke's. 11 Supper, religious talk, prayed. 12.15.

TUESDAY [MARCH] 20. 6.45 Prayed, tea, religious talk. 8 At home; with Charles, etc, necessary talk (religious). 9 At Agutter's, necessary business. 11 Writ to James Hervey, to George Whitefield, Seward, Ingham. 2 At home; necessary business; Hone came, religious talk. 3 At James Hutton's, religious talk, tea. 4.15 At Mr Hastings'. 5 Sang, etc. 6 At Mrs Wolf's, sister Thacker, etc, religious talk, sang. 7.15 At Mr Exall's, tea, religious talk. 8 Sang, etc (lively zeal, con). 10.30 Religious talk, prayed. 11.30.

WEDNESDAY [MARCH] 21. 6 Sang, prayed. 7 Read Prayers; chocolate; necessary talk (religious). 8.30 At Agutter's, writ to Cennick, to Mr Clayton. 12 Walked, meditated, prayed. 1 Writ to Clayton. 3.30 At home; necessary talk (religious). 4 At Mr Everard's, religious talk, tea. 5.30 At Mrs West's band, tea, prayed, sang. 7 At home; the leaders. 8 Fetter Lane. 10.30 At home; supper, religious talk, prayed. 11.30 Writ diary.

THURSDAY, MARCH 22. 6 Sang, meditated, read. 7 Read Prayers; chocolate. 8 Agutter's; Esther Hopson; writ to Dr Doddridge; religious talk with her. 9 Prayed. 10.15 Brown, sang, prayed. 10.30 He went for Lancashire; writ to Clayton. 12 Dinner. 12.30 At Mr Easy's, necessary talk (religious). 1 At Islington; at our House, necessary talk, sang. 2 At Mr Wilde's, Miss Crisp there, ate, religious talk, sang. 3.15 At Betty Hopson's, Esther there, tea, prayed. 4.30 At Mrs Thacker's band, religious talk, sang, prayed. 6.15 At James Hutton's, tea, religious talk, sang. 8 At the Savoy, sang, etc. 10 At Mr Gladman's, religious talk, prayed. 12 At home.

FRIDAY [MARCH] 23. 6.15 Sang, necessary talk, prayed. 7 Read Prayers; chocolate. 8 Agutter's, writ journal. 1.30 At Mrs Sellars', religious talk, tea. 2 At Mrs Herdson's, religious talk, tea, sang. 4 At Mrs Mills' band, tea, prayed. 5 At Mr Harris', tea, religious talk, prayed. 6 At the Room, sang, etc. 9.30 At home; supper, religious talk, prayed. 11.15.

SATURDAY [MARCH] 24. 5.45 Sang, prayed, necessary talk (religious). 7 Read Prayers; at James Hutton's, tea, religious talk. 9 At the Bishop of London's with Charles, religious talk. 10 At sister Wright's, tea, good talk (necessary). 11 At Agutter's, writ to ——. 12 Fetter Lane, sang, etc (twenty-two there). 2 At brother Clark's, dinner. 3 Fetter Lane, sang, etc (forty there). 5 At home; Miss Claggett there, religious talk, tea. 6 Fetter Lane, sang, etc. 7.15 At Mr Exall's, tea, religious talk. 8 Sang, etc. 11 At home; prayed. 11.15.

SUNDAY [MARCH] 25. 5.45 Dressed; St Ann's. 8.30 At home; prayed, sang. 9.45 At St Katherine's, meditated. 10.15 Read Prayers, preached. 1 At Mr Special's, religious talk with Nanny; dinner. 2.45 At the Marshalsea [Prison], read

Prayers, preached. 4.30 Tea. 5 At Mr Sims', sang, etc. 6.45 Tea, religious talk. 7.15 At brother Bell's, sang, etc. 10 At home; prayed. 11.15.

MONDAY, MARCH 26. 5.45 Sang, read Prayers. 6.45 At brother Hopson's, Esther, etc, sang, tea, religious talk, prayed. 9.30 At home; necessary talk (religious). 10 Necessary business. 11 With Exall at Islington, Garden, necessary talk. 12 Necessary business; corrected George Whitefield's sermon. 2.15 At Mrs Metcalf's, dinner; at Mrs Herdson's with her, tea, religious talk. 4.30 At Mrs May's, tea, sang, etc. 5.15 At Mary Hanson's band, religious talk, prayed. 6 At Mrs West's, sang, etc. 7.15 Tea, religious talk. 8 Gravel Lane, many angry! 8 Sang, etc (lively zeal, con). 10.30 At home; religious talk, prayed. 11.30.

TUESDAY [MARCH] 27. 6 Necessary talk (religious) with Okeley; tea, religious talk; James Hutton, prayed; Okeley went. 8 At Agutter's, writ to Charles Kinchin; corrected George Whitefield's sermon; necessary business. 12 At home; dressed; necessary talk (religious). 12.45 At Jewkes', necessary talk (religious); with Miss Kent; prayed. 1.15 Dinner, sang. 2.15 At Mrs Mosely's, Mrs Jenkins, religious talk. 3.15 At brother Williams', tea, religious talk. 4.30 At Mr Hastings', sang, etc (twenty there). 6 At Mrs Soane's, religious talk, prayed. 7.15 At Exall's, tea, religious talk. 8 Sang, etc (con). 10.30 At home; writ to Seward; necessary talk (religious). 11.15.

John 7:44; 8:45, 46.
Deuteronomy 32:49-52; 34:7 etc.
Acts 9:16; 8:2.

WEDNESDAY [MARCH] 28. 5.45 Sang; dressed. 6 Read Prayers; at Betty Hopson's, Mrs West, Esther, religious talk, tea, prayed. 9 At Agutter's, transcribed to Clayton; writ notes. 10.30 Prayed(+). 10.45 Sins!! prayed. 11 Necessary business. 11.30 Walked, meditated. 12 At Islington, necessary talk (religious). 1.15 At Mrs Sellars', the new band, religious talk, sang. 2 Religious talk with Patterson, prayed. 2.45 At Jewkes', with him at Mrs May's, necessary talk (religious). 3.15 At Jewkes'. 4 Mason there, tea, religious talk, prayed with Miss Kent. 5.15 At Mrs West's, tea, religious talk, prayed. 6.30 At home; necessary business. 7 The leaders, prayed, etc. 8 Fetter Lane; talk of my going to Bristol; lots, I going! prayed. 10.30 At home; supper, necessary talk (religious), prayed.

2 Samuel 4:11; 3:1.
2 Chronicles 28:27; 29:30.

THURSDAY [MARCH] 29. 5.15 Sang; necessary talk (religious); necessary business. 6.45 At Mrs Storer's, Mrs West, etc, prayed. 7.15 At James Hutton's, tea, religious talk; Betty and Esther [Hopson], Reed, Bray, etc, sang, prayed. 9.15 Set out with Charles, etc. 10 They went; prayed. 11 Meditated; read. 12 Met a man, religious talk. 1 At Egham, dinner, religious talk. 2.30 Set out; religious talk. 8.30 At Basingstoke; Mr Knight's, Cleve, Cowdry, etc, religious talk, tea. 9.30 Prayed, Bible, sang. 11.

FRIDAY, MARCH 30. 5 Religious talk. 5.45 Set out. 6.45 Dummer; religious talk with Hutchings, tea, prayed, sang. 9 Set out; sang, religious talk with Hutchings. 10 He went; meditated, prayed. 1 Newbury; dinner, religious talk. 2 Set [out], prayed, read. 3 Mostly religious talk. 3.45 At Hungerford, tea. 4.30 Set out; religious talk. 7 Marlborough. 8 Meditated; supper; writ diary; they [had] good talk. 9 Religious talk. 11.

SATURDAY [MARCH] 31. 5 Necessary talk; meditated. 5.45 Set out; meditated; prayed. 8.45 At Calne [MS reads Cane]; tea, man swore, reproved him. 9.45 Set out; meditated. 12 At Marshfield [MS reads Mashfield]; dinner. 3 Set out. 6 Prayed; horse quite tired. 7 At Bristol; at Mrs Grevil's [this will be 'home' in Bristol], George Whitefield, etc, prayed, sang, etc. 8 At Weavers' Hall, George Whitefield preached; sang, prayed. 9.30 At home; religious talk. 10 Supper, prayed, religious talk, sang. 11.30 Religious talk. 12.

SUNDAY, APRIL 1. 7 Dressed, religious talk, sang. 8 At the Bowling Green, George Whitefield preached! 10 At home; sang, tea, religious talk. 11.30 At Hanham Mount, George Whitefield preached. 1.45 At home; dinner. 2 At St Peter's, read Prayers, Sermon. 3.45 Writ diary; religious talk. 4.15 Set out; George Whitefield preached at Rose Green. 6.45 At Mr Allen's, tea, sang, prayed. 7.30 At Nicholas Street Society, sang, etc. 9.30 At home; religious talk, supper. 11 At Mr Deschamps' (thirty there), Communion, prayed, sang. 1.

MONDAY [APRIL] 2. 7 Sang, necessary talk (religious). 8.45 At Mrs ——; tea, religious talk, sang, prayed. 10 At home; George Whitefield read letters. 12 Dinner, prayed. 1 George Whitefield went [not to America; see 6/14, 6/20]; sang, necessary talk (religious). 2 Meditated; writ diary. 2.30 Writ to the brethren. 4 At the Glasshouse (three or four thousand). 6 At Mrs Norman's, tea, religious talk, sang. 7 At Baldwin Street Society, sang, etc. 9.15 At home; Easy there; supper, religious talk, prayed. 10.45.

TUESDAY [APRIL] 3. 5.45 Sang; dressed; writ orders for the bands. 8 Tea, religious talk; writ orders. 10.30 Newgate, read Prayers, preached (St John, chapter one). 12.30 At home; ended orders. 3 Writ diary; tea, religious talk. 4.30 Visited a sick man. 5 At Mrs Padmore's, sang, tea, religious talk, prayed. 7 At Nicholas St, sang, etc (con). 9 At home; supper, religious talk, prayed. 11.

WEDNESDAY, APRIL 4. 6 Sang, prayed. 6.30 Writ to Charles. 8 Tea, religious talk, prayed. 9 Writ to sister Emily, Simpson, brother Hall; writ to Mrs Vaughan. 10.45 Newgate, read Prayers, preached. 12.15 At home; religious talk to Wathen. 12.30 Prayed. 1 Writ to brother Samuel. 2 Religious talk. 3 At Mrs Norman's, tea, religious talk. 4 At Baptist Mills, preached (fifteen hundred there!). 6 At home; religious talk. 6.15 Writ to brother Samuel. 6.45 The band met! 8.30 At Mr Collet's. 9 Religious talk; supper, prayed. 10 At home; religious talk, prayed. 10.45.

THURSDAY [APRIL] 5. 5.45 Prayed, sang. 6.30 Corrected; read. 8 Coffee, religious talk. 9.30 Dressed; read. 10.30 Newgate, read Prayers, preached. 12.15 At home; religious talk (necessary). 12.30 Writ diary; prayed. 1 Writ to Esther Hopson; religious talk with many. 3 At Mrs Woodward's, Mrs Grevil, etc, tea, religious talk. 4 At Mrs Archer's, tea, religious talk. 5 At Castle Street Society, sang, etc. 7 Nicholas Street, sang, etc. 9 At home; supper, religious talk, sang, prayed. 10.30.

FRIDAY [APRIL] 6. 5.45 Sang. 6.30 Writ notes. 7.30 Read history of the Quakers. 8 Tea, religious talk. 9.15 Read. 10 Newgate. 12 Necessary talk. 12.15 Writ diary, sang, prayed. 1 Religious talk with man; visited. 3 At Williams', many there; Communion, tea, religious talk. 4.30 Prayed; visited. 5 At home; writ Journal. 6 At Baldwin Street, sang, etc (lively zeal, con). 8 At Mrs England's

[Lawford's Gate Society], sang, etc. 9.45 At home; supper, religious talk, sang, prayed. 11.15.

Matthew 26:47, 59.

2 Corinthians 5:10; 6:2, etc.

S<small>ATURDAY</small> [A<small>PRIL</small>] 7. 5.45 Sang; Greek Testament; prayed. 6.30 Writ Journal. 8 Tea, religious talk. 9 Journal. 10.15 Newgate. 12.30 Writ diary; at Baptist Mills; visited. 1.15 At home; read; Journal. 3 At Mrs Smith's, religious talk, prayed, tea. 4.15 At home; Journal. 5 At Mr Stedder's, religious talk, prayed. 6.30 At home; religious talk. 7 Weavers' Hall, sang, etc. 9 At home; supper, religious talk, sang, prayed. 11.15.

S<small>UNDAY</small> [A<small>PRIL</small>] 8. 6.15 Sang; dressed. 7 At the Bowling Green, preached. 8 At home; tea, religious talk; writ diary; dressed. 9.30 Set out with Mr Deschamps. 10.30 At Hanham. 11 Preached. 12.30 At Mr Deschamps', dinner, religious talk. 2 At St Peter's. 3 Read Prayers, Sermon. 4.15 At Rose Green, preached, prayed. 6.15 At Baldwin Street, sang, etc. 8 At home; supper; with the bands; lots; prayed. 9.30 Read Journal; prayed. 11.

M<small>ONDAY</small> [A<small>PRIL</small>] 9. 6 Sang, prayed. 6.30 Writ to Fetter Lane. 8 Tea, religious talk, sang. 9 Writ. 10.30 At Newgate. 12.15 At home; prayed; necessary business. 1 Writ to James Hutton, Edmunds, to Charles. 2 Dinner; Mrs Deschamps' band, necessary talk (religious), prayed. 3 Religious talk with soldiers, prayed. 3.30 At Mr Vauthry's, religious talk. 4 At the Brick-yard, preached (four thousand there). 5 At Mrs Williams' band, necessary talk (religious), prayed. 6.45 Ate, religious talk. 6.15 Visited. 6.30 At home; writ. 7 At Nicholas Street, sang, etc. 9 At home; writ. 9.30 Supper, religious talk, sang, prayed. 11.

T<small>UESDAY</small> [A<small>PRIL</small>] 10. 6 Prayed, sang. 6.30 Journal. 8 Tea, necessary talk (religious). 9 Journal. 10 Newgate. 12 At Mr Deschamps', dinner. 1 Set out with Mrs Grevil, Mr Deschamps. 4 At Bath, The Three Cups, John Feachem, tea, religious talk. 5 In the Meadow, preached (two thousand there). 6.30 At John's, religious talk, sang. 7 Preached in Gracious Street, prayed. 8.30 At the Inn, religious talk; Griffith Jones. 9 Supper, religious talk, read journal. 11 Prayed. 11.15.

W<small>EDNESDAY</small> [A<small>PRIL</small>] 11. 6 Necessary talk (religious), sang, prayed. 8.15 Mr Chapman, tea, religious talk, he went. 10 In the Meadow, preached, prayed. 12.15 Set out with them. 3 Horse fell. 3.30 At Mrs England's, religious talk, tea. 4 Baptist Mills, preached, prayed. 5.30 Visited. 6 At Mr Walwin's, tea, mostly religious talk, prayed. 7 At home; the female bands, religious talk, prayed. 8 At Baldwin Street, the male bands. 9 At home; supper, religious talk, sang, prayed. 11.15.

T<small>HURSDAY</small> [A<small>PRIL</small>] 12. 6 Prayed, sang. 6.30 Writ account of the bands. 8 Tea; Mrs Norman, Mrs Woodward, Mr Sadire, necessary talk (religious). 12.15 Walked. 12.45 At Mr Willis', sang, religious talk. 1.30 Dinner. 2.30 Walked to Rose Green. 3.45 At home; at Mr Thomas', Mr Collet, etc, religious talk, tea. 5.30 Castle Street Society. 7.15 Nicholas Street Society, sang, prayed (:, con). 9 At home; writ diary, religious talk, prayed. 11.15.

FRIDAY [APRIL] 13. 5.45 Dressed; read Prayers. 6.30 At Mr Tucker's, necessary talk (religious). 8 At home; tea, religious talk. 9 Journal. 12 Prayed; read. 1 Mrs Thornhill and six more, religious talk to each. 3 At Mrs Iscock's, tea, religious talk. 4.15 At Mr Labbè's, Mr Badham, etc, religious talk, tea. 5.45 Baldwin Street, sang, etc (lively zeal). 7.45 At Mrs England's, sang, etc (lively zeal, +). 9.15 At home; supper, religious talk, sang, prayed. 11.45.

SATURDAY [APRIL] 14. 5.45 Dressed. 6 Read Prayers. 6.45 Writ to Mr Tucker. 8 Tea, religious talk. 9 Journal. 11 Mr Taylor, etc. 11.15 At Mrs Thornhill's, religious talk with Misses. 12 At home; religious talk with Wathen, he convinced! religious talk with Mrs ——. 1 Writ diary. 2 Dinner, religious talk with many. 3 At Mrs Gibbs', he will not let me preach! 4 At the Poorhouse, preached, prayed. 5.30 At John Williams', tea, religious talk, sang. 7 At Weavers' Hall, sang, etc. 9 At home; religious talk, supper, prayed. 11.30.

SUNDAY, APRIL 15. 7 At the Bowling Green 8.30 Tea, religious talk. 9.30 Set out with Deschamps. 10.30 Hanham. 12.30 At Mr Deschamps', dinner, religious talk, sang. 1.30 At home; necessary talk (religious). 2 Newgate, read Prayers, preached. 3.45 At Mr Deschamps', tea. 4 Set out. 4.30 Rose Green. 6 At Mrs England's, sang, etc (lively zeal). 8.45 At Mr Allen's, religious talk. 8 At home; the women's Love-feast (nine there), supper, sang, ate, sang, prayed. 11.

MONDAY [APRIL] 16. 6 Prayed; journal. 8 Coffee. 9 Journal. 10 Religious talk with Quaker. 11.15 Writ to Fetter Lane. 1.45 Spoke to many. 3.30 Necessary talk (religious). 4 At the Brick-yard. 5.30 At Mrs Norman's, tea, religious talk, sang. 6 At Mrs England's, tea, the new band. 7 At Nicholas Street. 9 Writ diary. 9.30 Mrs Page, etc, ate, sang, prayed, sang. 12.

TUESDAY [APRIL] 17. 6 Prayed; journal. 8.15 Tea, religious talk. 9 Journal. 10 Sins of thought; Newgate, christened Lucretia Smith. 12.30 Prayed with the condemned men. 1 At home; prayed with Lucretia Smith, religious talk with her, with many. 3 The new female band, religious talk, prayed. 3.45 Tea. 4 Prayed with them; lots. 5 At a Society in the Lane [Back Lane]. 7 Baldwin Street, sang, etc. 9 Miss Cornish and three more! prayed, sang. 10 At home; religious talk, prayed. 11.30.

WEDNESDAY [APRIL] 18. 5.30 Sang; dressed. 6 Read Prayers; religious talk with two. 7 Journal. 8.15 Tea, Miss Cornish, etc, sang, religious talk. 9 Writ to George Whitefield, Seward, Mitchell. 10 Newgate. 12.15 Prayed. 1 Religious talk to many. 3.15 Tea, religious talk. 4 Baptist Mills (twenty-five hundred there). 5.15 At Mr Evans', necessary talk, tea. 6 At home; with the women. 7 With their bands, one received [justification]! 8 Baldwin Street, at the bands. 10 At home; supper, prayed. 11.15.

THURSDAY [APRIL] 19. 6.45 Sang; writ answer to Mr Tucker's *Queries*. 8 Tea; answer. 10 Newgate. 12 At home; meditated; prayed. 12.30 Religious talk to one, prayed. 12.45 Prayed. 1 Anthony Purver, religious talk. 1.30 Visited one sick. 2 Writ diary; religious talk with many. 3 Tea, religious talk with the condemned. 4.30 Writ; Griffith Jones; at Castle Street. 7 Nicholas Street. 9 At home; supper, religious talk, prayed. 11.

GOOD FRIDAY [APRIL 20]. 6 Prayed. 6.30 Ended [answer] to Mr Tucker. 8 Writ notes. 9 Sang, prayed. 10 All Saints. 11 Read Prayers, Sermon, Communion.

1.15 At home; sang, prayed. 2 St Philip's, read Prayers, Sermon. 3.30 At Mrs Norman's, tea, necessary talk (religious), sang. 5 Baldwin Street, Mrs Thornhill! 6 Lawford's Gate, Samuel Goodson, Ann Kolton. 9 At home; sang, supper, religious talk, prayed. 11.15.

EASTER EVE, APRIL 21. 6 Prayed. 6.30 Writ to Charles, James Hutton, West. 8 Tea; writ to Mrs Storer; necessary business. 10.30 At Mrs Thornhill's. 11 At our Society [probably Baldwin St., see JWJ and diary April 29, 1741], read letters, etc. 1 At Madam Deschamps', necessary talk (religious), to Mr and Mrs Elliot. 2 Baldwin Street. 4 At the Poorhouse. 5 At Anthony Williams', tea. 5.30 At our Society. 7.30 Weavers' Hall. 9.30 At home; religious talk, supper, sang, prayed. 12.30.

EASTER DAY, APRIL 22. 6.30 Dressed; meditated. 7.15 Newgate. 8.30 At home; tea, religious talk. 9.30 Set out with Mr Deschamps. 10.30 Hanham. 1 At Mr Deschamps', dinner. 2 Newgate. 4.45 At Mr Willis'; rain; preached, prayed. 6.30 Nicholas Street (lively zeal, +). 9 At home; supper. 10 Religious talk, prayed. 11.15.

MONDAY, APRIL 23. 5.45 Dressed. 6 Read Prayers; at Oldfield's, tea, sang, religious talk. 8 Set out with Wathen and twenty, sang, religious talk. 10.30 At Pensford, sang in the street. 11 In the House, sang. 11.30 In the Market-place, sang, prayed, preached. 1.15 Set out, religious talk. 3.15 At home; dressed; at Mrs Norman's, tea, religious talk. 4 At his brick-yard, preached (four thousand there), religious talk with one. 6 At Mrs England's Love-feast; tea, religious talk, sang. 7.15 Nicholas Street (lively zeal, +). 9 At home; supper, sang, prayed. 10.30.

TUESDAY, APRIL 24. 4.30 Dressed; at Mr Deschamps', tea, religious talk. 5.45 Set out with him; meditated. 7.45 Bath. 8 At Mr Dibble's, tea, religious talk. 9 In the field, preached, prayed. 10.15 At John's, religious talk; settled the bands. 11.30 At Mr Dibble's, preached. 12.30 Ate, religious talk. 1.15 Set out. 3.30 At Two-mile Hill [Kingswood], necessary talk (religious). 4 Preached; at the place for the School. 6.45 At home. 7 At Mrs Thornhill's, religious talk with Becky. 7.14 Baldwin Street (con), Bush received! 9.30 At home. 10 Supper; prayed. 11.

WEDNESDAY, APRIL 25. 6 Sang; writ upon predestination. 8 Tea; writ. 10.30 Newgate. 12.15 Walked with Purdy and Anthony Williams, necessary talk (religious). 1.45 Frenchay [MS reads French Hay]; at Anthony Purver's, dinner, religious talk. 3 He walked with us, religious talk. 4 Baptist Mills. 5.30 At home; religious talk with many. 6.30 Tea. 7 With the women, prayed, sang; at Mrs Thornhill's, religious talk. 8 At our Society. 9.30 At home; supper, religious talk, prayed. 11.

THURSDAY [APRIL] 26. 6 Prayed. 6.30 Writ to Fetter Lane. 8.15 Tea, religious talk. 9 Writ. 10.30 Newgate. 12 Appealed to God concerning predestination, Ann Davis. 1 At home; religious talk; writ diary; dinner, religious talk with many. 3.30 At Mr Page's, Miss Iscock. 4 Religious talk, tea. 4.30 At Mrs Ryan's, religious talk, prayed. 5 Castle Street (con). 7 Nicholas Street. 8 Hannah Cox. 9.15 At home; religious talk with Miss Gregory; with him! 10 Supper, religious talk, prayed. 11 Slept. 12 The fire; sang. 12.15.

FRIDAY, APRIL 27. 6 Prayed. 6.30 Writ to brother Bray, Nowers, G Chapman. 8

Tea, religious talk. 9 Writ to Newman, Waldron, Parker, Oxlee. 10.15 Newgate, Mary Robinson and ——. 1.30 Visited. 2 At home; religious talk to many. 3.15 Tea, religious talk. 4 At Mrs Hodges', tea, religious talk, prayed. 5 At Baldwin Street (con). 7 At Lawford's Gate. 9 At Mr Labbè's, supper, religious talk, tea. 10.45 At home; religious talk to Mrs Grevil. 12.

SATURDAY [APRIL] 28. 6 Prayed. 6.30 Sermon upon predestination. 8 Tea, religious talk. 9 Sermon. 10.15 Newgate. 12.30 At home; meditated, prayed. 1 Dinner, religious talk with many. 2.15 Sermon. 3 At Mrs Williams', many there, Communion. 4 At the Poorhouse. 5.15 Visited. 5.30 At home; sermon. 6 At Mr Jones', tea, religious talk. 7 Weavers' Hall. 9 At home; supper. 10 Religious talk; writ sermon. 11.

SUNDAY [APRIL] 29. 5.30 Prayed; writ. 7 Bowling Green, 'Free Grace' (four thousand there). 8 Tea; at Clifton, married four. 10.30 Hanham (three thousand there). 12 Visited. 12.30 At Mr Deschamps', dinner; Clifton, read Prayers, preached. 4.30 Rose Green, Galatians 3:22 (seven thousand there). 6 At Mrs England's, tea, religious talk. 7.30 Sang, etc. 8.30 At our Love-feast. 10 At home; religious talk. 11.

MONDAY [APRIL] 30. 6.15 Prayed. 6.30 Writ to Fetter Lane. 8.15 Tea, religious talk. 9 Writ. 10.30 Newgate, Mary Robinson and Mrs Davis. 12.15 Writ; religious talk. 12.30 Prayed. 1 At Mr Farley's, necessary talk. 2 Dinner. 2.45 At home; religious talk to many. 4 Brick-yard, 'Free Grace' (two struck, one comforted)! 5.30 Visited two. 6.15 At home. 7 Writ to Edmunds, Hodges. 7 Nicholas Street. 9 At Mr Bull's, Labbè there, religious talk; supper, prayed. 10.30 At home; Mrs Norman, etc, prayed, sang. 11.15.

TUESDAY, MAY 1. 6.30 Prayed; writ to Mrs Fox, Compton. 8 Tea. 8.45 Writ to James Mears, Sarah Hurst, Mrs Robinson, Mills. 10.15 Newgate. 12 Prayed. 12.30 Writ to brother Thompson. 1 Dinner, religious talk. 1 Religious talk. 2.15 Walked. 3 Read Vaughan Powell. 3.30 At Two-mile Hill, read Prayers. 4 Walked. 5 Visited; Vaughan Powell. 5 At the Back Lane, sang, etc. 7 At Baldwin Street (ten received [remission of sins])! 9.30 Supper, religious talk, sang. 11.

WEDNESDAY [MAY] 2. 6 Prayed. 6.30 Writ sermon. 8 Tea, religious talk. 8.45 Sermon. 9.30 Necessary talk (religious). 10.15 Newgate, one comforted. 12.30 At Mrs Page's, Jenny Worlock comforted. 1 Prayed, sang. 1.30 At John Haydon's, he very ill, prayed, he well! 3.30 Baptist Mills, at Mrs Shell's, tea, religious talk. 4 Preached (two thousand there), rain. 5 At John Haydon's, prayed. 5.30 At Mr Whitehouse's, religious talk, sang, tea; Mrs Thornhill, etc. 7 At the female bands, sang, prayed; Miss Cutler received. 8.15 Visited. 8.30 Baldwin Street. 9.15 At home; religious talk, prayed. 11 Religious talk (necessary) to Mrs Grevil. 11.45.

THURSDAY [MAY] 3. 7 Sermon. 8 Tea, necessary talk (religious). 9 Newgate. 11 Necessary talk (religious). 11.45 Set out in the coach with Mrs Grevil, Longden, Norman, sang, religious talk. 1.30 Anthony Purver's, Mr ((Warren)); dinner, he prayed, religious talk. 3.30 Set out. 4 Sang, religious talk. 5 Visited. 5.15 Castle Street. 7 Nicholas Street. 9 At home; religious talk to many. 9.45 Supper, religious talk, sang. 11.

FRIDAY [MAY] 4. 6.15 Prayed. 6.30 Sermon. 8 Tea, religious talk. 9 Sermon.

12.15 Prayed. 1 Visited. 1.45 At home; religious talk to many. 2.30 Sermon. 3 At Mrs Thomas', religious talk, tea, prayed. 4 At Mr Wiggington's, religious talk, sang, prayed. 5 Baldwin Street (+, lively zeal). 7 At Mrs England's, one received [remission of sins]. 9 Supper, read Rosewell. 11.30.

SATURDAY [MAY] 5. 6 Prayed. 6.30 Writ to Charles, and James Hutton. 8 Tea, religious talk. 9 Writ to George Whitefield, Seward, Hutchins. 10.15 Newgate. 12 At home; six Quakers, six of us, religious talk, prayed. 1 Dinner; visited several. 4 Bowling Green, 'Be still' (two thousand there). 5 Visited. 6 At Mrs Dagge's, religious talk, tea. 7 Weavers' Hall. 9 Supper, read, prayed. 11.30.

SUNDAY, MAY 6. 6 Prayed; dressed; religious talk. 7 Bowling Green, 'Little children' (seven thousand there). 8.30 At Mrs Willis', Communion, sang, tea, prayed with Miss Gotley. 10.30 Hanham, Galatians 3:22; visited. 12.30 Mr Deschamps', dinner. 1.45 Clifton, read Prayers, 1 Corinthians 1:30. 4.15 Mr Deschamps', tea. 4.45 Rose Green, Galatians 3 (five thousand there). 7 Baldwin Street. 9 At home; read; supper, religious talk. 11.

MONDAY, MAY 7. 6 At Baldwin Street (twelve there), prayed, sang. 7.30 At home; writ to Fetter Lane. 8 Tea, religious talk, prayed. 9 Set out. 11 Pensford, tea. 11.30 At Publow (four hundred there!), preached, prayed; set out. 3 At home; dressed; at Baldwin Street, prayed. 3.30 At Mrs Norman's, tea, religious talk. 4 Preached (four thousand there), Matthew 18:3; visited. 6 At home; writ. 7 Nicholas Street, one received. 9 At home; writ. 10 Supper, necessary talk (religious). 11.

TUESDAY [MAY] 8. 6 Prayed. 6.30 Writ to my mother, Bowes, Nowers, James Hutton. 8 Tea; writ to Mr Fox, C Graves. 10.15 Newgate. 12 At Mr Deschamps', dinner. 12.30 Set out; read. 3 At Bath; at John [Feachem]'s, necessary talk (religious); at Mr Dibble's. 4 Preached. 5.15 At Mr Merchant's, necessary talk (religious). 6 At Mr Dibble's, sang, etc. 7 Set out with Mr Deschamps; at home; necessary talk (religious). 11.

WEDNESDAY [MAY] 9. 4.15 Necessary talk (religious); tea. 5.15 At the inn with Mrs Grevil, sang, religious talk, prayed. 5.45 She went to London; walked, religious talk. 6.30 At home; slept. 8.45 Tea; writ to Charles. 10.30 Newgate. 12 At the Schoolroom; took seisin. 1 Writ to brother Samuel; religious talk to many. 3.30 Tea, religious talk. 4 Baptist Mills, Matthew 18:3 (two thousand there). 5 Visited many. 7 With the female bands. 8.15 Baldwin Street. 9 Writ diary; writ to brother Samuel. 9.30 Supper; read Rosewell. 11.

THURSDAY [MAY] 10. 6.15 Prayed. 6.30 Writ account of bands. 8.15 Tea; writ to brother Samuel. 10.30 At Newgate. 12 Meditated, prayed, religious talk to many. 1 Rosewell; dinner. 2 Religious talk to many. 3.30 At Mrs Brummidge's, tea, religious talk, sang. 4.45 At Mr Labbè's, religious talk. 5 Castle Street. 7 Nicholas Street. 9.15 At Mr Whittington's, supper, religious talk. 10 At home; sang, read. 11.

FRIDAY [MAY] 11. 6 Prayed. 6.30 Sermon. 8 Tea, religious talk (necessary). 9 Sermon. 10.15 Newgate. 12 Prayed, religious talk, sang. 1 Religious talk to many; sermon. 3 Set out; Clifton, necessary talk. 3.45 Buried. 4.30 At Mrs Deschamps', necessary talk (religious). 5 Baldwin Street. 7 Gloucester Lane, Miss Gotley! 9 At home; supper, necessary talk (religious). 11.

SATURDAY [MAY] 12. 6 Prayed. 6.30 Sermon. 8 Tea, religious talk. 9 Sermon. 10.30 Newgate; Mrs Labbè! 12 Laid the stone; prayed, sang. 12.45 Visited. 1 At home; dinner. 2 Sermon. 2.30 Visited. 3 At Mrs Williams', Communion (twelve there). 4 Bowling Green. 5.15 At Mr Labbè's, tea, religious talk. 6 Clifton; buried; spoke. 7 Weavers' Hall, three received. 10 At home; supper, religious talk, sang. 11.

SUNDAY, MAY 13. 6 Prayed; meditated; dressed. 7 Bowling Green, 1 Corinthians 13 (six thousand there). 8.30 Tea, religious talk. 9.30 Set out; meditated. 10.30 Hanham, Galatians 3 (four thousand there). 12 Visited. 12.30 At Mr Deschamps', dinner. 1 At home; necessary talk; meditated. 2 Clifton, read Prayers, John 4:13, 14. 4.30 At Mr Deschamps', tea, religious talk. 5 At Rose Green, Galatians 3 (six thousand there). 6.15 Came with Miss Burdock in the coach, religious talk. 7 At Mrs England's, sang, etc; M Simkin! 8.15 At home; the women's Love-feast, prayed, etc. 11.

MONDAY [MAY] 14. 6 Prayed. 6.30 Writ to Fetter Lane. 8 Tea, religious talk; sermon. 10.30 Newgate. 12 Visited. 12.45 At home; meditated, prayed; religious talk to many. 2 At Mrs Norman's, dinner. 3.30 Mrs Thornhill, religious talk. 4 Brick-yard (five thousand there), Matthew 18. 5 Visited many. 7 Nicholas Street (three [mourners comforted] there). 9.15 At Mrs Brummidge's, religious talk; supper, sang. 11.45.

TUESDAY [MAY] 15. 5 Dressed; walked with Mr Labbè and Purdy; Bedminster. 5.30 Christened Sara Labbè. 7.30 At Mr Jones', religious talk, tea. 9.30 At home; writ. 10.30 Newgate. 12 At our House. 12.30 At home; meditated; prayed. 1 Dinner, religious talk to some. 2 Set out. 3 At Two-mile Hill (four hundred there); preached. 4 Necessary talk (religious); christened. 5 At the Back Lane, sang, etc. 7 Baldwin Street, three comforted! 9.30 At home; supper. 10 Miss Gregory, etc, prayed; all comforted!. 11.

WEDNESDAY [MAY] 16. 6.15 Prayer. 6.30 Sermon. 8 Tea, religious talk. 9 Religious talk to Thomas Robins. 10.30 Newgate. 12 At our House; visited. 1.30 Religious talk; writ to George Whitefield. 2 At Mr Whitehead's, necessary talk. 3 Tea, religious talk. 4 Baptist Mills. 5 Visited. 5.30 At N Champion's, tea, necessary talk (religious). 6.45 At home; writ diary. 7 The female bands, sang, prayed. 8.30 Baldwin Street. 9.45 Supper; necessary talk (religious). 11.

THURSDAY [MAY] 17. 6.30 Prayed. 6.45 Sermon. 8.15 Tea, Mr Castle, etc, religious talk. 9 Sermon. 12 Prayed. 12.30 Mr England, etc, necessary talk of the Schoolhouse, Kingswood. 1 Dinner, religious talk to many. 3 At Mrs Thomas', tea, religious talk. 3.30 In the coach with her and Mrs Stephens, Purdy, and Wathen. 4 At Mrs Willis', prayed, sang. 4.45 Set out; at Mr Gotley's, necessary talk (religious) to Miss Rachel at the window. 5.15 Castle Street. 7 Nicholas Street. 9 At home; supper, prayed, religious talk. 10.30 Read Archbishop Tillotson. 11.

FRIDAY [MAY] 18. 6 Prayed. 6.30 Sermon. 8 Tea, religious talk; sermon. 11 Preached at the Dial; visited. 12.45 Prayed. 1 Religious talk to many. 2.30 Visited. 3 At Mr Martin's, tea, sang, religious talk. 4 At Mr Linnington's, tea, religious talk. 5 Baldwin Street. 7 At Mrs England's. 9.15 At home; supper, religious talk, prayed. 11.

SATURDAY [MAY] 19. 4.45 Dressed. 5 Set out. 6 Kingswood, necessary talk of the House; prayed. 8.45 At home; tea. 9.15 Read letters, etc. 11 Baldwin Street. 1 Dinner, necessary talk (religious). 2 Baldwin Street. 4 At the Bowling Green (two thousand there), 'Charity'. 5.15 Baldwin Street. 7 Weavers' Hall (two there [received]). 9.30 At home; supper, religious talk, prayed. 11.

SUNDAY [MAY] 20. 6.45 Dressed. 7 Bowling Green, 'Charity' (seven thousand there). 8.30 Set out to Clifton; married. 9.45 At Mr Deschamps'; set out. 10.30 Two thousand there, 'Charity'. 12 Visited. 12.30 At Mr Deschamps'; dinner. 2 Clifton, Luke 5:32. 4.15 At Mr Deschamps', tea, in the coach with Miss Smith, Cornish, Wiggington. 5.15 Rose Green, thunder, Ps. 29:3, 4 (fifteen hundred there). 7 Nicholas Street (three there [received]). 9.45 At home. 10 Supper, prayed. 11.

MONDAY [MAY] 21. 4.30 Dressed; at Mr Deschamps'. 5.15 Set out. 6 At Kingswood, laid the stone [cf 5/12], necessary talk (religious). 8.45 At Clifton; married; tea; Mr Hodges died. 10 At Mrs Deschamps', religious talk, tea. 11.30 At the Dial, preached. 12.15 Visited. 12.45 At home; religious talk to many; one freed [from sin]! 1.15 Dinner, religious talk to many. 3.30 At Mrs Norman's, religious talk. 4 Brick-yard, Ps. 46:10 (twenty-five hundred there, seven comforted)! 5.30 Visited many. 7 Nicholas Street, sang, etc. 8 Eleven comforted. 10 At Mr Page's, supper. 11 With Mrs ——, etc, all comforted. 1.

TUESDAY [MAY] 22. 6.30 Dressed; at Mr Deschamps', tea. 7.30 Set out with him and Mr Wiggington, religious talk. 10 Bath; dressed; at Mr Dibble's, necessary talk (religious); at John [Feachem]'s, religious talk, sang. 12 At Mr Chapman's, religious talk. 1 At Richard Merchant's, dinner, religious talk. 2.45 At Mr Dibble's, tea, religious talk. 4 At the Ham, Ephesians 5:14 (one thousand there). 5.30 Set out. 8 Baldwin Street. 9 At home; supper, religious talk. 10.30.

WEDNESDAY [MAY] 23. 6.45 Dressed; writ diary; writ to Mr Seward. 8.45 At Mrs Gotley's, religious talk, tea. 10.30 Newgate. 12.15 Visited. 12.45 At home; slept. 1.15 Religious talk to many. 2.30 Walked; at Mr Shell's, religious talk, tea. 4 Preached (two thousand there), Acts 28:6; [at Newgate?] Luke 18:6. 5.15 At Mr Champion's, tea, religious talk, prayed. 6.30 At home; writ. 7 The women, necessary talk (religious), prayed. 8.15 Baldwin Street, necessary talk (religious), sang. 9.15 At Mrs Deschamps', W Tolley, etc, sang, religious talk; supper. 11.30.

THURSDAY, MAY 24. 6.45 Dressed; at Richard Champion's (nine there), tea, religious talk, prayed. 9 Writ to brother Soane, Exall, Parker, P Sims, Mrs Grevil, Charles Delamotte. 12.30 Dinner. 1.30 Set out with Henry Dory. 3 Publow; Mr Jeffrys'; preached, Isaiah 53:5; at Mr Jeffrys'. 5.15 Set out, religious talk; meditated. 6.30 At brother Williams', tea, religious talk. 7.15 At Baldwin Street. 9.15 At home; supper, religious talk. 10.45.

FRIDAY [MAY] 25. 5.45 Prayed; meditated. 6.30 Sermon. 8 Tea, religious talk; sermon. 1 Religious talk to many. 2 Set out; *History of Puritans.* 3 At the Fishponds (one thousand there), Isaiah 53:5, 6. 5 In the coach, religious talk to Lucretia Smith, etc. 6.15 Baldwin Street. 7 Gloucester Lane. 9 At Mr White's, religious talk, supper, religious talk. 11.

SATURDAY [MAY] 26. 6 Prayed. 6.30 Sermon. 8 Tea, religious talk. 9 Sermon. 11

John Whitehead, prayed! 12.30 Sermon. 1 Dinner, religious talk to many. 3 At Mrs Williams', Communion (thirteen there). 4 Bowling Green (two thousand there), 'Charity'. 5 At Mrs Iscock's, tea; at Mrs Stephens'. Tea, religious talk, prayed. 6.30 At Mrs ——, tea, religious talk. 7 Weavers' Hall. 9 At Mr Wiggington's; Miss Burdock's, supper, religious talk, prayed. 11.30.

Sunday [May] 27. 6.30 Meditated; dressed. 7 Bowling Green (six thousand there), 'Charity' (con). 8.30 At Mr Deschamps', tea, religious talk. 9.15 At Mrs Willis', Communion (twelve there). 10.30 Hanham, Isaiah 53:5, 6 (twenty-five hundred there); visited. 12.30 At Mrs Deschamps', dinner; visited. 2 At home; writ diary. 2.30 At Christ Church. 4 At Mr Deschamps', tea, Rose Green (ten thousand there), Luke 9:55, 56 (three [comforted] there!). 6.45 At Mrs England's (eleven [comforted] there!). 10.30 At Mr Labbè's, religious talk, supper. 11.30.

Monday [May] 28. 6.15 Prayed. 6.30 Writ. 8 Tea, religious talk; writ to Fetter Lane. 11 Weavers' Hall (two [received remission of sins] there). 1 At home; dinner, religious talk to many. 3.30 Brick-yard (seven [received] there). 6.45 At Mr Labbè's, tea. 7 Baldwin Street (ten [received] there). 10.30 At home; supper. 11.15.

Tuesday [May] 29. 6 Prayed; ended sermon; corrected *Nicodemus*. 8 Tea, religious talk to Mr Fancourt. 9 *Nicodemus*. 12.30 Dinner. 1 Visited. 1.45 Set out; read Gill. 2.30 At our House, necessary talk. 3 Preached. 4 At James Burgess', necessary talk to many. 5.15 Back Lane. 7 Nicholas Street. 9 At Mrs Oldfield's, Mrs Thornhill, Miss Burdock, etc, religious talk; supper; sang, prayed. 11.15.

Wednesday [May] 30. 6 Prayed. 6.30 Read Ridgley. 8 Tea, religious talk. 9 Ridgley. 9.30 Walked to Mr Tindal's, religious talk. 10.45 Newgate, christened. 1 At home; religious talk to many. 2 At Mr Whitehead's, Mr Pitt; dinner, religious talk. 4 Baptist Mills (one [received] there!). 5 At Miss Shepherd's, religious talk, tea. 6 At Mrs Thornhill's, Miss Sally Burdock, tea, sang, prayed. 7 With the women. 8 Baldwin Street. 9 At first [band?], Mrs Davis', supper; Mrs Panou, etc, prayed, sang. 11.

Thursday [May] 31. 6 Prayed. 6.30 Writ notes. 8 Tea, necessary talk (religious). 9 Writ diary; writ notes. 9.30 Set out with Mr Wiggington, Mrs England, Davis, Labbè, Miss Smith, in the coach, sang, religious talk. 12 At Kings Weston Hill, prayed, sang. 12.45 Dinner. 1 Prayed. 2 Many came, preached. 3 Set out, sang, religious talk. 5 Castle Street. 7 Weavers' Hall. 9 At home; supper, necessary talk (religious). 10.30. 1 Sins!

Friday, June 1. 6 Prayed. 6.30 Writ accounts. 8 Tea, religious talk. 9 Writ notes. 10.30 Weavers' Hall. 12 At home; meditated. 11.15 Mr Farley, religious talk, sang, prayed. 11.45 Religious talk to many. 2.45 At Mr Linnington's; at Mrs Morgan's. 3 Tea, mostly religious talk, sang. 4 At the new Brick-yard (fifteen hundred there). 5.15 At Mr Marine's, religious talk. 6 At Mrs Norman's, Miss Burdock, tea, sang, religious talk. 7 Gloucester Lane. 9 At home; supper, religious talk. 10.45.

Saturday [June] 2. 5.45 Prayed. 6.15 Writ to Bray, Edmunds, Easy, J Chambers. 8 Tea, religious talk. 8.45 Religious talk to Miss Cornish, she in love with me! 10 Writ to Seward, Metcalf, Esther Hopson, Oxlee, Clapham, Miss Thacker, Holland, Charles Graves. 1 Dinner, religious talk to many; writ to Betty Hughes, James Mears. 3 At Mrs Williams', Communion (twelve there). 4 Bowling Green; writ diary; one thousand there, rain. 5.15 At home; writ. 5.45 At W[ido]w Davis', writ; tea, sang; Mrs Norman, etc. 6.30 Weavers' Hall (con). 8.45 At Mrs Thornhill's, Miss Burdock, religious talk. 9.15 Prayed (lively zeal, +). 10 At Mrs Linnington's, supper, religious talk, sang. 12.

Sunday [June] 3. 6.30 Dressed; meditated. 7 Bowling Green, 'Charity' (con!; seven thousand there). 9 At Mr Deschamps', tea; set out. 10.15 Hanham, Romans 3:19 (three thousand there); visited. 12.30 At Mr Deschamps', dinner. 1.15 At home; writ to George Whitefield, to James Hutton. 2.30 All Saints (+, con). 4.15 At Mr Deschamps', tea. 5 Rose Green (nine thousand there!), Romans 3:19. 7 At our Room. 9.30 At Lucretia Smith's, supper, religious talk. 12.

Monday, June 4. 6.45 Prayed; writ to Fetter Lane. 8.30 Tea, religious talk (necessary). 9 Writ. 10.30 Dressed; Ezra 8:21, 22; Ps. 9:16; 10:16; 17:16[BCP]; Weavers' Hall. 1 At home; dinner, religious talk to many. 3.45 At Mrs Norman's; at the Brick-yard, Isaiah 41:10. 5.30 At home; writ. 6 At Mrs Norman's, tea, religious talk. 6.45 Gloucester Lane. 8.45 At Mr Norman's, necessary talk (religious). 9 At Mr Marine's, Mrs Norman, Longden, Labbè, etc, supper, sang, prayed. 11.30.

Tuesday [June] 5. 6.15 Prayed; writ to Miss Burdock. 8 Tea, mostly religious talk; writ. 10 At Mr Deschamps'. 10.45 Set out, religious talk to Mr Eyres. 1.30 Bath. 2 At Mr Dibble's, dinner, religious talk. 3 At Richard Merchant's, necessary talk (religious). 4 Preached; Mr Nash! 5.45 Set out. 7 At our Room. 9 At Mrs Deschamps', Mr Tindal there, necessary talk (religious), sang, prayed. 10 At home; supper, religious talk. 11.15.

Wednesday [June] 6. 6.45 Prayed; writ to Mrs Fox and Sarah Hurst. 8 Tea, necessary talk (religious). 9 Writ to brother Gibbs, Shaw, Clark. 10.45 Newgate. 3 Christened! 12.45 At home; prayed. 1 Religious talk to many. 3 At Captain Williams', prayed, religious talk. 4 Baptist Mills (twenty-five hundred there), John 9. 5.15 At Mr Champion's, religious talk, tea, prayed. 6.30 At home; the leaders; with the women. 8 Baldwin Street. 9.15 At Mrs Thornhill's, religious talk. 9.45 With Mrs Cooper, she spoke! 11 At Mr Labbè's, supper. 12.

Thursday [June] 7. 7 Prayed. 7.15 Writ to brother Samuel. 8.15 Tea, religious talk. 9 Writ. 11 Writ to Miss Burdock. 12.30 Dinner, religious talk; writ. 1.45 Set out with Deschamps and Cornish, religious talk. 2.45 Pensford, at the Society, religious talk, sang. 3.15 Priestdown, Acts 16:30 (four hundred there). 4.45 At Mr Jeffrys', tea. 5.15 Set out, religious talk. 6.45 Weavers' Hall. 8.45 At brother Williams', sang, religious talk, supper, prayed. 11.15.

Friday [June] 8. 6.15 Prayer; writ to brother Hodges and Gould. 8 Tea, religious talk. 9.15 Writ notes. 10 At Mr Wiggington's, religious talk, he angry! 10.45 Weavers' Hall. 12 At Mrs Davis', religious talk. 12.45 At home; prayed. 1 Religious talk to many. 2.30 Set out. 3.15 At the Fishponds, Romans 3:19; visited. 5.15 At Mr Deschamps', tea. 5.45 At home; necessary talk (religious) to Mr Wiggington. 6.45 Gloucester Lane. 9 At Captain Williams', prayed;

supper, religious talk, prayed. 10.30 At home; Mrs Grevil, necessary talk (religious). 11.

SATURDAY [JUNE] 9. 5.45 Prayed. 6.15 Writ to Dr Isham. 8 Tea, religious talk; writ. 10.45 Read *History of Puritans.* 12.15 Meditated; prayed. 1 Dinner, religious talk to many. 2.30 Visited. 3 At Mrs Williams', Communion (ten there). 4 Bowling Green, John 9 (one thousand there). 5.15 At home; necessary talk (religious). 6 At Mrs Dissign's, tea, sang. 6.30 Weavers' Hall. 8.45 At brother Williams', writ to Sally Burdock. 9 At Mrs Davis', Miss Smith, Mrs Longden, Mrs Labbè, etc, sang, supper, prayed. 11.15 At home; necessary talk. 11.45.

SUNDAY [JUNE] 10. 6.15 Dressed; meditated. 7 Bowling Green (three thousand there), John 3:8. 9 At Mrs Willis', Communion (ten there); tea. 10.30 Hanham, Acts 2:1, 2, 3 (twelve hundred there). 12.30 At Mr Deschamps', dinner, religious talk. 1.30 At home; writ diary. 2 Ended my letter. 2.30 All Saints. 4.15 At Mr Deschamps', tea. 5 Rose Green (three thousand there), Acts 2:1, etc. 7 At the Room. 9 At home; the women's Love-feast. 10 Religious talk to Thomas Whitefield. 10.45.

MONDAY [JUNE] 11. 5.30 Prayed. 6 *Christian Perfection* [Law?] 8.15 Tea, religious talk; *Christian Perfection.* 10.45 Weavers' Hall. 12.15 At home; prayed. 1 Lots: I go to London; dinner, necessary talk (religious). 2.15 Writ diary. 3 Writ notes; religious talk (necessary) to many. 4 Brick-yard, Acts 20:26 (thirty-five hundred there). 5 At Mrs Norman's, many there, religious talk, tea, sang, prayed. 6.30 Set out with brother Deschamps, religious talk with Vaughan and Parsons. 7.45 They went, religious talk. 9 Marshfield; at the Crown, writ diary. 9.15 Necessary talk (religious). 9:45 Supper; writ to Miss Burdock. 11.

TUESDAY [JUNE] 12. 4 Set out; meditated; religious talk. 8.30 Marlborough; tea, religious talk. 10.30 Set out. 1:30 Woolhampton, religious talk, dinner. 3 Set out. 5 Met Kezzy, religious talk. 6.15 Hare Hatch, with three more. 7 Set out; meditated. 9.15 Slough; supper, necessary talk (religious). 11.

WEDNESDAY [JUNE] 13. 4.30 Dressed. 4.45 Set out. 8.30 At Mrs West's, Charles there; tea, religious talk. 9.30 Set out with Charles, religious talk. 11 Islington, read Prayers, Communion. 12.30 With my mother, necessary talk (religious). 2 At Mrs West's, dinner. 4 With the women; at Mr Bray's, Hutchins there, religious talk, tea, sang. 5.30 Fetter Lane [women]. 8 Fetter Lane [men]. 11 Supper.

THURSDAY, JUNE 14. 7.15 Dressed; religious talk. 8 At Mrs West's, mostly religious talk. 9.15 Set out; read George Whitefield's journal. 1 Blendon; dinner, religious talk with George Whitefield [not in America after all]. 4 Writ to brother Purdy; tea. 5 Set out. 6.45 Blackheath, preached (fifteen thousand there), 1 Corinthians 1:30. 8 At the Green Man, religious talk. 8 Read Seagrave's answer to Trapp. 9.30 Supper. 10 Sang; George Whitefield spoke. 11.30.

FRIDAY [JUNE] 15. 4.15 Dressed. 4.30 Set out with James Hutton, etc; read George Whitefield's journal. 6.30 At Mrs West's; slept. 8 At Nicholas Davis', Anthony Purver there. 9.15 At Mrs West's; at Mr Bray's; necessary business.

12.30 Islington, with my mother, religious talk. 3 At sister Hall's, necessary talk (religious). 4 At Mrs West's, tea, religious talk, sang. 5.15 At Mrs Mills', religious talk to Tompson. 6 At the Room, Wapping (twenty-six [comforted]). 11 At home; ate. 11.30.

SATURDAY, JUNE 16. 6.15 Dressed; necessary talk (religious). 7.15 St Dunstan's. 9 At home; religious talk to many; tea, religious talk to Hutchings, etc. 12 Fetter Lane. 2 At brother Clark's, dinner, religious talk. 3 Fetter Lane. 5 At sister Hall's with sister Kezzy, necessary talk. 6 Fetter Lane. 8 At home; Esther Hopson. 9 Supper. 9.30 Fetter Lane. 11 At home. 11.15 Sins of thought.

SUNDAY, JUNE 17. 5.45 Dressed; meditated. 6.45 Moorfields (seven thousand there), Isaiah 55. 8.45 At Mrs West's, tea, religious talk; Betty and Esther Hopson, sang. 9.30 At home; brother Shaw and Wolf, religious talk, prayed. 11 Writ diary; writ journal. 12.30 Read. 1 Dinner, religious talk. 2 At brother Patterson's, religious talk, prayed. 3 At Mrs Mills', religious talk, tea. 5.15 At Kennington Common, Isaiah 45:22 (fifteen thousand there). 7 Fetter Lane, women bands. 9.30 Our bands, religious talk, prayed. 10.30 At home; supper. 11.15.

MONDAY, JUNE 18. 4.30 Necessary talk (religious); chocolate. 5.45 Set out. 10 Colnbrook; tea, religious talk. 11 Set out. 3 Reading; dinner. 4 Set out. 6.45 Feacham [Thatcham?], religious talk to them. 7.15 Set out. 8.45 At an inn, walked, wrote diary. 9.15 Meditated; supper, religious talk. 10.30.

TUESDAY [JUNE] 19. 4 Dressed. 4.15 Set out. 8.15 Marlborough; tea, religious talk. 9.15 Set out. 11 Calne; dinner, religious talk. 12 Set out. 3 Marshfield, tea, religious talk. 4 Set out. 5 Cornish, etc, met us, religious talk. 6 At Anthony Williams', tea, religious talk, sang. 7 Bowling Green, Isaiah 45:22 (five thousand). 8.15 At home; religious talk to many. 9 Supper; Howell Harris, religious talk, prayed. 11.

WEDNESDAY [JUNE] 20. 6.30 Prayed; 2 Samuel 20:20. 7 Writ to George Whitefield. 8.30 Tea, religious talk. 10.30 Newgate. 12.45 At home; slept. 2 Writ diary; meditated. 3 Visited. 3.15 At Mrs Norman's, tea, religious talk. 4 Baptist Mills (twelve hundred there), Luke 22:31. 5.30 At Mr Labbè's, tea, religious talk. 6.30 At home; religious talk. 7 At Elizabeth Davis' with the women. 8 Baldwin Street, necessary talk (religious), prayed, all well! 10 Supper, religious talk. 11.15.

THURSDAY [JUNE] 21. 6 Religious talk to Mr Bailis. 8.15 Tea, religious talk. 9 Necessary business. 12.15 Meditated; prayed. 1 Dinner. 1.30 Set out; religious talk to Edward Smith. 3.15 Publow (one hundred fifty there), Isaiah 45:22. 4.30 At Mr Jeffrys'; set out; read George Whitefield's journal. 6 At home; writ diary; tea, religious talk. 6.45 At our Room ['the Schoolroom']. 9 At Miss Cutler's with Mary [Molly] Deacon's band, religious talk, prayed. 10 Supper, religious talk. 11 At home; religious talk. 11.30.

FRIDAY [JUNE] 22. 6 Prayed. 6.30 Writ to the society at Wells; necessary business. 8.15 Tea, religious talk. 9 At Mr Whitehead's, necessary talk. 10.30 At Mr Farley's, necessary talk (religious). 11 Weavers' Hall. 12.15 Visited. 1.45 At home; religious talk to some. 2.30 At Mrs Deschamps', tea; at the Fishponds, Isaiah 45:22. 5.15 At home; writ. 5.30 At Elizabeth Davis', Mrs Thornhill's band. 6.30 At Gloucester Lane (seven [comforted] there!). 9 Visited; at home; supper. 11.

SATURDAY [JUNE] 23. 6 Prayed. 6.30 Writ to ——. 8.15 Tea, religious talk. 9.15 Writ to Charles. 10 Mr Whitehead, etc, necessary talk. 10.30 Visited Mrs Page; writ. 12 Meditated; prayed; religious talk. 1 Dinner, religious talk to many. 3 At Mrs Williams', Communion (twelve there). 4 Bowling Green, 1 Corinthians 10:31 (two thousand there). 5.15 At home; tea, religious talk. 6 Writ to George Whitefield. 6.45 Weavers' Hall. 9 At Mr Cornish's, Mrs Labbè, etc; supper, religious talk, sang, prayed. 11.15.

SUNDAY, JUNE 24. 6.45 Dressed. 7 Bowling Green (five thousand there), 1 Corinthians 10:31. 8.45 At Mrs Willis', Communion (twelve there). 9.30 Tea. 10.15 Hanham, 1 Corinthians 10:31 (three thousand there). 12.30 At Mr Norman's, religious talk. 1 Dinner. 2.30 All Saints. 4.15 At Mrs Deschamps', tea. 4.30 Set out; the horse fell. 5.15 Rose Green, 1 Corinthians 10:31 (sixty-five hundred there). 7.15 At our Room. 10 At home; necessary talk (religious). 11.

MONDAY [JUNE] 25. 7 Writ to brother Ellis, brother Ingham. 8 Tea, religious talk. 8.45 Writ to Mr Abbott. 10.45 Weavers' Hall. 12.30 Religious talk to three; sins of thought. 1 Read journal. 1.30 Necessary business. 1.45 Dinner, religious talk to many. 3 Writ to Charles, to brother Parker. 4 Brick-yard, Revelation 1:11 (thirty-five hundred there). 5.15 At Miss Purnell's band, tea, religious talk, prayed. 6.15 At Mr Quin's, tea, religious talk. 6.45 Sang, etc (five [comforted]!). 8.45 At ——'s band! 9 At Mr Wiggington's, Miss Suky Burdock, religious talk, sang. 10.15 Supper, religious talk, sang, prayed. 11.15 At home; necessary talk (religious). 11.30.

TUESDAY [JUNE] 26. 6.45 Prayed; writ to brother Samuel. 8.15 Tea, religious talk. 9 Writ. 11.45 Set out with Mrs Thornhill, etc, religious talk. 12.30 At Mr Willis', sang, prayed. 1 Dinner, religious talk, sang. 2.15 At Mr Campbell's, ate, religious talk. 3 At the [School] house, necessary talk. 3.30 At the tree, Isaiah 55:11 (two hundred there). 5.15 At Mr Deschamps', tea. 6 Back Lane, sang, etc. 7 Horse-fair (three [comforted] there!). 9 At Miss Smith's band, prayed, religious talk, sang. 10 Supper, religious talk. 11.15.

WEDNESDAY [JUNE] 27. 6.30 Prayed; meditated. 7 Writ; read Law. 8 Tea, religious talk. 9 Read Gill. 10.45 Newgate; visited. 12.45 Meditated; slept. 1.15 Religious talk to many. 2.30 Writ to George Whitefield. 2.45 At Mrs Cooper's with Mr Labbè, religious talk, tea. 4 Baptist Mills, 1 Corinthians 10:22 (two thousand there). 5.15 At Mr Parker's, tea. 6 At Mrs Williams', religious talk, prayed. 7 At Mrs Davis' with the women, religious talk, prayed. 8 Baldwin Street, religious talk, prayed. 9.45 At home; supper, religious talk. 10.45 Prayed. 11.15.
[con, +]

THURSDAY [JUNE] 28. 6.30 Prayed. 6.45 Writ letters. 8 Tea, religious talk. 9 Letters. 12.30 Meditated; prayed. 1.30 Dinner. 1 Religious talk to many. 3 Visited; walked. 4.15 James Harding's, sang, prayed. 5 Walked, religious talk. 6 At Mr Deschamps', tea, religious talk. 6.30 At our Room. 8.30 With brother Wathen's band. 9 At Mrs Brummidge's, supper. 11.15.

FRIDAY [JUNE] 29. 6.30 Prayed. 6.45 Writ to George Whitefield; writ journal. 8

Tea, religious talk. 9 At Mr Lyne's, altered the les[son]. 10 Journal. 11 Weavers' Hall. 12.15 At home; meditated; prayed. 1 Religious talk to some. 2.30 At brother Purdy's, many there; tea, religious talk, sang. 3 Walked, religious talk. 4 James Harding's, religious talk, ate. 4.15 Preached, Acts 16:31. 5.30 Walked. 6.30 Gloucester Lane. 8.45 Supper. 9.30 With brother Giles' band. 10 Sang, prayed. 11 At home; religious talk to Mrs Grevil. 12.

SATURDAY [JUNE] 30. 6.15 Prayed; journal. 8 Tea, religious talk; journal. 10 At our Room; necessary talk! 11 At Mrs Williams', prayed, religious talk! 12.30 At home; meditated; prayed. 1 Religious talk with Mrs Thornhill; dinner. 2.15 Journal; writ diary. 2.45 At Mrs Williams', Communion (fourteen there). 3.30 At Miss Iscock's, religious talk. 4 Bowling Green (twelve thousand there), 1 Corinthians 10:23. 5.15 At Mrs Master's, necessary talk (religious). 5.45 At Mrs Davis', tea, religious talk. 6.30 Weavers' Hall (seventeen there). 8.30 Necessary talk to Mr Foy. 9 With John Brooks' band, religious talk, prayed. 9.30 At Mrs Deschamps', religious talk, supper, sang. 11.

SUNDAY, JULY 1. 6.30 Dressed; meditated. 7 Bowling Green, Ecclesiastes 7:16 (five thousand there). 8.15 Writ diary; at Mr Deschamps', tea, religious talk. 9 Set out. 10 Hanham, Luke 7:40. 11.45 At ——, religious talk, prayed (three [comforted] there!). 12.15 At Mr Deschamps', religious talk to Kitty; dinner, sang. 1 At home; writ diary; journal. 3.45 All Saints. 4.15 At Mr Deschamps', tea. 5 Rose Green, Luke 7:41 (fifty-five hundred there). 6.45 At our Room (five or six [comforted] there!). 9 At brother Palmer's band. 9.30 At Mr Thornhill's, her sisters there; necessary talk (religious), supper, religious talk. 11.30.

MONDAY [JULY] 2. 6.15 Prayed; meditated. 6.45 Journal. 8.15 Tea, religious talk. 9 Journal. 11 Weavers' Hall (one [comforted] there!). 12.15 Visited. 12.30 At home; meditated; prayed. 1 Writ. 1.30 Dinner. 2 Religious talk to many. 3 At Mrs Thomas', tea, religious talk; visited. 4 Brick-yard, Ecclesiastes 7:16 (three thousand there). 5.15 At Mrs Arthur's, tea, religious talk. 6 At Mrs Norman's, necessary talk (religious). 6.30 Gloucester Lane (eight [comforted] there!). 9 At Mr Castle's, religious talk to Mrs Rutter; supper, religious talk, sang. 11.15.

TUESDAY, JULY 3. 6 Prayed; meditated. 6.30 Writ to Dr Isham, etc. 8.15 Tea, religious talk. 9 Writ to 10 At Mr Deschamps', necessary talk (religious). 10.30 Set out with him and Cornish; meditated. 12.45 At John Feachem's; at Mrs Dibble's, necessary talk (religious). 1 At John's, Mrs Hamilton came; writ to James Hutton and Mrs Storer. 2 Dinner, religious talk, sang. 3.15 At Richard Merchant's, necessary talk (religious). 3.45 Sang, preached, Luke 5:32 (nine hundred there). 5 Set out; meditated. 7 At Mr Deschamps', tea. 7.15 At our Room. 8.30 At home; the boys' band. 9 At Henry Lucans', sang, supper, prayed. 11.15.

WEDNESDAY [JULY] 4. 6.30 Prayed. 6.45 Writ to Mr Deberdt. 8.15 Tea, religious talk. 9 Letter; letter. 10 Mrs Thornhill, religious talk. 11 Newgate, John 12. 12.30 Mr Castle and his son, religious talk. 12.45 Meditated; prayed. 1 Writ; religious talk to many. 3 At Mr Labbè's, tea, religious talk. 4 Baptist Mills, Ecclesiastes 7:16 (fifteen hundred there). 5 At Mrs Williams', religious talk, sang. 6.30 At home; writ. 7 At the women's bands. 8 At Baldwin Street, sang, prayed, necessary talk (religious), sang, prayed. 10 At home; supper, religious talk. 11.15.

T HURSDAY [J ULY] 5. 6 Prayed; meditated. 6.30 Writ. 8 Tea, religious talk. 9 Began the New Testament. 12.45 Necessary business. 1 Dinner, religious talk; New Testament. 2 Set out with Edward Smith, religious talk; meditated. 3.45 Publow, Luke 5:32 (five hundred there). 5 At Mr Jeffrys', tea, religious talk. 5.30 Set out; meditated; prayed. 6.30 At home; necessary business. 6.45 At our Room. 9 At brother Porter's; supper, religious talk, sang, prayed. 11.15.

F RIDAY [J ULY] 6. 6.45 Prayed. 7.15 New Testament. 8 Tea, religious talk. 9 New Testament. 10.30 Weavers' Hall. 11.45 At home; New Testament. 12.30 Religious talk to many. 1.30 At Mr Deschamps', tea, religious talk. 3.15 At Anthony Purver's, religious talk. 4.30 At the Fishponds, Luke 7:36, etc. 6 At Mr Quin's, religious talk, tea. 6.30 At home; with George Whitefield, necessary talk (religious). 7.30 Baptist Mills, George Whitefield preached. 9.15 At home; necessary talk (religious); supper. 10 Religious talk; prayed. 11 Writ diary.

S ATURDAY [J ULY] 7. 6.15 Prayed; writ accounts. 8 Read letters. 8.30 At Mr Labbè's with George Whitefield. 9 Religious talk, tea; Wathen came, necessary talk (religious). 12.15 At home; accounts. 1.15 Dinner, religious talk. 2 Religious talk. 3 At Mrs Williams' with George Whitefield (eighteen there). 4 Collected Prayers. 5 At Mr Deschamps', religious talk, tea. 6 At John Haydon's, religious talk. 7 At Baptist Mills; George Whitefield preached. 9 At home; supper. 10.30 Prayed, sang. 11.15.

S UNDAY, J ULY 8. 6.15 Dressed; meditated. 7 Bowling Green; George Whitefield preached. 9 At home; tea. 10 At Mrs Willis', Communion (thirty-two there). 11.30 Hanham; George Whitefield preached. 12.15 At Mr Deschamps', dinner, religious talk. 2.30 At home; religious talk. 3 St Nicholas's. 4.30 At home; many there, prayed. 5 Writ to Miss Burdock; writ diary. 6 At Mr Deschamps', tea, religious talk. 7 Rose Green (seventeen thousand there), George Whitefield preached. 9.30 At home; supper. 10 At the women's Love-feast, religious talk, prayed. 11.15.

M ONDAY [J ULY] 9. 5.45 Dressed; read Prayers. 6.45 Writ for the bands. 8.45 At Jenny's [Worlock?], religious talk, tea, prayed. 10 At home; writ. 1 At Mr Hodges', dinner, prayed. 2.30 At home; writ orders for the Society [see letter to George Whitefield]. 4.15 At Mrs Townsend's, tea, religious talk. 5.30 At home; writ to Mr Davidson, Oulton, James Hutton. 7 At the Brick-yard, George Whitefield preached. 9 At Mr Allen's, mostly religious talk; supper, mostly religious talk, prayed. 11.45.

T UESDAY [J ULY] 10. 6.45 Necessary talk (religious); writ notes. 8 Religious talk to some. 8.45 At Mr Wiggington's, tea, sang, religious talk. 12.30 Set out with George Whitefield, etc. 1.15 At J Burgess'; at the Schoolhouse, George Whitefield preached. 4.45 Set out. 5.45 At Bath; the White Hart, tea, sang. 7.30 George Whitefield preached. 9 At the inn; religious talk; supper. 10.15 George Whitefield went; prayed. 11.

W EDNESDAY [J ULY] 11. 7 Dressed; at Mr Dibble's, tea, religious talk. 8.15 George Whitefield preached. 9.30 Religious talk to many. 10 At Lady Cock's with Mrs Bridget, religious talk. 11 Set out; meditated. 1.15 At Mr Deschamps', tea. 2 At home; dressed; at Mrs Deschamps', dinner, religious talk; George Whitefield baptized Jane Rutter. 4 At Mrs Padmore's, tea. 5.30 Baptist Mills; George Whitefield preached. 7 At the women's bands. 8.15 Baldwin Street, religious talk, prayed [GW says they united the two leading societies together]. 9.30 At home; supper, religious talk, prayed. 11.15.

THURSDAY [JULY] 12. 6 Prayed; meditated. 6.30 Writ to Miss Burdock. 8.30 At Mrs Smith's, religious talk, tea, prayed. 10 At home; writ to Miss Burdock. 12 Journal. 1.30 At Mr Dagge's, dinner, religious talk. 3 At Mr Cutler's, prayed, tea, sang, prayed. 4.30 At Mrs Norman's, religious talk, tea. 6 At Mrs Page's, religious talk, prayed. 7 At the Bowling Green, George Whitefield, preached. 9 At Mr Porter's, supper, religious talk, sang, prayed. 10.30 I lay down; sins. 11.

FRIDAY, JULY 13. 6.30 Dressed; meditated. 7 Bowling Green; George Whitefield preached. 9 At Mr White's, necessary talk (religious). 10.15 At home; writ German. 12.30 Mr Chapman of Bath, religious talk. 12.45 Dinner; writ diary. 1.45 Sang; prayed with many; George Whitefield preached. 4 Set out; hard rain; sang, religious talk. 7.30 Thornbury, tea, religious talk. 8.15 George Whitefield preached (five hundred there). 9.30 Supper, religious talk, prayed. 11.

SATURDAY [JULY] 14. 6.15 Religious talk, sang, tea. 7.30 At Isaac Sharpless', tea, religious talk. 8.15 George Whitefield preached (six hundred there). 10 Set out; German verse. 12.30 At Cambridge, ate. 1.30 Set out; verse. 3.30 Gloucester; dressed. 4 Read Prayers. 5 At home; dinner; corrected George Whitefield's sermon. 7 George Whitefield preached (two thousand there). 9 At home; tea, religious talk, sang, prayed. 10.30 Lay down; sins of thought. 11.

SUNDAY [JULY] 15. 6 Sang; dressed. 7 At the Ground, preached (four thousand there), 1 Corinthians 1:30. 8.45 At the Bell, tea, religious talk. 10 At St Miles's [Michael's], Communion. 12.30 At home; dinner, religious talk. 2 At Mr Harris', religious talk, tea. 4 Read Prayers. 5 At the Ground, hard rain (three thousand there), Ezekiel 37:4. 7 At the Society. 9 Religious talk (necessary) to the members. 9.45 At Mr Harris', supper, many came, religious talk, prayed. 11.

MONDAY [JULY] 16. 6 Dressed; tea, religious talk. 7 Preached (twenty-five hundred there), Acts 16:30. 9 At home; religious talk to Mrs Wells. 9.30 Set out; verse. 12.30 Newport; dinner. 1.30 Set out; verse. 5.30 Bristol; at Mr Deschamps', tea, religious talk; at home; dressed. 7 At Brick-yard (three thousand there), Job 3:17. 8.15 At Mrs Norman's, necessary talk (religious). 8.30 At home; necessary talk (religious); writ diary. 9.30.

TUESDAY [JULY] 17. 4.45 Dressed. 5 At Mr Deschamps', tea. 5.30 Set out. 9 At Winsley; Mr Cottle's, religious talk, prayed, tea, sang. 10.30 Bradford; at Mr Rogers', necessary talk; at Mr Reed's, necessary talk (religious). 12 At Bearfield, [see Curnock, 2:243] 1 Corinthians 1:30 (one thousand there). 1 At Mrs Ballard's, religious talk. 2 Dinner, prayed. 4 At Bath, Acts 16:30 (twenty-five hundred there). 5 Set out. 7.45 At Mr Deschamps', ate. 8 At our Room. 9 At home; religious talk to some. 10.15.

WEDNESDAY [JULY] 18. 7.30 Prayed. 8.15 Tea, religious talk. 9 Writ journal. 11 Weavers' Hall. 12.15 At home; religious talk to many. 2 Journal. 2.45 Necessary business. 3 At Mrs Hooper's, Mr Labbè there, tea, religious talk, sang. 4.15 At

Mrs Lanning's, necessary talk (religious). 5 Baptist Mills, Ezekiel 37:3 (fifteen hundred there). 6.30 At home; supper. 7 With the women. 8 Baldwin Street. 9.45 At home; religious talk. 10 Lay down. 11.15 Slept.

THURSDAY [JULY] 19. 5.30 Dressed; read Prayers. 6.45 Prayed. 7 Writ notes; religious talk (necessary). 8 At Elizabeth Davis', religious talk, tea, prayed. 9 At the Room, necessary talk. 10 Visited. 11.30 At home; Miss Gotley, prayed, religious talk; sins. 12.15 Set out. 1.45 At Mr Jeffrys', dinner, necessary talk (religious). 2.45 At Mr Prig's, necessary talk. 3.45 At Priestdown, Hosea 14:4 (two hundred there). 5 At Mr Jeffrys', tea, religious talk. 5.30 Set out; verse. 6.30 At home; supper. 7 At our Room (one [comforted]!). 9 At home; writ to George Whitefield; writ diary. 10.

FRIDAY [JULY] 20. 5.30 Dressed; read Prayers. 7 Writ notes; necessary talk (religious). 8 At Miss Cutler's, tea, religious talk, prayed. 9.30 At home; writ notes; religious talk. 11 Weavers' Hall. 12.30 At Mrs Eyres', religious talk. 1 At home; religious talk to many. 2.30 At Mr Deschamps', tea, religious talk. 3 Set out, with Cennick, religious talk. 4 Fishponds, Hosea 14:4. 5 At Mrs England's, tea, religious talk. 5.45 Sang, etc (one [comforted]! N Burroughs!). 9 At home; brothers Wynn, Swain, Lewis, etc, prayed, religious talk; all well. 10.15.

SATURDAY, JULY 21. 5.30 Dressed; writ. 6 Read Prayers. 7 Writ to Edmonds; necessary talk (religious). 8 At Jenny's, prayed, religious talk, tea, prayed. 9.15 At home; writ to Mr Deberdt; to sister Patty. 12 Necessary talk (religious); meditated. 1 Dinner, religious talk to some. 2.30 Visited. 3.30 At Mr Labbè's, tea, religious talk. 4.45 Bowling Green (twelve hundred there), Matthew 5:1, etc. 6.30 At home; tea. 7 Weavers' Hall; N Roberts! 9.15 At home; religious talk; religious talk to Crawley. 11.15.

SUNDAY [JULY] 22. 6 Dressed; meditated. 7 Bowling Green, Matthew 5:3 (three thousand there; one [comforted] there! Nursman). 8.30 At Mr Deschamps', tea, religious talk. 9.15 At Mrs Willis', Communion (twenty-five there). 10.30 Hanham (twenty-five hundred there), Matthew 5:3; +. 12.30 At Mr Norman's, dinner, religious talk. 2.30 All Saints; Mr Tucker inducted. 4 At Mr Deschamps', tea. 4.45 Rose Green, Matthew 5:3 (five thousand there). 7 At the Room (two [comforted] there!). 8.15 At the Love-feast. 10 At home; necessary talk (religious) to Mrs Grevil. 11 Religious talk. 11.30.

MONDAY [JULY] 23. 5.45 Dressed; prayed. 6.45 Prayed. 7 Religious talk. 8 Tea, religious talk. 9 Writ to Deberdt. 10.30 Religious talk to Miss Oldfield. 11 Weavers' Hall (+). 12.30 At Mrs Stephens', dinner, religious talk. 1.30 At Mr Deschamps', prayed with N Roberts; visited. 2 At home; religious talk to some; sins. 3.15 Slept. 3.30 At Mr Lanning's, religious talk. 4.30 At Mrs Norman's, religious talk. 5 Brick-yard, Mark 4:26 (twenty-five hundred there). 6.15 At Mrs Deschamps', tea, religious talk. Gloucester Lane (one [comforted] there!). 9 First band. 10.15.

TUESDAY [JULY] 24. 5.30 Dressed; religious talk. 6 Read Prayers; prayed. 7 Writ. 8 At Ken Chandler's, Bush and Turner there, tea, religious talk. 9.30 At home; Mr Tindal, necessary talk (religious); religious talk to many. 1 Dinner, religious talk to many. 2.30 At Mr Deschamps', tea. 3 Set out with brother Purdy, religious talk. 4 At our House, preached, Ezekiel 37:3. 5.15 In a coach with

S Rutter, etc, religious talk. 6.15 At Mrs Deschamps', tea. 7.30 At Miss Cutler's band, religious talk. 7 Our Room. 8 At Miss Cutler's band, religious talk, prayed. 10 At home; mostly religious talk. 11.15.

WEDNESDAY, JULY 25. 5.30 Dressed; meditated. 6 Read Prayers; slept; necessary talk (religious). 8 At Mr Labbè's, religious talk. 8.30 At home; necessary talk (religious); tea; Mr Taylor of Bath. 9.30 Writ to Dr Stebbing. 11 Weavers' Hall. 12.30 Visited. 1 At home; religious talk to many; writ letter. 3 At Mrs Masters', necessary talk (religious); tea. 5 Baptist Mills (fifteen hundred there), Isaiah 40:1. 6 At John Brooks' band. 6.30 At Mr Deschamps', tea. 7 With the women. 8.15 With the men.10 At home; religious talk. 10.30.

THURSDAY [JULY] 26. 5.30 Dressed; meditated. 6 Read Prayers; prayed. 7 Letter. 8 Many here; tea, religious talk. 9.30 Letter. 12.45 At Mr Stanton's, dinner, religious talk. 2.15 At home; religious talk to some. 3 At Mr Deschamps', tea. 3.15 Set out; religious talk. 4 At the Cupolas, Hebrews 12:14 (two hundred there). 6.15 At home; religious talk. 7 At our Room. 9 At Mr Cutler's, religious talk to ——. 9.30 At brother West's band. 10.15 Sins of thought.

FRIDAY [JULY] 27. 5.15 Dressed; meditated; prayed. 6 Read Prayers; at Mrs Deffel's band, religious talk, prayed. 7.30 Tea, religious talk. 8.30 At home; religious talk to many. 9.15 Transcribed [letter] to Dr Stebbing; necessary talk to Mrs Masters. 11 Weavers' Hall. 12.30 At home; religious talk to some. 2 Writ to sister Patty. 3 Read Robert Barclay; sins of thought; Mr Richards of Brent, religious talk. 4 At Mr Davis'; some from Cardiff there, tea, religious talk. 5 At our House, necessary talk. 6 At Mr Darby's, tea, religious talk. 6.45 At Mrs England's (four [comforted] there!). 9 The band, religious talk, prayed. 10 At home; religious talk with Cennick. 10.30.

SATURDAY [JULY] 28. 5.30 Dressed; prayed. 6 Read Prayers; writ to Mr Oulton. 8 Mr Richards, Cartwright of Eynsham, etc, religious talk. 9 Religious talk to many. 10 Writ to Mr Hutchins, Kinchin, George Whitefield, Seward. 12.30 Dressed; at Mrs Harding's, dinner, religious talk. 2 At Mrs Iscock's. 2.30 At Mrs Williams' band, religious talk. 3 At Baptist Mills; Miss Smith, religious talk, tea, sang (Cennick there). 4 At Mrs Willis', Communion (fifteen there). 5 Bowling Green, Matthew 5:4 (three thousand there). 6.30 Writ diary; Weavers' Hall. 9.15 At home; tea, religious talk. 10.30.

SUNDAY, JULY 29. 6 Dressed; meditated. 7 Bowling Green (three thousand there), Matthew 5:4. 8.45 At Mr Deschamps', tea, religious talk. 10.15 Hanham (twelve hundred there), Matthew. 12.15 At Mr Deschamps', dinner, religious talk. 2.30 At home; religious talk. 3.30 All Saints. 4.30 At Mr Deschamps', tea. 5 Rose Green (four thousand there), Matthew 3. 7 At the Room. 9 At home; Captain Whitefield, religious talk. 10.45.

MONDAY [JULY] 30. 5.45 Dressed; prayed. 7 At Mrs Richardson's, tea, religious talk, prayed. 9 At Mrs Norman's, religious talk. 10 At home; Mr Stennet, religious talk. 11 Weavers' Hall. 12.15 At Mr Wiggington's, necessary talk (religious). 12.45 At home; religious talk. 1 Dinner, religious talk to many. 3 Writ to Miss Burdock. 4 At Mr Morris', tea, religious talk. 5 Brick-yard, 2 Corinthians 4 (fifteen hundred there). 6.15 At Mr Deschamps', tea. 7 At Mrs England's (two [seized] there!); at Mrs England's band. 10.15 At Mr Deschamps'. 10.30.

TUESDAY [JULY] 31. 4.15 Dressed; tea. 5 Set out with Purdy, religious talk. 8.15 At Winsley, religious talk. 9 Tirley [i.e., Turleigh]; at Mr Baskerville's, tea, religious talk. 10.15 At Bradford (twenty-five hundred there), Acts 16:30. 12.30 At Mr Baker's, dinner, religious talk. 1.15 At Mr Cottle's, prayed. 2.15 At Bath; John Feachem's, religious talk. 3.15 Tea; visited. 4 Acts 19:26, etc (one thousand there). 5.15 Set out; verse. 7.15 At Mr Deschamps', tea. 7.30 At the Room. 9.30 At brother Sayse's, with Mary Deacon's band. 10 Supper, religious talk, sang, prayed. 11.15.

WEDNESDAY, AUGUST 1. 6 Read Prayers; slept. 8 At Miss Taylor's, tea, religious talk, sang, prayed. 9.30 At home; writ notes; writ diary. 10.30 Visited. 11 Weavers' Hall; visited. 12.45 Slept. 1 Religious talk to brother Purdy and Cennick, sang. 2.30 Writ diary. 2.45 At Mrs Stephens', tea, religious talk. 3.30 At Mrs Grace's, Communion (nine there). 4 At Mrs Murray's, necessary talk (religious). 5 Baptist Mills, Hebrews. 6 At Mr Labbè's, tea, religious talk. 7 With the women. 8 Baldwin Street. 9.30 At Mr Labbè's; supper, religious talk, prayed. 11.

THURSDAY, AUGUST 2. 5.45 Dressed; read Prayers; walked to the Hot Well[s]. 8 At Mrs Page's, religious talk, tea, prayed. 9 Visited. 10.30 Writ journal. 12.30 Dressed; necessary business. 1 Dinner. 2.15 Set out with Purdy, religious talk. 3.30 Publow, Acts 2:26. 4.45 At Mr Jeffrys', tea. 5.15 Set out. 6.15 At home; tea, religious talk. 7 At our Room. 9 At brother Maxfield's band. 9.30 Religious talk. 10.15.

FRIDAY [AUGUST] 3. 5 Dressed; necessary talk (religious). 5.45 Mrs Longden went to Gloucester; read Prayers. 7 Writ. 8 At Mrs Turner's, tea, religious talk, prayed. 10 At home; necessary business. 11 Weavers' Hall; visited. 12.30 Religious talk to many. 2 Writ diary; religious talk. 2.45 At Mrs Deschamps', tea, religious talk. 4 At the Fishponds, Acts 26. 5.30 At Mr Deschamps', supper, religious talk. 6.15 At Mrs England's, religious talk. 7 Sang, etc. 9 At the second band. 10 At home; necessary talk (religious). 11.

SATURDAY [AUGUST] 4. 5.30 Dressed; meditated; read Prayers; prayed. 7 Journal. 8.15 At Betty Holder's. 9 Tea, religious talk, prayed. 9.30 At home; journal. 12.15 Prayed; dinner, religious talk to many. 2 At Mrs Williams', Communion (nine there). 2.45 At Mr Deschamps', religious talk. 3 Met Miss Burdock; at Mrs Shepherd's, religious talk, tea (gained no ground); parted! 5 Bowling Green, Matthew 5:5, 6 (two thousand there). 6.15 At Mrs Champion's, tea, religious talk. 7 Weavers' Hall (lively zeal; con). 9.15 At home; religious talk, prayed. 11.

SUNDAY [AUGUST] 5. 6 Dressed; prayed. 7 Bowling Green (three thousand there), Matthew 5:6. 8.30 At Mr Jones', tea. 9 At Mrs Willis' (fourteen there). 10.15 Hanham (twenty-five hundred there!), Matthew 5:5, 6. 11.45 At ——, religious talk, prayed. 1 At Mrs England's, dinner, sang. 2.15 At home; writ diary. 2.30 All Saints. 4 At Mrs Deschamps', tea. 5 Rose Green (twenty-five hundred there), Matthew 5:5, 6. 7 At the Room (six ill, three well [six deeply convinced of sin, three comforted]). 9.45 At the women's Love-feast. 11.15.

MONDAY [AUGUST] 6. 5.45 Dressed; read Prayers; religious talk to some; at Mr Turner's, tea, religious talk, prayed. 8.15 At Mrs Deschamps, Senior's; at Mrs

Panou's band. 9 Tea; Jenny Deschamps ill, prayed, sang. 10.30 At home; religious talk. 11 Weavers' Hall. 12 Writ to Miss B[urdock]. 1 At Mr Labbè's, dinner, sang, religious talk. 3.15 At home; letter. 4.45 At Mr Labbè's, tea. 5 Brick-yard, rain, Isaiah 55:10 (five hundred there). 6 Religious talk to Mrs Arthur; at Mrs Norman's, religious talk; at Mr Deschamps', tea. 7 Gloucester Lane; at first band. 9.30 Writ for Mrs Thornhill. 11.

TUESDAY, AUGUST 7. 5.30 Dressed; meditated. 6 Read Prayers; religious talk to some; at Mrs England's band. 8 Tea, religious talk. 9 At home; journal. 10.30 At Clifton; Mrs Hodges', tea, mostly religious talk. 11.30 Walked; meditated; prayed. 12.30 At home; necessary talk (religious); writ. 1 Dinner, religious talk to some. 3 At Mr Deschamps', tea; at the House. 4 Hebrews 10:38. 5.30 At Mr Deschamps', necessary talk (religious). 6.15 At Mr Davis', tea, religious talk. 7.45 At our Room. 9.30 At Miss Smith's band (two [comforted]!). 10 Sang, prayed, ate. 11.

WEDNESDAY, AUGUST 8. 5.30 Dressed; meditated; read Prayers; religious talk to some; writ. 8 At Mrs Morgan's, many there; tea, sang, prayed. 9.30 Writ journal. 11 Weavers' Hall. 12.15 At Mr Wiggington's, dinner, religious talk. 1.30 At home; religious talk to many. 2.15 Newgate, preached, prayed. 3.30 At Mrs Grace's, Communion (five there). 4 Visited; at T Haydon's with leaders. 5 Baptist Mills, Revelation 3 (Jenny Deschamps). 6 At Miss Gregory's; at Mrs Hooper's, tea, religious talk. 7 With the women. 8 Baldwin Street. 9.45 Religious talk. 10.30.

THURSDAY [AUGUST] 9. 4.45 Dressed; at Mr Wiggington's, coffee. 5.30 Set out with Mr Wiggington, Mrs Thomas, and Mrs Stephens. 9.30 At Wells. 10 Mr Sever's, ate, necessary talk (religious). 11 Preached, 1 Corinthians 1:30 (two thousand there). 12.30 At Mr Sever's, religious talk to some. 1 Dinner, sang, prayed. 2 Set out with Mrs Thomas and [Mrs] Stephens. 6 At Miss Wiggington's, tea, religious talk. 7 At the Room (three [comforted] there). 9.30 At home; with third band. 10.30.

FRIDAY [AUGUST] 10. 6 Read Prayers; religious talk to some; writ diary. 8 At Mrs Grimer's, tea, religious talk, prayed. 9.15 Visited. 10 At home; writ for Mrs Thornhill. 11 Weavers' Hall. 12.30 At home; religious talk to some. 1 Writ for Mrs Thornhill. 1.45 Visited; at Mr Whitehead's, ate, religious talk. 2.45 At home; necessary talk (religious). 3.15 At Mrs Padmore's, religious talk; tea, religious talk. 6.30 At Mr Deschamps', necessary talk (religious). 6.45 Gloucester Lane. 9.15 At home; religious talk. 10.30.

SATURDAY, AUGUST 11. 5.30 Dressed; prayed. 6 Read Prayers; necessary business; necessary talk (religious). 8 At Mr Stedder's, prayed. 9 Tea, religious talk, prayed. 9.30 At home; writ to Mr Griffiths; necessary talk (religious). 11 Nicholas Street; letters, etc. 1 At home; writ diary; dinner. 2 Baldwin Street. 4 At Mrs Williams' (ten there), Communion. 4.45 At Mr Labbè's, tea. 5 Bowling Green (three thousand there). 6 Baldwin Street; journal [mistake for preached?]. 7.15 Weavers' Hall (two [seized] there!). 9.15 At home; ate; John Feachem came, religious talk. 11.

SUNDAY [AUGUST] 12. 5 Writ to Miss Burdock. 6.30 Meditated; Bowling Green, Matthew 5:7 (four thousand there). 8.15 At Mr Deschamps', tea, religious talk.

9 At Mrs Willis' (twenty-one there), Communion. 10.15 Hanham, Matthew 5:7 (three thousand there). 12 Visited. 12.30 At Mr Taylor's, dinner, religious talk. 2 At home; writ diary. 3 Religious talk; All Saints; at Mr Deschamps', tea. 4.45 At Rose Green, Matthew 5:7 (four thousand there). 7 At the Room (four [seized] there!). 9.15 At home; religious talk to Miss Wotton. 10.15.

MONDAY [AUGUST] 13. 5.45 Dressed; read Prayers; at Mrs England's; at Mrs Deacon's band, religious talk, prayed, sang. 9.30 At home; necessary talk (religious); writ. 11 Weavers' Hall. 12.30 At home; religious talk; dinner; religious talk to some. 3 At Thomas Whitefield's, religious talk, prayed. 3.30 At Mrs Brummidge's. 4 Tea, religious talk; visited. 5 Brick-yard, Luke 10:42 (twenty-five hundred there). 6.30 At Mr Martin's, tea, religious talk. 7 Gloucester Lane (four [seized, one greatly comforted] there!). 9 At B Latcham's band, religious talk. 10 At Mr Deschamps', necessary talk (religious). 10.30.

TUESDAY [AUGUST] 14. 4.30 Tea; dressed. 5.30 Set out. 8.15 Freshford; Mr Gibbs', tea, religious talk. 10.30 Bradford (three thousand there), Luke 10:42. 12.30 At Turleigh; Mr Dixon's, dinner, religious talk, prayed. 3.30 Bath; John Feachem's, religious talk, tea. 4.30 Hebrews 10:38 (six hundred there). 5.45 Set out. 7.15 At Mr Deschamps', tea; at the Room (three [comforted] there!). 9.30 At home; religious talk. 10.15.

WEDNESDAY [AUGUST] 15. 5.45 Dressed; read Prayers; writ. 8 At Mr Wiggington, Senior's, tea, religious talk, prayed. 9.30 Writ for Mrs Thornhill. 10.45 At Miss Wiggington's, religious talk. 11 Weavers' Hall. 12.15 At home; religious talk to some; writ; religious talk. 2.30 At Mrs Smith's, tea, religious talk. 3 At Mrs Grace's, Communion (nine there). 4 Baptist Mills, 2 Corinthians 5:16 (twelve hundred there). 5 At leaders' meeting. 5.45 At Mrs Hooper's, tea, religious talk. 7 With the women's bands. 8 Baldwin Street. 9.15 At home; Captain Whitefield and Miss Johns, religious talk. 11.

THURSDAY, AUGUST 16. 5.45 Dressed; read Prayers; writ for Mrs Thornhill. 8 At Mrs Oldfield's, tea, religious talk, prayed. 9.30 At home; writ to the Mayor; writ diary. 10.15 Religious talk with the Bishop, the Dean there, religious talk. 12.15 At home; writ notes. 1 At Mr Norman's, dinner, religious talk. 2.30 Set out. 3.45 Publow, John 7:37, 38. 5 At Mr Jeffrys', tea, religious talk. 6.15 At home; tea. 7 At the Room. 9 At home; religious talk; with second band. 10.30.

FRIDAY [AUGUST] 17. 5.45 Dressed; read Prayers. 7 Journal. 8 At Mrs Purnell's, tea, religious talk, prayed. 9.30 At home; journal. 10.45 Weavers' Hall. 12.15 At home; journal. 1 At Baldwin Street, our bands here, prayed, sang. 3 At Mrs Turner's, tea, religious talk. 4 At the Fishponds, Luke 5:32. 5.30 At Mrs Deschamps', tea, religious talk. 6.15 At Mrs Lanning's, religious talk. 6.30 At Gloucester Lane (three [comforted] there). 8.30 At home; with the fifth band. 9.15 At Mr Wiggington, Senior's, supper. 10 Religious talk, prayed. 11.

SATURDAY [AUGUST] 18. 5.30 Meditated; dressed. 6 Read Prayers; journal. 8 At Mrs England's, Miss Purnell, etc, tea, sang, religious talk, prayed. 9.15 Visited. 9.30 At home; journal. 1 Dinner, religious talk to many. 3 At Mrs Williams', Communion (fourteen there). 4 Read Prayers. 5 At the Bishop's, Mr Sutton, Tucker, and the Chancellor, religious talk. 6.15 Bowling Green. 7.15 Weavers' Hall. 8.45 At home; ate. 9 Religious talk to many. 10.15.

SUNDAY [AUGUST] 19. 6 Dressed; meditated. 6.45 Bowling Green (five thousand there), Matthew 5:8. 8.15 At Mr Deschamps', tea. 9 At Mrs Willis' (twenty-two there), Communion. 10.30 Hanham (thirty-five hundred there), Matthew 5:8. 12.30 At Mr Deschamps', dinner. 2 At home; journal. 2.30 All Saints. 4.15 At Mr Deschamps', tea. 5.45 Rose Green (fifty-five hundred there). 7 At the Room; all well. 8.30 Baldwin Street; ate, religious talk (necessary), sang, prayed. 10 At home; Mr Richard Whitefield, religious talk. 11.

MONDAY, AUGUST 20. 5.45 Dressed; read Prayers. 7 At Mr Linford's, sang, religious talk. 8 Tea, sang, prayed. 9.30 At home; journal. 10 Necessary talk (religious) to many. 11 Weavers' Hall; at Bedminster, with Margaret Somerel, prayed, religious talk. 1 At home; religious talk, dinner. 2 Religious talk to many. 3.30 At Mrs Sage's, religious talk. 4 At Miss Wiggington's, tea, religious talk, prayed. 5 Brick-yard, Matthew 18 (thirty-five hundred there). 6.30 At Mrs Norman's, tea. 7 Gloucester Lane. 9 At Miss Latcham's and Mrs Highnam's and brother Oldfield's band. 10 At home; religious talk. 11 Prayed.

TUESDAY [AUGUST] 21. 5.45 Dressed; read Prayers; religious talk to some. 7.30 Journal. 8 At Mrs Highnam's, tea, religious talk, prayed. 9.15 At home; necessary talk (religious); writ to sister Patty and Miss Burdock. 12.45 Writ diary. 1 Religious talk to some. 1.45 Dinner; religious talk to many. 3 At Mr Deschamps', tea; set out; at the House. 4 Matthew 28:33. 5 At Mr Davis', religious talk, tea. 7 At the Room. 8.45 At Miss Smith's band; at home; religious talk. 11.

WEDNESDAY [AUGUST] 22. 5.30 Dressed; meditated; read Prayers; religious talk; at Miss Deffel's band. 8 At Mrs Latcham's, tea, religious talk, sang, prayed; Miss Bradshaw and Mrs England [filled with peace and joy]! 9.45 Necessary talk (religious). 11 Weavers' Hall. 12.15 At Margaret Somerel's, Communion (nine there). 1 At Miss Wiggington's, religious talk, dinner. 2 At home; religious talk to many. 3 At Mrs Townsend's, necessary talk (religious); tea. 4 Baptist Mills, Ecclesiastes 2:2 (one thousand there). 5.15 At Mr Deschamps', tea. 5.45 With the leaders. 6.15 At Mrs Grace's burying. 7 At the bands. 8 Baldwin Street. 9.30 At home; religious talk, prayed. 10.15.

THURSDAY [AUGUST] 23. 5.30 Dressed; meditated. 6 Read Prayers; writ to brother Ingham. 8 At Miss Bradshaw's, tea, religious talk. 9.15 Visited. 9.45 At home; writ to Mr Blackwell, Darracote, Reed. 1 At Mr Jones', dinner, religious talk. 2.15 At home; religious talk to some. 4 At Miss Gregory's, religious talk, tea. 5 At ——, tea, religious talk. 6 At Mrs Davis', religious talk. 4 Weavers' Hall. 9 At home; with second band, religious talk. 10.45 Read. 11 Sins!!!

FRIDAY, AUGUST 24. 5.30 Dressed; meditated; read Prayers. 7 At Mary Deacon's, religious talk, tea, sang. 8.30 At brother Sage's, tea, religious talk, prayed. 10 At home; writ to Mr Erskine. 11 Weavers' Hall. 12.15 At home; sang; meditated. 1 At Mrs England's, the bands met; prayed, sang. 3 At Mr Labbè's, tea, religious talk. 4 Visited. 4.30 At home; writ. 5.30 With Mrs Grevil, etc, tea. 6.45 Gloucester Lane. 8.30 At Mary Deacon's band. 9.30 At home; supper, religious talk. 11.

SATURDAY [AUGUST] 25. 5.30 Dressed; meditated; read Prayers. 7 Journal. 8 At K Chandler's, tea, religious talk, prayed. 9.30 At home; writ to Mr Davidson. 11

Journal. 12 Meditated; necessary talk (religious). 1 Dinner, religious talk. 2 Religious talk to some. 3 At Mrs Willis' (seventeen there), Communion. 4 At Mrs Cornish's, tea, religious talk. 5 Religious talk to Walter Chapman. 5 Bowling Green, Matthew 5:9. 6 At Mrs Eyres', religious talk. 6.45 Weavers' Hall. 9 At home; with the boys; supper, religious talk. 10.15.

SUNDAY [AUGUST] 26. 5.45 Meditated; dressed; prayed. 6.45 Bowling Green, Matthew 5:9 (four thousand there). 8.15 At Mr Deschamps', tea, religious talk. 9 At Mrs Willis', Communion (forty there). 10.15 Hanham (three thousand there), Matthew 5. 12.30 At Mr Deschamps', Mr and Mrs Jones, dinner, religious talk. 2 At home; meditated; religious talk. 2.30 All Saints. 4.15 At Mrs Deschamps', tea. 5 Rose Green (five thousand there), Matthew 5:9, 10, 11, 12. 7 At the Horse-fair. At home; supper, religious talk. 10.15. 11 Sins!

MONDAY [AUGUST] 27. 5.45 Dressed; read Prayers; at home; religious talk with some; writ. 8 At Mrs Page's, religious talk, tea, prayed. 9 At home; religious talk to some. 11 Weavers' Hall; meditated; prayed. 1 At Mrs England's, Thomas Robins, religious talk, dinner. 3.30 Visited. 4 At Mrs Padmore's, tea, religious talk. 5 Brick-yard, Luke 22:48 (twenty-five hundred there). 6 At Mrs Highnam's; at Miss Thomas', tea, religious talk. 7 Gloucester Lane. 9 At Miss Purnell's band. 10 At Mr Deschamps', ate, religious talk (necessary). 10.30.

TUESDAY, AUGUST 28. 4.30 Dressed; necessary talk; tea. 5.30 Set out; rain. 9 At Turleigh; Mr Dixon's, tea, religious talk, prayed. 10.30 Bradford, rain, Romans 14:17 (twenty-five hundred there). 12 At Mr Timbrel's, dinner, religious talk, prayed. 3.30 Bath; at John [Feachem]'s, religious talk. 4 Romans 4:4 (five hundred there). 5.30 Set out. 7.15 At Mr Deschamps', supper, Charles there! 7.30 At the Room. 9 At Thomas Whitefield's, supper, religious talk, prayed. 11.

WEDNESDAY [AUGUST] 29. 5.45 Dressed; read Prayers; religious talk with Charles. 8.15 At P Evans', tea, religious talk, sang, prayed. 9.15 At home; necessary talk (religious) with Charles. 11 Weavers' Hall. 12 Visited Mrs Linford, etc. 1 At home; religious talk to many. 3 At John Champion's, tea, religious talk, prayed. 4 Baptist Mills (twelve hundred there), Romans 14:17. 5.15 Met the leaders. 6 At Miss Purnell's, tea, religious talk, sang. 7 With the women. 8 Baldwin Street. 9 At home; supper, religious talk. 10.

THURSDAY [AUGUST] 30. 5.15 Necessary business; writ diary. 6 Set out with Charles, Deschamps, and Giles, sang, religious talk; lost the way. 10.45 Wells; at the Christopher, tea. 11.45 Acts 16:30 (two hundred there). 1.15 At Mr Sever's, dinner, religious talk. 2 Set out; necessary talk (religious); lost. 6.45 Sang, religious talk. 7 At Miss Wiggington's, tea, religious talk. 7.30 At the Room. 9.15 At Baldwin Street Society, sang, necessary talk, prayed. 10 At home; many there; religious talk; supper, sang, prayed. 11 At Mr Deschamps', religious talk. 11.30.

FRIDAY [AUGUST] 31. 5 Sang; tea, religious talk; many came, prayed. 6.30 Set out with brother Purdy. 7 Religious talk. 8.45 Marshfield; writ diary. 9 Tea, religious talk. 9.45 Set out. 12.30 Calne, dinner, religious talk. 1.30 Set out. 2 Storm. 4 Marlborough, tea, religious talk. 5 Set out; meditated. 7 Hungerford; writ diary; supper, religious talk. 9.

SATURDAY, SEPTEMBER 1. 5 Meditated; prayed. 5.30 Set out. 7.30 Overtook Fanny

Lucans and her father. 8 Woolhampton; they came, religious talk, tea. 9 Set out. 11 Reading; at Mrs Cennick's, religious talk, dinner, prayed. 1.30 Set out. 5 Rain. 5.15 Colnbrook, necessary talk (religious), supper. 8.

SUNDAY [SEPTEMBER] 2. 5.15 Prayed; meditated. 5.45 Set out. 9.15 At Mr Bray's, sang, tea, religious talk (necessary). 10.30 Read Prayers, Communion. 1.30 At Mrs Storer's, mostly religious talk, dinner, sang, prayed. 2.30 Prayed; Dr Heylin preached. 4.15 At brother Chapman's, tea, religious talk. 5.15 Kennington, Psalm 40:16. 6.15 Went with Sir Isaac Chard, etc, mostly religious talk. 8 Fetter Lane, women's Love-feast. 10.30 At home; religious talk, sang. 11.

MONDAY [SEPTEMBER] 3. 5.45 Dressed; read Prayers. 6.30 Necessary talk (religious). 7.15 At brother Hodges', tea, religious talk. 8 At Mr Hall's. Stonehouse there, necessary talk (religious) with them. 10 Necessary talk with sister Patty, sister Kezzy, etc. 12.45 Islington with sister Patty and sister Nancy. 1 At our House, necessary talk (religious). 2 At Mr Stonehouse's, dinner. 3 At my mother's, tea, religious talk, sang. 4.45 Southwark, visited. 6.45 At home; read notes; tea, religious talk. 8 At our band. 10.30 At home; religious talk, prayed. 11.15.

TUESDAY [SEPTEMBER] 4. 5.45 Dressed; prayed. 6.30 Necessary business. 8 At Mrs Mills', religious talk, tea, prayed. 11.15 At Mrs Storer's, necessary talk (religious). 12.15 At home; Audway came, religious talk. 1.15 At my mother's, religious talk, dinner; journal. 3 With Mrs Vaughan. 4 Tea, religious talk. 5 At N Tilson's band. 6 At home; Society. 8 At Mr Crouch's. 9.45 Tea, religious talk. 10.30 At home; ate, religious talk. 11.15.

WEDNESDAY [SEPTEMBER] 5. 6.15 Dressed; writ diary; religious talk to Hannah Knowles! prayed. 7.15 Religious talk to Miss Crisp, etc, prayed. 8.30 At Mr Bowes', tea, religious talk, prayed. 9.30 At Mrs Ewster's, religious talk, prayed, sang (Mrs Hamilton!). 11 Visited [poor woman]; Mrs Randal there, religious talk, prayed. 12.15 At home; writ diary. 2 Journal. 3 At Martha Soane's band, religious talk, tea, prayed. 4.45 At Mrs West's, religious talk. 5.30 Fetter Lane. 7 At home; the leaders. 8 Fetter Lane. 10.15 At home; supper, religious talk. 11.15.

THURSDAY, SEPTEMBER 6. 6 Dressed; writ. 6.30 Religious talk to some, prayed. 8 At Mrs Tenner's, religious talk, tea. 9.45 At Mrs Storer's, necessary talk (religious), tea; Mrs Ewster's, prayed. 11.30 At Miss Clark's, religious talk. 1 At home; necessary business; George Lowe, religious talk. 2 At brother Holland's, dinner; Shaw there, etc, religious talk. 4 At Mrs Talbot's, religious talk, coffee, prayed. 5.30 At Mr Birnham's. 6 At home; sang, etc. 8 Savoy, sang, etc. 10.15 At home; ate, religious talk. 11.

FRIDAY [SEPTEMBER] 7. 5.45 Dressed; read Prayers; religious talk to some. 8 At sister Johnson's, religious talk, sang, tea. 9.30 At home; journal. 10.30 At Mr Thorold's, Morgan there, Charles Delamotte, etc. 1 At home; ate; journal. 3 At Mrs Cripse's, religious talk, tea. 5 At my mother's, religious talk, tea. 5.30 At our House, sang, etc. 7.45 Fetter Lane, sang, etc. 9.45 At home; supper, religious talk, sang. 11 Sins of thought.

SATURDAY [SEPTEMBER] 8. 5.45 Dressed; read Prayers; religious talk to many. 8 At

Mrs Storer's, sister Nancy, etc, tea, religious talk, prayed. 10.30 At home; necessary business; journal. 12 Fetter Lane. 2 At Miss Clark's, dinner, religious talk. 3 Fetter Lane. 5 At home; tea. 6 Fetter Lane. 8 At Exall's, tea, sang, etc. 11.

SUNDAY [SEPTEMBER] 9. 6 Meditated; dressed; necessary talk (religious). 7 Moorfields, Acts 16 (ten thousand there). 8.15 At Bell, Junior's, tea, religious talk. 9 At home; necessary talk (religious) for brother Gibbs. 10 St Paul's, read Prayers, etc. 12.45 At Mr Cripse's, Mrs West, etc. 1 Dinner, religious talk, tea. 4 Set out with my mother, etc. 5 Kennington, Acts 16 (twenty thousand there). 7 Lambeth Marsh, sang, etc. 8.30 Fetter Lane, necessary talk (religious), prayed. 10.30 At home; supper. 11.

MONDAY [SEPTEMBER] 10. 6 Dressed; religious talk to many. 8 At Mrs Storer's, Mrs Ewster, etc, tea, religious talk, prayed. 10.15 At home; necessary talk (religious); writ. 1 At brother Clark's, religious talk, dinner; set out. 4 Plaistow, The Ship; Mr Bray, etc, tea, religious talk. 5 In the House, sang, etc. 6.30 At home; religious talk, sang. 7.30 At the House, sang, etc. 9 At home; supper, sang, prayed. 11.

TUESDAY, SEPTEMBER 11. 6 Dressed; meditated. 6.45 At the House, sang, etc. 8.30 Set out. 9.30 At Mr Bray's. 10 Tea, religious talk; writ orders. 1 At Mr Birnham's; Mr Mason, Lady Hume, etc, dinner, prayed. 3.30 At Exall's, necessary talk (religious). 4 At J Chambers', sang, etc. 6 At home; sang, etc. 8 Dowgate Hill, sang, etc. 10.15 At home; supper, religious talk. 11.

WEDNESDAY [SEPTEMBER] 12. 5.45 Dressed; read Prayers; religious talk to some. 8 At Mr Hopson's, necessary talk (religious), tea. 10 At home; brother Pattison, etc, prayed. 12 Read Barnes. 1 At Mr Wathen's, dinner; brother Hall and Mr Dobree, religious talk. 3.15 At home; Barnes. 3.45 The women leaders, necessary talk (religious). 5 At Mrs West's band, tea, religious talk. 6 Fetter Lane, sang, etc. 7.15 At home; leaders ((sang, etc)). 8 Fetter Lane. 10.15 At home; supper, religious talk. 11.

THURSDAY [SEPTEMBER] 13. 5.45 Dressed; read Prayers; religious talk to many. 8 At Mrs Eaton's, tea, mostly religious talk. 9 At Mr Howard's, tea, religious talk. 11.15 Religious talk to some; read. 12.45 Islington House, necessary talk (religious). 1.30 At my mother's, dinner, necessary talk (religious). 3 At brother Hall's, sister Wright and Kezzy, mostly religious talk. 3.30 At brother Hodges', sister Soane, etc, religious talk. 4 At sister Thacker's band, tea, religious talk, prayed. 5.30 At home; religious talk. 6 Sang, etc. 8 Fetter Lane, sang, etc. 10.30 At home; ate, religious talk. 11.

FRIDAY [SEPTEMBER] 14. 5.45 Dressed; read Prayers; religious talk to many. 8.15 At Mrs Mills', tea, religious talk, prayed. 10 At home; writ diary. 11 Journal. 3.30 Walked to Pancridge [St Pancras]. 4.30 At my mother's, religious talk, tea. 5.30 At the House; sang, etc. 8 Fetter Lane, sang, etc. 10 At home; supper, necessary talk (religious). 11.

SATURDAY [SEPTEMBER] 15. 5.45 Dressed; read Prayers; religious talk to many. 8 At brother Holland's, tea, religious talk. 8.30 At Mrs Denn's, necessary talk (religious), tea. 10 At home; journal; writ orders. 1 At Lady Hume's, religious talk; Will Delamotte, etc, dinner, sang, etc. 4 At Mrs Ewster's, tea, religious talk.

5 Visited. 6 Fetter Lane, sang, etc. 7.30 At Mr Exall's, tea, mostly religious talk. 8 Sang, etc. 10.15 At home; ate, religious talk, prayed. 11.

SUNDAY [SEPTEMBER] 16. 6 Meditated; dressed. 7 Moorfields, Acts 28:22 (ten thousand there). 9 At sister Wren's, tea, religious talk; at brother Holland's. 10 Coleman Street Church [St Stephen], Communion. 1 At Mrs West's, Mrs Cripse, etc, dinner, sang. 2.30 Dr Heylin's, read Prayers, Sermon. 5 Kennington, Acts 28. 7 Lambeth, sang, etc. 8.30 Fetter Lane, Love-feast. 10.30 Islington, necessary talk (religious). 11.15.

MONDAY, SEPTEMBER 17. 5 Dressed; sang; necessary talk (religious). 6 Prayed. 6.30 Necessary talk (religious). 7.30 Breakfast, necessary talk to many. 12.30 At brother Wilde's, dinner. 1.45 At home; necessary business. 2 At Mr Bowes', sang, etc; religious talk to some. 4.45 Plaistow, preached (three hundred there), Matthew 5:4. 7.30 Islington, my mother, etc; tea, religious talk, prayed, sang, read. 9.30 Writ diary; religious talk; read. 10.15.

TUESDAY [SEPTEMBER] 18. 5 Dressed; sang; necessary business. 6 Prayed; necessary talk (religious) to some; writ for the bands. 8 Tea, religious talk; writ. 10 Sins!; religious talk to many. 12 Nanny Smith, prayed. 1.30 At Mr Jones'; St Paul's; dinner, religious talk, sang. 3.30 At Mrs Soane's band, religious talk, tea. 4.15 J Chambers', sang, etc. 6 At Mr Bray's, sang, etc; tea. 8 At Mr Crouch's, sang, etc. 10 At Mr Bray's, supper. 10.45 At home; necessary talk (religious). 11.

WEDNESDAY [SEPTEMBER] 19. 5 Dressed; sang; meditated. 6 Prayed; writ notes. 7.30 Breakfast, religious talk to some. 9 Religious talk to sister Emily, to Mr Rowland, and Charles. 10.30 Necessary talk (religious); to Mr Stonehouse. 11 At my mother's, necessary talk (religious). 1.15 At Mrs Ewster's, dinner, religious talk. 2.15 At Mrs Storer's, Miss Bond and Temple, religious talk. 3.30 At Mrs West's, my mother, etc, tea, religious talk. 5.30 Fetter Lane. 7.30 At home; supper, necessary talk (religious) to Mr Piers and Mrs Okeley. 8 Fetter Lane. 10.15 At home. 10.45.

THURSDAY [SEPTEMBER] 20. 5 Dressed; meditated; prayed. 6 Prayed; writ. 7.30 Breakfast; writ; religious talk to many (Jane Vowell!). 12 Visited. 1.15 At Mr Stonehouse's, dinner, religious talk. 3 At Mr Bray's, necessary talk. 4 At Betty Thacker's, band, religious talk, tea, prayed. 5 At Mrs Storer's, Mrs Crouch there, Communion. 6 Turner's Hall, Mrs Crouch! 8 At Mr Bray's, sang, etc. 10.45 Religious talk to Mr Piers.

FRIDAY [SEPTEMBER] 21. 6.45 Dressed; necessary talk (religious); tea. 8.15 Bow. 10.15 At Mrs West's, tea, religious talk, prayed. 11.30 At Mrs Blackburn's, sang, prayed. 12.30 At Mrs Mills', religious talk to some, prayed. 1.30 Dinner. 3 At Mrs Dixon's band. 4.45 Islington, necessary talk (religious) to many. 5.30 Sang, etc. 8 Fetter Lane. 10.45 Islington.

SATURDAY [SEPTEMBER] 22. 5 Dressed; meditated; prayed. 6 Prayed; breakfast; writ; religious talk to many. 1 At The Three Cups, religious talk; dinner, prayed. 3.30 At Mr Sharp's, tea, religious talk, prayed. 5.45 Fetter Lane. 7.30 At Exall's, tea. 10 At Mr Bray's; at home. 10.45.

SUNDAY, SEPTEMBER 23. 5 Prayed; meditated. 6 Prayed. 6.45 Moorfields (ten thousand there), Romans 14. 8.30 At Mrs Darlington's, prayed, tea. 9.45 St Paul's. 12.30 At brother Dandy's, religious talk, dinner, religious talk, sang. 2.30 Dr Heylin's church. 5 Kennington (twenty thousand there), Luke 10:42. 6.30 Lambeth, sang, etc. 9.15 At Mr Bray's, supper. 10.45 At home.

MONDAY [SEPTEMBER] 24. 5 Prayed; dressed. 6 Prayed; [read] Barnes; writ. 7.30 Breakfast; writ to ((sister Emily)). 9 Religious talk to many; Sally Romley came. 12.30 At Mr Bray's, read. 1 Dinner, religious talk. 1.45 At Mr Bowers', sang, etc. 2.45 At Mr Bray's, religious talk, prayed, tea. 4.30 Plaistow, in the House, sang, etc. 7 At Mr Bray's, supper. 8.30 At Carnaby Market, sang, etc. 10.45 Islington.

TUESDAY [SEPTEMBER] 25. 5 Prayed; dressed; writ to Charles and Cennick. 6 Prayed; preached. 7 Breakfast. 8 Journal; religious talk to many (Fanny!). 11.15 At Mr Strahan's, necessary talk (none came). 12.15 At Mr Thornburgh's, Communion (fifteen there). 1.15 At Mr Pattison's marriage; dinner, sang, religious talk. 3.30 At Mrs Soane's, prayed. 4 St James's, sang, etc. 6 At Mr Bray's, sang, etc. 8 Winchester Yard, sang, etc. 10 Mrs MacCune brought me home, religious talk. 11.30.

WEDNESDAY [SEPTEMBER] 26. 5.15 Prayed; meditated. 6 Prayed; writ preface to Barnes; breakfast; preface. 9 Religious talk to many; Bray, Bowers, etc, prayed, sang. 11.30 Barnes. 12.45 At Mr Bray's, my mother there; dinner, religious talk. 3 Slept. 4 Religious talk. 4.30 At Mr West's, tea, religious talk. 5.45 Fetter Lane. 7.45 At Mr Bray's, tea, religious talk. 8 Fetter Lane. 11.45 At home.

THURSDAY [SEPTEMBER] 27. 5 Meditated; prayed. 6 Prayed; Barnes. 7.15 Breakfast; Barnes; religious talk to many. 12.15 Set out. 1 At P Sims', necessary talk (religious); dinner. 3 Deptford, sang, etc. 4.45 At Mrs ———'s, tea. 6 Turner's Hall. 8 At Mr Bray's, tea. 10 Supper, necessary talk (religious). 11.30 At home with Esther Hopson. 11.45.

FRIDAY [SEPTEMBER] 28. 5 Dressed; prayed; necessary talk. 6 Prayed; necessary talk (religious) with Oxlee, etc; breakfast. 8 Barnes; religious talk to many. 1.30 At Mrs Mills', religious talk, tea, prayed. 3 Visited. 4.15 At home; Mrs Ewsters, etc; tea. 8.15 Fetter Lane. 9.30 Mrs MacCune brought us home, religious talk. 11.

SATURDAY [SEPTEMBER] 29. 5 Dressed; meditated; prayed. 6 Prayed; necessary talk; necessary business. 7.30 Breakfast; writ to Bedder. 8 Benjamin Seward, etc, necessary talk (religious) to many. 1 At Mrs Prat's, Will Delamotte, Sparkes, etc, sang, religious talk; dinner. 3 Visited. 4 Newgate, with John Wright. 5 At Mr Bray's, tea, necessary talk (religious). 6 Fetter Lane. 8 Exall's, sang, etc. 9.45 Mrs MacCune brought me home. 11.

SUNDAY [SEPTEMBER] 30. 5.30 Dressed. 6.30 At Bell, Junior's, tea. 7 Moorfields (fifteen thousand there), Matthew 11:28; collected for Kingswood. 9.30 At Mr Bray's, tea. 10.15 Islington, read Prayers, etc. 12.30 At home; prayed; dinner, religious talk to many, to the children. 3.15 Prayed; at my mother's, necessary talk (religious). 5.15 Pancras (twelve thousand there), Acts 20:28. 7 Fetter Lane, the women. 10 At Mr Bray's, necessary talk (religious). 11 At home.

[MONDAY] OCTOBER 1. 5 Necessary business; prayed; religious talk to children;

sang, many here, prayed. 7 Set out with Purdy. 9 The Green Man; Mr Evans, tea, religious talk. 1.15 At Mr Crouch's, Mr Bedder, dinner, prayed, religious talk. 3 Set out. 7 At Mr Fox's, many there, tea, sang, etc. 9.30 Necessary talk (religious). 9.45.

TUESDAY [OCTOBER] 2. 7.30 Dressed; writ diary. 8.15 At Mr Bully's, tea, religious talk, prayed. 9.45 At Mrs Compton's, religious talk, prayed. 10.30 At Mrs Pricket's, religious talk, prayed. 11.15 At Mr Vesey's. 11.45 With Vaughn, mostly religious talk, dinner. 1 At Mrs Fox's, read; writ to Mrs Hamilton, Margaret Taylor. 2 Walked with Purdy. 3 At Mrs Plat's, necessary talk (religious). 4 At Mrs Fox's, tea, religious talk. 5.30 Read Prayers; at the Rector's, necessary talk (religious). 6.30 At Mrs Compton's, tea, religious talk, prayed. 7 At Mr Fox's, sang, etc (two [comforted] there! Hitchman). 9 At Mrs Ford's, supper, religious talk, prayed. 9.30 At Mr Fox's, with P Thurston's band. 10.45 Prayed. 11 Sins!!

WEDNESDAY [OCTOBER] 3. 7 Sang; writ. 8 Mrs Cleminger, Ford, etc, tea, religious talk. 9.30 Walked with Purdy. 10.30 At Mrs Fox's, religious talk to Sarah Hurst. 11 Prayed. 12 Mrs Cleminger, N Fox! 12 At Mr Bully's, dinner, prayed. 1.30 Set out with Purdy. 2.15 Stanton Harcourt, John Gambold not [there], religious talk, tea. 3.30 Set out. 6.15 Burford; Mr Mazy's [Mazine's?], necessary talk (religious). 7 1 Corinthians 1:30 (twelve hundred there). 9 Supper, sang, etc. 11.

THURSDAY [OCTOBER] 4. 6 Sang; meditated; tea. 7 Acts 16:30 (one thousand there). 8.45 At Mr Huntley's, tea, religious talk. 9.30 Set out. 10.45 At Westcote, Mr Morgan's, religious talk, prayed. 12 Set out. 3.15 Bengeworth, religious talk; Mr Taylor, tea. 5 Prayed, sang, explained 1 Corinthians 13. 7 At the Society, sang, etc. 9 At home; supper, prayed, religious talk, sang. 11.

FRIDAY [OCTOBER] 5. 6 Sang; meditated. 7 Prayed; religious talk to Mr Seward. 8 Luke 5:32. 9.15 Tea, religious talk. 11 Writ diary; religious talk. 12 At Mr Cartwright's, many there; religious talk, dinner. 1 Set out. 6 Gloucester, The Bell; with Mrs Longden and Mr Wiggington, supper, religious talk (necessary). 10 Prayed.

SATURDAY [OCTOBER] 6. 5.30 Dressed; prayed. 6 Set out. 8.30 Ebley; Mrs Ellis, religious talk, tea. 12 Garden; meditated. 12.30 Religious talk. 1.30 Dinner, religious talk. 2.45 Set out. 4.45 Gloucester, Romans 4:5 (one thousand there). 6.30 At inn; tea, necessary talk (religious). 7 At the Society. 8.45 At Mrs Harris', prayed with her. 9.30 At home; necessary talk; writ diary. 10.

SUNDAY [OCTOBER] 7. 6 Dressed; necessary business. 7 Romans 8:15 (three thousand there). 8.30 Tea; set out. 10.15 Randwick; read Prayers, Acts 16:30. 1 At Mr Ellis', Mr Rawlins there, dinner. 2.45 Randwick; read Prayers, Acts 16:31. 5.30 Stanley Borough (three thousand there), 1 Corinthians 1:30. 7.30 Ebley, religious talk, supper. 9 Matthew 5:2, 3. 10 Religious talk. 11.

MONDAY [OCTOBER] 8. 6 Dressed; tea, religious talk. 8.15 [Minchin] Hampton Common, Luke 7:42 (six thousand there). 10.15 At the inn; tea, religious talk; set out; read *Pilgrim's Progress*. 2.45 Sodbury, dinner. 4 Set out. 7 Bristol; Mr Deschamps', tea, prayed, religious talk to many. 8.45 Charles came, necessary talk (religious); at Mrs Grevil's, necessary talk (religious). 10 At Mr Deschamps'. 10.15.

TUESDAY [OCTOBER 9]. 5 Tea, necessary talk (religious). 5.45 Set out with Charles, etc. 9.30 Winsley; at Turleigh, tea, religious talk. 11 Bradford; Charles preached. 1.15 At Mr Palmer's, dinner. 2 Mr Reed, necessary talk (religious). 6.15 Bristol; at Mr Deschamps', tea. 7 At the Malt-house, sang, etc. 8.30 At home; supper, prayed. 10.30.

WEDNESDAY [OCTOBER] 10. 7 Sang, prayed, necessary talk (religious); necessary business. 9 At Mrs Brummidge's, tea, religious talk, sang. 10.15 At the House; at home; necessary business. 11 At the Malt-house, Charles explained. 12.30 At home. 1 Writ notes; religious talk to many. 3.15 At Mr Morris', tea, religious talk. 4 Baptist Mills, Hebrews 12:2 (fifteen hundred there). 5.30 At Elizabeth Clark's, tea, religious talk. 6 At John Haydon's with the leaders. 6.30 With the women. 8 With the men. 9.30 At home; supper; Betty Holder, etc, prayed! 10.30.

THURSDAY [OCTOBER] 11. 6 Prayed; necessary business. 7 Read Prayers; at Mrs Oldfield's, tea, religious talk, prayed. 9.45 At home; necessary talk; necessary business. 11 With Charles, etc. 1 At Mr Norman's, dinner, religious talk. 2.15 At home; religious talk to many; writ to Sally Burdock. 4 At Captain Whitefield's, Mr Sarney and Jekyl, religious talk, tea. 6.30 At the Malt-house, sang, etc. 8.45 At home; ate. 9 Sent for to Mr Battlesby, he came not. 9.45 At home; sins.

FRIDAY, OCTOBER 12. 4 Journal. 6 Slept. 6.45 Dressed; read Prayers. 7.45 At Margaret Evans', tea, religious talk, prayed. 9.30 At home; journal; religious talk to many. 11 Malt-house. 12 Visited Averel Spenser, prayed. 12.30 At home; religious talk to some. 1 At the Room, prayed. 3 At Mrs Labbè's, tea; in the coach, Miss Wiggington, Smith, and Mrs Labbè. 4 Fishponds, Matthew 12:22, etc. 5.15 In the coach, religious talk, sang. 6 At Mrs Deschamps', tea, religious talk. 6.30 Gloucester Lane, sang, etc. 9 At home; supper. 9.45.

SATURDAY [OCTOBER] 13. 4 Journal. 6.15 Slept. 6.45 Dressed; read Prayers. 7.30 Miss Wotton's, religious talk. 8.30 At Mrs Taylor's, Charles, tea, religious talk, prayed. 9.30 At home; writ to brother Harper, John Bray, Mr Rutter, sister Nancy; religious talk to many. 1 Dinner, religious talk. 2 Visited Averel Spenser. 2.30 At home; religious talk to some. 3 At Mrs Williams', Communion (twenty there); at Mrs Deschamps', tea, religious talk. 4 Bowling Green, Matthew 15:11, 12; Miss Wotton came, religious talk. 6 At Mr Wiggington's, tea, religious talk. 6.30 Malt-house (five there convinced). 8.45 At home; Captain Whitefield and Mr Jekyl, religious talk. 10.

SUNDAY [OCTOBER] 14. 4 Writ to sister Patty; writ diary. 5 Dressed; religious talk. 5.45 At Mrs Deschamps', tea. 6 In the coach with Mrs Hopkins, Okeley, etc, religious talk, sang. 7.45 Hanham. 8 Matthew 11:28 (fifteen hundred there). 9.30 At Mrs Willis', Communion (fifty-six there), prayed. 12.15 At Mrs England's, dinner, religious talk, sang. 1.30 At home; slept. 2 Christ Church. 3.45 Tea. 4 Bowling Green, 1 Corinthians 13:5 (six thousand there). 5.15 At Mrs Eyres', tea, religious talk. 6.45 At Averel Spenser's, prayed. 6 Malthouse, sang, etc; some comforted! 9.15 Love-feast, prayed. 9.30 At home. 9.45.

LONDON DIARY 2

15 October 1739—8 August 1741

(except 11 November 1739—12 April 1740)

Monday, October 15, 1739. 4.30 Writ to Fish; necessary business. 7 At Mr Deschamps', tea, religious talk (many there), sang, prayed. 8 Set out with Deschamps, Williams. 10 At the New Passage, wind high. 1 Chepstow. 2 At the Devauden, Walter Edwards, sang, dinner, religious talk. 3.45 Upon the Green, 1 Corinthians 1:30 (four hundred there). 5.30 At Mr Nexey's. 5.45 Matthew 5:3, sang, etc. 7.45 Religious talk. 8.45 Supper, religious talk. 11.

Tuesday [October] 16. 6.30 Dressed; prayed. 7.15 Tea, religious talk. 8 At the Green, Acts 16:30. 10 Set out. 1.30 Abergavenny; necessary talk (religious); dinner; writ diary. 3 Colossians 1:22, etc; necessary talk (religious); lots. 3.30 At Mr Waters', necessary talk (religious). 4.30 Acts 28:22 (one thousand there). 5 At Mr Waters', tea, religious talk. 7 At Mrs James', Acts 5:30, etc. 9 At Mr Waters', supper, religious talk, prayed. 10.30 Nanny, religious talk, prayed. 11.

Wednesday [October] 17. 6.15 Dressed; prayed; read *Life of Mr Henry*. 7 At Mrs James', religious talk, tea. 8 Acts 16:30 (seven hundred there). 9.30 At Mr Waters', necessary talk (religious). 10.30 Set out. 12.30 Usk; at the castle; dinner. 1 Matthew 18:11. 2.15 Set out. 3.30 Pontypool; Mr Griffiths not [there]; at the Cocking, tea. 4.15 At the school-steps, Acts 16:31 (six hundred there). 5.45 At Thomas Allgood's (many there). 6.15 Sang, etc. 8.30 Supper, religious talk. 10 Prayed.

Thursday [October] 18. 6.15 Dressed; prayed; writ diary. 7.15 Tea, religious talk. 8.15 Romans 4:5 (four hundred fifty there). 10 Set out. 12 Newport; dinner, religious talk (necessary). 1 Set out; religious talk. 3 Cardiff; at Mr Thomas Glascott's (many there), religious talk, tea. 5 At the Shire Hall, Acts 16:31. 6.30 At home; religious talk. 7 At the Shire Hall, Matthew 5:3, 4. 8.45 At home; supper. 9.15 At society here[?], religious talk, prayed. 11.

Friday, October 19. 6.30 Dressed; prayed. 7 Tea, religious talk. 8.15 Set out with Glascott, etc. 10.15 Newport, Acts 16:30. 12.30 Set out. 2.45 Cardiff; necessary talk (religious); ate. 3.45 Shire Hall, Romans 14:17! 5.15 At home; dinner. 6 At the Shire Hall, Matthew 5:5, etc. 9 At Mr Philips'; supper, religious talk, prayed. 11.15.

Saturday [October] 20. 6.30 Prayed; dressed. 7 At Mrs Howell's (many there); tea, religious talk, prayed. 8 Set out with Williams and Deschamps. 11.30 At the Rock; dinner. 12.45 Set out. 1.45 At the New Passage; writ diary. 4 Set out; religious talk. 5.30 At Mrs Grevil's, tea, Walter Chapman, religious talk. 6.10 At the Malt-house. 8.30 With Averel Spenser. 9 At home; supper, religious talk. 10.

SUNDAY [OCTOBER] 21. 4.30 Journal. 6 At Mr Deschamps', tea, religious talk. 6.15 Walked and visited. 7.30 At the House, Colossians 2:6 (two [comforted] there!). 10 At Mr Willis', Communion (thirty-nine there), prayed, sang. 12.15 At Mr Deschamps', dinner. 1.30 At home; journal. 2 Christ Church. 3.30 At home; tea. 4 Bowling Green, Colossians 2:6 (six thousand there). 5.15 Religious talk; at Mrs Eyres', religious talk. 6.15 Malt-house. 8.30 Religious talk to some. 9 At home; religious talk. 9.45.

MONDAY [OCTOBER] 22. 5 Prayed. 6 Read Prayers; writ to Edmonds. 8 At brother Davis', Miss Cutler, etc, tea, religious talk, prayed. 9.30 At home; necessary business. 12.45 At Mr Wiggington's. 1 Mrs Grevil and Charles there; dinner. 2 At home; writ to Miss Burdock; religious talk to many. 3 At Miss Wotton's, Mrs Highnam, etc, tea, religious talk. 4 Brick-yard, John 16, *ult* [to the end] (two thousand there). 5.15 At Mr Labbè's, tea, religious talk. 6 At Miss Gregory's, religious talk. 6.45 Gloucester Lane. 8.30 At home; supper, religious talk. 9.30.

TUESDAY [OCTOBER] 23. 4 Writ to John Bray, my mother, Spangenberg. 5.30 At Mr Deschamps', tea, religious talk. 6.15 Set out with Charles, religious talk (necessary). 7 Read Law on The New Birth. 9.15 Turleigh. 11 Bearfield, Romans 8:15 (three thousand there). 2 Bath; John Feachem's, tea, religious talk. 3 Set out. 5.30 At Mr Deschamps', tea, necessary talk (religious). 6.45 At Sally Jones', prayed, sang. 8.30 Betty Somers ill, prayed, sang. 9 Charles came, prayed, sang; both well! 12.15 Supper. 1.

WEDNESDAY [OCTOBER] 24. 6.30 Dressed; set out with Purdy. 7.30 At home; journal. 8 At sister Davis', B Morgan, etc, tea, religious talk, prayed. 9.30 At home; journal; sins! 11.30 Malt-house. 12.45 At home; religious talk to many. 3 At Mrs D——'s, tea, religious talk. 4 Baptist Mills, Romans 7:18. 5 Met the leaders. 5.30 At Mrs Hooper's, tea, religious talk. 6.15 With the women. 8 With the men. 9.45 Supper, religious talk. 10.30.

THURSDAY [OCTOBER] 25. 5 Prayed. 5.45 Journal. 7 Read Prayers; journal. 8.15 At Miss Thomas', tea, religious talk, prayed. 9.45 At home; journal. 11.30 Sheriff Barnes, necessary talk (religious); writ diary. 12 Religious talk to some. 12.15 With N Roberts, ill, prayed. 1.30 At Anthony Williams' dinner, religious talk. 3 With N Roberts, sang, prayed. 5 At home; writ to James Hervey. 5.30 Tea, religious talk. 6 Writ to Mrs Dutton. 7 With N Roberts (many there), sang, prayed. 12.15 At Mr Deschamps'.

FRIDAY [OCTOBER] 26. 6.45 Dressed; at home; writ. 7.30 Necessary talk; at the House. 8 At B Holder's, tea, religious talk, prayed. 9.30 At home; writ. 11 Malt-house. 12.15 At N Roberts', prayed! 12.45 At the House; prayed, sang. 3 Writ diary; tea, religious talk. 4 Journal. 5.45 At Mrs Stephens', tea, religious talk. 6.15 With N Roberts, prayed. 6.45 Gloucester Lane. 8.30 With N Roberts, prayed. 9 At home; supper. 10.

SATURDAY [OCTOBER] 27. 6 Prayed. 6.30 Dressed; read Prayers. 7.30 At home; tea; writ to brother Samuel, [Joshua] Read, Mills, Woods; sins; Oxlee. 12.30 With N Roberts! 1 At Mr Whitehead's, dinner, religious talk. 2.15 With Nanny Smith, ill, prayed. 3 Set out. 3.45 At Sally Jones'! 4 At Betty Somers', prayed. 6 She well! 8 At Mr Deschamps', tea. 8.30 At N Roberts', prayed, she well! 9.30 At home; religious talk. 10.

SUNDAY [OCTOBER] 28. 4 Writ journal. 5.45 Deschamps', tea. 6.30 Set out with Purdy. 9 Bath, Romans 14:17. 10.15 At the inn; John Feachem, religious talk. 11 Set out. 12 Turleigh; dinner, religious talk. 1.15 Burry-field [Bradford], Acts 20:26, 27 (ten thousand there). 3 Set out. 6.30 At Widow Jones', Cennick there. 7 Betty Somers, Lucy Clear, and Sally Jones ill, prayed, sang. 1.

MONDAY, OCTOBER 29. 6.45 Prayed; tea, religious talk. 9 At home; writ journal. 12.30 At Mrs Thomas', dinner, religious talk. 1.30 With N Roberts, prayed; she well. 2 Visited; at home; religious talk. 3.45 Brick-yard, Acts 28:22 (twenty-five hundred there). 5.15 Visited. 5.30 At home; Mrs Leport; tea, religious talk. 6.15 Visited; N Roberts, prayed. 7 At home; writ. 8.15 Supper, religious talk. 10.

TUESDAY [OCTOBER] 30. 5 Prayed. 6 Writ to Captain Whitefield. 7 Read Prayers; at Mrs Turner's band, tea, religious talk, prayed. 9.30 At home; necessary business. 12.15 Dressed; religious talk to some. 12.45 Visited N Roberts. 1.30 At Mr Willis', dinner. 2.45 At the House, Isaiah 53:5, 6. 5 At James Burgess', Sally Robins, Jones, Betty Somers, read Prayers. 6.15 At Mr Deschamps', tea, religious talk. 7 At the New Room. 8.30 At the United Society. 9.15 At Mrs Linnington's, supper, mostly religious talk. 11.

WEDNESDAY [OCTOBER] 31. 6 Prayed; read prayers. 7.45 At brother Sayse's, religious talk, prayed. 8.15 At the Room with Mary Deacon's band, religious talk, tea, prayed. 9.30 At Miss Lewis', with her band, religious talk, prayed. 10 At home; religious talk to some. 11 Malt-house, convincing. 12.45 At home; religious talk to many. 1.30 At Miss Gregory's, religious talk; at Miss Purnell's, religious talk, prayed. 2 Visited. 2.30 At Anthony Williams', Charles, etc, tea. 3.30 Baptist Mills (two thousand there), 2 Corinthians 2:11. 4.45 With Nanny Smith, prayed. 5 Visited; at sister Purnell's, religious talk. 5.30 At our Room; the women, religious talk (necessary), prayed; Miss Wotton, B Linford, B Oldfield, Miss Evans, Miss Smith, Miss Lowman, B Latcham (convinced). 8.30 With our men, necessary talk (religious), prayed. 9.15 With Miss Wotton, prayed. 9.45 Supper. 11 At home.

THURSDAY, NOVEMBER [1]. 4 Writ; dressed. 5.15 At Deschamps', tea (many there); prayed. 6.15 Set out with Purdy and Deschamps. 7 At Widow Jones', religious talk, prayed. 7.45 Set out, prayed. 9.45 Marshfield; writ diary; tea, religious talk. 11 Set out; prayed; sins; prayed; read Bunyan's *Life*. 2 Calne; dinner. 3 Set out; prayed; Bunyan. 5.30 Marlborough; Bunyan. 6 Tea; writ diary; journal; prayed. 8.

FRIDAY, NOVEMBER 2. 5 Dressed; read Prayers. 6 Set out; read *Pilgrim's Progress*. 8 Hungerford; tea. 9 Set out; *Pilgrim's Progress*. 11.45 Woolhampton. 12 Dinner. 1.30 Set out; read Bunyan of the law and works. 3.30 Reading; at the inn, necessary talk. 4 At Sally Cennick's. 5 Mrs Cennick not [there]; prayed, religious talk, tea; read my journal. 6.30 Many came, Acts 5! 8.30 Supper; journal, prayed. 11.

SATURDAY [NOVEMBER] 3. 5 Sang; tea, religious talk, prayed. 6.15 Set out; Bunyan. 9.30 Slough, tea. 10.30 Set out; Bunyan. 1 Brentford, dinner. 2 Set out. 4.15 At Mr Bray's, tea, religious talk with Mrs Turner! 5.30 Meditated; prayed. 6 Religious talk with Mr Bray. 8.15 Brown came; supper, religious talk; writ to Charles. 10.15.

SUNDAY [NOVEMBER] 4. 7 Fetter Lane. 7.30 Molther and Spangenberg came. 8 Spangenberg preached. 9 At Mr Bray's; tea, religious talk. 10.15 Islington. 11 Read Prayers, Communion. 1 At home; dinner, religious talk with Oxlee, etc, prayed. 2.30 With my mother, she better; tea, religious talk. 4.30 At Mr Bray's. 5 At Winchester Yard, John 5:5, 6. 6.45 Fetter Lane, religious talk, prayed. 9.15 Islington, supper, religious talk with brother Hall, Oxlee, etc, prayed. 10.

MONDAY [NOVEMBER] 5. 5 Meditated; prayed. 6 Prayed. 6.30 Necessary talk (religious) with Oxlee, Fern, and Mrs Hamilton, prayed. 8 At Mr Spangenberg's, tea, religious. 11.15 At my mother's, read journal. 12.30 Dinner; journal. 3.15 At sister Thacker's band, religious talk, sang. 4.30 Islington, necessary talk (religious). 5 Acts 15:7, 8. 7.30 Winchester Yard, many ill. 9.30 At Mr Bray's, supper. 10.30 At home.

TUESDAY [NOVEMBER] 6. 5 Prayed; writ diary. 6 Prayed, religious talk, sang. 7.30 At Mr Bray's. 8.15 At Mrs Mills'. 9 Tea, religious talk, prayed. 10.45 At Mr Bray's, Spangenberg came, religious talk. 12.15 He went; meditated; writ to Captain Whitefield and sister Nancy. 1.15 Dinner, religious talk. 3.30 At Margaret Clark's, necessary talk. 4 St James's, Acts 5. 5.15 At Margaret Clark's, tea, necessary talk (religious). 7 Dowgate Hill, Matthew 12. 9.30 At home; supper, religious talk. 10.

WEDNESDAY, NOVEMBER 7. 5 Meditated; prayed; writ diary. 6 Prayed; writ [Law's] *Christian Perfection;* necessary talk (religious) to some. 9 At my mother's, tea, religious talk. 10.15 At home; writ Law; sins. 1.45 At Mr Bray's, necessary talk. 2.15 At Mrs Claggett's, religious talk. 3.15 At sister Hodges' band, tea, religious talk, prayed. 5.15 Fetter Lane, Philippians 3:7; at Mr Bray's, tea, religious talk. 8 Fetter Lane. 10 Religious talk to Simpson. 11 At home.

THURSDAY [NOVEMBER] 8. 5 Meditated; prayed. 6 Prayed; writ Law. 7.30 Breakfast; Law; religious talk to some. 11 At Mrs Vaughan's band, religious talk, prayed; Mr Mills came. 1 At Miss Clark's; at Mrs MacCune's, dinner, religious talk, prayed. 3 At Mr Bray's, etc. 4 At Mrs Bell, Junior's, religious talk. 4.15 At Mary Cannon's, religious talk. 5 At Mrs Crouch's, tea, religious talk. 6 Turner's Hall, John 6:51. 8 Savoy Society, Ephesians 2:6. 9.45 At Mr Bray's, necessary talk (religious). 10.30 At home; necessary talk (religious) with sister Hamilton, etc. 10:45.

FRIDAY [NOVEMBER] 9. 5 Meditated; prayed. 6 Prayed; necessary talk (religious); journal. 9 At brother Holland's, tea, religious talk; Sympson there. 10.15 At Mrs Ewster's, religious talk, sang. 11 At James Hutton's, Charles Delamotte came, religious talk. 1 At home; at Mrs Drummond's with Brown, religious talk. 2.30 At sister Anderson's, Betty Hopson there, religious talk, tea. 4.15 Islington House (many there), tea, religious talk; 2 Peter 1. 7 At Mr Bray's, Mrs MacCune, supper. 8 Fetter Lane, Matthew 26. 9.45 At home. 10.

SATURDAY [NOVEMBER] 10. 5 Prayed; meditated. 6 Prayed; religious talk, prayed. 7.45 At Mr Bray's. 8 At James Hutton's, Spangenberg and Molther, religious talk, tea; Hall came, religious talk. 10 At Margaret Clark's, shaved; religious talk. 11.15 At Mr Bray's.

[A gap exists in this volume of the diary until June 1, 1740; a six-week fragment from another volume at Drew University begins with April 13, 1740:]

SUNDAY, APRIL 13, 1740. Prayed; dressed. 6 At Mrs Deschamps', tea, read. 7 The School, Romans 14:17. 8.45 Religious talk (necessary) to sister Reyon. 9.30 At Mrs Willis', Communion, prayed. 1 The band. 12.30 At Mrs Deschamps', dinner. 1.45 At home; the leaders, religious talk. 2.30 At Mrs Grevil's, religious talk. 3 Christ Church. 4.45 At Mrs Deschamps', tea. 5.30 Rose Green, Luke 2:14 (fifteen hundred there)! 7 Society. 9 Women's Love-feast, prayed! 10.30.

MONDAY [APRIL] 14. 4.30 Dressed; Mark 1; journal; tea; journal. 12 Religious talk to many. 2 At Mr Labbè's, dinner, religious talk. 4 At home; necessary business; at sister Halton's band, tea; at Miss Purnell's. 5 She, Miss Bradshaw, Nanny Smith. 7 Society, Hebrews 10:19. 9 Necessary talk (religious); journal. 10.

TUESDAY [APRIL] 15. 4.30 Dressed; Mark 1. 6 The women leaders. 8.30 Tea, religious talk to some. 9.30 Journal. 10 1 Peter 2. 12 Walked. 1 At Nanny Short's, Communion. 1.30 At Mr Wayne's, dinner, religious talk. 3 The School, Hebrews 10. 5.45 At Mrs Hooper's, tea, religious talk; writ diary. 7 Society, Ezekiel 36. 9 Journal. 10.

WEDNESDAY, APRIL 16. 4.30 Dressed; Mark 1; journal. 8 At Betty Bath's, tea, religious talk. 9 Journal. 12 Religious talk to many. 1 The leaders, prayed. 2.15 At Mr Davis', necessary talk to Barton; dinner, prayed. 3.30 At Mrs ((Barton's)) Hooper's, tea, religious talk. 4 At Mrs Martin's, tea, religious talk; visited some. 6 The women, many ill. 8 The men. 9.45.

THURSDAY [APRIL] 17. 4.30 Dressed; Mark 2; read Prayers; tea; journal. 10.30 At Miss Wiggington's, religious talk. 11 Luke 15! 12 Visited many. 1 Writ diary; religious talk to many. 2 At Mrs Thomas', dinner, religious talk. 3.30 Visited. 4 At Miss Jason's, Mr [and] Mrs Wayne, tea, religious talk. 5 At Mrs Moon's, religious talk. 6 At Captain Turner's, tea, religious talk. 7 Matthew 15. 8.30 Society, prayed, five ill. 9.45 Religious talk. 10.

FRIDAY [APRIL] 18. 4.30 Dressed; Mark 3; journal. 8 Tea; journal. 12 Religious talk to many; prayed. 3.15 At Mrs Grevil's, tea, religious talk. 5.15 At Mrs England's, tea, religious talk. 6.15 At Miss Cornish's, tea, religious talk. 7 Ezekiel 37:1, etc; many ill. 9 Journal. 10.

SATURDAY [APRIL] 19. 4.30 Dressed; Mark 3; read Prayers. 7 Journal; tea; journal. 11 Read letters. 1 At sister Perrin's, dinner, religious talk. 2 Letters. 4 At Mr Deschamps', tea. 5 At the School, the bands. 7 At Deschamps', supper. 7.30 At home; writ to Charles, Brown, Simpson. 10.

SUNDAY [APRIL] 20. 5 Dressed; at Mr Deschamps', tea, religious talk. 7 At the School, Exodus 14. 9.30 At Mrs Willis', Communion (sixty-one there!). 11.30 The bands. 12.30 At Mr Deschamps', dinner. 1.45 At home; religious talk with leaders. 2.30 All Saints. 4.30 At Mr Willis', Communion. 5 Rose Green (four thousand there), Romans 14:17! 7 At Mr Deschamps', tea. 7.30 Society; preached! many ill and well. 9.30 Religious talk to many. 10.30 Writ diary. 11.

MONDAY [APRIL] 21. 4.30 Dressed; Mark 3; prayed. 6.30 Chocolate; prayed, religious talk. 7.45 Set out with Nowers, Aldin, and Captain Turner; at Mrs Jones'. 9 Set out. 12 Chippenham; tea, religious talk, prayed. 1 They went back; Nowers and I. 4 Marlborough; coffee. 5 Set out; religious talk. 7 At Hungerford, The Bear; read hymns; supper; hymns. 9.15.

T UESDAY, A PRIL 22. 4 Dressed. 4.30 Set out. 7 Woolhampton; tea. 7.45 Set out. 10.30 At Hare Hatch; coffee. 11.30 Set out. 2 Colnbrook, dinner; slept. 3.30 Set out; religious talk to one. 7 At the Foundery, none at home; necessary business. 8.45 At Mr Garnault's, Charles came, religious talk, tea. 10.30.

W EDNESDAY [A PRIL] 23. 5.30 Dressed; necessary talk. 6 Charles preached. 7.15 Necessary talk (religious) to many. 8 Tea, necessary talk (religious). 9 At Mr Simpson's, religious talk. 10.45 At home; necessary talk (religious). 1.45 At Mrs Bolt's, Mrs Sparrow there; dinner, religious talk. 4 At sister Hall's; at brother Hodges', necessary talk (religious). 5.15 At brother Bowes', Matthew 4:1. 7 At Mrs Seaton's, tea. 8 At our Society. 10 At Mrs Seaton's, supper. 11.

T HURSDAY [A PRIL] 24. 5.30 Dressed; Charles preached; religious talk to some. 7.30 Tea, religious talk to many. 10 Islington; at Mrs Vaughan's, the bands. 2.15 At Mr Knolton's, Simpson, etc; dinner. 4 At Mr Horner's, tea, religious talk. 4.45 At sister Hodges', the band there; tea, religious talk. 6 1 Corinthians 15:36. 8 The United Society, religious talk, prayed. 10.30.

F RIDAY [A PRIL] 25. 5.30 Dressed; Mark 3 *ult* [the end]. 7.30 Religious talk to some; with sister Jack's band. 8.45 At brother Savage's, tea, religious talk. 10 At James Hutton's, Molther, etc, necessary talk (religious). 12 At home; religious talk to some. 2 Writ notes. 2.45 Visited. 3 At Mr Crouch's, brother Abbott and Humphreys, tea, religious talk. 4 At Margaret Taylor's, religious talk. 4.30 At Mrs Mills', the band, religious talk, tea, prayed. 6 At home; Ezekiel 37 (con). 8.15 At Mr Garnault's, supper, religious talk. 10.30.

S ATURDAY [A PRIL] 26. 5.30 Dressed; Mark *ult;* religious talk to some. 8 Humphreys and Abbott, tea, religious talk. 9.30 Writ for the bands. 1 Writ diaries; writ. 2 At Mr Witham's, dinner, religious talk. 3.30 At sister Soane's, religious talk, tea. 4.30 At sister Hall's, religious talk, prayed. 6.30 Foundery, Mark 4:36, Mrs MacCune, Green, Witham, Jackson, Crouch, Seaton, Miss Kent, Cutter, etc, prayed. 9 Writ to brother Mitchell, religious talk. 10.30.

S UNDAY, A PRIL 27. 6 Dressed; tea. 7 Psalm 47:10; the women, religious talk, prayed. 10 St Paul's. 1 At Mr Dawson's, dinner, prayed. 3 St Saviour's. 5 Kennington Common, Job 5:18. 7.45 ((Fetter Lane)) At Mrs Witham's, tea. 8.15 Society, Love-feast. 10 At Mrs Witham's, supper, religious talk. 11.

M ONDAY [A PRIL] 28. 5.45 Dressed; Charles preached. 8.15 At Mr Ibbison's, tea, religious talk. 10 At sister Hall's, prayed, religious talk. 11 At home; religious talk to many. 1.45 At Mrs Mason's, dinner. 3.30 At Mary Cannon's, religious talk. 4.45 At Bell, Senior's, tea, religious talk. 5.30 At sister Jackson's, the women. 6 Necessary talk (religious), prayed; my mother came. 7 Foundery, 2 Kings 5:13. 9.30 Religious talk to many. 10 Supper; at Mr Crouch's, prayed. 11.

T UESDAY [A PRIL] 29. 5.30 Dressed; tea. 6 1 Timothy 2:5; religious talk to many; writ diary. 8.30 At brother Cook's, tea, religious talk. 9.30 At brother Cheyne's, religious talk with Mrs Taylor. 11 At home; religious talk to many. 1 Writ to Purdy. 2 Mrs MacCune, Witham, Green, Seaton; dinner; their band. 4 Visited. 5.15 At Mr Hill's, tea, religious talk. 6.30 At Mr Crouch's. 8 Isaiah 51; twenty ill, three well. 9 Religious talk to many. 11 Sins.

W EDNESDAY [A PRIL] 30. 6 Foundery. 7.30 Religious talk to some. 8.30 At Sarah

Middleton's; tea, religious talk. 9.45 At Mr Stonehouse's; religious talk with him. 10.30 At sister Vaughan's. 11 The bands, religious talk, prayed! 12 Foundery; at Mr Bolt's. 1 Coach. 2 At Mrs Sparrow's; dinner, religious talk, tea. 5 Blackheath, John 3:3 (two thousand there). 7.45 At Mr Bray's, religious talk. 8 At Mrs Seaton's, tea. 8.15 [Fetter Lane] Society! 11 At Mr Garnault's with Charles Delamotte, necessary talk (religious). 12.

THURSDAY, MAY 1. 5.45 Dressed. 6 Foundery, Luke 22:19; religious talk to many. 8 Charles Delamotte, tea, religious talk. 10 At Mr Hilland's, religious talk, prayed! 11 At home; religious talk to many. 2 At Mrs West's, dinner, religious talk. 4 With Mary Cannon, religious talk. 5 At sister Bell's, religious talk. 5.30 At home; Mrs Green, etc, tea; necessary business. 6.30 John 19:33. 8.30 Society! 10 Religious talk to some. 10.45.

FRIDAY, MAY 2. 4.45 Dressed. 5 Necessary business; tea. 5.30 Many there, prayed. 6.15 Set out; religious talk with Mr Sadler. 9.30 Colnbrook; coffee, writ to Charles. 10.30 Set out. 1.30 Reading; at sister Cennick's. 2 Dinner, religious talk, prayed. 3 Set out. 5 Feacham [Thatcham]; tea. 5.45 Rode. 7.45 Hungerford; supper, writ. 9.30.

SATURDAY, MAY 3. 4.45 Dressed. 5 Rode. 7 Marlborough; tea. 8 Rode; verse. 10.15 Calne; coffee. 11 Rode; verse. 2.30 At Marshfield; dinner. 3.30 Rode. 6 Bristol; at Mr Deschamps', tea, religious talk. 7 At home; necessary business; religious talk to Brown, to Charles. 9 Supper, religious talk. 10.

SUNDAY, MAY 4. 4.45 Dressed; Cennick, necessary talk (religious); necessary business. 6 At Mr Deschamps', tea, religious talk. 7 At the School, 1 Corinthians 2:2. 9 At Mrs Cambourn's, their child ill; tea, prayed. 10 At Mrs Willis', Communion (fifty there!). 11.30 The band. 12.15 At Mr Deschamps', dinner. 1.15 At home; the leaders. 2.30 All Saints. 3.45 Visited. 4 At Mr Deschamps'; slept. 4.30 Tea. 5.15 At Rose Green (twelve hundred there), rain, 1 Corinthians 2:2. 7 At home; Society. 9 Religious talk to many. 9.30.

MONDAY [MAY] 5. 4 Writ notes. 5 Mark 4; journal. 7.30 Tea; journal. 12 Religious talk to many. 2 At Captain Turner's, dinner, religious talk, sang, prayed. 3 At home. 4 Religious talk to some. 5 At Mrs Masters', necessary talk. 5.45 At Mrs Grevil's; Miss Jason; tea, religious talk. 7 1 John 2:12; religious talk to many. 9.45.

TUESDAY [MAY] 6. 4 Journal; prayed. 5 Mark 4; the women leaders, necessary talk (religious), prayed; sins. 9 Journal. 10.30 Visited Margaret Evans, prayed. 11 Malt-house. 12.30 Walked. 1 At Nanny Short's; at Mr Wayne's, dinner. 3 At the School, Romans 8:2. 4.30 At Nanny Short's, Communion. 5.30 At Mr England's, tea, prayed. 6.30 At Susy Stephens', prayed. 7 Isaiah 51!; visited. 10.

WEDNESDAY [MAY] 7. 4.30 Dressed; prayed; Mark 4; read Prayers. 7 Tea; journal. 9.30 At sister Bath's, necessary talk (religious). 11.30 At home; religious talk to many. 1 The leaders, prayed. 3 At Mrs Hooper's, tea, religious talk. 4 Visited Mr Cutler. 4.45 At Mrs Harding's, tea, religious talk. 6 At home; the women. 7.30 The men. 9 At Mrs Hooper's, Mr Tomkins there; supper. 10.30.

THURSDAY, MAY 8. 4.30 Dressed; read notes. 5 Mark 4; religious talk to many. 7 Daniel Rowland, etc, tea, religious talk. 8.15 At Mrs Stafford's, prayed, tea, religious talk, prayed. 9.30 Visited. 10.15 With N Jeffrys, religious talk! 11

Malt-house! 12 Visited. 12.45 At home; religious talk to many. 2 At Mrs Norman's, dinner, religious talk. 4 At Mrs Williams', religious talk, prayed. 4.30 At Mrs England's, he dead. 5 Newgate, with C Cornick, necessary talk (religious), prayed; necessary talk (religious) to Mrs Dagge. 6 At Mr Henry Page's, religious talk, tea. 7 Acts 25! 8.30 Society, many ill. 10.45.

FRIDAY [MAY] 9. 4.45 Dressed; Mark 4; writ notes; religious talk to some. 6.30 Slept. 7 Tea; journal. 10 Miss Jason, necessary talk (religious). 10.30 Journal. 12 Religious talk to some. 1.15 Prayed. 3 Religious talk to some. 3.45 At Mrs Grevil's, tea, religious talk. 4.30 At Mrs Williams', Communion (sixteen there). 5 At Mary Purnell's, Miss Bradshaw, Nanny Smith, Betty Latcham ill! prayed. 6.30 At home; necessary business; writ diary; ate. 7 Acts 26! 9.15 Visited. Miss Cutler, he dead! religious talk, prayed. 9.45.

SATURDAY [MAY] 10. 4.30 Prayed; dressed; Mark 5; journal. 7 Chocolate; journal; sins! 11 Read Mr Erskine's books. 11.30 Religious talk to many. 1 Visited. 1.30 At Mrs Hooper's, dinner; visited. 3.30 Kingswood School, necessary talk. 4.30 The bands. 6.15 At Mr England's burying, religious talk. 8.15 At Miss Cutler's, religious talk. 9.15 At home; supper, religious talk to Purdy, etc. 10.15.

SUNDAY [MAY] 11. 4.45 Dressed; necessary talk (religious); at Mr Deschamps', tea. 6.45 At the School, Luke 2:10. 9 At Mr Willis', Communion (forty there!), prayed. 10 Sally Parsons, etc. 11 The band. 12 At Mr Jones', dinner. 1 At home; the leaders. 3.30 Visited Mrs Wright! Miss Lewis, tea. 4.30 At sister Reyon's, Communion. 5.15 Rose Green, Luke 2:10 (five thousand there). 6.45 At Mr Cutler's burying. 8.15 Society! 9 Women's Love-feast, prayed! many ill. 11.

MONDAY, MAY 12. 4.30 Prayed; dressed; Mark 5; read Prayers. 7 Religious talk to some; necessary talk; chocolate. 9 Corrected for Farley; writ to Charles. 12 At Mr Dawson's, Communion. 2 At Mr Labbè's, dinner, religious talk. 3.30 At home; necessary business. 4 At brother Aldin's, tea, religious talk. 5 At Mrs Grevil's with Miss Perrot, religious talk. 6.15 Tea, religious talk. 7 1 Peter 1:11! many ill; religious talk to some. 9.45.

TUESDAY [MAY] 13. 4.30 Prayed; dressed; Mark 5; the women leaders. 9 First band upon trial. 9 Tea, religious talk, prayed; writ diary. 11 At the Malt-room [Malt-house?], 1 Peter 3! 12 At sister Evans', Communion (sixteen there). 1.45 At Mr Willis', dinner, prayed. 2.15 Walked; read Erskine's *Account.* 3 At the School, 1 Peter 1:9. 4 Read Erskine. 4.45 At Mrs Jones', writ hymns. 7 Upton [Cheney]; at the Maypole, Acts 5:30; they beat pans! sang, prayed. 8.30 Visited Mrs Lawton, prayed. 9.15 At Mrs Jones', supper, religious talk. 10.15.

WEDNESDAY [MAY] 14. 4.45 Hymns; chocolate. 6 At the School, Matthew 12! 7.15 Writ hymns. 12 Went with sister Milsom to the Fishponds. 1 Visited; Communion. 2 At home; leaders, prayed. 3 Religious talk to many. 3.30 At Mrs Grevil's, Miss Jason, mostly religious talk, tea. 4.30 At Mrs Martin's, tea, religious talk. 5.30 Necessary business. 6 The women, religious talk, prayed! 7.30 The men, prayed. 9 At Mrs Grevil's, Miss Jason, supper. 10 With her alone, religious talk! 11.15.

THURSDAY [MAY] 15. 5 Mark 6; slept. 7 Tea; hymns. 10 At Mr Wiggington's, religious talk. 11 Malt-room, Psalm 68:18! 12.15 At sister May Taylor's, Mary

Deacon, religious talk, prayed. 1.15 At sister Turner's, dinner, religious talk. 2.30 At home; religious talk to many. 3.45 Visited sister Lockier. 4.15 At Mrs Pottam's, tea, religious talk. 5.30 At home; writ names of Society. 7 Acts 26! 8.45 Society. 10.30.

FRIDAY, MAY 16. 4.30 Prayed; dressed. 5 Mark 7; slept. 7 Tea; hymns; sins! 10 Religious talk to sister Peck; hymns. 12 Religious talk to many. 1 Prayed. 3 The leaders, necessary talk (religious). 3.30 At Mrs Grevil's, tea, religious talk. 4 At Mrs Williams', Communion (sixteen there). 5.15 Visited some. 7 Acts 26! 9 At Mr Blatchley's, Mrs Smyth, etc, necessary talk of the mortgage, made it. 11 Supper, religious talk. 11.30.

SATURDAY [MAY] 17. 4.45 Dressed; Mark 7; slept. 7 Tea; writ for the Society. 11 Read letters; prayed. 1 At Mrs Brummidge's; writ to Howell Griffiths; dinner. 2 Letters. 3.45 Read Erskine's *Account*. 4.45 At the School, religious talk (necessary). 5 The bands, prayed, religious talk, prayed. 6.30 At Mr Deschamps', tea, religious talk. 7 At home; writ diary; Erskine. 7.30 Writ to Charles; visited. 8.45 At home; necessary talk (religious). 10.

SUNDAY, MAY 18. 4.45 Meditated; dressed. 5.30 At Mr Deschamps', tea, religious talk. 6.30 At the School, 1 Peter 4:12. 9 At home; meditated; prayed. 10 Read Prayers at St James's, Communion (four hundred there). 1.30 At Mrs England's, dinner. 2.30 At home; the leaders. 4 At Miss Lewis', tea, religious talk. 5.15 Rose Green (six thousand there), 1 Peter 4:12. 7.30 Society, many ill. 9 Religious talk to some. 9.45.

MONDAY [MAY] 19. 4.30 Meditated; prayed. 5 Mark 8; read Prayers. 7 Religious talk to some; sister Rawlins' band. 8 Second band upon trial; tea, prayed. 9.30 Visited; religious talk. 11 Writ notes; religious talk to many. 2 Mary Bosher and Betty Stephens! 4.30 At sister Taylor's, Mary Deacon! 5.15 At sister Somerel's, he ill, Communion (twenty-six there). 6 At sister Witton's, tea, religious talk; Elizabeth Webb! 7 Society, Zechariah 3; religious talk. 10.

TUESDAY [MAY] 20. 4.30 Meditated; prayed; Mark 8. 6 The women leaders. 8.45 Tea; writ diary. 9.30 Writ notes. 10.30 At sister Elizabeth Turner's, religious talk. 11 Malt-room. 12 Visited some. 1 At Mrs Smith's, religious talk, dinner. 3.15 At the School, 1 Corinthians 1:30; visited. 5.30 At Miss Purnell's. 6 Tea, religious talk. 7 Hebrews 10:35! 9 At Felix Farley's, supper, religious talk. 10.45.

WEDNESDAY, MAY 21. 4.45 Dressed; Mark 9; slept. 7.30 Tea; writ to Charles; writ notes. 11.45 Religious talk to many. 1.15 The leaders. 3 Necessary talk (religious). 3.30 At Mrs Norman's. 4 Tea, religious talk. 5 Visited some; religious talk; Communion. 6 The women, many ill! 7.45 The men; Lucretia Smith! prayed. 10.45.

THURSDAY [MAY] 22. 4.30 Prayed; Mark 9; read Prayers. 7 At Mrs Hooper's, her band. 8 Tea, religious talk, prayed. 8.30 At home; writ diary; writ for the Society. 9.30 Mrs Grevil came, religious talk. 10 At sister Evans', Communion (twenty-one there). 11 Malt-room. 12.30 At home; religious talk to some. 1.45 At Mrs Stephens'; dinner, religious talk. 3.15 Visited some. 4.45 At N Arundel's. 5 Tea; Mrs Grevil, religious talk. 5.30 At sister Oldfield's, tea, religious talk. 6.30 Acts 27, many ill; Society, religious talk. 10.30.

FRIDAY [MAY] 23. 4.30 Prayed; dressed; Mark 10; writ. 7 The band; tea, religious talk, prayed. 9 Writ preface to journal. 11.30 Religious talk to some; necessary business. 1.15 Prayed! 3.15 Visited. 3.30 At Mrs Grevil's, tea, religious talk. 4.30 At Mrs Williams', Communion (twenty-two there). 5.15 At Mr Labbè's, Mrs Gotley there, tea, religious talk. 6.45 At home; necessary business. 7 Isaiah 51 *ult*, many ill; visited; ate; prayed. 10.15 Slept. 12 Sins.

SATURDAY [MAY] 24. 4.30 Prayed; Mark 9; read Prayers. 7 At P Evans' band, religious talk, prayed. 8.30 At sister Bath's, religious talk. 9 Writ journal. 10.45 Writ diary; writ to Charles. 12 Religious talk to many. 1.15 Walked; N Gotley met us! 2 At Mrs Hooper's, dinner, religious talk to Miss Gregory. 4 At the School, necessary talk (religious). 4.45 The bands; prayed, etc. 7.30 At Mr Deschamps', supper. 8 At Mr Labbè's; visited Suky. 8.30 At home; religious talk; writ diary. 9.15 Lay down. 10.

SUNDAY, MAY 25. 4.30 Meditated; dressed. 5.15 Mr Deschamps', tea, religious talk. 6.15 At the School, christened Jon[athan] Reeves. 6.45 John 16:8, 9! 9.15 At home; meditated; prayed. 10 Read Prayers; Communion. 1.30 At brother Wedmore's, dinner. 2.15 At home; the leaders. 4 At Mrs Oldfield's, Mr Oldfield there; tea, religious talk. 5.30 Rose Green, John 16:8, 9 (five thousand there). 7.30 Society, many ill! 8.45 Our Love-feast! 10.30.

MONDAY [MAY] 26. 4.30 Meditated; prayed; Mark 10! read Prayers; the band; tea, religious talk, prayed. 9 Religious talk to many. 10.30 At ——'s [Harding's; see JWJ], religious talk! 11.30 Malt-room. 12.30 Visited. 1 At Mr Grevil's, dinner. 2.30 Visited. 3.15 At Mrs Gotley's, religious talk. 4 At Mrs Stafford's, tea, religious talk, prayed. 5 The Society met, settled them. 7 Acts 2:4, many ill and well! 10.

TUESDAY [MAY] 27. 4.45 Dressed; Mark 10; the women leaders. 9 The band. 10.30 At Mrs Gee's, religious talk. 11 Malt-room! 1.30 At Mr Wayne's. 3 At the School, Acts 2:4! 5.45 At Miss Purnell's band. 6 Tea, religious talk, prayed! 7 Society, Acts 28! supper, religious talk to many. 10.

WEDNESDAY [MAY] 28. 4.30 Meditated; dressed; Mark 10; religious talk to some. 7 The band; tea, religious talk, prayed. 8.45 Religious talk to some. 9.30 Bedminster, Communion (sixteen there). 11 At home; religious talk to many. 1.30 The leaders, prayed! 3 Religious talk to many. 3.30 At Mrs Gotley's, tea, religious talk. 4 At Mr Martin's, tea, religious talk. 5 At Miss Nursman's band, religious talk. 6 The women. 8 The men. 9 Lucretia Smith! prayed. 10.45.

THURSDAY [MAY] 29. 4.45 Prayed; Mark 10; religious talk to many. 7 The band, religious talk, prayed. 9 Writ to Mr Richards of Kentisbeare [MS reads Kentsbeer] and Mr Matthews. 10.15 At sister Evans', Communion (twenty-four there). 11 Malt-room. 12.30 Visited. 1 At Mrs Walcom's, dinner, writ to Mrs James. 2.30 At Mrs Richardson's, tea, religious talk. 3.30 At Mrs Page's; Mr Porter's; Labbè's, etc. 5 At home; the band, tea, religious talk. 6 Acts 28! 8 Society; necessary business; prayed. 11.

[No entries for two days between diary fragment and resumption of other diary]

SUNDAY, JUNE 1. 5 Walked; meditated. 6.15 Tea, religious talk. 6.45 Hebrews 3:18, 19. 9 At Mrs Willis', Communion (one hundred fifteen there), prayed, some ill and well! 12.15 At Mrs Deschamps', dinner; at home; writ; the leaders. 4 At Mr Deschamps', tea. 5 Rose Green, Hebrews 3:18, 19 (seven thousand there!). 7 United Society, Ephesians 6; Grace Stephens, Molly Richardson, etc; visited; prayed. 11.30.

Monday [June] 2. 4 Necessary business; prayed; sang. 6.15 At Mr Deschamps', tea, religious talk. 6.45 Set out with brother Purdy and Nowers. 12.15 At Avon, religious talk. 1 Dinner, religious talk to Miss Gotley. 3.30 Tea, religious talk. 4.30 Set out with Mr [and] Mrs. 5 Miss Gotley, etc, religious talk with her. 6.30 Malmesbury. 7 At Mr Lyne's, with Mrs Lyne, religious talk. 7.30 At the Cross Hays, Hebrews 3:18, 19 (three hundred there). 8.45 At Mr Punter's, prayed. 9.15 At Mr Lyne's, supper, religious talk. 10.15 At Mr Punter's.

Tuesday [June] 3. 5 Dressed; necessary business; tea, religious talk. 6.45 Set out with Mr Canter, religious talk. 8.45 Purton, ate, religious talk. 9.45 Set out; religious talk. 11.15 Highworth; sins; tea. 12.15 Set out. 5 Oxford; at Mrs Fox's. 6 Necessary talk (religious); tea; slept. 7 Society, Hebrews 3:18, 19; religious talk to some. 9.45 At College. 10.

Wednesday [June] 4. 5 Necessary business. 6 Set out with Robson and Nowers. 8 At brother Gambold's, religious talk, tea, prayed. 11.45 Oxford; at College; sorted papers. 1.15 With Hutchins and Vesey. 1.30 At Viney's, Spaltzer, etc, necessary talk (religious). 3.15 At Mr Bully's, Gambold, Robson, etc; tea, religious talk. 4.15 At Mrs Compton's, religious talk; at Mrs Plat's, religious talk! 7 At Mr Fox's, 1 Peter 1:11! 9 Tea, necessary talk (religious). 10.30.

Thursday, June 5. 4 Dressed; necessary business. 5 Set out with Nowers and Purdy, religious talk. 7.15 Tetsworth; tea, religious talk. 8.15 Set out; religious talk. 10.30 At Mr Crouch's, religious talk, ate. 11 Simpson came! religious talk, prayed with a sick woman. 11.15 Set out. 1.30 Uxbridge, dinner. 2.30 Set out; religious talk. 5.30 At the Foundery. 6 Tea, necessary talk (religious). 6.30 Charles preached. 8.30 Supper; the Society, some ill! 11.

Friday [June] 6. 5.30 Dressed; meditated. 6 James 1:1, etc. 7 Necessary talk (religious); chocolate, necessary talk (religious). 9.30 Walked with Howell Harris, Charles, etc. 10.15 At Mr Stonehouse's with Molther, religious talk. 2 At home; Society, prayed, many ill. 3 With my mother, tea, religious talk. 5 Redriff [Rotherhithe], Ezekiel 33. 6.30 Wapping, 1 Peter 4; many ill! 8.30 At home; religious talk, supper. 10.15.

Saturday [June] 7. 5.15 Dressed; meditated. 6 James 1. 7 Chocolate, religious talk. 8.15 Writ diary. 9 Necessary business. 10 With Charles, Howell Harris, and Purdy at Mrs Ewster's, religious talk. 12.45 At brother Bell's, he not [there]. 1 At Mary Cannon's, religious talk. 2 At Mr Knolton's, Töltschig, etc, dinner, religious talk. 3.30 At brother Bell's, religious talk, tea. 5 At Bowes' Society, 1 Peter 4. 6 At brother Bray's, religious talk to them. 6.45 Tea, religious talk. 7.15 At home; writ. 8 The women bands, R Robinson! prayed. 10 Religious talk. 10.15 Sins.

Sunday [June] 8. 6 Dressed; writ diary; meditated. 7 Hebrews 3:18, 19. 8.30 Chocolate, religious talk. 9 Meditated; prayed. 10 St Paul's, Communion; one ordained. 1.45 At home; dinner; meditated; necessary talk; necessary business. 4 Meditated; writ. 5 Ezekiel 33. 7 The women's Love-feast; prayed, etc. 10.30.

MONDAY [JUNE] 9. 5.30 Dressed; religious talk (necessary). 6 James 1. 7 Religious talk to some; chocolate. 8 Writ names of Society; sins. 11 Religious talk to many. 2 At Mr Wilde's, dinner, religious talk. 3 Prayed, tea. 5.15 At home; religious talk with Jane Davis. 6.30 Hebrews 3:18, 19; many ill. 8.15 The women, religious talk, I prayed. 10 Religious talk to Hague, etc. 10.45.

TUESDAY [JUNE] 10. 5.45 Dressed; James 1. 7 Met the first band. 7.30 Brother Ingham came, religious talk, tea. 8.30 Religious talk with brother Ingham, etc. 12 Religious talk to many. 2.30 At Mr Garnault's, dinner. 4.30 At Mr Harris', tea, religious talk. 6 At Mr Crouch's, religious talk. 6.30 2 Corinthians 5; many ill. 9 At brother Bowes', the leaders. 10.30 At home; ate. 10.45.

WEDNESDAY, JUNE 11. 5.45 Dressed; James 1 with a band. 8 Ingham, etc, tea, necessary talk (religious). 9.30 Islington; at Mr Stonehouse's, Molther ill again! religious talk. 11.30 At home; religious talk to many. 3 At sister Ibbison's, tea, religious talk. 4.30 At sister Hodges', the band, tea, religious talk. 7 At home; supper. 8 At our Society, explained! 11.

THURSDAY [JUNE] 12. 5.45 Dressed; James 1; band. 8 Tea, religious talk. 9.30 Writ for Society; Howell Harris and brother Hall went. 12 Religious talk to many. 2.15 At Mr Watkins', dinner. 3.45 At home; writ for Society. 5.30 At sister Kewricks' [Kendrick's?], tea, religious talk! 6.30 At home; writ names. 8.15 Society, four ill; necessary talk, prayed. 10.30.

FRIDAY [JUNE] 13. 5.30 Religious talk; dressed; James 1; band. 8 Tea, religious talk. 9 Writ for Society. 11.15 Religious talk to many. 1 Many here; religious talk, prayed, many ill, one well! 4.15 At Mrs Mill's, tea, religious talk. 5.30 Redriff, Romans 4:5. 8 At home; supper, religious talk. 9.15 Religious talk with Mary Cannon and sister Johnson. 10.15.

SATURDAY [JUNE] 14. 5.30 Meditated; dressed; James 2. 7 The band. 8 Tea; necessary business; writ notes. 11 Read letters. 1 Necessary business. 1.30 At sister Ibbison's, dinner, religious talk, prayed. 3 At sister Hamilton's band, religious talk, sang, tea. 4.45 At brother Shaw's, religious talk. 6 At Mr Pellet's, religious talk. 7.30 At Mr Exall's, tea, religious talk. 8 Ezekiel 36. 9.45 At home; necessary talk (religious). 10.45.

SUNDAY [JUNE] 15. 5.30 Dressed; tea. 6.30 Charles preached. 8.30 Men and women leaders, settled role. 9.45 St Paul's. 12.30 At brother Dandy's, dinner, religious talk, sang. 2.30 At home; necessary business. 4.30 Tea, religious talk. 5 [no entry]. 7 At home; bands. 9.45 At Mrs Witham's, supper, religious talk. 11.15.

MONDAY [JUNE] 16. 5.30 Dressed. 6 James 2. 7 The band; chocolate; necessary business; religious talk with Ingham. 11 Necessary business. 12 Religious talk to many. 2.30 At sister Vaughan's, dinner, religious talk. 4.15 At the House; the bands, necessary talk (religious). 5 Ezekiel 36. 6.30 At Mr Crouch's, Matthew 5. 8 At my band. 9.15 At home; religious talk. 10.15.

TUESDAY, JUNE 17. 5.30 Meditated; James 2. 7 Journal; chocolate; writ journal; necessary talk. 12 Religious talk to many. 1.30 Dinner, religious talk to many. 4 Writ; religious talk. 5 At Betty Spring's, tea, religious talk, prayed. 6 Visited Mrs Ward, prayed, religious talk. 7 Visited brother Turner. 7.30 At home; the Society, religious talk, prayed. 10 Supper, necessary talk (religious). 11.15.

WEDNESDAY [JUNE] 18. 5.30 Prayed; James 2. 7 Journal; chocolate; journal; necessary talk. 12 Religious talk to some; Charles went to Bristol. 1 Religious talk to many; necessary talk (religious). 3.15 At sister Hodges'; at Mr Williams', tea, religious talk. 4.15 At sister Timberlake's, tea, religious talk. 5.15 At Mr Keen's. 6 Marylebone, Acts 5:30! 7.45 At home; supper. 8.30 Society; Ingham there. 10.30 At home.

THURSDAY [JUNE] 19. 5.30 Prayed; dressed; James 2; chocolate; journal. 11 Necessary talk (religious); journal. 12 Religious talk to many. 2 At Mr Bowles', dinner, religious talk. 4.15 At Deptford, Mrs Davis' [see JWJ, 6/9, 6/19], religious talk, prayed! 5.15 At Mr Church's, tea, religious talk. 6.30 The Foundery, Ephesians 6. 8 Supper; Society, Mr Acourt! prayed, religious talk. 10.45.

FRIDAY [JUNE] 20. 5.30 Prayed; dressed; James 2; chocolate; religious talk; Mr Wallis came. 8.45 Journal. 12 Religious talk to many. 1 Prayed. 3 At Mrs West's, tea, religious talk. 4 At Miss Kent's, tea, religious talk. 5 Redriff, John 3:7. 6.30 Wapping, Mark 3. 8 At Mrs Burton's, supper, religious talk. 9.45 At home; writ diary. 10.30.

SATURDAY [JUNE] 21. 5.30 Dressed; James 3; chocolate; journal. 12 Religious talk to many. 2 At Mrs Seaton's, Mrs MacCune, dinner, religious talk. 4 Visited; Communion. 5 Whitechapel, Matthew 5:2, 3, 4. 7.15 At home; supper; the women, religious talk, prayed. 10.15.

SUNDAY [JUNE] 22. 5.30 Prayed; tea; dressed. 6.30 Jeremiah 6:16. 8 The women leaders. 10 St Paul's. 1 At home; Elizabeth Ash, etc, dinner. 3 At Dr Heylin's church. 5 Kennington, 1 Peter 1:9. 7 At Mrs Seaton's, tea. 8 At the Love-feast! 10 At home; religious talk. 11.15.

MONDAY, JUNE 23. 5.30 Prayed; Matthew 5; journal; necessary business. 12 Religious talk to some. 2.30 At Mrs Vaughan's, tea, religious talk. 4.30 At the House, John 16. 7 At Mr Craven's, Isaiah 53:5, 6. 8 At Mr Dawson's, Mrs Mills there, supper, religious talk, prayed. 10.15 At home, religious talk. 11.

TUESDAY [JUNE] 24. 5.30 Prayed; Colossians 2; with a band. 8 Tea, religious talk; journal. 11 Religious talk to many. 2 At brother Milbourn's, tea, religious talk. 3.30 At Mr Bray's with brother Seward, necessary talk (religious). 5 At sister Spring's, religious talk; at Mrs ____'s, tea, religious talk. 6.30 At home; Hebrews 10[:35]. 8 Supper, religious talk; writ to Charles. 10.30.

WEDNESDAY [JUNE] 25. 5.30 Prayed; dressed; 2 Timothy 3. 7 Writ sermon; chocolate; writ to Miss Jason, sister Nancy, Mrs Dutton, Mr Birket, and Davidson. 12 Religious talk to many. 2 Dinner. 3 Walked to Deptford; at sister Church's, tea, religious talk. 5.30 Society, Hebrews 4:11. 8.15 At home; supper. 8.45 Society, religious talk, prayed. 10.45.

THURSDAY [JUNE] 26. 5.30 John 5:39; religious talk to many; tea; writ sermon; writ for Society. 12 Religious talk to many. 2 At Mr Garnault's, dinner, religious talk. 4 Visited. 4 At Mrs Cutter's, tea, religious talk. 5 At Mrs Westry's, tea, religious talk. 6.30 Mark 9, many ill. 8 Supper. 8.30 Society, Elizabeth Baddily! religious talk, prayed. 11.

FRIDAY [JUNE] 27. 5.30 Prayed; Luke 22:19; religious talk to many; writ notes; tea; writ notes. 12 Religious talk to many. 1.15 Prayed. 3.15 At Mr Craven's, necessary talk. 4.15 At Mr Jones', tea, religious talk. 5 Rag Fair, Ephesians 2:8; visited two. 7.45 At home; Seward, etc, religious talk. 8.15 He went; supper, religious talk. 10.

SATURDAY [JUNE] 28. 5.30 Dressed; Luke 22:19; religious talk to some; tea. 9 Necessary talk for brother Nowers! 9.30 Writ to Habersham, Burnside, Lindal, Brownfield, Mrs Fallowfield. 12 Religious talk to many. 2 At brother Hogg's, dinner, religious talk. 4.15 [Stoke] Newington; at sister Betteridge's, religious talk to J Bourn. 5.15 At Mr Spenser's, Mr Drake, etc, necessary talk. 5.30 Tea, religious talk. 6.30 Long Lane, Luke 18! 8.30 At home; supper, necessary talk (religious); necessary business. 10.30.

SUNDAY, JUNE 29. 5 Dressed; tea; meditated. 6.30 Moorfields, Titus 3:8; collected for the Negro school. 9 The leaders. 10 St Paul's. 1 At home; dinner. 1.30 The women leaders. 2.45 Dr Heylin's; at Mr Spenser's, tea. 5.15 Kennington, Titus 3:8! 7.30 At Mrs Beller's, supper, religious talk. 9 At home; the women! 11.

MONDAY [JUNE] 30. 5.30 Dressed; prayed; Romans 14:1; necessary talk (religious). 8 Tea; writ for Society. 12 Religious talk to many. 2 At sister Johnson's, dinner, religious talk. 4 Islington; at Mrs Scott's, necessary talk (religious), tea. 4.45 Matthew 18. 5.45 Southwark, Matthew 18; supper. 8.45 At home; prayed, religious talk. 10.

TUESDAY, JULY 1. 5.30 Prayed; 1 John 5:3; religious talk to many; tea; writ for Society. 11.30 Religious talk to many. 2.30 At brother Hobbins', dinner; with a sick woman. 4 Communion; visited. 5 At Betty Spring's, tea, religious talk. 6.30 Hebrews 7:25. 8 Necessary talk (religious), supper. 8.30 At Mr Bowes', necessary talk. 9.45 At home. 10.30.

WEDNESDAY [JULY] 2. 5.30 Prayed; 1 Timothy 2:4; religious talk to many. 8 Tea; writ preface to Hymns. 11.30 Religious talk to many. 3 At Miss Gilby's, tea, religious talk. 4.15 At Mr Osgood's, religious talk. 5 At Mr Keen's, tea, religious talk. 6 Marylebone, Romans 14:17. 7.30 At Mrs Lane's, religious talk. 8.30 At our Society. 9.30 At sister Westry's, religious talk, prayed. 10.30.

THURSDAY [JULY] 3. 5:30 Prayed; Ephesians 6:1; religious talk to many. 8 Tea; writ Preface. 12 Religious talk to many. 2 At Mr Nightingale's, dinner. 3.30 At Mrs Kendrick's, religious talk. 4 At Mrs Seaton's, the band, tea, religious talk. 5.30 At Mrs Reeves', tea, religious talk. 6.15 1 Corinthians 2:2. 8 Supper; Society! 10.30.

FRIDAY [JULY] 4. 5.30 Prayed; Matthew 6. 7 Writ preface. 11.30 Religious talk to many. 2.15 Prayed. 3 Religious talk to many. 4 Tea; at sister Kent's. 5.15 Redriff. 7 At sister Robinson's, religious talk. 8 At home; supper. 8.30 The leaders, religious talk, prayers; religious talk to Nanny Smith. 10.45.

SATURDAY, JULY 5. 5.30 Prayed; 2 Corinthians 4:1, 2; at Mr Garnault's; preface; sins. 8 Tea; preface. 10.30 At Charles Rivington's, religious talk. 11.30 At home; necessary business. 12 Religious talk to many. 2 At Mrs West's, religious talk; Seward, brother Hall, etc, dinner. 3.45 At Mrs Hunt's, her son! prayed.

4.15 At Mrs Hawthorn's, tea, religious talk. 6.15 Whitechapel Society, Luke 13:12. 8.15 At home; supper, religious talk; necessary business. 10 At brother Garnault's.

SUNDAY [JULY] 6. 7 Writ to many; tea. 9.30 At home; the men, prayed; St Paul's. 1 At home; dinner; the women leaders, religious talk (necessary). 3.30 Writ letters; tea. 5 Acts 2:19. 7 Women's Love-feast. 10.45.

MONDAY [JULY] 7. 5.30 Dressed; 1 John 5:1. 7 At Mr Garnault's; writ journal. 8.15 Tea; journal. 11.30 At home; necessary business; religious talk to many. 2 Dinner; visited. 3.45 Islington; at sister Vaughan's, religious talk. 4.15 With the band. 4.30 1 Peter 1:9. 6.30 At Mrs Dean's, tea, religious talk. 7 Long Lane, 1 Peter 9. 8.30 At home; supper, religious talk. 10.

TUESDAY [JULY] 8. 5.30 Dressed; James 3; at Mr Garnault's; writ for Society. 12 Religious talk to many. 2 At sister Horner's, dinner, religious talk, prayed. 3.15 At Mr Barnes', religious talk, tea. 5.15 At Nancy Morris', tea, religious talk. 6.15 Exodus 14:13. 8 Supper; Society, many ill! 10 Lay down. 12.15.

WEDNESDAY [JULY] 9. 5.30 Dressed; James 3; at brother Garnault's; journal; tea; journal. 11 At home; necessary business; religious talk to many. 2 Christened Elizabeth Ash, Rebecca Perkins, Susy Smithers. 4 At Mrs Sutherland's, tea, religious talk. 5.30 At home; supper. 8 Fetter Lane. 8.30 At brother Pattison's, christened his son. 9 Fetter Lane; explained! 11.

THURSDAY [JULY] 10. 5.30 Dressed; James 3; brother Garnault's; journal. 11.30 At home; religious talk to many. 2.30 At brother Dawson's, dinner, religious talk, prayed. 4 At sister Seaton's band, religious talk. 5 At sister Hogg's, tea, religious talk. 6 At home; preached. 7 Supper; Society. 8.30 Islington; brother Molther preached. 9.45 At home; necessary talk. 10.30.

FRIDAY, JULY 11. 5.30 Prayed; James 3; at brother Garnault's; journal. 8.30 Tea; journal. 11 At home; religious talk to many. 1 Prayed. 3 Tea; at Mrs West's, tea, religious talk. 5 Redriff, Matthew 5:20. 6.30 Wapping, Matthew 5:4. 8.30 At home; supper; the leaders. 10.15.

SATURDAY [JULY] 12. Prayed; dressed; James 3; at brother Garnault's; journal. 9 Tea, religious talk. 9.30 At home; writ notes. 11 Religious talk to many. 12 Read letters. 2 Dinner. 3 Letters. 5.15 Visited. 6 At Mr Spenser's, tea. 6.30 Long Lane, Ecclesiastes 7:16. 8.30 At home; supper. 9.30 Necessary business. 10.30.

SUNDAY [JULY] 13. 5.15 Dressed; tea, necessary talk. 6.30 Philippians 3. 8 The bands. 9.45 St Paul's. 12.45 At home; dinner. 1.45 At women leaders. 3.30 Writ notes. 5 Kennington, Luke 10:42; rain! 6.30 At brother Patterson's, religious talk. 7 At home; the women. 8 At brother Patterson's, his child. 9 At home; prayed, sang. 10.30.

MONDAY [JULY] 14. 5.30 Dressed; James 4; Garnault's, journal; writ to Charles. 8.30 Tea; journal. 12 Religious talk to many. 2.15 Dinner. 3.30 Islington, the bands! 4.30 I Corinthians 1:20, etc. 6.30 At Mrs Bolt's, tea. 7 Southwark, Philippians 3. 8.30 At home; supper; necessary business. 10.

TUESDAY [JULY] 15. 5.30 Dressed; James 4; Garnault's; journal. 8.30 Tea; journal. 12 At home; religious talk to many. 2 At Mrs Witham's, dinner, religious talk. 4.30 At home; writ to Miss Jason. 5.30 At sister Horner's; tea, religious talk. 6.30 1 Corinthians 6:11. 8 Fetter Lane! 11.

WEDNESDAY [JULY] 16. 5.30 Dressed; James 4; Garnault's; journal. 8.30 Tea; journal. 11.45 At home; religious talk to many. 2 Visited. 2.30 At home; dinner. 3.30 At Mrs Redford's, tea, religious talk. 4.45 At brother Hodges', religious talk. 5.30 At Mrs Lane's, tea, religious talk. 6 Marylebone, Hosea 14:4! 7.30 At sister Ibbison's, religious talk. 8.15 Fetter Lane, much talk. 11 At home; supper. 11.30.

THURSDAY, JULY 17. 5.30 Prayed; James 4; Garnault's; journal; tea. 9.15 Writ for Society. 12 Religious talk to many. 2.15 At Mr Mason's, dinner, religious talk! 4.15 At Mrs Witham's band, tea, religious talk. 5.30 At brother Bell's, many there, tea. 6.15 At home; Mark 9:23; Society! 10 Religious talk to some; prayed. 10.30.

FRIDAY [JULY] 18. 5.30 Dressed; James 5; Garnault's; journal; tea; journal. 10 At Mary Cannon's, religious talk. 11.15 At home; necessary business; religious talk to many. 1.15 Prayed. 3 Communion (nineteen there), agreed to leave the Society! 4 Tea; To —— Cox. 5.15 Redriff, 1 Corinthians 13. 6.30 Wapping, John 16:9; three ill! visited. 8.30 At home; supper. 9 Brother Hague, etc; religious talk; prayed. 10.15.

SATURDAY [JULY] 19. 5.30 Prayed; James 5; Garnault's; journal. 8.45 At N Roberts', tea, religious talk. 10.45 At sister Horner's, religious talk. 11.30 At home; religious talk to many. 2 At Mr Scott's, dinner, religious talk. 3 At home; Mr Doleman, religious talk. 4.15 Necessary talk (religious), tea. 5 At Mrs West's, tea, religious talk. 6.30 Long Lane! 8.30 At home; necessary talk (religious), supper, religious talk. 10.15.

SUNDAY [JULY] 20. 5.30 Dressed; tea; meditated. 6.30 Moorfields, 1 Thessalonians 1:4. 8.30 The leaders, religious talk, prayed. 10 Coleman Street Church; Communion. 12.30 At home; meditated; dinner. 1.30 Women leaders. 5 Kennington, Galatians 6. 7.15 At home; the women. 8.15 Fetter Lane; Love-feast; parted! 9.15 At home; the women. 11.15.

MONDAY [JULY] 21. 5.30 Dressed; 1 John 1. 7 Met two bands! 8.30 Visited. 9 At Mrs Redford's, tea, religious talk, prayed! 11 At home; necessary business; religious talk to many. 2 At brother Wilde's, dinner, religious talk. 3.30 The bands! 4.30 Zechariah 13. 6.30 At Mrs Bolt's, tea, religious talk. 7 Long Lane, Acts 1! 9 At home; religious talk. 10.15.

TUESDAY [JULY] 22. 5.30 Dressed; 1 John 1; met a band; religious talk to some. 8.30 At ——. 9 Visited. 11.30 At home; necessary talk (religious); necessary business; religious talk to many. 2 At Peter Sims', Chapman there! dinner. 3.30 Visited many. 5 At sister Hurtley's, tea; visited. 6.30 At home; Acts 1! supper. 8 Society [at the Foundery?], religious talk, prayed! 11.

WEDNESDAY [JULY] 23. 5.30 Prayed; 1 John 2:1; the band. 8.45 Tea, religious talk to some; visited. 11.45 Religious talk to many. 2.15 Took boat. 3.45 At Deptford; at Sarah Clavel's, tea, religious talk. 5 At the Barn, Romans 3:21! 7.45 At home; supper. 8.15 The bands, religious talk, prayed; brother Cawley went. 9.45 Necessary talk; necessary business. 10.30.

THURSDAY [JULY] 24. 5.30 Prayed; 1 John 2:2; the band. 9.30 At Mr Thorold's with Seward, James Hutton, etc, religious talk; Dr Doddridge came. 11 Molther, etc, religious talk. 12 Prayed. 1 At home; religious talk to some. 1.30 At Mr Wilkinson's, christened his son! 3 Dinner. 4.45 Visited; Communion. 5.30 At Mrs Seaton's, the band, tea, religious talk. 6.15 Acts 2. 8 Society! 10.15.

FRIDAY [JULY] 25. 5.30 Prayed; 1 John 2:3, 4; the band. 8.30 Tea, religious talk; necessary business. 9 Writ notes. 11.30 Religious talk to many. 1 Prayed. 3 Communion; at sister Gaskarth's. 4 Tea; visited. 5 Redriff, 1 John 3:1. 6.15 Wapping, Zechariah 13! visited. 8 At Mrs Burton's; supper, religious talk. 10.15.

SATURDAY [JULY] 26. 5.30 Prayed; 1 John 2. 7 The band. 8.30 At sister Ibbison's, tea, religious talk. 12 Mrs Seaton, MacCune, religious talk (necessary). 12 At home; religious talk to many. 2.15 At brother Lewin's, dinner, religious talk, sang. 4.15 At sister Kent's, religious talk. 4.30 At sister Wollard's, tea, religious talk. 5.15 At sister Woodruff's, tea, religious talk. 6.30 Long Lane, Acts 2. 8 Visited. 9 At home; supper, religious talk. 10.15.

SUNDAY [JULY] 27. 5.30 Dressed; tea. 6.30 Romans 4:5. 8.30 The leaders; religious talk, prayed; prayed with my mother. 10 Coleman Street Church. 12.45 At home; dinner. 1.30 The women leaders, religious talk, prayed. 3 Religious talk with Nancy Morris. 3.30 Tea, religious talk. 5 Kennington, 2 Corinthians 3:17. 7.15 At home; the women; supper, religious talk, prayed! 10.15.

MONDAY [JULY] 28. 5.30 Prayed; 1 John 2; the band. 8.30 At brother Garnault's; tea, religious talk. 9.45 At home. 10 Writ notes. 12 Religious talk to many. 3 At sister Vandrelst's, tea, religious talk. 4.30 Islington, 1 John 4:1, 2. 6.30 At Mrs Bolt's, tea, religious talk. 7 Long Lane, Acts 2; visited. 9.15 At home; supper, religious talk. 11.

TUESDAY, JULY 29. 5.30 Prayed; 1 John 2; the band. 8.30 At sister Waldron's, religious talk, tea, prayed. 10 At sister Aspernell's, tea, religious talk. 10.30 At home; necessary business. 11 Writ names. 12 Religious talk to many. 2.45 At Mr Craven's, dinner, necessary talk (religious). 6.30 At home; Acts 2. 7.45 Supper; the women bands! 10.30.

WEDNESDAY [JULY] 30. 5.30 Prayed; 1 John 2; the band; tea, religious talk. 9.15 Writ names. 12.15 Religious talk to many. 2 Christened three women, one man. 3.15 At sister Belvin's, tea, religious talk. 5 At Mrs ——'s, tea, religious talk. 6 Marylebone, 1 Timothy 2:4. 7.45 At home; supper, religious talk. 8.30 The bands. 10.15.

THURSDAY [JULY] 31. 5.30 Prayed; 1 John 2; the band. 8.15 Tea, religious talk. 9 Writ names. 12 Religious talk to many. 2.15 At Mrs West's, dinner. 3.45 At Mrs Sutherland's, tea, religious talk. 5.45 At sister MacCune's band. 6.15 Acts 2; supper. 8 Society, prayed. 9.45 Necessary talk (religious). 10.30.

FRIDAY, AUGUST 1. 5.15 Prayed; 1 John 2; the band. 8 At Mrs ——'s, tea, religious talk; visited. 10 At home; writ names. 11.45 Religious talk to many. 1.15 Prayed. 3 Communion. 4 At brother Price's, tea; at sister Mills', tea, religious talk. 5.15 Redriff, Hebrews 3 *ult.* 6.15 Wapping, Matthew 7:8! visited, prayed! 8.30 At home; supper, religious talk. 10.

SATURDAY, AUGUST 2. 5.15 Prayed; 1 John 2; religious talk; visited. 7.30 Brother Bell, Simpson, Knolton, Horn, tea, religious talk. 9 At sister Harrison's, Waldron's, religious talk, prayed. 10 At home; writ to Charles, sister Reyon, sister Gregory. 12 Religious talk to many. 2 At brother Sadler's, dinner, religious talk. 3.30 At Miss Malton's, religious talk, tea. 4.30 At Mr Barnes', tea, religious talk. 5.45 At Mr Chamberlain's, religious talk. 6.30 Long Lane, Acts 2. 8.30 At brother Crouch's, supper, religious talk; at home; necessary talk (religious). 10.30.

SUNDAY, AUGUST 3. 5.30 Meditated; tea, religious talk. 6.30 Galatians 6:3. 8 The leaders, religious talk, prayed. 9.30 Visited. 10 St Luke's, Communion. 1.30 At home; dinner, religious talk. 2.15 The leaders. 3.30 Visited sister Drable. 5 Kennington, Zechariah 12:10. 7 At home; the women's Love-feast; supper. 10.

MONDAY [AUGUST] 4. 5.15 Prayed; 1 John 3; the band. 8 At sister Harrison's, sister Waldron, etc, tea, religious talk, prayed. 10 At home; writ letters. 12 Religious talk to many. 2.15 At Mr Standex's, dinner, religious talk. 3.15 At Mrs Redford's, religious talk; at Mr Standex's, tea. 4.45 Islington, Isaiah 12! 6.15 At Mrs Coyet's, tea, religious talk. 7 Long Lane, Acts 2! 9.15 At home; supper. 10.

TUESDAY [AUGUST] 5. 5.15 Prayed; 1 John 3; religious talk to some. 7.30 Writ to Herrnhut. 8 Tea; writ. 11.15 Religious talk to many. 2.15 At Mrs Angel's. 3 Dinner, religious talk. 4 At sister Tanner's, religious talk, tea, prayed. 5 At brother Savage's, tea, religious talk. 6.30 At home; Acts 2!; supper. 8 B Hatfield, etc, ill; with them, religious talk, prayed. 11.

WEDNESDAY [AUGUST] 6. 5.15 Prayed; 1 John 3; writ to Herrnhut. 8 With the band, prayed. 8.15 Tea; letter. 11.30 Religious talk to many. 2 Christened Sarah Drable. 3 At brother Thornton's, tea; at the House, necessary talk. 5.15 At Mr Watkins', tea, religious talk. 6.15 At brother Thornton's; at Mrs Roberts'. 7.15 At home; supper, religious talk. 8 The bands, religious talk, prayed. 10.

THURSDAY [AUGUST] 7. 5.15 Prayed; 1 John 3; writ to Herrnhut. 7.45 Mrs MacCune, tea, religious talk. 9 Letter. 12 Religious talk to many. 2 At sister Coyet's, dinner, religious talk. 4 At St Paul's, tea, religious talk. 5 At Mrs Jones', tea. 6.15 Acts 4; religious talk to many. 8.15 Society. 10 Necessary talk (religious). 11.

FRIDAY [AUGUST] 8. 5.30 Prayed; 1 John 3; writ to Herrnhut. 8 Tea; brother Viney, religious talk. 10 Writ to George Whitefield, John Syms. 11.30 Religious talk to many. 2 Prayed. 3 Communion; tea. 4 With Mrs Scholey! 5.30 Wapping, John 15. 6.15 Visited; Communion. 7 At brother Price's, Matthew 1:23! 9 At home; supper, religious talk. 10.45.

SATURDAY, AUGUST 9. 5.30 Prayed; 1 John 3. 7 Religious talk to many. 8 At sister Middleton's, tea, religious talk. 9 At home; read letters; writ to George Whitefield, John Syms, and Charles. 12 Read the letters; many ill. 2 Dinner, religious talk. 3 Letters. 5 At Mrs Baddily's, tea, religious talk. 6 At Mr Craven's, religious talk (necessary). 6.30 Acts 3. 8.15 At home; supper; the Society. 10.

SUNDAY [AUGUST] 10. 5.30 Dressed; tea. 6.30 Galatians 6:3. 8 The leaders! 10 Coleman Street; Communion. 1 Dinner; the women leaders. 3.15 Religious talk with Nancy Morris; tea, religious talk with her. 5.15 Matthew 1:21. 6.45 Supper. 7.15 The women; some ill. 9.30 Religious talk. 10.

Monday [August] 11. 4.45 Prayed; 1 John 4. 7 Religious talk to some. 8 At Mrs Aspernell's, religious talk, tea, prayed. 9.30 At home; writ to Nanny Smith, sister Baddily, etc. 12 Religious talk to many. 2.15 Islington; at Mr Daniel's, dinner, religious talk. 3.30 With the band. 4.30 Romans 8:17, etc. 6 At Mrs Bolt's, tea, religious talk. 7 Long Lane, Acts 4! 8.45 At home; supper, religious talk. 10.

Tuesday [August] 12. 2.30 Prayed with many. 4.30 Slept. 5.45 Dressed; prayed; 1 John 4; religious talk to some. 8 Mr Chamberlain, religious talk, tea. 9.30 Writ to brother Richards, Miss Gregory, etc. 11.30 Religious talk to many. 2.30 Mrs Spenser, Craven, dinner, religious talk. 4 At Mrs Darlington's, tea, religious talk. 5 At Mrs Armsted's, tea, religious talk. 6.30 Acts 5! supper, religious talk to some. 10.

Wednesday [August] 13. 5.30 Prayed; 1 John 4; religious talk to many. 8 Mrs MacCune, etc, tea, religious talk. 9 Writ journal. 10 Visited Hannah Witham, religious talk, prayed. 11.30 At Mrs Sutherland's, religious talk. 12.30 At home; religious talk to many. 2.15 Christened John Padley and Joseph Paul. 4 At Mr Wallis', tea, religious talk. 5 At brother Clark's, tea, religious talk. 6 Marylebone, Acts 28:22. 8 At home; supper; the bands. 10.45.

Thursday [August] 14. 5.30 Prayed; 1 John 4; writ journal. 8 Tea; journal. 12 Dressed; religious talk to many. 2.15 At Mr Skey's, dinner, religious talk. 4.15 At brother Hodges', tea, religious talk. 6 At home; writ to Shrapnell; Acts 4. 7.30 Supper. 8 Society; many ill. 11.

Friday, August 15. 5.30 Dressed; 1 John 4; religious talk to some. 8 Tea, religious talk; journal; sins! 11.30 Dressed; religious talk to many. 1 Prayed; Communion. 3.45 At sister Gaskarth's, tea, religious talk. 4.45 At Mrs Harbottle's, tea. 5.30 Wapping, Hosea 13; three ill. 7 At brother Price's, religious talk; Acts 13; prayed! 9 At home; supper, religious talk. 9.45.

Saturday [August] 16. 5 Prayed; 1 John 4; religious talk to some; visited. 8 At sister Jackson's, tea, religious talk. 9.45 At home; journal. 10.30 Writ to Miss Jason, etc. 11.45 Religious talk to many. 2 At Mr Crouch's, religious talk, dinner. 3.30 At Mr Bird's, necessary talk (religious). 4 At sister Persal's, tea, religious talk. 5.15 At sister Martin's, religious talk. 6 At Mr Chamberlain's, tea, religious talk. 6.30 Long Lane, Acts 4. 8.30 At home; tea; women, prayed! 10 Supper. 10.45.

Sunday [August] 17. 5.30 Prayed; tea; meditated. 6.30 1 Corinthians 10:12! collection. 8.15 The leaders, religious talk, prayed. 10 Coleman Street, Communion. 1 Dinner; women leaders. 3.30 Tea; journal. 5 Zechariah 12:10! 7 The band; Love-feast! 10 Necessary talk (religious). 10.30.

Monday [August] 18. 5 Prayed; 1 John 5; religious talk to many. 8 Hoxton; sister Waldron's, tea, religious talk, prayed. 10 At home; writ letters. 12 Religious talk to many. 1 At sister Drable's, tea, religious talk. 3.45 Islington, religious talk to the band. 4.30 Matthew 18:29, etc. 5.30 At brother Scott's, tea, religious talk. 7 Long Lane, Acts 4; supper. 9.15 At home; necessary talk (religious). 10.

TUESDAY [AUGUST] 19. 5 Prayed; 1 John 5; religious talk to some; the band. 8 At home; tea, religious talk. 9 Writ to sister England, Robertson, Clancy, Lewis, Holder, Grace Stephens, brother Richards, etc. 12 Religious talk to many. 2.15 At brother Smagg's, dinner. 3.45 Visited sister Tubs, prayed. 4.15 At sister Haddock's, tea, religious talk. 5.30 At brother Spenser's, religious talk. 6.15 Acts 5! supper. 8 Society, prayed; fifteen ill. 11.

WEDNESDAY [AUGUST] 20. 5.45 Dressed: 1 John 5; religious talk to some; visited brother Waldon, prayed; and sister Bell, Junior. 8 At home; Higs and Cleland, tea, religious talk. 9.15 Writ notes. 10.30 Dressed; sins; religious talk to some. 12.45 In the coach with sister Seaton and Bolt. 8 At Mrs Sparrow's, dinner, religious talk, tea. 5.15 Deptford Room, Acts 13! 8.30 At home; the bands! 10.45.

THURSDAY [AUGUST] 21. 5.30 Prayed; 1 John 5; religious talk to many. 8 At Mrs Ridgeway's, tea, religious talk. 9.15 At home; journal; writ to brother Cennick, Richards, sister Bath, Miss Thomas. 12 Religious talk to many. 2 At brother Andrews', dinner. 3.15 At sister Gale's, tea, religious talk. 4.15 At sister Branch's, prayed. 5 At sister Brentford's, tea, religious talk. 6.15 Acts 5:30! 8 Society; many ill! 10.45.

FRIDAY [AUGUST] 22. 5.30 Prayed; 1 John 5; religious talk to some; visited brother Waldron, prayed. 8.15 At home; tea, religious talk. 9 Writ to Mrs Dutton; necessary business. 11.30 Religious talk to many. 1 Prayed; Communion (thirty there). 4.15 At sister Ibbison's, tea, religious talk. 6 At brother Jones', religious talk; visited! 7 Brother Price's; Hosea 11. 9 At home; supper. 10.

SATURDAY [AUGUST] 23. 5 Prayed; 1 John 5 *ult;* religious talk to many; tea, religious talk. 9 Writ to brother Richards, Mary Cannon, brother Cobb. 12 Religious talk to many. 2 At Mr Cennick's, dinner. 3.30 At Mr Doleman's; music. 5 At Billingsgate, tea, religious talk. 5.45 At sister Hatfield's, tea. 6.15 Long Lane, Acts 5! 8.30 At Mr Crouch's; supper, religious talk. 10.15.

SUNDAY [AUGUST] 24. 5.30 Dressed; tea; sick. 6.30 Ephesians 5:14; the leaders. 10 Coleman Street. 1 Dinner; the women leaders. 3.30 Slept. 4.30 At Mr Spenser's. 5.15 Kennington, Hosea 11. 7.15 The women, religious talk, prayed. 9 Supper. 9.45.

MONDAY [AUGUST] 25. 5.30 Prayed; 2 John; religious talk to some. 8 Hoxton; tea, religious talk; prayed; visited. 10 Journal. 12 Religious talk to many. 2.15 At sister Aspernell's, dinner, religious talk. 3.15 Visited. 3.45 At home; read Count Zinzendorf's sermons. 5 Visited; at Mrs Bolt's, tea; visited John Russel, prayed. 7 Acts 5. 8.45 At home; supper, religious talk. 10.

TUESDAY, AUGUST 26. 5.30 Prayed; 1 Peter 1; journal; tea; journal. 11.45 Religious talk to many. 2 At Mr Ball's, dinner. 4 At sister Barnes', tea, religious talk; visited. 6.30 Acts 6; supper. 8 The leaders, religious talk (necessary). 9 Religious talk (necessary) to some. 10.30.

WEDNESDAY [AUGUST] 27. 5.30 Prayed; 1 Peter 1; met band. 8 Tea; Mr Higs, Mrs Ridgeway, religious talk. 9 Read [Elisha] Cole on Predestination. 11.30 Writ diary; religious talk to many. 2 Christened Paul Chamberlain, David Jenkins, Sarah Hunlock, Kezia Smith. 4 Took coach with brother Flewit and Mrs Ash;

at Sarah Clavel's, tea. 5 At the Barn; Isaiah 12! 7.30 At home; supper. 8 The bands. 10.30.

THURSDAY [AUGUST] 28. 5.30 Prayed; 1 Peter 1; with the band. 8 At sister Ibbison's, tea, religious talk. 9.30 Nancy Morris and Susy Thomas came, religious talk. 10.45 At home; writ notes. 11.45 Religious talk to many. 2.15 At brother Dawson's, dinner, religious talk. 4 At Sweet Lewin's, tea, religious talk. 5 Visited; at sister Edward's. 6 Acts 7! 7.30 Society. 8 Supper; Society! 11.15.

FRIDAY [AUGUST] 29. 5.30 Prayed; 1 Peter 1; with the band. 8 At sister Aspernell's, tea, religious talk. 9.30 At home; necessary business. 11.30 Religious talk to many. 1 Prayed! Communion. 3.30 Religious talk to some. 4 Tea; ended Count Zinzendorf's sermons! 6.45 Rosemary Lane, 1 John 5:11! 8.45 At home; supper, religious talk. 10.

SATURDAY [AUGUST] 30. 5.30 Prayed; 1 Peter *ult;* religious talk to many. 8 Hoxton; at Mr Sweeting's, tea, prayed. 10 At home; necessary business. 12 Religious talk to many. 2 At Mrs Smith's, dinner, religious talk. 4 At Mr Wathen's, Mr Broughton, necessary talk. 5.15 At Mr Russel's, Communion. 6.15 Long Lane, Acts 6. 8 At home; supper; Society. 10.30.

SUNDAY, AUGUST 31. 5.30 Dressed; tea. 6.30 Mark 4:31. 8.15 Religious talk to many. 10 Coleman Street; Communion. 1 At home; dinner; the leaders. 3.15 At sister Horner's, tea, religious talk. 5 Kennington, 1 John 5:11. 7.15 At home; supper; the women's Love-feast. 9.30 Lay down.

MONDAY, SEPTEMBER 1. 3 Dressed. 3.30 Set out with brother Nicholson and Purdy. 7 Colnbrook; tea. 8 Set out. 11.30 Dinner. 1 Set out. 3 Feacham [Thatcham]; tea. 4 Set out. 6.30 Froxfield; dinner [sic], supper, necessary talk (religious). 9.

TUESDAY [SEPTEMBER] 2. 5 Dressed. 5.30 Set out. 7 Marlborough; tea, religious talk. 8 Rode; verse. 10.30 Calne; coffee, writ. 11.30 Rode; verse. 2.15 Marshfield; dinner. 3 Rode. 5.30 At Mr Deschamps'; at sister Highnam's. 6 At Mrs Hooper's; religious talk to Charles. 7 At the Room, Hosea 11! 8.15 With Charles, religious talk. 9.30 At home; slept.

WEDNESDAY [SEPTEMBER] 3. 4.45 Dressed. 5 Jude 3. 6 Read Prayers. 7 With Charles, religious talk. 8 Tea, religious talk. 9.15 At home; religious talk to many. 10.15 Susy Peck, necessary talk (religious)! 11.30 In the coach with Charles, religious talk. 1 At home; the leaders. 3 Betty Bush came, religious talk! with her at Mrs Hooper's and Cennick, necessary talk (religious). 4.30 Tea, religious talk. 5 At sister Harding's; Communion. 6 At home; the women, prayed. 7.45 Writ diary; the men. 10.

THURSDAY [SEPTEMBER] 4. 4.45 Dressed; Jude 3; the women leaders. 8.15 At Mrs Hooper's with Charles; tea, religious talk. 9 At home; religious talk to many. 11 Isaiah 12! 1 Visited. 1.30 At Mrs Grevil's, dinner, religious talk; brother Wedmore tried! 3.30 At sister England's, tea; at Mrs Labbè's, tea, religious talk. 5 Visited. 6.30 Hosea 12! Society. 10.

FRIDAY [SEPTEMBER] 5. 4.45 Dressed; Jude; read Prayers. 7.15 With Charles, religious talk. 8 Tea, religious talk. 9 Religious talk to many. 11 Coach with Charles; read journal. 1 Prayed. 3 At Jenny Worlock's band, tea, religious talk.

4.15 At sister Hooper's, Mrs Wayne, tea, sang. 5 At brother Cross', tea; Miss Cornish, religious talk; visited; with sister Holder's band. 6.15 Zechariah. 8 The bands. 10.

SATURDAY, SEPTEMBER 6. 4.45 Dressed; Jude. 6 Read Prayers. 7 Religious talk to many. 7.30 Tea, religious talk with Charles. 9 Religious talk to many. 11.30 Read letters. 1 At Mrs Stafford's, dinner, religious talk. 2 Letters. 4.30 Kingswood School, necessary talk (religious). 5 With the bands. 6.15 At Mr Deschamps', tea, religious talk. 6.45 Malt-room, Hosea! 8.15 At Captain Whitefield's, Mrs Grevil, etc. 9 Supper, mostly religious talk. 10.30.

SUNDAY [SEPTEMBER] 7. 4.45 Dressed; Galatians 6:3. 7 At the School, Galatians 6:3. 9.15 At Mrs Hooper's, tea, religious talk. 10 St Nicholas's; Communion. 1 At Mrs England's, dinner, religious talk. 2.30 At home; the leaders, necessary talk (religious). 4 Met two bands. 5 Mark 4:30. 7 Religious talk to many. 7.30 Society. 8.30 At Mrs Hooper's with Charles, supper. 9 At Mr Deschamps', necessary talk (religious). 9.30.

MONDAY [SEPTEMBER] 8. 3.15 Dressed; tea; sang. 4 Set out. 7.45 At Ford; tea, religious talk. 8.45 Rode. 11 Sins. 12.30 At a house; dinner. 1.15 Rode. 3.30 Hungerford; tea. 4.15 Rode. 6.45 Woolhampton; supper; writ diary. 8.30.

TUESDAY [SEPTEMBER] 9. 4.15 Dressed; necessary business. 5 Rode. 7.45 Hare Hatch; tea. 8.45 Rode. 12.15 Hounslow; dinner. 1.15 Rode. 3.30 At home; tea; necessary business; religious talk to brother Humphreys, etc. 6 Acts 8; supper; the leaders. 9.45.

WEDNESDAY [SEPTEMBER] 10. 5.15 Prayed; 1 Peter 2; religious talk to many. 8.45 At Dinah Reed's, tea, religious talk, prayed. 10.30 At home; necessary business; religious talk to many. 3.15 At brother Hodges', tea; at sister Hall's, religious talk. 4.30 Visited sister Timberlake! 5 Visited sister Leighton! 6 Visited sister Woodruff! 7.30 At home; supper. 8 The bands. 10.

THURSDAY [SEPTEMBER] 11. 4.45 Prayed, religious talk, prayed. 6 1 Peter 2. 7 With the band, religious talk. 8 [no entry]. 10 Writ notes. 11 Religious talk to many. 2 At Mrs Seaton's, Mrs MacCune, dinner, religious talk. 3.30 Visited Sweet Lewin! prayed. 4.30 Visited sister Crisp; Communion! 5.30 At home; religious talk (necessary). 6 Acts 9; Society. 10.15 Prayed.

FRIDAY [SEPTEMBER] 12. 5 Prayed, prayed. 6 1 Peter 2. 7 The band. 8 Mr Thomas Davidson and brother Mason, tea, religious talk. 9 Writ notes. 10 Religious talk to many. 1.15 Prayed. 3 Christened; Communion. 4.30 At brother Hall's; at brother Hodges', tea, religious talk. 6.45 Rosemary Lane, Romans 1:16. 8.45 At home; supper; visited. 10.15.

SATURDAY [SEPTEMBER] 13. 5 Prayed; 1 Peter 2; religious talk to some; writ to brother Richards. 8 At sister Aspernell's, tea, religious talk. 9.30 At home; writ notes. 10 Religious talk to some. 11 Read letters. 1 At sister Thew's, dinner, religious talk. 2 Read journal. 4.30 At Mrs West's, tea. 5.15 At Mrs Hawthorn's, tea, religious talk; visited sister Woodruff. 6.30 Long Lane, Acts 7. 8.15 At home; Society. 10.15.

SUNDAY [SEPTEMBER] 14. 5.15 Dressed; tea. 6.15 Romans 11:6. 8.15 The women leaders. 10 Coleman Street; Communion. 1 Dinner, necessary talk (religious).

2.30 St Benet Fink. 4.15 At Mrs Spenser's, tea. 5 Kennington, Romans 11:6. 7 At home; religious talk to the mob! supper. 8 The Love-feast! 10.

MONDAY [SEPTEMBER] 15. 5 Prayers; prayed; 1 Peter 2; religious talk to many. 8 At sister Waldron's, tea, religious talk. 10 At home; religious talk to many. 2 At Mr Dove's, dinner, religious talk. 3.30 At sister Sutherland's, tea, religious talk. 4.45 At sister Crouch's with Hannah, necessary talk (religious). 6 With sister Gaskarth, tea, religious talk. 7 Long Lane! 9 At home; supper, religious talk. 10.15.

TUESDAY, SEPTEMBER 16. 5 Prayed; 1 Peter 2; necessary talk (religious) to many. 8 At sister Vandome's, tea, religious talk. 10 At home; religious talk to many. 2.30 At Mr Stonehouse's. 3 Mr Simpson, there; dinner, religious talk. 4 Visited many. 5 At Mrs Edzard's, tea, religious talk. 6 Acts 10!! 7.30 Supper; Society! 10.30.

WEDNESDAY [SEPTEMBER] 17. 4.45 Writ for Society. 6 1 Peter 3; religious talk to many. 8 At sister Orange's, many there; religious talk, tea. 10 At home; visited. 11 Religious talk to many. 2 Read Account of Sarah Wight. 3 At brother Thornton's, tea, religious talk; at brother Hall's, necessary talk (religious). 5 At sister Timberlake's, prayed; at Mr Gould's, religious talk. 7.15 At home; supper. 8 The bands. 10.

THURSDAY [SEPTEMBER] 18. 5 Prayed; necessary business; 1 Peter 3; religious talk to many. 8.15 At Mr Burton's, Cock Lane; tea, religious talk, prayed; visited sister Smagg. 10.15 At home; necessary business; read [account of] Sarah Wight; religious talk. 2.15 At brother Buckmaster's, dinner, religious talk. 3.30 Visited. 4 At Sally Barnes', tea, religious talk; at sister Bennings', etc, prayed. 6 Acts 11!! supper; Society, Sally Dean, etc, ill. 12.30.

FRIDAY [SEPTEMBER] 19. 5.45 Dressed; 1 Peter 4; religious talk to many. 8.15 At sister Allar's, tea, religious talk. 10 At home; necessary business; with Sally Dean, prayed; religious talk to many. 1.15 Prayed; Communion; with sister Dean, prayed, tea. 5 At Mrs Burton's, Rag Fair, religious talk, prayed; visited. 6.30 Wapping, John 6:40. 8.15 At home; supper; with sister Dean, religious talk, prayed. 10.15.

SATURDAY [SEPTEMBER] 20. 5.15 Necessary talk (religious), prayed; 1 Peter 4; religious talk to many; visited. 8 Tea, religious talk. 9 With sister Dean, her sister, religious talk. 11.30 Religious talk to many; writ diary; religious talk. 2.15 At Mr Wathen's, dinner, religious talk. 4 With Tom Whitefield; visited some. 5 At sister Temple's, tea, religious talk. 6 Long Lane, Acts 8! 8 At home; supper, religious talk. 10.30.

SUNDAY, SEPTEMBER 21. 5.15 Dressed; tea. 6.30 Romans 11:6. 8 The women leaders. 10 With sister Dean. 10 Coleman Street; Communion. 1.15 Dinner. 1 With sister Dean, her brother and sister, religious talk. 3.30 Tea. 5 At Kennington, Romans 8:15! 7.15 At home; supper. 8 The women! 10.15.

MONDAY [SEPTEMBER] 22. 4.45 Dressed; necessary business. 5.30 Rode. 6.45 Deptford, Matthew 7. 8.15 My mother came; took coach. 10.30 At Mr Piers', tea, religious talk, sang. 12 Writ diary; John Tucker came, religious talk. 1.30 Dinner, religious talk. 3 My mother went; writ journal. 5 William Delamotte, tea, religious talk. 7 Luke 18:10. 9 Supper, religious talk. 10.30.

TUESDAY [SEPTEMBER] 23. 6.15 Dressed; journal. 7.15 Matthew 5:1-8. 8.45 Tea. 9.45 Journal. 2 Dinner. 3.30 Heard Mr Piers' sermon. 4 At the Poorhouse, religious talk, prayed. 5 At Mr Mason's, tea, religious talk, prayed. 7 In the church, read Prayers, Matthew 5:1-9. 9 At home; supper; read journal, prayed. 10.45 Sins!!

WEDNESDAY [SEPTEMBER] 24. 6 Prayed; journal. 7.30 Matthew 5:13, etc. 9 Tea; journal. 11.15 Read Prayers; Mrs Delamotte there! 12.30 Writ diary; necessary business. 1 Read with Mr Piers. 2.15 At Mrs Law's; dinner, religious talk. 3 Deptford; at brother Church's; religious talk to many. 4.15 Tea. 5 At the Barn, Matthew 1:22. 7.30 Bexley; necessary talk (religious). 8 Acts 13. 9 Supper, religious talk. 10.15.

THURSDAY [SEPTEMBER] 25. 6 Journal. 7.15 Matthew 5 *ult.* 9 Tea; journal. 2 Dinner. 3 Mr Piers read his sermon. 4 Journal. 4.45 Religious talk with Mrs Piers. 5.15 At Mrs Searles', tea, religious talk. 6.30 At home; journal, ended it. 7.15 1 John 5:12. 9 Supper, religious talk. 10.15.

FRIDAY [SEPTEMBER] 26. 5 Preface to journal. 7.15 Matthew 6. 9 Tea; preface. 11 Read Prayers. 12.15 Preface. 1.45 Heard his sermon. 3.30 At Mr Mason's, tea, religious talk, prayed. 5 His sermon. 6.30 Supper. 7 Read Prayers; Acts 16; sister Gaskarth, etc. 9 At home; religious talk. 10.30.

SATURDAY, SEPTEMBER 27. 5 Journal. 6.30 Sister Gaskarth, etc; tea, religious talk. 7.30 Matthew 7:16. 9 Journal. 11 Mr Piers ended his sermon. 12.30 Dinner. 1.15 At Mr Mason's, religious talk. 1.45 Rode. 3 At brother Church's, tea, religious talk. 4 Walked with Sarah Clavel, etc. 4.45 At Sarah Dean's, religious talk, tea. 6 Long Lane. 8.15 At home; necessary talk (religious). 10.15.

SUNDAY [SEPTEMBER] 28. 5 Dressed; tea. 6.15 Matthew 5:3. 8 The women leaders. 9.45 Necessary talk (religious). 10 Coleman Street; Communion. 1.15 At home; sister Nancy, dinner. 2 Writ for bands. 3.45 Tea. 5 Kennington, Acts 13! 7 At home; religious talk to the mob; prayed. 7.30 Supper; the women's Love-feast. 10.30.

MONDAY [SEPTEMBER] 29. 5 Religious talk; prayed. 6 1 Peter 4. 7 Religious talk to some. 7.15 At Mrs Skelton's; Communion, tea, religious talk. 9.15 At home; necessary business; writ notes. 11.30 Religious talk to many. 2 Dinner; religious talk to many. 4 Visited N Lewin; Sarah Dean. 5 Tea, religious talk, sang. 6.45 Long Lane. 8.45 At home; supper. 10.15.

TUESDAY [SEPTEMBER] 30. 5.15 Prayed. 6 1 Peter 4; religious talk to many; to Sarah Robinson. 8.30 At Mrs Scudamore's, tea, religious talk. 9.15 At Mr Freestone's, prayed! 10 At home; writ to Captain Whitefield; religious talk to many. 2.15 At Mr Strahan's; dinner. 4 At sister Peck's; Communion (twenty-one there); visited sister Richardson. 5.15 At sister Clowney's, tea, religious talk. 6 Acts 12! supper; the leaders. 10.30.

WEDNESDAY, OCTOBER 1. 5 Prayed; 1 Peter 4; religious talk to some. 8 Hoxton; tea, religious talk. 10 Writ notes. 11 Religious talk to many. 3 Visited; at sister Lewin's, tea; at Esther Kent's, tea, religious talk. 5 At Greyhound Lane, Acts 11:26. 7.15 At home; supper, religious talk. 8.30 Bands, religious talk, prayed. 10.45.

THURSDAY [OCTOBER] 2. 5.15 Prayed; 1 Peter 5; visited. 7.30 At home; necessary talk (religious). 8 At Nancy Morris', Simpson there! religious talk. 9.45 At home; writ notes; writ to Charles. 12 Religious talk to many. 2 At Mrs Johnson's, Sarah Dean, etc, dinner. 4 At brother Hodges'; at the House, necessary talk. 5.30 At sister Seaton's, tea, religious talk. 6.15 Acts 13; supper. 8 Society. 10 Necessary talk (religious). 10.45.

FRIDAY, OCTOBER 3. 5.30 Prayed; 2 Peter 1; religious talk to some; necessary business. 8 At brother ——'s, tea, religious talk. 10 At home; writ to brother Ingham. 11.30 Religious talk to many. 1.15 Prayed. 3 Communion (thirty-one there). 4.15 At sister Wollard's, tea, religious talk. 5 Redriff, 1 John 1. 6.15 Wapping, Luke 24. 8 At home; supper, religious talk. 10.

SATURDAY [OCTOBER] 4. [pointing hand in margin] 5.30 Dressed; prayed; 2 Peter 1; religious talk to some; necessary business; tea, necessary talk (religious). 9.30 Necessary business. 10 Writ diary; necessary business. 11 Letters. 1 At brother Frecquer's, tea; music. 6 Long Lane; at home; supper. 8.15 Society. 10.15.

SUNDAY [OCTOBER] 5. 5.30 Dressed; prayed; tea. 6.30 Matthew 5:4. 8 The women leaders. 10 St Luke's Church, Communion. 1.30 At home; dinner. 2.45 Sarah Dean, religious talk. 4 At sister Horner's, tea, religious talk. 5 Acts 11:26; supper. 7.30 The bands. 10.15.

MONDAY [OCTOBER] 6. 5.15 Dressed; necessary talk (religious). 6 2 Peter 1; religious talk to some. 8 At sister Harrison's, tea, religious talk, prayed. 9.45 At home; necessary business. 11 Religious talk to many. 3 At brother Bamford's, tea, religious talk. 4.15 Islington, Matthew 15. 6 At sister Loyd's, tea, religious talk. 7 Long Lane! 8.15 At sister Baddily's; supper, religious talk. 10.15.

TUESDAY [OCTOBER] 7. 5.15 Prayed; necessary talk with brother Webb. 6 2 Peter 1 *ult;* necessary talk (religious) to brother Webb. 8 At Mr Martin's, Cock Lane, tea, religious talk. 9.30 Writ to Mr Oulton, George Whitefield, Charles. 11 Religious talk to many. 3 At sister Ash's, tea, religious talk. 4.15 At Mrs Morgan's, tea, religious talk. 5.30 At home; necessary business. 6 Acts 13! 7.15 At the Baptist's Head. 8 The gentlemen met. 10.30.

WEDNESDAY [OCTOBER] 8. 5.30 Prayed; 2 Peter 2; religious talk to many. 8 At sister Ward's, tea, religious talk, prayed. 9.45 At home; journal. 11.15 Religious talk to many. 2.15 At Mr Craven's. 4 Deptford; brother Church's, tea. 5 At the Barn, 2 Corinthians 4:1. 7.30 At home; supper, religious talk. 8.30 The bands. 10.30.

THURSDAY, OCTOBER 9. 5.30 Prayed; 2 Peter 2; religious talk to many. 8.15 At sister Ibbison's, tea, religious talk. 9.45 At home; writ to Charles. 11.15 Religious talk to many. 2.15 At sister Allar's, dinner, religious talk. 4 At St Paul's; religious talk, tea. 5 At home; Mrs Morgan and Mr Hans, christened him. 6 Acts 14; supper. 8 Society; many ill! 10.30.

FRIDAY [OCTOBER] 10. 5.30 Prayed; 2 Peter 3; religious talk to some; visited. 8 At Mrs Jaggers', tea, religious talk. 9 At Sister Morris', religious talk. 9.45 At home; journal. 11.30 Religious talk to many. 1 Prayed; Communion. 4 At sister Mills', tea, religious talk. 5 Redriff, Hebrews 2:4. 6.30 At brother Price's, tea. 6.45 Hebrews 2. 8.15 At home; supper; religious talk with brother Cheyne. 10.30.

S<small>ATURDAY</small> [O<small>CTOBER</small>] 11. 5.15 Prayed; 2 Peter 3; religious talk to many. 8.30 At Dr Newton's, tea, religious talk. 10.15 At Mrs Skelton's, religious talk. 11 At home; religious talk to many. 2 At Mrs MacCune's, dinner, religious talk. 4 Matthew Clark, tea, religious talk. 6 Long Lane. 8 At home; supper. 9 The women; prayed. 10.30.

S<small>UNDAY</small> [O<small>CTOBER</small>] 12. 5.30 Prayed; tea. 6.30 Matthew 5:5! 8 The leaders. 10 St Paul's. 12.30 At home; journal. 1 Writ diary; dinner. 2.15 Visited. 3 Sarah Dean, tea. 4 Meditated, prayed. 5 Luke 11:21! 7.30 The men's Love-feast. 10 Necessary talk (religious). 10.30.

M<small>ONDAY</small> [O<small>CTOBER</small>] 13. 5.30 Prayed. 6 Matthew 1; religious talk to many. 8 At Mr Rut's, tea, religious talk. 9.45 At Mr Oswald's (two there), religious talk. 11.45 At home; religious talk to many. 3 Newington Green; at Mrs Clark's, religious talk, tea. 4.30 Islington, Matthew 12:26. 6 At brother Hodges'. 6.30 Carnaby Street, 1 John 5:11, 12. 8 At sister Keen's. 9 Supper, religious talk. 10.15 At home; necessary talk (religious). 11.

T<small>UESDAY</small> [O<small>CTOBER</small>] 14. 5.30 Prayed; Matthew 2; religious talk to some. 8 At sister Forder's, tea, religious talk. 9.30 At brother Kendrick's, religious talk. 10.30 At Mr Mazine's, religious talk! 12 At home; religious talk to many. 2.15 At brother Smith's, dinner, religious talk. 3.45 At sister Crouch's, religious talk; at Mrs Hill's, J Westry's, tea, religious talk. 5 At Mrs Bradley's, tea, religious talk. 6 Acts 15. 7.30 Supper; Society, religious talk. 10.30.

W<small>EDNESDAY</small>, O<small>CTOBER</small> 15. 5.30 Prayed; Matthew 3; religious talk to some. 8.30 At sister MacCune's, tea. 10.45 At the House, necessary talk. 12 At home; religious talk to some. 2 Christened three, Sarah Southgate, Elizabeth, and ——. 3 Communion. 4 Necessary business. 5 At sister Wollard's, tea, religious talk. 5.45 At Greyhound Lane, Ephesians 4. 7.30 At home; supper. 8 The bands. 9.15 Prayed; necessary talk. 9.45.

T<small>HURSDAY</small> [O<small>CTOBER</small>] 16. 4 Dressed; necessary talk; prayed. 5 Journal. 6 Matthew 3; religious talk; journal. 8 Necessary talk (religious) to Mary Daniel; tea, religious talk. 9 Journal; sins! 12.15 Religious talk to many. 2 At Mr Johnson's, Aldgate, dinner, religious talk. 3.15 At sister Persal's, tea, religious talk. 4.45 At Mr Witham's, tea, religious talk. 6 Acts 16; supper. 8 Society. 9.30 Prayed. 10.

F<small>RIDAY</small> [O<small>CTOBER</small>] 17. 4.30 Prayed. 5 Meditated; prayed. 6 Matthew 4. 7 Religious talk to some; with Sarah Dean. 8 Visited. 8.30 At brother Moreton's, tea, religious talk. 10 At home; journal. 12 Religious talk to many. 1 Prayed. 3 At brother Garnault's, tea; at Jane Church's; Communion! 5 Redriff, Matthew 3:2. 6.30 Rosemary Lane, Matthew 3:2. 8.15 At Mr Crouch's; supper, necessary talk (religious). 10.15.

S<small>ATURDAY</small> [O<small>CTOBER</small>] 18. 4:45 Prayed; prayed. 6 Matthew 4; religious talk to Brown and Knolton; tea. 8.30 Writ to Miss Jason, George Whitefield, etc. 12 Religious talk to many. 2.15 At Mrs Hawthorn's; dinner, religious talk. 4 At brother Windsor's; christened his son. 5 At Mrs West's, religious talk, tea. 6 Long Lane. 8 At home; supper. 9 Prayed. 9.45.

S<small>UNDAY</small> [O<small>CTOBER</small>] 19. 4 Dressed; prayed; necessary business; tea. 6.15 Matthew 5:6. 8 The leaders. 10 St Paul's; Communion. 12.45 At home; writ diary;

religious talk; dinner; religious talk with Betty Castle. 2.30 Visited brother Ball. 3 At home; read [account of] Sarah Wight. 4 Tea, religious talk. 4.30 Ephesians 5:1, 2! 6.30 With Sarah Dean. 7 Supper; the women. 9 Prayed. 9.45.

MONDAY, OCTOBER 20. 4.30 Prayed; prayed; Matthew 5. 7 Three bands met; religious talk, prayed. 9 At Mrs Wildbore's, tea, necessary talk (religious); visited Alice Morley. 10 Communion; Mr Mazine. 11.30 At home; necessary business. 12 Religious talk to many. 2 At sister Ibbison's, dinner. 4 At Mr Mazine, Junior's, necessary talk. 4.45 At Mrs Lane's, tea, religious talk; visited sister Leighton. 6.30 Short's Gardens, Romans 1! 9.15 At home; supper; prayed. 10.

TUESDAY [OCTOBER] 21. 4.15 Dressed; prayed; prayed. 5 Matthew 5. 7 The band. 8.15 At Mary Barraby's, tea, religious talk. 9 At home; writ to Charles, Elizabeth Baddily, Elizabeth Spring, Nanny Smith, Mary Thomas. 12 Religious talk to some. 2 At sister Edzard's, dinner, religious talk. 4 Visited Hobbins. 4.30 At home; Sarah Dean and Miss Reeves, tea. 6 Acts 17. 7.45 With the managers. 8.45 At home; sister Bird, brother Waldron, etc, ill! supper; prayed. 10.

WEDNESDAY [OCTOBER] 22. 4.15 Prayed; prayed. 6 Matthew 5; two bands. 8.15 Tea, religious talk. 9.45 At Mr Stonehouse's. 11.30 At Mr Mazine's. 12 At home; religious talk to many. 2 Christened two; Communion. 3 Tea; at sister Boatswain, Junior's, tea, religious talk. 5 Short's Gardens, Romans 1. 7.45 At home; supper. 8.15 The bands. 9.30 Prayed. 9.45.

THURSDAY [OCTOBER] 23. 4.15 Dressed; prayed; prayed. 6 Matthew 5; the band. 8.30 At sister Gillingham's, tea, religious talk, prayed. 9.45 At home; writ notes. 10 Dr Andrews, etc; at Mr Mazine's; the Infirmary. 11.30 At home; writ names. 12.30 Religious talk to many. 2 At Mr Harrison's, dinner, necessary talk. 4 At sister Bird's! tea. 5.15 At home; necessary business; necessary talk. 6 Acts 18; supper; Society; many ill; prayed. 10.

FRIDAY [OCTOBER] 24. 4.30 Dressed; prayed; prayed. 6 Matthew 5; the band. 8.30 At sister Aspernell's, tea, religious talk, prayed. 9.45 At home; writ for Society. 12 Religious talk to many. 1 Prayed; visited. 4 At sister Sparkes', tea, religious talk. 5.15 At sister Scolefield's. 6 At the House; at Mr Mazine's, necessary talk. 8.30 At home; supper; prayed. 9.45.

SATURDAY, OCTOBER 25. 4.30 Dressed; prayed; prayed. 6 Matthew 6; the band. 8 At sister Jackson's, tea, religious talk. 9.15 Visited; Communion. 10.45 Writ names. 12.15 Religious talk to many. 2 Visited; at Mrs Ketteridge's, dinner. 3.45 Visited sister Collins, etc. 4.45 At sister Ketteridge's, tea, religious talk. 6 Long Lane, Acts 12. 8 At home; supper; prayed. 9.45.

SUNDAY [OCTOBER] 26. 5 Dressed; tea. 6 Matthew 5:7, 8. 8 The leaders. 10 St Peter's, Cornhill; Communion. 1 At home; dinner; prayed. 2.15 At sister Taylor's, religious talk, tea. 4 At home; writ diary and meditated. 5 Acts 26:8! 7 Supper; the women's Love-feast. 9.45.

MONDAY [OCTOBER] 27. 4.30 Dressed; prayed; prayed. 6 Matthew 6; journal. 8 Tea. 9 Journal. 11 At brother Hobbins', christened Lydia Shepherd, prayed. 12.15 Religious talk to many. 2.45 At sister Vaughan's, dinner, tea. 4.30 At the House, Luke 24. 6.15 Short's Gardens, Romans 2. 9 At home; supper; prayed. 10.

TUESDAY [OCTOBER] 28. 4.30 Dressed; prayed; journal; prayed. 6 Matthew 6; journal. 7.30 With the band. 8 Tea; journal. 12 Religious talk to many. 2 At brother Smagg's, dinner. 3.30 At sister Southgate's, christened Ann ——. 4 At Mrs Bradley's, tea, religious talk. 5.15 At home; journal. 6 Acts 19; journal. 8 Supper; the leaders. 9.30 Prayed. 10.

WEDNESDAY [OCTOBER] 29. Dressed; prayed; prayed; writ. 6 Matthew 6; journal. 7.30 The band. 8 Tea; journal; sins. 11 Necessary talk (religious) to Mr Watkins, etc. 2 Christened Martha Smith; Communion. 3.30 At Mrs Mason, Senior's; religious talk to Miss Seward. 4 At brother Prig's, tea, religious talk. 5 Short's Gardens, Romans 2! 8 At home; supper; the bands; prayed. 10.

THURSDAY [OCTOBER] 30. 4.30 Prayed. 5 Writ upon Predestination. 6 Matthew 6! 7 Writ upon Predestination; the band. 8 Tea, necessary talk (religious). 9 Writ upon Predestination. 12 Religious talk to many. 2 At Mr Mason's, dinner, religious talk; visited. 4 At Coz [cousin?] Wilson's, tea, religious talk. 5.30 At home; writ. 6 Acts 20; supper; Society; prayed. 10.

FRIDAY [OCTOBER] 31. 4.30 Prayed; writ upon Predestination. 6 Matthew 7:10. 7 Writ; the band. 8 Tea, religious talk; writ upon Predestination. 12 Religious talk to many. 1 Prayed. 3 Visited Nanny Roberts, tea, prayed. 4.30 At Mr Keen's, necessary talk (religious). 5.15 Short's Gardens; Mrs MacCune, etc, tea, religious talk. 6 Romans 3. 8.30 At home; supper, religious talk, prayed. 10.

SATURDAY, NOVEMBER 1. [pointing hand in margin] 4.30 Prayed; prayed; meditated. 6 Matthew 7; the band. 8 Necessary talk (religious) to some. 9 tea; necessary business; writ to Charles. 12 Read letters. 2 At Mr Blake's, dinner. 3 Letters. 6 Long Lane, a storm! 8.30 At home; supper, religious talk, prayed. 10.

SUNDAY [NOVEMBER] 2. 4.30 Dressed; prayed; tea. 6 Matthew 5:10, etc. 8 The leaders. 9.15 Necessary talk (religious). 10 St Luke's; Communion. 1.15 At Mrs Pierce's, dinner. 3.30 At home; tea, religious talk. 4.30 Meditated. 5 Isaiah 49:15! 7 Supper; the women! 9.30 Prayed. 9.45.

MONDAY [NOVEMBER] 3. 4.30 Prayed; prayed. 6 Matthew 7 *ult;* the band. 8.15 Tea; necessary talk (religious). 9 With brother Purdy, etc. 9.45 Sorted things for the poor. 12.15 Religious talk to many. 2.30 Visited Nancy, prayed. 3 At Mrs Bolt's, dinner; Mrs Scott there. 4 Visited Mrs Hill. 4.30 At Mrs Bolt's, tea. 5.15 Short's Gardens; necessary business. 6 Romans 3. 7.30 Tea; the leaders. 9 Men and women leaders; prayed! 10.30 At home; supper. 11.

TUESDAY [NOVEMBER] 4. 4.15 Prayed; prayed. 6 Matthew 8; the band. 8 Tea, necessary talk (religious). 9.30 Writ notes. 10 Writ to Richards, etc. 12 Religious talk to many. 2 At brother Wilkinson's, dinner, religious talk. 3.30 At Mrs Happy's, tea, religious talk, prayed. 4 At brother Lewin's, tea, religious talk. 6 Acts 21. 7.45 Supper, necessary talk (religious). 9.15 prayed. 9.45.

WEDNESDAY [NOVEMBER] 5. 4.30 Prayed; prayed. 6 Matthew 9; the band. 8 Tea, religious talk. 9 Journal. 12 Religious talk to many. 2 The leaders, religious talk, prayed; Communion; prayed. 4 At brother Lewin's, dinner. 4.45 At Patty Kent's, tea, religious talk. 5.30 Greyhound Lane, Matthew 12:26; visited. 7.30 At home; supper. 8 The bands. 9.30 Prayed. 10.

Thursday [November] 6. 4.30 Prayed; prayed. 6 Matthew 9; the band. 8 Sister Morris, Francis, Hibbard, and Middleton, tea, religious talk. 12 Religious talk to many. 2 At Mrs Frognell's, dinner, religious talk. 4.30 At Mrs Sutherland's, religious talk, prayed. 5.15 At sister Aspernell's, religious talk. 6 Acts 22; supper. 8 Society! prayed. 10.15.

Friday [November] 7. 4.30 Prayed; prayed; Matthew 10; the band. 8 Mr Rogers and Mason, tea, religious talk. 10 Writ notes. 12 Religious talk to many. 1 Prayed. 3 Visited many. 4.30 At sister Belbin's, tea, religious talk. 5.30 At Short's Gardens, Romans 3. 8.15 At home; supper, religious talk, prayed. 10.

Saturday [November] 8. 4.30 Dressed; prayed; necessary talk (religious). 6 Matthew 10! visited Esther Owen; Communion. 8.30 At Coz Wilson's, tea, religious talk. 9.45 At home; writ to Charles; writ notes. 12 Religious talk to some. 2 At brother Windsor's, dinner, religious talk. 4 At brother Dawson's; at sister Woodruff's, tea, religious talk. 5.15 At sister Wilkinson's, tea. 6 Acts 13! 8 At home; supper. 8.15 The women. 10.15.

Sunday [November] 9. 4 Dressed; prayed; religious talk to some; tea. 6 Matthew 5:13, etc. 8 The leaders. 9 Religious talk to sister Morris. 10 St Peter's; Communion. 1 At home; dinner; visited. 2.45 At home; necessary business. 3.30 Tea, religious talk to many. 5 Isaiah. 7 Supper; the men's Love-feast! 9.30.

Monday [November] 10. 2 Dressed; tea; Mary Cannon, Nancy Morris, etc, prayed. 4 Rode with brother Nowers; verse. 7.45 Colnbrook, tea. 8.45 Rode; verse. 12 Reading; dinner. 1 Rode; verse. 5 Hungerford; writ; supper; prayed. 7.15.

Tuesday [November] 11. 5 Prayed; dressed. 6 Rode. 8 Marlborough; tea. 9 Rode. 11.45 Chippenham, dinner. 12.45 Rode; verse. 4.15 Bristol; at brother Deschamps', tea, religious talk. 5 At home; necessary business. 5.45 Isaiah 49:15! supper. 8 The bands, prayed! 9.15 Prayed. 9.30.

Wednesday [November] 12. 5 Dressed; prayed. 5.45 1 Timothy 2:4; the women leaders, necessary talk (religious), prayed. 9.15 Visited Miss Purnell, etc. 12.30 At home; necessary business. 1 The leaders, prayed. 2.30 At Mrs Hooper's, Mrs Norman, etc, religious talk, prayed. 3 At Mrs Norman's, tea, religious talk. 4.15 At home; first and second band. 6 The women; supper; the men, prayed! 9.30 Prayed.

Thursday [November] 13. 5 Dressed; prayed; Acts 7; third and fourth band. 8.45 At sister Highnam's, tea, religious talk. 10.15 Visited. 11 Malt-room, Luke 13! 12.30 Visited some. 1.30 At Mr Labbè's, dinner, religious talk to Suky, prayed. 3 At Mr Martin's, tea, religious talk. 4.15 At home; fifth and sixth band. 5.45 1 John 3; supper; Society. 9.30 Prayed. 10.

Friday [November] 14. 5 Dressed; prayed; 2 Peter 1:1-12! seventh and eighth band. 8.15 Tea, religious talk; necessary business. 9 Ninth and tenth band. 10 At sister Purnell's; Communion! visited. 12.30 At home; necessary business; prayed! 3 At Mrs Grevil's, tea, prayed with Mrs Parsons. 4 At home; eleventh and twelfth band. 5.15 Religious talk with sister Cennick, religious talk! 6 Romans 5:1-12. 8 Supper; religious talk, prayed; read. 10.

SATURDAY [NOVEMBER] 15. 5 Dressed; prayed; 2 Peter 1:1-12! eleventh and twelfth band. 8.30 At sister Highnam's, tea, religious talk. 10 At Mr Labbè's; Communion; visited. 11.30 At home; religious talk to some. 1 At Mrs Hooper's; writ diary; visited. 3 Kingswood; necessary talk with brother Cennick! 4.45 The bands, religious talk, prayed! 6 At Mrs England's; at sister Hooper's, tea, religious talk. 7 Malt-room, Luke 6. 8.45 Supper, necessary talk (religious). 10.

SUNDAY, NOVEMBER 16. 5 Dressed; prayed. 5.45 Ephesians 6:10; at Mr Deschamps', tea, religious talk. 8 Kingswood, 1 John 3:1, etc! 10 At our church [St James's]; Communion. 1.30 At sister England's, dinner; visited. 3.30 At sister England's with brother Richards, tea. 4.15 At home; writ diary. 4.45 Acts 13:30; society; prayed! 9.15 Necessary talk (religious); prayed. 9.45.

MONDAY [NOVEMBER] 17. 5 Dressed; prayed. 5.45 Romans 5:13, etc; thirteenth and fourteenth band. 8.30 At Mrs Stafford's, tea, religious talk, prayed. 10 At brother Richards'; Communion. 11.15 At home; religious talk to many. 1.30 At sister Stephens', dinner, religious talk. 3 At brother Morris', tea, religious talk. 4 At brother Darby's, tea, religious talk. 5 At home; with a band. 5.45 Romans 4:5. 7.45 The leaders, religious talk, prayed. 9.15 Read. 10.15.

TUESDAY [NOVEMBER] 18. 5 Dressed; prayed; Romans 7; fifteenth and sixteenth band. 8 Visited Mary Lockier; Communion. 9 At Mrs Norman's, tea, religious talk. 10 Visited. 11 Malt-room, Luke 6:40! 1.15 At Mr Wayne's, dinner. 2.30 At the School, Luke 6:40. 5.15 At Miss Cutler's, tea, religious talk. 6 2 Corinthians 7:1. 8 The schoolmasters, necessary talk (religious); supper. 10.

WEDNESDAY [NOVEMBER] 19. 5 Prayed; Romans 7; the bands. 8 At brother Lawton's, tea, religious talk. 10 At Captain Turner's. 10 At Peggy Davis', prayed. 11 Religious talk to many. 1.30 Prayed! 3 At brother Sayse's, tea, religious talk, visited. 4 Miss Purnell; at sister Hooper's, tea, religious talk; visited some. 6 At home; the women. 7.30 Supper; the men! 10.

THURSDAY [NOVEMBER] 20. 5 Charles came; prayed; Romans 9. 8 At sister Hooper's with Charles, religious talk. 9 Tea; Charles read journal. 10 At home; religious talk to some; writ diary. 11 1 Timothy 2:4; visited; Communion. 1.15 At Mr Farley's, dinner. 3 At sister Highnam's, religious talk, tea. 4.15 At sister Shrewsbury's, tea, religious talk. 5 At home; religious talk. 5.45 Hebrews 10:35. 7.30 Society. 8.45 At Mr Deschamps', necessary talk (religious), prayed. 9.30.

FRIDAY, NOVEMBER 21. 3 Tea; prayed. 4.15 Set out. 4.45 At sister Jones', religious talk, prayed. 5.15 Read verse. 8.30 Chippenham; tea, religious talk. 9.45 Rode; verse. 12.45 Marlborough; dinner, religious talk. 1.45 Rode; verse. 5.30 Woolhampton; read verse; supper, religious talk, prayed. 8.30.

SATURDAY [NOVEMBER] 22. 4 Dressed. 4.30 Rode; verse. 7.30 Hare Hatch; tea, religious talk. 8.45 Rode; verse. 12 Hounslow; dinner; writ. 1 Rode. 3.30 At home; read letters; tea, religious talk. 4.30 Necessary business; writ diary. 6 Writ to Charles; writ notes. 8 With Mary Gunning, prayed; at home. 9 Prayed. 9.30.

SUNDAY [NOVEMBER] 23. 4.45 Dressed; prayed; tea. 6 Matthew 5:16-20! 7.45 The women leaders. 10 St Peter's; Communion. 1 At home; dinner, religious talk. 2.30 Visited some. 3.30 At Mrs Witham's, Mrs MacCune, etc, tea, religious talk. 5 2 Kings 10:15; necessary talk; necessary business. 7.30 The women's Love-feast. 9.15 At Mary Gunning's, sang! 10.

MONDAY [NOVEMBER] 24. 4.30 Dressed; prayed; religious talk. 6 Matthew 10; the band. 8 Necessary business. 8.30 At sister Harrison's, many there, tea, prayed. 10 Visited sister Lewin. 10.30 Mr Mason, necessary talk (religious). 11 Corrected de Renty. 12 Religious talk to many. 2.45 At Walter Jones', dinner, religious talk. 4 At brother Broadmead's, married him. 4.45 At Short's Gardens; at brother Hodges', tea. 6 Short's Gardens, Romans 3. 8 The leaders, necessary talk (religious). 9 All the leaders, religious talk, prayed. 10.30 At home. 10.45.

TUESDAY [NOVEMBER] 25. 4.45 Dressed; prayed; meditated. 6 Matthew 11. 7.15 Walked with sister Jacks and Waldron; at Ratcliff Cross, sister Lane's, tea, religious talk, prayed. 11.15 At home; writ notes; religious talk to many. 1 With the spinners, prayed; religious talk to some. 2.15 At Mr Winsmore's, dinner, religious talk. 3.30 At Mrs Sisson's, religious talk. 4 At Mr Witham's, sister MacCune, etc. 4.30 At sister Brian's, tea, religious talk. 5.30 At home; in the School, prayed. 6 Acts 24! 8 With my mother. 9.30 Prayed. 10.

WEDNESDAY, NOVEMBER 26. 4.45 Dressed; prayed; meditated. 6 Matthew 11. 7 In the School, prayed; with the band. 8.15 At brother Gross', religious talk, tea. 9.30 Visited some. 10.45 At home; religious talk (necessary); religious talk to many. 2 Communion. 3 At Mrs Mackenzie's, tea, religious talk. 4.15 At sister Vandrelst's, tea. 5 Short's Gardens, Romans 3! 7.45 At home; supper. 8 The bands. 10.15.

THURSDAY [NOVEMBER] 27. 4.45 Dressed; prayed; meditated; prayed. 6 Matthew 12; in the School; the band. 8.15 At brother Cobb's, tea, religious talk. 9.30 At home; necessary business. 11 Journal. 12 Religious talk to some. 2.15 At Mr Ellis', dinner, prayed. 3.45 Visited. 4.15 At sister Sutherland's, tea, religious talk. 5.45 At home; School, Acts 25. 7.30 Necessary business. 8 Society! 9.45.

FRIDAY [NOVEMBER] 28. 4.45 Dressed; prayed; prayed. 6 Matthew 12; School; the band. 8.15 At sister Williams', tea, religious talk. 9.15 Visited. 9.45 At home; sins! journal. 11 Mr Allen of Kettering, religious talk. 12 Religious talk to many. 1.15 Prayed. 3.15 At sister Hall's, tea, religious talk. 4.15 At sister Scolefield's, christened her son. 5.15 At Short's Gardens; tea, religious talk. 6 Romans 3. 8.45 At home; supper; prayed. 9.45.

SATURDAY [NOVEMBER] 29. [pointing hand in margin] 4.30 Dressed; prayed; prayed. 6 Matthew 12; School; the band. 8.15 At Mrs Fox's, tea, religious talk. 9.30 At home; necessary business; writ notes. 12 Mr Benjamin Seward, etc, necessary talk (religious). 1 Prayed, sang. 2 At sister Horner's, dinner, religious talk. 2 Prayed; at sister Hawthorn's, tea, religious talk. 6 Long Lane, Acts 14. 8.15 At home; supper, religious talk, prayed. 9.15.

SUNDAY [NOVEMBER] 30. 4.15 Dressed; prayed; tea. 6 Matthew 5:20, etc; the leaders. 9.45 St Paul's; Communion; writ notes. 1 Dinner; visited some. 3.30 At home; tea, necessary talk (religious). 5 John 11:36; Mr MacCune, etc. 7 The women. 9 Prayed. 9.15.

MONDAY, DECEMBER 1. 4.30 Dressed; prayed; meditated. 6 Matthew 12; School; corrected; writ notes. 9 Journal. 12 Religious talk to many, to Nancy Morris, etc, tea. 4.30 At sister Ibbison's, brother Angel, etc. 5.30 Short's Gardens, tea. 6 Romans 4:5. 8 The leaders; brother Hall came, religious talk, prayed! 11 At home.

TUESDAY, DECEMBER 2. 4.45 Dressed; prayed; meditated; chocolate. 6 Matthew 12; School; religious talk to some. 8 Predestination. 12 School; religious talk to many. 2 At brother Syms', Marschall there, dinner, religious talk. 3.30 At home; necessary business. 4 Sister Middleton, etc, religious talk (necessary). 5 At sister Hunton's, sister Parker, and brother Hall, necessary talk (religious); tea. 6 Acts 26. 6 Read a sermon. 9.15 Prayed with many. 10.

WEDNESDAY [DECEMBER] 3. 4.30 Dressed; prayed; chocolate. 6 Matthew 13; School; with sister Hibbard. 8 Predestination. 11.30 Religious talk to many; School, religious talk. 2 Christened two [Ann Dorn and Elizabeth Baddily]! Communion. 4 Religious talk with sister Hibbard, etc. 4 Tea, religious talk. 5 Short's Gardens. 6.45 Tea, religious talk. 8 At home; the men, prayed! 10.15.

THURSDAY [DECEMBER] 4. 4.30 Prayed; dressed; chocolate. 6 Matthew 13; School, religious talk to some. 8 Predestination. 11.30 Religious talk to many. 2 At brother Dawson's, dinner, religious talk. 4.15 At home; necessary business; read Mrs Dutton's book; School. 6 Acts 26; necessary business. 8 Society! 10.

FRIDAY [DECEMBER] 5. 4.30 Dressed; prayed; chocolate. 6 Matthew 13; School; Predestination. 12 Religious talk to many. 1.15 Prayed! 3 Read letter from Herrnhut. 3.30 Tea; visited some. 5 Wapping, 2 Corinthians 4:1, etc! 6.45 Rosemary Lane, Romans 10:7, etc! 8.15 At home; supper; Mr Ellis, etc, necessary talk (religious), prayed. 10.

SATURDAY [DECEMBER] 6. 4.30 Dressed; prayed! meditated; chocolate. 6 Matthew 13; School; writ for Society. 11 At sister Aspernell's, religious talk! 12 At home; religious talk to many; School. 2 At Mr Doleman's, dinner, religious talk. 3.45 At the hospital. 4 At Guy's Hospital with sister Lincoln, Mr Chandler, prayed, religious talk! tea. 5.30 Visited. 6 Long Lane. 8 At home; the women, prayed. 10.

SUNDAY [DECEMBER] 7. 4.15 Dressed; prayed; tea. 6 Matthew 5:27, etc! the leaders. 10 St Luke's, Communion (three hundred communicants). 1.45 At home; dinner; prayed! 3 Visited brother Reeves, I prayed; tea. 4.30 At home; dressed; Romans 10:7! 7 The men's Love-feast. 10.

MONDAY, DECEMBER 8. 4.30 Dressed; prayed; chocolate. 6 Matthew 13; School. 7.30 Journal. 9 Writ names for Society; sins. 11.30 Religious talk to many. 3 At sister Middleton's, tea, religious talk. 4.30 At Mr Hall's, necessary talk (religious). 5.30 Short's Gardens, Romans 4 *ad fin* [to the end]. 8.15 At home; necessary business; prayed. 9.45.

TUESDAY [DECEMBER] 9. 4.30 Prayed; necessary business. 6 Matthew 14; School; writ notes; necessary business. 12 Religious talk to many; dinner. 3.30 At sister Edzard's, tea, religious talk; at sister Fox's, necessary talk (religious). 5.30 School. 6 Acts 26; the leaders. 10.

WEDNESDAY [DECEMBER] 10. 4.45 Dressed; prayed; necessary business. 6 Matthew 15; School; writ notes. 9 Tea, necessary talk; necessary business. 11 Visited. 12.30 At home; religious talk to many. 2.30 Communion. 4 Tea. 5 Short's Gardens, Romans 5! 7.45 At home; supper. 8.15 The bands. 10.15.

THURSDAY [DECEMBER] 11. 4.30 Prayed; dressed; religious talk to some. 6 Matthew 15; School; religious talk to some; necessary business. 9 Tea, necessary talk; necessary business. 11 Religious talk to many. 2.15 At sister Seaton's, dinner. 3.30 At Mr Hill's, sister Garneau's [Garnault's?], sister Aspernell's. 6 Acts 28; Society! religious talk to some. 10.15.

FRIDAY [DECEMBER] 12. 3 Dressed; tea, religious talk. 4.30 Set out with Mr Cennick, Nowers, Bond. 8.15 Colnbrook; tea, religious talk. 9.15 Rode; verse. 1 Reading; Sally Cennick, dinner, religious talk. 2.30 Rode; verse. 6.30 Hungerford; supper, necessary talk (religious). 8.30 Prayed.

SATURDAY [DECEMBER] 13. 4 Dressed; tea. 5.45 Rode. 11.45 Calne; dinner, religious talk. 1.15 Rode. 5.30 Bristol; at Mr Jones', necessary talk (religious). 7.30 At Mrs Hooper's, tea, religious talk. 8.30 Charles came, necessary talk (religious), prayed. 9.15 At home; necessary talk (religious), prayed. 10.

SUNDAY, DECEMBER 14. 5.30 Dressed. 6 Matthew 5:3; at Mr Deschamps', tea. 8.30 At the School; John 11:36! 9.45 At Mr Willis', Communion. 11.45 At Mrs England's, religious talk. 12.15 Dinner, religious talk. 2.15 At home; prayed with N Cole and Alice Philips. 3 Tea; necessary business. 4 John 11:36. 6.30 Kingswood; the men's Love-feast; prayed. 8.30 Religious talk with Nanny Davis and Ayling, prayed. 10.

MONDAY [DECEMBER] 15. 5.30 Read John Cennick's papers. 8 Matthew 5:3; at Mr Wayne's, tea, necessary talk (religious). 11 At home; necessary business; brother Griffith, etc. 12 Read notes. 2 At David Reynolds', dinner. 3.30 At home; read; necessary talk (religious). 5 Met three bands. 7 Matthew 5:4! 9 Religious talk to Nancy Ayling and Nanny Davis, prayed. 9.45.

TUESDAY [DECEMBER] 16. 5 Writ from Barclay. 8 Matthew 5:4; at Mrs Reed's, tea, religious talk. 11 At home; necessary business; Barclay. 12.30 at Mr Wayne's, religious talk, dinner. 2.30 School; James 1:4, 5! 4 Charles; religious talk to band. 6 Matthew 5:4! 7.45 Nanny, etc, religious talk, prayed. 10.

WEDNESDAY [DECEMBER] 17. 5 Barclay. 7.30 Tea. 8 Matthew 5:5, 6; at Mrs Cambourn's, Betty Bush, tea, religious talk. 11 At home; writ to Mr Hutchins, Mrs MacCune, Mr Evans, Humphreys. 1 Writ notes. 3 Tea; Nanny Davis, Ayling, and Richards, religious talk. 4 Barclay. 5.15 Band. 6 Brother John Cennick came; Matthew 5:7, etc. 7.30 Necessary talk (religious), religious talk with John Cennick! 9.15 Prayed. 9.45.

THURSDAY [DECEMBER] 18. 3.45 Barclay. 8 Matthew 5:9-16. 9.30 At Widow Jones', tea, sang. 11 At home; Barclay. 12.15 Brother Sayse came, religious talk. 2 At Mr Willis', Charles, Richards, etc, dinner, sang, prayed. 3.45 Visited. 4.45 At the School; Barclay. 6 Matthew 4! 7.30 Barclay; Anna Cennick, religious talk, prayed. 9.45.

FRIDAY [DECEMBER] 19. 3.45 Barclay. 8 Matthew 5:17, 18; religious talk to some; visited. 11 At brother Deschamps'; at sister Purnell's; at sister Hooper's, religious talk. 12 At the School; necessary talk (religious) with Charles. 1 Prayed. 2.30 At Dr Middleton's, necessary talk (religious). 3 At Mr Farley's, tea, sang. 5 At home; necessary business; writ diary. 6 Matthew 5:17, 18. 7.30 John Cennick, etc, necessary talk (religious), prayed. 9.30.

SATURDAY, DECEMBER 20. 3.45 Ended Barclay; tea; Sally Luton and Betty Lovel, religious talk. 8 Matthew 20; at Mrs Tippet's, coffee, religious talk; John Cennick, etc. 10.45 At home; Charles, John Cennick, T Beswick, Nowers, sisters Ayling and Davis, prayed, religious talk of Election! 2 At Charles Arthur's, dinner, sang. 4 At home; the bands. 5 Met a band; met another. 6.30 Writ. 7.15 Nanny Davis and Ayling, religious talk. 9 Prayed. 9.30.

SUNDAY [DECEMBER] 21. 4.45 Writ for the bands. 6.30 Two Nannys [Davis and Ayling], prayed; tea, religious talk; writ. 8 1 John 4:11. 9.15 At John Cennick's band. 10.30 At Mr Willis', religious talk, Communion. 12.30 At Mr Deschamps', dinner. 1 Visited Miss Pearse, brother Darby, N Cole. 2.15 At home; Mrs Norman, religious talk, tea. 3.45 Matthew 8:2, 3! 5.30 Society! 7 The bands of Kingswood and Bristol, Love-feast, sang, prayed. 11 At home.

MONDAY [DECEMBER] 22. 5 Necessary business; writ [for] bands. 7.15 Tea, religious talk. 8 Matthew 5:21, etc; visited David Reynolds. 10.30 At home; writ for bands. 1 At Mrs Hooper's, necessary talk (religious) with Charles; dinner. 2.15 At Captain Turner's, sang, prayed. 3 At sister Highnam's with Charles, religious talk, prayed. 5 Kingswood; met a band. 6 Matthew 5:20-28; met two bands. 8.30 With John Cennick, etc, necessary talk (religious). 9.15 Prayed. 9.45.

TUESDAY [DECEMBER] 23. 5 Writ to sister Seaton, Judith Matthews, and Sarah Mason. 7 At Mrs Jones', Charles there, religious talk; chocolate; Matthew 5:28. 10 At Mrs Bainton's, tea, religious talk, prayed; at sister Elizabeth Turner's. 11 1 Peter 4:1-4. 12 At sister Highnam's, Charles, etc, religious talk. 1 At Mr Deschamps' dinner. 2.30 At the School, Romans 15:1-6! 3.30 Tea, religious talk to J West, brother Ingham. 6 Matthew 5:31. 7.30 Writ to Mrs Dutton. 8.30 Religious talk, prayed. 9.30.

WEDNESDAY [DECEMBER] 24. 4.14 Corrected John Cennick's papers. 6.30 Prayed; tea, religious talk. 8 Matthew 5. 9 Corrected; necessary business. 3 Tea; corrected. 4.45 Mr Farley, etc, religious talk. 5.15 Met two bands; coffee, religious talk. 8.15 Sang, prayed. 12.15.

THURSDAY, DECEMBER 25. 12.15 Coffee; walked with many, sang. 2 Bristol; slept. 5 Luke 2:10. 6.30 Religious talk to some. 7.30 At brother Sayse's, tea, religious talk. 9 Visited. 9.45 Meditated. 10 St James's, Communion. 1.15 At Mr Thomas', dinner, religious talk, prayed. 2.30 At Mrs Hooper's with Lucretia Smith, sang, prayed. 3 At home; Mrs Norman, religious talk, tea. 4 Matthew 1:21! 5.45 Religious talk to some. 6.15 Society. 8 Religious talk to some. 9.

FRIDAY [DECEMBER] 26. 5 Dressed; Matthew 5:4! at Mr Deschamps', tea. 8 Kingswood, Matthew 5 *ult!* 9.15 Many here; made a case. 12.15 Dinner; walked. 2 Lay down; prayed, sang! 3.30 Sister Robertson and Purnell, etc, tea, religious talk, prayed; [read] Dr Edwards! 6 Matthew 5 *ult.* 7.30 Dr Edwards, ended it. 9 Prayed. 9.30.

SATURDAY [DECEMBER] 27. 4 Journal; writ to Charles; tea. 8 Matthew 6; necessary business; met a band. 11.45 At Mr Deschamps', ate. 12 Read letters. 2 At Mrs England's, dinner. 3.30 At the School; the bands. 6.15 At Mrs England's, tea, religious talk. 7 Malt-room, 1 Peter 4:4. 8.30 At home; the men leaders. 10.

SUNDAY [DECEMBER] 28. 5 Dressed. 5.30 Galatians 2:20; at Mr Deschamps', tea. 8 At the School, Galatians 2:20. 9.45 Necessary business; Communion with twenty-four. 12.15 Tea. 1 Christened John Hemming. 1.30 Met a band. 2 Ephesians 2:8. 4 At the Room, Ephesians 2:8. 6 Society. 7.30 At the School; the band! 9.30.

MONDAY [DECEMBER] 29. 3.15 Journal. 6.30 Sister Ayling, tea, religious talk; writ notes. 8 Matthew 6:10. 9.15 Two bands! 10 Miss Lowman, Mary Deacon, tea, religious talk. 11.15 Writ notes. 11.45 Visited Ralph Peacock. 1.15 At home; dinner; writ notes. 2.30 Matthew 6:11, etc. 5 At Mr Deschamps', tea; dressed; religious talk. 6 2 Corinthians 2:11. 9 At home; writ diary. 9.45.

TUESDAY [DECEMBER] 30. 4 Journal. 8 Matthew 6. 10.15 At Mrs Bainton's, religious talk, prayed. 11 1 Peter 4! 1 At Mr Wayne's, Mr Ford there, dinner. 2.15 Met a band. 3 Matthew 6. 5 At Miss Purnell's; at Mrs Hooper's, Lucretia Smith! tea. 6 Alice Philips buried! Luke 23; visited. 10 At the School.

WEDNESDAY, DECEMBER 31. 4 Journal. 8 Matthew 6. 10.30 Bristol; sins; necessary business; religious talk, prayed. 3 At sister Highnam's, tea, religious talk, prayed. 5.30 At home; many here. 6 The bands from Bristol, prayed! religious talk. 8 Coffee. 8.30 Prayed, etc! 12.45.

[THURSDAY] JANUARY 1, 1741. 6.30 Writ to Mr Wayne; tea, religious talk. 8 2 Corinthians 5:17! 11 Malt-room, 2 Corinthians 5:17! 2 At the School; dinner. 3 Necessary business; brother Richards, necessary talk (religious), tea; visited. 6 Philippians 2! Society. 10.

FRIDAY [JANUARY] 2. 5 Dressed. 5.30 Matthew 5:4; at brother Deschamps', tea. 8 At the School, Matthew 6 *ult!* 10.30 At the Room, religious talk to many. 1.15 Prayed; visited. 3 At Mr Labbè's, tea, religious talk, visited. 5.15 At the School; read notes. 6 Matthew 7; necessary business; read notes. 8.30 Necessary talk (religious) with two Nannys [Davis and Ayling]; prayed. 10.

SATURDAY [JANUARY] 3. 6 Writ to brother Humphreys, Purdy, Hutchings. 8 Matthew 7. 9 Writ to Mr Thorold, Webb. 10.30 Journal. 11 Writ for Society. 1.30 At Mr Willis', dinner, religious talk. 3.15 At the School, with Mr Vaughan, necessary talk. 3.30 A band. 4 The bands. 5.45 At sister England's, brother Humphreys there! at Mrs Deschamps', tea. 6.30 Revelation 14:13! sister [Elizabeth] Davis and [Anne] Cole buried. 10.30 At home.

SUNDAY [JANUARY] 4. 4.30 Writ for bands. 7 Tea; necessary talk (religious) to brother Bissicks; a band. 8 Philippians 3:13, 14. 9.45 Writ for the Society. 10.15 John Cennick and Humphreys, necessary talk (religious). 11 Communion (sixty there!). 12.15 At Mr Tippet's. 2 Matthew 6 *ult.* 4 Bristol; Philippians 3:13, 14; Society. 7 At the School; general Love-feast, spoke! prayed. 11.

MONDAY [JANUARY] 5. 6 Writ to sister Nancy, etc; tea. 8 Matthew 7:8, etc! 9.30 Writ for the bands. 1.30 At brother Arthurs', religious talk; dinner. 4 At home; writ notes. 5 Tea; met a band. 6 Matthew 7:10, etc! 7.30 Read Mrs Dutton's letters; prayed. 9.15.

TUESDAY, JANUARY 6. 4.15 Journal; tea, religious talk. 8 Matthew 7:13. 9.30 Religious talk to many. 10:30 Walked; visited; Mrs Bainton! 1 At Mr Wayne's, dinner. 2.45 School, Psalm 23! necessary talk (religious) to many; a band. 6 Matthew 7:14, etc. 7.30 Religious talk to many; read; prayed. 9.30.

W<small>EDNESDAY</small> [J<small>ANUARY</small>] 7. 4 Journal; writ to Charles; tea; visited W Sibs. 8 Matthew 7:16! 10.30 Bristol; at the Room; necessary talk (religious); necessary business. 1 The leaders, necessary talk (religious), prayed. 3 At Mrs England's, tea, religious talk. 4 Visited Jenny Connor! 4.30 At Captain Turner's, tea, religious talk. 5.30 At home; writ to Charles, Nanny Smith. 6 The women. 7.45 Supper; the men. 9.30 Prayed. 10.

T<small>HURSDAY</small> [J<small>ANUARY</small>] 8. 5 Dressed. 5.30 Matthew 5:6; the women leaders. 8.30 At sister Purnell's, tea, religious talk. 9.45 At home; religious talk to many. 11 Malt-room, 1 Peter 4:11! 12.30 At Mr Wiggington's, dinner, religious talk, prayed. 2 At Mrs Norman's, tea, religious talk. 3.30 At Mrs Bainton's funeral, Mr Oliver, etc. 5.30 At home; writ. 6 Psalm 23! Society! 9.45.

F<small>RIDAY</small> [J<small>ANUARY</small>] 9. 5 Dressed. 5.30 Matthew 5:7; the women leaders; necessary business. 8 At Mrs Grevil's, tea, necessary talk (religious). 9.15 At home; writ for Society. 10 Religious talk to many. 1 Prayed. 3 At Mrs Hooper's, tea, necessary talk (religious). 5.30 At home; writ for Society; Matthew 7. 6 Supper, necessary talk (religious). 9.15.

S<small>ATURDAY</small> [J<small>ANUARY</small>] 10. 4 Writ to some; writ for Society; tea. 8 Matthew 7:16. 9.30 Writ for Society. 12.15 Visited. 1.15 At Mr Willis', brother Cennick, Humphreys, etc, dinner. 3.15 At home; writ to Charles; the bands. 5 Tea; writ names. 6.30 Sister Robertson and Jane Williams; supper; writ. 9 Prayed. 9.15.

S<small>UNDAY</small>, J<small>ANUARY</small> 11. 4.15 Writ for Society; tea. 7 Met two bands. 8.15 Luke 6:40; necessary talk (religious). 10 Communion (seventy there!). 12 At brother Cennick's, Captain Turner, etc, dinner, religious talk. 2 Ephesians 2:8. 4 At the Room, Ephesians 2:8; Society! 6.15 At Mrs Jones'! 7.30 At home; the bands. 9 Nanny Davis, etc; supper, prayed. 10.

M<small>ONDAY</small> [J<small>ANUARY</small>] 12. 4.15 Writ to brother Cheyne, sister Morris, Aspernell, Thomas, Dean, my mother; dressed. 8 Matthew 7; necessary talk (religious). 10.30 At Mrs Jones'. 11 At home; writ to many. 1.15 At Captain Turner's, dinner, religious talk, prayed. 3 At sister Connor's, Communion. 4.30 At home; writ to Charles; tea; met a band. 6 Prayed; Psalm 89! 7.30 A band, Sarah Milsom! prayed. 8.45 Prayed. 9.15.

T<small>UESDAY</small> [J<small>ANUARY</small>] 13. 4 Journal; tea. 8 Matthew 7 *ult.* 9.30 Mr Labbè and Willis, necessary talk (religious). 10 John Feachem, religious talk. 1.15 At Mrs Wayne's, religious talk, dinner. 2.30 At the School; a band. 3 Matthew 7. 4.15 Rachel Gotley, etc, tea, religious talk. 5.15 Read notes. 6 1 John 1! 7.30 Nanny Davis with me, religious talk. 9.15 Prayed. 9.45 Sins!!

W<small>EDNESDAY</small> [J<small>ANUARY</small>] 14. 4 Journal; tea. 8 John 1:3, 4; necessary business. 10.30 At Mrs Jones', she well! 11 At Mr Deschamps', tea, religious talk (necessary). 11.30 At home; religious talk to many. 1.45 The leaders. 3 At Mrs Hooper's, necessary talk (religious), tea. 4.45 At home; necessary business. 5 Writ notes. 6 The women. 7.45 Supper. 8 The men. 10.

T<small>HURSDAY</small> [J<small>ANUARY</small>] 15. 5.15 Dressed; Matthew 5:7, 8; at Mr Deschamps', tea. 7.45 At the School; necessary business. 8 1 John 5:6, 7; necessary business. 10 At home; religious talk to some. 11 Malt-room, Psalm 8. 12.30 At Mr Pearse's, dinner, religious talk. 2.30 Visited sister Deacon and brother Black! 3 At Mr

George's, tea, prayed, religious talk. 4 At Mrs Stafford's, tea, religious talk. 5.15 At Mr Lillington's, tea, religious talk. 6 Hebrews 3:12! 7.45 Society. 10.

Friday [January] 16. 4.30 Dressed; religious talk. 5.30 Matthew 5:9, 10, etc. 7 At Mrs Deschamps', tea. 8 At the School, 1 John 1:8, 9, 10! 10 Visited Mary Hanny and Jane Connor. 10.30 At Mrs Martin's, tea, religious talk. 11 At home; religious talk to many. 1.15 Prayed. 3.30 At Rachel Gotley's, tea, religious talk. 5 At the School; writ accounts. 6 1 John 2:1, 2; Cennick there! 7.45 Supper, necessary talk (religious). 9 Sang.

Saturday, January 17. 4 Journal; tea. 8 1 John 2:3, etc. 9.30 A band. 10 Writ to Charles, to Mr Evans, Chapman of Bath, Yapping. 1.15 At William Kirby's, dinner, religious talk, prayed. 3 At home; necessary business; sister Hooper, etc, tea. 4.15 The bands. 6 At Mr Deschamps', tea. 7 At the Malt-room, 1 Peter 4 *ult!* 8.30 At home; necessary talk. 9.30 Prayed.

Sunday [January] 18. 4.45 Religious talk; dressed. 5.30 2 Corinthians [2:]11; at Deschamps', tea; Kingswood, 2 Corinthians [2:]11. 10 St James's! Communion. 1.30 At Mr Brummidge's, dinner. 2.30 The leaders, tea. 4 Hebrews 3:12! Society; all the bands, Love-feast. 10.15.

Monday [January] 19. 5 Dressed; Romans 14:1; tea; at the School, 1 John 2; brother Cennick, necessary talk (religious). 11 Necessary business; writ. 1.30 At brother Tilladam's, dinner. 3 At home; necessary business; necessary talk (religious). 4.30 At Bristol; visited some. 6 Psalm 23! Society! 9.30 At Mr Deschamps'. 10.

Tuesday [January] 20. 3 Tea; necessary talk (religious). 4 Set out with brother Grace. 9 Chippenham; tea, religious talk. 10 Rode. 1.45 Marlborough; dinner. 2.45 Rode; verse. 6.30 Newbury; writ; supper; prayed. 9.

Wednesday [January] 21. 4.15 Dressed; necessary business. 5 Rode. 8 Reading; tea. 9 Rode. 1 Slough; dinner. 2 Rode. 6 At the Foundery; with my mother, necessary talk (religious); supper. 8 The bands, religious talk, prayed. 10.

Thursday [January] 22. 5.30 Dressed; religious talk to Charles. 6 1 John 4:1, 2. 7 A band. 8.15 At brother Evans', tea, necessary talk (religious). 10.15 At home; necessary talk (religious) with many. 2.30 At brother Leighton's, dinner, religious talk. 4 At Mrs MacCune's, necessary talk (religious). 5.30 At home; necessary talk (religious). 6 Micah 7! Society, prayed! 10.15.

Friday [January] 23. 5.30 Dressed; necessary business. 6 1 John 4; a band. 8.15 Tea, necessary talk (religious) to many. 1 Prayed. 3 At sister Gaskarth's; tea; visited. 6 Short's Gardens, Romans 5:14, etc. 8 At Mrs MacCune's, necessary talk (religious); supper. 10.45 At home.

Saturday, January 24. [pointing hand in margin] 5 Meditated; necessary talk (religious). 6 1 John 4; a band. 8.15 Tea, religious talk (necessary) to many; writ notes. 11 Letters! prayed. 1 Dinner, religious talk. 2 Letters; prayed! 4.45 At sister Hawthorn's, tea, religious talk. 6 Acts 16. 8.15 At home; necessary talk (religious); prayed. 9.45.

Sunday [January] 25. 4.30 Dressed; prayed; tea. 6 Galatians 6:10! 8.30 The leaders. 9.45 St Paul's, Communion. 1.45 At home; dinner; prayed. 3.30 At brother Nightingale's, tea. 4 Hebrews 3:12! 6.45 The women. 9.15 Prayed.

MONDAY [JANUARY] 26. 4.30 Dressed; prayed. 6 1 John 4; a band. 8.15 At brother Cobb's, tea, religious talk. 9 With sister Aspernell; at sister Jackson's. 10.30 At home; necessary business. 11 Religious talk to many. 2.15 At brother Lewin's, dinner. 3 Visited. 4.15 At brother Lane's, tea, religious talk. 5.45 Short's Gardens; necessary talk. 6 Romans 6; at Mrs MacCune's, supper, religious talk. 11.

TUESDAY [JANUARY] 27. 4.30 Prayed; necessary talk (religious); meditated. 6 1 John 4; a band; tea; visited. 11 Religious talk to many; with Sarah Dean! 2.30 At brother Bond's, dinner, religious talk. 3.45 At brother Garnault's, tea, religious talk. 4.30 At sister Edzard's, religious talk, prayed! 5.30 At Mr Fox's, necessary talk (religious). 6 Psalm 23. 8 The leaders, necessary talk (religious), prayed. 10.

WEDNESDAY [JANUARY] 28. 4.30 Dressed; prayed; necessary talk (religious). 6 1 John 4; writ diary; religious talk (necessary); tea. 9 Brother Gambold came, brother Hall and Charles, religious talk! 11 Religious talk to many. 2.45 At Mrs Sutherland's; at Captain Griffith's, tea, necessary talk (religious). 5 Deptford, Psalm 23! 8 At home; religious talk with Charles; supper. 8.30 The bands. 9.45 Prayed. 10.

THURSDAY [JANUARY] 29. 4.45 Dressed; prayed. 6 1 John 4 *ult.* 7 A band. 8.15 At brother Wilde's. 9 Writ for Society. 11 Religious talk to many. 2 At brother Doleman's, dinner. 3.45 At Mrs Witham's, tea, religious talk. 5 At home; necessary talk; writ notes. 6 Romans 11:33! Society, religious talk. 10.15.

FRIDAY, JANUARY 30. 4.30 Dressed; prayed. 6 Luke 5:33; a band. 8.30 Mr Watkins, tea, religious talk; writ notes. 10.15 At sister Middleton's, tea. 11 At Charles'. 1.15 Prayed! 3 At sister Gilby's, tea, religious talk; visited. 4 At sister Martin's, tea, religious talk. 5 At Mrs Elbert's, religious talk. 6 Short's Gardens, Romans 6! 8 At Mrs MacCune's, supper, religious talk. 11.15 At home. 11.45.

SATURDAY [JANUARY] 31. 2.30 With Sarah Dean! 4.30 Slept. 5.30 Prayed. 6 1 John 5:1. 7 A band. 8 At sister Hunton's, tea, religious talk. 9.15 Writ to Charles, brother Nowers, Humphreys, Crooke. 11 Religious talk to many. 2.15 At Mrs Knight's, sister Peck's, sister Barrat's, tea, religious talk. 6 Long Lane, Acts 16:31. 8 At home; the women leaders! 10.

SUNDAY, FEBRUARY 1. 4.30 Dressed; prayed; tea. 6 Matthew 32, etc! 7.45 The leaders. 10 St Luke's, Communion. 1.45 At Mrs Clark's, dinner; at sister Isabell Johnson's, prayed! visited. 3.30 At brother Horner's, tea, religious talk. 4.15 At home; writ notes. 4.45 Hebrews 3 *ult!* 6.30 The women, necessary talk (religious), prayed. 7.45 The men's Love-feast. 10.

MONDAY [FEBRUARY] 2. 4.30 Dressed; prayed; 1 John 5; a band. 8 At sister Aspernell's, George Angel, etc, necessary talk (religious), tea. 10 At home; necessary business. 11 Religious talk to many. 2.30 At brother Bolt's, dinner. 3.30 At Mr Wynde's, necessary talk. 4.30 At brother Bolt's, tea, religious talk. 5 Visited Elizabeth Hurtley, Thomas Whitefield, prayed. 6 At Long Lane, necessary talk (religious). 7 Acts 17! 9.45 At home. 10.15.

TUESDAY [FEBRUARY] 3. 4.45 Prayed; necessary talk; 1 John 5; three bands. 8.15 Tea, necessary talk (religious); religious talk to some. 10 Writ to George Whitefield. 11 Religious talk to many. 2.15 At brother Cennick's, dinner. 4 At sister Barnes', religious talk; at sister Westry's, tea, religious talk. 6 Judges 3! 8 The leaders, prayed. 10.15.

Wednesday, February 4. 4.30 Prayed; necessary talk (religious). 6 Jeremiah 5:9! 8 The three bands. 9.30 Writ for brother Cennick, with Nanny Smith! 11 St Luke's. 1.30 Luke 13! 3 With Mrs MacCune, etc; coach. 4.45 At Mrs Sparrow's, prayed. 5.15 Deptford, John 11:36! 8.45 At home; supper. 9 The bands. 10.30.

Thursday [February] 5. 4.30 Dressed; prayed. 6 1 John 5; three bands. 8.15 Tea, religious talk (necessary). 9.15 Writ for Society. 11 Religious talk to many. 2 At Mrs Jeffrys', dinner, religious talk, prayed. 3.15 At brother Hogg's, tea, religious talk. 4 At sister Edzard's! tea, religious talk. 5.15 At home; writ notes. 6 Zechariah 13:6, etc! Society. 10.30.

Friday [February] 6. 4.30 Dressed; prayed. 5.15 John Haddock! 6 1 John 5:6! 7 Three bands. 8.30 At sister Orange's, tea, religious talk. 9.30 At home; writ diary. 10 Writ for the bands. 11 Religious talk to many. 2.15 Prayed. 3 Christened J Okey; Communion. 4 At brother Thomas Smith's, tea, religious talk. 5.15 Short's Gardens, necessary talk (religious). 6 Romans 6 *ult.* 8.30 At Mrs MacCune's, supper. 11 At home; Nanny Smith, religious talk! 12.30.

Saturday [February] 7. 4.45 Prayed; religious talk to some. 6 1 John 5:6! two bands. 8 At sister Ramsay's, many there, tea, religious talk. 9.15 Writ to Charles. 11 Religious talk to many. 2 At Peter Sims', dinner, religious talk. 3.30 At Betty Kent's, tea, religious talk. 4.30 At Sarah Dean's, tea, religious talk. 6 Long Lane, Acts 17! 8 Society, new members admitted; prayed! sister Kezzy came. 10.15.

Sunday [February] 8. 4.45 Dressed; prayed; tea, religious talk. 6 Ephesians 2:8; the leaders. 9.45 St Paul's; visited. 1 At brother Blake's, religious talk, dinner. 2.45 At home; writ diary; read George Fox's *Journal.* 4.15 With sister Kezzy, tea, religious talk. 4.45 Acts 17:34. 6.15 Supper, necessary talk (religious). 7 The women. 8.45 Nanny Smith, necessary talk (religious)! 10.15.

Monday [February] 9. 4.45 Prayed; religious talk. 6 1 John 5; the bands. 8.15 With sister Kezzy, tea, necessary talk. 9.15 Writ notes; religious talk to many. 2 With my mother, dinner. 3.30 At Mrs Lee's, Cannon Street, tea, religious talk. 4.45 At Mr Crouch's, Benjamin Seward came. 6 Visited Thomas Whitefield, prayed. 7 Long Lane, Acts 17! 9 At home; necessary talk (religious); Nanny Smith! 11.

Tuesday, February 10. 4.30 Dressed; prayed. 6 1 John 5:7. 7 Writ journal. 8.30 Tea, religious talk. 9 Writ journal; married Mr Daniel; journal. 2 At sister Edzard's, dinner, religious talk. 3.15 Visited Widow Frazier, prayed. 4 At sister Bowman's, religious talk, tea. 5 At home; necessary talk (religious). 6 Romans 1:16! 8 Necessary talk (religious); the leaders. 10.

Ash Wednesday [February] 11. 4.30 Dressed; prayed; religious talk. 6 Matthew 6:13; read John Cennick's hymns. 10 At sister Francis', religious talk. 11 St Luke's. 12.30 At home; necessary talk (religious). 1.15 Coach with sister Seaton and Nanny Smith. 3.15 At Mrs Sparrow's, religious talk, prayed, tea. 5 Romans 7. 8 At home; supper; the men, religious talk, prayed. 10.15.

THURSDAY [FEBRUARY] 12. 4.30 Dressed; prayed; religious talk to some. 6 1 John 5:7, 8, 9; corrected Haliburton. 8 Tea, necessary talk (religious); corrected Kempis. 11 Religious talk to many. 2 Dinner. 3.15 At brother Haddock's with Charles; tea, religious talk. 4.45 At home; religious talk with my mother. 5.15 At Mrs Scott's, tea, religious talk. 6 Charles preached; Society! 10.

FRIDAY [FEBRUARY] 13. 4.30 Dressed; prayed. 6 1 John 5:10, etc. 7 Corrected. 8 At sister Waldron's, tea, religious talk. 9.15 At home; Kempis. 1.15 Prayed! 3.30 At brother Hodges', tea, religious talk; visited. 5.30 Short's Gardens. 6 Mr Thomas Stephens, necessary talk of Georgia. 6 Romans 7. 8.30 At Mrs MacCune's, Charles there, supper, religious talk. 10.30.

SATURDAY [FEBRUARY] 14. 4.45 Dressed; prayed; 1 John 5:14, etc; Kempis. 8 Sister Jackson's with sister MacCune, etc. 9.30 Kempis. 2 At brother Dawson's with Robson, Charles, etc, dinner, religious talk. 3.45 At Mrs Lee's, tea. 5 At Sophy Combs', tea, religious talk. 6 Greyhound Lane, 1 John 5:11! 8.30 At home; necessary talk (religious). 9.45.

SUNDAY [FEBRUARY] 15. 4.45 Dressed; prayed; religious talk. 6 1 John 5:18. 7.45 The leaders, necessary talk (religious), prayed. 9 Meditated; prayed; St Paul's. 1 At sister Collins', dinner, religious talk. 2.45 At home; writ diary; tea; meditated. 4.45 1 John 2:2. 7 Women's Love-feast; Robson; prayed! 10.

MONDAY [FEBRUARY] 16. 4.30 Prayed; dressed; religious talk to some. 6 1 John 5 *ult!* prayed. 7.30 Religious talk to many. 8.30 At Nanny Morris', tea, religious talk. 9.30 Necessary talk (religious) with Charles. 10.30 Religious talk to many. 12.15 Dressed; at Sir John Ganson's, dinner, necessary talk. 3.45 At Mr Stephens', necessary talk of Georgia. 5 At Mrs MacCune's, tea. 7 Long Lane, Acts 18! 9.15 At home; necessary talk. 10.

TUESDAY [FEBRUARY] 17. 4.30 Dressed; tea. 5 Prayed. 5.45 Set out. 8.45 Gerrards Cross; tea. 9.30 Rode. 11.30 Stokenchurch; tea. 12.15 Rode. 2.45 At Mr Evans', necessary talk, dinner. 5 Walked, rain, dark, weary! prayed! 7 At Mr Gambold's, brother Hall there, religious talk, supper. 8.30.

WEDNESDAY [FEBRUARY] 18. 6 Religious talk, tea. 9 Writ diary; writ to Mr Hutchins; journal. 11 Read Prayers. 12.15 Dinner. 1.45 Walked. 6 Burford; Mr Bailey's, supper, religious talk, prayed. 10.

THURSDAY [FEBRUARY] 19. 6 Tea, religious talk, prayed. 7.30 Rode; verse. 11.30 Cirencester; religious talk, coffee. 12.15 Rode. 3.15 Malmesbury; at Mrs Lyne's, tea, religious talk. 6 Somerford; prayed; Luke 6:40! 9.45 At home; religious talk, prayed. 11.

FRIDAY [FEBRUARY] 20. 7 Tea, religious talk. 8:45 Rode. 12 [Chipping] Sodbury; dinner. 1 Rode. 4 At Mr Deschamps'; at sister Highnam's, religious talk (necessary). 5 Visited brother Richards. 6 Micah 7. 8 Necessary talk (religious). 9.15.

SATURDAY, FEBRUARY 21. [pointing hand in margin] 4.45 Dressed; necessary talk. 5.30 Acts 20:27. 7 Necessary talk (religious) to many; necessary business. 8.15 At Mrs Norman's, tea, religious talk. 9.15 At home; necessary business; necessary talk (religious) to some. 11.15 Letters. 1.15 Necessary business. 2 Necessary talk (religious) to some. 2.45 At Mr Wayne's, religious talk (necessary); dinner. 4.45 At the School; the bands, prayed! 6 At sister England's, tea; Malt-room, 1 Peter 5. 8.15 The leaders, necessary talk (religious). 10 Prayed.

SUNDAY [FEBRUARY] 22. 4.45 Dressed; necessary talk (religious); John 1:9. 7 At Mr Deschamps', tea. 8 Kingswood, 1 John 2:20. 9.30 Mr Wayne, John Cennick, Ann Ayling, Charles Arthurs, necessary talk. 12.15 At sister England's, prayed with brother Richards. 12.30 Dinner. 1.15 In the coach. 2.15 Micah 7:9. 4.30 At sister England's, tea, religious talk. 5 Judges 3:14! 6.15 Society. 7.15 Love-feast! 10.45.

MONDAY [FEBRUARY] 23. 5 Dressed; Romans 5:1. 7 At Mr Jones', coffee. 8.15 At the School, 1 John 2:12. 9.15 Sister Cambourn, etc, necessary talk (religious). 10.30 Necessary business; writ notes; read Gell. 1 At sister Cambourn's, coffee, religious talk (necessary). 2.15 At sister Bush's, necessary talk (religious), prayed. 4 At home; necessary business. 5 At sister England's, tea, religious talk, prayed. 6.15 Psalm 110:3. 8 The leaders, necessary talk (religious), prayed. 10.

TUESDAY [FEBRUARY] 24. 5 Dressed; John 16; at Nanny Smith's, tea, religious talk. 8 Kingswood, 1 John 2:14. 9.15 Necessary talk; writ notes. 12.30 At Mr Wayne's, necessary talk (religious), dinner. 2.30 1 John 2:14, etc; tea. 5 At sister England's, tea; Communion with brother Richards. 6.15 1 John 1:8. 9 The bands, prayed. 10.30.

WEDNESDAY [FEBRUARY] 25. 5. Dressed. 5.30 Romans 8:15; the women leaders. 8 At sister Perrin's, tea, religious talk. 9 Visited some. 10 Religious talk to many. 1 The women leaders, religious talk, prayed. 2 At sister Pottam's, dinner. 3 At Mrs Jones', tea, necessary talk (religious). 5 At Mrs Hooper's, tea, religious talk. 6 At home; the women. 8 The men! 10.

THURSDAY, FEBRUARY 26. 5 Dressed; necessary talk; Psalm 51; visited. 7.15 At Betty Gotley's, tea, religious talk. 8 At home; writ for Society; necessary business. 9.30 Religious talk to many. 11 Malt-room, 2 Peter 1! 12.15 Visited some. 1 With sister Webb, Communion. 1 At Mrs Norman's, dinner, religious talk. 3 At Mrs Smith's, tea, prayed. 4 At Maud Davis', religious talk. 5 At home; Mrs Jones, Page, etc, necessary talk; necessary talk (religious) to some. 6 Romans 8:1, etc; Society; 9.30 Writ diary; writ notes. 10.

FRIDAY [FEBRUARY] 27. 5 Dressed; prayed; Matthew 1:22; visited. 6.45 At Mr Deschamps', tea. 7.45 At the School; necessary business. 8 1 John 2:17, etc. 9 At Mr Arthur, Senior's, necessary talk (religious). 10.30 At home; religious talk to many. 1.30 Prayed. 3 Visited; with sister Gregory, tea, religious talk! 5 At Mr Willis'. 6 At the School; necessary business. 6.30.

SATURDAY [FEBRUARY] 28. 5 Writ to Charles, John Husband, brother Hutchins, Ingham; tea, religious talk. 8 1 John 3:1, etc. 9.15 Writ to Mr Meriton, brother Turner [of] St Ives. 11 Garden; meditated; walked. 12.30 Dinner; read notes; writ to sister Dutton. 2.45 With Betty Bush, necessary talk (religious). 4 Bands. 7 Malt-room, 2 Peter 1! 8.15 At home; tea, the stewards. 10.

SUNDAY, MARCH 1. 5 Dressed; Mark 4:27; at brother Deschamps', tea. 8 At the School, 1 John 3:10! 9.30 Charles Arthurs, etc, necessary talk (religious); Communion; 12 At sister Cambourn's, dinner. 1.30 At home; meditated. 2

Romans 10. 3.30 At Mr Jones', coffee. 4 Romans 10; Society. 7 Walked with many, religious talk, sang. 8 At the School; the bands, necessary talk (religious), prayed. 10.

MONDAY [MARCH] 2. 4 Writ upon Predestination. 7 Tea, religious talk. 8 1 John 3 *ult.* 9.30 Necessary business; Sally Perrin, etc, religious talk, coffee. 11 Nanny Smith, N Jeffrys, religious talk. 12 Predestination. 12.30 Tea; read notes. 2 Predestination. 4 Mr Lyne of Malmesbury; writ notes. 6 1 John 4. 7.45 Necessary talk (religious); prayed. 9.30.

TUESDAY, MARCH 3. 4 Dressed; walked. 5.30 2 Corinthians 5:17; tea. 8 At the School, 1 John 4. 9 Nanny Smith, Betty Gotley, etc [Elizabeth Gotley christened in early March]; writ notes. 1 At Mrs Ponting's, dinner, religious talk. 2.30 2 Corinthians 5:17! 4 A band. 5.15 Visited. 6 Mr Willis'. 6.15 At the Room. 8.30 Necessary talk with leaders. 10.

WEDNESDAY [MARCH] 4. 5 Dressed. 5.30 2 Timothy 2:5; at Mr Deschamps', chocolate. 7.30 At the School, 1 John 5. 9 Necessary business; Betty Baddily and Spring, tea, religious talk. 10 Writ to Charles, brother Humphreys, Mr Hutchins; necessary business. 3 Bristol; religious talk to a man. 3 At Mrs Vigors', tea, religious talk, prayed. 4.45 At sister Hooper's, sister Reyon, etc. 5.45 At home. 6 The women; supper; the men. 10.30.

THURSDAY [MARCH] 5. 5 Dressed. 5.30 Matthew 6:10; at Mr Deschamps', chocolate. 7.30 At the School, 1 John 5; Mrs Sparkes, tea, religious talk. 10 At home; religious talk. 11 2 Peter 1:10, etc; visited Kitty Davis, Communion. 1 At Mrs England's, dinner; visited many. 3.15 At home; meditated. 4 The women leaders. 6.15 Job 19:15; sister Goodman's band! 8 Society. 9.15 The stewards. 10.45.

FRIDAY [MARCH] 6. 5 Dressed; 1 Timothy 3 *ult;* at Mr Deschamps', tea. 7.30 At the School; necessary business. 10 At Mr Labbè's, religious talk. 11 At home; religious talk to many. 1.30 Prayed. 3 At sister Rawlins', sister England, etc. 4 Visited. 5.15 At the School; necessary talk (religious); coffee. 6.15 1 John 5:17! 8 Our bands! 9.45 Writ diary; necessary business. 11.

SATURDAY [MARCH] 7. 5 Writ for the Society. 7 Tea. 7.30 1 John 5 *ult!* necessary talk (religious) to Nanny Davis. 9.15 At brother Cennick's, tea, religious talk (necessary). 10 At home; writ for United Society. 1 Coffee; writ for Society. 3 Read. 4 The bands; we parted! 6.30 At sister England's, sister Spring and Baddily ill; tea; prayed. 7 2 Peter 1 *ad ult!* 8.30 Writ to Charles; writ notes. 10.30.

SUNDAY [MARCH] 8. 5 Dressed; 1 Corinthians 11; at sister England's, religious talk; at the School, James 3:1. 9.30 Our bands; Sarah Dyer christened. necessary talk (religious) to the bands. 10 Communion; prayed. 12.30 Coffee; read Glass; slept. 2 2 Timothy 2:23, 24. 3.45 At Mr Jones', dinner. 4 Acts 17:23! 5.45 Necessary business. 6 Society. 9 At the School. 9.15.

MONDAY, MARCH 9. 6 Dressed; writ diary; writ journal; tea. 7.15 1 Peter 1:9! necessary talk; journal. 1 At Mr Willis', religious talk, prayed. 2.15 At home; Mr Quin, Yapping, etc, religious talk, tea. 4.15 Journal. 6.30 Ephesians 1:13. 8 The leaders. 8.30 Supper; writ diary. 9.30.

TUESDAY [MARCH] 10. 4 Dressed; walked. 5.30 1 Corinthians 11. 7.30 Romans 8:15, etc. 9.15 Necessary business; writ for the bands. 12 Ended Glass. 1 Dinner; read. 2.30 1 Corinthians 9:21! 4.15 Walked; married. 5.15 At Nanny Smith's, tea, prayed. 6.15 1 Corinthians 9:21. 8 The leaders; necessary talk (religious); visited. 10.

WEDNESDAY [MARCH] 11. 5 Dressed; 1 Corinthians 14:15. 7.30 School; tea; 1 Corinthians 9:27! necessary business. 11 At the Room; religious talk to many. 1 The leaders, necessary talk (religious). 2.45 At sister Stephens', tea. 3.15 Visited many; prayed. 5.30 At Mrs Hooper's, tea, religious talk. 6 The women! supper; the men. 10.30.

THURSDAY [MARCH] 12. 5 Dressed. 5.30 [no entry]. 7.30 Romans 5:1. 10 At home; necessary talk (religious) to some. 11 2 Peter 2; visited. 1 At Mr Wiggington's, dinner, religious talk, prayed. 2.30 Visited many. 5 At Lucretia Wright's, Communion; visited. 6.30 John 4:17; Society. 10.15.

FRIDAY [MARCH] 13. 5 Dressed. 5.30 Psalm 27 *ult!* 7.15 At the School; tea; John 1:9; necessary business. 10 At home; necessary talk (religious) to some; writ notes. 1 Prayed! visited. 3.15 At Mr Hopkins', tea, religious talk. 4.30 Visited Mr Willis, prayed! religious talk. 5.45 At the School; necessary talk (religious); supper. 6.30 Matthew 14; the bands. 9.

SATURDAY [MARCH] 14. 5 Dressed; [writ upon] Predestination; tea, religious talk. 7.30 2 Peter 3; Predestination. 11 Visited sister Peacock, prayed; Susan Oddy, Communion. 1 At William Luton's, dinner; visited Hannah Clear, prayed! Hannah Davis, prayed! 3.30 At home; christened three children. 4 The bands, religious talk, prayed. 6.15 At Nanny Smith's, tea. 7 Malt-room, 2 Peter 3. 8.15 At home; the stewards, necessary talk (religious). 9.45.

SUNDAY, MARCH 15. 4.30 Dressed; Psalm 55:6, 7. 6.15 At sister Bracey's, tea, religious talk. 8 At the School, Psalm 55. 10 St James's, Communion. 1.15 In the coach. 2 At the School, Psalm 55. 3.45 At Mr Deschamps', dinner. 4.15 Psalm 55. 6 Society. 8 At the School; the Love-feast; prayed! 11.

MONDAY [MARCH] 16. 5.15 Writ to Charles, to Sarah Dean; tea. 7.15 Romans 4:7; necessary talk (religious) to some. 9.30 [Writ upon] Predestination. 12.15 Walked; at Charles Arthurs', brother Richards there, dinner. 2 Visited Hannah Davis and Hannah Clear, prayed! 5 At home; tea; writ to Mr Witham. 6.30 Exodus 14:13. The leaders. 9.45.

TUESDAY [MARCH] 17. 4 Coffee; walked. 5.30 Exodus 14:13. 7 At the School, tea. 7.30 Exodus 14:13. 9 Predestination. 11.30 Dressed; walked; visited. 1 At Mrs Reed's, dinner. 2.30 At the School, Genesis 18:25. 5 Visited; at Mr Labbè's, tea, necessary talk (religious). 6.45 Exodus 14. 8 The bands, necessary talk (religious), prayed. 9 The leaders. 10.

WEDNESDAY [MARCH] 18. 4.45 Dressed; Romans 4:7; at brother Deschamps', tea; at the School. 10 Visited; religious talk to some. 1 The leaders, prayed, necessary talk (religious)! 5 At sister Cowin's, Communion! 6 The women [start of penitents' bands], prayed! supper. 8 The men. 10.

THURSDAY [MARCH] 19. 4.45 Dressed; Revelation 7:13; at Miss Purnell's, tea, necessary talk (religious). 7.30 At the School, Revelation 7:13. 10 At home;

necessary talk (religious) to some. 11 Ezekiel 18; visited. 1.15 At brother Cross', dinner, religious talk, sang. 3 Visited Judith Williams! etc. 4 At Mrs Shrewsbury's, tea, religious talk. 5 At home; a band, necessary talk (religious). 6.30 James 3:2. 7.30 Writ diary; supper; Society, prayed! 11.

FRIDAY [MARCH] 20. 4.30 Dressed; religious talk. 5.15 Ecclesiastes 7:20; at sister Hooper's, tea. 7.30 At the School, Ecclesiastes 7:20. 10 At home; religious talk to many. 1.45 Prayed. 3 At sister Stephens', tea, religious talk; visited. 4 At sister Hooper's, sister Norman, etc, religious talk. 6 At the School; necessary business. 7 Slept. 7.30 With the bands, prayed! 8 With sister Robertson, Pottam, etc, tea. 8.45 1 Corinthians 2:6, prayed! 12.30.

SATURDAY [MARCH] 21. [pointing hand in margin] 6 Necessary business; tea, necessary talk (religious). 7.30 1 John 1. 8 Necessary business; necessary talk with many; writ notes. 11:15 Walked. 12 At the Room; letters. 2 At Mrs Vigors', dinner. 4 Christened two [John Davis and Elizabeth Thomas]; at sister Page's, tea, religious talk; visited; writ notes. 7 Malt-room, Ezekiel 33! 8.30 The stewards. 10.

SUNDAY [MARCH] 22. 4.45 Dressed; Philippians 3:13; at sister Rawlins', necessary talk (religious); tea. 8 At the School, Philippians 3:13! 9.30 Christened three [Elizabeth Haskins, Sarah Arthurs, Mary Prig]. 10 At bands, necessary talk (religious). 11 Communion! 1 At sister Cambourn's, dinner, prayed! 1 Isaiah 1:18! 4 At brother Deschamps', tea. 4.45 1 Corinthians 8:1. 6.30 Society! 10 At the School; sins!!

MONDAY [MARCH] 23. 6 Writ notes; tea, 7.30 2 Peter 1. 9 Journal. 1 Walked with sister Baddily and Smith; at Will Kirby's, dinner, religious talk. 3 At Hannah Davis', religious talk, prayed! 4.45 At sister Prig's, tea, religious talk. 5.30 At sister Love's, tea; christened a child. 6 Society; Luke 6:40! 8.45 At home; the leaders. 10.

TUESDAY [MARCH] 24. 4 Walked; 1 Corinthians 8:1; at Mr Deschamps', tea. 7.30 At the School, 2 Peter 1:9, etc; writ notes. 11.30 Visited Hannah Clear, Communion! 1 At Mr Wayne's, dinner, religious talk. 2.30 Visited. 3 At the School, 1 Corinthians 8:1. 5 At sister England's, necessary talk (religious), tea; visited. 6.45 Psalm 145:9! 8 Society. 9.45 At Mrs Deschamps'; necessary business. 10.15.

WEDNESDAY [MARCH] 25. 3.15 Tea, necessary talk (religious). 4.15 Set out. 8.45 Chippenham; tea. 9.30 Set out. 12.45 Marlborough; dinner. 2 Rode. 6 Woolhampton; read Haliburton; supper. 8 In bed; sins.

THURSDAY [MARCH] 26. 4 Necessary business; religious talk. 4.45 Rode. 6.45 Reading; tea. 7.30 Rode. 9.45 Maidenhead; tea, religious talk. 10.30 Rode. 12.30 Hounslow; dinner. 1.30 Rode. 4 At the Foundery; brother Charles, Hall, necessary talk (religious), tea. 6 Matthew 14:27; supper; Society. 9.15 In bed with brother Maxfield, religious talk. 10.

FRIDAY, MARCH 27. 6 Religious talk. 6.30 2 Corinthians 5:13, etc. 8.30 Tea; Society, necessary talk (religious). 10 St Luke's, Communion. 1 At home; Society; prayed. 3 Tea, necessary talk (religious) with Charles. 4 Writ diary; meditated; prayed. 4.30 Isaiah 1:18! 7.45 Supper; Society. 8.45 Religious talk with Charles, etc. 9.15 In bed with Charles; necessary talk (religious). 10.

S<small>ATURDAY</small> [M<small>ARCH</small>] 28. 5.15 Dressed; religious talk. 6 John 1:1, etc. 7.15 Necessary business; necessary talk (religious). 8 Spangenberg, Böhler, Marschall, and brother Hall, tea, religious talk. 10 At brother Whitefield's, necessary talk (religious)! 12.15 At home; religious talk to some. 1 Dinner; Sir John Ganson came, necessary talk; necessary business. 2.30 Read notes. 4.30 At sister Edzard's, tea, religious talk; visited Dickenson. 6 Acts 19. 8 At home; the bands; necessary talk (religious), prayed. 10.

S<small>UNDAY</small> [M<small>ARCH</small>] 29. 5 Dressed; necessary talk (religious). 6.30 Colossians 1:1, etc! 8.30 The leaders. 10 St Luke's, Communion. 2 At brother Hobbins' dinner, religious talk. 3 Visited. 3.30 At home; the men leaders. 4.45 1 Corinthians 1:30! 6.30 Supper. 7.15 The bands. 8 The Love-feast; George Whitefield and Cennick came, prayed! 10.15.

M<small>ONDAY</small> [M<small>ARCH</small>] 30. 4.45 The leaders; necessary talk (religious). 6.30 John 1:9, etc! 8.30 The three bands. 8.45 At brother Waldron's, religious talk, tea; visited. 11 Necessary talk (religious) to many. 3 Tea, religious talk. 4 Mr Hollis, prayed; Haliburton. 5.45 Ezekiel 18! 7.30 Religious talk to some; supper, necessary talk (religious). 9.15 Writ diary.

T<small>UESDAY</small> [M<small>ARCH</small>] 31. 5.15 Necessary talk (religious); necessary business. 6.30 John 1:13, etc. 8.30 Three bands. 10 At Dr Rowdon's, tea, religious talk. 11 At home; religious talk to many. 2.30 At sister Crouch's, dinner. 4 Visited; Communion. 5 At sister Crouch's, tea. 6 At home; Charles preached; necessary talk to Sir John Ganson. 8 The bands; necessary talk (religious), prayed. 10.15.

W<small>EDNESDAY</small>, A<small>PRIL</small> 1. 5.30 Necessary talk (religious). 6 John 2. 7.15 Three bands. 8.30 Tea; necessary business; sins. 9.45 Visited sister Wilde, prayed. 10 At home; religious talk to many. 2.30 Visited. 3 At the New Prison! 5 At home; C Metcalf, Charles, tea, religious talk. 6 Charles preached; supper. 8 The leaders; necessary talk (religious), prayed! 10.

T<small>HURSDAY</small>, A<small>PRIL</small> 2. 5.15 Necessary talk (religious); John 3; three bands. 8.30 Tea; necessary business. 10 Religious talk to brother Humphreys, to many. 2.45 At sister Allar's, dinner, religious talk; at sister England's. 4.45 At Mrs Motte's, tea, religious talk. 6 Habakkuk 3 *ult!* supper; Society. 10.

F<small>RIDAY</small> [A<small>PRIL</small>] 3. 2.30 Necessary business; slept. 3.30 Tea; Charles went; slept. 5.30 Dressed; necessary business. 6 John 3:8; three bands. 8.30 Tea, necessary talk (religious); necessary business. 10 Religious talk to many. 1 Prayed. 3 Visited Mrs Redford; Standex; at brother Thornton's, tea; at Mrs Lane's, tea. 6 Short's Gardens, Romans 7; at brother Hall's. 8.45 At home; supper. 9.30.

S<small>ATURDAY</small> [A<small>PRIL</small>] 4. 5.30 Dressed; necessary talk (religious). 6 John 3:14! three bands. 8.30 Tea; necessary business. 10.15 In the coach with George Whitefield, brother Hall, etc, religious talk. 12.30 At Mrs Sparrow's, necessary talk (religious), sang, dinner. 3 Coach; religious talk. 4.30 Visited; at Mrs Hawthorn's, tea, religious talk. 6 Long Lane, Acts 19. 8 The bands; prayed! 9.15 Sins.

S<small>UNDAY</small> [A<small>PRIL</small>] 5. 5 Prayed; tea, necessary talk (religious). 6.15 Philippians 3. 8.45 The women leaders. 10 St Paul's. 1 At brother Hall's, dinner. 2.30 At home; writ for bands. 4 Tea, religious talk. 4.30 Philippians 3! 6.30 Necessary talk (religious); supper. 7 The bands. 9.30 Brother Humphreys, religious talk, prayed. 10.30.

M ONDAY [A PRIL] 6. 5.15 Dressed; necessary talk (religious). 6 John 3 ((*ult*)); three bands. 8.30 At ((sister Williams')); tea, religious talk. 10 At home; Peter Böhler; religious talk to many. 2.45 At sister Baddily's, dinner; at sister Knight's, tea, religious talk. 5 At St Thomas's Hospital, spoke, prayed; at Guy's Hospital, religious talk, prayed. 6.30 Acts 20. 9.15 At home; necessary talk (religious) with brother Hall. 10.

T UESDAY [A PRIL] 7. 5 Dressed; prayed. 6 John 3 *ult;* the bands. 8.30 At sister Williams', tea, religious talk. 10 Necessary talk (religious) to many. 2.30 At brother Smatherst's, dinner! 4 At sister Barnes', tea, religious talk, prayed! 5 At Nancy Young's, tea, religious talk. 6 At home; Philippians 3! necessary business. 8 The bands. 10.30 Necessary talk (religious) with brother Hall. 11.

W EDNESDAY, A PRIL 8. 5 Dressed; prayed. 6 John 4; the bands. 8.15 At sister Price's, tea, religious talk. 9.15 Visited; Communion. 10 At home; writ notes; religious talk to some. 1.15 Writ diary; religious talk. 2 Christened Charles Bean. 4 Deptford; at brother Giles', christened. 5 At Charlton; brother Wollard's, religious talk, prayed. 5.45 Deptford, Ezekiel 36:20. 8 At home; supper. 8.30 At bands. 10.15.

T HURSDAY [A PRIL] 9. 5.15 Dressed; prayed. 6 John 4! the bands. 8.30 At Nanny Morris', tea, religious talk, prayed! 10 At home; religious talk to many. 2 At brother Nash's [Mash's?], dinner, religious talk, prayed. 3.30 At sister England's, tea, religious talk. 4.30 At home; brother Humphreys, religious talk. 6 Philippians 3; writ to Charles, to Nanny Smith. 8 Society. 10.

F RIDAY [A PRIL] 10. 5 Prayed; writ; religious talk. 6 John 4: 18, etc! 7 The bands. 8.15 At Mary Hilson's, tea, religious talk; visited sister Sutherland. 10.15 At home; religious talk to many. 1.15 Prayed! 3 Visited; at brother Hall's. 3 At Mrs Motte's; at Short's Gardens, necessary talk (religious); necessary business. 5 At Mrs Motte's, tea, religious talk. 6 Short's Gardens, Romans 8:1! 8 At Mrs MacCune's, Matthew Clark, religious talk, supper! 10.45 At home; sins.

S ATURDAY [A PRIL] 11. 5 Prayed; journal. 6 John 4 *ad ult;* journal. 8 Tea, Sir John Ganson, necessary talk. 9 Journal; rode.1.15 Walked; Short's Gardens; Vertue's, necessary talk. 2.30 At brother Dawson's, dinner, religious talk. 4.15 At sister Ketteridge's, tea, religious talk; Mrs Ball! at Mrs Mash's, religious talk. 6 Long Lane, Acts 20! the bands. 10.

S UNDAY [A PRIL] 12. 5 Necessary talk (religious); tea. 6.15 Ecclesiastes 7:20. 8.45 The leaders. 10 St Paul's. 1 At home; tea; writ notes. 3 The men leaders. 4.45 James 3:2! 7 Supper; the bands! 9.45 Necessary talk (religious). 10.

M ONDAY, A PRIL 13. 5 Prayed; necessary talk. 6 John 5; the bands. 8.30 At sister Aspernell's, tea, religious talk. 9.30 At home; necessary talk (religious) to many. 2.45 At Islington; Mrs Witham's, dinner. 4 ((At sister Ketteridge's, Mrs Ball there, religious talk, tea; At Mrs Mash's, religious talk)). 6.30 At Long Lane, Acts 20! 9 At home; necessary talk (religious). 10.

T UESDAY [A PRIL] 14. 5 Prayed; necessary talk (religious); writ. 6 John 5; the bands. 8.30 At sister Vandome's, tea, religious talk, prayed! visited! 10 At home; religious talk to many. 2.15 At brother Smagg's, dinner, religious talk. 4 At sister Malton's, tea, religious talk. 5 At sister Horner's, religious talk! 6 John 4:20! religious talk to Charles. 8.15 At bands! 10.

WEDNESDAY [APRIL] 15. 5 Prayed; necessary talk (religious). 6 John 5. 7.15 Set out. 9 At Lord Huntingdon's; with Lady Huntingdon, religious talk, tea. 12 Romans 5! 1.30 Religious talk with her. 2.30 Dinner, religious talk with her and him. 4.15 Rode. 6 Greyhound Lane, Ephesians 4 *ult.* 8 At home; supper. 9 The bands. 10.

THURSDAY [APRIL] 16. 5 Prayed; writ notes. 6 John 5. 7 The bands. 8 Spangenberg, tea, religious talk. 9.15 Read Poiret. 10 Charles Kinchin, necessary talk (religious). 11 Religious talk to many. 2 At brother Doleman's, christened his son. 4.30 Visited. 6 At home; Acts 2.27, etc; ate. 8 Society. 10.

FRIDAY [APRIL] 17. 5.15 Read Poiret. 6 John 5; the bands. 8.15 At brother Blake's, tea, religious talk. 9.15 Visited. 10.30 At home; religious talk to many. 1.30 Prayed! 3 At sister Prengnell's, tea, religious talk. 4.30 At Mrs Motte's, tea. 5.30 At Short's Gardens; Mrs Flemming's, tea, religious talk. 6 Romans 8:29, 30! 8.30 At Mrs MacCune's, supper, religious talk. 11.

SATURDAY, APRIL 18. [pointing hand in margin] 5.15 Dressed; necessary business. 6 John 5:35! 7 Writ upon Predestination. 8 Charles Kinchin came, tea, religious talk. 9 Writ. 12 Read letters. 2 Dinner, necessary talk (religious). 3 Letters. 5.15 At sister Bird's, tea, religious talk. 6 Long Lane, Acts 21. 8.15 The bands; prayed! 10.

SUNDAY [APRIL] 19. 5.15 Necessary business; tea, religious talk. 6.30 Psalm 55:5, 6. 8.45 The leaders. 10 St Paul's. 1.45 At brother West's, he married! 2.30 At home; writ; Society. 3 The men leaders. 4 Tea, religious talk. 4.45 Psalm 55. 6 Supper. 7.15 The bands; prayed! 10.

MONDAY [APRIL] 20. 5 Prayed; necessary business. 6 John 6; the bands; Böhler came. 8.15 At sister Broad's, tea, religious talk; visited. 10.30 At home; religious talk to many; dinner; religious talk to many. 2.45 Writ for Society. 4.30 At sister Miller's, tea, religious talk. 5.30 Visited. 6.30 Long Lane, Acts 22:9; at home; necessary business. 10 1 Samuel 30:19.

TUESDAY [APRIL] 21. 4.45 Necessary business; writ. 5.30 John 6. 6.30 Necessary talk (religious) to some. 7 Writ for the Society. 8.30 Tea, necessary talk (religious). 9 Writ for the United Society. 12 Writ to Charles, to brother Nowers. 2 At Mr Strahan's, dinner, mostly religious talk. 3.45 At Nancy Burton's, sister Barnes and Bowman, necessary talk (religious), tea. 5 At sister Horner's, tea, religious talk. 6 At home; necessary talk (religious). 6.30 Zechariah 4:6; religious talk to brother Baddily. 8 Society. 10 Sins.

WEDNESDAY [APRIL] 22. 4.45 Prayed; writ for Society. 5.30 John 6; the bands. 7.30 Writ for Society. 8.15 At Ruth Jaggers', tea, religious talk. 9.30 Writ for Society. 9.45 Religious talk to many. 2.30 Communion. 3 Visited. 3.30 At sister Ibbison's, tea, religious talk. 4.30 At sister Roberts', tea, religious talk; visited. 6 At sister Hall's. 7 At Short's Gardens, Romans 8:15! 8.15 At home; supper. 9 The bands! 10.30.

THURSDAY, APRIL 23. 5 Necessary business; necessary talk (religious). 5.30 John 6; the bands. 8.15 At Mary Burnet's, tea, religious talk. 10 Religious talk to many. 2 At Mrs Scott's, dinner, religious talk. 4 At brother Church's, tea, religious talk. 4.30 At the Barn, Luke 6:40. 6.45 At home; Isaiah 30:12. 8 Society. 10.

FRIDAY [APRIL] 24. 5 Prayed; necessary business; Knolton came, religious talk. 5.45 John 6 *ult.* 6.30 Religious talk to many. 7 The bands. 8.15 At brother Moreton's, tea, religious talk; visited! 9 At Suky Marriot's, tea, religious talk. 10.15 Religious talk to many. 1.30 Prayed! necessary talk (religious). 4 At Mrs Redford's, Communion. 5 At sister Hall's; at sister Scolefield's, tea. 5.30 At Mrs Stockdale's, religious talk; visited. 6.15 Short's Gardens, Romans 8:2! 8.15 At Mrs MacCune's, Matthew Clark, Miss Witham; supper; saw him! 11.

SATURDAY [APRIL] 25. 5 Prayed; necessary talk (religious). 5.30 John 7. 6.45 Writ for Society. 8.15 Tea, necessary talk (religious). 9 Writ. 10 Peter Böhler, necessary talk (religious)! 12 Writ to Charles; writ notes. 2 Coach with Mrs Scott, read upon Predestination. 4 Charlton; brother Wollard's, Communion. 4.45 Deptford, Philippians 3:13. 6.45 Long Lane, Acts 23. 8.30 At home; supper; the bands. 10.30.

SUNDAY [APRIL] 26. 5.15 Dressed; tea, religious talk. 6.15 Romans 8:29! the leaders. 10 St Paul's, Communion. 1 At Mrs Clark's, dinner, religious talk! visited. 2.45 At home; the leaders, tea. 5.30 Marylebone, Isaiah 1:18. 7 Short's Gardens; the bands. 10.30 At home; sins!

MONDAY [APRIL] 27. 5 Dressed; necessary talk (religious). 5.30 2 Corinthians 3:17; the bands. 8.15 At sister Angus'; tea, religious talk. 9.45 At home; religious talk to many. 2 Set out; in the chaise. 3.15 At Mary Clavel's, dinner, necessary talk (religious). 4 At the Barn, Romans 8:29! 7 Long Lane, Acts 24. 9 At home; supper, necessary talk (religious). 9.45.

TUESDAY APRIL 28. 5 Prayed. 5.30 2 Corinthians 3:17; writ to George Whitefield. 8.15 Tea, religious talk. 11 Writ to brother Humphreys and Charles. 1.30 Walked. 3 Deptford. 4 The Society, at brother Giles'. 4.45 In the boat. 6 At home; tea. 6 2 Corinthians 3:17; Society, read George Whitefield's, letter! prayed. 9.45.

WEDNESDAY [APRIL] 29. 5 Prayed. 5.30 1 Corinthians 9:21; the bands. 8 At sister Shaw's, tea, religious talk. 9.15 At home; writ notes. 10 Religious talk to many; Spangenberg, religious talk! 12 Went to Mr Marriot, prayed! 1.15 At home; religious talk to many; prayed. 2.45 At Mrs Nightingale's, dinner, religious talk. 4.30 At sister Haddock's, tea, religious talk; at sister Morison's. 6 Greyhound Lane, Ezekiel 36:25! 8 At home; the bands, prayed! 10.45.

THURSDAY [APRIL] 30. 5 Prayed; 1 Corinthians 9:21; the bands. 8.15 At sister Sweeting's, tea, religious talk. 9.15 At sister Aspernell's, Communion. 10 At home; religious talk to many. 2.15 At brother Wilkinson's, dinner, religious talk. 3.30 At sister Catison's, tea, religious talk, prayed! 5.15 At Mrs Doleman's, necessary talk (religious). 6 At home; necessary business. 6.30 1 Corinthians 9:21; necessary talk (religious). 8.30 Society. 10.15.

FRIDAY, MAY 1. 5 Dressed; prayed. 5.30 1 Corinthians 9:21; the bands. 8.15 At

Nanny Morris', religious talk, tea. 9.30 At sister Horner's, religious talk! 10 At home; religious talk to many. 1.30 Prayed. 2.45 Mr Bate of Deptford, necessary talk (religious); visited. 5 At sister Mann's, religious talk, tea. 6.15 Short's Gardens, Romans 8:4, etc. 9 At brother Bray's, Peter Böhler's Love-feast! seven of us. 10 Prayed. 10.45.

SATURDAY [MAY] 2. 5 Dressed; prayed; Romans 5:13; writ upon Predestination. 8 Spangenberg, Böhler, Nanny Morris, etc, tea, religious talk! 11.30 Writ upon Predestination. 1.30 Necessary business; dinner. 2.30 Visited some. 4 At Mr Lee's, tea, religious talk. 5 Visited; at the hospitals. 6.15 2 Corinthians 5:17. 8.15 At home; the bands. 10.30.

SUNDAY [MAY] 3. 5 Prayed; dressed; tea. 6 2 Corinthians 5:17. 8 The leaders. 10 St Martin's, Communion. 1 At Mr Keen's, Peter Böhler, dinner, religious talk. 2.30 Short's Garden; the leaders. 4.30 At sister Flemmer's [Flemming's?], tea, religious talk. 5.30 Marylebone [Fields], Micah 6:7! 7 At Short's Gardens; tea; the bands. 10 At home; sins.

MONDAY, MAY 4. 5 Prayed; John 7; the bands. 8 Sister Perrin, religious talk. 8.30 At Hannah Wainwright's, tea, religious talk. 9.15 Writ notes; religious talk to many. 2.30 At brother Garnault's, dinner, religious talk; visited; at Mr Hobbins, Senior's, tea, religious talk. 4.30 At sister Baddily's, Sally Loyd, necessary talk (religious). 5 At sister Hawthorn's, she ill, Communion! 6 Guy's Hospital, Betty Patrick. 6.45 Acts 25. 8.45 At home; read notes; supper. 10.15.

TUESDAY [MAY] 5. 5 Prayed; John 8; writ journal. 8 Tea, religious talk; journal. 12.15 Necessary business; read notes. 3 Deptford; brother Giles, dinner, necessary talk (religious). 3.45 The Dancing Room, 2 Corinthians 5:17. 6.30 At home; Ecclesiastes 12:1! 8.30 Writ to Charles; read his journal. 10.15.

WEDNESDAY [MAY] 6. 5 Prayed; John 8; the bands; sister Harrison's, tea, religious talk. 10 At home; religious talk to many. 1.15 The bands, prayed; —— christened! 3.15 Visited some. 5 At sister Esther Kent's, tea, religious talk. 6 Greyhound Lane, Luke 7 *ad fin.* 8 The bands. 10.

THURSDAY [MAY] 7. 5 Prayed; John 8; at sister Knight's, tea. 7.45 With sister Gaskarth. 9 In the chaise; read Bird. 10 Bexley; read Prayers, Communion. 1 At Mr Piers', read my letter to him; dinner, religious talk. 3 Chaise; read. 6.15 At home; tea; Psalm 145:9! Society! 10.15.

FRIDAY [MAY] 8. 5 Prayed; John 8; the bands. 8.15 At sister Sutton's, tea, religious talk. 9.45 At home; religious talk to many. 1.30 Prayed. 3 Visited; at brother Standex's, religious talk. 4.30 At sister Motte's, tea, religious talk. 5 Short's Gardens. 5.15 Romans 8:7-15. 8.30 At Mrs MacCune's, supper; prayed with him. 11.15.

SATURDAY, MAY 9. Ill. 6.30 Dressed; writ notes; read. 8 Tea; lay down. 9 Read. 1.30 Visited. 2 At Mr Wathen's, dinner, religious talk. 4.15 At Mr Hawthorn's, tea, religious talk. 6 Long Lane, 1 Corinthians 15. 8.15 At home; the Society. 10.

SUNDAY [MAY] 10. 6.15 Ill; Proverbs 23:26; the leaders. 9.15 Slept. 10.15 Communion. 11.15 Lay down; read. 12.30 Dinner; lay down. 2.15 The men leaders. 4.15 Tea. 4.45 1 Corinthians 8:1! 7 The Love-feast; prayed! well! 9.15.

MONDAY [MAY] 11. 5 Prayed; John 9; the bands. 8.15 Tea; read Poiret; writ notes. 10 Religious talk to many. 2 Dinner; religious talk to many. 3.45 Visited sister Harper, brother Martin, Joseph Johnson, Mrs Kent; Communion. 5.15 At Mrs Baddily's, tea. 6.15 Long Lane, Acts 26. 8.15 At home; supper; read notes. 9.30.

TUESDAY [MAY] 12. 5:15 Prayed; John 10; the bands. 8.30 Sister Perrin, Nanny Morris, etc. 9 Tea, religious talk; writ for Society. 11 Religious talk to many. 1.30 In the coach with Mrs Seaton and Bolt. 3 At brother Brown's, Deptford, dinner. 4 1 Corinthians 8:1. 6.30 At home; Luke 17:10! 8 The overseers of the poor. 10.

WEDNESDAY [MAY] 13. 5 Prayed; John 10; read notes. 8.30 In the coach with S Hawthorn and brother Merrick; read Poiret. 1 At Mr Hawthorn's, Mrs Hawthorn buried. 2 Dinner; tea, necessary talk (religious). 5 In the coach; Poiret. 8.15 At home; supper; the bands; Mr Hall! 10.30.

THURSDAY [MAY] 14. 5 Prayed; John 10; the bands. 8 At Mrs Flewit's, tea, religious talk. 9.30 Religious talk to many. 2.15 At Mr Cleland's, dinner, necessary talk (religious). 3.30 Visited many. 6.30 Luke 17:10! Society, Nanny Morris ill. 10.30.

FRIDAY [MAY] 15. 5 Prayed; John 10; bands. 8 At Nanny Morris', religious talk, prayed; Dr Newton's, tea, religious talk. 10 Religious talk to many. 1 Prayed! tea. 3.15 Visited many. 6.15 Short's Gardens, Romans 8! 8.45 At home; read notes. 10.

SATURDAY [MAY] 16. [pointing hand in margin] 5 Prayed; John 10; necessary talk (religious). 7 Writ notes. 8 Tea; writ to Charles, to Nowers; Peter Böhler, religious talk; writ. 12 Read letters; prayed! 2 Dinner. 3 Letters; prayed! 5 Visited. 7 Ratcliff Highway, Acts 2 *ult.* 9 At home; the bands. 10.

SUNDAY [MAY] 17. 5 Prayed; tea. 6 John 16:9, etc. 8 The leaders. 10 Communion. 1 At home; dinner; writ diary. 2.15 The leaders. 4 At Nanny Morris', Communion. 4.45 Charles Square, John 14. 6.30 At sister Waldron's, tea, religious talk. 7.15 The bands. 9 Mr Hall came, prayed. 10.15.

MONDAY [MAY] 18. 3.15 Necessary business. 4 Rode. 7.30 Colnbrook; tea. 9 Rode. 12.15 Reading; religious talk to strangers; dinner. 1.45 Rode. 6 Hungerford; supper; read. 8.

TUESDAY, MAY 19. 4 Necessary business. 4.30 Rode. 7.45 Marlborough; my horse lame; tea, necessary talk (religious). 9 Rode. 12.30 Chippenham; dinner. 1.30 Rode. 6 Kingswood School; Betty Bush, etc, prayed. 7 At Mr Deschamps'. 7.30 At the Room, prayed! 8.15 Society; prayed; supper. 10.

WEDNESDAY [MAY] 20. 6.45 Dressed; the women leaders. 8.30 At sister Downes', religious talk, tea, prayed. 9.30 At home; religious talk to many. 1.30 Prayed; at sister England's, prayed; at sister Cox's, Communion! 3 At Mrs Norman's, tea, religious talk. 4 The select band. 6 At the Room. 7 Supper; the bands, prayed! 10.

THURSDAY [MAY] 21. 4.30 Dressed; Micah 1:9, etc! 7 At brother Sayse's, tea, religious talk, prayed. 9 Necessary business. 9.30 Religious talk to many. 12.30

At Mr Willis', dinner. 2.30 Kendleshire, Habakkuk 3 *ult!* 5.30 At Mr Martin's, tea, religious talk. 6 Romans 8:29! 8.15 Supper. 9 Society. 10.

FRIDAY, MAY 22. 4.45 Dressed; Revelation 3; at Dr Bainton's, tea, necessary talk (religious). 8 Visited. 9 At home; necessary business; religious talk to many. 1.15 Prayed; at brother Hooper's, tea, religious talk; at sister England's, tea, religious talk; at sister Holder's. 6 Kingswood; necessary business; read notes. 8 Tea, religious talk. 8.30 Romans 8:29! prayed. 12.30.

SATURDAY [MAY] 23. 7 Dressed; tea. 8 Preached; visited many. 1 At Mrs England's. 2 Dinner, religious talk; visited. 5 Kingswood; the bands; prayed. 7.15 At the Room. 8 Necessary talk (religious); the stewards. 10 Walked. 11.30 School.

SUNDAY [MAY] 24. 6.30 Tea; the Kendleshire bands. 8 1 John 3:5; christened; the bands; Communion! 12.30 Sister Rawlins came. 1 At John Ashmishaw's, dinner, religious talk; visited in Kingswood. 4 At the Room; dressed. 5 Baptist Mills, Romans 8:29. 6 Charles there (five thousand there). 6.30 At Mrs Bessel's, tea. 7.30 At home; necessary talk (religious) with sister Purnell. 8 Society; prayed! 10 At brother Deschamps'; supper. 10.30.

MONDAY [MAY] 25. 3.15 Dressed; tea. 4.30 Rode with brother Nowers, religious talk. 8.15 Chippenham; tea. 9 Rode. 12.15 Marlborough; dinner. 1 Rode. 4.45 Newbury. 5.30 Rode. 8.30 Reading; supper. 9.30 Sins.

TUESDAY [MAY] 26. 5 Dressed. 5.45 Rode. 9 Windsor; at brother Larwood's, tea, necessary talk (religious). 11 At the Society Room, Ephesians 2:8! 12.30 At brother Larwood's. 1 Rode with him. 2.15 Colnbrook; religious talk. 3.15 Rode. 6 At home; tea. 6.45 Exodus 14:13. 8 The leaders, necessary talk (religious), prayed. 10.

WEDNESDAY [MAY] 27. 5 Dressed; prayed. 5.30 John 11; the bands. 8 At brother Wilkinson's, tea, religious talk; visited. 9.30 At home; slept. 10 Religious talk to many; writ to Mr Hutchins. 1 Dinner. 1.30 The bands, religious talk, prayed; visited. 4.30 At Mrs Fox's, tea, religious talk, prayed! 5.30 At sister Haddock's. 6 Greyhound Lane, Luke 16:2. 8 At home; supper; the bands. 10.

THURSDAY, MAY 28. 5 Dressed; John 11; the bands. 8 Tea; writ to Charles, George May, El Hudgson, etc. 12 Read notes. 2 At Mr Watkins', religious talk; dinner; prayed. 4 Visited many. 6 At home; tea. 6.30 Ephesians 4. 8 Society! 10.

FRIDAY [MAY] 29. 5 Dressed; prayed; John 11; at bands. 8.15 Hackney; at Mr Clare's [Clear's?], tea, religious talk. 9.30 At home; necessary talk (religious). 11 At brother Hall's. 12 Read Prayers; his child christened. 1 At brother Hall's, dinner, religious talk; brother Richards and Hales came. 3.15 At Mrs Motte's, religious talk, tea. 4.15 At Mrs MacCune's, with him, prayed! 5 Tea; at Mr Bridges'. 6.15 Short's Gardens, Romans 8:16! 8.30 At home; supper; visited Isaiah Allison, religious talk, prayed. 10.15.

SATURDAY, MAY 30. 5 Prayed; John 12; religious talk to some. 7 Corrected our hymns. 8 Tea; corrected. 1 Dinner; read notes. 3 Visited many. 5 At Mrs Hawthorn's, etc; at Sarah Perrin's, tea, religious talk. 6 Long Lane, Acts 26:24! 8 At home; the women! 10.

SUNDAY [MAY] 31. 5 Tea; necessary talk (religious). 6 Romans 9:18. 8 The leaders. 10 St Paul's, Communion. 1.30 At home; writ notes; etc; the leaders. 5 Hoxton, Philippians 3. 6.30 Sister Aspernell's, tea, religious talk. 7.30 The leaders. 10.

MONDAY, JUNE 1. 5 Prayed; dressed; John 12; the bands. 7.30 Rode. 9 Enfield Chase, tea, religious talk; Mr Hall came. 11 Set out. 12.30 At Mrs Witham's, dinner. 1.30 At home; religious talk to many. 3.15 Visited many. 6.30 Long Lane, Acts 26! 9 Deptford; supper; the Society, necessary talk (religious), prayed. 11.30.

TUESDAY [JUNE] 2. 3.30 Dressed; tea. 4.30 Rode in the chair with Merrick; read. 6 At Mr Piers', religious talk. 6.30 Zechariah 4:7, etc! 8 Tea, religious talk. 10 In the chair with him, necessary talk (religious). 12 At Mrs Maylor's, necessary talk (religious). 12.30 At Mrs Sparrow's, necessary talk (religious), dinner. 3.30 Deptford, Zechariah 4:7. 6.30 At home; Acts 26! supper. 8 The leaders. 10.

WEDNESDAY [JUNE] 3. 5 Prayed; dressed; John 13; the bands. 8.45 At Mr Vertue's. 11 At Mrs MacCune's, religious talk. 12 At sister Motte's, dinner. 1 At home; religious talk to some. 2 Christened many! [Mary Foster (age 19), Mary Patterson (age 6), Dorcas Walker (age 13), Will Davis, and Hannah Ryans.] 3 Communion! tea. 5 Visited. 6 Greyhound Lane, 2 Corinthians 6:1! 8 At home; supper; the bands. 10.

THURSDAY [JUNE] 4. 5 Prayed; dressed; John 13; the bands. 8 Tea; writ notes. 9 Religious talk to many. 3 Dinner. 4 Visited. 6 At home; tea; 2 Corinthians 6:1! 8 Supper; Society! 10.

FRIDAY [JUNE] 5. 5 Dressed; John 13; bands. 9 At Mr Vertue's. 12 At home; religious talk to many. 1.30 Prayed! 3 Tea, necessary talk (religious). 4 At James Hutton's, tea, religious talk. 5 At Mrs MacCune's; at brother Osgood's, tea, religious talk. 6.15 Short's Gardens, Romans 8. 8 At Mrs MacCune's; supper. 10.

SATURDAY [JUNE] 6. 5 Prayed; John 13; religious talk to many; writ journal. 8 At sister Wilde's, religious talk, tea. 9 Journal; necessary business. 12 Religious talk to many. 2.15 At brother Doleman's, dinner, religious talk; necessary business. 4 At sister Hughes', necessary talk (religious); visited. 5 At brother Windsor's, tea, religious talk. 6 Long Lane, Acts 28; Society! 10.

SUNDAY [JUNE] 7. 5 Religious talk to some; tea. 6 Hebrews 2:9. 8.30 The leaders. 10 St Paul's, Communion. 12.45 At brother Bond's, dinner. 2 At home; necessary business; the leaders. 4 Tea. 4.45 Charles Square, John 5:25, rain! 6.30 The Love-feast; prayed! 7.30 Rode. 9 Lady Huntingdon's, necessary talk (religious). 10.30 Supper. 11 Ephesians 2:8! 10 [sic].

MONDAY [JUNE] 8. 3.30 Dressed; tea, religious talk. 4.30 Set out in the chaise with Mr Howard. 9.30 Dunstable; tea. 11 Set out. 3.30 Newport Pagnell; coffee. 4.30 Set out. 8.30 Northampton; supper. 10.15.

TUESDAY [JUNE] 9. 4 Dressed. 4.45 Set out. 8.30 [Market] Harborough; tea. 9.30 Set out. 10.45 Leicester; Mr Craddock's, his son, necessary talk (religious). 1 Dinner. 3.30 Set out. 5.15 Markfield; Mr Ellis', necessary talk (religious); G Angel and Clapham, necessary talk (religious). 7 Walked; necessary talk (religious) to brother Angel. 8 Bagworth; at Mr Exon's, Matthew 24:42! 10.15

At home; necessary talk (religious), tea. 11.30 Prayed.

WEDNESDAY [JUNE] 10. 7 Writ to brother Maxfield; writ diary; tea, necessary talk (religious). 8.30 Romans 14:17. 10:30 At home; necessary talk. 11 Set out with David Taylor and Mr Howard. 1 [Long?] Whatton; ate, religious talk. 1.30 Walked, religious talk. 3 At Joseph Caladine's, religious talk, ate. 4.30 Walked; at George Morley's, prayed. 6 Ockbrook; at Mr Greaves', necessary talk (religious). 7.30 Heard Mr Simpson. 8 Exodus 14:13. 9.30 At Mr Greaves' tea, necessary talk (religious). 10 At Jane Cooper's, religious talk, prayed. 11.

THURSDAY [JUNE] 11. 5.15 Journal. 7 At Mr Greaves', tea, religious talk. 8.30 Ephesians 2:8. 11 Walked. 12.30 Smalley; with Mr Richardson, mostly religious talk. 2 Dinner, mostly religious talk. 3 Walked. 6 Nottingham; Mr Howe's, tea, religious talk; Peter Böhler and Charles Kinchin came. 8.30 Society, Acts 16:30. 10.15.

FRIDAY [JUNE] 12. 5.15 Journal. 7.15 Tea, necessary talk (religious). 8.30 Romans 14:17. 10 Walked with Mr Howe and Thomas. 11 They went. 2.30 Loughborough; Mrs Perkins came, tea, religious talk. 3.45 Walked. 4.45 At David Taylor's, religious talk, prayed. 6.30 Markfield; tea. 7.30 Isaiah 53:5, 6! 9.15 Necessary talk (religious); supper; prayed. 10.15.

SATURDAY [JUNE] 13. [pointing finger in margin] 5 Journal. 7 Tea, necessary talk (religious). 8.15 Romans 4:5. 10 Rode with David Taylor and brother Clapham. 12.30 Melbourne; at Mr Memry's; journal. 2 Dinner; upon the Common, Acts 5:30, etc. 4.15 Tea. 5 Rode. 6.30 Hemington; supper. 7 Acts 16:30! 9.15 At Mr Caladine's, religious talk, prayed! 10.30.

SUNDAY, JUNE 14. 4.45 Dressed; prayed. 5 Rode. 7 Nottingham; Mr Howe's, tea, religious talk. 8 At the Cross, John 5:25. 9.30 Religious talk to some. 10 Rode. 2 Markfield; necessary talk (religious). 3 Dinner. 4 Read Prayers. 5 Hosea 14:4. 6 At Mrs Bacon's, tea, religious talk. 7 Writ. 7.30 Luke 6! 9 At home; supper; prayed. 10.30.

MONDAY [JUNE] 15. 4 Dressed; tea; prayed. 5.30 Rode in the chaise; read Luther on the Galatians. 9.45 [Market] Harborough; journal; tea, religious talk. 11 Rode; Luther. 2.30 Northampton; read Ignatius. 3.30 In the chaise; Ignatius. 8.15 Husborne [Crawley]; journal. 9 Supper; prayed. 9.45.

TUESDAY [JUNE] 16. 4.15 Dressed; writ diary. 5.30 Rode; Ignatius. 9.15 St Albans; tea, necessary talk (religious). 11 Set out. 2 Enfield; Mrs Hutton and Mrs Spangenberg, read my journal, necessary talk (religious). 3.30 Rode. 5 London; at home; brother Nowers, necessary talk (religious); the leaders, tea, necessary talk (religious). 6.30 Galatians 5:6! 7.45 Supper; Society; prayed! 10.

WEDNESDAY [JUNE] 17. 5.15 Dressed; John 14:1-4! 7 Religious talk to many. 7.45 Necessary business; tea; visited. 9.30 Rode. 12.30 Uxbridge; tea. 1.30 Rode. 3.30 At Wycombe; brother Bedder's, tea, religious talk. 5 Rode. 7.30 Tetsworth; rode. 9.30 Oxford; at Mr Evans', supper, prayed. 11.

THURSDAY [JUNE] 18. 6 Necessary business; writ diary. 7.45 Tea, religious talk; writ to Nowers; read letters. 11 At College; at Mr Vesey's, necessary talk. 12 At home; necessary business; dinner; Mr Gambold, necessary talk (religious). 2.30 Writ to Charles; necessary business. 5 In the Grove; meditated; read letters;

read Prayers, Job 31! 6.15 At home; tea, religious talk. 7.15 At Mears' Society (fourteen there!), prayed! Luke 22. 8.45 At home; meditated; prayed. 9.30.

FRIDAY [JUNE] 19. 5.15 Meditated; writ notes. 6 Grove; meditated; read Prayers. 7.14 At home; writ to John Cennick. 8 Tea; writ to brother Ingham, Mr Ellis, Nanny Smith, Lady Huntingdon. 12 Writ plan for sermon. 3 Tea; sermon. 5 Grove; meditated; read Prayers. 6 Mr Allen of Kettering, necessary talk (religious). 7 Grove; read *Canones Concilii Tridentini;* meditated; prayed. 9.15 At home; prayed. 9.45 Sins!

SATURDAY [JUNE] 20. 5 Prayed. 5.15 Writ *genesis* upon Predestination. 7.30 Tea. 8.15 Read Prayers. 9 At the Rector's, necessary talk (religious), Mr Allen there. 10 *Genesis.* 12.45 Dinner. 1.15 *Genesis* upon Means of Grace. 4 Read Prayers. 5 *Genesis* upon Justification. 5 Tea; *genesis.* 7 Mark 8:19–9:1! visited Mrs Hitchman, religious talk, prayed. 8.15 With Richard Holmes, religious talk. 9 At home; prayed. 10.

SUNDAY [JUNE] 21. 5 Prayed; necessary business. 6.30 At Mrs Hitchman's, the band, necessary talk (religious), prayed. 8 Read Prayers. 9 At home; Mrs Ford, necessary talk (religious). 10 St Mary's. 11 Grove; *Concilii Tridentini.* 12.15 At home; dinner, religious talk. 2 St Mary's. 3 Grove; read. 4 Read Prayers; at the Rector's, tea. 5.15 At home; tea, religious talk. 6 Mears' Society, Isaiah 35:9. 7 Hall's Society, Exodus 14:13! 9 At home; ate, necessary talk (religious). 9.30 Sins. 10:30.

MONDAY [JUNE] 22. 5 Prayed; writ. 6 Grove; read Prayers. 7 At Mr Bully's, tea, religious talk, prayed. 8.15 At home; writ plan for Latin sermon. 12.30 Necessary business. 1 Dinner. 2 Writ plan. 4.30 Necessary business. 5 At Mrs Crisp's, tea. 5.30 Read Prayers. 6 At Mrs Ford's, tea, necessary talk (religious). 6.45 At Mr Bull's [Bully's?], necessary talk (religious). 7 At Mrs Mears', necessary talk (religious). 7.30 Malachi 3! 8.30 At home; sick. 9.45.

TUESDAY [JUNE] 23. 5.45 Dressed; prayed. 6.15 Read Prayers. 7 At home; sermon. 8 Tea, religious talk. 9 Sermon. 12.15 Dinner, religious talk. 1 Sermon. 4.30 Tea, religious talk. 5.15 Writ sermon. 7 At Mrs Hall's, 2 Corinthians 6:1. 9 At home; sang; writ diary. 9.30.

WEDNESDAY [JUNE] 24. 5 Prayed; sermon. 7.15 Tea, religious talk. 8 Read Prayers; in the Library, read Bishop Bull. 12.15 At home; sermon. 1 Dinner; in the Library, Bishop Bull. 4 Read Prayers; Bishop Bull. 6 At Mrs Hitchman's Love-feast, necessary talk (religious), prayed. 10.

THURSDAY [JUNE] 25. 5 Sermon. 6.15 Read Prayers. 7 At Mrs Compton's, tea, religious talk. 8.45 At home; sermon. 12.30 Dinner; sermon. 5 At Mrs Crisp's tea. 5.30 Read Prayers. 6 Necessary talk (religious) with Smith. 6.30 Necessary talk (religious) to Mr Bull[y]. 7 At Mrs Compton's, Romans 1, prayed; Society! 9.45.

FRIDAY, JUNE 26. 5 Sermon. 8 Tea; sermon. 3 Tea; sermon. 5.30 Read Prayers. 6 Supper; Grove. 7 At Mrs Hall's, Matthew 5:3! 8.45 At home; necessary business. 9.30.

SATURDAY [JUNE] 27. 3 Necessary business; tea. 4.15 Rode. 6.30 Tetsworth; tea, religious talk (necessary). 7.45 Rode. 10 At Mr Crouch's; tea, religious talk.

10.45 Rode. 12.45 Uxbridge; John Taylor, tea. 1.45 Rode. 4.15 At home; dinner, necessary talk (religious); slept. 6 The leaders. 6.30 Romans 3 *ult!* supper; Society! 10.15.

SUNDAY [JUNE] 28. 5.30 Dressed; necessary talk. 6 2 Corinthians 3:17! 8 The leaders; St Paul's. 1 At Mr Doleman's, dinner. 2.30 At home; religious talk (necessary) to Nanny Morris. 3 The leaders; tea. 5 Charles Square, Acts 26.27. 7 The bands! 8.30 Rode. 10 Lady Huntingdon's, Mr Wright. 11 Read Sermon. 12 Acts 13:37, etc! 2.

MONDAY [JUNE] 29. 3.30 Tea; rode. 5.30 At home; Ephesians 2:8! 7 Religious talk to many. 8.30 Tea; slept. 9.45 Rode. 12 Hounslow; dinner. 1 Rode. 2.15 Eton; religious talk, ate. 3 Luke 18:10, necessary talk (religious). 4.30 Rode with John Taylor, necessary talk (religious). 5.30 At ――, tea, religious talk. 6.30 Rode. 8.15 Wycombe; brother Bedder's, tea, religious talk, prayed. 9.45.

TUESDAY [JUNE] 30. 3.30 Tea, religious talk, prayed. 4.30 Rode. 9.30 At Mr Evans'; necessary business; slept. 12 Necessary business; dinner. 1.15 Slept. 3 Writ diary; journal. 5.45 Grove; meditated; read. 7 At Mrs Hall's, Matthew 5:4. 8.45 At home; necessary business. 9.15.

WEDNESDAY, JULY 1. 3 Dressed; necessary business. 4.15 Rode. 7.15 Farnborough; tea. 8 Rode. 11 Marlborough; Charles not there; tea; letter. 1.30 Rode. 5 At Wantage; tea. 6 Rode. 9 At home; supper; prayed. 10.

THURSDAY [JULY] 2. 5.30 Dressed; Grove; read Prayers. 7 At Mr Vesey's, tea. 8.15 At home; writ notes; writ to brother Nowers, to sister Emily. 10.30 Rode. 12 Read *Account of Religious Societies*. 12.45 At Combe; Mr Smith's, necessary talk (religious). 1.45 Dinner, necessary talk (religious). 3 Tea, necessary talk (religious). 4 Rode. 6 At home; tea, Gambold and Hall! 7 At Mrs Compton's, Romans 1. 8 Society! 9 At home; supper. 10.15.

FRIDAY, JULY 3. 5.45 Dressed; read Prayers. 7 At home; began sermon upon Acts 26. 8.30 Tea, necessary talk (religious). 9 Sermon. 1 Necessary business. 1.30 Sermon; writ to brother Ingham, to Mr Sandeman. 4 Mrs Plat, necessary talk (religious); tea; Mr Gambold, religious talk. 5.30 Read Prayers; ate. 6.15 Read Baxter's *Life*. 7 Mrs Hall's, Matthew 5:5, 6. 8 At Mr Bully's! at Mrs Hitchman's, necessary talk (religious). 9.15 At home; Mr ――; supper, religious talk, prayed. 10.45.

SATURDAY [JULY] 4. 6 Dressed; writ sermon; tea. 8 Read Prayers. 9 Writ sermon. 1 Necessary business; dinner. 2.15 Sermon. 4 Read Prayers. 5 Sermon; tea. 6 Mr Viney and Spaltzer, necessary talk (religious)! 8.30 They went; necessary talk (religious). 9 Prayed. 9.30.

SUNDAY [JULY] 5. 5 Sermon. 6.30 Tea; Christ Church, Communion. 9 In our Library, Bishop Bull. 12 Common Room, dinner. 12.45 Writ from Bishop Bull. 2 St Mary's. 3 Writ. 4 Read Prayers; writ. 6 At Mrs Hall's, Matthew 5:7, etc. 7 Mr Fulford. 7.30 At Mrs Mears, Romans 2. 8.30 At home; supper; Deborah Marcham, religious talk, prayed. 9.45.

MONDAY [JULY] 6. 5 Dressed; Library, Bishop Bull; read Prayers. 7 At Mrs Ford's, Viney, necessary talk (religious); tea. 8.30 Bishop Bull. 12 Dinner; read Episcopius. 5 Grove; meditated; read Prayers. 6 Waag, necessary talk; at home;

writ diary. 7 Read many things; necessary talk (religious), prayed. 9.30.

TUESDAY [JULY] 7. 5 Dressed; with Viney and Evans; washed. 6.30 At home; sermon. 7 Tea; sermon. 10 Smith came, corrected his sermon. 1 Dinner; John Taylor; necessary talk (religious). 2 Writ sermon. 5 Grove. 5.30 Read Prayers. 6 At home; tea, necessary talk (religious). 7 At Mrs Mears', Romans 2! 8.30 Read notes. 9 Prayed. 9.30.

WEDNESDAY [JULY] 8. 4.30 Sermon. 6 Grove; read Prayers. 7 At home; sermon; tea; sermon. 11 Corrected all the hymns. 2 Writ notes. 3 Tea; writ notes. 5.30 Read Prayers. 6 At home; tea; read notes. 9.30.

THURSDAY, JULY 9. 5 Writ [*genesis*] upon Predestination. 6 Read Prayers. 7 Tea, necessary talk (religious). 8.15 Bodley, writ notes. 11 In our Library, writ upon Predestination. 12 Dinner; Library. 2 Bodleian; writ. 5 Grove; read Prayers. 6 At home; tea. 7 At Mrs Compton's, Romans 2; Society; at home. 9.45.

FRIDAY [JULY] 10. 3 Dressed; tea. 4 Rode; read Tully's *Offices.* 7 Tetsworth; tea. 7.45 Rode; Tully. 11 At brother Bedder's; at Mr Hollis'; tea. 12 Rode; Tully. 3.30 Uxbridge; ended Tully; dinner. 5.45 Short's Gardens; tea, necessary talk (religious). 6.30 Acts 3:12, etc; 8.30 At home; supper, necessary talk (religious). 10.

SATURDAY [JULY] 11. [pointing hand in margin] 5.15 Dressed. 5.30 John 14; religious talk to some. 8 Rode with brother Nowers. 9.30 Enfield, Lady Huntingdon, tea, religious talk. 11.30 Rode. 1 At home; religious talk to many; dinner; religious talk to many. 4.30 At sister Horner's, tea, religious talk. 5.15 Visited Mrs Grey, Communion. 6.30 At home. 7 Hosea 2:11, etc; supper. 8.15 Society! 10.

SUNDAY [JULY] 12. 5.15 Dressed; Acts 16:31! 7.45 The leaders. 9.45 St Paul's, Communion. 1 At brother Nightingale's, prayed, religious talk. 1.30 At home; dinner. 2 The leaders. 4 Tea. 4.45 Charles Square, Micah 6! visited. 7 At home; the bands! 10.

MONDAY [JULY] 13. 5 Dressed; John 14. 7.30 At brother Kendrick's, necessary talk (religious). 8 Set out with him, necessary talk (religious). 10.30 Uxbridge; tea, necessary talk (religious). 11.30 Rode. 1.30 Wycombe; brother Bedder's, dinner, religious talk. 2.30 Rode. 4.30 Tetsworth; Tully *de Senectute;* tea. 5.15 Rode. 7.15 At Mrs Mears', Romans 2; Society. 8.30 At home; necessary business. 10.

TUESDAY [JULY] 14. 6 Dressed; sermon upon Perfection. 8 Tea; Mrs Stephens. 9 Sermon; sins. 12.30 Dinner. 1 Sermon. 5 Tea; Viney, Spaltzer. 6 Nanny Morris and Forder, necessary talk (religious). 6.45 Writ diary. 7.30 Read Calvin, necessary talk (religious). 9.30.

WEDNESDAY [JULY] 15. 2.30 Dressed. 3 Rode. 6 Burford; tea. 7 Rode. 9.15 Cirencester; tea, religious talk. 10.14 Rode. 12.45 Petty France; dinner. 1.30 Rode. 4 At Mr Deschamps'; at Mrs England's, tea, religious talk; visited some. 5.30 At home; necessary talk (religious) with brother Richards. 6 The women. 7.30 Supper; the men! 10.

THURSDAY, JULY 16. 4.30 Dressed; 1 Kings 22; the women leaders. 7 At sister

Stephens', tea, necessary talk (religious). 8.15 Necessary talk (religious) to many; slept. 11.15 Malt-room, Acts 10:34! 1 At Mrs Norman's, necessary talk (religious); dinner. 2.30 Visited some. 3.30 At home; read notes. 4.15 Visited some. 5.30 At sister Naylor's, tea, religious talk. 6.15 Visited Mrs Jelf, tea, religious talk. 7 Acts 3:12! 8.30 Society; prayed. 10.

FRIDAY [JULY] 17. 4.30 Dressed; 1 Kings 22! religious talk to some. 7 At sister Turner's, tea, religious talk. 8.15 At sister Pottam's. 9 At sister Purnell's, necessary talk (religious). 10 At home; writ. 11 Religious talk to many. 1.15 Prayed. 3 Religious talk to some. 4 Visited; walked. 6.30 Kingswood School; necessary business; Rachel Gotley, sister Baddily, tea, necessary talk (religious). 8 Prayed. 8.30 1 Corinthians 3; prayed. 12.30.

SATURDAY [JULY] 18. 7.15 Tea, religious talk. 8 Psalm 119:1, etc. 9.30 Writ journal. 11 Betty Bush, necessary talk (religious). 12.30 Walked. 1 At Mr Willis', dinner, religious talk. 3 At the School; Journal. 4.30 Writ preface to Dialogue. 6 Tea, religious talk to sister Steed. 7 Matthew 6:10. 8.45 At Mr Deschamps', supper. 9 At home; the stewards, necessary talk (religious). 10.15.

SUNDAY [JULY] 19. 4.30 Dressed; 2 Timothy 2:3. 6.15 Read Gell. 7 At Mr Deschamps', tea. 8 At the School, 2 Timothy 2:3. 9.30 Charles came, necessary talk (religious); read sermon. 12.30 At sister Cambourn's, dinner. 1.30 At home with Charles. 2 Read Bishop Bull. 2.15 Matthew 6:10. 4.15 Baptist Mills. 4 At Mrs Bessel's, tea, necessary talk (religious). 4.45 Acts 26:28! at Mrs Stafford's, tea, religious talk. 7 Society. 9.30 Necessary talk (religious) to many; at Mr Deschamps'. 11.

MONDAY [JULY] 20. 2.30 Dressed; chaise. 3 Rode with Charles, necessary talk (religious). 7.15 Malmesbury; at Mr Lyne's, tea, religious talk. 8.45 Rode; religious talk to stranger. 11 Highworth; tea. 12 Rode. 3 Oxford; at Mr Evans', writ notes; tea; slept. 6.30 At Mrs Compton's, Romans 3! 8.30 At home; supper; prayed. 9.15.

TUESDAY, JULY 21. 7 Dressed; writ sermon; tea; sermon. 12.30 Dinner; sermon. 4.30 At Mrs Stephens', tea. 5.45 At home; Calvin. 6.45 Mr Sarney, etc. 7 At Mrs Compton's Society! 9 At home; sang. 9.30.

WEDNESDAY [JULY] 22. 4.45 Dressed; ended sermon. 6 In our Library, Bishop Bull, etc; read Prayers. 7 Library, Bishop Bull. 12 Dinner; Library, Bishop Bull. 2 Read notes. 3.15 At home; dinner; tea; necessary business. 4.30 Walked; James Mears. 5.30 Met Nanny Morris, necessary talk. 6.30 Abingdon; at Mrs Gleed's, necessary talk (religious). 7 Acts 16. 9 Walked. 10.15 At Mr Evans', necessary talk (religious). 10.45.

THURSDAY [JULY] 23. 5 Dressed; writ upon Predestination, Dialogue. 6 Read Prayers; at the Rector's, read the sermon, religious talk. 8.30 At home; tea, religious talk. 9 Dialogue. 12.30 Dinner; Dialogue. 5.30 Tea; Dialogue. 7.15 Society! 8.45 At home; sang. 9 Writ. 9.30.

FRIDAY [JULY] 24. 4.30 Writ Dialogue. 6 Read Prayers. 7 At home; Dialogue. 8.30 Tea, necessary talk (religious). 9 [Read] Haggar; necessary talk (religious) to many. 2 At the Cross Inn with Mr Cline, dinner. 3 At home; Haggar. 4 Read my sermon; writ Haggar. 5.30 Mr and Mrs Bolt, tea. 6.30 Haggar. 7 Society. 8.30

At the Dolphin, Mrs MacCune, Motte, Miss Witham, etc. 9 All at Mr Evans', supper, prayed. 10.15.

SATURDAY [JULY] 25. 4.45 Dressed; prayed; writ notes. 6.45 Brother Nowers came, necessary talk (religious). 7.30 Tea; at the Dolphin. 8 In the Library; read Prayers. 9 Library. 10 Preached at St Mary's! 11 At home; writ upon Predestination. 1 Necessary talk (religious) with sister Hall. 2 Mrs MacCune, etc, dinner, necessary talk (religious). 4 Writ. 4.30 In the landau with them. 8.30 Stokenchurch. 9.45 Supper. 11.

SUNDAY [JULY] 26. 2.30 Dressed. 4.30 Set out. 9 Uxbridge; tea. 11 Set out. 2.30 At Mrs Motte's. 3.15 At home; dinner, necessary talk (religious) with Suky Harding, etc. 5 Hebrews 10:22. 7 Necessary talk (religious); the bands; Mrs Meriton! 10.

MONDAY, JULY 27. 5 Necessary talk (religious). 5.30 John 14 *ult!* visited. 7 With four bands. 8.15 Tea, necessary talk (religious). 9 Sorted things and papers. 12 Necessary talk (religious) to many. 4.15 At sister Frecquer's, necessary talk (religious); visited some. 6 At Hackney, by Shorehouse, Ephesians 2:8! 7 At Mr Clear's. 7.45 Necessary talk (religious). 8.30 At home; necessary talk (religious) with Suky Harding. 9.30 Nanny Smith. 10 Communion; necessary talk; slept. 12.

TUESDAY [JULY] 28. 5 Dressed; necessary talk (religious). 5.30 John 15! necessary talk (religious) to some. 7 The bands. 8.30 Religious talk (necessary). 9 *Order of Causes;* necessary business; writ notes. 12 Dinner; religious talk to many; visited. 5 At Nanny Morris', necessary talk (religious). 6.30 Judges 6:1! 7.30 Leaders. 8.45 Visited; with Mrs MacCune, religious talk, prayed! 9.45 At Mrs MacCune's, supper; writ. 11.15.

WEDNESDAY [JULY] 29. 4.30 Walked. 5.15 At home; slept. 5.45 John 15; the bands; necessary business. 9 *Order of Causes.* 12 Religious talk to many. 4 Visited; at sister Allar's, tea; visited. 6.30 Greyhound Lane, Luke 18:18! 8 At home; supper; the bands, religious talk, prayed. 10.45.

THURSDAY [JULY] 30. 5 Necessary talk (religious); John 14; visited. 7 The bands; tea. 9 Writ notes. 10 Writ diary; ended Haggar. 12 Necessary talk to many. 2.30 At Mrs Scott's, dinner, religious talk. 3.30 Visited many! 6.45'At home; Joshua 6. 8.30 Society! 11.

FRIDAY [JULY] 31. 5 Necessary talk (religious). 5.30 John 14 *ult;* the bands. 8.14 At brother Wilde's, tea, religious talk. 9 Writ Haggar; writ notes. 12 Religious talk to many. 1.45 Prayed! 3 At brother Nave's, tea, necessary talk (religious). 3.45 At sister Ibbison's, tea, religious talk. 5 At sister Motte's, brother Ingham there, tea. 6 Short's Gardens, Romans 8! visited Jane Muncy! 9 At home; supper. 10.

SATURDAY, AUGUST 1. 5 Dressed; John 15; necessary talk (religious) to brother Ingham. 8 Mr Meriton, necessary talk (religious), tea. 9 Writ Haggar; necessary talk (religious). 12 Necessary business; necessary talk (religious). 2 At brother Barrow's, dinner, religious talk. 4 At sister Paul's, tea, religious talk. 6 Long Lane, 1 John 1. 8 At home; supper; Society! 10.30.

SUNDAY, AUGUST 2. 5 Dressed; necessary talk (religious). 5.45 Romans 3 *ult.* 7 The leaders. 9 Tea; coach. 10 Wapping; Mr Meriton read Prayers. 11

Preached, 1 Kings 21 *ult;* Communion! 2.30 At home; dinner; the leaders. 5 John 21:5! 7.30 The bands. 10.

Monday [August] 3. 5 Dressed; John 16; the bands. 8 Tea, necessary talk (religious) to some. 9 Writ for bands. 12 Religious talk to many. 4.30 At Mrs Barnes', tea, religious talk. 5.30 Visited; Communion. 6.45 John 18:5! 8.15 At brother Frecquer's, necessary talk (religious); supper. 10.15.

Tuesday [August] 4. 5 Prayed; dressed; John 16; the bands 8.30 Rode. 9.45 Enfield; tea, religious talk with them. 12 Rode. 1.15 At home; writ to Nowers 2 Visited; at Mr Witham's, religious talk. 3.15 At brother Milbur's [Milbourn's?], tea, religious talk. 4.30 Visited sister Muncy. 5 Coach. 6 Chelsea, Ephesians 2:8! 9.15 At home; writ to Charles, Nanny Smith! 10.30.

Wednesday [August] 5. 5 Dressed; John 16; the bands. 8.30 Tea; brother Ingham, religious talk. 11 Writ notes. 12 Religious talk to many. 1.30 Prayed! 3.15 Visited. 6.15 Greyhound Lane, John 9. 8.15 At home; necessary talk (religious); supper. 8.30 The bands. 11.

Thursday [August] 6. 5 Dressed; John 16; the bands. 8.30 Mr Mash. 9.30 Writ. 10 Visited. 11.30 At home; writ to Charles. 12 Religious talk to many. 2.15 At brother Harley's, dinner; at sister Ervin's, tea; visited. 6.30 1 John 3:1! writ to John Taylor. 8.30 Society. 10.30.

Friday [August] 7. 5 Dressed; John 17; the bands. 8.30 Tea, necessary talk (religious). 9.30 Maxfield. 10 Writ for the bands. 12 Religious talk to many. 1.30 Prayed; visited. 4.30 Short's Gardens; tea, religious talk. 5.15 Revelation 14! 6 Buried Jane Muncy! 8 At Mrs MacCune's, supper, religious talk. 11 At home.

Saturday [August] 8. [pointing hand in margin] 6.30 Dressed; necessary business. 8.15 Tea, necessary talk (religious). 9 Brother Maxfield; necessary business. 12 Read letters. 2.30 At Mr Strahan's, dinner. 4 At James Hutton's, necessary talk; visited. 5.15 At sister Wollard's, tea, religious talk; visited some. 6.30 Long Lane, 1 John 2. 8.30 Society. 10.45.

[end of diary]

APPENDIX B

WESLEY'S INTERVIEW WITH BISHOP BUTLER,

August 16 and 18, 1739

The following dialogue is transcribed from a five-leaf holograph fragment of Wesley's journal in the Colman Collection, Methodist Archives, Manchester. Following Wesley's own practice, only the paragraphs containing his comments are enclosed in quotation marks. For additional comments on the background and context of this interview, see Frank Baker, 'John Wesley and Bishop Joseph Butler', in WHS 42 (May 1980):93-99.

[Thurs. 16.] Why sir, our faith itself is a good work. It is a virtuous temper of mind.

'My Lord, whatever faith is, our Church asserts, We are justified by faith alone. But how it can be called a good work I see not. It is the gift of God, and a gift that presupposes nothing in us but sin and misery.'

How, sir! Then you make God a tyrannical being, if he justifies some without any goodness in them preceding, and does not justify all. If these are not justified on account of some moral goodness in them, why are not those justified too?

'Because, my lord, they resist his Spirit; because they will not come unto him that they may have life; because they suffer him not to work in them both to will and to do. They cannot be saved because they will not believe.'

Sir, what do you mean by faith?

'My lord, by justifying faith I mean a conviction wrought in a man by the Holy Ghost that Christ hath loved *him* and given himself for *him*, and that through Christ *his* sins are forgiven.'

I believe some good men have this, but not all. But how do you prove this to be the justifying faith taught by our Church?

'My lord, from her Homily on Salvation, where she describes it thus: "A sure trust and confidence which a man hath in God, that through the merits of Christ his sins are forgiven, and he reconciled to the favour of God."'

Why, sir, this [is] quite another thing.

'My lord, I conceive it to be the very same.'

Mr. Wesley, I will deal plainly with you. I once thought Mr. Whitefield and you well-meaning men. But I can't think so now. For I have heard more of you—matters of fact, sir. And Mr. Whitefield says in his *Journal*, 'There are promises still to be fulfilled in me.' Sir, the pretending to extraordinary revelations and gifts of the Holy Ghost is a horrid thing, a very horrid thing.

'My lord, for what Mr. Whitefield says, Mr. Whitefield and not I is accountable. I pretend to no extraordinary revelations or gifts of the Holy Ghost—none but what every Christian may receive, and ought to expect and pray for. But I do not wonder your lordship has heard facts asserted which, if true, would prove the contrary. Nor do I wonder that your lordship, believing

471

them true, should alter the opinion you once had of me. A quarter of an hour I spent with your lordship before. And about an hour now. And perhaps you have never conversed one other hour with anyone who spoke in my favour. But how many with those who spoke on the other side! So that your lordship could not but think as you do.

'But pray, my lord, what are those facts you have heard?'

I hear you administer the sacrament in your societies.

'My lord, I never did yet, and I believe never shall.'

I hear, too, many people fall into fits in your societies, and that you pray over them.

'I do so, my lord. When any show by strong cries and tears that their soul is in deep anguish, I frequently pray to God to deliver them from it. And our prayer is often answered in that hour.'

Very extraordinary indeed! Well, sir, since you ask my advice, I will give it you very freely. You have no business here. You are not commissioned to preach in this diocese. Therefore I advise you to go hence.

'My lord, my business on earth is to do what good I can. Wherever therefore I think I can do most good, there must I stay so long as I think so. At present I think I can do most good here. Therefore here I stay.

'As to my preaching here, a dispensation of the gospel is committed to me, and woe is me if I preach not the gospel, wheresoever I am in the habitable world. Your lordship knows, being ordained a priest, by the commission then received I am a priest of the Church Universal. And being ordained as Fellow of a College, I was not limited to any particular cure, but have an indeterminate commission to preach the Word of God to any part of the Church of England.

'I do not therefore conceive that in preaching here by this commission I break any human law. When I am convinced I do, then it will be time to ask, "Shall I obey God or man?" But if I should be convinced in the meanwhile that I could advance the glory of God and the salvation of souls in any other place more than in Bristol and the parts adjoining, in that hour, by God's help, I will go hence; which till then I may not do.'

Fri. 17. Many of our society met, as we had appointed, at one in the afternoon, and agreed that 'all the members of our society should obey the Church to which we belong, by observing all Fridays in the year as days of fasting or abstinence.' We likewise [agreed] that as many of us as could, without prejudice to their necessary business, should meet every Friday and join in prayer from one to three o'clock.

Sat. 18. A note was sent me, part of which was as follows: 'While you are here, I must entreat you to be careful which way you go out of town. For there are two persons who have resolved to take your life.'

I immediately writ a line to each of those persons, desiring to know whether they were so resolved or not, and received an answer from each, disavowing any such thought. My time is in thy hand, O Lord! [Ps. 31:17 (BCP)]

In the afternoon I was sent for by the bishop. I went first to the College Prayers. Those words in the Psalms I could not but observe: 'If the Lord had not helped me, it had not failed but my soul had been put to silence. But when I said, My foot hath slipped, thy mercy, O Lord, held me up.' [Ps. 94:17-18 (BCP)]

Part of the First Lesson was: 'O son of man, I have set thee a watchman unto the house of Israel. Therefore thou shalt hear the word at my mouth, and warn them from me. . . . If thou warn the wicked of his way, to turn from it, if he do not turn from it, he shall die in his iniquity, but thou hast delivered thy soul.' [Ezek. 33:7-9]

In the Second Lesson were those words: 'Who is he that will harm you, if ye be followers of that which is good? But if ye suffer for righteousness' sake, happy are ye, and be not afraid of their terror, neither be ye troubled. . . . Having a good conscience, that whereas they speak evil of you, as of evil-doers, they may be ashamed that falsely accuse your good conversation in Christ!' [1 Pet. 3:13-16]

After service I went to the bishop, with whom were Mr. Tucker (minister of All Saints), Mr. Sutton (minister of St. Austin's), and the chancellor.

The conversation lasted about an hour. The most material part of it was to this effect:

(The bishop): Mr. Wesley, you have brought me a complaint in form against one of my clergy. You yesterday accused Mr. Tucker of affirming that there needs no atonement for original sin. Did you bring this complaint or did you not?

I answered, 'My lord, you wholly misstate the case. I did not bring any complaint in form. I only desired your lordship's advice how to proceed in a case of difficulty which I related.'

Nay, Mr. Wesley, you did bring it as matter of complaint. For when I said, 'You have no right to make complaint against my clergy,' you said you 'thought everyone had a right to complain against those who taught false doctrine.'

'But, my lord, did I not immediately add, "But I do not bring this as matter of complaint"?

'I cannot peremptorily say whether I said or not, "Mr. T[ucker] affirmed there needs no atonement for original sin." I told your lordship then, "I can't be exact as to the words." And when you said I "must be so, in bringing a complaint", I replied again, "I do not bring a complaint but desire direction for my private conscience."

'But this, my lord, was not the chief point I spoke of. But little was said upon it. The thing I insisted on then, as I do now, and which your lordship spoke largely upon, was this: Mr. T[ucker] affirmed, We are justified on account of our own righteousness. This I then maintained, as I do now, to be false doctrine and contrary to the doctrine of the Church of England.'

In answer to this his lordship read some paragraphs in Mr. T[ucker]'s sermon, all of which seemed to me to carry that sense, although it was not advanced in express terms. His lordship took occasion from them to offer several reasons why there must be something good in us before God could justify us, some morally good temper, on account of which God justified some and not others.

He then said, The sermon was a very good sermon, and there was no room to complain of it; and that (to speak in the mildest terms) I had been guilty of great want of candour and Christian charity. Mr. T[ucker] added that in preaching on that text ('Thou shalt bruise his head, and he shall bruise thy heel' [cf. Gen. 3:15]) he had no occasion to speak of the guilt of original sin, and therefore it was not his business to speak of the atonement for it. I asked, 'Sir, do you think it needs any? I will take your word.' To this he gave no answer.

Mon. 20. I preached at the Brick-yard to a much larger congregation than usual, on those words, 'Oughtest not thou to have had compassion on thy fellow-servant, as I had pity on thee?' [Matt. 18:33]

Wed. 22. I was with several that were in great sorrow and heaviness, two of whom, upon prayer made to God for them, were filled with peace and joy. In the afternoon I endeavored at Baptist Mills to guard the weak against the more dangerous extreme, levity of spirit or behaviour, from, 'I said of laughter, It is mad; and of mirth, What doth it?' [Eccles. 2:2]